MANAGEMENT AND ORGANISATIONAL BEHAVIOUR

'Laurie Mullins is to be commended for presenting a model textbook, the contents of which he has set out with great clarity and succinctness'
British Journal of Administrative Management

'Clearly laid out and thus easy to follow. The book will be of great value to students'
IIM Newscast

'Makes a significant British contribution to compete with the far greater number of transatlantic offerings'
The Leadership and Organisation Development Journal

'For each topic the author gives first class value, with in-depth coverage highlighting ways of making better use of human resources'
Office and Information Management International

'It succeeds in covering in one volume a wide field of study, and is particularly strong in areas relating to those management processes and organisational factors which influence the performance of people at work'
Administrator

About the author

Laurie Mullins is a principal lecturer in the Department of Business and Management in The Business School, University of Portsmouth, where he specialises in Managerial and Organisational Behaviour, and Managing People at Work. He is subject leader for Behavioural and Human Resource Management areas, a member of the Employment Relations Research Group and also has a keen interest in the Gender in Employment Research Group.

He initially worked as a mechanical engineering and naval architecture apprentice before undertaking a career change to work in local government administration, in industry and in academic administration. For a number of years he was also a member of, and an instructor in, the Territorial Army. By part-time study he qualified as a Company Secretary and Administrator and completed a Diploma in Management Studies, before gaining a Masters degree from the Department of Occupational Psychology, Birkbeck College, London. He is also a member of the Institute of Management and of the Institute of Administrative Management.

Laurie has been a regular contributor of numerous articles in a variety of professional journals and is author of *Hospitality Management: A human relations approach*, published by Longman. He has undertaken a range of consultancy work, and acted as adviser and tutor for a number of professional and educational bodies including UNISON Education. He has considerable experience as an external examiner for university degree and postgraduate courses, and for professional organisations. Recently, he completed a year's academic exchange as visiting professor in the Management Department, University of Wisconsin–Whitewater, USA.

MANAGEMENT AND ORGANISATIONAL BEHAVIOUR

FOURTH EDITION

LAURIE J MULLINS

Principal Lecturer
The Business School
University of Portsmouth

PITMAN PUBLISHING

London · Hong Kong · Johannesburg
Melbourne · Singapore · Washington DC

To my wife, Pamela
with a special mention for Kerrie and Tracey
and for Francesca

PITMAN PUBLISHING
128 Long Acre, London WC2E 9AN
Tel: +44 (0)171 447 2000
Fax: +44 (0)171 240 5771

A Division of Pearson Professional Limited

First published in Great Britain 1985
Second Edition 1989
Third Edition 1993
Fourth Edition 1996

© L J Mullins, 1985, 1989, 1993, 1996
© Chapter 4 Linda Hicks 1993, 1996
© Chapter 5 L J Mullins and Linda Hicks 1993, 1996

A CIP catalogue record for this book can be obtained from the British Library.

ISBN 0 273 61598 X

10 9 8 7 6 5 4 3 2

Typeset by Pantek Arts, Maidstone, Kent.
Printed and bound in Great Britain

CONTENTS

PART 4

CONTEXT OF THE ORGANISATION

PART 5

MANAGEMENT AS AN INTEGRATING ACTIVITY

ABOUT THIS BOOK

This book presents a **managerial approach to organisational behaviour**. It is concerned with interactions among the structure and operation of organisations, the process of management and the behaviour of people at work. *The underlying theme of the book is the need for organisational effectiveness and the importance of the role of management as an integrating activity.*

The aims of this book are to:

- relate the study of organisational behaviour to that of management;
- provide an integrated view embracing both theory and practice;
- point out applications of behavioural science within work organisations and implications for management action;
- indicate ways in which organisational performance may be improved through the better use of human resources.

It is hoped that the book will appeal to students at undergraduate, graduate or post experience level in business or management, or on related professional courses. It is also hoped that the book will appeal not only to those aspiring to a managerial position but to practising managers and supervisors who wish to expand their knowledge of the subject area.

The book is written with a minimum of technical terminology and the format is clearly structured. Each chapter contains a short introduction, learning objectives, a synopsis of key points, review and discussion questions, detailed notes and references, and assignments(s) and /or case(s).

Whilst a prior knowledge of behavioural science would prove useful to the reader, it is not assumed. Neither is such knowledge a necessary prerequisite for an understanding of the concepts and ideas discussed in this book.

No single book could hope to cover adequately all aspects of what is a wide and essentially multi-disciplinary field of inquiry, and it is not the intention to attempt to cover all aspects of individual or social behaviour. It is regrettable but inevitable therefore that some topics are excluded or given only limited coverage and it is not possible to meet fully the preferences of all readers. In order to attain a reasonable depth, this book concentrates on selected topics of particular relevance to problems of organisation and management in work situations, and which meet the needs of the intended audience.

There are, of course, related areas of specialisms such as human resource management (HRM) which also bear upon management action and organisational effectiveness. Part 7 of the book, The Personnel Function, aims at broadening the scope of the subject matter beyond the concerns of traditional Organisational Behaviour texts and is a distinctive feature of this book. However it is not the intention to attempt to compete with specialist HRM books. Rather, Chapters 18 and 19 serve to recognise the importance of the context in which the process of management and organisational behaviour takes place and to provide an overview and signpost some main HRM areas of interest.

The concepts and ideas presented in this book provide a basis on which to formulate a critical appraisal of contrasting perspectives on the structure, operation and management of organisations, and interactions among people who work in them. Hopefully this will encourage more awareness of, and sensitivity to, the organisational factors and management processes influencing the behaviour and performance of people at work.

THE FOURTH EDITION

Once again, it has been very pleasing to receive the many complimentary and positive comments from reviewers and users of the previous edition. These comments have been most appreciated and provided the encouragement for, and basis of, the fourth edition.

The fourth edition retains the same underlying theme, aims and approach. It also carries forward the same basic framework but with changes to the titles of Chapters 10 and 17. There are also some changes to the sequencing and ordering of certain sections.

Each chapter now starts with a section called 'Worth thinking about'. It is hoped that readers will find this an interesting and thought-provoking introduction and a discussion focus for the topic areas.

There is considerable new material and in particular greater attention is given to specific areas including organisational culture, ethics and values in organisations, organisational power, stress at work, and the introduction of new technology.

There is a general review, update and extension of material. The rationalisation of the text recognises the need for improved efficiency and improved business competitiveness. It also reflects how the general movement towards flatter structures, flexible working and greater employee involvement has placed increasing emphasis on an integrating rather than a hierarchical/controlling style of management.

There are additional cases and assignments, and practical examples. There are revised and updated procedures from Abbey National and Marks & Spencer, and details of a joint UK/US study of organisational change through teambuilding at Boots The Chemist.

There are more than 200 updated, revised or new references.

Continuing attention to the overall layout, style and presentation of the book should further enhance the appeal of this fourth edition to the reader.

An *Instructor's Manual* is available to lecturers adopting this textbook. A set of paper masters for OHPs is also available.

There is an accompanying *Student Workbook* by Karen Meudell and Tony Callen which has been written to complement this book. The workbook incorporates many of the assignments and activities in the book and also provides numerous new and additional exercises.

There is also a companion book of case studies, *Cases in Organisational Behaviour*, edited by Derek Adam-Smith and Alan Peacock, Pitman (1994). The framework for the order of the cases broadly follows the structure of *Management and Organisational Behaviour* and can be used in conjunction with this book. The following matrix identifies the major topics covered by the cases and possible links with other aspects of management and organisational behaviour.

Matrix showing relationship of cases to organisational behaviour topics in *Cases in Organisational Behaviour*

Case number	1	2	3	4	5	6	7	8	9	10	11	12	13	14	15	16	17	18	19	20	21	22	23	24	25	26	27
PART 1 Management and Organisational Behaviour	●	●	●			◐	◐		◐	◐						◐	◐										
PART 2 The Individual Groups and Leadership		◐	◐	●	●	●	●	●						◐				◐	◐		◐						
PART 3 Context of the Organisation	◐	◐							●	●	●	●	●			◐											◐
PART 4 Organisational Processes					◐						◐		◐	●	●	●	●		◐	◐		◐		◐			
PART 5 The Personnel Function				◐														●	●	●	●	●	◐	◐		◐	◐
PART 6 Improving Organisational Performance			◐	◐			◐	◐		◐		◐			◐							◐	●	●	●	●	●
Suitable for role-play activities		✔			✔								✔	✔	✔				✔	✔	✔	✔		✔			

● Main topic ◐ Supporting topic

PLAN OF THE BOOK

PART 1 – MANAGEMENT AND ORGANISATIONAL BEHAVIOUR		
Chapter 1 The Nature of Organisational Behaviour	Chapter 2 Approaches to Organisation and Management	Chapter 3 The Organisational Setting

PART 2 – THE INDIVIDUAL	
Chapter 4 Individual Differences	Chapter 5 The Process of Perception

PART 3 – GROUPS AND LEADERSHIP		
Chapter 6 The Nature of Groups	Chapter 7 Group Processes and Behaviour	Chapter 8 The Nature of Leadership

PART 4 – CONTEXT OF THE ORGANISATION		
Chapter 9 Organisational Goals and Objectives	Chapter 10 Organisation Structure and Design	Chapter 11 Contingency Approach to Organisation and Management

PART 5 – MANAGEMENT AS AN INTEGRATING ACTIVITY	
Chapter 12 The Nature of Management	Chapter 13 Managerial Behaviour and Effectiveness

PART 6 – ORGANISATIONAL PROCESSES			
Chapter 14 The Nature of Work Motivation	Chapter 15 Job Satisfaction and Work Performance	Chapter 16 The Nature of Delegation	Chapter 17 The Nature of Organisational Control

PART 7 – THE PERSONNEL FUNCTION	
Chapter 18 Personnel and Employee Relations	Chapter 19 Staffing the Organisation

PART 8 – IMPROVING ORGANISATIONAL PERFORMANCE	
Chapter 20 Organisation Development	Chapter 21 Management Development and Organisational Effectiveness

GUIDE TO YOUR STUDY
OF THE BOOK

The book adopts an applied approach to help in the search for the most appropriate ways of improving organisational performance and effectiveness. The objective analysis of organisations is supported, where appropriate, by a more prescriptive stance. For example, in Chapter 10 the underlying need to establish a framework of order and system of command by which the work of the organisation is undertaken demands that attention be given to certain basic principles and consideration of structure.

Although the main focus of attention is the private enterprise business organisation, reference is made to other types of organisations for the purpose of comparisons and examples. General principles and prescriptions apply equally to all types of work organisations which achieve their goals and objectives through the process of management.

It is possible that the more practically minded reader may wish to concentrate greater attention on the latter parts of certain chapters. However, even a cursory examination of earlier sections of the chapter will help provide an understanding of underlying studies upon which discussion of practical applications is based.

You are invited to test your knowledge and understanding of the contents by attempting the review and discussion questions at the end of each chapter. These questions provide a basis for revision and review of progress. You are also invited to undertake the assignment(s) and/or case(s) at the end of each chapter. The questions, assignments and case studies provide an opportunity to relate ideas, principles and practices to specific work situations, to think and talk about major issues, and to discuss and compare views with colleagues.

The notes and references given at the end of each chapter are to encourage you to pursue further any issues of particular interest. A simple numbering system has deliberately been choosen in order to keep the main text uncluttered and easier to follow, to provide more detailed and specific referencing, and because this system appears to be favoured by most readers.

Higher education is changing rapidly with initiatives such as semesterisation and modularisation. This book provides comprehensive coverage of a wide range of topic areas related to the effective use of human resources within the work situation. Although there is a logical flow to the sequencing of topic areas, each Part and each chapter of the book is self-contained. Main sections are identified clearly within each chapter and there are detailed headings and sub-headings. Accordingly an important and distinctive feature of this book is that it is likely to be suitable across a range of different but related modules and units, and will help to provide an integrated approach to your studies.

You are encouraged to complement your reading of the book by drawing upon your own experience of work organisations. Search for and study examples of management and organisational behaviour. Look for good and bad examples of

management activities and practices, and consider reasons for their apparent success or failure. Compare critically the practical examples given in the text and appendices with the procedures and practices in your own organisation.

Consider the manner in which concepts and ideas presented in this book can best be applied in particular work situations. Contemporary examples from your own observations should help further your interest in the subject area and illustrate practical applications to real-life situations.

In acknowledgement and appreciation

A very special tribute is due to my wife Pamela, children and family. I am deeply appreciative of their continuing interest, encouragement and support in completing this fourth edition.

A particular acknowledgement and thank you to my colleagues: Linda Hicks for Chapter 4 on individual differences, the section on gender dimensions in organisations and other contributions to Chapter 5; Tom McEwan for the section on values in organisations in Chapter 9; David Preece for the section on managing new technology in organisational contexts in Chapter 20; and Ray French for contributions of international aspects of management and organisational behaviour in a number of chapters.

Thanks to Richard Wagner of the Management Department, University of Wisconsin–Whitewater, USA, John Campbell of Executive and Staff Training Limited and Julian Page of Boots the Chemist for the account of organisational culture change and teambuilding in Chapter 20.

I also wish to record my thanks and appreciation for the help and support received from the following:

> Gordon Oliver, and colleagues in the Department of Business and Management, University of Portsmouth. Special thanks for their interest and encouragement to Karen Meudell, Derek Adam-Smith, David Goss, Marjorie Corbridge, Stephen Pilbeam.
>
> Philip Voller for the illustrations which introduce each Part of the book.
>
> Those managers who have kindly provided me with information and given permission to reproduce material in this book.
>
> Simon Lake, Penelope Woolf, Lisa Howard and colleagues at Pitman Publishing.

We are all influenced by the thoughts and ideas of other people which tend to drift into the subconscious and are not always distinguished clearly from one's own. I have attempted to give references for sources of work by other writers but apologise to any concerned if acknowledgement has inadvertently not been recorded.

ACKNOWLEDGEMENTS FOR ASSIGNMENTS AND CASE STUDIES

Chapter 1 – the case study 'Eric and Kipsy' is reprinted with permission from Porter, L. W., Lawler, E. E. and Hackman, J. R., *Behavior in Organizations*, McGraw-Hill, New York (1975) pp. 3–14.

Chapter 3 – 'Our Organizational Society: Your Association with Organizations' is reprinted with permission from Kast, F. E. and Rosenzweig, J. E., *Experiential Exercises and Cases in Management*, McGraw-Hill, New York (1976) pp. 13–15.

Chapter 5 – 'Inference–observation' exercise is reprinted with permission from Haney, W. V., *Communications and Interpersonal Relations: Text and Cases*, Sixth edition, Irwin, Illinois (1992) p. 231–3.

Chapter 6 – The copyright of the case study 'Hovertec PLC' rests with my colleague Tom McEwan, University of Portsmouth, and is reprinted with permission.

Chapter 7 – 'Wilderness Survival: A Consensus-Seeking Task' is reprinted from J. William Pfeiffer and John E. Jones (eds), *The 1976 Annual Handbook for Group Facilitators*, San Diego, CA: Pfeiffer & Company (1976) pp. 19–25 and is used with permission.

Chapter 8 – 'Least Preferred Co-worker (LPC) Scale' is reprinted from *A Theory of Leadership Effectiveness*, McGraw-Hill (1976), p. 41, with the permission of the author, Professor F. E. Fiedler, University of Washington.

'T–P Leadership Questionnaire: An Assessment of Style' is reprinted from J. William Pfeiffer and John E. Jones (eds), *A Handbook of Structured Experiences for Human Relations Training*, Vol. 1, San Diego, CA: Pfeiffer & Company (1974) pp. 7–12 and is used with permission. The questionnaire was adapted from Sergiovanni, Metzcus, and Burden's revision of the Leadership Behavior Description Questionnaire, Copyright (1969) by the American Educational Research Association and reprinted by permission of the publisher.

Chapter 9 – The case study 'Square Deal PLC' is reprinted with permission from *The Institute of Administrative Management*, Diploma in Administrative Management Examination Paper, Summer 1983.

Chapter 10 – The case study is adapted from that written originally by my colleague, the late John Cluett, and published in *Administrative Management*, Vol. 29, no. 3, November 1979. It is used with the permission of The Institute of Administrative Management.

Chapter 12 – The case study 'What is Management?' is reprinted with permission of the authors from *Further Case Studies in Hotel Management*, by R. Doswell and P. Nailon, Barrie and Jenkins (1977) pp. 15–26.

Chapter 13 – 'Principle of Supportive Relationships Questionnaire' is reprinted with permission from R. Likert, *The Human Organization – Its Management and Value*, McGraw-Hill, New York (1976) pp. 48–9.

Case Study 1 is reprinted with permission from *The Institute of Chartered Secretaries and Administrators*, Management Principles Pilot Paper, *Administrator*, December 1993.

Chapter 14 – 'Motivation: A Feedback Exercise' is reprinted from J. William Pfeiffer and John E. Jones (eds), *The 1973 Annual Handbook for Group Facilitators*, San Diego, CA: Pfeiffer & Company (1973) pp. 43–5 and is used with permission.

Chapter 15 – The case study 'The Wide Open Spaces' is reprinted with permission from J. Chilver, *People, Communication and Organisation*, Pergamon Press (1984) pp. 118–19.

Case Study 2 is reprinted with permission from *The Institute of Chartered Secretaries and Administrators*, Management: Principles and Policy Examination Paper, June 1985.

Chapter 16 – I have been unable to trace the original author of the case study 'The Enthusiastic Delegator'.

Chapter 17 – The case study 'The Omega Organisation' is reprinted with permission of *The Institute of Chartered Secretaries and Administrators*, Management: Principles and Policy Examination paper, June 1987.

Chapter 18 – Case Study 2 is reprinted with permission from *The Institute of Chartered Secretaries and Administrators*, Management: Principles and Policy Examination Paper, December 1992.

Chapter 19 – The case study 'Sixth Time Lucky' is reprinted with permission from J. Chilver, *People, Communication and Organisation*, Pergamon Press (1984) pp. 116–17.

The case study 'Wessex Computers' is reprinted with permission from *The Institute of Administrative Management*, Certificate in Administrative Management Examination Paper, Summer 1983.

Chapter 20 – The case study 'The Wakewood Organisation' is reprinted with permission from *The Institute of Chartered Secretaries and Administrators*, Management: Principles and Policy Examination Paper, December 1986.

Chapter 21 – The assignment is adapted from material prepared by John Bourn for a *UNISON* distance learning course and is used with permission of The Education Officer.

LAURIE J MULLINS

Part 1

MANAGEMENT AND ORGANISATIONAL BEHAVIOUR

1 THE NATURE OF ORGANISATIONAL BEHAVIOUR

The scope for the examination of behaviour in organisations is very wide. There is a multiplicity of interrelated factors which influence the behaviour and performance of people as members of a work organisation. It is important to recognise the role of management as an integrating activity and as the cornerstone of organisational effectiveness. People and organisations need each other. The manager needs to understand the main influences on behaviour in work organisations and the nature of the people–organisation relationship.

 Learning objectives

To:

- Explain the meaning and nature of organisational behaviour;

- Provide an introduction to a behavioural approach to management;

- Detail main interrelated influences on behaviour in work organisations and explain the nature of behavioural science;

- Recognise contrasting perspectives of organisations and the need for an international approach;

- Explain the importance of management as an integrating activity;

- Assess the importance of the psychological contract;

- Appreciate the complex nature of the behaviour of people in work organisations.

Worth thinking about

In understanding behaviour and managing people at work it is worth remembering the 'bag of gold' syndrome. However hard you try or whatever you do there are some people who you just cannot please: they will always find something to moan about. Give them a bag of gold and they will complain that the bag is the wrong colour.

THE MEANING OF ORGANISATIONAL BEHAVIOUR

We live in an organisational world. Organisations of one form or another are a necessary part of our society and serve many important needs. The decisions and actions of management in organisations have an increasing impact on individuals, other organisations and the community. Organisations play a major and continuing role in the lives of us all, especially with the growth of large-scale business organisations and the divorce of ownership from management. It is important, therefore, to understand how organisations function and the pervasive influences which they exercise over the behaviour of people.[1]

The behaviour of people

Organisational behaviour is concerned with the study of the behaviour of people within an organisational setting. It involves the understanding, prediction and control of human behaviour and the factors which influence the performance of people as members of an organisation.[2] There is a close relation between organisational behaviour and management theory and practice. Some writers seem to suggest that organisational behaviour and management are synonymous, but this is something of an over-simplification because there are many broader facets to management. **Organisational behaviour does not encompass the whole of management; it is more accurately described in the narrower interpretation of providing a behavioural approach to management.**

In most cases the term 'organisational behaviour' is, strictly, a misnomer: rarely do all members of an organisation, except perhaps very small organisations, behave collectively in such a way as to represent the behaviour of the organisation as a whole. In practice we are referring to the behaviour of individuals, or sections or groups of people, within the organisation. For example, when we talk about a 'caring organisation' we are really talking about the philosophy, attitudes and actions of top managers and/or departmental managers, or possibly an individual manager.

Nevertheless, the wording 'organisational behaviour' has become widely accepted and is found increasingly in textbooks and literature on the subject. The term 'organisational behaviour' is a convenient form of shorthand to refer to the multiplicity of interrelated influences on, and patterns of, behaviour of people within organisations.[3]

A framework of study

The behaviour of people, however, cannot be studied in isolation. It is necessary to understand interrelationships with other variables which together comprise the total organisation. To do this involves consideration of interactions among the formal structure, the tasks to be undertaken, the technology employed and methods of carrying out work, the process of management and the external environment.

The study of organisational behaviour embraces therefore an understanding of:

- the behaviour of people;
- the process of management:
- the organisational context in which the process of management takes place;
- organisational processes and the execution of work; and
- interactions with the external environment of which the organisation is part.

This provides us with a basic, but convenient, framework of study. (*See* Fig. 1.1.)

**Fig. 1.1
A basic framework of study**

INFLUENCES ON BEHAVIOUR IN ORGANISATIONS

The variables outlined above provide parameters within which can be identified a number of interrelated dimensions – the individual, the group, the organisation, and the environment – which collectively influence behaviour in work organisations.

The individual

Organisations are made up of their individual members. The individual is a central feature of organisational behaviour and a necessary part of any behavioural situation, whether acting in isolation or as part of a group, in response to expectations of the organisation, or as a result of influences of the external environment.

Where the needs of the individual and the demands of the organisation are incompatible, this can result in frustration and conflict. It is the task of manage-

ment to provide a working environment which permits the satisfaction of individual needs as well as the attainment of organisational goals.

The group

Groups exist in all organisations and are essential to their working and performance. The organisation is comprised of groups of people and almost everyone in an organisation will be a member of one or more groups. Informal groups arise from the social needs of people within the organisation. People in groups influence each other in many ways, and groups may develop their own hierarchies and leaders.

Group pressures can have a major influence over the behaviour and performance of individual members. An understanding of group structure and behaviour complements a knowledge of individual behaviour and adds a further dimension to organisational behaviour.

The organisation

Individuals and groups interact within the structure of the formal organisation. Structure is created by management to establish relationships between individuals and groups, to provide order and systems and to direct the efforts of the organisation into goal-seeking activities. It is through the formal structure that people carry out their organisational activities in order to achieve aims and objectives.

Behaviour is affected by patterns of organisation structure, technology, styles of leadership and systems of management through which organisational processes are planned, directed and controlled. The focus of attention, therefore, is on the impact of organisation structure and design, and patterns of management, on the behaviour of people within the organisation.

The environment

The organisation functions as part of the broader external environment of which it is part. The environment affects the organisation through, for example, technological and scientific development, economic activity, social and cultural influences and governmental actions.

The effects of the operation of the organisation within its environment are reflected in terms of the management of opportunities and risks and the successful achievement of its aims and objectives. The increasing rate of change in environmental factors has highlighted the need to study the total organisation and the processes by which the organisation attempts to adapt to the external demands placed upon it.

Contrasting but related approaches

These different dimensions provide contrasting but related approaches to the understanding of human behaviour in organisations. They present a number of alternative pathways for the study of the subject and level of analysis. It is possible, for example, to adopt a **psychological** approach with the main emphasis on the individuals of which the organisation is comprised. Psychological aspects are important but, by themselves, provide too narrow an approach for the understanding of management and organisational behaviour. Our main concern is not with the complex detail of individual differences and attributes *per se* but with the behaviour and management of people within an organisational setting.

It is also possible to adopt a **sociological** approach concerned with a broader emphasis on human behaviour in society. Sociological aspects can be important. A number of sociology writers seem set on the purpose of criticising traditional views of organisation and management. Many of the criticisms and limitations to

which such writers refer are justified and help promote healthy academic debate. Unfortunately, however, much of the argument tends to be presented in the abstract and lacking in constructive ideas on how, in practical terms, action could be taken to improve organisational performance.

BEHAVIOURAL SCIENCE – AN INTERDISCIPLINARY APPROACH

The study of organisational behaviour cannot be undertaken entirely in terms of a single discipline. It is necessary to provide an interdisciplinary, behavioural science approach. (*See* Fig. 1.2.)

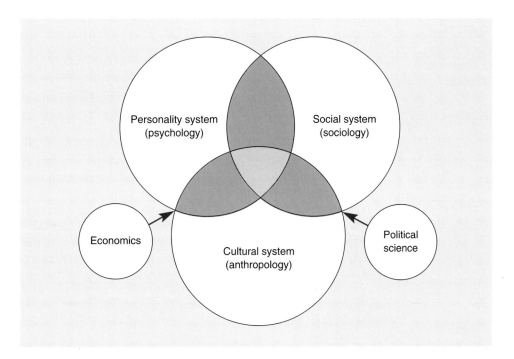

Fig. 1.2
Behavioural science – an interdisciplinary approach

The wording 'behavioural science' has no strict scientific definition. It may be used as a collective term for the grouping of all the social sciences concerned with the study of people's behaviour. However, it is now more frequently used to refer to attempts to apply a selective, interdisciplinary approach to the study of human behaviour. **In particular, the term is often taken as applying more narrowly and specifically to problems of organisation and management in the work environment.**

Three main disciplines

There are areas of overlap among the various social sciences, their sub-divisions and related disciplines such as economics and political science. However, the study of behaviour can be viewed in terms of three main disciplines – psychology, sociology and anthropology. All three disciplines have made an important contribution to the field of organisational behaviour.

7

- **Psychologists** are, broadly speaking, concerned with the study of human behaviour, with traits of the individual and membership of small social groups. The main focus of attention is on the individual as a whole person, or what can be termed the 'personality system', including for example perception, attitudes and motives.
- **Sociologists** are more concerned with the study of social behaviour, relationships among social groups and societies, and the maintenance of order. The main focus of attention is on the analysis of social structures and positions in those structures, for example the relationship between the behaviour of leaders and followers.
- **Anthropologists** are more concerned with the science of mankind and the study of human behaviour as a whole. As far as organisational behaviour is concerned the main focus of attention is on the cultural system, the beliefs, customs, ideas and values within a group or society, and the comparison of behaviour among different cultures – for example, the importance to Muslim women of wearing trousers to work. People learn to depend on their culture to give them security and stability, and they can suffer adverse reactions to unfamiliar environments.

Contribution of behavioural science

The contribution of relevant aspects of psychology, sociology and anthropology aid our understanding of the behaviour of people in work organisations, and underpin the field of organisational behaviour.

Behavioural science attempts to structure organisations in order to secure the optimum working environment. It is concerned with reconciling the needs of the organisation for the contribution of maximum productivity, with the needs of individuals and the realisation of their potential. Emphasis is on the application of relevant aspects of psychological and sociological theory and practice, and cultural influences, to problems of organisation and management in the work situation.

You should not be confused by use of the word 'theory'. Most rational decisions are based on some form of theory. Theory contains a message on how managers might behave. This will influence attitudes towards management practice and lead to changes in actual behaviour. **Theory helps in the building of generalised models applicable to all organisations. It further provides a conceptual framework and gives a perspective for the practical study of the subject.** Thus theory and practice are inseparable. Together they lead to a better understanding of factors influencing patterns of behaviour in organisations and applications of the process of management.

CONTRASTING PERSPECTIVES OF ORGANISATIONS

Organisations are complex social systems which can be defined and studied in a number of different ways. A significant approach to this broad perspective on the nature of organisations and organisational behaviour is provided by *Morgan*. Through the use of metaphors, Morgan identifies eight different ways of viewing organisations, as: machines, organisms, brains, cultures, political systems, psychic prisons, flux and transformation, and instruments of domination.

According to Morgan, these contrasting metaphors aid the understanding of the complex nature of organisational life and the critical evaluation of organisational phenomena.[4]

- **Machines** – this suggests that organisations can be designed as if they are machines with orderly relations between clearly defined parts. Viewing organisations as machines can provide the basis for efficient operation in a routine, reliable and predictable way. This form of bureaucratic structure provides form, continuity and security. However, it may have adverse consequences and limit the development of human capacities. Organisations viewed as machines function better in a stable and protected environment.

- **Organisms** – the organisation is seen as behaving like a living system. In the same way that biological mechanisms adapt to changes in their environment so organisations, as open systems, adapt to the changing external environment. Organisations operating within a turbulent and dynamic environment require an adaptable type of structure.

- **Brains** – viewing organisations as brains involves thinking about the organisation as inventive and rational, and in a manner that provides for flexibility and creative action. The challenge is to create new forms of organisation capable of intelligent change and that can disperse brainlike capacities.

- **Cultures** – this sees organisations as complex systems made up of their own characteristic sets of ideology, values, rituals, and systems of belief and practice. Attention to specific aspects of social development helps to account for variations among organisations.

- **Political systems** – in the sense that ways must be found to create order and direct people, organisations are intrinsically political. They are about authority, power, superior–subordinate relationships and conflicting interests. Viewing organisations as political systems helps in an understanding of day-to-day organisational life, the wheeling and dealing, and pursuit of special interests.

- **Psychic prisons** – this views organisations as psychic phenomena created and sustained by conscious and unconscious processes. Organisations and their members are constrained by their shadows or 'psychic prisons' and become trapped by constructions of reality. Their inherited or created mythical past places constraints on the representation of the organisation to the outside world. Viewing organisations as psychic prisons provides an understanding of the reality and illusions of organisational behaviour.

- **Flux and transformation** – the universe is in a constant state of flux embodying characteristics of both permanence and change. Organisations can be seen as in a state of flux and transformation. In order to understand the nature and social life of organisations, it is necessary to understand the sources and logic of transformation and change.

- **Instruments of domination** – in this view organisations are associated with processes of social domination, and individuals and groups imposing their will on others. A feature of organisations is asymmetrical power relations that result in the pursuit of the goals of the few through the efforts of the many. Organisations are best understood in terms of variations in the mode of social domination and control of their members.

The metaphors are not fixed categories

Although the concern of this book is with a managerial approach to organisational behaviour, these contrasting metaphors provide an interesting perspective on how to view organisations. They provide a broader view of the dynamics of organisational behaviour, and how to manage and design organisations. However, Morgan points out that these metaphors are not fixed categories and are not mutually exclu-

sive. An organisation can be a mix of each, and predominantly a combination of two or three metaphors. Also, these combinations may change over a period of time.

ORGANISATIONAL EFFECTIVENESS

Every work organisation is concerned with being effective, especially now in a difficult economic environment and in the face of fierce world competition. Organisational effectiveness should be the concern of everyone within the organisation. Upon the attainment of its goals and objectives will rest the success and ultimate survival and future of the organisation.

Gauging the effectiveness, or success, of an organisation is, however, not an easy task; it entails analysing both a definitive structure of organisation and the structure caused by human intervention.[5] For example, *Handy* identifies over 60 factors that impinge on any one organisational situation and which illustrate the complicated nature of the study of organisational effectiveness.[6] The nature of organisational effectiveness is discussed in Chapter 21.

The criteria for measuring 'success' may differ from one type of organisation to another. (*See*, for example, the discussion on management in private enterprise and public sector organisations in Chapter 12.) Success may also be short-lived and successful organisations today may well be less successful in the future.[7]

However, from studies of successful organisations, both in America and Britain, one central element becomes clear – **the importance of achieving productivity through the effective management of people, and their commitment to, and involvement with, the organisation**. According to *Lord Sieff* (formerly Chairman and Chief Executive of Marks & Spencer), for example, the promotion of good human relations at work and efficient management are two aspects of the same thing.[8]

ORIENTATIONS TO WORK

People differ in the manner and extent of their involvement with, and concern for, work. From information collected about the work situation, organisational participation and involvement with work colleagues, and life outside the organisation, *Goldthorpe et al.* identified three main types of orientation to work; instrumental, bureaucratic and solidaristic.[9]

- Individuals with an **instrumental orientation** defined work not as a central life issue but in terms of a means to an end. There is a calculative or economic involvement with work, and a clear distinction between work-related and non-work-related activities.
- Individuals with a **bureaucratic orientation** defined work as a central life issue. There is a sense of obligation to the work of the organisation and a positive involvement in terms of a career structure. There is a close link between work-related and non-work-related activities.
- Individuals with a **solidaristic orientation** defined the work situation in terms of group activities. There is an ego involvement with work groups rather than

with the organisation itself. Work is more than just a means to an end. Non-work activities are linked to work relationships.

Different work situations

Some people may well have a set motivation to work, whatever the nature of the work environment. However, different work situations may also influence the individual's orientation to work. For example, the lack of opportunities for team-work and the satisfaction of social expectations may result in an instrumental orientation to work, and a primary concern for economic interests such as pay and security. In other situations where there are greater opportunities to satisfy social needs, membership of work groups may be very important, and individuals may have a more solidaristic orientation to work.

MANAGEMENT AS AN INTEGRATING ACTIVITY

Fig. 1.3 Management as the cornerstone of organisational effectiveness

Whatever the individual's orientations to work, it is through the process of management that the efforts of members of the organisation are co-ordinated, directed and guided towards the achievement of organisational goals. **Management is therefore the cornerstone of organisational effectiveness, and is concerned with arrangements for the carrying out of organisational processes and the execution of work.** (*See* Fig. 1.3.)

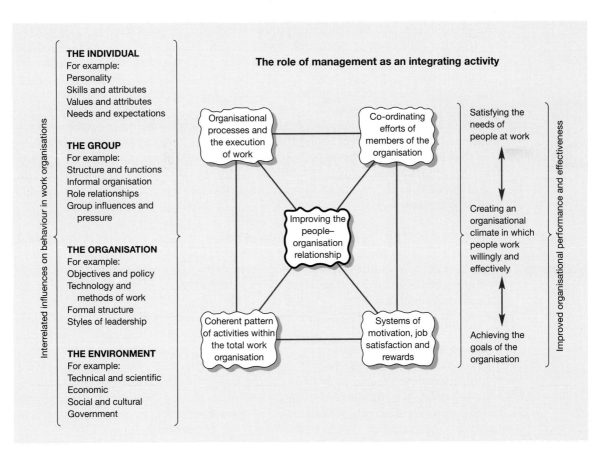

According to *Drucker*, it is management that enables the organisation to contribute a needed result to society, the economy and the individual.

> Management is tasks. Management is a discipline. But management is also people. Every achievement of management is the achievement of a manager. Every failure is a failure of a manager. People manage rather than 'forces' or 'facts'. The vision, dedication and integrity of managers determine whether there is management or mismanagement.[10]

There are many aspects to management in work organisations, but the one essential ingredient of any successful manager is the ability to handle people effectively. The manager needs to be conversant with social and human skills, and have the ability to work with and through other people. Without people there can be no organisation and no meaningful activity. **Behind every action or document in an organisation there are people.**

Patterns of human behaviour

It is the responsibility of management to manage. But organisations can only achieve their aims and objectives through the co-ordinated efforts of their members. It is the job of management to get things done through other people. This involves the effective management of human resources. However, it is important always to remember that it is people who are being managed and people should be considered in human terms. Unlike physical resources, people are not owned by the organisation. People bring their own perceptions, feelings and attitudes towards the organisation, systems and styles of management, their duties and responsibilities, and the conditions under which they are working.

Human behaviour is capricious, and scientific methods or principles of behaviour cannot be applied with reliability. Patterns of behaviour are influenced by a complex combination of individual, social and cultural factors. Tensions, conflicts and politics are almost inevitable, as are informal structures of organisation and unofficial working methods.

We need to remind ourselves of the human aspects of the organisation and the idiosyncratic behaviour of individuals. For example *Egan* refers to the importance of the shadow side of the organisation: that is, those things not found on organisation charts or in company manuals – the covert, and often undiscussed, activities of people which affect both the productivity and quality of working life of an organisation.[11]

The people–organisation relationship

In the belief of the author, the majority of people come to work with the **original** attitude of being eager to do a good job, and desirous of performing well and to the best of their abilities. Where actual performance fails to match the ideal this is largely a result of how staff perceive they are treated by management and the management function.

Many problems in the people–organisational relationship arise not so much from what management does, but **the manner in which it is done**. Often, it is **not so much the intent but the manner of implementation** that is the root cause of staff unrest and dissatisfaction. For example, staff may agree on the need to introduce new technology to retain the competitive efficiency of the organisation, but feel resentment about the lack of pre-planning, consultation, retraining programmes, participation in agreeing new working practices and wage rates, and similar considerations arising from the manner of its introduction.

Therefore, a heavy responsibility is placed on managers and the activity of management – on the processes, systems and styles of management. Accordingly, how managers exercise the responsibility for, and duties of, management is important. Attention must be given to the work environment, and appropriate systems of motivation, job satisfaction and rewards.

It is difficult to think of any aspect of the functioning of the organisation, or behaviour of people, which does not concern, or relate back to, management in some way. For example, even personality clashes between two individual members of staff could possibly be traced back to management procedures for recruitment and selection, induction, socialisation and training, delegation or the level and style of supervision. And clearly the personality clashes are likely to affect the attitudes and work performance of the members concerned, and also affect the morale of other staff.

Providing the right balance

Management should, therefore, endeavour to create the right balance between the interrelated elements which make up the total organisation, and to weld these into coherent patterns of activity best suited to the external environment in which the organisation is operating. Consideration must be given to developing an organisational climate in which people work willingly and effectively.

People and organisations need each other. **Attention should be focused, therefore, on improving the people–organisation relationship.** Management is an integral part of this relationship. It should serve to reconcile the needs of people at work with the requirements of the organisation. Management is essentially an integrating activity which permeates every facet of the operations of the organisation.

Style of management

The style of management adopted can be seen as a function of the manager's attitudes towards people, and assumptions about human nature and behaviour. *McGregor*, for example, put forward two sets of suppositions – Theory X and Theory Y.[12] The central principle of Theory X is based on direction and control through a centralised system of organisation and the exercise of authority. In contrast, the central principle of Theory Y is based on the integration of individual and organisational goals. These underlying philosophies will influence a whole range of managerial behaviours and strategies. (Theory X and Theory Y approaches are discussed in Chapter 13.)

The general movement towards flatter organisation structures, flexible working and greater employee involvement has placed increasing emphasis on an integrating rather than a hierarchical/controlling style of management.

THE PSYCHOLOGICAL CONTRACT

One significant aspect of the relationship between the individual and the organisation is the concept of the psychological contract. This is not a written document, but implies a series of mutual expectations and satisfaction of needs arising from the people–organisation relationship. It involves a process of giving and receiving by the individual and by the organisation. The psychological contract covers a range of expectations of rights and privileges, duties and obligations, which do not form part of a formal agreement but still have an important influence on people's behaviour.[13]

Individuals' expectations

The nature and extent of individuals' expectations vary widely, as do the ability and willingness of the organisation to meet them. It is difficult to list the range of implicit expectations that individuals have, and they change over time, but they may include that the organisation will, for example:

- provide safe and hygienic working conditions;
- make every reasonable effort to provide job security;
- attempt to provide challenging and satisfying jobs and reduce alienating aspects of work;
- adopt equitable personnel policies and procedures;
- allow staff genuine participation in decisions which affect them;
- implement best practice in equal opportunity policies and procedures;
- provide reasonable opportunities for personal development and career progression;
- treat members of staff with respect;
- demonstrate an understanding and considerate attitude towards personal problems of staff.

These expectations are notwithstanding any statutory requirements placed upon the organisation. Instead, they relate more to the idea of a social responsibility of management, which is discussed in Chapter 9.

The organisation's expectations

The organisation will also have implicit expectations of its members, for example:

- to accept the ideology of the organisation;
- to work diligently in pursuit of organisational objectives;
- not to abuse goodwill shown by management;
- to uphold the image of the organisation;
- to show loyalty;
- not to betray positions of trust;
- to observe reasonable and acceptable standards of dress and appearance.

The organisational side of the psychological contract places emphasis on expectations, requirements and constraints which often differ from, and may be in conflict with, an individual's expectations. For example, *French et al.* suggest the following list of organisational expectations and requirements:

1. Achieving organisational goals that are different from the personal goals of individual members.
2. Having sufficient involvement, commitment, and initiative from organisational members.
3. Requiring individuals to take certain organisational roles.
4. Having people perform certain tasks effectively and efficiently.
5. Requiring participants to accept authority and to assume responsibilities.
6. Achieving the integration and co-ordination of activities.
7. Requiring adherence to policies, rules and procedures.
8. Attaining responsiveness to leadership and influence.
9. Developing sufficient loyalty to maintain the organisation as a social system.[14]

Process of balancing

It is unlikely that all expectations of the individual or of the organisation will be met fully. There is a continual process of balancing, and explicit and implicit bargaining. The nature of these expectations is not defined formally, and although the

14

individual member and the organisation may not be aware consciously of them, they still affect relationships between them and have an influence on behaviour.

The psychological contract is a useful concept in examining the socialisation of new members of staff to the organisation. According to *Kotter*, for example, early experiences have a major effect on an individual's subsequent career in an organisation, and influence job satisfaction, attitude and level of productivity. The extent of the matches between individual and organisational expectations also influences the willingness of people to stay with the organisation and of the organisation to continue to employ them.[15]

THE NEED FOR AN INTERNATIONAL APPROACH

At the end of the twentieth century managers are facing major changes in the business environment. Often these are of a significant nature which cause them to reassess their strategies, policies and styles. For example, in the last 20 years managers have had to operate within a context of major advances in technology, an increasingly educated workforce, and an ever greater stress upon quality of goods and services.

Many commentators consider that the business environment is becoming more international or 'global'. The following factors are frequently cited as possible explanatory factors which underlie this trend:

- improvements in international communication facilities leading, for example, to the 24-hour financial market;
- international competitive pressures – for example the emergence of the 'Pacific rim' nations as stronger trading entities;
- even more powerful multinational corporations which, by definition, operate outside of national boundaries;
- the collapse of former communist societies such as the USSR and its satellite states in Eastern Europe, offering potentially huge new markets and supply of labour;
- the development of new integrated trading blocs such as NAFTA (the North American Free Trading Association) and the European Union single market.

Stewart suggests two major reasons for an interest in national differences in management. One is the need to learn from others, particularly from more successful foreign competitors. The other is the need to understand how to work effectively with people from other countries.[16]

Cultural similarities and differences

In the light of these developments it is not surprising to find many theories which attempt to outline and explain cultural similarities and differences among societies. This comparative focus is not new. *Turton*, for example, records that even 150 years ago, comparisons were being made between British and North American or Western European business cultures.[17]

The concentration upon the practices and attitudes of other countries is not simply an academic pursuit. Rather, it should be seen as an attempt to secure improved organisational performance based on **lessons from abroad**. This most practical concern may explain the longevity of comparative studies, given the long-term variability

of national economic performance. At the present time, the following issues are of particular concern to those who control and manage work organisations.

- How should one negotiate or deal more generally with people from other cultures?
- Do work organisations differ significantly across the world in terms of structure and growth patterns?
- In what ways do diverse systems of industrial relations influence the employer–employee relationship in different societies?

There are of course many other questions which may preoccupy those involved in international business. For example: how should one negotiate when buying or selling products and services? and how should one 'place a product' in the overseas market? But these questions lie outside the scope of this book. Our concern is with national differences relating to the effective management of people. **In particular, attention will be focused on the impact of Britain's membership of the European Union.**

BRITAIN AND THE SINGLE EUROPEAN MARKET

A major example of the international context is the passing of the Single European Act in 1987. This was intended to complete the move towards a single market which began with the birth of the (then) European Economic Community in 1956. The implications of this Act are massive. From 31st December 1992, all 12 (now 15) national states form one single, de-regulated market. All non-tariff barriers will have disappeared which will result in the free flow of capital, goods, services and labour. Mutual recognition of academic and vocational qualifications means that employees will be free to work in any member country.

Harmonisation of employment practices

Increasingly, therefore, work organisations may seek to recruit employees from other societies. From a survey of six thousand organisations in various EU states, *Lockhart* found that 20 per cent of UK organisations were already recruiting internationally. Up to 26 per cent of public sector organisations were found to be active in this respect.[18] Clearly, a development of this magnitude may require a pan-European strategy. It will most definitely necessitate an understanding of perceptions among staff in the overseas environment. A key question therefore becomes: does culture influence work attitudes?

It may also be that increased European integration will result in harmonisation of employment practices and conditions. At the Maastricht summit in December 1991, a 'social chapter' dealing with individual employment rights, including a minimum wage, was proposed and subsequently signed by 11 of the member states. The British delegation secured an 'opt out' clause on these matters. The extent to which such issues should be harmonised across Europe is likely to remain a matter of controversy.

It can be seen, therefore, that one piece of legislation may influence very significantly the way in which people are managed. (*See also* the discussion in Chapter 18 on personnel and employee relations.)

THE INFLUENCE OF NATIONAL CULTURE

'Culture' is a notoriously difficult concept to pin down. It is all too easy to assume that differences among societies may be attributed to culture *per se*, with no attempt to delve into reasons which lie behind these differences. *Robbins* notes that 'most people are unaware of just how their culture will affect them. Culture is like fish to water. It is there all the time but the fish are oblivious to it.'[19] This does not, of course, mean that culture is an irrelevant concept. But clearly it is dangerous to ask people how and why their culture operates.

In explaining the recent economic success of Japan, many commentators have adopted a **historical** perspective and have located current practices firmly in the past. For example, *French* records that the German system of co-determination – the practice of involving employees in decision-making – has its roots in the earliest period of industrial development in that country.[20] It is thus doubtful whether personnel policies and practices can always be transplanted easily from one country to another. However, the emergence in recent years of Japanese quality circles in western organisations appears to have been achieved without too much criticism. (The applications of quality circles are discussed in Chapter 15.)

Welford and Prescott provide a model of the cultural environment of any society which is shown in Fig. 1.4.[21] It may thus be seen that culture is a multifaceted concept. While we could never hope to have a deep knowledge of each feature of any society we come into contact with, the model does nonetheless provide us with a suggested framework for further study of the society in question.

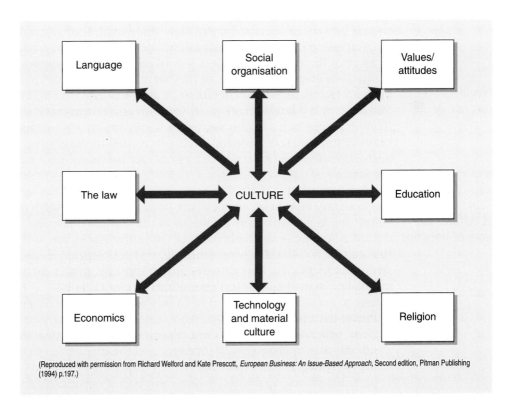

Fig. 1.4
Cultural
environment

(Reproduced with permission from Richard Welford and Kate Prescott, *European Business: An Issue-Based Approach*, Second edition, Pitman Publishing (1994) p.197.)

The study of culture

Other writers who have sought to conduct comparative research into workplace differences have frequently used the **matched pair** method of comparison. This involves selecting organisations which are similar in size, product or service provided, and ownership pattern. Therefore any differences which can be observed can be isolated and subjected to further analysis to see whether they are culturally derived. An example of this methodological tradition is the work of *Maurice, Sorge and Warner* which is looked at in Chapter 11.

In summary, culture is a difficult concept to identify but may nonetheless be real and of potentially great importance in the study of organisational behaviour. For the purpose of definition, it may be usefully conceived as **a distinctive pattern of values and beliefs which are characteristic of a particular society or sub-group within that society**. These values and beliefs are likely to have been transmitted by previous generations through the process of socialisation such as family influence and/or formal education. In a curious sense we may be viewed as carrying culture around with us.

Note: We have concentrated here upon the possible impact of **national** culture. The concept of corporate culture views work organisations as mini-societies with distinctive characteristics of their own. This idea of organisational culture is examined in Chapter 20.

CULTURE AND ORGANISATIONAL BEHAVIOUR

In the past, it has been assumed that there are indeed significant differences in organisations across the world which can be attributed to culture. However, one should be wary of overstating this view since some academic research now points to a somewhat different conclusion.

Some of the work of the Aston School points to **convergence** of organisational culture. For example, the work of *Hickson et al.* suggests that there is a relationship between factors such as size/technology and structure which transcends culture. A bureaucracy is a bureaucracy in all societies and bureaucratic structures are more likely to occur in particular sectors of the economy.[22] On a more general level, many commentators have followed *Kerr et al.*[23] in suggesting that industrial or post-industrial societies would in any case become more alike as they developed in the future.

Four dimensions of culture: the work of Hofstede

The contrary argument, that culture does matter when studying organisational behaviour, is perhaps more prevalent at the current time. *Geert Hofstede* has conducted a large-scale research study of IBM subsidiaries across the world. Arguing that culture is **collective programming**, which does indeed affect behaviour, Hofstede has identified four dimensions of culture: power distance; uncertainty avoidance; individualism; and masculinity.[24] (*See* Table 1.1.)

- **Power distance** is essentially used to categorise levels of inequality in organisations, which Hofstede claims will depend upon management style, willingness of subordinates to disagree with superiors, and the educational level and status accruing to particular roles. Countries which displayed a high level of power distance included France, Spain, Hong Kong and Iran. Countries as diverse as Germany,

Table 1.1. Classification of cultures by dimensions

I: More developed Latin	II: Less developed Latin	
high power distance	high power distance	
high uncertainty avoidance	high uncertainty avoidance	
high individualism	low individualism	
medium masculinity	whole range on masculinity	
Belgium	Colombia	
France	Mexico	
Argentina	Venezuela	
Brazil	Chile	
Spain	Peru	
	Portugal	
	Yugoslavia	

III: More developed Asian	IV: Less developed Asian	V: Near Eastern
medium power distance	high power distance	high power distance
high uncertainty avoidance	low uncertainty avoidance	high uncertainty avoidance
medium individualism	low individualism	low individualism
high masculinity	medium masculinity	medium masculinity
Japan	Pakistan	Greece
	Taiwan	Iran
	Thailand	Turkey
	Hong Kong	
	India	
	Philippines	
	Singapore	

VI: Germanic	VII: Anglo	VIII: Nordic
low power distance	low power distance	low power distance
high uncertainty avoidance	low-to-medium uncertainty avoidance	low-to-medium uncertainty avoidance
medium individualism	high individualism	medium individualism
high masculinity	high masculinity	low masculinity
Austria	Australia	Denmark
Israel	Canada	Finland
Germany	Britain	The Netherlands
Switzerland	Ireland	Norway
South Africa	New Zealand	Sweden
Italy	USA	

(From 'International Perspectives', Unit 16, Block V, Wider Perspectives, *Managing in Organizations*, The Open University (1985) p.60.)

Italy, Australia and the USA were characterised as low power distance societies. Britain also emerged as a low power distance society according to Hofstede's work.

- **Uncertainty avoidance** refers to the extent to which members of a society feel threatened by unusual situations. High uncertainty avoidance is said to be characteristic in France, Spain, Germany and many of the Latin American societies. Low-to-medium uncertainty avoidance was displayed in The Netherlands, the Scandinavian countries and Ireland. In this case Britain is said to be 'low-to-medium' together with the USA, Canada and Australia.

- **Individualism** describes the relatively individualistic or collectivist ethic evident in that particular society. Thus, the USA, France and Spain display high individualism. This contrasts with Portugal, Hong Kong, India and Greece which are low individualism societies. Britain here is depicted as a high individualism society.
- **Masculinity** is the final category suggested by Hofstede. This refers to a continuum between 'masculine' characteristics such as assertiveness and competitiveness; and 'feminine' traits such as caring, a stress upon the quality of life and concern with the environment. High masculinity societies included the USA, Italy, Germany and Japan. More feminine (low masculinity) societies included The Netherlands and the Scandinavian countries. In this case Britain was located within the high masculinity group.

Evaluation of Hofstede's work

Hofstede's work is by no means beyond criticism. The dimensions consist of generalised categories and no allowance is made for regional differences. By concentrating on one organisation – an example of the 'matched pair' methodology – Hofstede restricts the scope of his work. Some may find the definitions of terms such as 'masculinity' and 'femininity' unconvincing and provocative. Nonetheless, Hofstede's work represents an attempt to understand work-related differences and to account for these by reference to preferred management styles. Ultimately, readers will assess the value of his work in the light of their own experiences and interpretations of the business world. They may also reflect upon the history of their own countries and those of others, and consider whether it may provide an explanation of Hofstede's categories.

Cultural variance and workplace behaviour

Another Dutch writer, *Fons Trompenaars*, has also attempted to make a direct link between cultural variance and workplace behaviour. Trompenaars identifies seven areas in which cultural differences may affect aspects of organisational behaviour.[25]

- Relationships and rules. Here societies may be more or less **universal**, in which case there is relative rigidity in respect of rule-based behaviour, or **particular**, in which case the importance of relationships may lead to flexibility in interpretation of situations.
- Societies may be more oriented to the **individual** or **collective**. The collective may take different forms; the corporation in Japan, the family in Italy or the Catholic Church in the Republic of Ireland. There may be implications here for such matters as individual responsibility or payment systems.
- It may also be true that societies differ to the extent it is thought appropriate for members to show emotion in public. **Neutral** societies favour the 'stiff upper lip' while overt displays of feeling are more likely in **emotional** societies. Trompenaars cites a survey in which 80 employees in each of various societies were asked whether they would think it wrong to express upset openly at work. The numbers who thought it wrong were 80 in Japan, 75 in Germany, 71 in the UK, 55 in Hong Kong, 40 in the USA and 29 in Italy.
- In **diffuse** cultures, the whole person would be involved in a business relationship and it would take time to build such relationships. In a **specific** culture such as the USA the basic relationship would be limited to the contractual. This distinction clearly has implications for those seeking to develop new international links.

- **Achievement**-based societies value recent success or an overall record of accomplishment. In contrast, in societies relying more on **ascription**, status could be bestowed on you through such factors as age, gender or educational record.
- Trompenaars suggests that societies view *time* in different ways which may in turn influence business activities. The American dream is the French nightmare. Americans generally start from zero and what matters is their present performance and their plan to 'make it' in the future. This is 'nouveau riche' for the French, who prefer the 'ancien pauvre'; they have an enormous sense of the past.
- Finally it is suggested that there are differences with regard to attitudes to the **environment**. In western societies, individuals are typically masters of their fate. In other parts of the world, however, the world is more powerful that individuals.

Trompenaars' work is based on lengthy academic and field research. It is potentially useful in linking the dimensions of culture to aspects of organisational behaviour which are of direct relevance, particularly to people approaching a new culture for the first time.

THE STUDY OF MANAGEMENT AND ORGANISATIONAL BEHAVIOUR

The use of separate topic areas is a recognised academic means of aiding study and explanation of the subject. In practice, however, the activities of an organisation and the job of management cannot be isolated neatly in discrete categories. The majority of actions are likely to involve a number of simultaneous functions that relate to the total processes of management.

Consider, for example, a manager briefing departmental staff on an unexpected, important and urgent task which has to be undertaken. Such a briefing is likely to involve consideration of goals and objectives, organisation structure, management system, process of delegation, systems of communication, leadership style, motivation and management control systems. The behaviour of the staff will be influenced by a combination of individual, group, organisational and environmental factors.

Topic studies in organisational behaviour should not be regarded, therefore, as entirely free-standing. Any study of organisation and management inevitably covers several aspects, and each study can be used to a greater or lesser extent to confirm generalisations made about particular topic areas. The use of the same studies to illustrate different aspects of management and organisational behaviour serves as useful revision and reinforcement, and helps to bring about a greater awareness and understanding of the subject.

No single, right answer

By now, you will probably be aware that a feature of the study of management and organisational behaviour is the invariable difficulty in identification of a single solution to a particular problem. The absence of one, right answer can make study of the subject complex and frustrating. But the area of study can also be interesting and challenging, stimulating creative thought and ideas, and it can be related to your own work experience.

A useful model for the study of management and organisational behaviour is to see the organisation as an open system; this is discussed in Chapter 3. The open system approach views the organisation within its broader, external environment and places emphasis on multiple channels of interaction. It provides a means of viewing the total organisation and of embracing different dimensions of analysis. The open system model provides a perspective for a managerial approach to organisational behaviour. It helps in the search for the most appropriate ways of influencing the behaviour of people within an organisational setting.

THE USE OF CASE STUDIES[26]

Case studies are becoming increasingly popular as a part of the study of management and organisational behaviour. There are a variety of types of case studies and they may be presented in a number of different ways. Case studies range from, for example, a brief account of events which may be actual, contrived or a combination of both; 'armchair' cases based on hypothetical but realistic situations, and developed to draw out and illustrate particular points of principle; to complex, multi-dimensional cases giving a fuller descriptive account of actual situations in real organisations. The term 'case study' may be extended to include critical incident analysis, role-play and the in-tray (or in-basket) exercise, although these are more methods of training.

A case study may require you to work on an individual basis or it may involve group work. It may also specify that you are to assume a particular role, for example as financial controller, manager or consultant.

Objectives of use of case studies

Whatever the nature or form of case studies, a major objective of their use is usually the application of theoretical knowledge to practical situations and/or the integration of knowledge drawn from a number of related disciplines or areas of study. Case studies are basically problem analysis and decision-making exercises. They provide a test of the ability to distinguish real issues from less significant matters. There is unlikely to be a single, right answer.

Case studies, therefore, provide the participants with an opportunity to demonstrate analytical ability, logical thinking, judgement and persuasiveness and skills of communication in the presentation of answers. If the case study is undertaken as a group exercise it provides, also, a means of assessing both the performance of the group as a whole and the ability of individuals to work effectively as members of the group.[27]

Guidelines on tackling case studies

The level and depth of analysis, and the type of answer required, will depend upon the particular case study and the reasons for its use. However, despite variations in the nature and format of case studies it is possible to suggest general guidelines on how to tackle them.

(i) Read the whole of the case study. Try to get a 'feel' for what it is about and note what the question(s) ask(s) you to do. Check on the time allowed.

(ii) Read the case study a second time. Look at the material carefully and try to identify with the situation. Check again on exactly what you are required to do and instructions on how to present your answer. For example, if a report

is called for, your answer should be presented in proper report form. Check whether you are to assume a specific role and if your answer is to be directed at a specified audience, for example a senior manager, the board of directors or a committee.

(iii) If there are a number of different parts to the case study you should apportion available time and 'weight' your answers accordingly.

(iv) Approach your analysis of the case study with an open mind. Be conscious of any bias or prejudice you may have and avoid any predispositions which may influence your perception of the case material. Do not jump to hasty or unfounded conclusions. Do not formulate firm opinions or solutions until you have collated all the available evidence.

(v) Adopt a brainstorming approach and take the case apart by exploring all reasonably possible considerations. Remember there may be a number of separate problems with separate causes and a number of alternative courses of action.

(vi) You may need to search for hidden meanings and issues which are not at first readily apparent. Do not, however, make things unnecessarily complicated. Do not take the 'obvious' for granted and do not neglect simple responses which help to provide a satisfactory answer to the question as worded.

(vii) A particular feature of case study work is that you are likely to have only limited information. You should, therefore, make a point of studying all the details given in the case material, first, to make certain of the facts; and second, to identify what deductions or inferences can be drawn from these facts. You may feel it necessary to make certain assumptions. If so, these assumptions should follow *reasonably* from the case material and serve only to help clarify the situation. Even if you are not specifically requested to do so, it is recommended that you make clear any necessary assumptions as part of your answer.

(viii) The case study may set out deliberately to present a tangle of information, events or situations which need to be unravelled in order to clarify links and relationships, and to distinguish causes from effects, and symptoms from problems. Concentrate on what you see to be the more important matters as opposed to any irrelevant detail or possible red herrings which may confuse the real issues.

(ix) In your analysis of the case material you may find it helpful to emphasise key words or phrases, including emotive language and actions. You may also find it helpful to:
- list the people involved and draw a pen picture of them from the available information; and
- trace the sequence and timing of events which have led to the present situation.

The use of margin notes, underlining, numbering and/or lettering, colours or highlighting pens may all be useful but you should be careful not to make your analysis confused or too complicated.

(x) Where appropriate, relate your analysis of the case material to your theoretical studies, general points of principle and the work of leading writers. It is always valuable to be able to draw upon practical experience but make sure it is relevant to the particular circumstances. You may still be able to make use of knowledge gained from experience not related directly to the case study,

but avoid the temptation to distort your perception of the situation as described to suit your own personal experience.

(xi) Bearing in mind the question, clearly identify existing or potential difficulties or problem areas and indicate where you see the need for most urgent action. Where you have identified a number of possible courses of action indicate your recommended priorities. Bear in mind also practical considerations such as timing, cost and existing personalities. Where appropriate give reasons in support of your recommendations.

(xii) Draw up a plan of key points as the basis of your answer.

(xiii) The use of visual displays such as diagrams, charts or tables may enhance the presentation of your answer. But make sure such visual displays are accurate and clear and relate directly to your analysis of the case material, and to the question as worded. Every visual display should be given a meaningful title, and serve to help the reading and interpretation of your answer. Do not be tempted to use visual displays for their own sake or to spend too much time on an over-elaborate display at the expense of more important matters.

(xiv) Allow time to read through and check your work.

The case study method is now well established in the teaching of business and management studies. Adam-Smith and Peacock have produced an excellent collection of up to date case studies grounded in real-life organisations which broadly follow the structure of, and can be used in conjunction with, this book.[28]

SYNOPSIS

■ Organisations play a major and continuing role in the lives of us all, especially with the growth of large-scale business organisations. The decisions and actions of management in organisations have an increasing impact on individuals, other organisations and the community. It is important, therefore, to understand how organisations function and the pervasive influences they exercise over the behaviour of people.

■ The behaviour of people in work organisations can be viewed in terms of inter-related dimensions relating to the individual, the group, the organisation and the environment. The study of organisational behaviour cannot be understood fully in terms of a single discipline. It is necessary to provide an interdisciplinary behavioural science approach drawing on selected aspects of psychology, sociology and anthropology.

■ Organisations are complex social systems which can be defined and studied in a number of different ways. One approach is to view organisations in terms of contrasting metaphors. Gauging the effectiveness or success of an organisation is, however, not an easy task, although one central element is the importance of achieving productivity through the effective management of people.

It is becoming increasingly important for managers to adopt an international approach and one significant development is the European Union. Managers need to recognise the importance of national culture to the study of organisational behaviour.

■ It is through the process of management that efforts of members of the organisation are co-ordinated, directed and guided towards the achievement of organisational objectives. Management is therefore the cornerstone of organisational effectiveness, and is concerned with arrangements for the carrying out of organisational processes and the execution of work. How managers exercise the responsibility for, and duties of, management is important. Attention should be focused on improving the people–organisation relationship. Management is essentially an integrating activity which permeates every facet of the operations of the organisation.

■ One particular aspect of the relationship between the individual and the organisation is the concept of the psychological contract. This is not a formal, written document but implies a series of mutual expectations and satisfaction of needs arising from the people–organisation relationship. It involves a process of giving and receiving by the individual and by the organisation. There is a continual process of explicit and implicit bargaining. The nature of expectations has an important influence on behaviour in work organisations.

■ The activities of an organisation and the job of management cannot be isolated neatly in discrete categories. The majority of actions are likely to involve a number of simultaneous functions that relate to the total process of management.

The use of case studies is becoming increasingly popular as part of the study of management and organisational behaviour. A major objective of their use is usually the application of theoretical knowledge to practical situations and/or the integration of knowledge drawn from a number of related disciplines or areas of study.

 Review and discussion questions

1 Explain your understanding of (i) the nature of organisational behaviour; and (ii) the meaning of behavioural science.

2 Suggest main headings under which can be identified interrelated factors which influence behaviour in work organisations. For each of your headings give examples from your own organisation.

3 Discuss how organisations may be viewed in terms of contrasting metaphors. Explain how you would apply these metaphors to an understanding of your own organisation.

4 Why is it increasingly important for managers to adopt an international approach? Explain the importance of national culture to the study of organisational behaviour.

5 Discuss the role of management as an integrating activity. Give your own views on the responsibility of management and the manner in which you believe this responsibility should be exercised.

6 Explain the nature of the people–organisation relationship. Why is it important to distinguish between the 'intent' and the 'implementation' of management decisions and actions?

7 Explain what is meant by the 'psychological contract'. List (i) the personal expectations you have of your own organisation; and (ii) what you believe to be the expectations of the organisation. To what extent are these lists of expectations compatible?

8 Discuss what you believe are particular difficulties presented by the study of management and organisational behaviour. Where possible give practical examples based on your own experience.

 Assignment

A first step in understanding human behaviour and the successful management of other people is to know and understand yourself. For this simple exercise you are asked to select *any one* of the following shapes that you feel is 'YOU'.

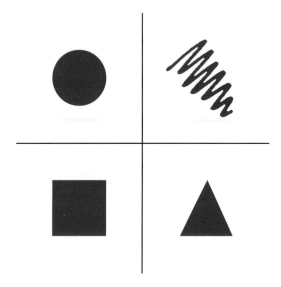

(Reproduced with permission from C. Rowe *The Management Matrix: The Psychology of Interaction*, Alfred Waller Limited (1992).)

After you have made your selection discuss in small groups the reasons which prompted you to choose that particular shape. How much agreement is there among members of your group? You should then consider and discuss the further information provided by your tutor.

CASE STUDY

Eric and Kipsy

Consider the plight of Eric

Eric is a new manager of product information for a national firm which wholesales electrical components. He's proud because he was assigned a 'tough' office right out of management training. He's challenged because he can see as clearly as everyone else in the office that the work is not getting done on time – and that mistakes are far above the 2 per cent target. And he's scared because he finds himself utterly incapable of figuring out what he ought to do to make things better.

The office is a new, one-storey building in a wooded suburban location – complete with carpeting on the floor and Muzak in the walls. The people are 35 female employees, ranging from recent high school graduates in their first job to experienced middle-aged housewives. And the job is to provide salesmen in the field with current information about price, availability, and delivery times of an exceptionally large inventory of electrical equipment and supplies.

Eric spent his first day on the job – some three months ago now – just watching and listening. While in management training, he had thought a lot about how he would handle that first day. He knew that everyone in the office would be as eager to find out what he was like as he was to learn about them and their jobs. And he wanted to make a good impression.

But Eric finally decided not to put on any false faces. The fact was that he knew virtually nothing about the people he would be managing, or the kind of work they did. So why, he asked himself, act otherwise? Besides, if the people saw that he was genuinely interested in listening to them and learning from them, perhaps that would help establish good mutual rapport between him and his people. So he would just watch, and listen, and try to learn in his first few days on the job.

The first day was fun. Soon after arriving and being introduced to the four first-level supervisors, he asked to be 'plugged in' to one of the complicated-looking operating consoles at which the women received calls from the field. A green light would blink on the console, and the information clerk would be connected to the salesman in the field – all taken care of by an out-of-sight computer, which assigned calls sequentially to the waiting clerks. The salesman would ask for information about the availability of a certain piece of equipment. The clerk would then look up the stock number of that item in a large catalogue at her side and punch the number into a keyboard on the console. Immediately, the computer would present full information about stocks and delivery times of that item on an electronic display panel on the console, and the clerk would relay the appropriate information to the salesman. When the call ended, the green light would extinguish itself, and the clerk would then wait for the light to flash again, signalling the arrival of a new call.

Eric was fascinated by both the efficiency of the operation and the pleasantness of the surroundings. His biggest worry at that point was that everything was so efficiently designed that he, as manager, would not have anything to do with his time.

He soon learned how wrong he was. When, on his second day at the office, he began to attack a pile of paperwork on his desk, he found messages from nearly a dozen field salesmen, all wanting him to return their calls. Each of these salesmen, it turned out, had a significant complaint about the product information service –

and some were obviously quite angry. Eric managed to maintain a calm, responsive stance toward the complaining salesmen, but he also felt his stomach tightening as he heard what they had to say. By the day's end, he had made a list of three general problems which seemed both frequent enough and serious enough to warrant his immediate attention and action:

1. Salesmen often were unable to get through quickly to information clerks. Since salesmen's calls usually were made from customer offices, this meant that they were left holding the telephone of a client for up to ten or fifteen minutes waiting for a clerk – while both the salesman and the customer became increasingly impatient.
2. Errors were excessive. Salesman after salesman reported that, on the basis of information provided by the clerks, they would promise delivery of materials on a specific date at a specific price – only to hear later from an irate customer that the materials had not been delivered or that the price was different from that quoted or (all too often) both.
3. The clerks were often abrupt and unfriendly to the salesmen when they called. According to more than one salesman, the clerks acted as if they were being imposed upon, rather than providing the salesmen with help in carrying out the company's business.

In the next week, as Eric attempted to track down the reasons for these difficulties, other problems came to light. First, absenteeism and turnover were extremely high. Part of the reason, it appeared, for the excessive delays was that 15 to 20 per cent of the clerks were unlikely to show up for work on any given day – especially Monday and Friday – and that up to an hour's tardiness was not uncommon. This created call 'backups' on the computer. The computer, of course, calmly held the calls for as long as necessary, oblivious as only a machine can be to the rise in tempers in the customer's office.

When absenteeism was particularly high on any given day, part-time employees would be called to fill in. Many of these individuals were not entirely familiar with the job and often did not remember some of the procedures to be used in looking up equipment numbers in the catalogue – resulting in wrong catalogue numbers and erroneous information being given to the customers. Worse, even experienced clerks had a high error rate. Eric's hope that the error problem was in the computerised information displayed on the clerks' consoles rather than a fault of the clerks themselves was clearly misplaced. And since reports of errors arrived weeks after the information had been provided (when orders failed to arrive on the customer's premises, or arrived with unexpected prices), it usually was impossible to determine who had made the mistake or why.

Finally, quite contrary to the impression he had received his first day, Eric learned that loafing on the job not only was widely practised among the clerks, but had indeed been developed into a rather elegant art form. It turned out that the clerks had devised ingenious ways to 'busy out' their consoles (i.e., to manipulate the console in order to provide the computer with a 'busy' indication when in fact the console was free). All a clerk needed to do, then, when she wanted a break from work, was to busy out her console and, if a supervisor happened to be nearby, act as if she were listening intently to a salesman on her headset.

Worse, there appeared to be a highly efficient system of informal communication among the clerks, which alerted everyone when a supervisor was about to

appear on the scene (or was monitoring calls surreptitiously from the private listening room). This informal network also was heavily used for creative co-ordination of 'personals' (i.e., brief relief from work to use the rest room) and for making sure that none of the clerks were violating the generally accepted norms about how hard one should work on a given day.

Given his own observations and impressions, Eric was not surprised when, a few weeks after he had taken over management of the office, he was visited by the regional vice-president of the company. The vice-president informed him that sales were falling companywide, and that at least part of the problem had to do with the quality of the information with which salesmen were being provided. Eric's operation was one of the most critical points of co-ordination in the entire company, he said, and it was important to everyone in the company that Eric reduce both the error rate and the number of delays salesmen currently were experiencing. The vice-president said he had enormous confidence in Eric's managerial ability, that he was sure the problems would be remedied quickly, and that he viewed Eric's future in the company with great optimism.

Eric panicked.

Within two days he had instituted a crash programme to increase efficiency, reduce call-in delays, and slash the error rate. He held a half-day meeting with his four first-level supervisors, impressing upon them the urgency of the situation and the need for them to work with their people, individually if necessary, to improve service. He held an evening meeting with all staff members (with everyone receiving both refreshments and overtime pay), at which he announced a set of officewide performance goals, and encouraged each employee to do her best to help achieve the new goals. He even had one of the supervisors construct four large signs reading Increase Efficiency (each with a line drawing of a smiling face under the words), which were placed on the four walls of the operating area.

Beginning the day after the kick-off meeting, all supervisory personnel (himself included) were to spend at least three hours a day on the floor, helping the employees improve their efficiency, making spot checks for errors, and generally doing anything possible to smooth the flow of work.

The first two days under the new programme seemed to go reasonably well: the average waiting time for incoming calls dropped slightly, spot checks of errors showed performance to be close to an acceptable level, and everyone seemed to be working hard and intently. No longer, for example, did the employees take time to look up from their work and smile or exchange a few words when Eric entered the room. That bothered him a bit because he always had enjoyed chatting with the clerks, but he accepted the loss of the smiles as a small price to pay for the increases in efficiency he hoped for.

On the third day disaster struck. Eric did not notice until midmorning that someone had carefully lettered IN before Efficiency on each of the four posters – and the smiles on the line drawings' faces had been extended into full-fledged, if subtly sarcastic, grins. Worse, everyone seemed to be studiously ignoring both the posters and him. Even the first-level supervisors said nothing to him about the posters – although Eric noticed that the supervisors, like the clerks, collected in pairs and threes for animated conversation when they were not aware of his presence. When he walked out into the operating area to start his three-hour stint, all eyes looked away and stayed there. He had never felt so completely alone.

That evening Eric stayed after everyone else had left; he removed the posters

and pondered what to do next. With possibly one or two exceptions, he was sure that the people who worked for him were decent human beings. And he knew that he himself was only trying to do his job, to get performance back up to standard. As he had told the employees at the kick-off meeting, this was in the best interest of everybody: the customers, the salesmen, the clerks, himself. So why the hostility toward him and his programme?

Gradually he began to suspect that the problems he had confronted – high errors and delays, excessive absenteeism and turnover – were merely outcroppings of some more basic difficulty. Perhaps, he thought, he had attacked the symptom rather than the disease.

But what was the disease? He considered each of the possibilities. He knew that there was a lot of complaining about the pay and the inflexibility of the hours. But the pay was actually very good, higher than for almost any other non-skilled job available to females in the suburban area – and every year there was a raise for everyone, which almost always was greater than the increase in the cost of living.

The hours were a problem, he knew. But even those employees who complained the most knew that he had tried mightily to convince the regional office to let him introduce a flexible scheduling plan that would allow the employees to better co-ordinate their personal and work lives. He had been told that company policy dictated an 8:30 to 5:00 workday and that hours (just like all other personnel policies) were centrally controlled in the interest of companywide efficiency and regularity. Eric didn't like the decision (he felt he needed to be given much more personal authority to be able to run his own operation effectively). He did, however, understand that there was some need for central co-ordination of policy, and he thought that the employees also should be able to see the necessity for it. The hours, he decided, could not conceivably be the root of all the difficulties.

He considered briefly the possibility that the employees were simply not capable of doing the work at satisfactory levels of speed and accuracy. But he knew that could not be the case: all had passed a company-administered ability test before they were hired and all had gone through a rigorous training programme which covered every contingency a person conceivably could face as an information clerk. Besides, the job was not all that difficult; he personally suspected that even the requirement of a high school diploma was superfluous, that anybody who could read and write could handle the job without significant difficulty. No, lack of ability was not the core of the problem.

Indeed, as Eric reflected further, it seemed that the reverse could be true: that perhaps the job was so simple and routine that the clerks were bored – and therefore chose to be absent a lot and to loaf whenever they could on the job. But surely the high pay and the pleasantness of the work setting should more than compensate for any such feelings of boredom. Also, holding errors below 2 per cent could provide a real challenge. And besides, loafing on the job would itself probably be more boring than working.

Supervision? It seemed most unlikely that this was the root of the difficulty. Each of the four supervisors had been information clerks themselves (although in the old days, when there was no computer and you had to look everything up in a set of reference manuals), and they knew the job inside out. Moreover, he knew from talking with the supervisors that they were genuinely committed to spending as much time as needed to help each clerk do as good a job as possible. Eric had observed each of them working on the floor many times, and there was no ques-

tion in his mind about how much time and energy they spent in assisting and developing individual clerks.

Then what? Maybe, he finally concluded, the key was Kipsy. Kipsy had been a thorn in his side (the supervisors agreed) ever since Eric started the job. Although she herself had been working as a clerk for less than a year, she already had emerged as one of the informal leaders of the workforce. Eric found himself agreeing with one of his supervisors who had suggested over coffee one morning that Kipsy alone created as many problems as any other dozen clerks taken together. He was 99 per cent confident, for example, that it was she who had mutilated his signs. And he recently had been hearing rumblings that Kipsy was informally talking up the possibility of the clerks unionising, probably even affiliating with some national outfit that had no understanding of the local situation.

He had tried to talk with her once. She had showed up unannounced at his office one day, with a long list of complaints about him and the work. His approach had been to listen and hear her out, to see what was troubling her, and then to do something about it – for her own sake, as well as for her supervisor and the company. Thinking back now, however, the main thing he remembered about the conversation (if you could call it a conversation) was her incredible anger. He was perplexed that he could not remember specifically what it was that she had been so mad about. Eric did recall telling her, as the conversation ended, that if she worked hard and effectively on her job for a year or two she would become eligible for enrolment in a company-run training course for a higher paying job. But again, he could not recall whether or not that had interested her.

In any case, it was clear that Kipsy was the link pin in the informal network among the clerks – and if they were turning against him and the company, you could be pretty sure that she was right in the middle of it. The question, though, was what to do about it. Fire her? In a very important sense, that would be admitting defeat – and publicly. Talk to her again? That probably would result in nothing more than his getting another load of hostility dumped in his lap, and that he didn't need.

Eric was in trouble, and he knew it. He realised it first when he could not think of a good way to repair the damage that his new motivational programme apparently had created. But he knew it for sure when he found that he was no longer thinking about work except when he was actually at his desk in the office and had to do so. When he started this job he had expected to become totally immersed in it; indeed, he had wanted to be. But now he was psychologically fleeing from his job as much as the clerks seemed to be fleeing from theirs.

Consider the plight of Kipsy

Kipsy has been an information clerk in Eric's office for almost a year. In that year she has become increasingly frustrated and unhappy in her work – and she doesn't know quite what to do about it. Things certainly have not worked out as she had expected them to. She had applied for the job because a friend told her that the company was a great place to work, that the pay was excellent, and that the people she would be working with were friendly and stimulating. Moreover, it was well known that the company was growing and expanding at a fast clip. That, Kipsy concluded, meant that there was a good chance for advancement for anyone who showed some initiative and performed well on the job.

Advancement was important. Throughout her high school years, Kipsy had always been seen as a leader by her classmates, and she had enjoyed that role

much more than she had let on at the time. Her grades had been good, mostly As and Bs, and she knew if she had pushed a bit harder she could have gotten almost all As. But she had decided that participation in school activities, doing after-school volunteer work, and (importantly) having friends and learning from them was just as important as grades. So she had deliberately let the grades slip a little.

The man who interviewed Kipsy for the job was extremely nice – and what he said about the job confirmed her high hopes for it. He even took her into the room filled with the complicated-looking consoles and let her watch some of the people at work. It seemed like it would be great fun – though perhaps a little scary – working with all that computerised equipment. She didn't know anything at all about computers.

When they returned to the hiring area from their visit to the console room, Kipsy's employment tests had been scored. The interviewer told her that she had scored in the top 10 per cent of all applicants for the job, that all signs pointed to a great future for her in the company, and that she could start training the next day if she wanted. Kipsy accepted the job on the spot.

Training for the job was just as exciting as she had expected it to be. The console seemed awfully complicated, and there was no end to the special requests and problems she had to learn how to deal with. The other people working on the job also were very nice, and Kipsy soon had made many new friends.

But after a few weeks the fun wore off. The kinds of difficult problems she had been trained to solve on the console seemed never to occur. Instead, the calls began to fall into what Kipsy experienced as an endless routine: the green light flashes, the salesman gives the name of a piece of equipment, you look it up in the book and punch the number on the keyboard, you recite the information displayed by the computer back to the salesman, and the green light goes off. Then you wait, maybe only a second, maybe five minutes, for the light to go on again. And you never know how long you are going to wait, so you can never think or read or even carry on an uninterrupted conversation with the girl next to you. It was, Kipsy decided, pretty awful.

Worse, many of her new friends were quitting. The rumour was that nearly 80 per cent of the people on the job quit every year, and Kipsy was beginning to understand why. Neither she nor any of her friends knew of anybody who had been promoted to management or to a better job from the ranks of the console operators, at least not in the last couple of years. And Kipsy was smart enough to realise that in time the whole operation would be automated – with salesmen punching in their requests for information directly from the field – at which time, she surmised, she and everyone else who had stuck out the job in hopes of something better would be laid off.

The only good thing about the job, she concluded, was that she was becoming the informal leader of the work group – and that had its moments. Like the time one of the girls had her planned vacation postponed on short notice, supposedly because absenteeism was so high that everyone had to be available for work merely to keep up with the flow of incoming calls. The girl (and two of her friends) had come to Kipsy and asked what she could do about it. Kipsy had marched straight away into the manager's office with the girl, asked for an explanation, and got him to agree to let her take the vacation as planned. That felt awfully good.

But such moments were too infrequent to keep her interested and involved – so she found herself making up interesting things to do, just to keep from going crazy. She developed a humorous list, Rules for Handling Salesmen, which she surrepti-

tiously passed around the office, partly in fun but also partly to help the new girls (there always were a lot of new girls) learn the tricks necessary to keep from getting put down by the always-impatient, sometimes-crude salesmen. She also found that girls having difficulties on the job (again, usually the new workers) often came to her rather than to the supervisors for help – which she gladly gave, despite the obvious disapproval of the supervisors. She even found herself assuming the role of monitor for the group, prodding girls who were not doing their share of the work, and showing new girls who were working too hard the various tricks that could be done to keep the pace of work at a reasonable level (such as 'busying out' the machine, when you just couldn't take any more and needed a break).

That was all fun, but as she reflected on it, it just didn't compensate for the basic monotony of the work or for the picky, almost schoolmarmish attitude of the supervisors. So she was buoyed up when she heard that a new manager was coming, fresh out of school. The rumour mill had it that he was one of the top young managers in the company, and she decided he surely would shake things up a bit as soon as he found out how miserable it was for people who worked in the office.

Eric's first few days on the job confirmed her high hopes for him: he seemed genuinely interested in learning about the job and in hearing what changes people had to suggest. And he talked directly to the people doing the work, rather than keeping safely out of sight and listening only to what the schoolmarms said people thought and felt. All to the good.

Her opinion about Eric's managerial abilities dropped sharply a few weeks later, however, by what came to be known around the office as the 'flexible hours fiasco'. Kipsy and two other girls had come up with a proposal for prescheduling work hours so that there would be substantially more flexibility in the hours each person would work. The plan was designed so that management would know at least two days ahead of time who would be coming in when. The only cost to the company would be some additional clerical time spent on actually doing the scheduling, and Kipsy had gotten agreement from almost everyone in the office to share in the clerical tasks, on their own time.

Eric had seemed receptive to the plan when Kipsy first presented it to him, and said only that he would have to check it out with higher-ups before instituting it. Nothing more was heard about the plan for about two weeks. Finally Eric called Kipsy into his office and (after a good deal of talking around the issue) reported that 'the people upstairs won't let us do it'.

Kipsy's respect for Eric plummeted. Rather than give a flat no, he had wiggled around for two weeks, and then lamely blamed the decision on 'the people upstairs'. She knew very well that the manager of an office could run his office however he pleased, so long as the work got done. And here was Eric, the bright new manager on the way up: he wouldn't go along with an employee-initiated proposal for making their life at work more bearable; he refused to take personal responsibility for that decision; and he even had the gall to ask Kipsy to help 'explain to the girls' how hard he had tried to get the plan approved, and how sad he was that it had been turned down. Kipsy's response was a forced smile, an elaborately sympathetic 'Of course I'll help', and a quick escape from his office.

She took the Monday of the next week off, to think about whether or not she should quit and try to find a better job. At the end of the day, she made up a list of what she wanted from her work, what she was getting, and whether or not things would improve if she stuck with the job:

My wants	Am I getting them?	Hope for improvement
1. Good pay	OK, not great	Little, till my hair turns grey
2. Interesting people	Fine	No change, except friends keep leaving
3. Interesting work	Dismal	Zero
4. Chance to show initiative and personal responsibility	None	No hope
5. Chance to contribute to an organisation I believe in	Low	Ha!

The next day, Tuesday, she took her list and went to see Eric. After listening to a fatherly lecture on the importance of not missing work, especially on Mondays when the work load was heaviest, she began to tell him how upset she was. She told him that the only thing she got from working hard on the job was a backache every evening. She told him she had been misled about the chances for promotion on the job. And she asked him, as politely as she knew how, what he would suggest she do.

Eric's response blew her mind. There was a new programme, he said, in which people who did well on entry-level jobs for a few years could apply for advanced training in a technical specialty. This training would be done at company expense and on company time, and would qualify her for a promotional-type transfer whenever openings in her chosen specialty developed. If she worked hard and was rated high on the quarterly supervisory assessments, Eric said, he would be prepared to nominate her for the advanced training. But it was important, he emphasised, that she behave herself – no unnecessary absences, high work productivity, good ratings by her supervisors. Otherwise, she certainly would not be selected by 'the people upstairs' for the new programme.

Something snapped. What kind of a fool did he think she was? How long did he expect she would be willing to wait for a 'chance to be nominated' for some foggy 'technical training programme'? She started telling him, no holds barred now, no false politeness, exactly what she thought of the job, of the supervisors, even of the way he was running the office. And the more she talked, the madder she got – until finally she got up, almost in tears, and ran out leaving behind only the reverberations of a well-slammed door.

She was ashamed later, of course. She knew she would be, and she was. But she also was too embarrassed to go up to Eric and apologise. Which was too bad, because she suspected that behind it all Eric was probably a decent man, and maybe even somebody she could learn to like and respect – if only he would let himself be human once in a while. But she knew there was nothing she could do to change the way Eric did his job; the first move clearly had to be his. It could be a long wait, Kipsy decided. In the meantime she would come to work, try to

minimise her backaches and upsets, and continue to think about finding another job. Of one thing she was sure: no more 'bright ideas' for improving things at the office would come from her; that got you nothing but grief. And no longer was she going to worry so much if she happened to misremember a catalogue number or accidentally disconnect a salesman. If all they wanted was a machine, that was all they were going to get.

Kipsy found herself much less able to be cavalier about her work than she had thought she could be. As hard as she tried not to care when she made errors, the distressing fact was that mistakes still *did* bother her. And she still felt like an unreconstituted sinner when she was a few minutes late for work.

It took the 'increase efficiency' programme to finally break her completely. It was not to be believed: an evening meeting, complete with supposedly inspirational messages from all the bosses about how we all had to pitch in and help the company make more money; grade school posters on all the walls imploring people to work harder; and, to top it all off, all the bosses, even Eric, standing around hours at a time looking over everybody's shoulders, day after day.

Did Eric really believe that treating people like children would make them work harder? She could have told him straight out beforehand that the programme would make things worse rather than better. But of course he didn't ask.

Kipsy went on the offensive. She knew it was wrong, but she also knew she had to do *something* to preserve her sanity. Her first target was the signs; she and another girl stayed late in the rest room and, when everybody else had left, carefully changed the lettering of the signs to read 'Increase INEfficiency', and turned the smiling face on each sign into an obviously sarcastic grin. Kipsy also began discussing with the other girls the possibility of forming a club, which would be partly social but which could possibly develop into a vehicle for doing some hard-nosed bargaining with Eric.

It didn't work. Changing the signs, after the initial thrill, only made her feel more guilty. And even though virtually everyone in the office shared her dismay about the monotony of the work and was as upset as she about Eric and his 'increase efficiency' programme, nobody was very excited about forming a club. Some thought it wouldn't have any impact and would be a waste of time; others thought it sounded like the first step towards unionisation, which they didn't want. So the club idea died.

Kipsy was depressed. What should she do? Quit? Her preliminary explorations had not yet turned up any jobs which were much better – and most paid less than this one. Besides, to quit would be to admit publicly her inability to change anything in the office. She was supposed to be the leader of the girls in the office; she shouldn't become just one more tally towards the 80 per cent a year who left.

Talk to Eric again? She seriously doubted that he would listen to one word she said. And she doubted equally seriously that she could keep herself from blowing up again at him – which would accomplish nothing and help no one.

Shut up and stick it out? That was what she had been trying for the last three months. Without noticeable success.

What, then?

(a) Analyse the issues of organisational behaviour which are raised in this case study.

(b) Suggest solutions to the problems faced by Eric and Kipsy.

Notes and references

1. A summary of some merits in understanding organisational behaviour theory and the role of management is given in Mullins, L. J. 'The Organisation and the Individual', *Administrator*, vol. 7, no. 4, April 1987, pp. 11–14.
2. See, for example: Luthans, F. *Organisational Behaviour*, Sixth edition, McGraw-Hill (1992).
3. For further details of recurring themes in organisational behaviour and premises about life in organisations see, for example: Porter, L. W., Lawler, E. E. and Hackman, J. R. *Behaviour in Organisations*, McGraw-Hill (1975).
4. Morgan, G. *Images of Organization*, Sage (1986).
5. Dunderdale, P. 'Analysing Effective Organisations', *Professional Manager*, September 1994, pp. 23–5.
6. Handy, C. B. *Understanding Organizations*, Fourth edition, Penguin (1993).
7. Stewart, R. *Managing Today and Tomorrow*, Macmillan (1991).
8. Sieff, Marcus (Lord Sieff of Brimpton) *Management The Marks & Spencer Way*, Fontana Collins (1991).
9. Goldthorpe, J. H. *et al. The Affluent Worker*, Cambridge University Press (1968).
10. Drucker, P. F. *Management*, Pan Books (1979) p. 14.
11. Egan, G. 'The Shadow Side', *Management Today*, September 1993, pp. 33–8.
12. McGregor, D. *The Human Side of Enterprise*, Penguin (1987).
13. See, for example, Schein, E. H. *Organizational Psychology*, Third edition, Prentice-Hall (1988).
14. French, W. L., Kast, F. E. and Rosenzweig, J. E. *Understanding Human Behaviour in Organisations*, Harper and Row (1985) pp. 42–3.
15. Kotter, J. P. 'The Psychological Contract: Managing the Joining-Up Process', *California Management Review*, vol. 15, no. 3, 1973, pp. 91–9.
16. Stewart, R. *Managing Today and Tomorrow*, Macmillan (1991).
17. Turton, R. *Behaviour in a Business Context*, Chapman and Hall (1991).
18. Lockhart, T. 'Human Resource Management in the Single European market', *MBA Review*, December 1990, pp. 17-21.
19. Robbins, S. *Essentials of Organizational Behaviour*, Third edition, Prentice-Hall (1992) p. 14.
20. French, R. 'The Development and Structuring of Personnel Departments in Britain and West Germany', Unpublished PhD thesis, Nottingham Polytechnic, 1985.
21. Welford, R. and Prescott, K. *European Business: An Issue-Based Approach*, Second edition, Pitman (1994).
22. Hickson, D., McMillan, C., Azumi, K. and Horvath, D. 'Grounds for Comparative Organisation Theory: Quicksands or Hardcore?' in Lammers, C. and Hickson, D. (eds) *Organisations Alike and Unlike*, Routledge and Kegan Paul (1979).
23. Kerr, C., Dunlop, J. T., Harbison, F. and Myers, C. A. *Industrialism and Industrial Man*, Penguin (1973).
24. Hofstede, G. *Culture's Consequences: International Differences in Work-Related Values*, Sage Publications (1980).
25. Trompenaars, F. *Riding The Waves of Culture*, Nicholas Brealey (1993).
26. Based on Mullins, L. J. 'Tackling Case Studies', *Student Administrator*, vol. 1, no. 5, June 1984.
27. See, for example: Easton, G. *Learning From Case Studies*, Second edition, Prentice-Hall (1992).
28. Adam-Smith, D. and Peacock, A. (eds) *Cases in Organisational Behaviour*, Pitman (1994).

2 APPROACHES TO ORGANISATION AND MANAGEMENT

Management is a discursive subject and much has been written about it. The study of organisations and their management has, therefore, to proceed on a broad front. No single approach to organisation and management provides all the answers. It is the comparative study of the different approaches which will yield benefits to the manager. The study of organisations, their structure and management is important for the manager. Identification of major trends in management and organisational behaviour, and the work of leading writers, provide a perspective on concepts and ideas discussed in more detail in other chapters.[1]

 Learning objectives

To:

- Explain the relationships between management theory and practice;

- Identify major trends in the development of organisational behaviour and management thinking;

- Contrast main features of different approaches to organisation and management;

- Evaluate the relevance of these different approaches to the present-day management of organisations;

- Assess the value of the study of management theory and different approaches to organisation and management;

- Recognise the relationship between the development of theory, behaviour in organisations and management practice;

- Provide a basis for consideration of aspects of management and organisational behaviour discussed in following chapters.

Worth thinking about

'All these different theories and ideas about organisations and management, but what practical value do they have?' . . . 'How else would you attempt to learn about the complexities of management and organisational behaviour? Without some framework of study it would be like trying to catch water in a sieve.'

MANAGEMENT THEORY

Writing on organisation and management, in some form or another, can be traced back thousands of years.[2] However, the systematic development of management thinking is viewed, generally, as dating from the end of the nineteenth century with the emergence of large industrial organisations, and the ensuing problems associated with their structure and management.

A central part of the study of organisation and management is the development of management thinking and what might be termed management theory. The application of theory brings about change in actual behaviour. Managers reading the work of leading writers on the subject might see in their ideas and conclusions a message about how they should behave. This will influence their attitudes towards management practice. As *McGregor* puts it:

> Every managerial act rests on assumptions, generalizations, and hypotheses – that is to say, on theory. Our assumptions are frequently implicit, sometimes quite unconscious, often conflicting; nevertheless, they determine our predictions that if we do *a*, *b* will occur. Theory and practice are inseparable.[3]

Importance of management theory

The study of management theory is important, therefore, because:

- What leading writers say is an important part of the study of management;
- It is necessary to view the interrelationships between the development of theory, behaviour in organisations and management practice;
- An understanding of the development of management thinking helps in understanding principles underlying the process of management;
- Knowledge of the history helps in understanding the nature of management and organisational behaviour, and reasons for the attention given to main topic areas;
- Many of the earlier ideas are of continuing importance to the manager and later ideas on management tend to incorporate earlier ideas and conclusions.

DEVELOPMENTS IN MANAGEMENT AND ORGANISATIONAL BEHAVIOUR

It is helpful, therefore, to trace major developments in management and organisational behaviour, and what has led to the concentration of attention on such topics as structure, motivation, groups, leadership and organisation development.

Miner makes the point that the more that is known about organisations and their methods of operation, the better the chances of dealing effectively with them. Understanding may be more advanced than prediction, but both provide the opportunity to influence or to manage the future. Theory provides a sound basis for action.[4] However, if action is to be effective, the theory must be adequate and appropriate to the task and to improved organisational performance. It must be a 'good' theory.

In order to help identify main trends in the development of organisational behaviour and management theory it is usual to categorise the work of writers into various 'approaches', based on their views of organisations, their structure and management. This provides a framework in which to direct study and focus attention on the progression of ideas concerned with improving organisational performance.

A framework of analysis

There are, however, many ways of categorising these various approaches. For example, *Skipton* attempts a classification of eleven main schools of management theory.[5] Whatever form of categorisation is adopted it is possible to identify a number of other approaches, or at least sub-divisions of approaches, and cross-grouping among the various approaches. The choice of a particular categorisation is therefore largely at the discretion of the observer.

The following analysis will revolve around a framework based on four main approaches of:

**Fig. 2.1
Main approaches to organisation, structure and management**

- Classical
- Human Relations
- Systems
- Contingency (*See* Fig. 2.1)

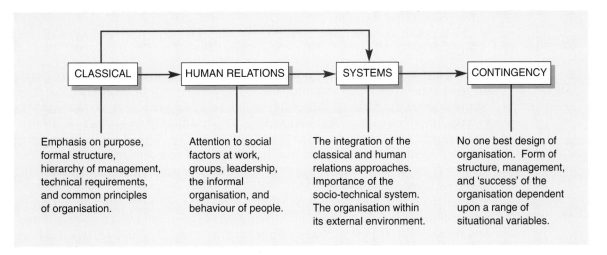

THE CLASSICAL APPROACH

The classical writers thought of the organisation in terms of its purpose and formal structure. They placed emphasis on the planning of work, the technical requirements of the organisation, principles of management, and the assumption of rational and logical behaviour. The analysis of organisation in this manner is associated with work carried out initially in the early part of this century, by such writers as *Taylor, Fayol, Urwick, Mooney and Reiley*, and *Brech*.

A clear understanding of the purpose of an organisation is seen as essential to understanding how the organisation works and how its methods of working can be improved. Identification of general objectives would lead to the clarification of purposes and responsibilities at all levels of the organisation, and to the most effective structure. Attention is given to the division of work, the clear definition of duties and responsibilities, and maintaining specialisation and co-ordination. Emphasis is on a hierarchy of management and formal organisational relationships.

Sets of principles

The classical writers (also variously known as the formal or scientific management writers – although scientific management is really only a part of the classical approach) were concerned with improving the organisation structure as a means of increasing efficiency. They emphasised the importance of principles for the design of a logical structure of organisation. Their writings were in a normative style and they saw these principles as a set of 'rules' offering general solutions to common problems of organisation and management.

Most classical writers had their own set of principles but among the most publicised are those of *Fayol* and *Urwick*. Fayol recognised there was no limit to the principles of management but in his writing advocated fourteen.[6] Urwick originally specified eight principles, but these were revised to ten in his later writing.[7] (*See* Chapters 10 and 12.)

Mooney and Reiley set out a number of common principles which relate to all types of organisations. They place particular attention on:

- **The principle of co-ordination** – the need for people to act together with unity of action, the exercise of authority and the need for discipline;
- **The scalar principle** – the hierarchy of organisation, the grading of duties and the process of delegation;
- **The functional principle** – specialisation and the distinction between different kinds of duties.[8]

Brech attempts to provide a practical approach to organisation structure based on tried general principles as opposed to the concentration on specific cases or complex generalisations of little value to the practising manager. He sets out the various functions in the organisation and the definition of formal organisational relationships.[9] Although clearly a strong supporter of the formal approach in some of his views such as, for example, on the principle of span of control, Brech is less definite than other classical writers and recognises a degree of flexibility according to the particular situation.

Brech does, however, place great emphasis on the need for written definition of responsibilities and the value of job descriptions as an aid to effective organisation and delegation. This work builds on from the ideas of earlier writers, such as

Urwick, and provides, therefore, a comprehensive view of the classical approach to organisation and management.

Evaluation of the classical approach

The classical writers have been criticised generally for not taking sufficient account of personality factors, and for creating an organisation structure in which people can exercise only a limited control over their work environment. The idea of sets of principles to guide managerial action has also been subject to much criticism. For example, *Simon* writes: 'Organisational design is not unlike architectural design. It involves creating large, complex systems having multiple goals. It is illusory to suppose that good designs can be created by using the so-called "principles" of classical organisation theory.'[10] Research studies have also expressed doubt about the effectiveness of these principles when applied in practice.[11]

However, although the work of the classical writers is sometimes regarded as an out-of-date approach it does focus attention on important factors in the study of organisation and management. Technical and structural factors are important considerations in improving organisational performance. Yet, whilst attention to formal structure is important, it is also necessary to consider the people who work within the structure.

The classical approach attempts to provide some common principles applicable to all organisations. These principles are still of some relevance in that they provide general guidelines to the structuring and efficiency of organisations. They provide a useful starting point in attempting to analyse the effectiveness of the design of organisation structure. But, the application of these principles must take full account of:

● the particular situational variables of each individual organisation; and
● the psychological and social factors relating to members of the organisation.

Major sub-groupings

Two major 'sub-groupings' of the classical approach are:

(i) Scientific management, and
(ii) Bureaucracy.

SCIENTIFIC MANAGEMENT

Many of the classical writers were concerned with the improvement of management as a means of increasing productivity. At this time emphasis was on the problem of obtaining increased productivity from individual workers through the technical structuring of the work organisation and the provision of monetary incentives as the motivator for higher levels of output. A major contributor to this approach was *F. W. Taylor* (1856–1917) – the 'father' of scientific management.[12] Taylor believed that in the same way that there is a best machine for each job, so there is a best working method by which people should undertake their jobs. He considered that all work processes could be analysed into discrete tasks and that by scientific method it was possible to find the 'one best way' to perform each task. Each job was broken down into component parts, each part timed, and the parts rearranged into the most efficient method of working.

<table>
<tr><td>

**Principles
to guide
management**

</td><td>

Taylor was a believer in the rational–economic needs concept of motivation. He believed that if management acted on his ideas, work would become more satisfying and profitable for all concerned. Workers would be motivated by obtaining the highest possible wages through working in the most efficient and productive way. Taylor was concerned with finding more efficient methods and procedures for co-ordination and control of work. He set out a number of principles to guide management. These principles are usually summarised as:

</td></tr>
</table>

- The development of a true science for each person's work;
- The scientific selection, training and development of the workers;
- Co-operation with the workers to ensure work is carried out in the prescribed way;
- The division of work and responsibility between management and the workers.

In his famous studies at the Bethlehem Steel Corporation, Taylor, who was appointed as a management consultant, applied his ideas on scientific management to the handling of pig iron. A group of 75 men were loading an average of $12\frac{1}{2}$ tons per man per day. Taylor selected a Dutch labourer, called Schmidt, who he reported to be a 'high-priced' man with a reputation for placing a high value on money, and a man of limited mental ability. By following detailed instructions on when to pick up the pig iron and walk, and when to sit and rest, and with no back talk, Schmidt increased his output to $47\frac{1}{2}$ tons per day. He maintained this level of output throughout the three years of the study. In return Schmidt received a 60 per cent increase in wages compared with that paid to the other men.

One by one other men were selected and trained to handle pig iron at the rate of $47\frac{1}{2}$ tons per day and in return they received 60 per cent more wages. Taylor drew attention to the need for the scientific selection of the workers. When the other labourers in the group were trained in the same method only one in eight was physically capable of the effort of loading $47\frac{1}{2}$ tons per day, although there was a noticeable increase in their level of output.

**Reactions
against
scientific
management**

There were strong criticisms of, and reaction against, scientific management methods from the workers who found the work boring and requiring little skill. Despite these criticisms Taylor attempted to expand the implementation of his ideas in the Bethlehem Steel Corporation. But fears of mass redundancies persuaded the management to request Taylor to moderate his activities. However, Taylor's belief in his methods was so strong that he would not accept management's interference and eventually his services were dispensed with.

Scientific management was applied for a time in other countries with similar criticisms and hostile reactions. The ideas of scientific management were also adopted in the American Watertown Arsenal despite the lingering doubts of the controller. He was not convinced about the benefits of paying bonuses based on methods which reduced time taken to complete a job; also the workers reacted unfavourably to time and motion studies, and he was fearful of a strike. The controller eventually gave way, however, and the approach of scientific management was adopted – to be followed almost immediately by a strike of moulding workers. The strike at Watertown Arsenal led to an investigation of Taylor's methods by a House of Representatives Committee which reported in 1912.

The conclusion of the committee was that scientific management did provide some useful techniques and offered valuable organisational suggestions, but gave

production managers a dangerously high level of uncontrolled power. The studies at Watertown Arsenal were resumed but the unions still retained an underlying hostility towards scientific management. A subsequent attitude survey among the workers revealed a broad level of resentment and hostility, by both union and non-union members, to scientific management methods. Arising from this report Taylor's methods of time study were banned in defence establishments by the Senate.

Functional foremen

Taylor also put forward the idea of functional foremanship under which workers would be responsible simultaneously to eight different, specialist first line supervisors. The eight supervisors were divided into two groups: **Planning**, concerned with (i) order of work, (ii) instruction cards, (iii) time and costing and (iv) discipline; and **Performance**, concerned with (v) gang boss, (vi) speed boss, (vii) repair boss and (viii) inspector. The idea of functional foremen represented a practical application of the idea of specialisation and the belief that each person's work should, as far as possible, be confined to a single leading function. However, such an arrangement gives rise to problems of co-ordination, role conflict and unity of command. The idea of functional foremanship appears not to have become very popular and to have had little application in practice.

Taylorism as management control

There has also been considerable interest in 'Taylorism' as representing a system of management control over workers. Taylor placed emphasis on the content of a 'fair day's work' and on optimising the level of workers' productivity. A major obstacle to this objective was 'systematic soldiering' and what Taylor saw as the deliberate attempt by workers to promote their own best interests and to keep employers ignorant of how fast work, especially piece-rate work, could be carried out.

According to *Braverman*, scientific management starts from the capitalist point of view and method of production, and the adaptation of labour to the needs of capital. Taylor's work was more concerned with the organisation of labour than with the development of technology. A distinctive feature of Taylor's thought was the concept of management control.[13] Braverman suggests that Taylor's conclusion was that workers should be controlled not only by the giving of orders and maintenance of discipline, but also by removing from them any decisions about the manner in which their work was to be carried out. By division of labour, and by dictating precise stages and methods for every aspect of work performance, management could gain control of the actual process of work. The rationalisation of production processes and division of labour tends to result in the de-skilling of work and this may be a main strategy of the employer.[14]

RELEVANCE OF SCIENTIFIC MANAGEMENT

While Taylor's work is often criticised today it should be remembered that he was writing at a time of industrial reorganisation and the emergence of large, complex organisations with new forms of technology. Taylor's main concern was with the efficiency of both workers and management. He believed his methods of scientific management would lead to improved management–labour relations, and contribute to improved industrial efficiency and prosperity.

Taylor adopted an instrumental view of human behaviour together with the application of standard procedures of work. Workers were regarded as rational, economic beings motivated directly by monetary incentives linked to the level of work output. Workers were viewed as isolated individuals and more as units of production to be handled almost in the same way as machines. Hence, scientific management is often referred to as a machine theory model.

The work of Taylor continues to evoke much comment and extreme points of view. For example, *Rose* suggests that:

> It is difficult to discuss the 'contribution' of F. W. Taylor to the systematic study of industrial behaviour in an even-tempered way. The sheer silliness from a modern perspective of many of his ideas, and barbarities they led to when applied in industry, encourage ridicule and denunciation.[15]

The theme of inefficiency

Rose argues that Taylor's diagnosis of the industrial situation was based on the simple theme of inefficiency. Among his criticisms are that Taylor selected the best workers for his experiments and assumed that workers who were not good at one particular task would be best at some other task. There is, however, no certainty of this in practice. Taylor regarded workers from an engineering viewpoint and as machines, but the one best way of performing a task is not always the best method for every worker.

The reduction of physical movement to find the one best way is not always beneficial and some 'wasteful' movements are essential to the overall rhythm of work. Rose also argues that the concept of a fair day's pay for a fair day's work is not purely a technical matter. It is also a notion of social equity and not in keeping with a scientific approach.

On the other hand, however, *Drucker* claims that:

> Frederick Winslow Taylor may prove a more useful prophet for our times than we yet recognize...Taylor's greatest impact may still be ahead...the under-developed and developing countries are now reaching the stage where they need Taylor and 'scientific management'...But the need to study Taylor anew and apply him may be the greatest in the developed countries.[16]

According to Drucker, the central theme of Taylor's work was not inefficiency but the need to substitute industrial warfare by industrial harmony. Taylor sought to do this through: higher wages from increased output; the removal of physical strain from doing work the wrong way; development of the workers and the opportunity for them to undertake tasks they were capable of doing; and elimination of the boss by the duty of management to help the workers.

Drucker also suggests that Taylor's idea of functional foremen can be related to what is now known as matrix organisation (matrix organisation is discussed in Chapter 10). Support for Drucker's views appears to come from *Locke* who asserts that much of the criticism of Taylor is based on a misunderstanding of the precepts and that many of his ideas are accepted by present-day managers.[17]

Impetus to management thinking

Whatever the opinions on scientific management, Taylor and his disciples have left to modern management the legacy of such practices as work study, organisation and methods, payment by results, management by exception and production control. The development of mass assembly line work, invented by Henry Ford in 1913 ('Fordism') and which dominated production methods in western economies can be seen to have many common links with the ideas of scientific management.[18]

The principles of Taylor's scientific approach to management appear still to have relevance today. We can still see examples of Taylorism alive and well, and management practices based on the philosophy of his ideas. As an example, Figure 2.2. shows a 'Hanger Insertion Programme' for a large American department store.

Whatever else Taylor did, at least he gave a major impetus to the development of management thinking and the later development of organisational behaviour. It is difficult to argue against the general line of Taylor's principles but they are

KEY IDEAS

Hanger Insertion

- The new programme involving the process of hanging merchandise on hangers efficiently and effectively

The purposes of this new programme:

- To assist the stores in better customer service – by having the merchandise ready to go on the floor, saving space in the stockroom, and creating customer goodwill.
- To increase the units per hour produced.
- To perform the job duties as efficiently and effectively as possible.

TECHNIQUES

- Keep the necessary items needed in your range. All supplies should be within arm's reach. For example, place the trash bin next to you, have your hanger supply near you. You should not need to take any steps.

- For ANY prepack, Unpack merchandise in the prepack or unpack enough of the prepack in the amount to be placed on the trolley, tearing the plastic off of the entire group.
 Lay the merchandise out on the unpack table, and if applies, unfold each piece, removing tissue etc.
 Insert the hangers and hang *the entire group* of merchandise at once.

- When removing hangers from the merchandise, have the merchandise in a group on the unpack table; remove these hangers working from the front to the back.

- When inserting hangers, as a group, insert working from the back to the front of the group on the unpack table. Hang pieces as a group.

- If merchandise is bulky, Leave merchandise folded, **remove all of the plastic at once**, insert hangers for merchandise unpacked, hang all pieces on the trolley, then remove at the same time all excess plastic, clips etc.

- When possible, it is more efficient to remove **all** the plastic at once after the merchandise is hung.

- When hanging pants, skirts, etc., slip the hanger over both sides of the piece of merchandise and push metal clips down at the *same* time. This will alleviate additional steps.

- When pants are in plastic and hangers have to be removed, hang them first, take pants off hangers, lay on table, throw away plastic, insert hangers.

- When having to button pants, skirts, etc., take the top of the button through the hole first. This makes the process flow easier and more efficient.

- Put your supply of hangers in the cover of a tote and place on the table next to you.

- Each trolley must have the same number of garments. Each space between the pegs doesn't.

Fig. 2.2
Hanger Insertion
Programme – an
example of scientific
management

subject to misuse. What is important is the context and manner in which such principles are put into effect. For example, there is arguably one best way *technically* to perform a job. But account needs to be taken of human behaviour. People tend to have their preferred way of working and the need for variety. Provided work is carried out safely and to a satisfactory standard and completed on time, to what extent should management *insist* on the 'one best way'?

It seems that Taylor did not so much ignore (as is often suggested) but was more unaware of the complexity of human behaviour in organisations and the importance of the individual's own feelings and sentiments, group working, managerial behaviour and the work environment. However, we now have greater knowledge about social effects within the work organisation, and about the value of money, incentives, motivation, and job satisfaction and performance.

BUREAUCRACY

A form of structure to be found in many large-scale organisations is bureaucracy. Because of its importance in the development of organisation theory it is often regarded as a sub-division under the classical heading and studied as a separate approach to management and the organisation of work. The ideas and principles of the classical writers were derived mainly from practical experience. Writers on bureaucracy, however, tend to take a more theoretical view.

Weber, a German sociologist, showed particular concern for what he called 'bureaucratic structures', although his work in this area came almost as a side issue to his main study on power and authority.[19] He suggested that 'the decisive reason for the advance of bureaucratic organisation has always been its purely technical superiority over any other form of organisation'. Weber pointed out that the definition of tasks and responsibilities within the structure of management gave rise to a permanent administration and standardisation of work procedures notwithstanding changes in the actual holders of office.

The term 'bureaucracy' has common connotations with criticism of red tape and rigidity, though in the study of organisations and management it is important that the term is seen not necessarily in a deprecative sense but as applying to certain structural features of formal organisations. Weber analysed bureaucracies not empirically but as an 'ideal type' derived from the most characteristic bureaucratic features of all known organisations. He saw the development of bureaucracies as a means of introducing order and rationality into social life.

Main characteristics of bureaucracies

Weber did not actually define bureaucracy but did attempt to identify the main characteristics of this type of organisation. He emphasised the importance of administration based on expertise (rules of experts) and administration based on discipline (rules of officials).

- The tasks of the organisation are allocated as official duties among the various positions.
- There is an implied clear-cut division of labour and a high level of specialisation.
- A hierarchical authority applies to the organisation of offices and positions.

- Uniformity of decisions and actions is achieved through formally established systems of rules and regulations. Together with a structure of authority this enables the co-ordination of various activities within the organisation.
- An impersonal orientation is expected from officials in their dealings with clients and other officials. This is designed to result in rational judgements by officials in the performance of their duties.
- Employment by the organisation is based on technical qualifications and constitutes a lifelong career for the officials.[20]

The four main features of bureaucracy are summarised by *Stewart* as specialisation, hierarchy of authority, system of rules, and impersonality.

- **Specialisation** applies more to the job than to the person undertaking the job. This makes for continuity because the job usually continues if the present job-holder leaves.
- **Hierarchy of authority** makes for a sharp distinction between administrators and the administered, or between management and workers. Within the management ranks there are clearly defined levels of authority. This detailed and precise stratification is particularly marked in the armed forces and in the civil service.
- **System of rules** aims to provide for an efficient and impersonal operation. The system of rules is generally stable, although some rules may be changed or modified with time. Knowledge of the rules is a requisite of holding a job in a bureaucracy.
- **Impersonality** means that allocation of privileges and the exercise of authority should not be arbitrary, but in accordance with the laid-down system of rules. In more highly developed bureaucracies there tend to be carefully defined procedures for appealing against certain types of decisions. Stewart sees the characteristic of impersonality as the feature of bureaucracy which most distinguishes it from other types of organisations. A bureaucracy should not only be impersonal but be seen to be impersonal.[21]

CRITICISMS OF BUREAUCRACY

Weber's concept of bureaucracy has a number of disadvantages and has been subject to severe criticism.

- The over-emphasis on rules and procedures, record keeping and paperwork may become more important in its own right than as a means to an end.
- Officials may develop a dependence upon bureaucratic status, symbols and rules.
- Initiative may be stifled and when a situation is not covered by a complete set of rules or procedures there is a lack of flexibility or adaptation to changing circumstances.
- Position and responsibilities in the organisation can lead to officious bureaucratic behaviour. There may also be a tendency to conceal administrative procedures from outsiders.
- Impersonal relations can lead to stereotyped behaviour and a lack of responsiveness to individual incidents or problems.

Lack of attention to the informal organisation

Weber's work has been criticised on the grounds that there is lack of attention to the informal organisation and the development of groups with goals of their own, and inadequate recognition of conflict in organisations. *Crozier*, in his study of two French bureaucratic systems, views bureaucracies not so much as static technical systems but as dynamic social systems.[22] Individuals have goals of their own and they devise ways of improving their position in the power struggle within organisations. Formal rules and the rigidity of the system will never fully remove this power struggle. There will always be areas of uncertainty which groups will want to claim and preserve for themselves. Crozier's view of bureaucracies as social systems with individuals having their own goals and expectations, and pursuing their own strategies, provides a link with the social action approach which is discussed later in this chapter.

Restriction of psychological growth

One of the strongest critics of bureaucratic organisation, and the demands it makes on the worker, is *Argyris*.[23] He claims that bureaucracies restrict the psychological growth of the individual and cause feelings of failure, frustration and conflict. Argyris suggests that the organisational environment should provide: a significant degree of individual responsibility and self-control; commitment to the goals of the organisation; productiveness and work; and an opportunity for individuals to apply their full abilities.

When these ideas are related to the main features of bureaucracy discussed above, such as specialisation, hierarchy of authority, system of rules and impersonality, it is perhaps easy to see the basis of Argyris's criticism.

A similar criticism is made by *Caulkin* who refers to the impersonal structure of bureaucracy as constructed round the post rather than the person and the ease with which it can be swung behind unsocial or even pathological ends. 'The overemphasis on process rather than purpose, fragmented responsibilities and hierarchical control means that it's all too easy for individuals to neglect the larger purposes to which their small effort is being put.'[24]

Bureaucratic dysfunction

Another area of criticism comes from writers who question Weber's concept of bureaucracy as an ideal type, and as highly functional with everything neatly in its place and contributing to the smooth running of the organisation. These writers are usually referred to under the heading of 'bureaucratic dysfunction' and include *Merton, Selznick* and *Gouldner*.

Merton refers to the development of 'bureaucratic personality' and fixation on rules and lack of adaptability as an unintended consequence of bureaucracy. There is also a tendency to 'goal displacement' where the means become ends in themselves and more important than the actual goals which the organisation is intended to achieve.[25]

Selznick also draws attention to the vulnerability of bureaucracies to goal displacement. Increased specialisation, and delegation and independence given to experts, can lead to the unintended consequences of the emergence of sub-groups with their own goals at variance with the goals of the organisation.[26]

Gouldner distinguishes three types of bureaucracy:

- **Mock** – where rules are formulated by an outside body but ignored by both managers and workers;
- **Representative** – where rules are formulated by management together with participation of the workers, and are considered to be reasonable;
- **Punishment-centred** – where rules are formulated by one party but not accepted as legitimate by other parties.[27]

Gouldner also studied the unanticipated consequences of a bureaucratic system in a gypsum mine ('wildcat strike') and the effects of introducing tighter supervision and formal controls over the workers in order to increase efficiency. The workers responded by attempting to resist the changes, by reducing the amount of work they did and by submitting a wage claim. Although the wage claim was settled there were continuing problems at the plant which culminated in a wildcat strike.

EVALUATION OF BUREAUCRACY

By their very nature, bureaucracies are likely to attract criticism. Much of this criticism is valid, but much also appears to be unfair comment. In any case, whatever the validity of the criticism, **it is difficult to envisage how modern large-scale organisations could function effectively without exhibiting at least some of the features of a bureaucratic structure.**

Public sector organisations

In the case of public sector organisations in particular there is a demand for uniformity of treatment, regularity of procedures and accountability for their operations. This leads to adherence to specified rules and procedures which limit the degree of discretion exercised by management, and to the keeping of detailed records.

It is interesting to note that, despite the criticisms of bureaucracy, people in their dealings with public sector organisations often call for what amounts to increased bureaucracy, even though they may not use that term. One can frequently see letters to newspapers, for example, that call for a letter of law and a clearer set of rules in dealings with benefit claims from government departments instead of decisions made on the opinion of a particular manager in a particular office.

The need for flexibility

The growth of bureaucracy has come about through the increasing size and complexity of organisations and the associated demand for effective administration. The work of the classical writers has given emphasis to the careful design and planning of organisation structure and the definition of individual duties and responsibilities. Effective organisation is based on structure and delegation through different layers of the hierarchy. Greater specialisation and the application of expertise and technical knowledge has highlighted the need for laid-down procedures.

Bureaucracy is founded on a formal, clearly defined and hierarchical structure. But with rapid changes in the external environment there is an increasing need to organise for flexibility. *Peters and Waterman*, for example, found that excellent American companies get quick action just because their organisations are fluid, and have intensive networks of informal and open communications.[28]

STRUCTURALISM

Sometimes the work of Weber is associated with the ideas of writers such as Karl Marx under the sub-heading of the structuralism approach, which is a synthesis of the classical (or formal) school and the human relations (or informal) school.[29] A major line of thought was that the earlier approaches were incomplete and lack

adequate theoretical assumptions and background. The structuralism approach provides a radical perspective of social and organisational behaviour.[30] Greater attention should be given to the relationship between the formal and informal aspects of the organisation, and the study of conflict between the needs of the individual and the organisation, and between workers and management. Structuralism is sometimes associated as part of a broader human relations approach, discussed below.

THE HUMAN RELATIONS APPROACH

The main emphasis of the classical writers was on structure and the formal organisation, but during the 1920s, the years of the great depression, greater attention began to be paid to the social factors at work and to the behaviour of employees within an organisation – that is, to human relations.

The Hawthorne experiments

The turning point in the development of the human relations movement ('behavioural' and 'informal' are alternative headings sometimes given to this approach) came with the famous Hawthorne experiments at the Western Electric Company in America (1924–32), and the subsequent publication of the research findings.[31]

The researchers included people from the National Research Council, the Harvard Business School and the Massachusetts Institute of Technology. Among the people who have written about the Hawthorne experiments was *Elton Mayo* (1880–1949) who is often quoted as a leader of the researchers. However there appears to be some doubt as to the extent to which Mayo was actually involved in conducting the experiments and his exact contribution to the human relations movement.[32]

There were four main phases to the Hawthorne experiments:

- the illumination experiments;
- the relay assembly test room;
- the interviewing programme;
- the bank wiring observation room.

The illumination experiments

The original investigation was conducted on the lines of the classical approach and was concerned, in typical scientific management style, with the effects of the intensity of lighting upon the workers' productivity. The workers were divided into two groups, an experimental group and a control group. The results of these tests were inconclusive as production in the experimental group varied with no apparent relationship to the level of lighting, but actually increased when conditions were made much worse. Production also increased in the control group although the lighting remained unchanged. The level of production was influenced, clearly, by factors other than changes in physical conditions of work. This prompted a series of other experiments investigating factors of worker productivity.

The relay assembly test room

In the relay assembly test room the work was boring and repetitive. It involved assembling telephone relays by putting together a number of small parts. Six women workers were transferred from their normal departments to a separate area. The researchers selected two assemblers who were friends with each other. They

then chose three other assemblers and a layout operator. The experiment was divided into 13 periods during which the workers were subjected to a series of planned and controlled changes to their conditions of work, such as hours of work, rest pauses and provision of refreshments. The general environmental conditions of the test room were similar to those of the normal assembly line.

During the experiment the observer adopted a friendly manner, consulting with the workers, listening to their complaints and keeping them informed of the experiment. Following all but one of the changes there was a continuous increase in the level of production. (*See* Table 2.1.) The researchers formed the conclusion that the extra attention given to the workers, and the apparent interest in them shown by management, was the main reason for the higher productivity.

Table 2.1 Relay assembly test room experiment

Period	Length in weeks	Conditions	Results
1	2	records kept on assembly line work	base rate established
2	5	operators enter test room, no other changes	production up slightly
3	8	payment rate changed to give higher reward for individual effort	production up
4	5	two five-minute rests, one morning and one afternoon	production up
5	4	rest breaks lengthened to ten minutes each	production up
6	4	six five-minute rest breaks	operators complain that too many breaks make them lose the rhythm of the work; production up a little
7	11	fifteen-minute morning break and ten-minute afternoon break; company provides refreshments	production up
8	7	work stops at 4:30 instead of 5:00; rest breaks as in period 7	production up
9	4	work stops at 4:00; rest breaks as in period 7	total daily production down slightly but hourly rate up
10	12	same as period 7	production up
11	9	Saturday work eliminated; rest breaks as in period 7	production up
12	12	same as period 3; no breaks	production drops slightly at first, then rises
13	31	same as period 7; but company supplies only coffee	production breaks all records

(From K. London, *The People Side of Systems*, McGraw-Hill (1976) p. 67.)

The interviewing programme

Another significant phase of the experiments was the interviewing programme. The lighting experiment and the relay assembly test room drew attention to the form of supervision as a contributory factor to the workers' level of production. In an attempt to find out more about the workers' feelings towards their supervisors

and their general conditions of work, a large interviewing programme was introduced. More than 20 000 interviews were conducted before the work was ended because of the depression.

Initially, the interviewers approached their task with a set of prepared questions, relating mainly to how the workers felt about their jobs. However, this method produced only limited information. The workers regarded a number of the questions as irrelevant; also they wanted to talk about other issues than just supervision and immediate working conditions. As a result, the style of interviewing was changed to become more non-directive and open-ended. There was no set list of questions and the workers were free to talk about any aspect of their work.

The interviewers set out to be friendly and sympathetic. They adopted an impartial, non-judgemental approach and concentrated on listening. They did not take sides or offer opinions, but if necessary would explain company policy and details of, for example, benefit schemes. The interviewers made verbatim notes of the interview, but it was made clear that everything said was in confidence. No identification was to be given on the notes and no personal details revealed to management.

Arising from this approach, the interviewers found out far more about the workers' true feelings and attitudes. They gained information not just about supervision and working conditions, but also about the company itself, management, work group relations and matters outside of work such as family life and views on society in general. Many workers appeared to welcome the opportunity to have someone to talk to about their feelings and problems, and to be able to 'let off steam' in a friendly atmosphere. The interviewing programme was significant in giving an impetus to present-day personnel management and the use of counselling interviews, and highlighting the need for management to listen to workers' feelings and problems.

The bank wiring observation room

Another experiment involved the observation of a group of 14 men working in the bank wiring room. It was noted that the men formed their own informal organisation with sub-groups or cliques, and with natural leaders emerging with the consent of the members. The group developed its own pattern of informal social relations and 'norms' of what constituted 'proper' behaviour. Despite a financial incentive scheme where the workers could receive more money for the more work produced, the group decided on a level of output well below the level they were capable of producing.

Group pressures on individual workers were stronger than financial incentives offered by management. The group believed that if they increased their output management would raise the standard level of piece rates. The importance of group 'norms' and informal social relations are discussed in Chapter 6.

EVALUATION OF THE HUMAN RELATIONS APPROACH

The human relations approach has been subjected to severe criticism. The Hawthorne experiments have been criticised, for example, on methodology and on failure of the investigators to take sufficient account of environmental factors – although much of this criticism is with the value of hindsight. The human relations writers have been criticised generally for the adoption of a management perspective, their 'unitary frame of reference' and their over-simplified theories.[33]

Other criticisms of the human relations approach are that it is insufficiently scientific, and that it takes too narrow a view. It ignores the role of the organisation itself in how society operates.

Sex power differential

There are a number of interpretations of the results of the Hawthorne experiments, including the possible implications of the 'sex power differential' between the two groups. In the relay assembly room where output increased the group was all female, whilst in the bank wiring room where output was restricted the group was all male. The workers in the relay assembly test room were all young unmarried women. All except one were living at home with traditional families of immigrant background. In the work environment of the factory the women had been subjected to frequent contact with male supervisors and therefore 'the sex power hierarchy in the home and in the factory were congruent'. It is suggested, therefore, that it was only to be expected that the women agreed readily to participate with management in the relay assembly test room experiment.[34]

Importance of the Hawthorne experiments

Whatever the interpretation of the results of the Hawthorne experiments, they did generate new ideas concerning the importance of work groups and leadership, communications, output restrictions, motivation and job design. They placed emphasis on the importance of personnel management, and gave impetus to the work of the human relations writers. The Hawthorne experiments undoubtedly marked a significant step forward in providing a further insight into human behaviour at work and the development of management thinking. The Hawthorne experiments are regarded as one of the most important of all social science investigations and are recognised as probably the single most important foundation of the human relations approach to management and the development of organisational behaviour.

Humanisation of the work organisation

Whereas supporters of the classical approach sought to increase production by rationalisation of the work organisation, the human relations movement has led to ideas on increasing production by humanising the work organisation. The classical approach adopted more of a managerial perspective, while the human relations approach strove for a greater understanding of people's psychological and social needs at work as well as improving the process of management. It is usually regarded as the first major approach to organisation and management to show concern for industrial sociology.

The human relations approach recognised the importance of the informal organisation which will always be present within the formal structure. This informal organisation will influence the motivation of employees who will view the organisation for which they work through the values and attitudes of their colleagues. Their view of the organisation determines their approach to work and the extent of their motivation to work well or otherwise.

Human relations writers demonstrated that people go to work to satisfy a complexity of needs and not simply for monetary reward. They emphasised the importance of the wider social needs of individuals and gave recognition to the work organisation as a social organisation and the importance of the group, and group values and norms, in influencing individual behaviour at work. It has been commented that the classical school were concerned about 'organisations without people', and the human relations school about 'people without organisations'.

NEO-HUMAN RELATIONS

Certainly there were shortcomings in the human relations approach, and assumptions which evolved from such studies as the Hawthorne experiments were not necessarily supported by empirical evidence.

For example, the contention that a satisfied worker is a productive worker was not always found to be valid. However, the results of the Hawthorne experiments and the subsequent attention given to the social organisation and to theories of individual motivation gave rise to the work of those writers in the 1950s and 1960s who adopted a more psychological orientation. The major focus of concern was the personal adjustment of the individual within the work organisation, and the effects of group relationships and leadership styles. This group of writers is often (and more correctly) categorised separately under the heading of 'neo-human relations'. The works of these writers are examined in more detail in subsequent chapters but are summarised broadly here.

The work of Maslow

A major impetus for the neo-human relations approach was the work of *Maslow* who, in 1943, put forward a theoretical framework of individual personality development and motivation based on a hierarchy of human needs.[35] The hierarchy ranges through five levels from, at the lowest level, physiological needs, through safety needs, love needs, esteem needs, to the need for self-actualisation at the highest level. Individuals only advance up the hierarchy as each lower-level need is satisfied. Although Maslow did not originally intend this need hierarchy to be applied necessarily to the work situation it has, nevertheless, had a significant impact on management approaches to motivation and the design of work organisation to meet individual needs. The work of Maslow provides a link with the earlier human relations approach.

Some leading contributors

Among the best-known contributors to the neo-human relations approach are *Herzberg* and *McGregor*. Herzberg isolated two different sets of factors affecting motivation and satisfaction at work. One set of factors is those which, if absent, cause dissatisfaction. These are 'hygiene' or 'maintenance' factors which are concerned basically with job environment. However, to motivate workers to give of their best, proper attention must be given to a different set of factors, the 'motivators' or 'growth' factors. These are concerned with job content.[36]

McGregor argued that the style of management adopted is a function of the manager's attitudes towards human nature and behaviour at work. He put forward two suppositions called Theory X and Theory Y which are based on popular assumptions about work and people.[37]

Other major contributors to the neo-human relations approach include *Likert*, whose work includes research into different systems of management;[38] and *Argyris*, who considered the effects of the formal organisation on the individual and psychological growth in the process of self-actualisation.[39]

The neo-human relations approach has generated a prolific amount of writing and research not only from original propounders, but also from others seeking to establish the validity, or otherwise, of their ideas. This has led to continuing attention being given to such matters as organisation structuring, group dynamics, job

satisfaction, communication and participation, leadership styles and motivation. It has also led to greater attention to the importance of interpersonal interactions, the causes of conflict and recognition of 'industrial relations' problems.

THE SYSTEMS APPROACH

More recently, attention has been focused on the analysis of organisations as 'systems' with a number of interrelated sub-systems.

The classical approach emphasised the technical requirements of the organisation and its needs – 'organisations without people'; the human relations approaches emphasised the psychological and social aspects, and the consideration of human needs – 'people without organisations'.

The systems approach attempts to reconcile these two earlier approaches and the work of the formal and the informal writers. Attention is focused on the total work organisation and the interrelationships of structure and behaviour, and the range of variables within the organisation. This approach can be contrasted with a view of the organisation as separate parts. The systems approach encourages managers to view the organisation both as a whole and as part of a larger environment. The idea is that any part of an organisation's activities affects all other parts.

Systems theory

Systems theory is not new and has been used in the natural and physical sciences for a number of years. One of the founders of this approach was the biologist *Ludwig von Bertalanffy* who used the term 'systems theory' in an article published in 1951, and who is generally credited with having developed the outline of General Systems Theory.[40] The systems approach to organisation has arisen, at least in part, therefore, from the work of biologists, and *Miller and Rice* have likened the commercial and industrial organisation to the biological organism.[41]

Using a General Systems Theory (GST) approach *Boulding* classified nine levels of systems of increasing complexity according to the state of development and knowledge about each level.[42] Organisations are complex social systems and are more open to change than lower-level simple dynamic or cybernetic systems. Boulding felt there were large gaps in both theoretical and empirical knowledge of the human level and the social organisations level of systems, although some progress has now been made with recent theories of organisational behaviour.

The business organisation as an open system

The business organisation is an open system. There is continual interaction with the broader external environment of which it is part. The systems approach views the organisation within its total environment and emphasises the importance of multiple channels of interaction. Criticisms of earlier approaches to organisation are based in part on the attempt to study the activities and problems of the organisation solely in terms of the internal environment.

The view of the organisation as an open system is examined in Chapter 3.

The socio-technical system

The systems approach views the organisation as a whole and involves the study of the organisation in terms of the relationship between technical and social variables within the system. Changes in one part, technical or social, will affect other

parts and thus the whole system. The concept of the organisation as a 'socio-technical' system directs attention to the transformation or conversion process itself, to the series of activities through which the organisation attempts to achieve its objectives. The socio-technical system is concerned with the interactions between the psychological and social factors and the needs and demands of the human part of the organisation, and its structural and technological requirements.

Longwall coal-mining study

The idea of socio-technical systems arose from the work of *Trist* and others, of the Tavistock Institute of Human Relations, in their study of the effects of changing technology in the coal-mining industry in the 1940s.[43] The increasing use of mechanisation and the introduction of coal-cutters and mechanical conveyors enabled coal to be extracted on a 'longwall' method.

Shift working was introduced with each shift specialising on one stage of the operation – preparation, cutting or loading. However, the new method meant a change in the previous system of working where a small self-selecting group of miners worked together, as an independent team, on one part of the coalface – the 'single place' or 'shortwall' method.

Technological change had brought about changes in the social groupings of the miners. It disrupted the integration of small groups and the psychological and sociological properties of the old method of working. There was a lack of co-operation between different shifts and within each shift, an increase in absenteeism, scapegoating and signs of greater social stress. The 'longwall' method was socially disruptive and did not prove as economically efficient as it could have been with the new technology.

The researchers saw the need for a socio-technical approach in which an appropriate social system could be developed in keeping with the new technical system. The result was the 'composite longwall' method with more responsibility to the team as a whole and shifts carrying out composite tasks, the reintroduction of multi-skilled roles and a reduction in specialisation. The composite method was psychologically and socially more rewarding and economically more efficient than the 'longwall' method.

The technology approach

The concept of socio-technical systems provides a link between the systems approach and a sub-division, sometimes adopted – the technology approach. Writers under the technology heading attempt to restrict generalisations about organisations and management, and emphasise the effects of varying technologies on organisation structure, work groups and individual performance and job satisfaction. This is in contrast with the socio-technical approach which did not regard technology, *per se*, as a determinant of behaviour.

Under the heading of the technology approach could be included the work of such writers as *Walker and Guest* (effects of the assembly-line production method on employee behaviour);[44] *Woodward* (relationships between application of principles of organisation and business success);[45] *Sayles* (relationship between technology and the nature of work groups);[46] and *Blauner* (problems of 'alienation' in relation to different work technologies).[47]

THE CONTINGENCY APPROACH

The classical approach suggested one best form of structure and placed emphasis on general sets of principles while the human relations approach gave little attention at all to structure. In contrast the contingency approach showed renewed concern with the importance of structure as a significant influence on organisational performance. The contingency approach, which can be seen as an extension of the systems approach, highlights possible means of differentiating among alternative forms of organisation structures and systems of management. There is no one optimum state. For example, the structure of the organisation and its 'success' are dependent, that is contingent upon, the nature of tasks with which it is designed to deal and the nature of environmental influences.

The most appropriate structure and system of management is therefore dependent upon the contingencies of the situation for each particular organisation. The contingency approach implies that organisation theory should not seek to suggest one best way to structure or manage organisations but should provide insights into the situational and contextual factors which influence management decisions. Contingency models of organisation and management are discussed in Chapter 11.

OTHER APPROACHES TO THE STUDY OF ORGANISATIONS

The four-fold framework of classical, human relations, systems and contingency approaches provides a helpful categorisation. But the study of organisations, their structure and management is a broad field of inquiry. Depending on the views and preferences of the writer, other possible main approaches include decision-making and social action.

THE DECISION-MAKING APPROACH

The systems approach involves the isolation of those functions most directly concerned with the achievement of objectives and the identification of main decision areas or sub-systems. Viewing the organisation as a system emphasises the need for good information and channels of communication in order to assist effective decision-making in the organisation.

Recognition of the need for decision-making and the attainment of goals draws attention to a sub-division of the systems approach, or a separate category, that of the decision-making (or decision theory) approach. Here the focus of attention is on managerial decision-making and how organisations process and use information in making decisions.

Successful management lies in responding to internal and external change. This involves the clarification of objectives, the specification of problems, and the search for and implementation of solutions. The organisation is seen as an infor-

mation-processing network with numerous decision points. An understanding of how decisions are made helps in understanding behaviour in the organisation. Decision-making writers seek to explain the mechanisms by which conflict is resolved and choices are made.

Some leading writers

Leading writers of the decision-making approach include *Barnard*, *Simon*, and *Cyert and March*. The scope of the decision-making approach, however, is wide, and it is possible to identify contributions from engineers, mathematicians and operational research specialists in addition to the work of economists, psychologists and writers on management and organisation.

Barnard stressed the need for co-operative action in organisations. He believed that people's ability to communicate, and their commitment and contribution to the achievement of a common purpose, were necessary for the existence of a co-operative system.[48] These ideas were developed further by Simon. He sees management as meaning decision-making and his concern is with how decisions are made and how decision-making can be improved. Simon is critical of the implication of man as completely rational and proposes a model of 'administrative man' who, unlike 'economic man', 'satisfices' rather than maximises. Administrative decision-making is the achievement of satisfactory rather than optimal results in solving problems.[49]

Economic models of decision-making, based on the assumption of rational behaviour in choosing from known alternatives in order to maximise objectives, can be contrasted with behavioural models based not so much on maximisation of objectives as on short-term expediency where a choice is made to avoid conflict and within limiting constraints. Managers are more concerned with avoiding uncertainties than with the prediction of uncertainties.[50]

SOCIAL ACTION

Social action represents a contribution from sociologists to the study of organisations. Social action writers attempt to view the organisation from the standpoint of individual members (actors) who will each have their own goals, and interpretation of their work situation in terms of the satisfaction sought and the meaning that work has for them. The goals of the individual, and the means selected and actions taken to achieve these goals, are affected by the individual's perception of the situation. Social action looks to the individual's own definition of the situation as a basis for explaining behaviour. Conflict of interests is seen as normal behaviour and part of organisational life. According to *Silverman*, 'The action approach...does not, in itself, provide a theory of organisations. It is instead best understood as a method of analysing social relations within organisations'.[51]

Criticisms of earlier approaches

A main thrust of social action is the criticism of earlier approaches to organisation and management, and of what is claimed to be their failure to provide a satisfactory basis for the explanation or prediction of individual behaviour. For example, criticism is directed at approaches which focused on the goals and needs of the organisation, rather than on considerations of the effectiveness of an organisation in meeting the needs of its individual members.

The human relations approaches have been criticised because of their focus on generalised theories of good management, group psychology, and the suggestion of needs common to all individuals at work. The technology approach has been criticised for attributing feelings of alienation to the nature of technology and the status of work groups, rather than an analysis which focused on concern for the individual's expectations of, and reactions to, work. The systems approach has been criticised for failure to examine the orientation of individual members to the organisation, the different expectations people have of their work or ways in which the environment influences expectations of work.

Unitary or pluralistic view

Important contributors to a social action approach include *Goldthorpe* (industrial attitudes and behaviour patterns of manual workers)[52] and *Fox*. In a research paper written for the Royal Commission on Trade Unions and Employers' Associations (the Donovan Report), Fox suggests two major ways of perceiving an industrial organisation – a 'unitary' approach and a 'pluralistic' approach.[53]

With the **unitary approach** the organisation is viewed as a team with a common source of loyalty, one focus of effort and one accepted leader. The **pluralistic approach** views the organisation as made up of competing sub-groups with their own loyalties, goals and leaders. These competing sub-groups are almost certain to come into conflict.

The unitary and pluralistic perspectives of the organisation are discussed in Chapter 18.

Action theory

A theory of human behaviour from an 'action approach' is presented by *Bowey*.[54] She suggests that action theory, systems theory and contingency theory are not necessarily incompatible approaches to the understanding of behaviour in organisations. It would be possible to take the best parts of the different approaches and combine them into a theory that would model empirical behaviour, and also facilitate the analysis of large numbers of people in organisations. Bowey goes on to present such a theory as a particular form of an action theory approach. According to Bowey, action theory is not capable of dealing with the analysis of the behaviour of a large number of people in organisations. Her theory is based, therefore, on three essential principles of action theory, augmented by four additional concepts taken from systems theory.

The three essential principles of action theory are summarised as:

- sociology is concerned not just with behaviour, but with 'meaningful action';
- particular meanings persist through reaffirmation in actions;
- actions can also lead to changes in meanings.

Additional concepts

Bowey suggests that these three principles apply mainly to explanations of individual, or small-scale, behaviour. She gives four additional concepts, taken from systems theory, on which analysis of large-scale behaviour can be based. These concepts are redefined in accordance with an action approach.

- **Role** – this is needed for the analysis of behaviour in organisations. It explains the similar action of different people in similar situations within the organisation, and the expectations held by other people.
- **Relationships** – this is needed to explain the patterns of interaction among people and the behaviours displayed towards one another.

- **Structure** – the relationships among members of an organisation give rise to patterns of action which can be identified as a 'transitory social structure'. The social factors, and non-social factors such as payment systems, methods of production and physical layout, together form the behavioural structure.
- **Process** – human behaviour can be analysed in terms of processes, defined as 'continuous interdependent sequences of actions'. The concept of process is necessary to account for the manner in which organisations exhibit changes in structure.

The three principles of action theory, together with the four additional concepts from systems theory, provide an action approach to the analysis of behaviour in organisations. Bowey goes on to illustrate her theory by case studies of five different types of organisations, all in the restaurant industry.

A NUMBER OF DIFFERENT APPROACHES

We can now see that within the broad four-fold classification of classical, human relations, systems, and contingency approaches it is possible to identify a number of other approaches or at least sub-divisions of approaches. So far we have identified a possible nine-fold classification: classical (including scientific management); bureaucracy; human relations; neo-human relations; systems; technology; contingency; decision-making; and social action – and if structuralism is included, we have a ten-fold classification. This classification could be extended still further. For example, another more recent categorisation sometimes identified as a separate approach is management science – with emphasis on quantitative analysis, mathematical models, operational research and computer technology.

It is possible then to distinguish a number of different approaches to the study of organisation and management, although there is no consensus on the categorisation of these different approaches or on the identification of the various contributors to one particular approach. (*See* Fig. 2.3.)

RELEVANCE TO MANAGEMENT AND ORGANISATIONAL BEHAVIOUR

The different possible categorisations are not necessarily a bad thing – they illustrate the discursive nature of management. The possible sub-divisions and cross-groupings help illustrate the many factors relevant to the study and practice of management and organisational behaviour. Discussion on the various categorisations of approaches and the identification of individual writers within a particular approach can provide a useful insight into the subject.

Positive advantages

Whatever form of categorisation is adopted the division of writers on organisation and management into various approaches offers a number of positive advantages.

- It is helpful to students in the arrangement and study of their material.
- It provides a setting in which to view the field of management, and to consider the contribution of individual writers.

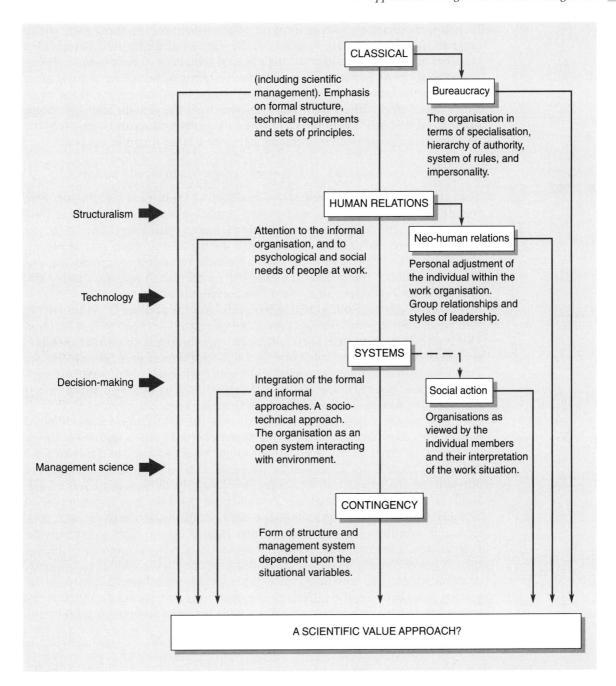

The diagram contains the following elements:

CLASSICAL

(including scientific management). Emphasis on formal structure, technical requirements and sets of principles.

Bureaucracy

The organisation in terms of specialisation, hierarchy of authority, system of rules, and impersonality.

HUMAN RELATIONS

Attention to the informal organisation, and to psychological and social needs of people at work.

Neo-human relations

Personal adjustment of the individual within the work organisation. Group relationships and styles of leadership.

SYSTEMS

Integration of the formal and informal approaches. A socio-technical approach. The organisation as an open system interacting with environment.

Social action

Organisations as viewed by the individual members and their interpretation of the work situation.

CONTINGENCY

Form of structure and management system dependent upon the situational variables.

Structuralism

Technology

Decision-making

Management science

A SCIENTIFIC VALUE APPROACH?

Fig. 2.3
An outline of developments of approaches to organisation and management

- It traces the major lines of argument developed by writers seeking to advise practising managers on how they might improve performance.
- It provides a framework in which the principles enunciated can be set, and against which comparisons with management practice can be made.
- It helps in organisational analysis and in the identification of problem areas. For example, is the problem one of structure, of human relations, or of the socio-technical process?

- It enables the manager to take from the different approaches those ideas which best suit the particular requirements of the job. For example, in dealing with a problem of structure the ideas of the classical writers or of contingency theory might be adopted. When there is a problem relating to personnel management ideas from the human relations movement might be of most value. If the problem is one of environmental influence insights from the systems approach might prove most helpful. For problems of a more quantitative nature ideas from the decision-making approach or from management science might be applicable.

Caveats to be noted

There are, however, a number of important caveats which should be noted.

- The various approaches represent a progression of ideas, each building on from the other and adding to it. Together they provide a pattern of complementary studies into the development of management thinking. The different approaches are not in competition with each other and no one approach should be viewed as if it were the only approach, replacing or superseding earlier contributions. Many ideas of earlier writers are still of relevance today and of continuing importance in modern management practice.
- Any categorisation of individual writers into specific approaches is inevitably somewhat arbitrary and not all writers can be neatly arranged in this manner. This is only to be expected. Such writers are expounding their current thoughts and ideas in keeping with the continual development of management theory and changes in management practice. The comment made about some management writers that they are saying different things at different times might therefore be taken more as a compliment than as a criticism.
- Even when there is agreement on the nature of the contribution from different writers, the actual division into varying approaches may take a number of different forms. In other words, whilst there might be acceptance of the need for a framework there is no agreement on its shape. Different authors have adopted different formats in which to set out the developments in management thinking.
- Some of the literature categorises management thinkers into divisions called 'schools'. The use of this term suggests a clarity of distinction between each division and a uniformity of beliefs within each division. This is perhaps an exaggeration. The distinction between these so-called schools is not clear-cut and there is not necessarily a consistency of thinking among the various contributors in each division. The term 'approaches' to management is more indicative of the obscure lines between the different categorisations and, paradoxically, it is the suggestion of vagueness which, arguably, makes it a more appropriate term to use.

CHANGES IN MANAGEMENT THINKING

In a review of management theory and practice, *Heller* contrasts British and American thinking with methods employed by the Japanese.[55] In the 1960s western managements showed a total lack of curiosity about competition from Japan. British and European managers were still obsessed by the American example. The Japanese built hugely on what they had borrowed from the USA. But the Japanese also practised and perfected what management scientists often only preached.

Although British management has failed to live up to Japanese standards, professional standards among managers in Britain have improved greatly over the past 25 years. The potential of a widening Europe and the Japanese penchant for locating more plants in Britain provide the best reasons for brighter future prospects.

25 years of management thinking

Heller also cites the London Business School and 12 changes in management thinking over the 25 years, 1966–91.

1. In 1966 London and Manchester Business Schools opened. Today an annual 5000 MBAs graduate from British institutions.
2. In 1966 the prevailing management view was that America knew best. Today management education is international.
3. In 1966 business was predominantly national in scope. Today managers adopt a more international perspective.
4. In the 1960s management theory emphasised technology *or* psychology. Today, it is more pluralistic in approach.
5. In the 1960s systems theory dominated management. Today business school teaching is based on practice.
6. In the 1960s managers were seen as superstars of planning and control. Today we accept that they spend more time talking and listening.
7. In the 1960s the human resources of enterprise were ignored. Today people are an acknowledged part of business.
8. In the 1960s IT was seen as the great panacea. Today it is more realistically viewed as a strategic tool needing management.
9. In the 1960s management theory rested on the idea of consensus. Today's key concept is power.
10. In the 1960s business schools emphasised endless analysis of the competitive position. Today they plan for new markets.
11. In the 1960s the interests of shareholders, staff and the community were thought incompatible. Today the needs of all must be satisfied.
12. In the 1960s most managers were male. Today we increasingly acknowledge the diversity of gender and race.

TOWARDS A SCIENTIFIC VALUE APPROACH?

It might be that the study of organisations, their structure and management is moving towards a more scientific approach. Management science can assist managers in the analysis of complex problems that are subject to quantitative constraints and in the optimisation of decisions to such problems. It may also assist in the establishment of broad theory. However, many operational problems in organisations relate to the nature of human behaviour and the people–organisation relationship, and do not lend themselves to the application of a scientific answer.

There are no definitive or final solutions to the problems of organisations. The nature of work organisations and the environment in which they operate is becoming increasingly complex and subject to continual change. But at least we do understand more about the dynamics of management and organisational behaviour as a basis for the analysis of human behaviour in organisations.[56]

Research findings

The research findings on organisational behaviour are still inconclusive and contradictory but, according to *London*, there are a number of general features which can be identified.

- Modern organisations have failed to provide individuals with adequate outlets for creativity and self-actualisation, thus causing alienation and conflict.
- Conflict and tension, in themselves, are not necessarily undesirable. The nature of conflict needs to be understood so it can be utilised to help improve organisational performance.
- Organisation structures can be designed to allow individuals full scope for self-actualisation, and at the same time facilitate achievement of organisational goals and objectives.
- Different individuals have different levels of skills and ambitions. Managers must be able to manage if the organisation is to achieve its goals and objectives.
- Modern management has become too democratic. Without evoking excesses of Taylorism, there must be a return to more authoritarian attitudes of management.[57]

Balance between philosophy and science

Miner, however, suggests that although the degree of commitment to the scientific value system is increasing, as yet there is insufficient research to move the field entirely into science, completely divorced from philosophy. At present management theory is clearly in the 'schools' phase. As discussed earlier, it is possible to argue over the use of the term 'schools'. But whatever terminology is used, and whatever the state of our knowledge, the message from Miner is clear: '...schools of management thought are very much a reality, and the management student who approaches the field without at least a minimal understanding of them does so at some risk'.[58]

BENEFITS TO THE MANAGER

Whatever the balance between philosophy and science, a knowledge and understanding of management theory will help with the complexities of management in modern work organisations. No single approach to organisation and management provides all the answers. It is the comparative study of different approaches which will yield benefits to the manager.[59]

There are many aspects to management. There are no simple solutions, no one best way to manage. The study of organisations, their structure and management is important for the manager and an indispensable part of the job.

SYNOPSIS

- The study of organisation and management has to proceed on a broad front. A central part of this study is the development of management thinking and what might be termed management theory. In order to help identify main trends in the development of management thinking and organisational behaviour, it is usual to categorise the work of leading writers into various 'approaches' based on their views of organisations, their structure and management. This provides a framework in which to direct study and focus attention.

■ Our analysis has revolved around a framework based on four-fold categorisation of classical, human relations, systems, and contingency approaches. The classical writers placed emphasis on purpose and structure, on the technical requirements of the organisation, and on the assumption of rational and logical behaviour. The human relations writers emphasised the importance of the informal organisation and the psychological and social needs of people at work. The systems approach attempts to integrate the work of the classical and human relations writers. Attention is focused on the interactions between technical and social variables. The organisation is seen in continual interaction with the external environment. Contingency theory highlights possible means of differentiating between alternative forms of structures and systems of management.

■ This four-fold categorisation provides a useful starting point for the identification of main trends in the development of management thinking. It provides a framework in which to focus attention on different aspects of management theory and practice, and the development of organisational behaviour. Within this framework, however, it is possible to identify a number of other approaches or sub-divisions of approaches.

■ Among other possible main approaches are decision-making and social action. The decision-making approach emphasises the need for good information and channels of communication. Social action writers attempt to view the organisation from the position of individual members who will each have their own interpretation of the work situation in terms of the satisfaction sought and the meaning that work has for them.

■ Whatever form of categorisation is adopted, the division of writers on organisation and management into various approaches offers a number of advantages. For example, it helps in organisational analysis and the identification of problem areas. It enables the manager to take from the different approaches those ideas which suit best the particular requirements of the job. There are, however, a number of caveats which should also be noted.

■ It might be that the study of organisations is moving towards a more scientific value approach. But whatever the balance between philosophy and science, a knowledge of management theory will help with the complexities of management in modern work organisations. It is necessary to view the interrelationships among the development of theory, behaviour in organisations and management practice.

Review and discussion questions

1 Identify, and outline briefly, major trends in approaches to organisation and management since the beginning of this century.

2 Assess critically the relevance of scientific management to present-day management in organisations. Illustrate your answer with reference to your own organisation.

3 To what extent is there anything positive to be said for bureaucratic structures? Select a large-scale organisation of your choice and suggest ways in which it displays characteristics of a bureaucracy.

4 What are the main conclusions that can be drawn from the Hawthorne experiments? Discuss critically the relevance of these experiments for management and organisational behaviour today.

5 Summarise the main features of the neo-human relations approach to organisation and management. How does it differ from other approaches?

6 Evaluate the application of the systems approach to the analysis of work organisations. Suggest an example of a work situation in which the systems approach might be appropriate.

7 Contrast approaches to improving organisational performance based on attention to technical and structural requirements, with those based on concern for psychological and social factors.

8 Explain what is meant by a social action approach. Assess critically the practical relevance of 'action theory'.

9 Discuss the extent to which the study of the development of management theory has any practical value to the manager. What caveats should be noted?

10 Which *one* of the different approaches to organisation and management would you select as most relevant to the analysis of a particular work situation? Give a detailed assessment of the contributions and limitations of your selected approach.

 ## Assignment

In self-selecting groups of three or four, visit a work organisation of your choice, preferably one that is well known to at least one member of your group.

(i) Investigate those features of the structure, management and operations of the organisation which are characteristic of:
 (a) scientific management; and
 (b) bureaucracy.
 Comment critically on what you believe to be the practical effects of your set of characteristics, and give examples in support of your comments.
(ii) For the same, or a different, organisation:
 comment critically, with supporting examples, on the extent to which applications of the human relations approach to organisation and management have been applied in practice.

Notes and references

1. This chapter is based in parts on a development of the author's articles: Mullins, L. J. 'Approaches to Management', *Management Accounting*, vol. 57, no. 4, April 1979, pp. 15–18, and Mullins, L. J. 'Some Further Approaches to Management Theory', *Management Accounting*, vol. 58, no. 3, March 1980, pp. 30–3.

2. See, for example: George, C. S. *The History of Management Thought*, Second edition, Prentice-Hall (1972).

3. McGregor, D. *The Human Side of Enterprise*, Penguin (1987) p. 6.

4. Miner, J. B. *Theories of Organizational Behaviour*, Dryden Press (1980).

5. Skipton, M. D. 'Management and the Organisation', *Management Research News*, vol. 5, no. 3, 1983, pp. 9–15.

6. Fayol, H. *General and Industrial Management*, Pitman (1949). See also: Gray, I. *Henri Fayol's General and Industrial Management*, Pitman (1988).

7. Urwick, L. *Notes on the Theory of Organization*, American Management Association (1952).

8. Mooney, J. D. and Reiley, A. C. *The Principles of Organization*, Harper and Bros (1939); revised by Mooney, J. D., Harper and Row (1947).

9. Brech, E. F. L. *Organisation: The Framework of Management*, Second edition, Longman (1965).

10. Simon, H. A. *Administrative Behaviour*, Third edition, Free Press (1976) p. xxii.

11. Woodward, J. *Industrial Organization: Theory and Practice*, Second edition, Oxford University Press (1980).

12. Taylor, F. W. *Scientific Management*, Harper and Row (1947). Comprises Shop Management (1903), Principles of Scientific Management (1911) and Taylor's testimony to the House of Representatives' Special Committee (1912).

13. Braverman, H. *Labor and Monopoly Capital*, Monthly Review Press (1974).

14. For a study of employers' labour relations policies, including comments on the work of Braverman, see: Gospel, H. F. and Littler, C. R. (eds), *Managerial Strategies and Industrial Relations*, Heinemann Educational Books (1983).

15. Rose, M. *Industrial Behaviour*, Penguin (1978) p. 31. See also: Rose, M. *Industrial Behaviour*, Second edition, Penguin (1988) Chapter 2.

16. Drucker, P. F. 'The Coming Rediscovery of Scientific Management', *The Conference Board Record*, vol. XIII, June 1976, pp. 23–7. Reprinted in Drucker, P. F. *Towards the Next Economics and Other Essays*, Heinemann (1981).

17. Locke, E. A. 'The Ideas of Frederick W. Taylor: An Evaluation', *Academy of Management Review*, vol. 7, no. 1, January 1982, pp. 14–24.

18. For a discussion on 'Fordism', see for example: Fincham, R. and Rhodes, P. S. *The Individual Work and Organization*, Second edition, Weidenfeld and Nicolson (1992).

19. Weber, M. *The Theory of Social and Economic Organization*, Collier Macmillan (1964).

20. Blau, P. M. and Scott, W. R. *Formal Organizations*, Routledge and Kegan Paul (1966).

21. Stewart, R. *The Reality of Management*, Second edition, Pan Books (1986).

22. Crozier, M. *The Bureaucratic Phenomenon*, Tavistock Publications (1964).

23. Argyris, C. *Integrating the Individual and the Organization*, Wiley (1964).

24. Caulkin, S. 'Faceless Corridors of Power', *Management Today*, January 1988, p. 65.

25. Merton, R. K. *Social Theory and Social Structure*, Revised edition, Collier Macmillan (1968).

26. Selznick, P. *TVA and the Grass Roots*, Harper and Row (1966).

27. Gouldner, A. W. *Patterns of Industrial Bureaucracy*, Free Press (1954), and *Wildcat Strike*, Harper and Row (1965).

28. Peters, T. J. and Waterman, R. H. *In Search of Excellence*, Harper and Row (1982).

29. For example, see: Etzioni, A. *Modern Organizations*, Prentice-Hall (1964) p. 41.

30. See for example: Aktouf, O. 'Management and Theories of Organizations in the 1990s: Towards a Critical Radical Humanism?', *Academy of Management Review*, vol. 17, no. 3, 1992, pp. 407–31.

31. There are many versions of the Hawthorne experiments. Among the most thorough accounts is Roethlisberger, F. J. and Dickson, W. J. *Management and the Worker*, Harvard University Press (1939). See also: Landsberger, H. A. *Hawthorne Revisited*, Cornell University Press, Ithaca (1958).

32. See, for example: Rose, M. *Industrial Behaviour*, Second edition, Penguin (1988).

33. Silverman, D. *The Theory of Organisations*, Heinemann (1970).

34. Stead, B. A. *Women in Management*, Prentice-Hall (1978) p. 190.

35. Maslow. A. H. 'A Theory of Human Motivation', *Psychological Review*, vol. 50, no. 4, July 1943, pp. 370–96.

36. Herzberg, F. W., Mausner, B. and Snyderman, B. B. *The Motivation to Work*, Second edition, Chapman and Hall (1959).

37. McGregor, D. *The Human Side of Enterprise*, Penguin (1987).

38. Likert, R. *New Patterns of Management*, McGraw-Hill (1961). See also: Likert, R. *The Human Organization*, McGraw-Hill (1967), Likert, R. and Likert, J. G. *New Ways of Managing Conflict*, McGraw-Hill (1976).

39. Argyris, C. *Understanding Organizational Behavior*, Tavistock Publications (1960) and *Integrating the Individual and the Organization*, Wiley (1964).

40. Bertalanffy, L. von. 'Problems of General Systems Theory: A New Approach to the Unity of Science', *Human Biology*, vol. 23, no. 4, December 1951, pp. 302–12.

41. Miller, E. J. and Rice, A. K. *Systems of Organization*, Tavistock Publications (1967).

42. Boulding, K. 'General Systems Theory – The Skeleton of Science', *Management Science*, vol. 2, no. 3, April 1956, pp. 197–208.

43. Trist, E. L. *et al. Organizational Choice*, Tavistock Publications (1963).

44. Walker, C. R. and Guest, R. H. *The Man on the Assembly Line*, Harvard University Press (1952). See also: Walker, C. R., Guest, R. H. and Turner, A. N. *The Foreman on the Assembly Line*, Harvard University Press (1956).

45. Woodward, J. *Industrial Organization: Theory and Practice*, Second edition, Oxford University Press (1980).

46. Sayles, L. R. *Behaviour of Industrial Work Groups*, Wiley (1958).

47. Blauner, R. *Alienation and Freedom*, University of Chicago Press (1964).

48. Barnard, C. *The Functions of the Executive*, Oxford University Press (1938).

49. Simon, H. A. *The New Science of Management Decision*, Revised edition, Prentice-Hall (1977).

50. Cyert, R. M. and March J. G. *A Behavioural Theory of the Firm*, Second edition, Blackwell (1992).

51. Silverman, D. *The Theory of Organisations*, Heinemann (1970) p. 147.

52. Goldthorpe, J. H. *et al. The Affluent Worker*, Cambridge University Press (1968).

53. Fox, A. *Industrial Sociology and Industrial Relations*, HMSO (1966).

54. Bowey, A. M. *The Sociology of Organisations*, Hodder and Stoughton (1976).

55. Heller, R. 'The Change Managers', *Management Today: 25th Anniversary Issue*, 1991, pp. 12–16.

56. See, for example: Klein, S. M. and Ritti, R. R. *Understanding Organizational Behavior*, Second edition, Kent Publishing (1984) Chapter 1.

57. London, K. *The People Side of Systems*, McGraw-Hill (1976).

58. Miner, J. B. *Management Theory*, Macmillan (1971) p. 145. See also: Miner, J. B. *Theories of Organizational Behaviour*, Holt, Rinehart and Winston (1980) Chapter 1.

59. For a critical account on competing views about organisation theory and its applications, see: Perrow, C. *Complex Organizations*, Second edition, Scott, Foresman (1979). For a discussion of British and American ideas on conceiving and selling management theory, see: Foster, G. 'Management's Missing Ideas', *Management Today*, March 1980, pp. 72–5, 152–6.

3 THE ORGANISATIONAL SETTING

The application of organisational behaviour and the process of management take place not in a vacuum but within the context of a particular organisational setting. The organisation is a complex social system and is the sum of many interrelated variables. The operations of the organisation are influenced by the external environment of which it is part. The manager needs to understand the nature of organisations and the main features which affect the structure, management and functioning of the work organisation.

 Learning objectives

To:

- Explain the nature of organisations, and distinguish between the formal and the informal organisation;

- Describe the basic components of an organisation;

- Distinguish alternative types and classifications of organisations, and relate different organisations to these classifications;

- Examine the organisation in terms of an open systems model;

- Analyse organisations on the basis of interrelated sub-systems;

- Appreciate the influence of technology in work organisations and the impact of information technology;

- Recognise the importance of the organisational setting.

Worth thinking about

'If the process of management takes place within an organisational setting, and no two organisations are the same, then what use are general models of organisation theory? I am only concerned with what happens in my own organisation.' . . . 'Yes, but so then is every other student – hence the need for generalised models!'

THE NATURE OF ORGANISATIONS

All organisations have some function to perform. Organisations exist in order to achieve objectives and to provide satisfaction for their members. Organisations enable objectives to be achieved that could not be achieved by the efforts of individuals on their own. Through co-operative action, members of an organisation can provide a synergistic effect. There are many different types of organisations which are set up to serve a number of different purposes and to meet a variety of needs.

Organisations come in all forms, shapes and sizes. Consider the diversification among such organisations as, for example:

Firm of accountants	Hotel
School	Leisure centre
Retail shop	Quarry works
Local authority	Government department
Airport	Pharmaceutical company
Motor car manufacturer	Bank
Hospital	Nationalised industry

The structure, management and functioning of these organisations will all vary because of differences in the nature and type of the organisation, their respective goals and objectives, and the behaviour of the people who work in them.

Let us now consider just two types of organisations towards the opposite ends of a possible continuum – say a maximum security prison and a university largely concerned with research – as a framework in which to focus attention.

We can appreciate readily that although both types of organisation will be concerned with the basic activities of organisation and management their goals and objectives, actual procedures and methods of operation, structure, systems and style of management, and orientation and behaviour of members will differ considerably.

Common factors in organisations
Despite the differences among various organisations there are, however, at least three common factors in any organisation:

- people,
- objectives,
- structure.

It is the interaction of **people** in order to achieve **objectives** which forms the basis of an organisation. Some form of **structure** is needed by which people's interactions and efforts are channelled and co-ordinated. To which we can add a fourth factor –

● management.

Some process of **management** is required by which the activities of the organisation, and the efforts of its members, are directed and controlled towards the pursuit of objectives. (*See* Fig. 3.1.)

The actual effectiveness of the organisation will be dependent upon the quality of its people, its objectives and structure, and the resources available to it. There are two broad categories of resources:

● non-human – physical assets, materials and facilities; and
● human – members' abilities and influence, and their management.

The interrelationship of people, objectives and structure, together with the efficient use of available non-human and human resources, will determine the success or failure of the organisation and the extent of its effectiveness.

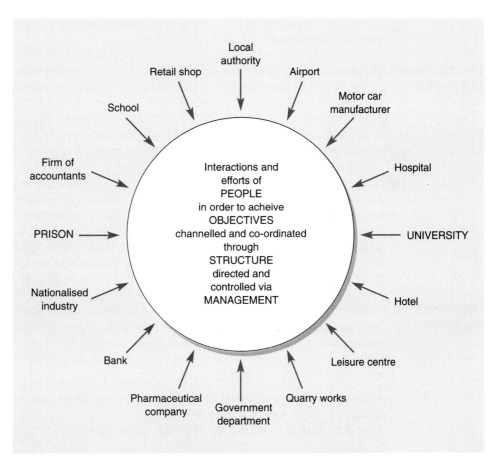

Fig. 3.1
Common factors in organisations

FORMAL AND INFORMAL ORGANISATIONS

The formal organisation

The formal organisation can be distinguished from the informal organisation. The difference between the formal and the informal organisation is a feature of the degree to which they are structured.

A **formal organisation** has been defined by *Schein* as 'the planned co-ordination of the activities of a number of people for the achievement of some common, explicit purpose or goal, through division of labor and function, and through a hierarchy of authority and responsibility'.[1] An organisation is a pattern of roles and a blueprint for their co-ordination. The object of co-ordination is activities, not people. The formal organisation can exist independently of the membership of particular individuals.

The formal organisation is:

- deliberately planned and created;
- concerned with the co-ordination of activities;
- hierarchically structured with stated objectives, the specification of tasks, and defined relationships of authority and responsibility.

An organisation chart, for example, gives a representation of the formal structure. Other examples of the formal organisation are rules and regulations, policy manuals, standing orders, and job descriptions.

The organisation as a coalition

The formal organisation can be seen as a coalition of individuals with a number of sub-coalitions.[2] Membership of the coalition will be dependent upon the type of organisation but could include, for example, managers, administrators, workers, elected representatives, appointed officials, volunteers, shareholders, suppliers, trade union officials, leaders of interest groups, customers, clients, patrons, donors, specialists, consultants, and representatives of external agencies.

It is difficult to define specific, permanent boundaries for an organisational coalition. However, by focusing on participants over a given period, or participants concerned with particular decision-making processes, it is possible to identify the main members of a coalition. Strategies adopted by particular sectional interests or sub-coalitions will sometimes be part of the formal organisation structure, for instance, in the pursuit of manifest managerial goals; and sometimes related to the informal structure, for example, heads of department vying with each other for limited resources, or workers indulging in restrictive practices.

The informal organisation

Within the formal structure an informal organisation will always be present. The informal organisation arises from the interaction of people working in the organisation, their psychological and social needs, and the development of groups with their own relationships and norms of behaviour, irrespective of those defined within the formal structure.

- The informal organisation is flexible and loosely structured.
- Relationships may be left undefined.
- Membership is spontaneous and with varying degrees of involvement.

Group relationships and norms of behaviour exist outside the official structure and the informal organisation may, therefore, be in conflict with the aims of the

formal organisation. A summary of differences between the formal and the informal organisation is given in Table 3.1.

Table 3.1 **Comparison of formal and informal organisation**

Characteristic	*Formal organisation*	*Informal organisation*
1. Structure		
A. Origin	Planned	Spontaneous
B. Rationale	Rational	Emotional
C. Characteristics	Stable	Dynamic
2. Position terminology	Job	Role
3. Goals	Profitability or service to society	Member satisfaction
4. Influence		
A. Base	Position	Personality
B. Type	Authority	Power
C. Flow	Top-down	Bottom-up
5. Control mechanisms	Threat of firing, demotion	Physical or social sanctions (norms)
6. Communication		
A. Channels	Formal channels	Grapevine
B. Networks	Well defined, follow formal lines	Poorly defined, cut across regular channels
C. Speed	Slow	Fast
D. Accuracy	High	Low
7. Charting the organisation	Organisation chart	Sociogram
8. Miscellaneous		
A. Individuals included	All individuals in work group	Only those 'acceptable'
B. Interpersonal relations	Prescribed by job description	Arise spontaneously
C. Leadership role	Assigned by organisation	Result of membership agreement
D. Basis for interaction	Functional duties or position	Personal characteristics, ethnic background, status
E. Basis for attachment	Loyalty	Cohesiveness

(Adapted and reproduced with permission from: J. L. Gray and F. A. Starke *Organizational Behavior: Concepts and Applications*, Fourth edition, Merrill Publishing Company, an imprint of Macmillan Publishing Company (1988) p. 432.)

FUNCTIONS OF THE INFORMAL ORGANISATION

The informal organisation can serve a number of important functions.

- It provides satisfaction of members' social needs, and a sense of personal identity and belonging.
- It provides for additional channels of communication; for example, through the 'grapevine' information of importance to particular members is communicated quickly.

- It provides a means of motivation, for example, through status, social interaction, variety in routine or tedious jobs, and informal methods of work.
- It provides a feeling of stability and security, and through informal 'norms' of behaviour can exercise a form of control over members.
- It provides a means of highlighting deficiencies or weaknesses in the formal organisation, for example, areas of duties or responsibilities not covered in job descriptions or outdated systems and procedures. The informal organisation may also be used when formal methods would take too long, or not be appropriate, to deal with an unusual or unforeseen situation.[3]

The informal organisation, therefore, has an important influence on the morale, motivation, job satisfaction and performance of staff. It can provide members with greater opportunity to use their initiative and creativity in both personal and organisational development. Covert and informal activities may also have economic consequences for the organisation in terms of added values and/or costs that escape ordinary accounting procedures.[4]

The importance and nature of groups, and reasons why people form into groups, both formal and informal, are discussed in Chapter 6. At this stage, however, we are concerned with consideration of the formal organisation (although in practice it is not always possible to distinguish clearly between formal and informal organisations). We are not concerned with what is sometimes referred to as the social organisation. Social organisations are groups or institutions, such as the family or friends, where human behaviour is socially organised and where members share common beliefs or interests. Social organisations arise from the interaction of individuals. There are no specially defined hierarchical structures and no explicit organisational goals.

BASIC COMPONENTS OF AN ORGANISATION

Any organisation can be described, broadly, in terms of an operating component and an administrative component.[5]

The **operating component** comprises the people who actually undertake the work of producing the products, or providing the services.

The **administrative component** comprises managers and analysts, and is concerned with supervision and co-ordination.

Developing this description, we can analyse the work organisation in terms of five basic components: the operational core; operational support; organisational support; top management; and middle management. (*See* Fig. 3.2.)

- The **operational core** is concerned with direct performance of the technical or productive operations and the carrying out of actual task activities of the organisation; for example, people putting together parts on an assembly line, teaching in a classroom, treating a patient, cooking meals in a hotel, serving in a bank, repairing a hole in the road.
- **Operational support** is concerned indirectly with the technical or productive process but closely related to the actual flow of operational work; for example, people working in quality control, work study, progress planning, storekeeping, works maintenance, technical services.

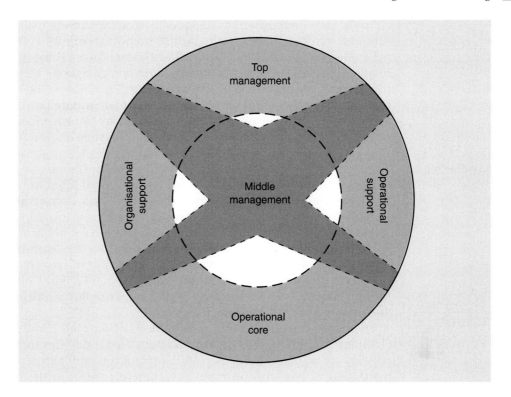

Fig. 3.2
Five basic
components of
an organisation

- **Organisational support** is concerned with provision of services for the whole organisation, including the operational core, but which are usually outside the actual flow of operational work; for example, people working in personnel, medical services, canteen, management accounting, office services.
- **Top management** is concerned with broad objectives and policy, strategic decisions, the work of the organisation as a whole and interactions with the external environment; for example, managing director, governors, management team, chief executive, board of directors, council members.
- **Middle management** is concerned with co-ordination and integration of activities; and providing links with operational support staff and organisational support staff, and between the operational core and top management.

PRIVATE AND PUBLIC SECTOR ORGANISATIONS

Organisations can, traditionally, be distinguished in terms of two generic groups:

- private enterprise organisations; and
- public sector organisations.

The distinction can be made on the basis of ownership and finance, and the profit motive. Private enterprise organisations are owned and financed by individuals, partners, or shareholders in a joint stock company. The main aim is of a *commercial* nature such as profit, return on capital employed, market standing or sales level.

Public sector organisations include, for example, municipal undertakings and central government departments, which do not have profit as their goal. Municipal undertakings such as local authorities are 'owned' by the ratepayers and financed by rates, government grants, loans and charges for certain services. Central government departments are 'state owned' and financed by funds granted by parliament. Public sector organisations do not distribute profits. Any surplus of revenue over expenditure may be reallocated by improved services or reduced charges. The main aim is a *service to* and the well-being of *the community*.

Privatisation

The extent of the state ownership of public sector operations, or of their 'privatisation', and the balance between commercial and social interests, are determined by the government of the day. In recent years, the Conservative government embarked upon a major 'denationalisation' programme involving the selling off of shares and subsidiaries, and increasing competition for public monopolies. There has been a vigorous policy of creating freedom from state control and the transfer of business undertakings to private hands (privatisation) involving such organisations as, for example, British Petroleum, National Freight Corporation, Jaguar, British Telecom, British Aerospace, British Gas, Rolls-Royce, British Airways, British Steel, water authorities and electricity boards.

There are other public sector organisations whose aims involve both a commercial interest and a service interest. Nationalised industries such as coal and the railways are, at present, run as public corporations with autonomy on day-to-day management, but with ultimate government control in the national interest. These public corporations are required to make efficient use of their resources by ensuring a given minimum rate of return on their investments and to charge prices based on the actual cost of supplying goods or services to certain groups of consumers. But provision may also be made for certain activities to be undertaken on social grounds as a service to the community even though these activities might be run at a financial loss.

There have also been increasing moves to encourage contracting-out of certain local authority services and putting them to compulsory competitive tender. Examples include cleansing services, vehicle maintenance, catering, parks services, refuse collection and social services transport. A greater degree of competition has also been introduced, for example, in the supply of communications apparatus, and removal of restrictions on passenger road transport to allow increased competition among coach and bus operators. The exposure to competition and demands for economical and high quality service has prompted the demand for local authorities to replace administration with business management.

The increasing scale of privatisation and the blurring of commercial interests and social interests have led to an alternative classification of organisations:

- **profit**; and those clearly
- **not-for-profit.**

Not-for-profit organisations include on one hand charities, private societies and most religious organisations, and on the other hand National Health Service hospitals, universities, prisons, and most government and local authority departments.

However, even in not-for-profit, public sector organisations there has been increased government pressure to ensure cost-effectiveness, investment by private sector involvement, and efficiency and economy in their operations.

TYPES OF AUTHORITY AND ORGANISATIONS

In one of the earliest studies of formal organisations, *Weber* distinguished three types of authority: **traditional**, **charismatic** and **legal–rational**.[6] These types of authority are based on the form of control regarded as legitimate by subordinates, and their acceptance of the power of superiors. The three types of authority relate to different types of organisations.

- In **traditional organisations**, authority is legitimised by custom and a long-standing belief in the natural right to rule, or is possessed by traditional ('proper') procedure. Examples would be the authority of the pope, kings or queens or a paternalistic employer.
- In **charismatic organisations**, authority is legitimised by belief in the personal qualities of the leader; authority is based on the leader's strength of personality and inspiration. Winston Churchill might be quoted as an example. The practical need for some routine, for procedures and systems and for economic support means that if the movement is to continue it must become organised. On the impending demise of the charismatic leader the movement might collapse unless a 'legitimate' heir is found. This process tends to transform a charismatic organisation into either a traditional organisation or a bureaucratic organisation.
- In **bureaucratic organisations**, authority is based on the acceptance of the law of formal rules and procedures, and on impersonal principles. There is a legal–rational authority which stems from hierarchical position in the organisation and not from personality. Examples are the armed forces and the authority of government ministers or a college principal.

The concept of legal–rational authority is of most interest to us because most business organisations, particularly large-scale ones, tend to be of the bureaucratic type of structure, although there are variations in degree. Bureaucracy, as applying to certain structural features of organisation, is the most dominant type of formal organisation.

THE CLASSIFICATION OF ORGANISATIONS

In order to relate the study of management and organisational behaviour to one particular type of organisation as distinct from another, it is necessary to group similar types of organisations together. This enables generalisations to be made on the basis of certain characteristic features of organisations within a particular grouping. Organisations can be distinguished by, for example, their nature and type; goods or services provided; size; aims and objectives; and the people who are employed by or who work in them. Organisations can, therefore, be classified in a number of ways and different writers have emphasised particular features of organisations.

Classification by major purpose A common classification of organisations is by their major purpose. This leads to a distinction between, for example:

- business firms (economic organisations);
- armies, trade unions and police forces (protective organisations);

- clubs and societies (associative organisations);
- local authorities and hospitals (public service organisations); and
- churches (religious organisations).

Further distinctions could be made, for example, into political organisations, educational organisations, military organisations and voluntary organisations.

Such a distinction tends to lack refinement and not all organisations fit simply into one classification. Many universities combine research with teaching. Some hospitals are concerned as much with training and/or research as with treatment of patients. One could debate the main purpose of a prison; is it, for example, corrective, protective, penal or educational? The main purpose of a trade union is seen, presumably, as protection of the interests of its members through their wages and working conditions, but many trade unions also have strong social, educational and political interests.

Many organisations serve more than one goal; but although they are multi-purpose organisations it is usual to be able to identify one predominant goal (or purpose) by which the organisation can be classified, however crude this classification may be. It is, however, of interest to note the comment by *Etzioni* that 'To the extent that such things can be measured, it appears that many multi-purpose organisations tend to serve each of their goals separately and all of them together more effectively and efficiently than single-purpose organisations of the same category'.[7]

PRIME BENEFICIARY OF THE ORGANISATION

Blau and Scott propose a classification on the basis of the prime beneficiary.[8] Four groups of persons involved in a relationship with any organisation are categorised into:

- The members, or rank and file participants;
- The owner or managers of the organisation;
- The clients or, more generally, the 'public-in-contact' who are technically 'outside' the organisation yet have regular direct contact with it;
- The public at large, that is, the members of the society in which the organisation operates.

Organisations are then classified on the basis of who benefits, that is, which of the four categories is the prime beneficiary of its operations. Four types of organisation are identified on this basis:

- **Mutual-benefit associations**, where the prime beneficiary is the membership, such as political parties, trade unions and professional associations;
- **Business concerns**, where the owners are the prime beneficiaries, such as industrial and other firms privately owned and operated for profit;
- **Service organisations**, where the client group is the main beneficiary, such as hospitals, schools and welfare agencies;
- **Commonweal organisations**, where the prime beneficiary is the public-at-large, such as central government departments, the armed services and the police.

Problems associated with each type of organisation

It is emphasised that the prime beneficiary is not necessarily the only beneficiary. Each of the various groups who make a contribution to an organisation do so only in return for certain benefits received.

Blau and Scott suggest that special problems are associated with each type of organisation.

In **mutual-benefit organisations** the main problem is that of providing for participation and control by the membership, and of maintaining internal democracy.

In **business concerns** the central problem is that of maximising operational efficiency in a competitive environment.

In **service organisations** the problem is reconciling conflict between professional service to clients and administrative procedures.

In **commonweal organisations** the important problem is ensuring democratic procedures by which they are held accountable to the public for their actions.

Difficulty in finding a comprehensive classification

It is not easy to find a comprehensive classification into which all organisations can be simply and satisfactorily categorised; and a degree of generalisation, assumption and qualification is required. However, the classification of Blau and Scott provides a useful typology of organisations. An alternative form of classification is provided by *Katz and Khan*.

PRIMARY ACTIVITY OF THE ORGANISATION

The *Katz and Khan* classification is based on 'genotypic (first-order) factors' and on 'second-order factors'.[9] In terms of the genotypic function, which is the primary activity of the organisation as a sub-system within the larger society, there are four broad types of organisations:

- **Productive or economic** – concerned with the creation of wealth, the manufacture of goods, and the provision of services for the public;
- **Maintenance** – for example, schools and churches, concerned with the socialisation of people to fulfil roles in other organisations and in society;
- **Adaptive** – for example, research establishments, concerned with the pursuit of knowledge and the development and testing of theory;
- **Managerial or political** – for example, government departments, trade unions and pressure groups. These are concerned with adjudication, co-ordination and control of physical and human resources and other sub-systems.

Object-moulding or people-moulding

Organisations can then be described in terms of second-order factors. Among other things these factors relate to structure; the system of intrinsic or extrinsic rewards to attract and retain members and to achieve satisfactory performance from them; and the nature of the throughput – the transformation or processing of objects or the moulding of people as the end product of the organisation. A distinction can be made between

- **object-moulding organisations** and
- **people-moulding organisations**.

Object-moulding organisations are concerned with physical or material objects as the nature of work being carried out, for example, a manufacturing plant, a coal-mine or an oil company.

People-moulding organisations are concerned with human beings as the basis of the nature of work being carried out, for example, a school or a leisure centre. In people-moulding organisations a further distinction can be made between

(i) people-processing organisations, for example, an employment agency or a social security benefit office; and

(ii) people-changing organisations, for example, a mental hospital or an open prison.

THE ORGANISATION AS AN OPEN SYSTEM

We have seen that organisations differ in many important respects. But they also share common features. Organisations can be viewed as open systems which take inputs from the environment (outputs from other systems) and through a series of activities transform or convert these inputs into outputs (inputs to other systems) to achieve some objective. (*See* Fig. 3.3.)[10]

In terms of this open systems model the business organisation, for example, takes in resources such as people, finance, raw materials and information from its environment; transforms or converts these; and returns them to the environment in various forms of outputs such as goods produced, services provided, completed processes or procedures in order to achieve certain goals such as profit, market standing, level of sales or consumer satisfaction.

A common point of reference There are, of course, differences in the activities and methods of operation of the various forms of business organisations. There will also be differences between business organisations of the same type, for example, in relation to their size and scale of activities. However, adopting the systems view of organisations, we can identify principles and prescriptions of organisation and management that apply

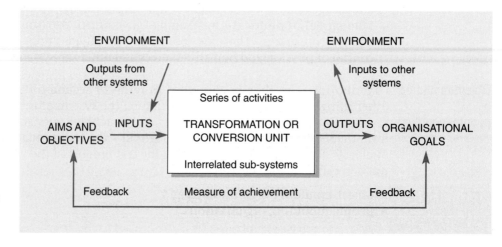

Fig. 3.3
The open systems model of organisations

to business organisations in general. Differences in the application and operation of these principles and prescriptions as between one business organisation and another is largely a matter only of degree and of emphasis.

Using this systems model the same form of analysis can be applied to all types of organisations. Viewing organisations as systems provides a common point of reference and enables us to take a general approach to the study of organisations, to analyse them and to derive general principles and prescriptions.[11]

An example of the open systems model applied to the environment systems division of a major heating and ventilation company is given in Fig. 3.4.

Fig. 3.4
An example of the open systems model

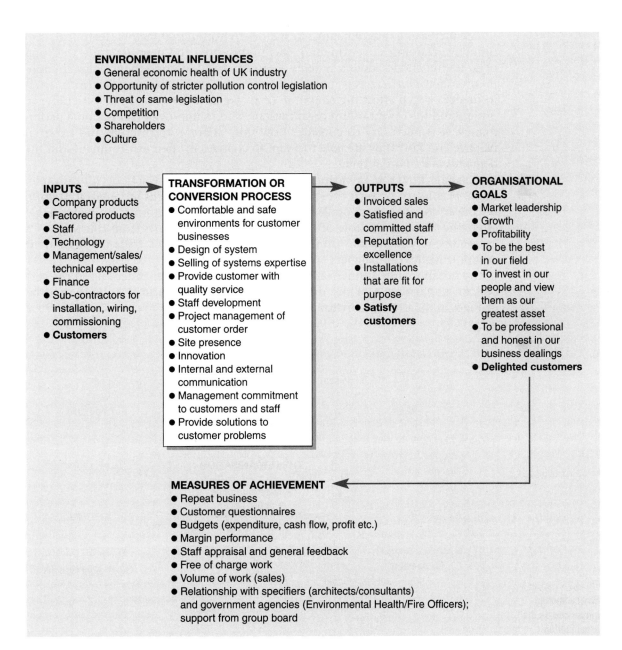

ENVIRONMENTAL INFLUENCES
- General economic health of UK industry
- Opportunity of stricter pollution control legislation
- Threat of same legislation
- Competition
- Shareholders
- Culture

INPUTS
- Company products
- Factored products
- Staff
- Technology
- Management/sales/ technical expertise
- Finance
- Sub-contractors for installation, wiring, commissioning
- **Customers**

TRANSFORMATION OR CONVERSION PROCESS
- Comfortable and safe environments for customer businesses
- Design of system
- Selling of systems expertise
- Provide customer with quality service
- Staff development
- Project management of customer order
- Site presence
- Innovation
- Internal and external communication
- Management commitment to customers and staff
- Provide solutions to customer problems

OUTPUTS
- Invoiced sales
- Satisfied and committed staff
- Reputation for excellence
- Installations that are fit for purpose
- **Satisfy customers**

ORGANISATIONAL GOALS
- Market leadership
- Growth
- Profitability
- To be the best in our field
- To invest in our people and view them as our greatest asset
- To be professional and honest in our business dealings
- **Delighted customers**

MEASURES OF ACHIEVEMENT
- Repeat business
- Customer questionnaires
- Budgets (expenditure, cash flow, profit etc.)
- Margin performance
- Staff appraisal and general feedback
- Free of charge work
- Volume of work (sales)
- Relationship with specifiers (architects/consultants) and government agencies (Environmental Health/Fire Officers); support from group board

Interaction with environment

The structure, management and functioning of an organisation is not only determined by internal considerations and choices, but is also strongly influenced by a range of external, environmental factors.

The business organisation is an open system. That means that it is open to, and in continual interaction with, the external environment of which it is part. In order to be effective and maintain survival and growth, the organisation must respond to the opportunities and challenges, and the risks and limitations, presented by the external environment. Changes in the environment will affect inputs, and changes in inputs will affect the transformation or conversion process and hence the outputs. The open systems approach views the organisation within its total environment and emphasises the importance of multiple channels of interaction.

The increasing rate of change in major environmental factors (technical, economic, social and governmental) has highlighted the need to study the total organisation and to adopt a systems approach. In addition to these major environmental factors, there is a multiplicity of constantly changing environmental influences which affect the operation of an organisation (*see* Fig. 3.5). In order to understand the operations of organisations, and to improve organisational performance, it is necessary to consider how they achieve an internal and external balance and how they are able to adapt to changes in their environment and the demands placed upon them.

Consider how the operations of a large comprehensive school, for example, might be affected by such external influences as: government proposals for reform of education; changing population trends; advances in information technology; changing views of the role of education in society; reports from Her Majesty's Inspectors; representations from employer's associations and trade unions; parent groups; equality campaigners.

Organisational performance and effectiveness will be dependent upon the successful management of the opportunities, challenges and risks presented by changes in the external environment.

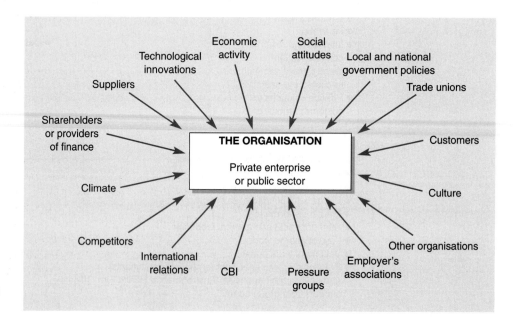

Fig. 3.5 Environmental influences on the organisation

THE COMPARATIVE STUDY OF ORGANISATIONS

All organisations need clear aims and objectives which will determine the nature of inputs, the series of activities to achieve outputs and the realisation of organisational goals. Feedback about the performance of the system, and the effects of its operation on the environment, are measured in terms of achieving the aims and objectives.

Basic principles of organisation and management apply in any series of activities in any organisation.

- Attention must be given to the design of a suitable structure.
- The common elements of management – clarification of objectives, planning, organising, directing and control – apply to a greater or lesser extent in all cases.
- Essential administrative functions must be carried out in all types of organisation.

These common features make possible the application of general principles of management and organisational behaviour, and the meaningful study of organisation theory.

Characteristic features of particular organisations

Whilst general principles and prescriptions apply to all organisations, differences in their aims and objectives, organisational goals, and environmental influences will result in differences in the input–conversion–output process and in the series of activities involved in this process. The nature of inputs, the throughputs, and the form of the outputs will emphasise characteristic features of a particular organisation. These features highlight alternative forms of structure, management, methods of operation, and behaviour of people employed by or working in different types of organisations.

The study of organisations as open systems serves, therefore, to indicate both the common features of organisations and the main distinguishing features between different types of organisations. It provides a useful framework for the comparative study of organisations. The systems view of organisations enables managers to view their own organisation in perspective, and to compare it in meaningful terms with other types of organisations.[12]

ORGANISATIONAL SUB-SYSTEMS

Whatever the type or classification of organisations, the transformation or conversion of inputs into outputs is a common feature of all organisations. Within the organisation (system) as a whole, each of the different transformation or conversion activities may themselves be viewed as separate sub-systems with their own input–conversion–output process interrelated to, and interacting with, the other sub-systems.

The analysis of an organisation could perhaps be based upon the departmental structure as sub-systems. However, this could lead to an investigation concentrating on blinkered, sectional interests, rather than on the need to adopt a corporate approach. It is not just a question of whether individual departments are operating efficiently. The important point is the interrelationships and co-ordination of sub-systems in terms of the effectiveness of the organisation as an integrated whole.

83

The interrelationship and interdependence of the different parts of the system raise the question of the identification of these sub-systems. What are the boundaries that distinguish one sub-system from other sub-systems, and from the system as a whole? In practice the boundaries are drawn at the discretion of the observer and sub-systems are identified according to the area under study. These sub-systems may be identified, therefore, in a number of different ways, although there is a degree of similarity among the alternative models.

Socio-technical system

The work of *Trist* and others of the Tavistock Institute of Human Relations, in their study of changing technology in the British coal-mines, gave rise to the idea of the socio-technical system.[13] The socio-technical system is concerned with the transformation or conversion process itself, the relationships between technical efficiency and social considerations and the effect on people. It was observed that new methods of work and changes in technology disrupted the social groupings of the miners, and brought about undesirable changes to the psychological and sociological properties of the old method of working. As a result, the new method of work was less efficient than it could have been despite the introduction of new technology.

The researchers saw the need for a socio-technical approach in which an appropriate social system could be developed in keeping with the new technical system. They suggested that there are three sub-systems common to any organisation:

- the **technological** sub-system;
- the sub-system of **formal role structure**;
- the sub-system of **individual members' feelings or sentiments**.

This form of analysis is taken a stage further by *Kast and Rosenzweig* who see the organisation as an open, socio-technical system with five major sub-systems.[14]

- **Goals and values** – the accomplishment of certain goals determined by the broader system and conformity with social requirements.
- **Technical** – the knowledge required for the performance of tasks, and the techniques and technology involved.
- **Psychosocial** – the interactions of individuals and groups, and behaviour of people in the organisation.
- **Structure** – the division and co-ordination of tasks, and formal relationships between the technical and psychosocial sub-systems.
- **Managerial** – covering the whole organisation and its relationship to the environment, setting goals, planning, structure and control.

Interrelated sub-systems

An alternative model is suggested by *Hersey and Blanchard*, who identify four main interrelated sub-systems.[15]

- **Human/social** focuses on the needs and motivations of members of the organisation and styles of leadership.
- **Administrative/structural** focuses on authority and responsibility, and the structure within the organisation.
- **Informational/decision-making** focuses on key decisions and information needs necessary to keep the organisation operational.
- **Economic/technological** focuses on the work to be undertaken and its cost-effectiveness related to the goals of the organisation.

Another useful model is that of *Leavitt* who suggests the organisation consists of four main elements – task, structure, information and control, and people – which interact with each other and with the external environment.[16]

- **Task** – involves problem-solving and improving organisational performance.
- **Structure** – refers to patterns of organisation, authority and responsibility, and communications.
- **Information and control** – techniques for controlling and processing information, such as accounting techniques.
- **People** – involves attitudes and interpersonal relations.

THE ANALYSIS OF WORK ORGANISATIONS

However these sub-systems are identified, it is the task of management to co-ordinate the sub-systems, and to ensure that the activities of the organisation as a whole are directed towards the accomplishment of its goals and objectives. We can suggest, therefore, five main interrelated sub-systems as a basis for the analysis of work organisations. (*See* Fig. 3.6.)

- **Task** – the goals and objectives of the organisation. The nature of inputs and outputs, and the work activities to be carried out in the transformation or conversion process.
- **Technology** – the manner in which the tasks of the organisation are carried out and the nature of work performance. The materials, systems and procedures, and equipment used in the transformation or conversion process.
- **Structure** – patterns of organisation, lines of authority, formal relationships and channels of communication among members. The division of work and co-ordination of tasks by which the series of activities are carried out.
- **People** – the nature of the members undertaking the series of activities: such as their attitudes, skills and attributes; needs and expectations; interpersonal relations and patterns of behaviour; group functioning and behaviour; informal organisation and styles of leadership.
- **Management** – co-ordination of task, technology, structure and people, and policies and procedures for the execution of work. Corporate strategy, direction of the activities of the organisation as a whole and its interactions with the external environment.

The attention given to organisational sub-systems can be related to developments in management thinking and organisational behaviour (discussed in Chapter 2). The classical approach emphasised the structural and the managerial sub-systems and the development of general principles of organisation. The human relations approach emphasised the psychological and sociological aspects and gave attention to the importance of people in the organisation and such factors as the social needs of individuals, motivation and group behaviour.

The systems approach focuses attention on the organisation as a whole, as a socio-technical system, and considers the interrelationships between the different sub-systems and the importance of environmental influences. The contingency approach concentrates on situational factors as determinants of alternative forms of organisation and management.

A broader view of the organisation's activities

We have seen that an open systems approach is an attempt to view the organisation as a purposeful, unified whole in continual interaction with its external environment. The organisation (system) is composed of a number of interrelated parts (sub-systems). Any one part of the organisation's activities affects other parts. Managers cannot afford to take a narrow, blinkered view. They need to adopt a broader view of the organisation's activities. Managers should recognise the interrelationships between various activities and the effects that their actions and decisions have on other activities.

Using the above framework of five main interrelated sub-systems – task, technology, structure, people, management – provides a useful basis for the analysis of organisational performance and effectiveness.

**Fig. 3.6
Organisational
sub-systems**

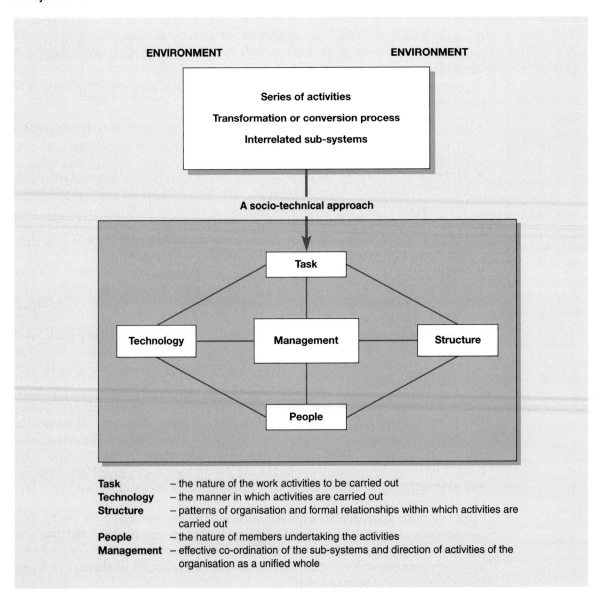

Task	– the nature of the work activities to be carried out
Technology	– the manner in which activities are carried out
Structure	– patterns of organisation and formal relationships within which activities are carried out
People	– the nature of members undertaking the activities
Management	– effective co-ordination of the sub-systems and direction of activities of the organisation as a unified whole

The manager must realise that in order to improve organisational effectiveness attention should be focused on the total work organisation and on the interrelationships between the range of variables which affect organisational performance. The organisation is best viewed as an open system and studied in terms of the interactions between technical and social considerations, and environmental influences. Changes in part of the system will affect other parts and thus the whole organisation. **The open systems approach provides a perspective in which to compare and contrast different types of organisations and their methods of operation.**

CONTINGENCY MODELS OF ORGANISATION

The analysis of organisational effectiveness requires an understanding of relationships within the organisation's structure, the interrelated sub-systems and the nature of its external environment.

Irrespective of the identification of sub-systems, the nature and scale of the series of activities involved in converting inputs to outputs will differ from one organisation to another in terms of the interrelationships between technology, structure, methods of operation, and the nature of environmental influences. 'Contingency' models of organisation highlight these interrelationships and provide a further possible means of differentiation between alternative forms of organisation and management.

The contingency approach takes the view that there is no one best, universal form of organisation. There are a large number of variables, or situational factors, that influence organisational performance. Contingency models can be seen as an '*if–then*' form of relationship. *If* certain situational factors exist, *then* certain organisational and managerial variables are most appropriate. Managers can utilise these models to compare the structure and functioning of their own organisation. Contingency models are examined in Chapter 11.

THE INFLUENCE OF TECHNOLOGY

The systems and contingency approaches have drawn attention to the importance of technology in the structure, management and functioning of work organisations.

It is important to note that the meaning of technology is interpreted broadly to include both:

* the physical aspects of machines, equipment, processes and work layout (machine technology) involved in the transformation or conversion process; and
* the actual methods, systems and procedures involved (knowledge technology) in carrying out the work of the organisation and transforming or converting inputs into outputs.

There is a close interrelationship between the machine side of technology and the specialist knowledge side of technology.[17]

The nature of technology can, therefore, be applied to the analysis of all organisations. For example, in a university the machine side of technology would

include: blackboards or whiteboards; overhead projectors; computers; televisions and video recorders, closed circuit television; scientific and engineering equipment; library facilities. The knowledge side of technology would include: lectures, seminars and tutorials; case studies; role-playing; practical laboratory work; visiting speakers; project and assignment work; examinations.

The work processes of a university, and other educational establishments, give rise to the specialist study of educational technology.[18] A university will receive inputs of students and, through the process of educational technology, 'transform' them and return them as outputs into the broader society.

Technology and the behaviour of people

The nature of technology can influence the behaviour of people in work organisations in many ways including, for example, the following.

- It influences the specific design of each member's pattern of work including the nature and variety of activities performed, and the extent of autonomy and freedom of action.
- It affects the nature of social interactions, for example the size and nature of work groups, the extent of physical mobility and of contacts with other people. A person working continuously on a single, isolated machine in a mass production factory will have very limited social interactions compared with, say, a team of receptionists in a large conference hotel.
- It can affect role position and the nature of rewards. People with higher levels of specialist technical knowledge and expertise such as engineers or systems analysts tend to receive higher status and pay than machine operators on an assembly line.
- It can impose time dimensions on workers and may require set times for attending to operations and a set pace of work; for example, the mechanical pacing of work on a mass-production assembly line.
- It can result in distinguishing features of appearance; for example, the requirement to wear a standard uniform or protective clothing, compared with a personal choice of smart clothes.[19]

The general climate of the organisation

Technology is a major influence on the general climate of the organisation and the behaviour of people at work. For example, according to *Huczynski and Buchanan*:

> The organization of work around a given technology can be used to control labour costs, to control decision making, to control the relative status of different groups in an organization and to control promotion and career prospects. Managers may be able to manipulate employees in these ways by appealing to the technological determinist argument: 'We have to do this because the technology demands it.' Technological determinism may thus be used to justify unpopular management decisions and render them safe from effective challenge.[20]

The nature of technology is also a potential source of tension and stress and affects motivation and job satisfaction: this is discussed in Chapter 15.

The systems approach should serve to remind managers that activities managed on the basis of technical efficiency alone are unlikely to lead to optimum improvements in organisational performance. It is important to maintain the balance of the socio-technical system. Changes to the work organisation as a result of new developments in technology must take account of human and social factors as well as technical and economic factors.

INFORMATION TECHNOLOGY

The importance of the effective management of technical change has been highlighted by recent and continuing developments in information technology. Although the term 'information technology' originated in the computer industry, it extends beyond computing to include telecommunications and office equipment. Advances in technical knowledge, the search for improved economic efficiency and government support for information technology have all prompted a growing movement towards more automated procedures of work.

The impact of information technology demands new patterns of work organisation, especially in relation to administrative procedures. It affects the nature of individual jobs, and the formation and structure of work groups. There is a movement away from large-scale, centralised organisation to smaller working units. Processes of communication are increasingly linked to computer systems with the rapid transmission of information and immediate access to other national or international offices. Improvements in telecommunications mean, for example, that support staff need no longer be located within the main 'production' unit. Modern methods of communication may reduce the need for head office clerical jobs.

Changes wrought by information technology relate to the nature of the management task itself. Information technology bears heavily on the decision-making processes of the organisation and increasingly forms an essential part of management information and corporate strategy.[21]

The nature and conditions of work

The growth of information technology means that individuals may work more on their own, from their personal work stations or even from their own homes, or work more with machines than with other people. One person may be capable of carrying out a wider range of activities. There are changes in the nature of supervision and in the traditional hierarchical structure of jobs and responsibilities. Computer-based information and decision support systems provide an additional dimension of structural design. They affect choices such as division of work, individual tasks and responsibilities. The introduction of information technology undoubtedly transforms, significantly, the nature of work and employment conditions for staff.

Advances in technical knowledge tend to develop at a faster rate than, and in isolation from, consideration of related human and social consequences. For example, fatigue and low morale are two major obstacles to the efficiency of staff. Research is now being conducted into possible health hazards such as eye strain, backache, general fatigue and irritability for operators of visual display units. This concern has prompted union proposals for recommended working practices for VDU operators. The Trades Union Congress has called for regular health checks and eyesight tests for operators, and a 20-minute break every two hours.

MANAGING TECHNICAL CHANGE

Failure to match technical change to the concomitant human and social considerations means that staff may become resentful, suspicious and defensive. People's cognitive limitations, and their uncertainties and fears, may result in a reluctance to accept change.

The psychological and social implications of technical change, such as information technology and increased automation, must not be underestimated. New ideas and innovations should not be seen by members of staff as threats. The manager has to balance the need for adaptability in meeting opportunities presented by new technology with an atmosphere of stability and concern for the interests of staff. The manner in which technical change is introduced into the organisation will influence people's attitudes to work, the behaviour of individuals and groups, and their level of performance.[22]

An understanding of human behaviour

Continued technical change is inevitable and likely to develop at an even greater rate. Managers must be responsive to such change. Information technology and automation create a demanding challenge. The systems nature of organisations emphasises the interrelationships among the major variables or sub-systems of the organisation. The implementation and management of technological change needs to be related to its affect on the task, the structure and the people.[23]

Managers need to develop working practices based on an accurate understanding of human behaviour and the integration of people's needs with organisational needs. *Charsley*, for example, emphasises the point that 'It is prudent therefore to remember that it is extremely dangerous to place more importance on the workers' tools than the workers themselves'.[24]

It is important to avoid destructive conflict, alienating staff including managerial colleagues, or evoking the anger and opposition of unions. At the same time, it is important to avoid incurring increasing costs or a lower level of organisational performance caused by delays in the successful implementation of new technology. What needs to be considered is the impact of technical change on the design of the work organisation, and the attitudes and behaviour of staff.[25] It will be necessary for managers and supervisors to develop more agile skills in organisation. This calls for the effective management of human resources and a style of managerial behaviour which helps to minimise the problems of technical change. (The management of conflict and organisational change is discussed further in Chapter 20.)

ORGANISATIONAL GOALS

Whatever the form and structure of the transformation or conversion process, the activities of an organisation are directed towards some end, some organisational goal. A goal is a future expectation: it is something the organisation is striving to accomplish. The goals of an organisation will determine the nature of its outputs and the series of activities through which those outputs are achieved. Organisational goals and objectives are discussed in Chapter 9.

SYNOPSIS

■ The application of organisational behaviour and the process of management take place not in a vacuum but within the context of an organisational setting. Organisations come in all forms, shapes and sizes. However, despite the differences among various organisations there are at least three common factors in any organisation:

people, objectives and structure. To which can be added a fourth factor – management. The qualities of these factors determine organisational effectiveness.

■ The formal organisation can be distinguished from the informal organisation and from the social organisation. The formal organisation is deliberately planned and created, and is concerned with the co-ordination of activities. Five basic components of a formal organisation are: operational core, operational support, organisational support, top management and middle management. The informal organisation arises from the interaction of people. It serves a number of important functions and has an influence on the morale, motivation, job satisfaction and performance of staff.

■ There are many different types of organisations which are set up to serve a variety of needs. Organisations can, traditionally, be distinguished in terms of two generic groups: private enterprise and public sector. The increasing rate of privatisation has led, however, to a blurring of commercial interests and service to the community. In order to relate the study of management and organisational behaviour to one particular type of organisation as distinct from another, it is necessary to group similar types of organisations together.

■ The structure, management and functioning of organisations will differ according to their nature and type, aims and objectives, and the behaviour of people who work in them. Organisations differ in many important respects but they also share common features. Business organisations can be viewed as open systems in continual interaction with the external environment of which they are part. Within the organisation as a whole there are a number of sub-systems interrelating to and interacting with each other. Contingency models of organisation draw attention to interrelationships among technology, structure, methods of operation and environmental influences.

■ The systems and contingency approaches have drawn attention to the importance of technology in work organisations. The nature of technology can influence the behaviour of people at work in many ways. The impact of technical change has been highlighted by recent developments in information technology and automation. It is important to maintain the balance of the socio-technical system. This calls for effective management of human resources and a style of managerial behaviour which helps to minimise problems of technical change.

? Review and discussion questions

1 Why do organisations exist? What are the common factors in any organisation?

2 Distinguish between the formal and the informal organisation, and explain their main characteristics. What functions are served by the informal organisation?

3 Explain the basic components of a work organisation. Support your answer with examples from your own organisation.

4 Contrast various organisations, including your own, in terms of classifications based on: (i) prime beneficiary and (ii) primary activity.

5 Discuss critically the extent to which differences among various organisations limit the value of the study of management and organisational behaviour.

6 Explain the organisation as an open system. What is meant by organisational sub-systems and how might they be identified? Illustrate each of these sub-systems by reference to your own organisation.

7 Assess the practical value to both the student and the manager of adopting an open systems view of organisational analysis.

8 Discuss the importance of technology in the structure, management and functioning of work organisations. Give practical examples of how the nature of technology can influence the systems nature of organisations.

 Assignment 1

OUR ORGANISATIONAL SOCIETY: YOUR ASSOCIATION WITH ORGANISATIONS

Learning objectives

1. To identify some of the important organisations in your life.
2. To determine relevant, specific characteristics of organisations.
3. To describe some of the important functions of management in organisations.

Advance preparation

Read the Overview and Procedure Sections. Complete the form 'Profile of Organisations'.

Overview

Undoubtedly, you have had recent experiences with numerous organisations. Ten to fifteen minutes of reflective thinking should result in a fairly large list of organisations. Don't be misled by thinking that only large organisations, such as your college or General Motors, are relevant for consideration. How about the clinic with the doctor(s), nurse(s) and secretary/bookkeeper? Or the corner garage or service station? The local tavern, McDonald's and the neighbourhood theatre are all organisations. You should not have any difficulty in listing a number of organisations with which you have had recent contact.

The second part of the exercise, however, gets tougher. You are asked to describe several of the key characteristics of the organisations that you have listed. One of the major issues in studying and describing organisations is deciding *what* characteristics or factors are important. Some of the more common characteristics considered in the analysis of organisations are:

1. Size (small to very large);
2. Degree of formality (informal to highly structured);
3. Degree of complexity (simple to complex);
4. Nature of goals (what the organisation is trying to accomplish);

5. Major activities (what tasks are performed);
6. Types of people involved (age, skills, educational background, etc.);
7. Location of activities (number of units and their geographic location).

You should be able to develop a list of characteristics that you think are relevant for each of your organisations.

Now, to the third, final, and most difficult task. Think about what is involved in the *management* of these organisations. For example, what kinds of functions do their managers perform? How does one learn the skills necessary to be an effective manager? Would you want to be a manager in any of these organisations?

In effect, in this exercise you are asked to think specifically about organisations you have been associated with recently, develop your own conceptual model for looking at their characteristics, and think more specifically about the managerial functions in each of these organisations. You probably already know a great deal more about organisations and their management than you think. This exercise should be useful in getting your thoughts together.

Procedure

Step 1
Prior to class, list up to ten organisations (e.g., work, living group, club) in which you have been involved or with which you have had recent contact.

Step 2
Enter five organisations from your list on the form 'Profile of Organisations'.
a. List the organisation.
b. Briefly outline the characteristics that you consider most significant.
c. Describe the managerial functions in each of these organisations.

Step 3
During the class period, meet in groups of five or six to discuss your list of organisations, the characteristics you consider important, and your descriptions of their management. Look for significant similarities and differences across organisations.

Step 4
Basing your selections on this group discussion, develop a list entitled 'What We Would Like to Know about Organisations and Their Management'. Be prepared to write this list on the board and to share your list with other groups in the class.

PROFILE OF ORGANISATIONS		
Organisation	*Key characteristics*	*Managerial functions*
1. _____		
2. _____		
3. _____		
4. _____		
5. _____		

Assignment 2

With the aid of a diagram, depict your own organisation, or some other organisation well known to you, in terms of an open systems model.

a Indicate, clearly:
 – main aims and objectives;
 – inputs;
 – the nature of the transformation or conversion process;
 – outputs;
 – measurements of effectiveness in achieving organisational goals.

b Give specific examples of ways in which the structure, management and functioning of the organisation are affected by external environmental influences.
 How effective is the organisation in adapting to changes in its external environment?

c Analyse the transformation or conversion process in terms of main interrelated sub-systems. (Use a model or framework of your own choice.)
 How effective are the interactions and interrelationships among the sub-systems? Provide practical examples to support your views.

d Comment critically on the *effectiveness of management* in co-ordinating the sub-systems and directing the activities of the organisation as a unified whole towards the accomplishment of its goal and objectives. Give specific examples in support of your comments.

Notes and references

1. Schein, E. H. *Organizational Psychology*, Third edition, Prentice-Hall (1988) p. 15.
2. Cyert, R. M. and March, J. G. *A Behavioral Theory of the Firm*, Second edition, Blackwell (1992).
3. For a detailed account of the nature and function of the informal organisation, see: Gray, J. L. and Starke, F. A. *Organizational Behavior: Concepts and Applications*, Fourth edition, Charles E. Merrill (1988).
4. Egan, G. 'The Shadow Side', *Management Today*, September 1993, pp. 33–8.
5. Mintzberg, H. *The Structuring of Organizations*, Prentice-Hall (1979).
6. Weber, M. *The Theory of Social and Economic Organization*, Collier Macmillan (1964).
7. Etzioni, A. *Modern Organizations*, Prentice-Hall (1964) p. 14.
8. Blau, P. M. and Scott, W. R. *Formal Organizations*, Routledge and Kegan Paul (1966).
9. Katz, D. and Khan, R. L. *The Social Psychology of Organizations*, Second edition, Wiley (1978).
10. A summary of the systems view of organisations, and its value in distinguishing between private and public organisations, is given in: Mullins, L. J. 'The Organisation – A Systems View', *Professional Administration*, vol. 11, no. 2, February 1981, pp. 20–2.
11. See, for example: Mullins, L. J. *Hospitality Management: A Human Resources Approach*, Second edition, Pitman (1995).
12. For an interesting collection of readings on the systems view of organisations see: Lockett, M. and Spear, R. (eds) *Organizations as Systems*, Open University Press (1980).
13. Trist, E. L. *et al. Organizational Choice*, Tavistock Publications (1963).

14. Kast, F. E. and Rosenzweig, J. E. *Organization and Management*, Fourth edition, McGraw-Hill (1985).

15. Hersey, P. and Blanchard, K. *Management of Organizational Behavior*, Sixth edition, Prentice-Hall (1993).

16. Leavitt, H. J. *Managerial Psychology*, Fourth edition, University of Chicago Press (1978).

17. For a fuller discussion on the meaning of technology, see: Kast, F. E. and Rosenzweig, J. E. *Organization and Management*, Fourth edition, McGraw-Hill (1985).

18. See, for example: Davies, I. K. *The Management of Learning*, McGraw-Hill (1971).

19. Developed from French, W. L., Kast, F. E. and Rosenzweig, J. E. *Understanding Human Behavior in Organizations*, Harper and Row (1985) pp. 321–2.

20. Huczynski, A. A. and Buchanan, D. A. *Organizational Behaviour: An Introductory Text*, Second edition, Prentice-Hall (1991) pp. 306–7.

21. See, for example: Moynihan, E. 'Information Technology Strategy for the Administrator', *Administrator*, October 1990, pp. 7–9.

22. See: Mullins, L. J. 'Information Technology – The Human Factor', *Administrator*, vol. 5, no. 5, September 1985, pp. 6–9.

23. See, for example: Wilson, B. 'The Challenge of Change', *Industrial Management and Data Systems*, November/December 1987, pp. 19–22.

24. Charsley, W. F. 'The Human Factor in Office Automation', *Office and Information Management International*, vol. 2, no. 9, March 1989, p. 21.

25. See, for example: Gretton, I. 'Striving to Succeed in a Changing Environment', *Professional Manager*, July 1993, pp. 15–17.

Part 2

THE
INDIVIDUAL

4 INDIVIDUAL DIFFERENCES

Linda Hicks

Organisations consist of people working together. Individuals offer different perceptions, learning experiences and attitudes to their working world. Differences between individuals on the basis of personality or gender can be a source of developing creativity or the root of conflict, frustration and inevitable organisational problems. It is one of the tasks of management to recognise individual potential and harness talent to achieve organisational goals. Managers need to be aware of the factors affecting individual differences and their own assumptions and attitudes

 Learning objectives

To:

● Outline the importance of the individual's contribution to the organisation and factors affecting behaviour and performance;

● Examine the major difficulties of studying personality and the approaches taken by psychologists;

● Apply the key issues of personality studies to the work organisation with particular reference to personality assessment;

● Detail the significance of attitudes, their functions, change and measurement, with particular reference to culture of organisations;

● Apply the principles of attitude change to the workplace;

● Evaluate the principles of learning theories and the process of learning, and applications to organisational behaviour;

● Recognise the importance of an understanding of individual and social behaviour.

Worth thinking about

O.K. so it is important to understand that managing is all about people, and every person is an individual in his or her own right. But many theories and models about behaviour appear to apply to people in general. So to what extent should we be concerned with differences among individuals rather than with similarities among people?

INDIVIDUAL BEHAVIOUR IN ORGANISATIONS

One of the major paradoxes of organisational life is the maintenance of individuality and self-responsibility alongside the creation of co-operation and conformity. Managers expect their employees to work with others and be willing to obey; but at the same time expect to see evidence of personality, creativity and independence. Balancing individual needs and goals with group co-operation and conformity can be a major cause of tension, and yet is one of the most important tasks of management.

Selecting staff who will conform to organisational goals yet offer valuable individuality is a key to an organisation's health and effectiveness. The criteria used to reject or accept applicants are a major indicator of an organisation's values and beliefs. The selection process has been described as a 'cultural sieve'[1] and as an important method of control.[2] Indeed Tom Peters[3] has suggested that organisations need to review their selection requirements and instead of checking that every minute of every day is accounted for when appointing applicants they should consider applicants who have 'broken out' from the mould, rebelled from the system and thus demonstrated original thought. Peters regards such personal qualities as key attributes for leading-edge organisations.

However, this individualistic approach contrasts with the notion that organisations need team players who will be co-operative and conforming. As soon as the new recruits begin their employment a 'psychological contract' is struck which forms the basis for the obedience and conformity expected of the employees by the company. The manager's responsibility is to ensure that the socialisation process enables the new recruits to quickly learn the rules of the system. Rewards, if given at this stage, for correct behaviour and attitudes, will promote conformity and provide further incentives for the individuals to match the organisation's needs. (The recruitment and selection of staff is discussed in Chapter 19.)

Recognition of individuality

Recognition of good performers and performance is an essential part of the process of management. Managing people in organisations requires not only an understanding of the employees, but also a recognition of the culture of the organisation; for some organisations, creativity and individuality may be the last thing they would want to see between 9 and 5, but for others these characteristics are essential.

A discussion of individual behaviour in organisations is therefore riddled with complexity and contradictions. Managers are required to be competent at selecting the individuals who will be valuable to the organisation. They need to be observant

about the individuals who are performing well and have the potential to develop within the organisation. Finally managers need to know themselves and understand their own uniqueness and the impact their personality has on others.

Organisation change and individual differences

The speed at which organisations are undergoing change places almost continuous pressure on individuals at work. The paradox that change is now a 'constant feature' in organisational life has become a key feature in recent academic journals. Being able to manage the process of change is a necessity for all managers regardless of the type and nature of the organisation. Managing some areas of change, such as the development of computer skills (e.g. the transfer of skills when learning a new software package), may be relatively straightforward. The management of cataclysmic change, for example when organisations are taken over or merged, requires more sensitive handling. Knowledge of some of the fundamental issues relating to individual differences is essential for managers during these periods of change when there is the implicit requirement of a change in attitudes and beliefs. Such changes may lead to new mind-sets, new attitudes and new perceptions which enable people to cope and adjust to the different world. At these times effective management is vital; managers will be expected to understand the strains that their employees feel during times of change, but at the same time be able to deal with their own stress levels.

This part of the book addresses the ways in which it is possible to differentiate between individuals. Personality, the heart of individual differences, is explored first in this chapter. The emotional demands required by organisations of their employees are identified and discussed. There then follows an examination of the importance and functions of attitudes. An understanding of the ways in which people learn is fundamental to an appreciation of individual differences and is considered towards the end of this chapter. The process of perception and the impact of gender differences are examined in Chapter 5. All of these aspects are studied in the light of the impact they have on individual behaviour in organisations, and applications of psychological theory and concepts to the world of work.

Note: It would also have been legitimate to include motivation within this chapter, as individuals differ significantly with regard to their needs, their ambitions and the ways in which they satisfy their goals. However, the way which organisations choose to reward, or punish, their staff also differs and directly affects motivation. Therefore this topic is discussed in detail, as part of organisational processes, in Chapter 14.

PERSONALITY

It is possible to differentiate between individuals in terms of the following criteria:

- types/traits;
- gender;
- abilities;
- physique;
- development aspects;
- motivation;
- attitudes;
- perception;
- social and cultural aspects.

All of these characteristics shape our sense of self. So in one way we all share the same 'humanness'. Some of us share the same gender type or the same personality dimensions; we may have the same ability levels or share similar socio-economic backgrounds, but our uniqueness stems from the dynamic ways in which these features combine.

Dynamics – the key to understanding personality

Psychologists tend to specialise and focus on one of the features listed on page 101. Clearly, this is essential for the dedicated research required but, when applying theories to people at work, it is important to remember that a holistic view should be taken which takes into account the dynamic processes. The application of theory into the world of work is not always easy and some students find the process confusing when the theory does not match with their own experiences. Psychological investigations emphasise the complexity and variety of individual behaviour and insist that simple answers and explanations are generally inadequate. Students may therefore have to adjust their attitudes and perceptions about the world and for some students this experience may be uncomfortable. The study of personality provides an excellent example of some of the complexities involved in applying psychological theory in practice.

Let us consider two individuals who share similar characteristics. They are both 24 years old, and have lived in the same area; both have a first class honours degree in engineering and they have identical personality assessment profiles. However, we would still predict differences with regard to their attitude and performance in the workplace. In addition, differences would be predicted in the ways that they interacted with others and in the ways that others interacted with them. If one of the engineers was female a further set of assumptions might start to appear. It is not only the features themselves which identify individuals as being different but also their interaction. The complexities of the process pose a number of interesting questions which psychologists have tried to solve and in this context it is not surprising perhaps that differing theories and ideas have evolved. (*See* Tables 4.1 and 4.2.)

Figure 4.1 identifies the links between the dynamics of personality and life's experiences.

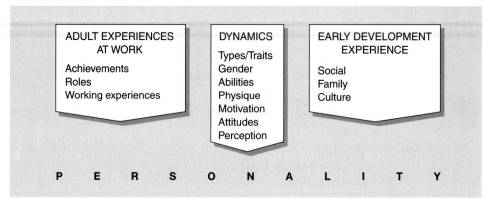

Fig. 4.1
To what extent does our personality remain constant?

Table 4.1

Dilemma 1 – The role of early experiences. To what extent is our personality constant throughout life?	
Solution (a)	*Solution (b)*
If we consider the two young engineers described above it could be argued that their personality is a culmination of experiences. Their personality has been shaped by the people around them from their very earliest years. Early family life – the relationship between family members, the size of the family, the rewards and punishments exercised by their parents would have had an influence on the type of person they are now. In other words the environment and early learning experiences have contributed to their personality development.	Perhaps the young engineers have a core-inherited part of their personality which has remained resistant to change. The way in which they have responded to the world has remained consistent with their true 'self'.

Table 4.2

Dilemma 2 – Assessment of personality. Is it possible to 'measure' an individual's personality?	
Solution (a)	*Solution (b)*
Identifying an individual's personality typically refers to distinguishing traits or types. For instance, Joe is an introvert (type); he is placid, quiet and reflective. John, however, is an extrovert (type); he is excitable, sociable and loud. Personality traits are usually identified by what people do, the behaviour they exhibit. This is the way that all of us would normally describe another's personality. Some psychologists, in place of watching behaviour, ask questions about behaviour which the individual answers on a paper questionnaire. They would assert that asking a person to report on the way they feel or behave is a legitimate way of assessing personality. These self-reporting questionnaires would then be subject to quantitative methods. Thus psychologists have made it possible to quantify the strength of a person's trait and to enable comparisons to be made with others. Such information then becomes a basis for prediction. Given that a person has a high score on extroversion it would be possible to predict the way in which the individual might behave in a given situation. These measuring techniques are subject to some controversy.	Do people always reveal their true 'self'? Is it possible that circumstances may force them to behave in a way that is unlike their 'typical' behaviour? Or do people choose to act in a certain way because they think it is appropriate? Is it possible to measure a 'strength' of a trait? Can people reliably report on their own behaviour or is there a real difference between what people say and what people do? Instead of requiring individuals to respond to set questions it may be more appropriate to use open-ended techniques. This ensures that individuals use their own definitions, and allows for greater understanding about their motivations and causes of behaviour.

Uniqueness and similarities

The dilemmas described in Tables 4.1 and 4.2 focus on two major issues of prime importance in the study of personality. First, is personality a constant throughout our lifetime, which remains resistant to change and circumstances? Second, to what extent can we measure and compare individuals on the basis of their personality? This second question assumes that it is possible to distinguish personality characteristics in the first place. Psychologists have produced various theories to solve both these dilemmas and one of the ways of making sense of these theories is to see them working at different levels of depth. (*See* Fig. 4.2.)

LEVEL 3 ☺ ☺ ☺ ☺ ☺ ☺ ☺ ☺ ☺ ☺ ☺ ☺ ☺ UNIVERSAL HUMAN FEATURES	*Psychologists' Research Interests* Common human aspirations
LEVEL 2 ☺ ☺ ☺ ☺ ☺ ☺ ☺ ☺ SOME SHARED FEATURES – GENDER; ABILITY	Identification, Measurements, comparison [Nomothetic]
LEVEL 1 ☺ UNIQUE COMBINATION OF FEATURES	'Self' – Unique interaction with the world [Idiographic]

Fig. 4.2
Different levels of personality research

Studying individual differences therefore presents a set of interesting problems for psychologists. A review of the theories in the next section will show that they often work at one of the levels shown in Fig. 4.2, resulting in differing approaches and emphasis.

This section will discuss two major approaches to the study of personality and their handling of the dilemmas of constancy and assessment. Applications of personality studies to organisations and their management will be discussed at the end of the section.

NOMOTHETIC AND IDIOGRAPHIC APPROACHES

Broadly speaking, personality studies can be divided into two main approaches which have been labelled nomothetic and idiographic.

Nomothetic approaches

Nomothetic approaches are primarily concerned with the collection of group data. This means that such theorists accumulate evidence with regard to the identification of personality traits; producing effective measurements of the traits in order to draw comparisons between individuals. Being able to predict behaviour is a major aim and outcome of this approach. Researchers closely align themselves to studies which are 'scientific' in a positivistic sense. (The term positivism refers to the branch of science which is exclusively based on the objective collection of observable data – data which are beyond question.) Such an approach transfers methods used in natural sciences to the social world.

Nomothetic approaches tend to view environmental and social influences as minimal and view personality as consistent, largely inherited and resistant to change. Although they would not diminish the difficulties that measuring personality brings, nomothetic approaches would claim that it is possible to measure and predict the ways in which personality types would behave given certain circumstances, and are able to support their claims with research findings.[4]

Nomothetic approaches would: solve dilemma 1 with solution (b); solve dilemma 2 with solution (a); and focus on level 2 as described in Fig. 4.2.

Idiographic approaches

Idiographic approaches are concerned with understanding the uniqueness of individuals and the development of the self concept. They regard personality development as a process which is open to change. They regard individuals as responding to the environment and people around them, and see the dynamics of the interactions as playing a critical part in shaping personality. The measurement of traits is seen as largely inappropriate in that one person's responses may not be comparable to another's. Furthermore they would suggest that personality assessment is not a valid method of understanding the unique ways in which a person understands and responds to the world. The depth and richness of a person's personality can not be revealed in superficial paper-and-pencil questionnaires. Furthermore, the categories defined by psychologists are too narrow in scope and depth.

Idiographic approaches would: solve dilemma 1 with solution (a); solve dilemma 2 with solution (b); and focus on level 1 as described in Fig. 4.2.

Complementary approaches

Some researchers do not fit easily into either of these two broad approaches. *Freud*, for instance, is idiographic in the sense that he is interested in the self and its development, but his theory does not allow for personality growth and change after childhood.[5] *Kelly*'s Personal Construct Theory also bridges the two approaches.[6] His theory will be explored later in this chapter.

The approaches can be seen as complementary; indeed, it could be argued that different foci are important in understanding the many complicated facets of personality.

THEORETICAL APPROACHES: NOMOTHETIC

Two main theories discussed under this approach are:

- Eysenck's theory of main personality types; and
- Cattell's identification of personality traits.

EYSENCK

Hans Eysenck followed a tradition of writers by applying four basic types introduced by Hippocrates: melancholic; sanguine; phlegmatic; and choleric. Eysenck's approach was influenced by the positivistic tradition; his aim was to produce objective evidence of personality differences using large samples of the population. By investigating 700 servicemen he was able to use rigorous statistical data to test his hypotheses.[7] His findings supported the notion that there were two major differences which could be measured:

Individuals in Eysenck's theory could, therefore, be one of four main personality types. The type would lead to a predisposition of traits which would, itself, lead to the likelihood of certain behaviours. For instance, a person typed as an extrovert would be responsive and outgoing and in a new social situation s/he would predictably initiate conversation among a group of strangers.

Eysenck's theory and his subsequent Personality Inventory allowed identification of a personality type. From this description it was possible to predict likely behaviours. Eysenck had a clear view about the constancy of personality. He believed that personality was largely inherited and that introverts and extroverts are born with differing physiological tendencies. Furthermore he argued that the personality we are born with is largely unalterable by environmental influences.

Supporting research evidence

Although it could be argued that Eysenck's theory is too simplistic in terms of the number and range of types proposed, this theory has an impressive amount of supporting research evidence. His approach has immediate appeal to managers in organisations who are concerned with predicting the future behaviour of their employees either for selection or promotion.

One of his earlier studies indicated that stable introverts were generally found among the most successful businessmen. Stability seemed to be manifest regardless of the type of work the managers did but their degree of extroversion seemed to vary, depending on the nature of their work. It is therefore not surprising to find that the use of psychometric tests has grown substantially over the past decade and that the majority of large companies use occupational tests.[8] (Further information about testing is given on page 113.)

CATTELL

Cattell's work has striking resemblances to that of Eysenck in the methods that he used to study personality. He used quantitative, objective techniques in order to analyse his data (although he used a different factor analytic measure), and fol-

lowed traditional scientific procedures in order to understand the basic dimensions of personality.[9] Cattell used three main sources for the collection of personality data.

(i) L-data (Life record data). Ratings by trained observers.
(ii) Q-data (Self-rating questionnaire). Responses to a questionnaire which measured personality traits. (Cattell 16PF Questionnaire.)
(iii) T-data (Test data). Observations collected in specific situation tests.

Personality factors

The data collected were factor-analysed by Cattell resulting in the identification of two main types of personality traits.

- **Surface traits**, those traits which seem to cluster together consistently; and
- **Source traits**, which seem to underlie and determine the traits which are likely to 'surface' into behaviour.

Cattell identified 16 personality factors (or source traits). (*See* Table 4.3.)[10]

Table 4.3

Factor	High score	Low score
A	Outgoing	Reserved
B	More intelligent (abstract thinker)	Less intelligent (concrete thinker)
C	Higher Ego Strength Emotionally stable	Lower Ego Strength Emotionally unstable
E	Dominant	Submissive
F	Surgency (optimistic)	Desurgency (pessimistic)
G	Stronger superego strength (conscientious)	Weaker superego strength (expedient)
H	Parmia (adventurous)	Threctia (timid)
I	Presmia (tender-minded)	Harria (tough-minded)
L	Protension (suspicious)	Alaxia (trusting)
M	Autia (imaginative)	Praxernia (practical)
N	Shrewdness	Artlessness (unpretentious)
O	Insecure – guilt-proneness	Self-assured
Q1	Radicalism	Conservatism
Q2	Self-sufficiency	Group dependence
Q3	High self-concept control (controlled)	Low self-concept control (casual)
Q4	High ergic tension (tense, frustrated)	Low ergic tension (relaxed, tranquil)

(Adapted from Cattell, R. B. and Kline, P. *The Scientific Analysis of Personality and Motivation*, Academic Press (1977) Table 4.1, pp. 44–5.)

Unlike Eysenck, he did not 'type' individuals but used 'traits' as his main personality descriptor (although there is high correspondence between Cattell's second-order factors and Eysenck's 'types'). They also differed with regard to the determinants of personality: Eysenck viewed the inherited physiological basis as the main determinant whereas Cattell was more interested in taking social factors into account when understanding an individual's personality. Both theorists have contributed to a lively debate about personality structure and its measurement, and in doing so have advanced the selection techniques available to managers.[11]

THEORETICAL APPROACHES: IDIOGRAPHIC

Idiographic approaches emphasise the development of the individual and of individuals' views of themselves – their self concept. Supporters of idiographic approaches are critical of the nomothetic approach which attempts to categorise individuals on the basis of group data. They argue that the techniques used to collate the group data are questionable and the outcome inappropriate to an understanding of personality. For the idiographic researchers personality is expressed through the experiences and development of the individual. It cannot be understood outside a social context and has to be studied in the light of individuals' own perceptions of their world. Idiographic researchers would always take into account the social circumstances of the person and in particular the relationships with others, family life and social conditions. The following theories are typical examples of the idiographic approach:

- *Carl Rogers'* theory claims that personality is embedded within personal relationships. He emphasised the importance of fulfilment and psychological growth, placing at the centre people's knowledge of their own feelings. For Rogers, the expression of emotion was critical in freeing up people's autonomy and creativity in the quest for self-actualisation. The process of becoming a person requires the ability to give and receive unconditional regard – the warmth and respect for the *person*, who they *are*, regardless of how they behave.[12]
- *G. H. Mead* was unable to separate the notion of an individual's personality from the concept of society. He claimed that 'A person is a personality because he belongs to a community, because he takes over the institutions of that community into his own conduct'.[13] As individuals we can only have a sense of self in relation to others. He proposed the idea that the self has two components: one which is spontaneous and unique (I), and the other which is learnt through exposure to society (me).
- *C. Cooley*, like Mead, emphasised the importance of early development and socialisation. He believed the emotion and sensation that we hold of 'self' was instinctive but was developed by experience. His phrase 'the looking-glass self' suggests that we come to know ourselves through our relationship with others and their reactions to us.

ERIKSON

Erik Erikson's theory is a good example of the idiographic approach. He viewed personality development as continuing throughout life. He was interested in the effect of experiences on the development of the self concept and how different individuals resolved personal conflicts.[14]

Although he recognised the importance of early childhood in establishing certain basic concepts of trust, autonomy and initiative, he disagreed with *Freud*'s emphasis on the effects of early development. (*See* section below.)

Tensions and conflicts

For Erikson, all eight stages of life produce different tensions and conflicts which have to be resolved. (*See* Table 4.4.)

Successful resolution produces a healthy personality, whereas difficulties in earlier stages may produce problems later on. Erikson's theory not only makes considerable sense in terms of face validity (i.e. the 'feel-good' factor) but also links with other research indicating that managers' motivations and goals change with age. *Hunt*, for instance, identified nine different career/life stages.[15]

Table 4.4

Stage 1	Trust	v	Mistrust	1st year
Stage 2	Autonomy	v	Doubt	2–3 years
Stage 3	Initiative	v	Guilt	4–5 years
Stage 4	Industry	v	Inferiority	6–11 years
Stage 5	Identity	v	Role confusion	12–18 years
Stage 6	Intimacy	v	Isolation	Young adult
Stage 7	Generativity	v	Self-absorption	Middle age
Stage 8	Integrity	v	Despair	Old age

(Adapted from Erikson, E. H. *Identity and The Life Cycle*, Norton (1980) Worksheet Table Appendix.)

OTHER THEORETICAL APPROACHES

Other significant theoretical approaches include:

- **Psychoanalytic approaches** – Sigmund Freud and neo-Freudians; and
- **Cognitive approaches** – George Kelly

FREUD

A discussion on personality would not be complete without a mention of *Sigmund Freud* (1856–1939). His psychoanalytic approach emphasised the importance of:

- early childhood experiences, particularly parental relationships and dealing with trauma;
- different levels of consciousness and the influence of the unconscious mind on behaviour;
- understanding the 'whole' person in relation to their past.[16]

Early childhood experiences were seen by Freud as paramount in understanding the adult personality. He described the development of all individuals as one which progressed through a number of stages: (i) oral; (ii) anal; and (iii) phallic. An inner force (or libido) was also identified. This libido was seen by Freud as a universal human characteristic which provides the necessary life energy for progression through the developmental stages. Each stage was also characterised by an internal struggle of domination by three personality structures called the id, ego and superego (*see* Fig.4.3) as well as external conflict with outside relationships. These conflicts and tensions, rooted into the past and repressed within the unconscious, were seen by Freud as key to the understanding of adult personality.

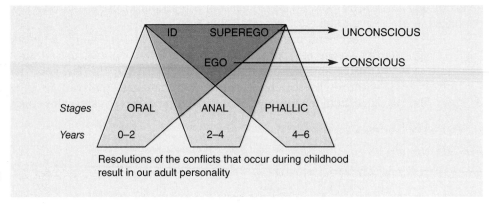

Fig. 4.3
Representation of
Freud's personality
theory, development
and structure

Freud's theory has been heavily criticised on the grounds that:

- it is not replicable and his arguments were circular;
- samples used were atypical;
- it is subjective and unscientific;
- a heavy emphasis on early childhood makes it highly deterministic; and
- it disregards later development and changes.

His theory should, however, be seen in its historical context and in terms of its impact upon the development of later theories and ideas.

Applications to organisational behaviour

With regard to organisational behaviour, Freud's theory still has much to offer with respect to understanding stress at work. When the going gets tough it is easy to slip into habitual ways of responding that have been learned as children. Within the working context such behaviour may be seen as inappropriate and yet bring immediate relief or comfort to the individual. Instances include regressing into temper tantrums or gaining relief by excessive eating or drinking and can be seen to protect the ego from a painful memory or unwanted impulse. Freud labelled these defence mechanisms. The most readily observable ones in the workplace include:

- **Regression** – adopting childhood patterns of behaviour;
- **Fixation** – inflexible and rigid behaviour or attitudes;
- **Rationalisation** – elaborate 'covering-up' of ideas/motives;
- **Projection** – attributing feelings and motives to others.

(*See also* the discussion on frustrated behaviour in Chapter 14.)

In summary, Freud saw adult personality as being largely determined by the strength of inner drives and impulses and the resolutions of these tensions within early childhood experiences. Freud's overwhelming interest lay in understanding the conflicts that exist for the person and how people come to terms with their anxieties and tensions. His interest therefore lay in understanding the whole person and not in identifying traits or types.

Neo-Freudians

Freud produced a generation of scholars who developed his ideas to produce their own theories and models of personality development. Although of course rooted in Freudian thinking the neo-Freudians have deviated from Freud in important respects. Two of the most significant are *Karen Horney* and *Melanie Klein*.

- Although *Karen Horney* accepted certain principles of Freud's theory with regard to unconscious motivation, she disagreed with the predominance of sexual forces and her theory suggests far more optimism than Freud's.[17]
- *Melanie Klein* encouraged the study of the sources of anxiety. She suggested that the principal source of anxiety was the fear of the death instinct. She posited that early childhood is a critical time for the formulation and development of lifelong mental attitudes.

JUNG

Carl Jung's theory is of particular significance in that it bridges Freudian ideas with modern approaches of personality test design. His theory identifies life energy as concerned with hopes and goals of the future and not just of the past. Unlike Freud, Jung describes three levels of personality:

- conscious level (daily reality);
- an unconscious level (contains our own unique complexes); and
- a collective unconscious (store of universal and evolutionary experiences).

Jung identified four universal aspects of our personality which he referred to as archetypes which we all share. For instance, according to Jung we all strive for self-actualisation; have a darker self; have both masculine and feminine qualities; and have a persona, a role we can play.[18]

Personality functions and attitudes

However, it was Jung's identification of personality functions and attitudes which has been applied to the rigours of systematic testing by *Isabel Briggs-Myers and Katherine Briggs*.[19] Jung identified differences between individuals in terms of their libidinal energy which could flow outwards to the external world (extrovert) or inwards to their inner world (introvert). Personality differences would also be manifest through differing cognitive functions of thinking, feeling, sensation and intuition. The Myers-Briggs Type Indicator (MBTI) is based on these theoretical constructs with the additional dimension of style of living. The personality types are shown in Table 4.5.

The MBTI has promoted considerable research interest, particularly with regard to the correlation between personality type, occupations and management style.

COGNITIVE THEORY: KELLY'S PERSONAL CONSTRUCT THEORY

Kelly's theory of personal constructs does not just consider personality development; it considers the whole person in terms of their perceptions, attitudes, goals. For Kelly, personality is the individual's way of construing and experimenting with their world. Kelly was critical of separating the study of personality apart from the 'whole' person:

Table 4.5 Characteristics frequently associated with each type

	Introverts	*Extroverts*		
Intuitive types	**INTJ** Usually have original minds and great drive for their own ideas and purposes. In fields that appeal to them, they have a fine power to organize a job and carry it through with or without help. Skeptical, critical, independent, determined, sometimes stubborn. Must learn to yield less important points in order to win the most important. **INFJ** Succeed by perseverance, originality, and desire to do whatever is needed or wanted. Put their best efforts into their work. Quietly forceful, conscientious, concerned for others. Respected for their firm principles. Likely to be honored and followed for their clear convictions as to how best to serve the common good.	**INTP** Quiet and reserved. Especially enjoy theoretical or scientific pursuits. Like solving problems with logic and analysis. Usually interested mainly in ideas, with little liking for parties or small talk. Tend to have sharply defined interests. Need careers where some strong interest can be used and useful. **INFP** Full of enthusiasms and loyalties, but seldom talk of these until they know you well. Care about learning, ideas, language, and independent projects of their own. Tend to undertake too much, then somehow get it done. Friendly, but often too absorbed in what they are doing to be sociable. Little concerned with possessions or physical surroundings.	**ENTP** Quick, ingenious, good at many things. Stimulating company, alert and outspoken. May argue for fun on either side of a question. Resourceful in solving new and challenging problems, but may neglect routine assignments. Apt to turn to one new interest after another. Skillful in finding logical reasons for what they want. **ENFP** Warmly enthusiastic, high-spirited, ingenious, imaginative. Able to do almost anything that interests them. Quick with a solution for any difficulty and ready to help anyone with a problem. Often rely on their ability to improvise instead of preparing in advance. Can usually find compelling reasons for whatever they want.	**ENTJ** Hearty, frank, decisive, leaders in activities. Usually good in anything that requires reasoning and intelligent talk, such as public speaking. Are usually well informed and enjoy adding to their fund of knowledge. May sometimes appear more positive and confident than their experience in an area warrants. **ENFJ** Responsive and responsible. Generally feel real concern for what others think or want, and try to handle things with due regard for the other person's feelings. Can present a proposal or lead a group discussion with ease and tact. Sociable, popular, sympathetic. Responsive to praise and criticism.
Sensing types	**ISTJ** Serious, quiet, earn success by concentration and thoroughness. Practical, orderly, matter-of-fact, logical, realistic, and dependable. See to it that everything is well organized. Take responsibility. Make up their own minds as to what should be accomplished and work toward it steadily, regardless of protests or distractions. **ISFJ** Quiet, friendly, responsible, and conscientious. Work devotedly to meet their obligations. Lend stability to any project or group. Thorough, painstaking, accurate. Their interests are usually not technical. Can be patient with necessary details. Loyal, considerate, perceptive, concerned with how other people feel.	**ISTP** Cool onlookers – quiet, reserved, observing and analyzing life with detached curiosity and unexpected flashes of original humor. Usually interested in cause and effect, how and why mechanical things work, and in organizing facts using logical principles. **ISFP** Retiring, quietly friendly, sensitive, kind, modest about their abilities. Shun disagreements, do not force their opinions or values on others. Usually do not care to lead but are often loyal followers. Often relaxed about getting things done, because they enjoy the present moment and do not want to spoil it by undue haste or exertion.	**ESTP** Good at on-the-spot problem solving. Do not worry, enjoy whatever comes along. Tend to like mechanical things and sports, with friends on the side. Adaptable, tolerant, generally conservative in values. Dislike long explanations. Are best with real things that can be worked, handled, taken apart, or put together. **ESFP** Outgoing, easygoing, accepting, friendly, enjoy everything and make things more fun for others by their enjoyment. Like sports and making things happen. Know what's going on and join in eagerly. Find remembering facts easier than mastering theories. Are best in situations that need sound common sense and practical ability with people as well as with things.	**ESTJ** Practical, realistic, matter-of-fact, with a natural head for business or mechanics. Not interested in subjects they see no use for, but can apply themselves when necessary. Like to organize and run activities. May make good administrators, especially if they remember to consider others' feelings and points of view. **ESFJ** Warm-hearted, talkative, popular, conscientious, born cooperators, active committee members. Need harmony and may be good at creating it. Always doing something nice for someone. Work best with encouragement and praise. Main interest is in things that directly and visibly affect people's lives.

Introverts · *Extroverts*

(Reproduced by special permission of the Publisher, Consulting Psychologists Press, Inc., Palo Alto, CA 94303 from *Myers-Briggs Type Indicator Report Form* by Isabel Briggs-Myers. Copyright © 1976 by Consulting Psychologists Press, Inc. All rights reserved. Further reproduction is prohibited without the Publisher's written consent. *Myers-Briggs Type Indicator* and MBTI are registered trademarks of Consulting Psychologists Press, Inc.)

The castrating effect of separating personality off as a mini-psychology in its own right is perhaps best seen in the curiously named study of 'individual differences', which in fact turns out to be the study of group sameness. As a result we have focused on the establishment of general dimensions, at some point along which all individuals can be placed, rather than on a study of the dimensions which each individual develops in order to organise his own world.[20]

For Kelly it was critical to take data from one individual person (idiography) and to employ a technique which could cope with the qualitative nature of the data to be collected. He developed the Repertory Grid which was able to measure an individual's construct of the world. Kelly was thus able to employ a clear and valid measure within an idiographic approach. This was an important advance in idiographic techniques and the repertory technique has become increasingly important as a research tool. It enables the person to use his/her own constructions of the world but in such a way that they are comparable and measurable.

Illustration of Kelly's repertory grid technique

An example of the repertory grid technique is provided from a case study by *Fiona Wilson*. The research examined the impact of computer numerical control (CNC) technology in the engineering industry. Its main objective was to explore the effect of new technology on the responses of both craftsmen and managers in two differing companies. One of the research measures used to explore the subjective experiences of the workers was Kelly's Repertory Grid. Wilson describes it as a 'formalised conversation' and says that 'It is an attempt to stand in others' shoes, to see their world as they see it, to understand their situation, their concerns'.[21]

Using this technique, Wilson was able to measure the workers' own feelings and motivations, and to understand the impact that technology had on their job, their skills and sense of self worth. She noted in her conclusion that the strategic decisions made by the two companies in their utilisation of the new technology made a direct and measurable impact on the perception and attitudes of the craftsmen. An example of the repertory grid is given in Table 4.6. (*See* Assignment 1 at the end of this chapter for an application of the repertory grid.)

APPLICATIONS WITHIN THE WORK ORGANISATION

Organisations regard personality as being of key significance in their decision-making and it would be rare for organisations not to take the personality of a candidate into consideration at a selection interview. For some organisations, personality is the major criterion for selection or rejection. The hospitality industry, for example, is replete with research studies demonstrating the potency of personality.[22] So how do organisations assess a candidate's personality?

The interview remains the most usual method of selection, but there is an increasing use of objective psychometric measures. Such growth in psychometric testing is significant and a number of studies have demonstrated its growing popularity.[23] Concern has been expressed about the use and misuse of psychological instruments and there is a continuing debate within psychological circles with regard to the validity of these measures.[24] *Anastasi* has stated that 'The construction and use of personality inventories are beset with special difficulties over and above common problems encountered in all psychological testing. The question

Table 4.6 An example of a first repertory grid

1	CNC job	Skilled turner's job	Ideal job (professional footballer)	Job I would enjoy (electrician, own business)	Job I would not enjoy (a job on an oil rig)	Job I would hate (miner)	7
Boring	3	4	7	7	2	1	Interesting
Unskilled	2	5	7	6	2	2	Skilled
Not physically demanding	4	5	7	2	7	7	Physically demanding
Gives no job satisfaction	2	5	7	6	2	2	Gives job satisfaction
Unsafe working conditions	5	3	5	6	2	1	Safe working conditions
Dirty work conditions	4	2	6	7	2	1	Clean work conditions
A job in which I am not respected	2	5	7	7	2	2	A job in which I am respected
A job with no challenge	3	6	7	7	3	3	A challenging job
A job in which I do not reap the gains	2	2	7	7	2	2	A job in which I reap the gains
A job where I am tied to one place	2	3	7	7	1	2	A job where I am free to move about

of faking and malingering is far more acute in personality measurement than in aptitude testing.'[25]

Recent critics have accused consultants and practitioners of inappropriate use of personality assessments and claim low validity between non-work-related personality assessments and work performance.[26] *Goss* suggests that the use of personality assessments not only is an infringement of the individual's privacy but also leads to unfortunate organisational consequences with 'cloning' as on outcome. Such techniques can be perceived as a form of social engineering and an insidious form of organisational control.[27]

Aware of these problems, the British Psychological Society has produced guidelines and codes of practice for users of psychometric tests and a number of studies positively support the use of personality assessments as an aid to selection decisions.[28] Furthermore, evidence is emerging to show that where personality questionnaires have been specifically designed and related to work characteristics,

prediction and validity scores are much higher.[29] (*See also* Chapter 19.)

Despite reservations concerning personality questionnaires, they can be particularly valuable if individuals complete them for their own benefit and development. As an introduction in a self-awareness programme, personality questionnaires can initiate discussion about individual differences. In these situations there is no judgement about better or worse characteristics or matching of individuals to personnel specifications; rather the discussion centres on the value of individual differences and the strengths which each personality type can bring to the working situation.

Producing a good team of people requires understanding of the team's strengths and weaknesses. A balanced team with complementary personalities, skills and abilities is ideal. Personality questionnaires can therefore be the first part of this process – an audit of strengths and weaknesses – followed by group training exercises designed to enable a situation which encourages the development of strengths to complement and balance the weaknesses of the team. An effective team at work should be aware of the division of their strengths and weaknesses. 'None of us is perfect; but a group of people, whose strengths and talents complement each other, can be.'[30]

Early leadership studies attempted to identify the personality traits in an effort to establish differences between the leaders and the followers. These studies were unsuccessful in finding recurring personality traits among leaders. More recent approaches have established ways of analysing the dynamics of the situation/ leader/group. (*See* Chapter 8 for further details.) The interaction between personality and expected role behaviour is certainly an interesting area of study. Although personality is a powerful determinant of a manager's effectiveness, account must also be taken of the social rules and expectations within the workplace. There is no doubt that in some organisations these expectations are very forceful and insist upon behaviour which conforms to cultural demands. In some roles the individual's personality is in danger of being undermined. For instance, it would be a surprise to meet an introverted, quiet and reflective Head Chef in a major hotel or a paramedic who was frantic, nervy and hysterical.

STRESS AND THE INDIVIDUAL

Organisational change, the recurrent theme of the 1990s, has produced its casualties at both organisational and individual level resulting in stress and trauma. The costs of stress at national, organisational and individual levels are well known. *Cooper* has indicated the high incidence of stress throughout organisations irrespective of job and seniority and has suggested that 'every job has its own stress fingerprint'.[31] Research also indicates that personality plays its part in the stress process. Individuals who have a personality classified as Type A are more likely to suffer from heart disease under severe stress than individuals with a Type B personality.[32]

Stress is individually defined; one person's stress can be another's excitement and energiser. Everyone has a range of comfort within which they can feel steady and safe. Stress occurs when the individual feels that they are working outside this comfort zone. Individual differences are significant in determining the stage at which an individual feels discomfort. Although stress may activate people (for some it may be immobilising) into action with possible positive behavioural consequences, the physiological impact upon the person should not be forgotten. Headaches, muscular

tension, fatigue and hypertension have been cited as effects of stress.[33] Stress is a complex topic; it is intrinsically tied into an individual's perceptual system and as such can be seen as a subjective phenomenon, but it can also be objectively defined in terms of a physiological measure. It should also be seen within the social context as it is society which largely prescribes and defines the causes of stress, or stressors. It should be noted that there is a perverse sense of status within organisations about the value of stress; for instance a librarian complained bitterly that her role was regarded as low stress, implying that jobs given 'high stress position' also rank high in prestige.

Coping with stress is dependent upon the identification of stressors and the ability to be able to enact action. *Cooper* and others[34] have identified six major sources of stress at work:

- intrinsic to the job: working conditions, shift work, etc.;
- role in the organisation: overload; underload;
- relationships at work, particularly with the boss;
- career development, mid-life being a critical stage;
- organisational structure and climate; the extent of rules and regulations;
- home–work interface; particularly the growth of dual-career families.

(Stress at work is also discussed in Chapter 15.)

Because the nature of human stress is complex and socially and culturally bound it is interesting to reflect on its possible developments. Is it the case that during the 1990s stress predominates because our expectations are still bound within the bureaucratic organisations of earlier decades of work? Personal life commitments are significantly tied into full employment and a career for life (with a 25-year mortgage and easier credit arrangements) and yet evidence is growing of organisations' requirements for shorter and more flexible working patterns. Perhaps, with an increasing awareness of the changing nature of work patterns and a reorganisation of the interface between work and home, stress may be reduced or at the very least may be perceived in new ways. Are the 1990s at the cusp of new changes where a new generation may have differing expectations and may adapt their lives to suit a new order and style?

ATTITUDES

There are no limits to the attitudes people hold. Attitudes are learned throughout life and are embodied within our socialisation process. Some attitudes (such as religious beliefs) may be central to us – a core construct – and may be highly resistant to any change, whereas other, more peripheral attitudes may change with new information or personal experiences. Specific events, particularly traumatic ones such as redundancy, may have a dramatic effect on our attitudes.

What are attitudes?

So what are attitudes and how can they be distinguished from beliefs and values?

- **Attitudes** can be defined as providing a state of 'readiness' or tendency to respond in a particular way.[35]
- **Beliefs** are concerned with what is known about the world; they centre on what 'is', on reality as it is understood.
- **Values** are concerned with what 'should' be and what is desirable.

Gross suggests that 'to convert a belief into an attitude, a "value" ingredient is needed which, by definition, is to do with an individual's sense of what is desirable, good, valuable, worthwhile and so on'. It has been suggested by Gross that whereas 'adults may have thousands of beliefs, they may have only hundreds of attitudes and a few dozen values'.[36] *Hofstede* defines values as 'broad tendency to prefer certain states of affairs over others'.[37]

The functions of attitudes

Katz has suggested that attitudes and motives are interlinked and, depending on an individual's motives, attitudes can serve four main functions.

- **Knowledge**: One of the major functions is to provide a basis for the interpretation and classification of new information. Attitudes provide a knowledge base and framework within which new information can be placed.
- **Expressive**: Attitudes become a means of expression. They enable individuals to indicate to others the values that they hold and thus to express their self-concept and adopt or internalise the values of a group.
- **Instrumental**: Held attitudes maximise rewards and minimise sanctions. Hence, attitudes towards other people (or objects) might be held because of past positive (or negative) experiences. Behaviour or knowledge which has resulted in the satisfaction of needs is thus more likely to result in a favourable attitude.
- **Ego-Defensive**: Attitudes may be held in order to protect the ego from an undesirable truth or reality.[38]

Prediction of behaviour

Is it possible to predict behaviour if we know an individual's attitude?

Research suggests the answer is 'No'. It seems that we do not always behave in a way that is true to our beliefs; what we say and what we do may be very different. Such evidence indicates that attitudes can be revealed not only in behaviour but also by the individual's thoughts (although these may not be revealed in public) and by feelings, the strength of which demonstrates the extent to which the attitude is a core or peripheral construct.

A classic study by *La Piere* illustrates this point. Visiting American hotels and restaurants with a Chinese couple, La Piere found no sign of prejudiced attitudes in the face-to-face situation, but there were marked racist attitudes in the follow-up attitude survey. He found complete contradictions between public and private attitudes.[39]

These findings have important implications for the study of attitudes and reveal two important issues for the psychologist and manager.

Issue 1: Attitudes cannot be seen; they can only be inferred.

Given that the attitudes employees hold are important for morale and the effectiveness of organisations, it is important that there is confidence in the measurement techniques used to assess the strength of attitudes. As attitudes are inferred, heavy reliance is placed therefore on the accuracy of assessment. Although there are a number of different techniques which could be used to measure attitudes, the two most common techniques are **direct observation** and **self-reporting techniques**.

All of us observe others and assess attitudes on the basis of their communication style (both verbal and non-verbal) and their behaviour. This is an example of an informal approach; unsystematic, spontaneous and based on our understanding of social cues. We may be wrong in our judgement. Students who turn up late for classes, slouch on their seat and do not ask questions may still hold very positive

attitudes towards organisational behaviour. Managers may also be erroneous in their assumptions and beliefs about their colleagues (both subordinates and superiors). Their beliefs may never have been tested out – merely assumed to be correct.

Organisations which assess their employees' attitudes by using attitude questionnaires (self-reporting techniques) are attempting to systematically gauge and measure these assumptions. Attitude questionnaires are time-consuming to design and administer. The questions asked, their relevance, style and length are all important variables in the validity of the questionnaire. So, too, is the honest completion of questionnaires.

Making public people's private attitudes may also have its dangers as expectations of change may be envisaged. If these do not occur, disappointment and low morale may be the result.[40] (*See also* the discussion on the Johari window in Chapter 7.)

Attitude questionnaires are used by many companies as a barometer for the attitudinal climate of organisations and as such enable managers to be in touch with employees' views and feelings.

Issue 2: Attitudes are often shared within organisations and as such are embodied in the culture of organisations.

This does not imply that attitudes are constructed just within the organisations. Classic research has shown the influence of the wider community in the formation of orientations towards work. Differences in class/orientation may elicit a range of loyalties and possibly produce opposing perceptions of commitment, loyalty and co-operation.

For example, *Salaman* states that 'the commitment and co-operation of worker members of the organisation is frequently regarded by senior management as problematic and uncertain' and suggests that consensus and control has to be achieved by the selection and manipulation of attitudes, values and knowledge.[41] Thus, counter-cultures are recognised as having a powerful influence on the maintenance of an organisation's integrity. *Kanter* suggests that people within counter-cultures who change their orientation and identify with organisational values face criticism and hostility from their peer group.[42]

Thus research suggests that attitudes are not just individually formed but arise out of interaction with others. They are often 'locked-in', often regarded as obvious, mere common sense, and are so much taken for granted that they may be overlooked. Sharing the belief system of others also has affective outcomes. If people feel that they belong and are included it enables them to feel good about working in an organisation. If, on the other hand, people do not feel part of the organisation – if they feel that they do not share the dominant attitudes and beliefs – negative emotional consequences are likely to result. Studies of token women in management support these ideas.

ATTITUDES, MANAGERS AND CULTURE

Although the role, power and responsibility of managers vary from organisation to organisation, all managers regardless of status contribute to the maintenance of the organisation's culture. In one sense the position of manager is a formal recognition of success and as such managers play a key role in personifying the culture. It has

been suggested that managers and their culture are inseparable from each other and that managers consistently influence and affect the perceptions and attitudes of their subordinates.[43] Organisations may initiate rituals and ceremonies to encourage and maintain certain attitudes and beliefs.[44] Many attitudes and ideas become permanent and unchallengeable, making them highly resistant to change.[45]

A shared understanding

Research by *Hicks* in the hotel industry revealed that irrespective of personal circumstances (age, gender, education, social class) managers had been exposed to a process which had 'encultured' them to a shared understanding of the industry, resulting in common attitudes on a range of topics. Attitudes towards their management trainees were found to be significant with regard to the trainees' development; such high expectation ensured broad training opportunities and the use of their own personal network of contacts to ensure their protégés' success. The significance of positive attitudes of managers towards their trainees cannot therefore be over-emphasised.[46]

ATTITUDE CHANGE

The permanency of attitudes clearly has implications for attitudinal change. At the beginning of this section it was pointed out that whereas peripheral attitudes may easily change with new information or experiences, central attitudes tied into other cognitive systems may be much more difficult to shift.

Theories on attitude change stress the importance of balance and consistency in our psyche.

- *Heider*, for example, suggests that not only would we find it uncomfortable to hold two conflicting attitudes, but to do so would motivate us to change one of the attitudes in order to reach a balanced state.[47]
- Cognitive dissonance is the term given to the discomfort felt when we act in a way that is inconsistent with our true beliefs. Like balance theory, it suggests that we are motivated to reduce its impact.[48]

The process of attitude change is dependent on a number of key factors, the most important being:

- why an attitude is held in the first place
- why it should change;
- what the benefits are and to whom;
- what the outcomes are if it does not change.

Considerable research has demonstrated the importance of the following variables in a programme of attitude change:

- the persuader's characteristics;
- presentation of issues;
- audience characteristics;
- group influences;
- outcome of attitude change (reward or punishment).

The implementation of change

The last decade has produced tumultuous change for employees and their managers. It would be rare indeed to find an organisation which has not experienced some degree of change in structure, product, processes, philosophy, culture or ownership. The way in which these changes are implemented can have a dramatic impact on the attitudes of staff. Research has shown that when organisations merge, even when they appear to be compatible in terms of their style and philosophy, stress and negative attitudes can result.[49] The affective component of attitudes therefore should not be underestimated; neither should its relationship with a host of other variables concerned with the motivation and morale of individuals at work. *Morgan* suggests that managers require increasing skill and competence in dealing with the 'emerging waves and challenges'. He believes that organisations and their managers need to 'develop the attitudes and skills that facilitate proactive management' and that special attention will need to be devoted to 'mobilise the energies and commitments of people through the creation of shared values and shared understandings'.[50]

LEARNING

Imagine these scenarios:

- a student listening in a lecture theatre;
- a young person falling off a bicycle;
- a nurse receiving instruction on new equipment;
- a trainee watching the manager deal with an irate customer;
- a young football fan attending a match for the first time.

The major feature these situations have in common is that learning has taken or is about to take place. There is clearly nothing world-shattering about these scenarios, neither are they restricted to learning institutions but they demonstrate the nature of learning as a continuous, automatic and often social process. Although there are times when individuals will deliberately and consciously 'learn' and 'study', for the most part learning takes place without any necessary deliberations, nor any assessments to find out how much has been learned.

A discussion on learning inevitably involves an examination of change and how it takes place. Learning is an all-embracing term which covers changes of an enduring and persistent nature. As the situations above demonstrate, learning includes not only knowledge and skills but also attitudes and social behaviour.

Individual differences occur because of the active and dynamic nature of the learning process. Individuals are not just vessels which are filled with knowledge; they are active participants who interact and relate to the world around them. Their ability to learn is an effect of their innate potential and their social experiences.

It is self-evident that learning will be influenced by how motivated an individual is and by the attitudes held. These attitudes may themselves be affected by the rewards and punishments received in past situations, and by the culture and close environment within which the individual lives.

THE PROCESS OF LEARNING

It can be seen, therefore, that learning links the individual to the social world and is both a personal and social experience. (*See* Fig. 4.4.) Learning is a natural, spontaneous process which can be observed in the play of young children as they imitate and model their behaviour and attitudes on the people around them. Although learning has a consequence for the individual's understanding it should not be forgotten that learning is frequently a shared experience. Sometimes this process may be deliberate as, for example, in the parent–child relationship when parents are attempting to socialise the child into acceptable ways of behaving, or in organisations where employees are taught opening phrases to say when answering the telephone. At other times learning happens as a natural consequence of living in and adapting to the world.

Formal learning settings can therefore be seen as special situations which can be distinguished from other forms of social learning. Formal learning – based in institutions – is typically concerned with the acquisition of knowledge or skills (although attitude change often accompanies such changes). Individuals are often tested, graded and deemed to have passed (or failed) a preconceived and agreed standard. Such a process is ingrained in our society and is used as a basis for distinguishing between individuals.

How do people learn?

Are there similarities in the learning process regardless of whether the situation is informal or formal?

Theories of learning have their roots in the history of psychology and some of the earliest experimental psychologists focused their attention on animal learning. These theorists based their ideas on positivistic traditions and were keen to develop *laws* of learning. They were only interested in behaviour which could be objectively measured, and they designed experiments which maximised their control and the validity of their results.

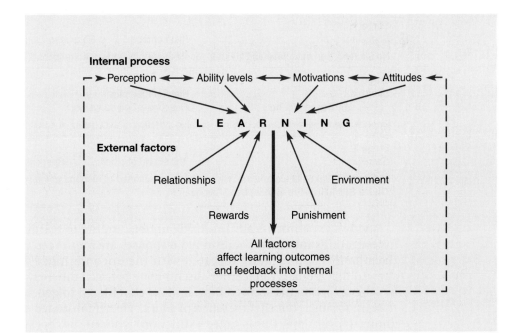

Fig. 4.4
A simplified view of the learning process

BEHAVIOURISM

A school of psychology called **behaviourism** developed out of these early research studies. As the name suggests, researchers were interested in behaviour – action that could be observed, measured and controlled, rather than ideas and thoughts in people's minds which were invisible and impossible to measure.

Leading behaviourists include the following:

- *J. B. Watson*'s **law of exercise and association**;
- *I. Pavlov*'s theory of **classical conditioning**;
- *E. Thorndike*'s work on the **outcomes of learning**;
- *B. F. Skinner*'s thesis of **operant conditioning.**

The law of exercise and association

J. B. Watson developed the law of exercise and association. This refers to the process which occurs when two responses are connected together and repeatedly exercised. Watson was particularly interested in the study of fixed habits and routines.[51]

CLASSICAL CONDITIONING

I. Pavlov, working in Russia, produced a theory concerned with 'classical conditioning'.[52] His laboratory experiments demonstrated how reflexes, such as salivation, could respond to a new situation and new stimulus. He found, for example, that dogs would salivate to a bell if this was repeatedly associated with the arrival of a plate of food. The dog had learned to associate the sound of the bell with the food and thus had been conditioned to respond in a particular way – in this example by salivating. (*See* Table 4.7.)

Table 4.7 Classical conditioning

Stage 1	
Stimulus: Plate of food......	*Response:* Dog salivates.
No learning – an automatic and 'natural' reaction – an unconditioned response.	
Stage 2	
Stimulus: Plate of food plus the sound of a bell......	*Response:* Dog salivates.
Repeated over many trials. Dog is in a learning situation of associating the bell with the onset of food.	
Stage 3	
Stimulus: The sound of a bell......	*Response:* Dog salivates.
Learning has taken place and the dog has been conditioned to respond to the sound of the bell. Thus a S(timulus)–R(esponse) bond has been made.	

Pavlov's experiments advanced the understanding of learning by his various investigations into how conditioned responses are reinforced or strengthened if the stimulus is constantly repeated with the unconditioned response. He also showed that animals can learn to discriminate between different tones of bells and in other experiments showed how animals could learn to generalise and respond to bells of similar but slightly different sound. He demonstrated that responses will diminish over time (this is called extinction) without the repeated connection of the stimulus with the unconditioned response.

These laws of learning which Pavlov established in his animal laboratory are applicable to human learning in the 1990s and a discussion of their applications is given at the end of this section.

The outcomes of learning

E. L. Thorndike's work drew attention to the outcomes of learning.[53] He watched animals in new learning situations and observed that animals learn by trial and error. Although there was no evidence of insight in the first place, their behaviour was affected by the success of the outcomes. If an action was successful (for example, if it led to the reward of food), then it was more likely to be repeated. He called this **the law of effect**.

OPERANT CONDITIONING

B. F. Skinner advanced the ideas of Thorndike to produce a thesis of operant conditioning.[54] Skinner's experiments on animals showed the effects of rewards and punishment on animal learning. He proved that a response would be learned when the animal associated the behavioural response to a reward, or reinforcement as Skinner termed it. (*See* Table 4.8.)

Table 4.8 Operant conditioning

A hungry animal is placed in a box – called the Skinner Box – empty except for a lever and food container.
Stage 1 *Stimulus*: Lever in a box...... *Response*: By trial and error the animal presses the lever. The lever releases a pellet of food.
Stage 2 *Stimulus*: Lever in a box...... *Response*: Lever pressed *for* the pellet of food. The animal has learned to respond to the lever for the reward of food and thus a S(timulus)–R(esponse) bond has been made.

In subsequent trials the animal did not require the trial and error stage; it immediately pressed the lever to receive the reward. Conditioning had therefore been achieved.

Skinner experimented with the reinforcement process. What would happen if the animal was not rewarded on each trial? What effect would partial reinforcement have on the rate of learning? He found that this strengthened the Stimulus–Response bond and the behaviour was more resistant to extinction. The reward seemed to hold even greater importance.

Negative reinforcement was also shown to be powerful. These experiments were still concerned with the Stimulus–Response bond but the reward was the prevention or stopping of something painful or nasty. For instance, if the animal had been placed in a box and received an electric shock unless it jumped into a box when the light came on, the animal quickly learned to jump. If, by responding in a particular way it prevented something nasty or uncomfortable happening, negative reinforcement was said to occur.

Punishment, however, is very different in kind as this is trying to break the S–R bond. So, for instance, if the animal pressed the lever and received an electric shock it would be punished for pressing the lever and thus would quickly learn not to respond.

APPLICATIONS OF THEORIES OF CONDITIONING

Even though the conditioning experiments in the animal laboratory are very simple it is possible to apply the theories to human situations. For example, classical conditioning (whereby responses are connected together automatically) can be illustrated in the following examples:

- a driver's foot might come off the accelerator at the sight of a police car even though the speed limit is not being broken;
- a patient's blood pressure might automatically go up in the dentist's waiting room on hearing the sound of the drill.

Behaviour modification

Operant conditioning (whereby responses are learned because of their outcome) can be illustrated by a variety of learning situations from learning skills and sports to learning how to behave. Behaviour modification is the term given when behaviour is gradually shaped and reinforced by rewards as the person comes closer to the end objective. Learning occurs incrementally with the task divided into sub-goals each with their own reward. Sometimes shaping occurs away from the main business, in training centres where peer assessment and reward can also act as further encouragement for the 'shaping' process. As the trainee's behaviour becomes modified, expectations will alter and enlarge and praise (reinforcement) will be given less.

Many schools use a form of behaviour modification particularly in the earliest years. Some psychiatric hospitals have advanced the shaping techniques to evolve a 'token economy system' for certain long-stay patients to encourage certain behaviour patterns. Tokens are issued when behaviour conforms to the required pattern and these tokens can then buy various privileges.

Vital aspects of organisational behaviour

It is possible to understand, therefore, how people can become conditioned to react in certain ways. We all have our own habits, routines and ways of doing things (although we may vary in terms of our tolerance if we have to change our ways!) which may have been learned by past praise and reinforcement. Learning the skills and knowledge required in a job and the social ways of behaving are vital aspects of organisational behaviour. Consider a new young employee who acts inappropriately not because of belligerence but because s/he had never been shown, in a systematic way, the 'correct and appropriate' responses. In behaviourist terms, the appropriate S–R bond had not been learned.

A further advancement of behaviourist ideas, developed by *Miller and Dollard*, focused on social learning. Basically, they examined the factors affecting imitation learning and noted that behaviour was more likely to be copied if rewards were given.[55] Imitating, or modelling as it is called, can be seen to be a very important part of the socialisation process and it is therefore no surprise that a number of studies have focused their attention on children. However, there are many

instances of modelling in organisations: the trainee watching the supervisor, the young manager observing senior managerial behaviour. Aspects of the role model's behaviour may be incorporated into the trainee's own behaviour patterns and style.

However, rewards are only one part of the learning process. The observed managerial behaviour will also be assessed by the more junior manager (the junior may decide NOT to use the manager as a role model). The assessment requires judgement; it is not simply a response to a situation based on association. Human behaviour offers far greater complexity than an animal's hungry response pattern. Arguably the behaviourist school enhanced knowledge of learning processes and their theories are capable of explaining many simple learning situations but, by themselves, they are not able to account for the complexity of differing situations that individuals face nor for the variety of individual responses given.

LIMITATIONS OF THE BEHAVIOURIST SCHOOL

From the 1930s cognitive psychologists have advanced a number of arguments with respect to the limitations of the behaviourist school.

Areas of learning special to humans

By concentrating only on observable behaviour it could be argued that theories are seriously restricted, and the areas of learning which are particular and special to humans (e.g. speech and complex thought) are thus evaded. Individuals have goals and plans not readily observable which might affect the learning process. So too, an individual's personality, perceptions, and motivations will also play their part in helping or hindering the learning process. Past learning and experiences, whether positive or negative, might also impinge upon the rate of learning. *Gallwey*, in his 'inner game' books, discusses the role of the inner world of ego personalities affecting the quality of performance, the level of enjoyment and the rate of learning.

> Once I became aware of Self 1, it grew increasingly obvious that this judgmental little voice barking away like a drill sergeant inside my head was not the best thing for my tennis game. Self 1 was more of a hindrance than the great help he wanted me to think he was. Thereafter I began looking for ways to decrease the interference of Self 1 and to see what happened if I trusted the potential of Self 2.[56]

Experimental laboratories can only cope with controllable and generally simple experiments rather than skills which are learned over a period of time and which are more complex by nature.

Rewards and reinforcements given in the process of learning may be simple to define when dealing with a hungry animal but become increasingly difficult to identify when dealing with groups of individuals. For instance, the reward of money might satisfy some individuals whilst others might prefer the achievement of a certificate or the knowledge that they have reached their own target.

Account of cognitive factors

Behaviourism cannot easily explain the natural curiosity that humans have and the great desire to learn, to make sense of their environment and to feel competent in activities. Neither can it explain the extent of incidental learning which takes place, whereby individuals learn by chance. For instance, my youngest son, a

125

keen footballer, learned the geography of the UK and town locations quite incidentally through his passionate interest in the sport.

Thus, cognitive factors have to be taken into account to understand how people learn. Observing changes in behaviour is only a part of the learning process. To understand how and why people learn attention must be given to a myriad of individual factors. People learn not only by association and rewards but by having knowledge of their results and by receiving feedback. The achievement of their desired aims and goals motivates and drives people to learn. This has led theorists and educationalists to consider the ways in which people learn through experience.

COGNITIVE THEORIES

Two of the earliest cognitive theorists investigated animal learning in the 1920s and 1930s. *Kohler* argued that chimpanzees were able to solve a problem through the use of insight. He placed fruit out of reach of the chimpanzees but with a stick within reach. He believed that the chimpanzees had actually worked out what they needed to do and that the process of learning was more complex than a simple stimulus–response association.[57]

Tolman showed that rats were capable of cognitive behaviour in a series of experiments in which he investigated animal learning. He disagreed with the behaviourists and their simple notions of S–R learning because his findings indicated that the rats had learned an image of the maze (a cognitive map) which they would use at a latter time. [58]

Piaget, a Swiss psychologist, directed interest and attention to human learning and showed through a series of careful observations that childhood is made up of four major stages of intellectual growth:

- sensory-motor period: birth to 2 years;
- pre-operational thought: 2 years to 7 years;
- concrete operations: 7 years to 11 years;
- formal operations: 11 years to 15 years.

Although there may be differences in the time that children may take to pass through all the stages, Piaget's theory offers a tight coherent perspective of the maturation of intellectual thought and development. Piaget also encouraged studies to consider the cyclical nature of learning and the ways in which children and adults adjust to and accommodate their environments.[59]

For many cognitive theorists learning is viewed as a form of information processing with three stages:

- an active perception stage which gives attention to stimuli from the environment;
- a second mentally active stage which makes sense of the information;
- finally, a restructuring and storage phase.

Rather than learning being seen as the acquisition of discrete information some researchers argue that the most significant process is the building of holistic frameworks or 'scaffolds', as suggested by Glaser.[60] The type and build of differing scaffolds may be a useful way of viewing individual differences in learning effectiveness.

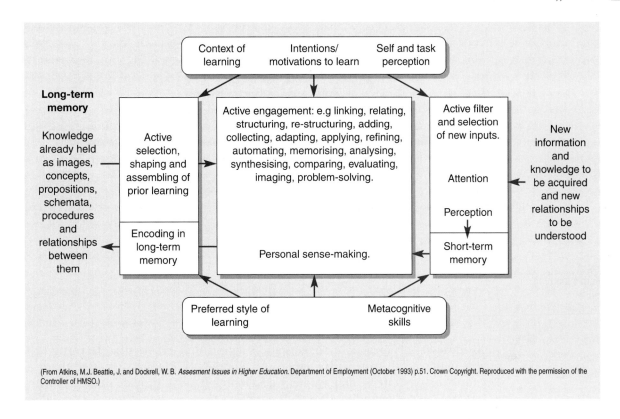

(From Atkins, M.J. Beattie, J. and Dockrell, W. B. *Assesment Issues in Higher Education.* Department of Employment (October 1993) p.51. Crown Copyright. Reproduced with the permission of the Controller of HMSO.)

**Fig. 4.5
A cognitive model
of learning**

Discussion continues with regard to the nature of these mental structures and the extent to which general cognitive skills can be applied.

A cognitive model of learning is given in Fig 4.5.[61]

THE NATURE OF LEARNING

The cyclical nature of learning

Some cognitive theorists have emphasised the cyclical nature of learning and its active nature. *Davis*, for example, claims that 'experiential learning is an integration and alteration of thinking and doing'.[62] *Kolb*'s learning cycle is typical of this approach.[63] (*See* Fig. 4.6.)

This approach emphasises the importance of the synthesis between individuals' behaviour and actions, and the evaluation of their experiences. The individual's goals and aims (often in the form of a learning contract) are focused as being crucial. Reflection of what has been learned in order to experiment with new situations and to become aware of new possibilities is a vital part of the learning process.

Action learning

Kolb's learning cycle is the very essence of action learning. Learners are not able to be passive recipients; they are forced into a situation which demands that they reflect and evaluate their actions. This encourages individuals to become lifelong learners and to be central in the learning process. It is no surprise therefore that

127

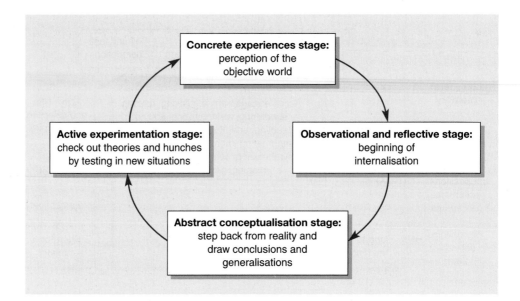

**Fig. 4.6
Kolb's learning
cycle**

Kolb addresses his ideas to managers and suggests that experiential learning will enable managers to cope with change and complexity. He has suggested that: 'A key function of strategic management development...is to provide managers with access to knowledge and relationship networks that can help them become life-long learners and cope with the issues on their continually changing agendas'.[64] Kolb and his colleagues continue by suggesting that partnerships between education and industry create feedback loops which enable an interaction between ideas and action and create a lifelong attitude towards learning.

Cognitive styles Kolb has also advanced ideas about the different ways in which people learn, recognising their different cognitive styles. He describes four main learning styles (Convergent, Divergent, Assimilative and Accommodative) which have particular characteristics and whose strengths lie in differing situations. He suggests that individuals have a preference for learning in certain styles, and thus understanding and knowing one's style will go some way in helping the learning process.

Learning cultures Recent writers suggest that hand in hand with experiential learning should be the creation of learning cultures. The recognition that organisations have to be able to cope with constant change and complexity requires a learning climate in which the new order of things can be understood. Such a climate allows for disagreement and conflict by seeing differing perspectives as energising debate and innovation. Making mistakes is seen as an opportunity for review and modification rather than looking for someone or something to blame. *Garratt* regards the creation of a learning organisation as having positive and liberating consequences which include not only enabling organisational efficiency and effectiveness but significantly the generation of a 'healthier and more cheerful organisation'.[65]

LEARNING THEORY APPLIED TO STUDY SKILLS

These illustrations combine findings from both cognitive and behaviourist schools. There are three fundamental features:

- good organisation;
- active planned sessions; and
- psychological preparation.

Organisation

Material is more easily learned when it is associated and organised in as many and varied ways as possible. In addition to your written and organised notes, use other senses such as: visual sense – draw maps, plans and posters; auditory sense – make and play back revision cassette tapes. Using resources effectively (time, library, tutors) is perhaps self-evident but clearly essential.

Active planned sessions

Learning is enhanced when you distribute your workings sessions and avoid cramming. It is sensible to allow reasonable time breaks and recall sessions. Being constantly active in your learning, ensuring that you understand the material and that you are not passively re-writing notes without thinking them through, is also critical. Constantly testing your knowledge and reviewing material is good practice.

Psychological preparation

Setting targets and goals is important for readiness to learn and cutting down procrastination time. Setting your own psychological contract by aiming to achieve a goal, being clear about what you are planning to learn and then rewarding yourself when you have reached the target, has also proved successful. The environment also promotes this readiness to learn and sitting in the same room or at the same desk can encourage a positive learning attitude. Being positive, getting rid of anxiety and emotional factors, may be the most difficult but is probably the most important part of this preparation process.

APPLICATIONS OF LEARNING THEORY TO ORGANISATIONS

The list below is not exhaustive but identifies some of the major areas where it is possible to apply the theories of learning.

Self development
- Learning what to 'do' (for example, skills and knowledge).
- Learning how to 'be' (role behaviour).
- Learning the ropes (socialisation process and culture) and the social rules (norms and attitudes).

Development of others
- Personal development – training others and developing their potential (including skills of mentoring, assessing, advising).
- Policy development – developing policies for 'learning organisations'; coping with changes and development; enabling 'loose', creative and lateral thinking.

129

SYNOPSIS

- Variety is the spice of life. Organisations need to capture and utilise this variety in the people they employ. By working together individuals will create a society which will generate its own accepted ways of behaving. Managers, however, in order to perform their role, will need to ensure that this created work society matches the goals of the organisation. The first point of analysis of this work society is the individual member.

- Encouraging and developing each member at work is essential for individual and organisational health and is a major task of management. Recognising and improving individual talent and potential is critical to ensure that the many roles and functions of an organisation are achieved effectively. However, differences between individuals can also be the source of problems and conflict. Personality clashes may occur; differences of attitudes and values may lead to polarisation and discrimination.

- One of the important aspects of the education of managers is in terms of self-development and self-awareness. An understanding of their own characteristics, strengths and weaknesses may lead to an appreciation of others' personalities. Although psychologists do not agree in terms of the relative importance of certain factors, there is much to be gained from both nomothetic and idiographic approaches. Personality assessment techniques have been found to be helpful in terms of self-knowledge and discovery as well as adding to the rapidly enlarging repertoire of assessment centres. In mentoring an individual's development, an understanding of the causes of behaviour and past experiences can be helpful in terms of future planning.

- Assessment of attitudes is vital in selecting potential employees and future managers, and yet informal measures of observation are frequently used. Given the difficulties of attitude measurement and doubts associated with predicting behaviour, such assessment is fraught with problems. Managers may hold incorrect assumptions and beliefs about their colleagues. Without a gauge to measure these attitudes, ineffective management decisions may be made. Attitudes can take on a permanency which is maintained by the culture of the organisation and thus be very resistant to change. Moreover, the power of attitudes should be recognised particularly with regard to influencing newer members of the organisation and their development.

- Learning is a feature of all human activity and encouraging a learning environment is the responsibility of management. Change is one of the common features of organisations over the last decade and the rate of change shows no sign of slowing down. It is important both for individuals' health and for the organisation's health to enable people to develop their own strategies and contracts for coping with change. Reflection and evaluation are critical aspects of this process. Praise

130

and encouragement have long been established in the classic theories of learning as leading to more positive, effective outcomes than punishment and criticism. However, many managers would seem not to use these basic principles of learning in organisations, as shown by the oft-spoken phrase 'my manager only notices my mistakes'.

■ The differing approaches taken by psychologists offer complementary perspectives from which to analyse individual behaviour. This analysis is developed further in the following chapter which examines the importance of the perceptual process and the impact of gender differences on organisational behaviour.

Review and discussion questions

1 List the major ways in which it is possible to differentiate between individuals. For each of the headings compare and contrast with members of your study (or working) group.

2 To what extent has your personality changed over the last ten years? Prepare a case to support either the nomothetic or idiographic approach.

3 Why has personality assessment grown in significance over the last few years? Discuss the advantages and disadvantages.

4 What do you understand by the term 'defence mechanism' and how helpful is it to an understanding of organisational behaviour? Using either your college or work organisation, detail examples of defence mechanisms that you have observed.

5 Why do we hold attitudes? Discuss how attitudes are formed, measured and changed.

6 Discuss the power and influence of managerial attitudes. Use examples from your organisation.

7 Critically assess the extent to which experiments on animals enhance our understanding of the learning process.

8 Assess critically the importance of an understanding of individual differences in the light of continuing organisational change. In your answer give priority to the maintenance of individuals' well-being.

 Assignment 1

Using Kelly's repertory grid technique and Wilson's framework (Table 4.6 in the text) complete your own **personal construct grid**.

The repertory grid is a method for exploring personal construct systems. A grid is made up of three components: the elements; the constructs (which are the ways in which the person differentiates between the elements); and an assessment value (or score).

The elements

Answer the following:

1 the job I do now;
2 the job I used to do (where appropriate);
3 an ideal job;
4 a job I would enjoy;
5 a job I would not enjoy; and
6 a job I would hate.

The constructs

Write your answer at the top of each column. Now, select two elements (for example 1 and 2) and compare with a third (for example 6). State the way in which the two elements are alike, and different from the third. Write your answer in the rows. These are your constructs.

For example, I am now a lecturer (element 1) and I used to be a personnel officer (element 2), and a job I would hate would be a factory operative (element 6). The ways in which I see elements 1 and 2 as alike, and different from 6, are in the intellectual demands of the jobs.

Select different triads until you have exhausted all possible constructs.

Scoring the constructs

Examine each construct in relation to the elements (jobs) you have described. Score between 7 (high) and 1 (low).

Now compare

(i) Your pattern of scores for element 1 and element 3. What does this tell you about your current career and motivation?
(ii) Your pattern of scores with the grid completed by an engineering craftsman as shown in the section in the text on personality. (*See* Table 4.6.)
(iii) Your constructs and elements with other colleagues.

Assess the strengths and weaknesses of using the repertory grid technique.

 Assignment 2

The following situations are not untypical of problems which a manager might face.

Situation 1

Brenda Porter is a trainee accountant in a small firm of chartered accountants. She had been employed by Balance Brothers for 18 months and had been attending college part-time during this period. Mr Balance had hopes that Brenda would stay with the firm for five years or more. He was very pleased with the way Brenda had settled into the company; she was hard-working, cheerful and willing to help. She was also becoming particularly competent at using some new software they had recently purchased. However, he had noticed over the last few weeks that Brenda's attitude was beginning to change.

Brenda was not entirely happy. She found a lot of the work rather tedious and menial, and only seemed to really enjoy the time she had working on the computer. She was having second thoughts about a career in accountancy and had taken a couple of days off for interviews on the pretence that she was ill. This particular Friday, she had come into work 30 minutes late. Mr Balance decided to have a word with Brenda.

Situation 2

Mark Grant has been an accountant with you for the past six years. Currently he is facing a period of domestic problems. His wife had a second baby a month ago and is now having to return to hospital for a minor operation. His elder daughter has contracted chicken pox. Consequently Mark has had a long period of irregular work. Although sympathetic with his problems, you are facing staff shortage at an extremely busy time of year and other staff have been staying at work late to keep up with the level of work. How will you attempt to resolve the problem?

Either

(a) Act out the two scenarios and discuss the outcomes. How did the two actors respond? How much empathy and understanding was shown? Did you agree with the result?

and/or

(b) Write a short account of how you, as a manager, would respond to each of the situations.

Notes and references

1. Turner, B. *Exploring the Industrial Sub-culture*, Macmillan (1977).
2. Salaman, G. 'Organisations as Constructions of Social Reality', in Salaman, G. and Thompson, K. (eds) *Control and Ideology in Organisations*, MIT Press (1983).
3. Video 'Management Revolution and Corporate Reinvention', BBC for Business (1993).
4. Eysenck, H. J. *The Structure of Human Personality*, Methuen (1960).
5. Freud, S. *New Introductory Lectures on Psychoanalysis*, Penguin (1973).
6. Kelly's theory as described by Bannister, D. and Fansella, F., in *Inquiring Mind: The Theory of Personal Constructs*, Penguin (1971).
7. Eysenck, H. J. *Eysenck on Extroversion*, Crosby, Lockwood Staples (1973).
8. Mabey, B. 'The Majority of Large Companies Use Occupational Tests', *Guidance and Assessment Review*, vol. 5, no. 3, 1989.
9. Personality tests have been debated by: Bartram, D. 'Addressing The Abuse of Personality Tests', *Personnel Management*, April 1991, pp. 34–9; and Fletcher, C. 'Personality Tests: The Great Debate', *Personnel Management*, September 1991, pp. 38–42.
10. Cattell, R. B. and Kline, P. *The Scientific Analysis of Personality and Motivation*, Academic Press (1977).
11. Howarth, E. 'A Source of Independent Variation: Convergence and Divergence in the Work of Cattell and Eysenck', in Dreger, R. M. (ed.) *Multivariate Personality Research*, Claiton (1972).
12. Rogers, C. *A Way of Being*, Houghton Mifflin (1980).
13. Mead, G. H. *Mind, Self and Society*, University of Chicago Press (1934) pp. 152–64.
14. Erikson, E. H. *Identity and Life Cycle*, Norton (1980).
15. Hunt, J. W. *Managing People at Work: A Manager's Guide to Behaviour in Organisations*, Third edition, McGraw-Hill (1992).
16. Freud, S. *New Introductory Lectures on Psychoanalysis*, Penguin (1973).
17. Horney, K. *The Collected Works of Karen Horney*, Norton (1963).
18. Jung, C. G. *Analytical Psychology: Its Theory and Practice*, Routledge and Kegan Paul (1968). See also: Jacobi, J. *Psychology of C. G. Jung*, Seventh edition, Routledge and Kegan Paul (1968).
19. Briggs-Myers, I. *Introduction to Type*, Oxford Psychologists Press (1987); and Hirsch, S. K. and Kummerow, J. *Introduction to Type in Organisations*, Oxford Psychologists Press (1990).
20. Kelly's theory as described by Bannister, D. and Fansella, F., in *Inquiring Mind: The Theory of Personal Constructs*, Penguin (1971) pp. 50–1.
21. Wilson, F. 'Deskilling of Work? The Case of Computer Numerical Control in the Engineering Industry, Case 4', in McGoldrick, J. (ed.) *Business Case File in Behavioural Science*, Van Nostrand Reinhold (1987).
22. Stone, G. 'Personality and Effective Hospitality Management', Paper presented at the International Association of Hotel Management Schools Symposium, Leeds Polytechnic, Autumn 1988; and Worsfold, P. A. 'Personality Profile of the Hotel Manager', *International Journal of Hospitality Management*, vol. 8, no. 1, 1989, pp. 55–62.
23. Bartram, D. 'Addressing the Abuse of Psychological Tests', *Personnel Management*, April 1991, pp. 34–9; Newell, S. and Shackleton, V. 'Management Selection: A Comparative Survey of Methods Used in Top British and French Companies', *Journal of Occupational Psychology*, vol. 64, 1991, p. 23.
24. Kline, P. 'The Big Five and Beyond', Conference Paper given at the British Psychological Society Occupational Psychology Conference, University of Warwick, January 1995.
25. Anastasi, A. *Psychological Testing*, Macmillan (1988) p. 560.
26. Blinkhorn, S. and Johnson, C. 'The Insignificance of Personality Testing', *Nature*, 348, 1990, pp. 671–2.

27. Goss, D. *Principles of Human Resource Management*, Routledge (1994).
28. Rice, G. H., Jnr and Lindecamp, D. P. 'Personality Types and Business Success of Small Retailers' *Journal of Occupational Psychology*, 62, 1989, pp. 177–82.
29. Gibbons, P., Baron, H., Nyfield, G. and Robertson, I. 'The Managerial Performance and Competences', Conference Paper given at the British Psychological Society Occupational Psychology Conference, University of Warwick, January 1995.
30. Platt, S. with Piepe, R. and Smythe, J. *'Teams': A Game to Develop Group Skills,* Gower (1988).
31. Cooper, C. 'Papering Over the Cracks: Individual Strategies or Organizational Interventions in Dealing with Stress at Work', Conference Paper given at the British Psychological Society Occupational Psychology Conference', University of Warwick, January 1995.
32. Rosenmann, R., Friedman, F. and Straus, R. 'A Predictive Study of CHD', *Journal of the American Medical Association*, vol. 189, 1964, pp. 15–22; and Warr, P. and Wall, T. *Work and Well-Being*, Penguin (1975).
33. Melhuish, A. *Executive Health*, Business Books (1978).
34. Cooper, C., Cooper, R. D. and Eaker, L. H. *Living with Stress*, Penguin (1988); Cartwright, S. and Cooper, C. L. *No Hassle! Taking the Stress out of Work*, Century (1994).
35. Ribeaux, P. and Poppleton, S. E. *Psychology and Work*, Macmillan (1978).
36. Gross, R. D. *Psychology: The Science of Mind and Behaviour*, Edward Arnold (1987).
37. Hofstede, G. *Culture's Consequences: International Differences in Work-Related Values*, Sage (1980).
38. Katz, D. 'The Functional Approach to the Study of Attitudes', *Public Opinion Quarterly*, 21, 1960, pp. 163–204.
39. La Piere, R. T. 'Attitudes versus Action', *Social Forces*, 13, 1934, pp. 230–7.
40. Sykes, A. J. M. 'The Effect of a Supervisory Training Course in Changing Supervisors' Perceptions and Expectations of the Role of Management', *Human Relations*, 15, 1962, pp. 227–43.
41. Salaman, G. 'Organisations as Constructions of Social Reality', in Salaman, G. and Thompson, K. (eds) *Control and Ideology in Organisations*, MIT Press (1983).
42. Kanter, R. M. *Men and Women of the Corporation*, Basic Books (1977).
43. Schein, E. H. *Organisational Culture and Leadership*, Jossey-Bass (1985).
44. Peters, J. and Waterman, R. H. *In Search of Excellence*, Harper and Row (1982).
45. Hofstede, G. *Culture's Consequences: International Differences in Work-Related Values*, Sage (1980).
46. Hicks, L. Gender and Culture: A Study of the Attitudes Displayed by Managers in the Hotel Industry, Unpublished doctoral thesis, University of Surrey, 1991.
47. Heider, F. 'Attitudes and Cognitive Organization', *Journal of Psychology*, 21, 1946, pp. 107–12.
48. Festinger, L. A. *A Theory of Cognitive Dissonance*, Row, Peterson and Co. (1957); Reissued by Stanford University Press and Tavistock Publications (1962).
49. Cartwright, S. and Cooper, C. L. 'The Psychological Impact of Merger and Acquisitions on the Individual', Paper presented at The British Psychological Society Occupational Psychology Conference, Liverpool, January 1992.
50. Morgan, G. 'Emerging Waves and Challenges: The Need for New Competencies and Mindsets', in Henry, J. (ed.) *Creative Management*, Sage (1991) pp. 283–93.
51. Watson, J. B. *Behaviourism*, J. B. Lippincott (1924).
52. Pavlov, I. *Conditioned Reflexes*, Oxford University Press (1927).
53. Thorndike, E. L. *The Fundamentals of Learning*, Teachers College, New York (1932).
54. Skinner, B. F. *Science and Human Behaviour*, Macmillan (1953); and Skinner, B. F. *About Behaviourism*, Jonathan Cape (1974).
55. Miller, N. E. and Dollard, J. C. *Personality and Psychotherapy*, McGraw-Hill (1950).

56. Gallwey, W. T. *The Inner Game of Golf,* Jonathan Cape (1981) p. 19.
57. Kohler, W. *The Mentality of Apes,* Harcourt Brace and World (1925).
58. Tolman, E. C. *Purposive Behaviour in Animals and Men,* The Century Co.: Appleton-Century-Crofts (1932).
59. Piaget, J. *The Language and Thought of the Child,* Harcourt Brace and Co. (1926).
60. Glaser, R. 'Learning Theory and Instruction', Paper for International Congress of Psychology 1992, cited in *Assessment Issues in Higher Education* (Report produced for the Department of Employment) by Atkins, M. J., Beattie, J. and Dockrell, W. B. (1993).
61. Atkins, M. J., Beattie, J. and Dockrell, W. B. *Assessment Issues in Higher Education* (Report produced for the Department of Employment, October 1993).
62. Davis, L. *Experience-based Learning Within the Curriculum,* Council for National Academic Awards, (1990).
63. Kolb, D. A. *Experiential Learning: Experience as the Source of Learning and Development,* Prentice-Hall (1985).
64. Kolb, D. A., Rubin, I. M. and McIntyre, J. M. *Organizational Psychology: An Experiential Approach to Organizational Behaviour,* Prentice-Hall (1984).
65. Garratt, B. *The Learning Organization,* Harper Collins (1994) p. 128.

5 THE PROCESS OF PERCEPTION

Laurie Mullins and Linda Hicks

We all have our own picture of the world, and the extent to which we share this world with others is a complex and dynamic process. It is vital that managers are aware of their own perceived reality and of perceptual differences between individuals that may cause organisational problems. A particularly important aspect of perception is the significance of gender. Managers need to understand the importance of perception including the dimension of gender.

 Learning objectives

To:

- Examine the process of perception;

- Explain internal and external factors which influence the process of perceptual selection;

- Identify problems, distortions and bias with particular regard to the perception of people;

- Examine the links between perception and communications and the importance of understanding the interaction process;

- Examine gender dimensions in organisations and the participation of men and women in the workforce;

- Provide an understanding of women's position and status in the organisational world;

- Recognise the importance of the study of perception and gender.

Worth thinking about

Managers require an understanding of perception in order to help judge the behaviour and intentions of other people. It is not unreasonable to argue that there is no such thing as reality – only the individual's perception or interpretation of reality. How, then, can managers avoid organisational problems which result from perceptual differences?

THE PERCEPTUAL PROCESS

The significance of individual differences is particularly apparent when focusing on the process of perception. This is a characteristic feature of behaviour which has particular importance to the manager. We all see things in different ways. We all have our own, unique picture or image of how we see the 'real' world. We do not passively receive information from the world; we analyse and judge it. We may place significance on some information and regard other information as worthless; and we may be influenced by our expectations so that we 'see' what we expect to see. Perception is the root of all organisational behaviour; any situation can be analysed in terms of its perceptual connotations. Consider, for instance, the situation where a member of the management team has sent a memorandum to section heads asking them to provide statistics of overtime worked within their section during the past six months and projections for the next six months. Mixed reactions could result:

- One section head may see it as a reasonable and welcomed request to provide information which will help lead to improved future staffing levels.
- Another section head may see it as an unreasonable demand, intended only to enable management to exercise closer supervision and control over the activities of the section.
- A third section head may have no objection to providing the information, but be suspicious that it may lead to possible intrusion into the running of the section.
- A fourth head may see it as a positive action by management to investigate ways of reducing costs and improving efficiency throughout the organisation.

Each of the section heads perceives the memorandum differently based on their own experiences. Their perceived reality and understanding of the situation provokes differing reactions.

Individuality

We are all unique; there is only one Laurie Mullins, and one Linda Hicks, and there is only one of you. We all have our own 'world', our own way of looking at and understanding our environment and the people within it. A situation may be the same but the interpretation of that situation by two individuals may be vastly different. For instance, a lively wine bar may be seen as a perfect meeting place by one person, but as a noisy uncomfortable environment by another. One person may see a product as user-friendly but another person may feel that it is far too simplistic and basic. The physical properties may be identical in terms of how they 'are', but they are perceived quite differently because each individual has imposed upon the object/environment their own interpretations, their own judgement and evaluation.

Selectivity in attention and perception

It is not possible to have an understanding of perception without taking into account its sensory basis. We are not able to attend to everything in our environment; our sensory systems have limits. The physical limits therefore insist that we are selective in our attention and perception.

Organisation and judgement

Early pioneer work by psychologists has resulted in an understanding of universal laws which underlie the perceptual process. It seems that we cannot help searching for meaning and understanding in our environment. The way in which we categorise and organise this sensory information is based on a range of different factors including the present situation (and our emotional state), and also our past experiences of the same or similar event.

Some information may be considered highly important to us and may result in immediate action or speech; in other instances the information may be simply 'parked' or assimilated in other ideas and thoughts. The link between perception and memory processes becomes obvious. Some of our 'parked' material may be forgotten or, indeed, changed and reconstructed over time.[1]

Assumptions

We should be aware of the assumptions that are made throughout the perceptual process, below our conscious threshold. We have learnt to take for granted certain constants in our environment. We assume that features of our world will stay the same and thus we do not need to spend our time and energy seeing things afresh and anew. We thus make a number of inferences throughout the entire perceptual process. Although these inferences may save time and speed up the process they may also lead to distortions and inaccuracies.

Perception as information processing

It is common to see the stages of perception described as an information processing system: information (stimuli) (Box A) is selected at one end of the process (Box B), then interpreted (Box C), and translated (Box D), resulting in action or thought patterns (Box E), as shown in Fig. 5.1.

Inferences and assumptions

However, it is important to note that such a model simplifies the process and although it makes it easy to understand (and will be used to structure this chapter) it does not give justice to the complexity and dynamics of the process. In certain circumstances we may select information out of the environment because of the way we categorise the world. In other words, arrows should also lead back from Box E to Box A.

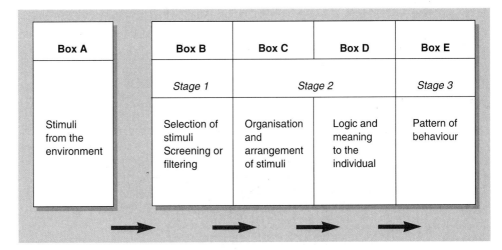

Fig. 5.1
Perceptions as information processing

Box A		Box B	Box C	Box D	Box E
		Stage 1	*Stage 2*		*Stage 3*
Stimuli from the environment		Selection of stimuli Screening or filtering	Organisation and arrangement of stimuli	Logic and meaning to the individual	Pattern of behaviour

For instance, if a manager has been advised by colleagues that a particular trainee has managerial potential the manager may be specifically looking for confirmation that those views are correct. This process has been known as 'top-down', because the cognitive processes are influencing the perceptual readiness of the individual to select certain information. This emphasises the active nature of the perceptual process. We do not passively digest the information from our senses, but we actively attend and indeed, at times, seek out certain information.

MEANING TO THE INDIVIDUAL

The process of perception explains the manner in which information (stimuli) from the environment around us is selected and organised, to provide meaning for the individual. Perception is the mental function of giving significance to stimuli such as shapes, colours, movement, taste, sounds, touch, smells, pain, pressures and feelings. Perception gives rise to individual behavioural responses to particular situations.

Despite the fact that a group of people may 'physically see' the same thing, they each have their own version of what is seen – their perceived view of reality. Consider, for example, the image (published by W. E. Hill in *Puck*, 6 November 1915) shown in Fig. 5.2.

What do you see? Do you see a young, attractive, well-dressed woman? Or do you see an older, poor woman? Or can you now see both? **And who can say with certainty that there is just the one, 'correct' answer?**

Internal and external factors

The first stage in the process of perception is selection and attention. Why do we attend to certain stimuli and not to others? There are two important factors to consider in this discussion: first, internal factors relating to the state of the individual; second, the environment and influences external to the individual. The process of perceptual selection is based, therefore, on both internal and external factors.

Fig. 5.2

INTERNAL FACTORS

Our sensory systems have limits, we are not able to see for 'miles and miles' (unlike the classic song by 'The Who'). Neither are we able to hear very low or very high pitched sounds. All our senses have specialist nerves which respond differentially to the forms of energy which are received. For instance, our eyes receive and convert light waves into electrical signals which are transmitted to the visual cortex of the brain and translated into meaning.

Our sensory system is geared to respond to changes in the environment. This has particular implications for the way in which we perceive the world and it explains why we are able to ignore the humming of the central heating system, but notice instantly a telephone ringing. The term used to describe the way in which we disregard the familiar is 'habituation'.

Sensory limits or thresholds

As individuals we may differ in terms of our sensory limits or thresholds. Without eyeglasses some people would not be able to read a car's number plate at the distance required for safety. People differ not only in their absolute thresholds, but also in their ability to discriminate between stimuli. For instance, it may not be possible for the untrained to distinguish between different grades of tea but this would be an everyday event for the trained tea taster. This implies that we are able to learn to become more discriminatory and are able to train our senses to recognise small differences between stimuli. It is also possible for us to adapt to unnatural environments and learn to cope.[2]

We may also differ in terms of the amount of sensory information we need to reach our own comfortable equilibrium. Some individuals would find loud music at a party or gig uncomfortable and unpleasant, whereas for others the intensity of the music is part of the total enjoyment. Likewise, if we are deprived of sensory information for too long this can lead to feelings of discomfort and fatigue. Indeed, research has shown that if the brain is deprived of sensory information then it will manufacture its own and subjects will hallucinate.[3] It is possible to conclude therefore that the perceptual process is rooted to the sensory limitations of the individual.

Psychological factors

Psychological factors will also affect what is perceived. These internal factors, such as personality, learning and motives, will give rise to an inclination to perceive certain stimuli with a readiness to respond in certain ways. This has been called an individual's perceptual set. (*See* Fig. 5.3.)

Differences in the ways individuals acquire information has been used as one of four scales in the Myers-Briggs Type Indicator (discussed in Chapter 4). They distinguish individuals who 'tend to accept and work with what is given in the here-and-now, and thus become realistic and practical' (sensing types), from others who go beyond the information from the senses and look at the possible patterns, meanings and relationships. These 'intuitive types' 'grow expert at seeing new possibilities and new ways of doing things'. Myers and Briggs stress the value of both types, and emphasise the importance of complementary skills and variety in any successful enterprise or relationship.[4]

Personality and perception have also been examined in the classic experiments by *Witkin et al.* on field dependence/independence. Field dependent individuals were found to be reliant on the context of the stimuli, the cues given in the situa-

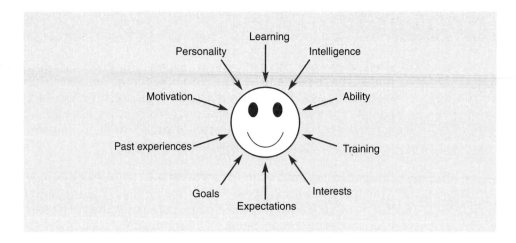

Fig. 5.3
Factors affecting an individual's perceptual set

tion, whereas field independent subjects relied mainly on their own internal bodily cues and less on the environment. These experiments led Witkin to generalise to other settings outside the psychological laboratory and to suggest that individuals use, and need, different information from the environment to make sense of their world.[5]

The needs of an individual

The needs of an individual will affect their perceptions. For example, a manager deeply engrossed in preparing an urgent report may screen out ringing telephones, the sound of computers, people talking and furniture being moved in the next office, but will respond readily to the smell of coffee brewing. The most desirable and urgent needs will almost certainly affect an individual perceptual process.

The 'Pollyanna Principle' claims that pleasant stimuli will be processed more quickly and remembered more precisely than unpleasant stimuli. However, it must be noted that intense internal drives may lead to perceptual distortions of situations (or people) and an unwillingness to absorb certain painful information. This will be considered later in this chapter.

Previous experiences

Learning from previous experiences has a critical effect throughout all the stages of the perceptual process. It will affect the stimuli perceived in the first instance, and then the ways in which those stimuli are understood and processed, and finally the response which is given. For example, it is likely that a maintenance engineer visiting a school for the first time will notice different things about it than a teacher attending an interview or a child arriving on the first day. The learning gained from past experiences colours what is seen and processed.

Our language plays an important role in the way we perceive the world. Our language not only labels and distinguishes the environment for us but also structures and guides our thinking pattern. Even if we are proficient skiers, we do not have many words we can use to describe the different texture of snow; we would be reliant on using layers of adjectives. The Inuit, however, have 13 words for snow in their language. Our language is part of the culture we experience and learn to take for granted. Culture differences are relevant because they emphasise the impact of social learning on the perception of people and their surroundings.

EXTERNAL FACTORS

The knowledge of, familiarity with or expectations about, a given situation or previous experiences, will influence perception. External factors refer to the nature and characteristics of the stimuli. There is usually a tendency to give more attention to stimuli which are, for example:

- large;
- moving;
- intense;
- loud;
- contrasted;
- bright;
- novel;
- repeated; or
- stand out from the background.

Any number of these factors may be present at a given time or situation. It is therefore the **total pattern** of the stimuli together with the **context** in which they occur that influence perception. For example, it is usually a novel or unfamiliar stimulus that is more noticeable, but a person is more likely to perceive the familiar face of a friend among a group of people all dressed in the same style uniform.

The sight of a fork-lift truck on the factory floor of a manufacturing organisation is likely to be perceived quite differently from one in the corridor of a university. The word 'terminal' is likely to be perceived differently in the context of, for example: (i) a hospital, (ii) an airport or (iii) a computer firm.

Consumer psychologists and marketing experts apply these perceptual principles with extraordinary success for some of their products.

ORGANISATION AND ARRANGEMENT OF STIMULI

The Gestalt School of Psychology led by Max Wertheimer claimed that the process of perception is innately organised and patterned. They described the process as one which has built-in field effects. In other words, the brain can act like a dynamic, physical field in which interaction among elements is an intrinsic part. The Gestalt School produced a series of principles, which are still readily applicable today. Some of the most significant principles include the following:

- figure and ground;
- grouping; and
- closure.

Figure and ground

The figure–ground principle states that figures are seen against a background. The figure does not have to be an object; it could be merely a geometrical pattern. Many textiles are perceived as figure–ground relationships. These relationships are often reversible as in the popular example shown in Fig. 5.4.

143

Fig. 5.4

What do you see? Do you see a white chalice (or small stand shape) in the centre of the frame? Or do you see the dark profiles of twins facing each other on the edge of the frame? Now look again. Can you see the other shape?

The figure–ground principle has applications in all occupational situations. It is important that employees know and are able to attend to the significant aspects (the figure), and treat other elements of the job as context (background). Early training sessions aim to identify and focus on the significant aspects of a task. Managerial effectiveness can also be judged in terms of chosen priorities (the figure). Stress could certainly occur for those employees who are uncertain about their priorities, and are unable to distinguish between the significant and less significant tasks. They feel overwhelmed by the 'whole' picture.

Grouping

The grouping principle refers to the tendency to organise shapes and patterns instantly into meaningful groupings or patterns on the basis of their proximity or similarity. Parts that are close in time or space tend to be perceived together. For example, in Fig. 5.5(a), the workers are more likely to be perceived as nine independent people; but in Fig. 5.5(b), because of the proximity principle, the workers may be perceived as three distinct groups of people.

(a) (b)

Fig. 5.5

Taxi firms, for example, often use the idea of grouping to display their telephone number. In the example below which of the following numbers, (a), (b) or (c), is most likely to be remembered easily?

265 265	265265	26 52 65
(a)	(b)	(c)

Similar parts tend to be seen together as forming a familiar group. In the following example there is a tendency to see alternate lines of characters – crosses and noughts (or circles). This is because the horizontal similarity is usually greater than the vertical similarity. However, if the page is turned sideways the figure may be perceived as alternate noughts and crosses in each line.

×	×	×	×	×	×	×	×
o	o	o	o	o	o	o	o
×	×	×	×	×	×	×	×
o	o	o	o	o	o	o	o

It is also interesting to note that many people when asked to describe this pattern refer to alternate lines of noughts and crosses – rather than crosses and noughts.

There is also an example here of the impact of cultural differences, mentioned earlier. The author recently undertook a teaching exchange in the USA and gave this exercise to a class of American students. Almost without exception the students described the horizontal pattern correctly as alternate rows of crosses and noughts (or zeros). The explanation appears to be that Americans do not know the game of 'noughts and crosses' but refer to this as 'tic-tac-toe'.

Closure

There is also a tendency to complete an incomplete figure; to (mentally) fill in the gaps and to perceive the figure as a whole. This creates an overall and meaningful image, rather than an unconnected series of lines or blobs.

Fig. 5.6

(Reproduced with permission from Morgan C. T. and King R. A., *Introduction to Psychology*, Third edition, McGraw-Hill (1966) p. 343.)

In the example in Fig. 5.6[6] most people are likely to see the blobs as either the letter B or the number 13, possibly depending on whether at the time they had been more concerned with written material or dealing in numbers. However, for some people, the figure may remain just a series of eleven discrete blobs or be perceived as some other (to them) meaningful pattern/object.

According to Gestalt theory, perceptual organisation is instant and spontaneous. We cannot stop ourselves making meaningful assumptions about our environment. The Gestaltists emphasised the ways in which the elements interact and claimed that the new pattern or structure perceived had a character of its own, hence the famous phrase: 'the whole is more than the sum of its parts'.

PERCEPTUAL ILLUSIONS

Here are some examples to help you judge your own perceptive skills.
In Fig. 5.7 try reading aloud the four words.

M – A – C – D – O – N – A – L – D

M – A – C – P – H – E – R – S – O – N

M – A – C – D – O – U – G – A – L – L

M – A – C – H – I – N – E – R – Y

Fig. 5.7

It is possible that you find yourself 'caught' in a perceptual set which means that you tend to pronounce 'machinery' as if it too was a Scottish surname.
In Fig. 5.8[7] which of the centre, black circles is the larger – A or B?

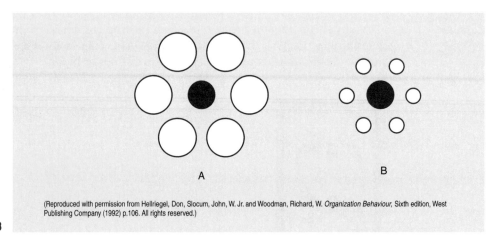

A B

Fig. 5.8

Although you may have guessed that the two centre circles are in fact the same size, the circle on the right (B) may well **appear** larger because it is framed by smaller circles. The centre circle on the left (A) may well **appear** smaller because it is framed by larger circles.
Finally, in Fig.5.9[8] which of the three people is the tallest?
Although the person on the right may **appear** the tallest, they are in fact all the same size.
The physiological nature of perception has already been discussed briefly but it is of relevance here in the discussion of illusions. Why does the circle on the right in Fig. 5.8 look bigger? Why does the person on the right look taller in Fig. 5.9? These examples demonstrate the way our brain can be fooled. Indeed we make assumptions about our world which go beyond the pure sensations our brain receives.[9]

Fig. 5.9 (Reproduced with permission from Luthans, F. *Organizational Behavior*, Sixth edition, McGraw-Hill (1992) p. 66.)

BEYOND REALITY

Perception goes beyond the sensory information and converts these patterns to a three-dimensional reality which we understand. This conversion process, as we can see, is easily tricked! We may not be aware of the inferences we are making as they are part of our conditioning and learning. The Stroop experiment illustrates this perfectly.[10] (*See* Assignment 1 at the end of this chapter.)

The impossible triangle

An illustration of the way in which we react automatically to stimuli is the illusion of the impossible triangle. (*See* Fig. 5.10.)

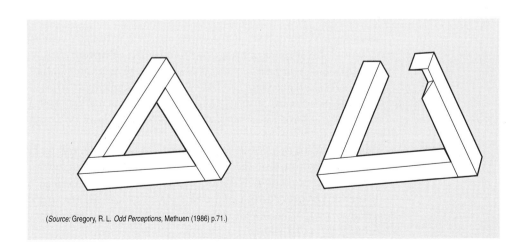

**Fig. 5.10
The impossible triangle**

(*Source:* Gregory, R. L. *Odd Perceptions*, Methuen (1986) p.71.)

Even when we know the triangle is impossible we still cannot help ourselves from completing the triangle and attempting to make it meaningful. We thus go beyond what is given and make assumptions about the world, which in certain instances are wildly incorrect.

Psychologists and designers may make positive use of these assumptions to project positive images of a product or the environment. For instance, colours may be used to induce certain atmospheres in buildings; designs of wallpaper, or texture of curtains, may be used to create feelings of spaciousness or cosiness. Packaging of products may tempt us to see something as bigger or perhaps more precious.

Person perception

Perceptual distortions and inaccuracies may not only affect our perception of the environment but also affect our perception of people. Although the process of perception is equally applicable in the perception of objects or people, there is more scope for subjectivity, bias, errors and distortions when we are perceiving others. The focus of the following section is to examine the perception of people, and to consider the impact this has on the management and development of people at work.

PERCEIVING OTHER PEOPLE

The principles and examples of perceptual differences discussed above reflect the way we perceive other people and are the source of many organisational problems. In the work situation the process of perception and the selection of stimuli can influence a manager's relationship with subordinate staff. Some examples might be as follows.

- the way in which a manager may think of a number of staff: either working in close proximity; or with some common feature such as all clerical workers, all management trainees or all black workers; as a homogeneous group rather than a collection of individuals each with their own separate identity and characteristics;
- the extent to which allowance is made for flexibility and tolerance given for personal initiative, imagination or individual action by staff; rather than insistence on continuity, formal regulations or set procedures;
- the degree to which unanimity is perceived, and decisions made or action taken in the belief that there is full agreement with staff when, in fact, a number of staff may be opposed to the decision or action.

A manager's perception of the workforce will influence attitudes in dealing with people and the style of managerial behaviour adopted. The way in which managers approach the performance of their jobs and the behaviour they display towards subordinate staff are likely to be conditioned by predispositions about people, human nature and work. An example of this is the style of management adopted on the basis of McGregor's Theory X and Theory Y suppositions, which is discussed in Chapter 13.

The perception of people's performance can be affected by the organisation of stimuli. In employment interviews, for example, interviewers are susceptible to contrast effects and the perception of a candidate is influenced by the rating given to immediately preceding candidates. Average candidates may be rated highly if they follow people with low qualifications, but rated lower when following people with higher qualifications.[11]

The dynamics of interpersonal perception

The dynamics of person perception cannot be overestimated. Unlike the perception of an object which just exists, another individual will react to you and be affected by your behaviour. This interaction is illustrated in the following quotation:

> You are a pain in the neck and to stop you giving me a pain in the neck I protect my neck by tightening my neck muscles, which gives me the pain in the neck you are.[12]

The interaction of individuals thus provides an additional layer of interpretation and complexity. The cue which we may attend to, the expectation we may have, the assumptions we may make, the response pattern that occurs, leave more scope for errors and distortions. We are not only perceiving the stimulus (that is, the other person) but we are also processing their reactions to us, and therefore we are only one part of this process.

Thus person perception differs from the perception of objects because:

- it is a continually dynamic and changing process; and
- the perceiver is a part of this process who will influence and be influenced by the other people in the situation.

Fig. 5.11 Cycle of perception and behaviour

(*See* Fig. 5.11.)[13]

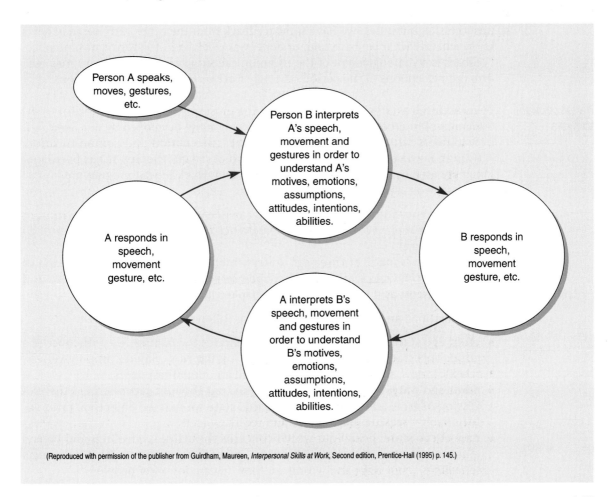

(Reproduced with permission of the publisher from Guirdham, Maureen, *Interpersonal Skills at Work*, Second edition, Prentice-Hall (1995) p. 145.)

Setting and environment

Person perception will also be affected by the setting, and the environment may play a critical part in establishing rapport. For example, next time you are involved in a formal meeting consider the following factors which will all influence the perceptual process.

- **Why?** Purpose of and motives for meeting. Emotional cost to parties.
- **Who?** Status/role/age/gender/ethnic group/appearance/personality/interests/attitudes. Previous encounters.
- **When?** Time of meeting.
- **Where?** Environment/culture.
- **How?** Past experience. Rapport.

PERCEPTION AND COMMUNICATION

It is difficult to consider the process of interpersonal perception without commenting on how people communicate. Communication and perception are inextricably bound. How we communicate to our colleagues, boss, subordinates, friends and partners will depend on our perception of them, on our 'history' with them, on their emotional state, etc. We may misjudge them and regard our communication as unsuccessful, but unless we have some feedback from the other party we may never know whether what we have said, or done, was received in the way it was intended. Feedback is a vital ingredient of the communication process. The feedback may reaffirm our perceptions of the person or it may force us to review our perceptions.

Transactional analysis

Transactional analysis (or TA) is one of the most popular ways of explaining the dynamics of interpersonal communication. Originally developed by *Eric Berne*, it is now a theory which encompasses personality, perception and communication. Although Berne used it initially as a method of psychotherapy it has been convincingly used by organisations as a training and development programme.[14]
 TA has two basic underlying assumptions:

- all the events and feelings that we have ever experienced are stored within us and can be replayed, so we can re-experience the events and the feelings of all our past years;
- personality is made of three ego states which are revealed in distinct ways of behaving. The ego states manifest themselves in gesture, tone of voice and action, almost as if they are different people within us.

Berne identified and labelled the ego states as follows:

- **child ego state**: behaviour which demonstrates the feelings we remember as a child. This state may be associated with having fun, playing, impulsiveness, rebelliousness, spontaneous behaviour and emotional responses.
- **adult ego state**: behaviour which concerns our thought processes and the processing of facts and information. In this state we may be objective, rational, reasonable – seeking information and receiving facts.
- **parent ego state**: behaviour which concerns the attitudes, feelings and behaviour incorporated from external sources, primarily our parents. This state refers to feelings about right and wrong and how to care for other people.

He claimed that the three ego states were universal, but the content of the ego states would be unique to each person. We may be unaware which ego state we are operating in and may shift from one ego state to another. All people are said to behave in each of these states at different times. The three ego states exist simultaneously within each individual although at any particular time any one state many dominate the other two.

We all have a preferred ego state which we may revert to: some individuals may continually advise and criticise others (the constant Parents); some may analyse, live only with facts, and distrust feelings (the constant Adult); some operate with strong feelings all the time, consumed with anger, or constantly clowning (the constant Child). Berne emphasised that the states should not be judged as superior or inferior but as different. Analysis of ego states may reveal why communication breaks down or why individuals may feel manipulated or used.

Berne insists that it is possible to identify the ego state from the words, voice, gestures, and attitude of the person communicating. So for example it would be possible to discern the ego state of a manager if he/she said the following:

'Pass me the file on the latest sales figures.'
'How do you think we could improve our safety record?'
(**Adult ego stage**);

'Let me help you with that – I can see you are struggling.'
'Look, this is the way it should be done; how many more times do I have to tell you...?'
(**Parent ego state**);

'Great, it's Friday. Who's coming to the pub for a quick half?'
'That's a terrific idea – let's go for it!'
(**Child ego state**).

A dialogue can be analysed not only in terms of the ego state but also whether the transaction produced a complementary reaction or a crossed reaction. By complementary it is meant whether the ego state was an expected and preferred response, so for instance if we look at the first statement, 'Pass me the file on the latest sales figures', the subordinate could respond: 'Certainly – I have it here' (Adult ego stage), or 'Can't you look for it yourself? I only gave it to you an hour ago' (Parent ego state).

The first response was complementary whereas the second was a crossed transaction. Sometimes it may be important to 'cross' a transaction. Take the example 'Let me help you with that – I can see you are struggling' (Parent ego state). The manager may have a habit of always helping in a condescending way, making the subordinate resentful. If the subordinate meekly accepts the help with a thankful reply this will only reinforce the manager's perception and attitude, whereas if the subordinate were to respond with 'I can manage perfectly well. Why did you think I was struggling?', it might encourage the manager to respond from the Adult ego state and thus move his/her ego position.

Knowledge of TA can be of benefit to employees who are dealing with potentially difficult situations.[15] In the majority of work situations the Adult–Adult transactions are likely to be the norm. Where work colleagues perceive and respond by adopting the Adult ego state, such a transaction is more likely to encourage a rational, problem-solving approach and reduce the possibility of emotional conflict. Given the incidence of stress in the workplace, analysis of communication may be one way of understanding such conflict. By focusing on

the interactions occurring within the workplace TA can aid the understanding of human behaviour. It can help to improve communication skills by assisting in interpreting a person's ego state and which form of state is likely to produce the most appropriate response. This should lead to an improvement in both customer relations and management–subordinate relations. TA can be seen therefore as a valuable tool in which we can understand social situations and the games that people play both in and outside work organisations.

TA emphasises the strong links between perception and communication and illustrates the way in which they affect each other. But it does not answer how we construct our social world in the first place, what we attend to and why, or why we have positive perceptions about some people and not others. To answer these questions we can concentrate on the stages of the perceptual process – both selection and attention, and organisation and judgement – and apply these to the perception of people.

SELECTION AND ATTENTION

What information do we select and why? The social situation consists of both verbal and non-verbal signals. The non-verbal signals include:

- bodily contact;
- proximity;
- orientation;
- head nods;
- facial expression;
- gestures;
- posture;
- direction of gaze;
- dress and appearance;
- non-verbal aspects of speech.

Verbal and non-verbal signals are co-ordinated into regular sequences, often without the awareness of the parties. The mirroring of actions has been researched and is called 'postural echoing'.[16] There is considerable evidence to indicate that each person is constantly influencing the other, and being influenced.[17]

Cook has suggested that in any social encounter there are two kinds of information which can be distinguished:

- **static information** – information which will not change during the encounter: for example, colour, gender, height and age; and
- **dynamic information** – information which is subject to change: for example, mood, posture, gestures and expression.[18]

Impression management

In some situations we all attempt to project our attitudes, personality and competence by paying particular attention to our appearance, and the impact this may have on others. This has been labelled 'impression management'[19] and the selection interview is an obvious illustration. Some information is given more weight than other information when an impression is formed. It would seem that there are central traits which are more important than others in determining our perceptions.

One of these central traits is the degree of warmth or coldness shown by an individual.[20] The timing of information also seems to be critical in the impressions we form. For example, information heard first tends to be resistant to later contradictory information. In other words, the saying 'first impression counts' is supported by research and is called 'the primacy effect'.[21] It has also been shown that a negative first impression is more resistant to change than a positive one.[22] However, if there is a break in time we are more likely to remember the most recent information – 'the recency effect'.

ORGANISATION AND JUDGEMENT

The ways in which we organise and make judgements about what we have perceived is to a large extent based on our previous experiences and learning. There are cultural differences in the way that body language is perceived and interpreted.

It is also important at this point to be aware of the inferences and assumptions we make which go beyond the information given. We may not always be aware of our pre-set assumptions but they will guide the way in which we interpret the behaviour of others. There has been much research into the impact of implicit personality theory.[23] In the same way that we make assumptions about the world of objects, and go beyond the information provided, we also make critical inferences about people's characteristics and possible likely behaviours.

A manager might well know more about the 'type of person' A – a member of staff who has become or was already a good friend, who is seen in a variety of social situations and with whom there is a close relationship – than about B – another member of staff, in the same section as A and undertaking similar duties, but with whom there is only a formal work relationship and a limited social acquaintance. These differences in relationship, information and interaction might well influence the manager's perception if asked, for example, to evaluate the work performance of A and B.

Judgement of other people can also be influenced by perceptions of such stimuli as, for example:

- role or status;
- occupation;
- physical factors and appearance; and
- body language, for example inferences drawn from posture, invasions of personal space, the extent of eye contact, tone of voice or facial expression.

The importance of body language

Body language is of particular significance. This is because in our face-to-face communications with other people the message about our feelings and attitudes come only 7 per cent from the words we use, 38 per cent from our voice and 55 per cent from body language including facial expressions. Significantly, when body language such as gestures and tone of voice conflicts with the words greater emphasis is likely to be placed on the non-verbal message.[24]

Body language may be a guide to personality but errors can easily arise if too much is inferred from a single message rather then a related cluster of actions. And there are of course many cultural variations in body language.[25] As an example, when talking to another person the British tend to look away spasmodically, but Norwegians typically look people steadily in the eyes without altering their gaze.

153

Perceptual judgement applies particularly to perceptions about other people. A person may tend to organise perception of another person in terms of the 'whole' mental picture of that person. Perceptual judgement is influenced by reference to related characteristics associated with the person and the attempt to place that person in a complete environment.

In one example, an unknown visitor was introduced by the course director to 110 American students, divided into five equal groups.[26] The visitor was described differently to each group as:

(i) Mr England, a student from Cambridge;
(ii) Mr England, demonstrator in psychology from Cambridge;
(iii) Mr England, lecturer in psychology from Cambridge;
(iv) Dr England, senior lecturer from Cambridge;
(v) Professor England from Cambridge.

After being introduced to each group, the visitor left. Each group of students was then asked to estimate his height to the nearest half inch. They were also asked to estimate the height of the course director after he too left the room. The mean estimated height of the course director, who had the same status for all groups, did not change significantly among groups. However, the estimated height of the visitor varied with perceived status: as ascribed academic status increased, so did the estimate of height. (*See* Table 5.1.)

Table 5.1 Estimated height according to ascribed academic status

Group	Ascribed academic status	Average estimated height
(i)	Student	5' 9.9"
(ii)	Demonstrator	5' 10.14"
(iii)	Lecturer	5' 10.9"
(iv)	Senior lecturer	5' 11.6"
(v)	Professor	6' 0.3"

(Adapted from Wilson, P. R. 'Perceptual Distortion of Height as a Function of Ascribed Academic Status', *Journal of Social Psychology*, no. 74, 1968, pp. 97–102.)

It seems therefore that part of the process of perceiving other people is to attribute characteristics to them. We judge their behaviour and their intentions on past knowledge, and in comparison with other people we know. It is our way of making sense of their behaviour. This is known as attribution theory.

ATTRIBUTION THEORY

A more recent approach to the study of motivation is attribution theory. Attribution is the process by which people interpret the perceived causes of behaviour. The initiator of attribution theory is generally recognised as *Heider*, who suggests that behaviour is determined by a combination of **perceived** internal forces and external forces.[27]

- **Internal forces** relate to personal attributes such as ability, skill, amount of effort or fatigue.
- **External forces** relate to environmental factors such as organisational rules and policies, the manner of superiors, or the weather.

Behaviour at work may be explained by the **locus of control**, that is whether the individual perceives outcomes as controlled by themselves, or by external factors. Judgements made about other people will also be influenced strongly by whether the cause is seen as internal or external.

Basic criteria in making attributions

In making attributions and determining whether an internal or external attribution is chosen, *Kelley* suggests three basic criteria: distinctiveness, consensus and consistency.[28]

- **Distinctiveness**: how distinctive or different was the behaviour or action in this particular task or situation compared with behaviour or action on other tasks or situations?
- **Consensus**: is the behaviour or action different from, or in keeping with, that displayed by most other people in the same situation?
- **Consistency**: is the behaviour or action associated with an enduring personality or motivational characteristic over time, or an unusual one-off situation caused by external factors?

Kelley hypothesised that people attribute behaviour to internal forces or personal factors when they perceive **low distinctiveness, low consensus** and **high consistency**. Behaviour is attributed to external forces or environmental factors when people perceived **high distinctiveness, high consensus**, and **low consistency** (*see* Fig. 5.12).

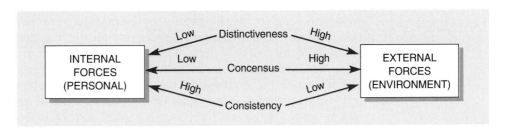

Fig. 5.12 Representation of attribution theory

An example of these criteria related to a student who fails a mid-sessional examination in a particular subject is given in Table 5.2.[29]

Table 5.2 Example of criteria in making attributions

	Distinctiveness	*Consensus*	*Consistency*
Internal attribution	Student fails all mid-sessional examinations	Student is the only one to fail	Student also fails final examination
External attribution	Student gains high marks on other mid-sessional examinations	All students in the class get low marks	Student obtains a good mark in final examination

(Adapted and reproduced with permission from Mitchell, Terence R. *People in Organizations*, Second edition, McGraw-Hill (1982) p. 104.)

Classification of attributions

An additional consideration in the evaluation of task performance within an organisational setting is whether the cause of behaviour was due to 'stable' or 'unstable' factors.

- **Stable factors** are ability, or the ease or difficulty of the task.
- **Unstable factors** are the exertion of effort, or luck.[30]

The combination of internal and external attributions, and stable and unstable characteristics, results in four possible interpretations of a person's task performance (*see* Table 5.3).

Table 5.3 Classification of possible attributions for performance

	Internal attributions	External attributions
Stable factors	ABILITY	TASK DIFFICULTY
Unstable factors	EFFORT	LUCK

Implications of attribution theory

Employees with an internal control orientation are more likely to believe that they can influence their level of performance through their own abilities, skills or efforts. Employees with an external control orientation are more likely to believe that their level of performance is determined by external factors beyond their influence.

Studies appear to support the idea that staff with an internal control orientation are generally more satisfied with their jobs, are more likely to be in managerial positions, and are more satisfied with a participatory style of management, than staff with an external control orientation.[31] As a generalisation it might be implied that internally controlled managers are more effective than those who are externally controlled. However, this does not appear to be always the case.[32]

People with a high achievement motivation may perceive that successful performance is caused by their own internal forces, and their ability and effort, rather than by the nature of the task or by luck. If members of staff fail to perform well on their tasks they may believe that external factors are the cause, and as a result may reduce the level of future effort. On the other hand, if staff perform well but the manager perceives this as due to an easy task or to luck, the appropriate recognition and reward may not be given. If the staff perceive that good performance was due to ability and/or effort the lack of recognition and reward may well have a demotivating effect.

DEALINGS WITH OTHER PEOPLE

There are a number of well documented problems which arise when perceiving other people. Many of these problems occur because of our limitations in selecting and attending to information. This selectivity may occur because:

- we already know what we are looking for and are therefore 'set' to receive only the information which confirms our initial thoughts;

or

- previous training and experience have led us to short-cut and only see a certain range of behaviours;

or

- we may group features together and make assumptions about their similarities.

The Gestalt principles apply equally well to the perception of people as to the perception of objects. Thus we can see, for example, that if people live in the same geographical area, assumptions may be made about not only their wealth and type of accommodation but also their attitudes, their political views and even their type of personality.

PERCEPTUAL DISTORTIONS AND ERRORS

We have seen that differences in perception result in different people seeing different things and attaching different meanings to the same stimuli. Every person sees things in his or her own way and as perceptions become a person's reality this can lead to misunderstandings.

The accuracy of interpersonal perception and the judgements made about other people are influenced by:

- the nature of the relationship between the perceiver and the other person;
- the amount of information available to the perceiver and the order in which information is received;
- the nature and extent of interaction between the two people.[33]

There are four main features which can create particular difficulties and give rise to perceptual problems, bias or distortions, in our dealings with other people. These are:

- stereotyping;
- the halo effect;
- perceptual defence; and
- projection.

STEREOTYPING

This is the tendency to ascribe positive or negative characteristics to a person on the basis of a general categorisation and perceived similarities. The perception of that person may be based more on certain expected characteristics than on the recognition of that person as an individual. It is a form of typecasting.

Stereotyping is a means of simplifying the process of perception and making judgements of other people, instead of dealing with a range of complex and alternative stimuli. It occurs when an individual is judged on the basis of the group to which it is perceived that person belongs. When we see all people belonging to a particular group as having the same characteristics we are stereotyping individuals. Pre-judgements are therefore made about an individual without ever really knowing whether such judgements are accurate; they may be wildly wrong.

Examples of common stereotyping may be based on:

- nationality – e.g., all Germans are orderly and industrious;
- occupation – e.g., all accountants are boring;
- age – e.g., all young people are unreliable, no old person wants to consider new ideas;
- physical – e.g., all people with red hair have fiery temperament;
- education – e.g., all graduates are clever;
- social – e.g., all unemployed people are lazy;
- politics – e.g., all Labour voters are in favour of strong trade unions, all Conservative voters support privatisation.

Although stereotyping condenses the amount of information that we need to know and thus enables us to cope with a vast information flow, the consequences of attributing incorrect characteristics are extremely negative.

Social implications

Stereotyping infers that all people within a particular perceived category are assumed to share the same traits or characteristics. A significant social implication of stereotyping is therefore the perception held about particular groups of people based on, for example:

- gender;
- race;
- disability;
- religious belief;
- age.

(By way of an example the illustrative case at the end of this chapter focuses on the effects of stereotyping women.)

A major danger of stereotyping is that it can block out accurate perception of the individual or individual situation.[34] Stereotyping may lead to potential situations of prejudice or discrimination. An example might be the perception of people with HIV or AIDS.[35]

Stereotyping may work either negatively or favourably for a particular group of people. For example a sizeable number of employers still maintain negative and inaccurate stereotypes about the capabilities and training of older workers.[36] However, B&Q, the UK's largest home-improvement chain, have claimed improved profit figures partly because of the older age profile of their employees: they have a policy of staffing certain stores with people over 50 years of age.

THE HALO EFFECT

This is the process by which the perception of a person is formulated on the basis of a single favourable or unfavourable trait or impression. The halo effect tends to shut out other relevant characteristics of that person. Some examples might be as follows.

- A candidate for employment who arrives punctually, is smart in appearance and friendly may well influence the perception of the selectors, who then place less emphasis on the candidate's technical ability, qualifications or experience for the job.

- A new member of staff who performs well in a first major assignment may be perceived as a likely person for promotion, even though that assignment is not typical of the usual duties the member of staff is expected to undertake.
- A single trait, such as good attendance and time-keeping, may become the main emphasis for judgement of overall competence and performance, rather than other considerations such as the quantity, quality and accuracy of work.

A particular danger with the halo effect is that, where quick judgements are made on the basis of readily available stimuli, the perceiver may become 'perceptually blind' to subsequent stimuli at variance with the original perception, and (often subconsciously) notice only those characteristics which support the original judgement.

The rusty halo effect

The process may also work in reverse: **the rusty halo effect**. This is where general judgements about a person are formulated from the perception of a negative characteristic. For example, a candidate is seen arriving late for an interview. There may be a very good reason for this and it may be completely out of character. But on the basis of that one particular event the person may be perceived as a poor time-keeper and unreliable. Another example may be a new member of staff who performs poorly in a first major assignment. This may have been due to an unusual set of circumstances and not typical behaviour, but the person may still be perceived as a bad appointment.

PERCEPTUAL DEFENCE

This is the tendency to avoid or screen out certain stimuli that are perceptually disturbing or threatening. People may tend to select information which is supportive of their point of view and choose not to acknowledge contrary information. For example, a manager who has decided recently to promote a member of staff against the advice of colleagues may select only favourable information which supports that decision and ignore less favourable information which questions that decision.

PROJECTION

Attributing, or projecting, one's own feelings, motives or characteristics to other people is a further distortion which can occur in the perception of other people. Judgements of other people may be more favourable when they have characteristics largely in common with, and easily recognised by, the perceiver. Projection may also result in people exaggerating undesirable traits in others that they fail to recognise in themselves.

Perception is distorted by feelings and emotions. For example, a manager who is concerned about possible redundancy may perceive other managers to be even more concerned. People have a tendency to perceive others less favourably by projecting certain of their own feelings or characteristics to them. As another example, supervisors may complain that their manager did not work hard enough to secure additional resources for the department, when in fact the supervisors failed to provide the manager with all the relevant information and statistics.

Protection for ourselves

Discussed by *Freud* in his description of defence mechanisms, projection is a way in which we protect ourselves from acknowledging that we may possess undesirable traits and assign them in exaggerated amounts to other people. For instance, a manager who considers all subordinates as insincere may be projecting one of the manager's own characteristics.

Perception of 'self' and how people see and think of themselves, and evaluate themselves, are discussed in Chapter 7.

THE PERCEPTUAL PARADOX

These problems with people perception arise because of the selectivity which exists in the perceptual process. We do not enjoy living in a world where uncertainty abounds and our perceptual system works to minimise our energy consumption. We do not have to start every day afresh – we have our store of memories and experiences to guide us.

The paradox is that this process is also our downfall. Errors and bias are inherent in such a system. Although exhortations can be made for us to become more aware of our own biases and to take more time in making judgements we are working against our normal quick-fire perceptual system.

ILLUSTRATIVE EXAMPLE – PERCEPTION OF WOMEN

The perceptual process has been outlined as selective and subjective: we perceive the world in our own terms and expect the world to 'fit' into our constructs. Throughout our development we have learned to distinguish what is important and significant (figure) from information which is additional and contextual (ground). This process is repeated when we join new organisations or have a new job within the same organisation. Fitting into the organisation involves selecting information which is necessary from that which is less significant. At times, the process can be distorted and we can also be 'tricked' into seeing the world in particular ways.

Beliefs about women and their roles

One of the most common stereotypes is to view women in terms of their biology and reproductive abilities. Unlike men, beliefs about women and their roles focus outside the workplace rather than inside. For instance, the prospect of women marrying and having children leads people to question their permanency as employees, and results in organisations viewing their engagement as high risk, with a low return on investment in their training.

In middle years the additional responsibilities of having children are often assumed to be the major role of women. This leads to further beliefs regarding their assumed lack of time and ambition for senior positions. Women, for a period stretching over twenty years, could be perceived as less reliable, less promotable and less ambitious than men.

Instead of stereotyping women and viewing them as a group with identical life patterns, it would clearly be more equitable to judge women individually. This

would seem particularly relevant as statistics reveal that nearly two-thirds of women at work who leave to have a baby are economically active within nine months of childbirth.[37]

Stereotypes about women employees

In the workplace, there are many commonplace stereotypes about women employees. Women may be perceived as: an 'earth-mother'; a counsellor figure; a 'pet' brightening up the place; a 'seductress'; a sex object; an 'iron maiden'; a man-hater.[38] In addition, women who have made it to the top have to face other pressures concerned with their visibility and uniqueness. The token woman has to contend with additional interest because of her gender and she may be excluded from social activities and male 'chat'.

Some studies have focused on the behavioural characteristics of men and women, and have noted that women may be caught in a 'double bind'. If they show typical feminine characteristics it is thought they do not have the ambition to go further; whereas if they demonstrate assertiveness and determination they can be considered to be too aggressive, pushy and masculine.

Understanding the organisational process

Although some organisations may discriminate, it is the view of the authors that perceptions of women are not always calculated: they are often made automatically and without conscious thought – in much the same way as we may be tricked by visual illusions. In fact, perceptual illusions are a very appropriate way of understanding the organisational processes affecting women.

The 'Ames Room' is relevant for this purpose.[39] This is a room of an irregular size with one of the far corners at a greater distance than the other, although the room is arranged and decorated so that it gives the appearance of being rectangular. If two people of the same size stand in diagonally opposite corners, one in the furthest corner, and the other in the near corner, a visual illusion occurs whereby our perception of depth is 'tricked' to see the farthest away looking dramatically smaller. (*See* Fig. 5.13.)

By analogy it is possible to see the room as representing the culture of the organisation surrounded by beliefs and traditions, rather like pictures on the wall. They seem reasonable, logical and appropriate. The individual standing at the farthest corner of the room could be seen as the female, the nearest the male. Both people are in the room surrounded by the culture; but one, the male, is nearest and most visible. He is perceived differently and advantageously, whereas the woman is perceived in a relatively inconsequential way. If the woman stays at the back of the room in an ancillary position, or leaves the room altogether, she is reinforcing the beliefs around the walls.

Some women, however, do become managers and these exceptional women would then join the male corner and would seem to become larger in size and more visible. However, the perceptual distortion is complete because the lone woman could legitimately be viewed as a 'trick', as an illusion. For the males, their position fits and they have only to prove their merit for a management post, and not that they are different from the norm. Their success will feed back into the system and reaffirm the beliefs that are held.

Applications to the organisational setting

This illusion can be applied to any organisational setting. *Hicks* found, for example, that even in hotels, which mirror the domestic world of women and should suit perfectly the alleged skills of women, a male ethic resides.[40] The female manager is atypical, a deviation from the norm, and women can be seen to be the

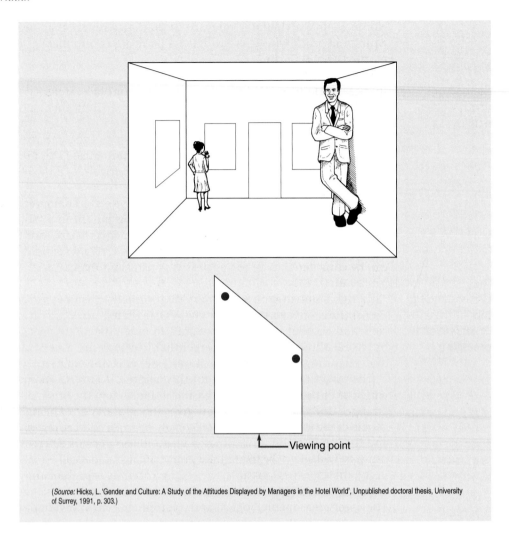

(*Source:* Hicks, L. 'Gender and Culture: A Study of the Attitudes Displayed by Managers in the Hotel World', Unpublished doctoral thesis, University of Surrey, 1991, p. 303.)

Fig. 5.13
The Ames Room

disadvantaged gender group. Men and women are perceived very differently. Young, male trainees are expected and encouraged to do well, it is considered 'normal'; whereas young women and their assumed needs are less likely to fit into the demands of the industry. Young women are expected to diversify and specialise in roles considered suitable for their gender such as personnel or public relations.

For any organisation to be effective it is imperative that the staff are competent to do their work and satisfy the 'psychological contract' (discussed in Chapter 1). One part of the role of managers is to select and train those people who they predict will perform successfully on the job, and then to monitor and assess their competence for future promotion. Accordingly, it clearly seems important for managers to be aware of their own prejudices and assumptions concerning women. By opening channels and encouraging and developing all staff, trust might be fed back into the system from which equity could begin and stereotypes might end.

GENDER DIMENSIONS IN ORGANISATIONS

The common stereotyping of women draws attention to a particular aspect of people perception in the work organisation – that of gender. This section examines the participation of men and women in the workforce, and in particular reviews the position and status of women.

A review of statistical evidence reveals that the places where women work have not changed substantially and remain different in kind from male occupations. In essence, women are working in occupations which reflect their perceived role in society, and they are generally found servicing and caring for others. It is recognised that many organisations are adopting equal opportunity policies and are seriously examining whether they are fulfilling the potential of all their staff. However, statistics reveal that progress is slow and the number of women holding senior managerial positions is still insignificant.

Recent reports have indicated that a 'glass ceiling' exists in many organisations, preventing women from rising to the top. Changes were suggested by the Hansard Society Commission relating not only to working structures and practices which are seen as inflexible, but also to 'outmoded attitudes about the roles of women'.[41] The tone of the report could be described as liberal with an emphasis on egalitarianism and potential resource wastage. It suggested ways in which the domestic role of women could be tackled more successfully in tandem with a managerial career, and as such it did not challenge societal expectations of the dual role of women.

The report shows a mood of optimism and discusses good practices, and indicates that changes can happen when intention and action prevail. It should be noted, however, that the Commission found informal practices and unintentional insensitivities as being highly significant in limiting women's opportunities. Reported changes were ones of improvement rather than any dramatic redress of women's position. Given the difficulties already discussed in attitude change, and the pervasiveness of organisational culture in maintaining beliefs and values, such an optimistic approach might be seen as unrealistic.

A report which surveyed the progress of women on the Boards of the Times Top 200 companies revealed the slow pace of change. Although the number of women on the Boards had risen (from 11 per cent in 1989 to 25 per cent in 1993) the actual number of women executives remained low. The number of women in part-time and non-executive posts was considerably higher than in executive appointments (of the 57 appointments only 11 were executive).[42] The authors conceded that the glass ceiling was being penetrated but at a very slow pace and with women executives still a rare sight in the city and in business generally.

HISTORICAL PERSPECTIVE

It is commonly felt that women's participation in the labour force has been increasing steadily. The increase in the number of married women working since the Second World War has been identified as a significant change and *Lewis* asserts that the older married woman is the typical female worker.[43] Historians have iden-

163

tified that going to work changed the notion of work as something that was public, paid and therefore seen to be valuable.

Interestingly, in the nineteenth century occupations that women were engaged upon were very similar to their household tasks: 35 per cent of working women were servants; 19.5 per cent textile workers; 15.6 per cent dressmakers. For men at that time work was not only more variable but generally higher paid. The textile industries, for example, provided certain lower paid jobs for women and there were few opportunities for training for higher paid work.

The social class of women

Many craft guilds excluded women except for the wives of master craftsmen. The social class of the women had a determining effect on whether they would work or not. 'A lady must be a real lady and nothing else' was typical of the attitudes held. The government's publicity encouraging women to work for the 'War Effort' was focused particularly on the middle classes who had not been employed and the First World War marked the beginning of their inclusion into the labour force.

However, these work opportunities were short-lived as men returning to work demanded their jobs and women were encouraged to retreat into their previous domestic positions. *Lewenhak* reports that women who refused to take domestic work offered to them at the Labour Exchange had their benefits stopped and the marriage bar, relaxed during the war years, was once more re-established.[44]

Women's participation in the labour market was transformed once more as a result of the Second World War. This provided women with greater occupational opportunities which had been positively discouraged at other times. However, many employers de-skilled jobs, divided the labour and offered lower wages to women.

Pattern of women's employment

Although there have been noticeable changes in the pattern of women's employment and a substantial change in the number of women working, little has changed in the structure of their employment. There are four main recurrent themes.

- Women have occupied different positions from men not only in content (horizontal segregation) but also in power and responsibility (vertical segregation). This pattern has been constant over time.
- The jobs that women have occupied (and are still occupying) mirror the domestic/servicing, caring functions. This pattern has been encouraged by both government and employers in the policies that have been enacted over the century.
- The value and status placed on these occupations have been low: occupations concerned with domestic work are usually unpaid (housework) or low paid.
- Women's role outside the workplace is inextricably bound with their role life in the domestic sphere.

One theme of variation is evident, however: the number of women in occupations has fluctuated over the century with an upsurge of numbers during wartime. A pattern of working has been established, defined as 'bi-modal', whereby women enter the labour force, leave and re-enter at an older age.[45]

UNDERSTANDING WOMEN'S POSITION AND STATUS

Why should men's and women's working experiences be so different? Why should the dogma of 'a woman's place is in the home' still prevail? Five explanations are presented. These should not be seen as competitive but as all contributing to the understanding of women's position and status in the organisational world. The explanations are:

- economic theories;
- psychological sex differences;
- the socialisation process;
- orientations and motivations towards work; and
- working practices.

ECONOMIC THEORIES

Two major economic theories seek to explain and predict labour patterns of women's employment:

- human capital theory; and
- dual labour market theory.

Human capital theory

The main tenet of human capital theory is that to have the benefit of choices in the workplace, individuals are required to make a substantial investment – for example, in education and training.[46] Human capital theory predicts that women will acquire less schooling and training than men, and will have less time to reap rewards of investment. Whatever skills they had learned will be outdated during their period at home.

The interrupted pattern of women's employment therefore decreases the incentives for both women and employers to engage in their training. Although this may explain the position for some it does not explain the position of women who *do* invest their time in education and training. Neither does it explain the disparities in earnings which exist between men and women where *neither* have committed themselves to education and training.

Dual labour market theory

Dual labour market theory argues that the labour market is divided into two separate markets: the primary market consisting of jobs with career prospects, high wages and stable employment; and the secondary market whose jobs are dead-end, low paid and with poor prospects. Research evidence shows that women, and ethnic groups, are over-represented in the secondary market.[47] *Loveridge and Mok* suggest that women comprise an 'outgroup' and are treated as such, and form the basis of an industrial reserve providing the source of additional labour when society requires it.[48]

Although these explanations are rich in detail they leave unexplored the origin of women's roles as looked at by psychologists and sociologists.

PSYCHOLOGICAL SEX DIFFERENCES

Is it the case that men and women follow different occupational routes because these match their particular sex type? Significantly, it has been found that the male species are far more vulnerable physically. For example, *Gross* comments that 'there is no doubt that males are, biologically, the weaker sex!'[49]

In their classic review of this subject, *Maccoby and Jacklin* claimed support for differences between males and females in terms of visuo-spatial ability, mathematical ability and aggressiveness (male scores higher); and verbal ability (female scores higher). But they also explored a number of myths which surround sex differences and concluded there were more similarities than differences between the sexes.[50]

Biological differences

Studies focusing on biological differences remained unsupported without the inclusion of inter-relational factors. The reciprocal effect that babies and parents have on each other provides fascinating data on the preferential treatment that parents give their babies depending on their sex. It has been found that mothers are less responsive to boys crying than girls, even at the age of three weeks.[51] Studies have also shown the different interpretative connotations placed on behaviour which fits the stereotype of active, energetic boy, and passive, nurturing girl.[52]

One conclusion to draw is that biology alone cannot explain differences in women's position. Attention must be focused on social issues, and the influence and impact of the socialisation process.

THE SOCIALISATION PROCESS

The family consists of a number of psychologically intense and powerful social relationships in which it is possible to see how little girls and little boys learn their gender, identity and role. The definition of gender, what it is and what it means to family members, is reinforced from external agencies (for example, the media and school) so that messages concerning gender are continuously being processed and reaffirmed. As *Barrett* has said: 'gender identity is not created once and for all at a certain point in the child's life but is continually recreated and endorsed, modified or even altered, substantially through a process of ideological representation'.[53]

One study demonstrated the overriding effect of societal influences on a child's gender role learning. The trivia, tiny events and language all created a particular picture and image which established a gender consciousness. Many studies support the notion that everyday language and events identify, acknowledge and maintain the dependent, subordinate position of women.[54]

Gender shaping

Gender shaping occurs in education in overt forms of schooling, for example curriculum; and in the 'hidden' patterns of behaviour such as teachers' values and expectations. Evidence indicates that girls traditionally prefer to study humanities rather than science and achieve a higher number of passes in these preferred subjects. Even in newer subjects such as computing, boys have dominated.[55] It has also been shown that girls achieve better results in single-sex schools, and are

more likely to continue their education at a further level and in areas normally dominated by men.[56]

The hidden curriculum supports the notion of male dominance which the administrative hierarchy reaffirms. It is more likely that children will be taught by a woman in their younger years but the school will be managed by a man. At secondary level the pastoral caring role is more likely to be undertaken by a woman, the science and engineering subjects by a man, and the school managed by a man. However, women predominate in peripheral roles such as cleaners, dinner attendants and cooks.

Girls and boys show different tendencies to report performance and potential: it has been found that girls are more likely to underestimate their own ability; whereas boys overestimate and exaggerate theirs.[57]

ORIENTATIONS AND MOTIVATIONS TOWARDS WORK

It is perhaps salutary to recognise that women workers have tended to be overlooked within many of the classical studies on orientation and motivation. Early studies tended to focus entirely on men (for example, the work of *F. W. Taylor*); or avoid an interpretation of gender divisions (recall, for example, the discussion in Chapter 2 on sex power differential in the Hawthorne experiments).

There is also a common, underlying suggestion that for 'he' one may also assume 'she'. For example, *Alban-Metcalfe* commented that anyone reading the management literature may well 'gain the impression that the managerial population is hermaphrodite since the vast majority of studies (which transpire when examined) have been based upon exclusively male samples which are interpreted as if the findings apply equally to females and males'.[58]

Decisions about working

Early studies by *Hunt* revealed that decisions about working revolved around women's primary responsibility for home care. Differences in motivations among the sampled women depended on the life stage which they had reached. Hunt claimed it was not possible to discuss motivation without taking into account the social context of work and home.[59]

There may also be pressure upon women to give 'legitimate' reasons for wanting to work. *Marshall* discusses the double bind for women.[60] Although it is seen to be acceptable for women to say they need the money (and therefore have little choice but to work) such a reason suggests that women do not desire to satisfy their own personal developmental needs. Thus, women may be seen as not holding work values concerning a high level of organisational commitment. However, if women are seen to be overly ambitious then they must be neglecting their primary role in society as a woman.

Some writers claim that men's and women's motivations are the same, although there is partial support for the notion that women perceive their career differently and have a different sense of time.[61]

WORKING PRACTICES

Is it the case that men and women experience different working practices? This idea contradicts the view that organisations are neutral and objective endeavours but suggests that work itself has a masculine blue print. Recent research has suggested that the following practices seem to have gendered bias:

- recruitment and selection;
- informal communication;
- career development; and
- attitudes.

Recruitment and selection

Investigations into (supposedly) neutral personnel procedures have found that informal criteria based on gendered stereotypes are maintained in selection decisions.[62] It has been suggested that there is a gap between the rational procedures of specifying scientifically the job, and the informal evaluation of recruiting candidates and evaluating their suitability.[63]

Informal communication

Informal communication within organisations has also been studied and it has been shown that advice from 'gatekeepers' affect women's opportunities and their perceptions of themselves. For example, one study reported that males and females received different career advice.[64] In another study, young female lawyers were subjected to greater scrutiny than male applicants in terms of their motivation and attitude.[65]

Career development

The socialisation period has been found to have a marked effect on subsequent performance and work-related values. The formation of appropriate bonds between individuals and the group are crucial in order that the new member feels involved and accepted by the organisation. Exclusion from a group has far-reaching effects for information transmission, decision-making and eventual career progression.[66]

Training opportunities are vital for personal development and career success. Studies in various industries indicate that women are frequently not encouraged to study; or they are encouraged to study in functional specialisms (such as personnel management or public relations) rather than in mainstream managerial activities.[67]

Attitudes

Paternalistic attitudes also reveal that male managers frequently think it 'best' not to send a woman on an assignment or ask her to attend late meetings. Although intentions might be well-meaning, the lack of opportunities for women to be placed in challenging or risky situations places them at a disadvantage *vis-à-vis* men.

Kanter illustrates the pervasiveness of status levelling whereby women's status is levelled down and men's levelled up.[68] Thus a woman answering the telephone will usually be assumed to be the secretary, whereas a man will be assumed to be the boss. Token women have particular difficulties in that they are forced to play a role which is constrained by male rules and strategies. They are often excluded from informal relations, and thus from important informal networks and communication.[69]

The term 'homosociability' has been coined by Kanter for the process whereby members of the same sex are preferred, promoted and developed. Inevitably in most organisations this equates with male development. It is often a pleasure for

senior managers to mentor and develop a younger person with whom they can identify. If this notion is taken together with research that suggests the informal relations and networks within organisations play a powerful part in determining career opportunities, then young men are placed in an advantaged position.

POSITIVE APPROACHES

Reviews and articles explaining the position and status of women typically conclude with exhortations to organisations to introduce and promote schemes which would positively help and support women. The logic of introducing such schemes is based on good business sense in that women represent an untapped human resource. There has been considerable media hype about the progress of women at work and yet this is not revealed in the latest statistics. Improving the 'lot' of women can also provoke resentment from men.

Perhaps the most positive approach to take is for an organisation to acknowledge the changing working pattern of all employees and to consider the best working practices for managing a diverse workforce. This should not be done mechanically but by analysis of the organisation and its workforce. Organisations need to analyse, consciously debate and question their unwritten assumptions and expectations in order to reveal prejudices inherent in the culture of their organisations. Analysis of the way in which culture is expressed in all its trivial detail would lead to an understanding of perceptions and attitudes. Until a full analysis is completed it remains doubtful if more egalitarian practices will develop.

Employees should go through a three-stage process of auditing existing policies, setting measurable goals and making a public commitment from top management to achieving them. Organisations choose their own goals in line with their business objectives.[70] Such an investment in time and people enables the most appropriate working practices to be created so that people are able to balance their lives.

SYNOPSIS

■ The process of perception links individuals to their social world. Although we all see the world through our own 'coloured spectacles' we also have the opportunities to share our experiences with others. By learning others' perspectives and by widening our understanding of how others may see the world, depth and variety is encouraged and problems of bias and distortion become minimised.

■ For managers, an understanding of perception is essential to ensure that they are aware of the problems which can arise from the process of perceptual selectivity. The process of perception is innately organised and patterned. The organisation and arrangement of stimuli is influenced by three important factors: figure and ground; grouping; and closure.

■ Part of the process of perceiving other people is to attribute characteristics to them. We judge their behaviour and intentions on past knowledge and in comparison with other people we know. Perception gives rise to individual behavioural

responses in given situations. The importance of communication and the way we interact with others cannot be overestimated as our well-being and morale can be affected by the nature of these social experiences.

■ There are a number of difficulties which arise with interpersonal perception. Four main features which may give rise to perceptual distortions or errors are: stereotyping; the halo effect; perceptual defence; and projection. In the work situation perceptual differences reflect the way we perceive other people and are the source of many organisational problems.

■ The perceptual process is selective and subjective. One particularly important example is the perception of women. Five explanations which all contribute to the understanding of women's position and status in the organisational world are: economic theories; psychological sex differences; the socialisation process; orientations and motivations to work; and working practices. The common stereotype of women draws attention to the importance of gender dimensions in organisations.

■ It would appear that gender issues are inherent in the culture of organisations. Perceptions of gender are not necessarily deliberate or overt but are often expressed in tiny, trivial and covert ways. The accumulation of these gendered perceptions and expressions leads to a process which in its effects is biased in favour of males. Change and more egalitarian practices are unlikely to come about until organisations analyse and consciously question their unwritten assumptions and expectations.

 Review and discussion questions

1 Explain your understanding of the process of perception. Why is the study of perception important in the study of management and organisational behaviour?

2 Discuss those factors which affect selection and attention in the process of perception. Give examples of how perceptual selectivity is the source of organisational problems.

3 Explain the most significant principles which influence the organisation and arrangement of stimuli. Provide your *own* example of each of these principles.

4 What factors influence the judgements we make of other people? Explain the main distortions or errors in interpersonal perception. Support your answer with practical examples.

5 Explain the principles of attribution theory and its importance to, and implications for, management. Apply the principles to your own working life.

6 Transcribe a short dialogue you have had with a colleague, friend, or boss and analyse the responses in Transactional Analysis terms.

7 Consider a situation where you felt there was a communication breakdown and evaluate the extent to which TA helps you to understand the process.

8 Analyse the evidence which suggests that men's and women's motivations and attitudes to work are different.

9 During the period of one week, review the media (television and radio, advertisements, films, newspapers and magazines) for evidence of traditional male and female stereotypes. In a group discussion evaluate the impact and power of these stereotype8s.

10 List recommendations you would make to young women about to embark on a management career. Consider the differences you would make if you were to advise young men. Compare your list with others in your group.

Assignment 1

Stroop – illustrative experiment

(i) Write two vertical lists of 20 colour names in felt tip pen. For the first list use the correct colour pen for the colour word you are writing (for example, blue pen for the word blue). Repeat some of the colours but place them in random order.

(ii) For the second list use different colour pens for the colour word (for example, use a red pen for the word blue).

(iii) Now ask a colleague to read out loud the *colour* that the word is written in (not the word itself). Compare the amount of time it takes your colleague to read out the two lists. The second list probably not only took longer, but had more mistakes and more hesitations.

William Stroop, who first conducted this experiment, noted that the task interferes with expected behaviour. It is difficult to stop yourself from reading the word (the result of our early learning) which in this case directly impairs performance.

Assignment 2

Inference – observation

1. Read the following short story.
2. Then read the 15 statements about the story and check each to indicate whether you consider it true, false or ?
 'T' means that the statement is *definitely true* on the basis of the information presented in the story.
 'F' means that it is *definitely false*.
 '?' means that it may be either true or false and that you cannot be certain which on the basis of the information presented in the story. If any part of a statement is doubtful, mark it '?'.
3. Answer each statement in turn. Do not go back to change any answer later and do not re-read any statements after you have answered them.

4. After you have completed checking all 15 statements, work in small groups of three to five and discuss your individual answers. How much agreement is there among members of your group? On what basis did members of your group give different answers and how did their perception of the statements about the story differ?

 Do not change any of your first individual answers. However, if as a result of your group discussion you would now give a different answer to any of the statements, note this alongside your original answer.

The story

A businessman had just turned off the lights in the store when a man appeared and demanded money. The owner opened a cash register. The contents of the cash register were scooped up, and the man sped away. A member of the police force was notified promptly.

Statements about the story

1. A man appeared after the owner had turned off his store lights.	T	F	?
2. The robber was a man.	T	F	?
3. The man who appeared did not demand money.	T	F	?
4. The man who opened the cash register was the owner.	T	F	?
5. The store owner scooped up the contents of the cash register and ran away.	T	F	?
6. Someone opened a cash register.	T	F	?
7. After the man who demanded the money scooped up the contents of the cash register, he ran away.	T	F	?
8. While the cash register contained money, the story does *not* state *how much*.	T	F	?
9. The robber demanded money of the owner.	T	F	?
10. A businessman had just turned off the lights when a man appeared in the store.	T	F	?
11. It was broad daylight when the man appeared.	T	F	?
12. The man who appeared opened the cash register.	T	F	?
13. No one demanded money.	T	F	?
14. The story concerns a series of events in which only three persons are referred to: the owner of the store, a man who demanded money, and a member of the police force.	T	F	?
15. The following events occurred: someone demanded money, a cash register was opened, its contents were scooped up, and a man dashed out of the store.	T	F	?

Notes and references

1. Bartlett, F. C. *Remembering Cambridge*, Cambridge University Press (1932).
2. Kohler, I. 'The Formation and Transformation of the Visual World', *Psychological Issues*, 3, 1964, pp. 28–46, 116–33.
3. Bexton, W., Heron, W. and Scott, T. 'Effects of Decreased Variation in the Sensory Environment', *Canadian Journal of Psychology*, vol. 8, 1954, pp. 70–6.
4. Briggs-Myers, I. *Introduction to Type*, Oxford Psychologists Press (1987).
5. Witkin, H. A., Lewis, H. B., Hertzman, M., Machover, K., Meissner, P. P. and Wapner, S. S. *Personality Through Perception*, Harper and Row (1954).
6. Morgan, C. T. and King, R. A. *Introduction to Psychology*, Third edition, McGraw-Hill (1966) p. 343.
7. Hellriegel, D., Slocum, J. W. and Woodman, R. W. *Organizational Behaviour*, Sixth edition, West Publishing Company (1992) p. 106.
8. Luthans, F. *Organizational Behaviour*, Fifth edition, McGraw-Hill (1989) p. 152.
9. For further examples of perceptual teasers, see Tosi, H. L., Rizzo, J. R. and Carroll, S. J. *Managing Organizational Behaviour*, Third Edition, Blackwell (1994).
10. Stroop, J. R. 'Studies of Interference in Serial Verbal Reactions', *Journal of Experimental Psychology*, vol. 4, no. 18, 1935, pp. 643–62; and Penrose, L. S. and Penrose, R. 'Impossible Objects: A Special Type of Illusion', *British Journal of Psychology*, part 1, February 1958.
11. Wexley, K. N., Yukl, G. A., Kovacs, S. Z. and Sanders, R. E. 'Importance of Contrast Effects in Employment Interviews', *Journal of Applied Psychology*, 56, 1972, pp. 45–8.
12. Laing, R. D. *Knots*, Penguin (1971) p. 30.
13. Guirdham, M. *Interpersonal Skills at Work*, Second edition, Prentice-Hall (1990) p. 55.
14. Berne, E. *Games People Play*, Penguin (1966).
15. See, for example: Stewart, I. and Jaines, V. *TA today: A New Introduction to Transactional Analysis*, Life Space Publishing (1987).
16. Kendon, A. 'Some Functions of Gaze Direction in Social Interaction', *Acta Psychologica*, 26, 1967, pp. 22–63.
17. Mehrabian, A. *Nonverbal Communication*, Aldine Atherton (1972).
18. Cook, M. *Interpersonal Perception*, Penguin (1971).
19. Goffman, E. *The Presentation of Self in Everyday Life*, Penguin (1971).
20. Asch, S. E. 'Forming Impressions on Personality', *Journal of Abnormal and Social Psychology*, 41, 1946, pp. 258–90.
21. Miller, N. and Campbell, D. T. 'Recency and Primacy in Persuasion as a Function of the Timing of Speeches and Measurements', *Journal of Abnormal and Social Psychology*, 59, 1959, pp. 1–9.
22. Hodges, B. 'Effect of Volume on Relative Weighting in Impression Formation', *Journal of Personality and Social Psychology*, 30, 1974, pp. 378–81.
23. Gahagan, J. *Interpersonal and Group Behaviour*, Methuen (1975).
24. Mehrabian, A. *Tactics of Social Influence*, Prentice-Hall (1970).
25. See, for example: Green, J. 'Can You Read Other People's Body Talk?' *Administrator*, February 1994, pp. 8–9.
26. Wilson, P. R. 'Perceptual Distortion of Height as a Function of Ascribed Academic Status', *Journal of Social Psychology*, no. 74, 1968, pp. 97–102.
27. Heider, F. *The Psychology of Interpersonal Relations*, John Wiley and Sons (1958).
28. Kelley, H. H. 'The Process of Causal Attribution', *American Psychologist*, February 1973, pp. 107–28.
29. Mitchell, T. R. *People in Organizations: An Introduction to Organizational Behaviour*, Third edition, McGraw-Hill (1987).
30. Bartunek, J. M. 'Why Did You Do That? Attribution Theory in Organizations', *Business Horizons*, September–October 1981, pp. 66–71.

31. Mitchell, T. R., Smyser, C. M. and Weed, S. E. 'Locus of Control: Supervision and Work Satisfaction', *Academy of Management Journal*, September 1975, pp. 623–31.

32. Durand, D. E. and Nord, W. R. 'Perceived Leader Behaviour as a Function of Personality Characteristics of Supervisors and Subordinates', *Academy of Management Journal*, September 1976, pp. 427–38.

33. For a more detailed analysis of the accuracy of interpersonal perception and problems in judgement of others, see: Krech, D., Crutchfield, R. S. and Ballachey, E. L. *Individual in Society*, McGraw-Hill (1962).

34. For a fuller discussion see, for example: McKenna, E. F. *Business Psychology and Organisational Behaviour*, Lawrence Erlbaum (1994).

35. See, for example: Atkin, A. 'Positive HIV and AIDS Policies at Work', *Personnel Management*, December 1994, pp. 34-7.

36. Taylor, P. and Walker, A. 'Employers and Older Workers' *Employment Gazette*, vol. 101, no. 8, August 1993, pp. 371–8.

37. *Equal Opportunities Review*, no. 54, March/April 1994, Industrial Relations Services, London, p. 3.

38. Cooper, C. and Davidson, M. *High Pressure: Working Lives of Women Managers*, Fontana (1982).

39. Ames, A. 'Visual Perception and the Rotating Trapezoidal Window', *Psychological Monographs*, vol. 65, no. 7, 1951.

40. Hicks, L. 'Gender and Culture: A Study of the Attitudes Displayed by Managers in the Hotel World', Unpublished doctoral thesis, University of Surrey, 1991.

41. Hansard Society Commission Report, *Women at the Top*, The Hansard Society (1990).

42. Holton, V., Rabberts, J. and Scrives, S. (Ashridge Management Research Group), 'Women on the Boards of Britain's Top 200 Companies: A Progress Report', *The Occupational Psychologist*, no. 24, April 1995.

43. Lewis, J. *Women in England 1870–1950*, Wheatsheaf Books (1984).

44. Lewenhak, S. *Women and Work*, Macmillan (1980).

45. Hakim, C. *Occupational Segregation*, Research Paper No. 9, Department of Employment, November 1979.

46. Amsden, A. (ed.) *Papers in the Economics of Women and Work*, Penguin (1980).

47. Smith, J. and Ward, M. *Women's Wages and Work in the Twentieth Century*, Rand (1984).

48. Loveridge, R. and Mok, A. 'Theoretical Approaches to Segmented Labour Markets', *International Journal of Social Economics*, no. 7, 1980.

49. Gross, R. D. *Psychology: The Science of Mind and Behaviour*, Edward Arnold (1987).

50. Maccoby, E. and Jacklin, C. *The Psychology of Sex Differences*, Stanford University Press (1974).

51. Donelson, E. *Sex Differences in Developmental Perspective*, Homewood Learning Systems (1975).

52. Condry, S. and Condry, J. C. 'Sex Differences: A Study of the Eye of the Beholder', *Annual Progress in Child Psychiatry and Child Development*, 1977, pp. 289–301.

53. Barrett, M. *Women's Oppression Today*, Verso (1980) p. 206.

54. Garbucker, M. *There's A Good Girl*, The Women's Press (1988).

55. Newton, P. 'Computing: An Ideal Occupation for Women', in Cozens, J. F. and West, M. (eds) *Women at Work*, Open University Press (1991).

56. Shaw, J. 'Finishing School: Some Implications of Sex-Segregation Education', in Barker, D. L. and Allen, S. (eds) *Sexual Division and Society: Process and Change*, Tavistock (1976).

57. Rosenkrantz, P., Vogel, S., Bee, H. and Broverman, D. 'Sex Role Stereotypes and Self-Concepts in College Students', *Journal of Consulting and Clinical Psychology*, 32, 1968, pp. 287–95.

58. Alban-Metcalfe, B. 'Attitudes to Work: Comparison by Gender and Sector of Employment', *The Occupational Psychologist*, no. 3, December 1987, p. 8.

59. Hunt, A. *A Survey of Women's Employment*, HMSO (1968).

60. Marshall, J. *Women Managers: Travellers in a Male World*, Wiley (1984).
61. *Ibid.*
62. Collinson, D. *Managing to Discriminate: A Multi-Sector Study of Recruitment Practices*, EOC Research Report (1986).
63. Webb, J. 'The Politics of Equal Opportunity: Job Requirements and the Evaluation of Women's Suitability', Paper presented at The Psychology of Women at Work International Research Conference, London, 1988.
64. Terborg, J. 'Women in Management: A Research Review', *Journal of Applied Psychology*, vol. 62, no. 6, 1977, pp. 647–64.
65. Podmore, D. and Spencer, A. 'Joining the Professionals: Gender Issues in Recruitment and Careers of Solicitors', Case 5, in McGoldrick, J. (ed.) *Business Case File in Behavioural Science*, Van Nostrand Reinhold (1987).
66. Kanter, R. M. *Men and Women of the Corporation*, Basic Books (1977).
67. *Equal Opportunities for Women in the Civil Service,* HMSO (1983).
68. Kanter, R. M. *Men and Women of the Corporation*, Basic Books (1977).
69. Cooper, C. and Davidson, M. *High Pressure: Working Lives of Women Managers*, Fontana (1982).
70. *Employment News*, Department of Employment Group, no. 207, June 1992.

Part 3

GROUPS AND LEADERSHIP

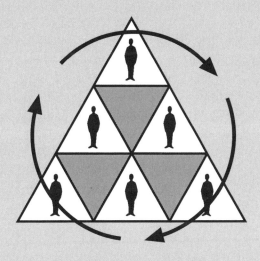

6 THE NATURE OF GROUPS

Groups are a major feature of organisational life. The organisation and its sub-units are made up of groups of people. Most activities of the organisation require at least some degree of co-ordination through the operation of group working. An understanding of the nature of groups is vital if the manager is to influence the behaviour of people in the work situation. The manager must be aware of the impact of groups and their effects on organisational performance.

 Learning objectives

To:

- Explain the meaning and nature of groups;

- Distinguish between formal and informal groups;

- Explain the main reasons for the formation of groups;

- Examine factors which influence group cohesiveness and performance;

- Assess the impact of technology on the attitudes and behaviour of work groups;

- Analyse the nature of role relationships and role conflict;

- Appreciate the importance of groups for effective organisational performance.

Worth thinking about

'I recognise that groups are an integral part of the work organistion but I do value my individuality and the right of self-expression.' . . . 'That shouldn't be a problem. After all the skill of management is to make full use of people's individuality for the mutual benefit of the group as a whole.' . . . 'Oh, I see – I think.'

THE MEANING AND IMPORTANCE OF GROUPS

Individuals seldom work in isolation from others. Groups are a characteristic of all social situations and almost everyone in an organisation will be a member of one or more groups. Work is a group-based activity and if the organisation is to function effectively it requires good teamwork. The working of groups and the influence they exert over their membership is an essential feature of human behaviour and of organisational performance. The manager must use groups in order to achieve a high standard of work and improve organisational effectiveness.

Definitions of a group

There are many possible ways of defining what is meant by a group. The essential feature of a group is that its members regard themselves as belonging to the group. Although there is no single, accepted definition most people will readily understand what constitutes a group. A popular definition defines the group in psychological terms as:

> **any number of people who (1) interact with one another; (2) are psychologically aware of one another; and (3) perceive themselves to be a group.**[1]

Another useful way of defining a work group is a collection of people who share most, if not all, of the following characteristics:

- a definable membership;
- group consciousness;
- a sense of shared purpose;
- interdependence;
- interaction; and
- ability to act in a unitary manner.[2]

Essential feature of work organisations

Groups are an essential feature of the work pattern of any organisation. Members of a group must co-operate in order for work to be carried out, and managers themselves will work within these groups. People in groups influence each other in many ways and groups may develop their own hierarchies and leaders. Group pressures can have a major influence over the behaviour of individual members and their work performance. The activities of the group are associated with the process of leadership (which is discussed in Chapter 8). The style of leadership adopted by the manager has an important influence on the behaviour of members of the group.

The classical approach to organisation and management tended to ignore the importance of groups and the social factors at work. The ideas of people such as *F. W. Taylor* popularised the concept of the 'rabble hypothesis' and the assumption that people carried out their work, and could be motivated, as solitary individuals unaffected by others. The human relations approach, however, gave recognition to the work organisation as a social organisation and to the importance of the group, and group values and norms, in influencing behaviour at work.

The general movement towards flatter structures of organisation, wider spans of control, and reducing layers of middle management, together with increasing empowerment of employees, all involve greater emphasis on the importance of group working.[3]

INFLUENCES ON BEHAVIOUR AT WORK

The power of group membership over individual behaviour and work performance was illustrated clearly in the famous Hawthorne experiments at the Western Electric Company in America,[4] already referred to in Chapter 2.

One experiment involved the observation of a group of 14 men working in the bank wiring room. It may be remembered that the men formed their own sub-groups or cliques, with natural leaders emerging with the consent of the members. Despite a financial incentive scheme where workers could receive more money the more work they did, the group decided on 6000 units a day as a fair level of output. This was well below the level they were capable of producing. Group pressures on individual workers were stronger than financial incentives offered by management.

Group values and norms

The group developed its own pattern of informal social relations and codes and practices ('norms') of what constituted proper group behaviour.

- **Not to be a 'rate buster'** – not to produce at too high a rate of output compared with other members or to exceed the production restriction of the group.
- **Not to be a 'chiseller'** – not to shirk production or to produce at too low a rate of output compared with other members of the group.
- **Not to be a 'squealer'** – not to say anything to the supervisor or management which might be harmful to other members of the group.
- **Not to be 'officious'** – people with authority over members of the group, for example inspectors, should not take advantage of their seniority or maintain a social distance from the group.

The group had their own system of sanctions including sarcasm, damaging completed work, hiding tools, playing tricks on the inspectors, and ostracising those members who did not conform with the group norms. Threats of physical violence were also made, and the group developed a system of punishing offenders by 'binging' which involved striking someone a fairly hard blow on the upper part of the arm. This process of binging also became a recognised method of controlling conflict within the group.

Another finding of the bank wiring room experiment was that the group did not follow company policy on the reporting of production figures. It was company policy that each man's output should be reported daily by the supervisor. How-

ever, the workers preferred to do their own reporting, and in order to remain in favour with the group the supervisor acquiesced to this procedure. On some days the men would actually produce more than they reported to 'build up' extra units for those days when they produced less than reported. Although actual production varied the group reported a relatively standard amount of output for each day. The men would also exchange jobs with each other even though this was contrary to management instructions.

Socio-technical system

The systems approach to organisation and management also gave recognition to the importance of groups in influencing behaviour at work. The concept of the organisation as a socio-technical system is concerned with the interactions between the psychological and social factors, as well as structural and technical requirements. Again, it may be remembered that technological change in the coal-mining industry had brought about changes in the social groupings of the miners.[5]

New methods of working disrupted the integration of small self-selecting groups of miners who worked together as independent teams. The change had undesirable social effects and as a result the new method did not prove as economically beneficial as it should have done with the new technology. The result was a 'composite' method of working with more responsibility taken by the team as a whole. The composite method proved to be not only more rewarding socially to the miners but also more efficient economically than the previous new method of working. (The importance of autonomous work groups as a feature of job design is discussed in Chapter 15.)

WORK PATTERN OF ORGANISATIONS

Groups, therefore, help shape the work pattern of organisations, and the attitudes and behaviour of members to their jobs. The formation and operation of work groups, and the behaviour of their members, has an important significance for the manager. *Likert*, for example, has developed a theory of organisation based on work groups. In his discussion of group processes and organisational performance he concludes that 'Group forces are important not only in influencing the behavior of individual work groups with regard to productivity, waste, absence and the like, they also affect the behavior of entire organisations'.[6]

Overlapping group membership

Likert suggests that organisations function best when members act not as individuals but as members of highly effective work groups. He proposes a structure based on overlapping group membership with a **'linking-pin' process** by which the superior of one group is a subordinate member of the next group. The superior is, therefore, the linking-pin between a group of subordinates and the next authority level group (Fig. 6.1).

A structure of vertical overlapping groups helps to develop a committed team approach and would improve the flow of communication, co-ordination and decision-making. The use of the overlapping group structure together with a participative style of management form part of the criteria for System 4 management, discussed in Chapter 13.

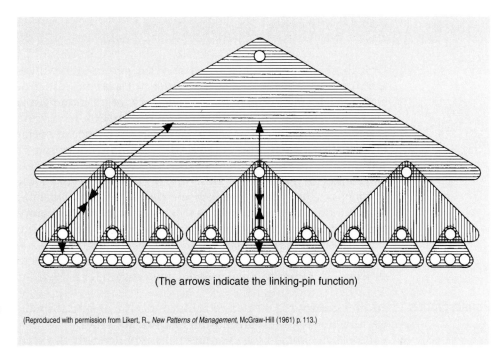

(The arrows indicate the linking-pin function)

(Reproduced with permission from Likert, R., *New Patterns of Management*, McGraw-Hill (1961) p. 113.)

**Fig. 6.1
Overlapping group
structure and the
linking-pin**

**Horizontal
linking-pin**

Likert also recognises the position of subordinates serving as horizontal linking-pins (Fig. 6.2) between different groups, such as functional or line work groups, and product-based work groups.[7]

Likert recognises that sooner or later the subordinate is likely to be caught in a conflict between membership of both groups and the provision of information for decision-making. He suggests that both groups would need to be involved in group decision-making to resolve differences and that this is more likely to occur with System 4 management.

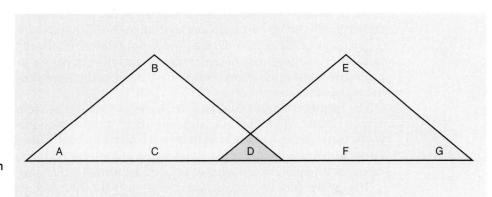

**Fig. 6.2
D is a member of
both groups and
acts as a linking-pin
for horizontal
communication**

183

FORMAL AND INFORMAL GROUPS

Groups are formed as a consequence of the pattern of organisation structure and arrangements for the division of work, for example the grouping together of common activities into sections. Groups may result from the nature of technology employed and the way in which work is carried out, for example the bringing together of a number of people to carry out a sequence of operations on an assembly line. Groups may also develop when a number of people of the same level or status within the organisation see themselves as a group, for example departmental heads of an industrial organisation, or chief officers of a local authority.

Groups are deliberately planned and created by management as part of the formal organisation structure. But groups will also arise from social processes and the informal organisation. The informal organisation arises from the interaction of people working within the organisation and the development of groups with their own relationships and norms of behaviour, irrespective of those defined within the formal structure. This leads to a major distinction between formal and informal groups.

Formal groups

Formal groups are created to achieve specific organisational objectives and are concerned with the **co-ordination of work activities**.

People are brought together on the basis of defined roles within the structure of the organisation. The nature of the tasks to be undertaken is a predominant feature of the formal group. Goals are identified by management, and certain rules, relationships and norms of behaviour established.

Formal groups tend to be relatively permanent, although there may be changes in actual membership. However, temporary formal groups may also be created by management, for example the use of project teams in a matrix organisation.

Formal work groups can be differentiated in a number of ways, for example on the basis of membership, the task to be performed, the nature of technology, or position within the organisation structure.

Informal groups

Within the formal structure of the organisation there will always be an informal structure. The formal structure of the organisation, and system of role relationships, rules and procedures, will be augmented by interpretation and development at the informal level. **Informal groups** are based more on personal relationships and agreement of group members than on defined role relationships. They serve to satisfy psychological and social needs not related necessarily to the tasks to be undertaken. Groups may devise ways of attempting to satisfy members' affiliation and other social motivations which are lacking in the work situation, especially in industrial organisations.

The membership of informal groups can cut across the formal structure. They may comprise individuals from different parts of the organisation and/or from different levels of the organisation, both vertically and diagonally, as well as from the same horizontal level. An informal group could also be the same as the formal group, or it might comprise a part only of the formal group. (*See* Fig. 6.3.)

The members of an informal group may appoint their own leader who exercises authority by the consent of the members themselves. The informal leader may be chosen as the person who reflects the attitudes and values of the members, helps to resolve conflict, leads the group in satisfying its goals, or liaises with manage-

ment or other people outside the group. The informal leader may often change according to the particular situation facing the group. Although not usually the case, it is possible for the informal leader to be the same person as the formal leader appointed officially by management.

An example of informal groups

A lack of direction and clear information flow within the formal structure can give rise to uncertainty and suspicion. In the absence of specific knowledge, the grapevine takes on an important role, rumours start and the informal part of the organisation is highlighted, often with negative results. A typical example concerned an industrial organisation which was in a highly competitive market and was experiencing a drop in sales. Two top managers had suddenly lost their jobs without any explanation to members of staff and there were board meetings seemingly every other day. Although there was no specific information or statements from top management the general feeling among the staff was that whatever was about to happen it was most unlikely to be good news.

At lunchtime three junior members of staff, one female and two male, each from different departments, were having a chat. With a half smile the female member said to the others that she could well be seeing a lot more of both or at least one of them before long. She said that she had heard, unofficially, from her manager that the department was about to be awarded a very profitable order. She surmised that the other departments, which she had also heard had lost their parts of the same contracts and not had many orders recently, would have to integrate into the successful department with the possible loss of certain jobs. The other two members both believed this and talked about it within their own departments as if it was a fact. The result? Even more uncertainty throughout the organisation, increased gloom and distraction from the task. In fact no such integration did take place, only a minor restructuring of the organisation with no direct loss of jobs other than through voluntary early retirement. However it proved very difficult for top management to effectively quash the rumour and restore trust and morale.

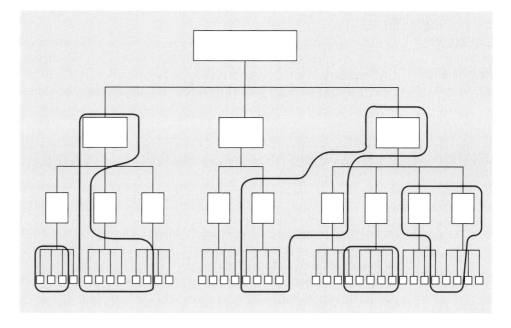

Fig. 6.3
Examples of informal groups within the formal structure of an organisation

REASONS FOR FORMATION OF GROUPS

Individuals will form into groups, both formal and informal, for a number of different reasons relating to both work performance and social processes.

- **Certain tasks can be performed only through the combined efforts of a number of individuals working together.** The variety of experience and expertise among members of the group provides a synergetic effect which can be applied to the increasingly complex problems of modern organisations.
- **Groups may encourage collusion between members** in order to modify formal working arrangements more to their liking, for example by sharing or rotating unpopular tasks. Group membership therefore provides the individual with opportunities for initiative and creativity.
- **Groups provide companionship and a source of mutual understanding and support from colleagues.** This can help in solving work problems, and also to mitigate against stressful or demanding working conditions.
- **Membership of the group provides the individual with a sense of belonging.** The group provides a feeling of identity, and the chance to acquire role recognition and status within the group.
- **The group provides guidelines on generally acceptable behaviour.** It helps to clarify ambiguous situations such as, for example, the extent to which official rules and regulations are expected to be adhered to in practice, the rules of the game, and what is seen as the correct actual behaviour. The informal organisation may put pressure on group members to resist demands from management on such matters as, for example, higher output or changes in working methods. Group allegiance can serve as a means of control over individual behaviour. The group may discipline individuals who contravene the norms of the group; for example, the process of 'binging' in the bank wiring room, mentioned above.
- **The group may provide protection for its membership.** Group members collaborate to protect their interests from outside pressures or threats.

Expectations of group membership Individuals have varying expectations of the benefits from group membership. Group are a potential source of motivation and of job satisfaction, and also a major determinant of effective organisational performance. It is important, therefore, that the manager understands the reasons for the formation of groups and is able to recognise likely advantageous or adverse consequences for the organisation.

GROUP COHESIVENESS AND PERFORMANCE

Social interaction is a natural feature of human behaviour but ensuring harmonous working relationships and effective teamwork is not an easy task. The manager's main concern is that members of a work group co-operate in order to achieve the results expected of them. Cohesive groups do not necessarily produce a higher level of output. Performance varies with the extent to which the group accepts or rejects the goals of the organisation. Also, with a very high level of cohesiveness and attention to social activities, there may even be a fall in output.

The level of production is likely to conform to a standard acceptable as a norm by the group and may result in maintaining either a high or a restricted level of output.[8] However, cohesive groups may result in greater interaction between members, mutual help and social satisfaction, lower turnover and absenteeism, and often higher production.[9]

Co-operation among members is likely to be greater in a united, cohesive group. Membership of a cohesive group can be a rewarding experience for the individual and can contribute to the promotion of morale.

Members of a high-morale group are more likely to think of themselves as a group and work together effectively. **Strong and cohesive work groups can, therefore, have beneficial effects for the organisation.**

Factors affecting cohesiveness

In order to develop the effectiveness of work groups the manager will be concerned with those factors that contribute to group cohesiveness, or that may cause frustration or disruption to the operation of the group.

The manager needs to consider, therefore, both the needs of individual members of staff, and the promotion of a high level of group identity and cohesion.

There are many factors which affect group cohesiveness and performance, which can be summarised under four broad headings, as shown in Fig. 6.4.

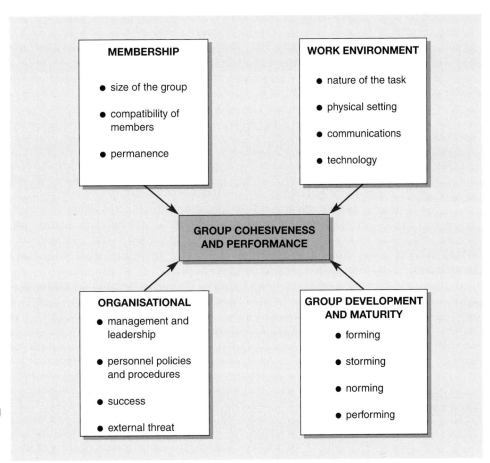

Fig. 6.4
Factors contributing to group cohesiveness and performance

(i) **Membership**
- size
- compatibility
- permanence

(ii) **Work environment**
- nature of task
- physical setting
- communications
- technology

(iii) **Organisational**
- management and leadership
- personnel policies and procedures
- success
- external threat

(iv) **Group development and maturity**, for example:
- forming
- storming
- norming
- performing.

MEMBERSHIP

Size of the group

As a group increases in size, problems arise with communications and co-ordination. Large groups are more difficult to handle and require a higher level of supervision. Absenteeism also tends to be higher in larger groups. When a group becomes too large it may split into smaller units and friction may develop between the sub-groups.

It is difficult to put a precise figure on the ideal size of a work group. Much will depend upon other variables, but it seems to be generally accepted that cohesiveness becomes more difficult to achieve when a group exceeds 10–12 members.[10] Beyond this size the group tends to split into sub-groups. A figure of between five and seven is often quoted as an apparent optimum size for full participation within the group.[11]

Compatibility of the members

The more homogeneous the group in terms of such features as shared backgrounds, interests, attitudes and values of its members, the easier it is usually to promote cohesiveness. Variations in other individual differences, such as the personality or skills of members, may serve to complement each other and help make for a cohesive group. On the other hand, such differences may be the cause of disruption and conflict. Conflict can also arise in a homogeneous group where members are in competition with each other. Individual incentive payment schemes, for example, may be a source of conflict.

Permanence of group members

Group spirit and relationships take time to develop. Cohesiveness is more likely when members of a group are together for a reasonable length of time, and changes occur only slowly. A frequent turnover of members is likely to have an adverse effect on morale, and on the cohesiveness of the group.

WORK ENVIRONMENT

The nature of the task

Where workers are involved in similar work, share a common task, or face the same problems, this may assist cohesiveness. The nature of the task may serve to bring people together when it is necessary for them to communicate and interact regularly with each other in the performance of their duties, for example members of a research and development team.

Even if members of a group normally work at different locations they may still experience a feeling of cohesiveness if the nature of the task requires frequent communication and interaction; for example, security guards patrolling separate areas who need to check with each other on a regular basis. However, where the task demands a series of relatively separate operations or discrete activities, for example on a machine-paced assembly line, it is more difficult to develop cohesiveness. Individuals may have interactions with colleagues on either side of them but little opportunity to develop a common group feeling.

Physical setting

Where members of a group work in the same location or in close physical proximity to each other this will generally help cohesiveness. However, this is not always the case. For example, in large open-plan offices staff often tend to segregate themselves from colleagues and create barriers by the strategic siting of such items as filing cabinets, bookcases or indoor plants. The size of the office and the number of staff in it are, of course, important considerations in this case. Isolation from other groups of workers will also tend to build cohesiveness. This often applies, for example, to a smaller number of workers on a night shift.

Communications

The more easily members can communicate freely with each other the more likelihood there is of group cohesiveness. Communications are affected by the work environment, by the nature of the task, and by technology. For example, difficulties in communication can arise with production systems where workers are stationed continuously at a particular point with limited freedom of movement. Even when opportunities exist for interaction with colleagues, physical conditions may limit effective communication. For example, the technological layout and high level of noise with some assembly line work can limit contact between workers. Restrictions on opportunities for social interaction can hamper internal group unity.

Technology

We can see that the nature of technology and the manner in which work is carried out has an important effect on cohesiveness, and relates closely to the nature of the task, physical setting and communications. Where the nature of the work process involves a craft or skill-based 'technology' there is a higher likelihood of group cohesiveness. But, as mentioned above, with machine-paced assembly line work it is more difficult to develop cohesiveness. Technology also has wider implications for the operation and behaviour of groups and therefore is considered in a separate section below.

ORGANISATIONAL FACTORS

Management and leadership

The activities of groups cannot be separated from management and the process of leadership. The form of management and style of leadership adopted will influence the relationship between the group and the organisation, and is a major determinant of group cohesiveness. In general terms, cohesiveness will be affected by such things as the manner in which the manager gives guidance and encouragement to the group, offers help and support, provides opportunities for participation, attempts to resolve conflicts, and gives attention to both employee relations and task problems.

Personnel policies and procedures

Harmony and cohesiveness within the group are more likely to be achieved if personnel policies and procedures are well developed, and perceived to be equitable with fair treatment for all members. Attention should be given to the effects that appraisal systems, discipline, promotion and rewards, and opportunities for personal development have on members of the group.

Success

The more successful the group, the more cohesive it is likely to be; and cohesive groups are more likely to be successful. Success is usually a strong motivational influence on the level of work performance. Success or reward as a positive motivator can be perceived by group members in a number of ways. For example, the satisfactory completion of a task through co-operative action; praise from management; a feeling of high status; achievement in competition with other groups; benefits gained, such as high wage payments from a group bonus incentive scheme.

External threat

Cohesiveness may be enhanced by members co-operating with one another when faced with a common external threat, such as changes in their method of work, or the appointment of a new manager. Even if the threat is subsequently removed, the group may still continue to have a greater degree of cohesiveness than before the threat arose. Conflict between groups will also tend to increase the cohesiveness of each group and the boundaries of the group become drawn more clearly.

GROUP DEVELOPMENT AND MATURITY

The degree of cohesiveness is affected also by the manner in which groups progress through the various stages of development and maturity. *Bass and Ryterband* identify four distinct stages in group development: mutual acceptance and membership; communication and decision-making; motivation and productivity; and control and organisation.[12]

- **First stage – developing mutual acceptance and membership.** Members have an initial mistrust of each other and a fear of inadequacies. They remain defensive and limit their behaviour through conformity and ritual. The priority is with questions of likes and dislikes, and power or dependency of group members.

- **Second stage – communication and decision-making.** Once members have learned to accept each other they begin to express their feelings and conflicts. Norms of procedure are established and there is acceptance of legitimate influence over the group. Members develop a liking, or at least a sense of caring for each other. There are more open communications and reactions. More constructive problem-solving and decision-making behaviour strategies develop.
- **Third stage – motivation and productivity.** Problems of members' motivation have been resolved. Members are involved with the work of the group. They co-operate with each other instead of competing. Members are motivated by intrinsic rewards to achieve a high level of productivity.
- **Fourth stage – control and organisation.** The final stage of group development. Work is allocated by agreement and according to the members' abilities. Members work independently and the organisation of the group is flexible and adaptable to new challenges.

Group development and relationships

An alternative, and more popular, model by *Tuckman* also identifies four main successive stages of group development and relationships: forming, storming, norming and performing.[13]

- **Stage 1 – forming.** The initial formation of the group and the bringing together of a number of individuals who identify, tentatively, the purpose of the group, its composition and terms of reference.

 At this stage consideration is given to hierarchical structure of the group, pattern of leadership, individual roles and responsibilities, and codes of conduct. There is likely to be considerable anxiety as members attempt to create an impression, to test each other, and to establish their personal identity within the group.
- **Stage 2 – storming.** As members of the group get to know each other better they will put forward their views more openly and forcefully. Disagreements will be expressed and challenges offered on the nature of the task and arrangements made in the earlier stage of development. This may lead to conflict and hostility.

 The storming stage is important because, if successful, there will be discussions on reforming arrangements for the working and operation of the group, and agreement on more meaningful structures and procedures.
- **Stage 3 – norming.** As conflict and hostility start to be controlled members of the group will establish guidelines and standards, and develop their own norms of acceptable behaviour.

 The norming stage is important in establishing the need for members to co-operate in order to plan, agree standards of performance and fulfil the purpose of the group. This co-operation and adherence to group norms can work against effective organisational performance. It may be remembered, for example, that, in the bank wiring room experiment of the Hawthorne studies, group norms imposed a restriction on the level of output of the workers.
- **Stage 4 – performing.** When the group has progressed successfully through the three earlier stages of development it will have created structure and cohesiveness to work effectively as a team. At this stage the group can concentrate on the attainment of its purpose and performance of the common task is likely to be at its most effective.

POTENTIAL DISADVANTAGES OF STRONG, COHESIVE GROUPS

If the manager is to develop effective work groups then attention should be given to those factors which influence the creation of group identity and cohesiveness. But strong and cohesive groups also present potential disadvantages for management. The goals of the group may be at variance with the goals of the organisation. Again, for example, in the bank wiring room experiment, group norms and pressures on individual members led to restrictions on production and a low level of output.

Once a group has become fully developed and created cohesiveness, it is more difficult for the manager successfully to change the attitudes and behaviour of the group. It is important that the manager should attempt to influence the group during the norming stage when members are establishing guidelines and standards, and their own norms of acceptable behaviour. When a group has become fully developed and established its own culture it is more difficult to change the attitudes and behaviour of its members.

Inter-group conflict

Strong, cohesive groups may develop a critical or even hostile attitude towards people outside the group or members of other groups. This can be the case, for example, when group cohesiveness is based on common status, qualifications, technical expertise or professional standing. Group cohesiveness may result in lack of co-operation with, or opposition to, non-members. As a result, resentment and inter-group conflict may arise to the detriment of the organisation as a whole.

In order to help prevent, or overcome, unconstructive inter-group conflict, the manager should attempt to stimulate a high level of communication and interaction between the groups, and to maintain harmony. Rotation of members among different groups should be encouraged.

On the other hand, inter-group rivalry may be deliberately encouraged as a means of building stronger within-group cohesiveness.[14] The idea is that a competitive element may help to promote unity within a group. However, inter-group rivalry and competition need to be carefully handled by the manager. Groups should not normally be put in a situation where they have to compete for resources, status or approval.[15]

The manager should attempt to avoid the development of 'win–lose' situations. Emphasis should be placed on overall objectives of the organisation and on superordinate goals. These are goals over and above the issues at conflict and which, if they are to be achieved, require the co-operation of the competing groups.

CHARACTERISTICS OF AN EFFECTIVE WORK GROUP

The characteristics of an effective work group are not always easy to isolate clearly. The underlying feature is a spirit of co-operation in which members work well together as a united team, and with harmonious and supportive relationships. This may be evidenced when members of a group exhibit:

- a belief in shared aims and objectives;
- a sense of commitment to the group;
- acceptance of group values and norms;
- a feeling of mutual trust and dependency;
- full participation by all members and decision-making by consensus;
- a free flow of information and communications;
- the open expression of feelings and disagreements;
- the resolution of conflict by the members themselves; and
- a lower level of staff turnover, absenteeism, accidents, errors and complaints.

Understanding group behaviour

The effective management of work groups requires an understanding of the psychological and social influences on behaviour within organisations. *Allcorn* distinguishes between defensive and non-defensive work groups, and provides a typology based on four differing sets of culture.[16] (*See* Table 6.1.)

• homogenised	**Defensive groups.** They provide collective and
• institutionalised	individual defences against anxiety that results
• autocratic	from group membership.
• intentional	Deals with group participation in a **non-defensive** way. The type of group that is desirable in the workplace.

Changing the culture of a group

Attempting to change the culture of a defensive group into that of an intentional group in not easy. The intervention strategy is likely to be perceived as threatening to members of the group. Allcorn suggests that successful intervention involves the comparisons of perceptions and understandings in order to provide a thoughtful summary of the group's perceptions which is accepted by the members. This requires sensitivity to the anxiety of group members and the forces that mitigate against change. Members need to understand the actions associated with the intentional group as a basis for establishing and maintaining an intentional culture.

Allcorn reminds us that: 'individual and group behaviour is highly complex, difficult to understand and even more difficult to manage'. It is important to further develop group-process skills.

The analysis of behaviour in groups, group processes and group dynamics are discussed in Chapter 7.

THE EFFECTS OF TECHNOLOGY ON WORK GROUPS

The nature of technology and the work flow system of the organisation is a major determinant of the operation of groups, and the attitude and behaviour of their members. Low morale and a negative attitude towards management and the job are often associated with a large number of workers undertaking similar work.

A number of different studies have drawn attention to the relationship between technology and work groups. For example, *Walker and Guest* referred to effects of technology on work groups. The character or type of group is determined largely by the technological requirements of the organisation. They found that the technological layout and pacing of work by the assembly line operation was a source of dissatisfaction to the workers.[17]

Table 6.1. A typology of work groups

The cultures of the four workplace groups			
Homogenised Group	*Institutionalised Group*	*Autocratic Group*	*Intentional Group*
All members have equal **status**, with no clear individual **roles**.	Each member is assigned a particular **role** and **status**, and given guidelines for changing the role and status.	All members are assigned **roles** with **status**, but no clear guidelines are provided for self-advancement.	All members assume and accept **roles** and **status** based on the needs of the group and the leader.
No **leader** is acknowledged to exist or permitted to arise.	**Leadership** is designated by the group's operating structure.	The **leader** is viewed as omnipotent and is clearly in control of the group.	A permanent **leader** may be found among the members or **leadership** may be passed among members based on each person's unique ability to lead the group at the time.
Autonomous behaviour such as the offering of ideas is either attacked or not supported by others.	**Autonomous behaviour** such as the offering of ideas is controlled by procedures.	**Autonomous behaviour** such as the offering of ideas may be rewarded or punished by the leader, who may offer no reasons for his or her decision.	**Autonomous behaviour** is acknowledged as valuable as long as it contributes to the group's purpose.
Members are unable to find a **direction for the group**.	The **direction of the group** is limited by the organisation structure.	All skills for **directing the group** are held by the leader.	Members actively participate in offering **direction** to the group.
The group acts as though time and the environment has been temporarily suspended, and as if there were nothing more than the group's experience.	**The group acts as though** the organisation were in control of events and the process, and as if work were to be accomplished as planned.	**The group acts as though** the leader will take care of everything if he or she is permitted to do so.	**The group acts as though** all members were responsible for the group's work and leadership.
Some group members may be **singled out and stigmatised** for their willingness to express their feelings and thoughts. They may be coaxed into increasing emotionalism until they are rendered incompetent and discarded.	Some group members may be **singled out and praised** for participating in the group as expected, or they may be **publicly punished** for deviating.	Some members may be **singled out for rewards** for actions the leader finds supportive, or **punished for deviations** from the leader's expectations.	Contributions of members are **acknowledged by the group** as a whole.
Little **work on the group's task** is accomplished and no plans are made to do any work.	**Work on the group's task** is accomplished as specified by the organisational work process.	**Work on the group's task** as specified by the leader is accomplished according to the leader's instructions.	**Work on the group's task** becomes the responsibility of all the members with no one individual (including the leader) assuming complete responsibility for the work.

(continued)

Table 6.1. *(continued)*

Membership experience in the four workplace groups			
Homogenised Group	*Institutionalised Group*	*Autocratic Group*	*Intentional Group*
Members fear the consequences of speaking out and taking action.	**Members fear the consequences of speaking out** in other than the prescribed manner, and of taking independent action without prior approval.	**Members fear the consequences of speaking out** without some idea of the leader's likely response, and of taking independent action without the leader's consent.	**Members are eager to offer their points of view** regarding the group's work.
Helplessness is experienced, as others are attacked by group members.	**Helplessness** is experienced, as those who deviate are attacked.	**Helplessness** is experienced because little can be done to change the leader's mind or to influence events.	**Helplessness** is not an element of group membership experience.
Members feel **security** in being unnoticed.	Members feel that **safety** lies in following the rules.	Members feel **unsafe** and **insecure** because the leader may become dissatisfied with them unexpectedly.	The group offers a sense of **safety and security** to its members.
Members feel that they and the group have lost their **purpose**.	Members feel that they have lost their individual **purpose** in the face of the predominance of the group's goals.	Individuals lose their sense of personal **purpose** in the face of the all-powerful leader.	Members experience a sense of **purpose** because they and their contributions are acknowledged by the group.
Frustration is evident, in that members feel as if nothing can be done to help the situation. No ideas are generated to improve the group's performance.	**Frustration** occurs, as members feel that nothing can be done to change the organisation.	**Frustration** develops because group members cannot solve problems that stem from the leader's direction and style.	**Frustrations** over the group's progress and direction are openly discussed.

Scott undertook a study of a large steel plant which appeared to have an unusual history of assimilating large-scale technical change with the minimum of resistance or overt conflict despite problems with demarcations, wage differentials and redundancies.[18] One of the main reasons for this was the nature of the work groups. Operators worked in close co-operation with group members. The groups were 'self-regulating', they allocated functions to their members and established a hierarchy of skill and authority based on seniority. New members of the group started at the lower level of the hierarchy and worked their way up. They felt it to be in their long-term interests to stay with the organisation and to remain in the same group.

**Production
systems and
group behaviour**

The type of production system determines the nature of work groups and the manner in which they conduct themselves. On the basis of a study of 300 work groups in a number of different industrial organisations, *Sayles* identified four main types of group, each with distinctive technological features and characteristic patterns of behaviour: apathetic, erratic, strategic and conservative.[19]

- **Apathetic groups.** Tended to be relatively low skilled, and poorly paid. Members performed a range of different functions with little task interdependence. There was a lack of enthusiasm, little sense of internal unity, lack of a clearly defined leader, individual rather than group problems, low morale. Tended to accept management decisions with few pressure devices. Members felt suppressed and discontented.
- **Erratic groups.** Also tended to be low skilled and with low status. Members performed identical or very similar tasks requiring frequent interaction with each other. Work was often physically demanding. Tended to be unpredictable. Developed occasional cohesion. Mixed relationship with management, but easily inflamed in handling grievances. Tended to have authoritarian leadership.
- **Strategic groups.** Relatively skilled, well paid and self-assured. Usually a good production record. Generally individual jobs but with a high degree of interaction and internal group unity. Jobs were often important to management. Tended to be active and influential with continual union participation and pressure on management. Shrewd in use of grievance procedures and in improving their own position.
- **Conservative groups.** Skilled workers with high status. Mainly individual operation. Wide dispersion throughout the organisation and low level of interaction, but strong sense of identity and a reasonable degree of internal unity. Tended to be conservative in negotiations but exert strong pressure for specific objectives, for example maintenance of traditional differentials and wage levels. Often associated with professional bodies and tended to be ambivalent regarding trade unions.

There was a marked similarity of behaviour among the different types of groups with similar technological features across a wide range of industrial settings. The work organisation and production technology determines the type of work group that emerges, and restricts the form of action taken by the group. Sayles suggests that the relationship between work groups, management and the form of grievance behaviour, and the collective activity of the group, is influenced by five major variables:

- relative position of the group on the internal promotion ladder;
- relative size and importance of the group;
- similarity of jobs within the group;
- extent to which the work is indispensable to the functioning of the department or organisation; and
- precision with which management can measure the workload and work pace for the group.

These variables are determined largely by the nature of technology. Technology also influences the differentiation of the task and division of work, and the internal social structure of the group. The greater the task differentiation and the more complex the internal structure of the group, the less likely the effects of grievance behaviour.

Differences in behaviour of social groupings

Lupton undertook a study of the organisation of two contrasting workshops at different companies termed Wye and Jay.[20] Wye Garment Company made waterproof garments and also embraced other manufacturing activities. The workers were mainly female. Jay's Electrical Components was founded originally for the manufacture of equipment for the generation and transmission of electricity. The workers were mainly male.

In both companies there were clear social groupings, but marked differences in their behaviour. At Wye the social groupings had no influence on the work situation, they appeared to accept management norms and there was no solidarity or control aimed at determining the level of output or earnings.

At Jay's the social groupings coincided with the work groups and actually shaped their pattern. They established norms of output, sanctions to control individual behaviour, and an informal division of labour which affected output and earnings. In attempting to explain the differences in the pattern of behaviour between the two workshops, Lupton examined a number of factors such as the sex of the workers, the wage payment system, external conditions, and technology and the work organisation.

At Wye there was a detailed breakdown of operations, the work flow was based on the individual, and jobs had a short time-span. At Jay's there was no detailed breakdown of operations, the production unit was based on the section, and each job had a reasonably long time-span with opportunity for manipulation. There was more scope for the workers and more opportunity for worker control. Lupton suggests that the layout of the job, the work flow pattern, the method of job allocation and the time-span of the operational cycle, are important to a comparative analysis of the degree of control which can be exercised by the workers.

Technology and alienation

The nature of technology and the work organisation can result in a feeling of alienation, especially among manual workers. Factors which have been shown to affect alienation include the extent to which the work of the individual or the group amounts to a meaningful part of the total production process, and the satisfaction which workers gain from relationships with fellow workers and group membership.

In a study of assembly line and other factory work, *Goldthorpe* found that the technology was unfavourable for the creation of work groups.[21] However, he also found a group of workers who, although alienated, were still satisfied. Membership of a meaningful work group was not necessarily an important source of job satisfaction. The workers, all married men, aged between 21 and 46, were not interested in maintaining close relationships with fellow workers or supervisors. Their earnings were well in excess of the average manual wage at the time – they were 'affluent' workers.

Goldthorpe recognised, however, that in other situations where there is the opportunity for teamwork, the workers will have greater social expectations and the membership of work groups may be very important to them.

Technology and group behaviour

Technology is clearly a major influence on the pattern of group operation and behaviour. The work organisation may limit the opportunities for social interaction and the extent to which individuals are able to identify themselves as members of a cohesive work group. This in turn can have possible adverse effects on attitudes to work and the level of job satisfaction. In many assembly line production systems, for example, relationships between individual workers are

determined by the nature of the task, the extent to which individual jobs are specified, and the time cycle of operations.

In recent years there have been attempts to remove some of the alienating aspects of mass production and assembly line work by increasing the range of tasks and responsibility allocated to small groups. These attempts include greater use of self-regulating work groups and of group technology.[22]

Group technology involves changes to the work flow system of production. With the traditional 'functional layout' of production, lines of similar machines or operations are arranged together so that components are passed back and forth until all activities are completed. However, with 'group technology' production, the work flow system is based on a grouping of workers and a range of machines. This enables work groups to perform series of successive operations using a group of machines on a family of similar components.

Impact of information technology

You may recall from our discussion in Chapter 3 that the impact of information technology demands new patterns of work organisation, and affects the formation and structure of groups. Movement away from large-scale centralised organisation to smaller working units can help create an environment in which workers may relate more easily to each other. Improvements in telecommunications mean, for example, that support staff need no longer be located within the main production unit. On the other hand, modern methods of communication mean that individuals may work more on their own, or even from their own homes, or work more with machines than with other people.[23]

ROLE RELATIONSHIPS

In order that the organisation can achieve its goals and objectives the work of individual members must be linked into coherent patterns of activities and relationships. This is achieved through the 'role structure' of the organisation.

A 'role' is the expected pattern of behaviours associated with members occupying a particular position within the structure of the organisation. It also describes how a person perceives their own situation.

The concept of 'role' is important to the functioning of groups and for an understanding of group processes and behaviour. It is through role differentiation that the structure of the work group and relationships among its members are established. The development of the group entails the identification of distinct roles for each of its members. Some form of structure is necessary for teamwork and co-operation. The concept of roles helps to clarify the structure and to define the pattern of complex relationships within the group.

The formal organisational relationships (line, functional, staff or lateral) which are discussed later in Chapter 10 can be seen as forms of role relationships. These individual authority relationships determine the pattern of interaction with other roles.

The role, or roles, that the individual plays within the group is influenced by a combination of

- **situational factors**, such as the requirements of the task, the style of leadership, position in the communication network; and
- **personal factors** such as values, attitudes, motivation, ability and personality.

The role that a person plays in one work group may be quite different from the role that person plays in other work groups. However, everyone within a group is expected to behave in a particular manner and to fulfil certain role expectations.

A person's role-set

In addition to the role relationships with members of their own group – peers, superiors, subordinates – the individual will have a number of role-related relationships with outsiders, for example members of other work groups, trade union officials, suppliers, consumers. This is **a person's 'role-set'**. The role-set comprises the range of associations or contacts with whom the individual has meaningful interactions in connection with the performance of their role. (*See* Fig. 6.5.)

Role incongruence

An important feature of role relationship is the concept of **'role incongruence'**. This arises when a member of staff is perceived as having a high and responsible position in one respect but a low standing in another respect. Difficulties with role incongruence can arise from the nature of groupings and formal relationships within the structure of the organisation. There are a number of work-related relationships, such as doctor and nurse or senior manager and personal assistant, which can give rise to a potential imbalance of authority and responsibility.

A classic account of role incongruence can be seen in *Whyte's* study of the American restaurant industry.[24] The chefs, who regarded themselves as of high status and were generally recognised as such by the staff, resented being 'told' what to do by the waitresses who were generally regarded to be of lower status. As a result arguments resulted, disrupting performance. The conflict of status was resolved by the introduction of an ordering process by which the chefs received customers' orders without the appearance of taking instructions from the lower status waitresses.

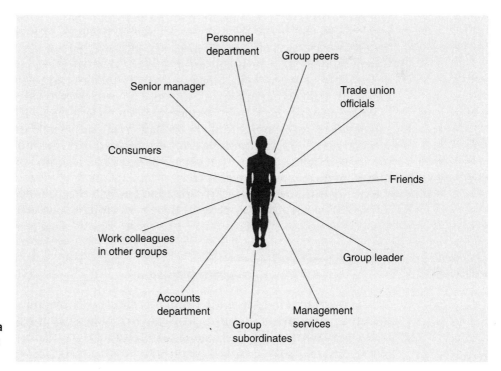

Fig. 6.5
Representation of a possible role-set in the work situation

Difficulties with role incongruence can also arise in line-staff relationships: for instance, a relatively junior member of the personnel department informing a senior departmental manager that a certain proposed action is contrary to the policies of the organisation. Another example with staff relationships is where a person establishes him or herself in the role of 'gatekeeper' to the boss,[25] for instance where a comparatively junior personal assistant passes on the manager's instructions to one of the manager's more senior subordinates or where the personal assistant attempts to block a more senior member of staff having access to the manager.

Problems over role incongruence can also lead to the possibility of role stress; this is discussed later in this chapter.

Role expectations

Many **role expectations** are **prescribed formally** and indicate what the person is expected to do and their duties and obligations. Formal role prescriptions provide guidelines for expected behaviours and may be more prevalent in a 'mechanistic' organisation. Examples are written contracts of employment, rules and regulations, standards, policy decisions, job descriptions, or directives from superiors. Formal role expectations may also be derived clearly from the nature of the task. They may, in part at least, be defined legally, for example under the Health and Safety at Work Act, or as with the obligations of a company secretary under the Companies Acts, or the responsibilities of a district auditor under the Local Government Acts.

But not all role expectations are prescribed formally. There will be certain patterns of behaviour which although not specified formally will none the less be expected of members. These **informal role expectations** may be imposed by the group itself or at least communicated to a person by other members of the group. Examples include general conduct, mutual support to co-members, attitudes towards superiors, means of communicating, dress and appearance.

Members may not always be consciously aware of these informal expectations yet they still serve as important determinants of behaviour. Under this heading could be included the concept of a psychological contract which was discussed in Chapter 1. The psychological contract implies a variety of expectations between the individual and the organisation. These expectations cover a range of rights and privileges, duties and obligations which do not form part of a formal agreement but still have an important influence on behaviour.[26]

Some members may have the opportunity to determine their own role expectations, where, for example, formal expectations are specified loosely or only in very general terms. Opportunities for **self-established roles** are more likely in senior positions, but also occur within certain professional, technical or scientific groups, or where there is a demand for creativity or artistic flair. Such opportunities may be greater within an 'organic' organisation and will also be influenced by the style of leadership adopted, for example where a *laissez-faire* approach is adopted.

ROLE CONFLICT

The concept of role focuses attention on aspects of behaviour existing independently of an individual's personality. Patterns of behaviour result from both the role and the personality. Role conflict arises from inadequate or inappropriate role definition and needs to be distinguished from personality clashes. These arise from

incompatibility between two or more people as individuals even though their roles may be defined clearly and understood fully.

In practice, the manner in which a person actually behaves may not be consistent with their expected pattern of behaviours. This inconsistency may be a result of role conflict. Role conflict as a generic term can include:

- role incompatibility;
- role ambiguity;
- role overload; and
- role underload.

These are all problem areas associated with the creation of role expectations. (*See* Fig. 6.6.)

Role incompatibility

**Fig. 6.6
Role relationships and conflicts**

Role incompatibility arises when a person faces a situation in which simultaneous different or contradictory expectations create inconsistency. Compliance with one set of expectations makes it difficult or impossible to comply with other expectations. The two role expectations are in conflict. A typical example concerns the person 'in the middle', such as the supervisor or section head, who faces opposing expectations from workers and from management.

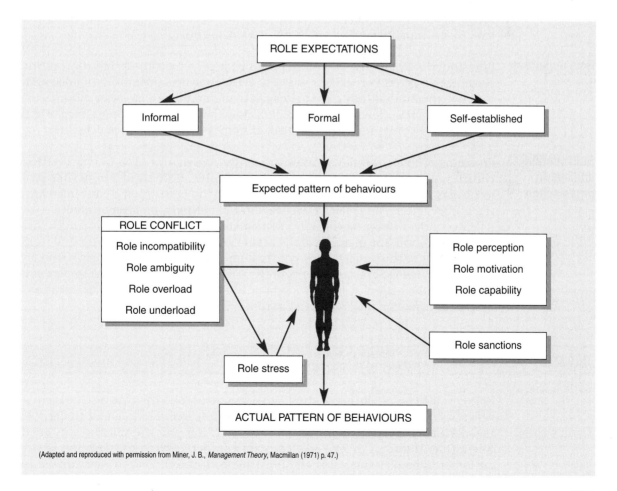

(Adapted and reproduced with permission from Miner, J. B., *Management Theory*, Macmillan (1971) p. 47.)

Another example might be the situation of a manager who believes in a relaxed, participative style of behaviour more in keeping with a Theory Y approach, but whose superior believes in a Theory X approach and expects the manager to adopt a more formal and directive style of behaviour.

Role ambiguity

Role ambiguity occurs when there is lack of clarity as to the precise requirements of the role and the person is unsure what to do. The person's own perception of their role may differ from the expectations of others. This implies that insufficient information is available for the adequate performance of the role.

Role ambiguity may result from a lack of formally prescribed expectations. It is likely to arise in large, diverse groups or at times of constant change. Uncertainty often relates to such matters as the method of performing tasks, the extent of the person's authority and responsibility, standards of work, and the evaluation and appraisal of performance.

Role overload

Role overload is when a person faces too many separate roles or too great a variety of expectations. The person is unable to meet satisfactorily all expectations and some must be neglected in order to satisfy others. This leads to a conflict of priority.

Some writers distinguish between role overload and work overload. Role overload is seen in terms of the total role-set, and implies that the person has too many separate roles to handle. Where there are too many expectations of a single role, that is, a problem of quantity, this is work overload.[27]

Role underload

Role underload can arise when the prescribed role expectations fall short of the person's own perception of their role. The person may feel their role is not demanding enough and that they have the capacity to undertake a larger or more varied role, or an increased number of roles. Role underload may arise, for example, when a new member of staff is first appointed, or from the initial effects of delegation.

Role conflict and matrix organisation

Problems of role conflict can often arise from the matrix form of organisation (which is discussed in Chapter 10) and, for example, from the use of flexible project teams. Where staff are assigned temporarily, and perhaps on a part-time basis, from other groups this creates a two-way flow of authority and responsibility.

Unless role differentiations are defined clearly this can result in conflicting expectations from the manager of the person's own functional grouping, and from the manager of the project team (role incompatibility). It can also lead to uncertainty about the exact requirements of the part the person is expected to play as a member of the project team (role ambiguity). The combinations of expectations from both managers may also result in role overload.

ROLE STRESS

Role conflict can result in role stress. An example of role stress can also be seen in *Whyte*'s study of the American restaurant industry (referred to above under role incongruence). A number of waitresses found the job very stressful and they cried often. One reason for this was the constant conflict between the demands of the customer to be served quickly and pressure from the chefs who were unable to

produce the food in time. The waitresses were caught between two incompatible expectations and were pulled both ways.

In a survey of a representative sample of 725 male industrial workers in America, *Kahn* found widespread feelings of role conflict and role ambiguity.[28] Forty-eight per cent of the sample reported experience of role conflict, for example between the demands of management and the unions, or between the requirements of superiors and subordinates. Fifteen per cent reported this as a frequent and serious concern. Thirty-five per cent reported having been disturbed by lack of clarity about the scope and responsibilities of the job. Twenty-nine per cent were concerned about what co-workers expected of them. Thirty-two per cent expressed feelings of tension arising from uncertainty about their superior's evaluation of them. A review of research by *Filley and House* into the consequences of role conflict concluded that job satisfaction is lower and there is an adverse effect on the level of individual performance.[29]

Although a certain amount of stress may **arguably** be seen as a good thing, and especially at managerial level helps to bring out a high level of performance, it is also potentially very harmful. Stress is a source of tension, frustration and dissatisfaction. It can lead to difficulties in communication and interpersonal relationships and can affect morale, effectiveness at work and health.[30]

Role stress, then, is a major influence on job satisfaction and work performance. It will be discussed further in Chapter 15.

Reducing role conflict and role stress

Greater attention is now given to health problems that are classified as stress-related.[31] There is increasing evidence concerning illnesses, such as cardiovascular diseases, and social problems, for example marriage breakdowns, which can have stress as a factor. Decreasing efficiency resulting from work stress is also extremely costly to organisations. It is important, therefore, that managers make every effort to minimise the causes of stress.

There are a number of ways in which management might attempt to avoid or reduce role conflict, and the possibilities of role stress.

- Increase specification and clarity of prescribed role expectations, for example through written statements on objectives and policy, use of manuals and set procedures, introduction of appropriate rules, and detailed job descriptions. However, such measures may be resented by staff. They may restrict the opportunity for independent action and personal development, giving rise to even more role conflict.
- Improved recruitment and selection and the careful matching of abilities, motivation, interests and personalities to the demands of a particular role.
- Attention to induction and socialisation programmes, job training and retraining, staff development and career progression plans.
- Medical examinations and health screening to give early indications of potential stress-related problems.
- The creation of new roles or assimilation of existing roles. The reallocation or restructuring of tasks and responsibilities. The clarification of priorities, and the elimination or downgrading of minor roles.
- Giving advance notice and explanation of what is likely to happen, for example of an expected, additional heavy workload which must be completed urgently. Where possible and appropriate provide an opportunity for practice or experience.

- Attention to factors which may help improve group structure and group cohesiveness, and help overcome inter-group conflict.
- Change in management system and leadership style, for example the move towards System 4 management, or the possible use of Management by Objectives. (*See* Chapter 13.)
- Review of organisation structure, information flow and communication networks, for example members of staff being answerable to more than one superior. Bureaucratic interference and poor delegation are all common causes of work stress, whereas greater autonomy and the introduction of autonomous work groups can result in a marked reduction in stress.[32]

Other influences on behaviour

Even if there is an absence of role conflict and role stress, a person's actual behaviour may still be inconsistent with their expected pattern of behaviours. *Miner* gives three reasons that may account for this disparity.[33]

- The person does not perceive their job in the way the role prescriptions specify. This is a form of role ambiguity but may arise not because the role prescriptions themselves are unclear, but because the person misunderstands or distorts them.
- Motivation is lacking, and the person does not want to behave in the way prescribed.
- The person does not have the capabilities – knowledge, mental ability or physical skills – required to behave in the way the role prescriptions specify.

Application of sanctions

Organisations apply a number of both positive and negative sanctions as inducements for members to contribute and behave in accordance with their prescribed roles. Typical examples are: an increase in salary or wages; promotion; a sideways or downwards move in the organisation structure; the threat of dismissal.

There are also a number of less direct sanctions which may be adopted. These include: the size of office or work area; the allocation of unpopular tasks; giving opportunities for paid overtime work; level of supervision; the amount of information given or the extent of consultation; granting or withholding privileges.

Role sanctions may also be applied through the operation of the informal organisation. Members of the group may impose their own sanctions and discipline individuals who contravene the norms of the group or expected standards of behaviour.

SYNOPSIS

■ Groups are a major feature of human behaviour and of organisational performance. Members of a group must co-operate with one another for work to be carried out. Groups help shape the work pattern of organisations, and the attitudes and behaviour of members regarding their jobs. Groups develop their own values and norms of behaviour. Organisations function best when members act not as individuals, but as members of highly effective work groups.

■ Groups are formed as a consequence of the pattern of organisation structure and arrangements for the division of work. There are two main types of groups at work, formal and informal. Formal groups are deliberately planned and created by

management as part of the organisation structure, and to achieve specific organisational objectives. They are concerned with the co-ordination of work activities. Informal groups are based on personal relationships and develop irrespective of the formal structure. Informal groups serve to satisfy members' psychological and social needs. Groups are formed, therefore, for a number of reasons relating to both work performance and social processes.

■ The manager's main concern is that members of a work group co-operate with one another. Factors which affect group cohesiveness can be considered under the broad headings of: membership; work environment; organisational; and group development and maturity. Membership of strong and cohesive groups can be a rewarding experience for the individual and have beneficial effects for the organisation.

■ There are, however, potential disadvantages and the manager should attempt to prevent unconstructive inter-group conflict. On the other hand, inter-group rivalry may be deliberately encouraged as a means of building stronger within-group cohesiveness. The effective management of work groups requires an understanding of the psychological and social influences on behaviour within organisations.

■ The nature of technology and the work flow system of the organisation is a major influence on the operation of groups, and the manner in which they conduct themselves. There may also be differences in behaviour between social groupings. The nature of technology can be unfavourable for the creation of work groups and a source of alienation, especially for manual workers. The impact of information technology is likely to lead to new patterns of work organisation, and affect the formation and structure of groups.

■ The concept of 'role' is important to the functioning of groups, and for an understanding of group processes and behaviour. It is through role differentiation that the structure of work groups and relationships among members is established. Role expectations may be established formally, they may be informal or they may be self-established. Inadequate or inappropriate role definition can result in role conflict including: role incompatibility, role ambiguity, role overload and role underload. Role conflict can result in role stress. It is important that the manager makes every effort to minimise role conflict and the causes of role stress.

 Review and discussion questions

1 What is a group? Explain the importance of group values and norms, and give practical examples from within your own organisation.

2 Explain what is meant by a 'linking-pin' process of group membership. Illustrate your answer with a simple diagram.

3 Distinguish between formal and informal groups. What functions do groups serve in an organisation?

4 Identify different stages in group development and maturity. What other factors influence the cohesiveness of work groups? Give examples by reference to a work group to which you belong.

5 Assess the impact of technology as a determinant of group behaviour and perfor- mance. What action might be taken by management to help remove some of the alienating aspects of technology?

6 What is meant by the role structure of an organisation? Construct a diagram which shows your own role-set within a work situation. Give examples of informal role expectations to which you are, or have been, a party.

7 Explain different forms of role conflict which can result in role stress. Give an account of a work situation in which you have experienced role conflict/role stress. As man- ager, what action would you have taken in an attempt to rectify the situation?

8 What are the characteristics of an effective work group? As a manager, how would you attempt to develop effective group relationships and performance?

 ## Assignment 1

Obtain, or prepare, a chart depicting the formal groupings within your organisation or a large department of the organisation.

(i) Using this chart identify clearly the *informal* groups that exist within the formal structure.

(ii) Discuss ways in which these informal groups aid, or conflict with, the work of the organisation/department.

(iii) Explain the extent to which management recognise the influence of the informal groups.

(iv) What conclusions do you draw from this assignment?

 Assignment 2

Attempt, *preferably*, to observe a small group or project team at work; *alternatively*, recall the working of any small group of which you have recently been a member.

(i) (a) Explain the extent to which the group progressed through the stages of: forming; storming; norming; performing.

(b) Complete the following grid by giving a tick in the appropriate box to denote each contribution by individual members.

Names of group members (or reference numbers)

Forming					
Storming					
Norming					
Performing					

(ii) (a) Give examples of the group values or norms which constituted 'proper' behaviour of group members.

(b) Explain sanctions applied to those members who did not conform to the group norms and the apparent effectiveness of these sanctions.

(iii) Explain the factors which influenced the cohesiveness of the group.

(iv) Give your views, with supporting reasons, on:

(a) the apparent satisfaction derived by individuals from membership of the group; and

(b) the effectiveness of the group as a whole.

▌C A S E S T U D Y

Hovertec plc

Background information

Hovertec plc is a large public company which has been manufacturing civilian and military helicopters for nearly 50 years. The company is very successful in its field and during 19xx/19xx achieved total sales of over £280 million. Profits before taxation exceeded £16½ million. Hovertec plc employs over 6000 people, most of whom work in three manufacturing plants which are situated in South-West England, Scotland and Northern Ireland.

The company has developed two main types of helicopters since the Second World War. These are the 'Falcon' range of small helicopters, which are sold to civilian operators, and the 'SX/Hawk' range of small and large military helicopters which are produced for government defence projects. Some export orders of 'SX/Hawk' helicopters are manufactured for NATO countries and other friendly countries. The precise number and size of Ministry of Defence contracts is not published and is regarded as classified information by Hovertec plc.

Nevertheless, it is possible to gain some insight into the close relationship between the Ministry of Defence and the company from the details of the research and development (R&D) expenditure which is published in the Hovertec plc Annual Report and Accounts. During 19xx/19xx, the R&D expenditure exceeded £43 million, of which £13 million was 'raised from private venture expenditure', £2.5 million was 'funded in civilian helicopter sales prices' and £28 million was 'covered by classified research contracts'. All the research and development projects, as well as all the military and some civilian contracts, are undertaken at the largest plant in South-West England. The remaining civilian helicopter contracts are shared between the two smaller factories in Scotland and Northern Ireland.

The manufacture of a helicopter

Without going into technical details, the manufacture of a helicopter can be divided into five interconnected processes:

(i) *The power unit*, which 'drives' the helicopter like an engine drives a motor car.

(ii) *The helicopter loom*, which is an inter-woven collection of between 1200 and 2000 insulated copper wires and electrical cables, connecting the power unit with the various 'control' switches, dials, buttons and levers in the cockpit and passenger/crew compartment, and can be compared, in human terms, with the function of the spinal cord in linking the brain with the arms and legs, etc.

(iii) *The external rotor blades*, which are mounted over the cockpit and passenger/crew compartment, and also above the tail of the helicopter.

(iv) *The cockpit and passenger/crew compartment*, which has a different layout, services and accessories (viz. electronic weapon systems), depending on whether the helicopter is intended for civilian or military purposes.

(v) *The superstructure or 'shell'*, which encases the helicopter in a similar manner to the 'bodywork' on a motor car.

Although the latest technology is used in these production and assembly processes, the manufacture of a complete helicopter is a relatively slow process, taking three weeks for a civilian unit and four weeks for the larger, more sophisticated military helicopter. The main 'bottleneck' in the process is the long time taken to assemble the helicopter loom and complete the 1200–2000 connections between the power unit and the numerous helicopter systems and services.

Assembling a helicopter loom

Because of the complexity of the task and the high risk of error, the assembly of each helicopter loom is normally carried out by one loom technician who takes up to two weeks (ten working days) to assemble a complete loom unit. Production output is maintained by a team of 24 loom technicians who work in two shifts of 12 technicians per shift. The loom technicians are all qualified maintenance fitters who have received extensive training from the company in loom-assembly procedures. They are the highest-paid section of the workforce after the supervisors and management, and they receive other benefits, such as membership of the company pension scheme, free BUPA medical insurance and additional holiday entitlement which is related to length of service with the company.

All of these technicians are men, aged between 36 and 50 years with between 8 and 15 years' service with the company. Many were recruited from either the Royal Navy or the Army Engineering Corps, where they received their basic training as maintenance fitters. This form of recruitment is adopted, firstly, because the loom technicians help to assemble both civilian and military helicopters and possible security risks have to be minimised on Ministry of Defence contracts. Secondly, the majority of Hovertec plc managers possess Army or Naval backgrounds and strong links are maintained with the armed services.

Perhaps the one striking difference between the working conditions at the Hovertec plc factory in South-West England and those at their previous employment in the Armed Services is that all the loom technicians belong to a trade union which is recognised by the company, although in practice the Hovertec plc management frequently circumvent the union representatives by informing the workforce directly of changes in procedures, policy, etc., using 'briefing' procedures.

An improved helicopter loom-assembly method

The 19xx company Corporate Plan concluded that: 'Because of the constricting squeeze on defence projects and on the finances of civilian helicopter operators, which appears likely to continue until the world recession ends and general demands picks up, future activity in the three factories will be at a lower level during the next two to three years than seemed likely a few years ago'.

A detailed cost-cutting exercise was introduced on the strength of this plan, with particular emphasis on the helicopter loom workshop. For example all overtime working was withdrawn in September 19xx. Meanwhile, the Research and Development Laboratories had devised a radically new method of assembling helicopter looms which, under pilot-scheme conditions, reduced the assembly time from two weeks (ten working days) to two working days. The new method had the added advantage of allowing unskilled labour to be employed and resulted in a saving of assembly costs.

Instead of one technician assembling a single loom, by following a blueprint in a painstaking way, the new method relies upon a team of five operatives working

together and following a sequence of 'instructions' provided by a computer. The 1200–2000 insulated copper wires and electrical cables are previously 'colour coded' in terms of the ten main helicopter operating systems. Each operative is given responsibility for two sets of colour-coded wires and cables and is required to thread the leads of one colour through the loom, one at a time, by following a 'map' which is set out on a personal visual display unit.

The total computerised layout, which appears on a separate large screen, resembles a coloured map of the London Underground system. For example, as one operative threads each blue electrical cable through the loom, a blue light flicks on as each correct 'station' is reached. If an error is made, the appropriate light fails to appear and a buzzing alarm sounds continuously until the mistake is corrected and the correct 'route' is re-established. At the same time, the computer-directed system can also be used for the other 'colour-coded' electrical connections and the team is therefore able to assemble the loom simultaneously, without slowing down or interfering with each other's work.

Further trials conducted by the Research and Development Laboratories indicated that small groups of five female workers achieved, on average, 40 per cent higher productivity than similar teams of male operatives. The highest productivity was consistently achieved under laboratory conditions by a team of 16-to-17-year-old female school-leavers, who were permitted to choose their working partners and were also allowed to change from one 'colour code' to another whenever they became bored with one colour or started to make errors. This team was given ten-minute 'rest pauses' every hour to change 'colour codes' and was supervised by a member of the Research and Development Laboratory team, who also collected data on the group's productivity, etc.

Proposed changes in the helicopter loom workshop

Within six months, a decision was taken by the Hovertec plc senior management to transfer the new computerised system pilot-scheme to the loom workshop on a three-months' trial basis. Management informed the workforce about the proposed trials beforehand and the loom technicians accepted the proposed change after receiving a personal assurance that no redundancies would occur as a result of the trials. The company wrote to their trade union about ten days later, during the week when the trials began, to inform them of the new situation; and also pointed out that the trials would allow full-time employment to be offered to five female school-leavers, who would otherwise be out of work.

Outcome of the trials

Within two weeks of the new computerised system being installed, three of the five girls in the work group handed in their notice because of continual abuse from and arguments with the loom technicians. Productivity fell far below the expected targets on every day after the first loom was completed (in four days). The cause of low productivity was invariably due to breakdowns of equipment (loss of VDU pictures was the most frequent fault) which, according to the Research and Development Department, was the direct result of vandalism. A serious argument broke out on one occasion between a loom technician and the Research and Development Supervisor, who had earlier asked the technician to leave the VDU area and return to his own work area, and the outcome was that disciplinary action had to be taken against the loom technician.

Three days later, the trade union representing the loom technicians advised the company that the men were unwilling to work alongside the girls on classified defence contracts in future. The reason given was that the girls were considered to be irresponsible and were more of a 'security risk' than the service-trained loom technicians. Management were swift to point out that none of the girls possessed any expertise in engineering or electronic systems and, in fact, three of the girls were close relatives of different loom technicians.

Output in the loom workshop fell during April and May and the company began to fall behind on outstanding defence contracts. A senior Ministry of Defence official visited the plant in South-West England to advise senior management of the 'Whitehall View' that the new computerised loom assembly trials should be suspended on all defence contract helicopters until further notice.

(a) Using your knowledge of different approaches to organisation and management, comment on the Research and Development Laboratory trials carried out by Hovertec with the team of young, female workers.

(b) Discuss the conditions which contributed to the cohesiveness of the loom technicians as a work group.

(c) What factors might explain the difficulties between the group of loom technicians and the team of female workers?

(d) What action would you propose should be taken by the management of Hovertec?

Notes and references

1. Schein, E. H. *Organizational Psychology*, Third edition, Prentice-Hall (1988) p. 145.
2. Adair, J. *Effective Teambuilding*, Gower (1986).
3. See, for example: Davidow, W. H. and Malone, M. S. *The Virtual Corporation*, Harper Collins (1993).
4. Roethlisberger, F. J. and Dickson, W. J. *Management and the Worker*, Harvard University Press (1939).
5. Trist, E. L. *et al. Organizational Choice*, Tavistock Publications (1963).
6. Likert, R. *New Patterns of Management*, McGraw-Hill (1961) p. 38.
7. Likert, R. *The Human Organization*, McGraw-Hill (1967).
8. Seashore, S. E. *Group Cohesiveness in the Industrial Work Group*, Institute for Social Research, University of Michigan (1954).
9. Argyle, M. *The Social Psychology of Work*, Second edition, Penguin (1989).
10. See, for example: Jay, A. *Corporation Man*, Penguin (1975). In an amusing historical account of the development of different forms of groups, Jay suggests that ten is the basic size of human grouping.
11. See, for example: Handy, C. B. *Understanding Organizations*, Fourth edition, Penguin (1993).
12. Bass, B. M. and Ryterband, E. C. *Organizational Psychology*, Second edition, Allyn and Bacon (1979).
13. Tuckman, B. W. 'Development Sequence in Small Groups', *Psychological Bulletin*, vol. 63, 1965, pp. 384–99.
14. See, for example: Staw, B. M. 'Organizational Psychology and the Pursuit of the Happy/ Productive Worker', *California Management Review*, vol. 28, no. 4, Summer 1986, pp. 40–53.
15. For example, see: Schein, E. H. *Organizational Psychology*, Third edition, Prentice-Hall (1988).
16. Allcorn, S. 'Understanding Groups at Work', *Personnel*, vol. 66, no. 8, August 1989, pp. 28–36.
17. Walker, C. R. and Guest, R. H. *The Man on the Assembly Line*, Harvard University Press (1952).
18. Scott, W. H. *et al. Technical Change and Industrial Relations*, Liverpool University Press (1956).
19. Sayles, L. R. *Behavior of Industrial Work Groups*, Wiley (1958).
20. Lupton, T. *On the Shop Floor*, Pergamon Press (1963).
21. Goldthorpe, J. H. *et al. The Affluent Worker*, Cambridge University Press (1968).
22. See, for example: Grayson, D. *Self Regulating Work Groups – An Aspect of Organisational Change*, ACAS Work Research Unit, Occasional Paper, no. 146, HMSO (July 1990).
23. For example, see: Kinsman, F. 'The Virtual Office and The Flexible Organisation', *Administrator*, April 1994, pp. 31–2.
24. Whyte, W. F. *Human Relations in the Restaurant Industry*, McGraw-Hill (1948).
25. See, for example: Lerner, P. M. 'Beware the Gatekeeper', *Amtrak Express*, July/August 1994, pp. 14–17.
26. See, for example: Schein, E. H. *Organizational Psychology*, Third edition, Prentice-Hall (1988).
27. See, for example: Handy, C. B. *Understanding Organizations*, Fourth edition, Penguin (1993).
28. Kahn, R. L. *et al. Organizational Stress*, Wiley (1964).
29. Filley, A. C. and House, R. J. *Managerial Process and Organizational Behavior*, Scott Foresman (1969).

30. See, for example: *Managers Under Stress: A Survey of Management Morale in the 90s*, The Institute of Management (December 1993).
31. Rockledge, S. 'The Human Cost of Bad Management', *Administrator*, vol. 7, no.1, January 1987, p. 13; Ridd, J. 'Hidden Costs of Work Stress', *The British Journal of Administrative Management*, October/November 1994, pp. 14–15.
32. Hall, K. and Savery, L. K. 'Stress Management', *Management Decision*, vol. 25, no. 6, 1987, pp. 29–35.
33. Miner, J. B. *Management Theory*, Macmillan (1971).

7 GROUP PROCESSES AND BEHAVIOUR

If the manager is to make the most effective use of staff, then it is important to have an understanding of group processes and behaviour. It is necessary to understand the nature of group functions and roles, and factors which influence their performance and effectiveness. Attention must be given to the analysis of behaviour of individuals in group situations. The manager must be aware of the functioning and operation of work groups.

 Learning objectives

To:

- Explain interactions among members of a group and patterns of communication networks;

- Examine methods of analysing behaviour of individuals in group situations;

- Distinguish different functions and member roles in the study of group behaviour;

- Explain the use of frameworks of behavioural analysis in groups;

- Assess the nature of group performance and effectiveness;

- Explain the nature and value of group dynamics;

- Recognise the importance of understanding the functioning and operation of work groups.

Worth thinking about

Walking along a corridor you see a small group of colleagues apparently sharing a joke. As you approach the group they all start to laugh. You ask a person at the back of the group who is laughing loudly what the joke was all about. The person replies: 'Sorry, I don't really know, Chris speaks softly and I couldn't catch what was said.'

INTERACTIONS AMONG MEMBERS

In order to help improve the performance of the organisation it is necessary to understand the nature of human relationships and what goes on when groups of people meet.[1] Working in a group is likely to be both a psychologically rewarding, but also a potentially demanding, experience for the individual. Group performance and the satisfaction derived by individuals are influenced by the interactions among members of the group. As an example, Table 7.1 gives an unsolicited commentary from five final-year business studies degree students after completing a group-based assignment.

Table 7.1 Unsolicited commentary from students after completing a group-based assignment

WHAT WE FEEL WE HAVE LEARNT FROM WORKING IN A GROUP
1. We learnt that we had to listen to everybody's points of view and take these into consideration.
2. We found that we had to be prepared to make certain sacrifices and adopted a democratic decision process. However, if an individual felt very strongly about a specific point and persisted with a valid argument then this had to be included.
3. We often felt frustrated.
4. It was time-consuming and difficult to schedule meetings due to differences in timetables and preferences in working hours.
5. We learnt that it is good to pool resources because this increased the overall standard of the piece of work. We feel this was only because we all set high personal standards and expected these from our fellow group members. We learnt that it is possible to work in other less productive groups where individual levels of achievement may decrease.
6. We learnt that it is better to work in a smaller and not a larger group, as there is a tendency for individual ideas to be diluted.
7. Groups formed on the basis of friendship alone are not as effective as groups formed with work as the major influence. The former tend to be unproductive.
8. We found that it was good to get positive response, encouragement and feedback from team members. Likewise, it was demotivating to receive a negative response.
9. We learnt a lot about our individual personalities.
10. We benefited from sharing personal experiences from our industrial placements.
11. It is important to separate work and personal relationships.

MEMBERSHIP OF SUCCESSFUL TEAMS

If groups are to be successful and perform effectively there must be a spirit of unity and co-operation. Members of a group must work well together as a team. Following years of research and empirical study, *Belbin* concludes that groups composed entirely of clever people, or of people with similar personalities, display a number of negative results and lack creativity. The most consistently successful groups comprise a range of roles undertaken by various members. The constitution of the group itself is an important variable in its success.[2]

Eight key team-roles

For a fully effective group, there are eight useful types of contribution – or team-roles. Belbin describes 'team-role' as a pattern of behaviour characteristic of the way in which one team member interacts with another where performance serves to facilitate the progress of the team as a whole. The eight key team-roles are:

- Company Worker (CW);
- Chairman (CH);
- Shaper (SH);
- Plant (PL);
- Resource Investigator (RI);
- Monitor-Evaluator (ME);
- Team Worker (TW);
- Completer-Finisher (CF).

An explanation of these team-roles is given in Table 7.2.

The eight types of people identified are useful team members and form a comprehensive list. These are the key team-roles and the primary characters for successful teams. Creative teams require a balance of all these roles and comprise members who have characteristics complementary to one another. Belbin claims that good examples of the eight types would prove adequate for any challenge, although not all eight types are necessarily needed. Other members may be welcome for their personal qualities, for example a sense of humour, but experience suggests there is no other team-role that it would be useful to add.

Back-up team-roles and functional roles

The most consistently successful teams were 'mixed' with a balance of team-roles. The role that a person undertakes in a group is not fixed and may change according to circumstances. Individuals may have a 'back-up team-role' with which they have some affinity other than their primary team-role. If certain roles were missing members would call upon their back-up roles. Team-roles differ from what Belbin calls 'functional-roles'. These are the roles that members of a team perform in terms of the specifically technical demands placed upon them. Team members are typically chosen for functional roles on the basis of experience and not personal characteristics or aptitudes.

Revised list of team-roles

In a follow-up publication Belbin discusses the continued evolution of team-roles which now differ in a few respects from those identified in earlier research.[3] Two roles are renamed, largely for reasons of acceptability: 'Co-ordinator' replaces 'Chairman'; and 'Implementer' replaces 'Company Worker'. The most significant

Table 7.2 Useful people to have in teams

Type	Symbol	Typical features	Positive qualities	Allowable weaknesses
Company worker	CW	Conservative, dutiful, predictable.	Organising ability, practical common sense, hard-working, self-discipline.	Lack of flexibility, unresponsiveness to unproven ideas.
Chairman	CH	Calm, self-confident, controlled.	A capacity for treating and welcoming all potential contributors on their merits and without prejudice. A strong sense of objectives.	No more than ordinary in terms of intellect or creative ability.
Shaper	SH	Highly strung, outgoing, dynamic.	Drive and a readiness to challenge inertia, ineffectiveness, complacency or self-deception.	Proneness to provocation, irritation and impatience.
Plant	PL	Individualistic, serious-minded, unorthodox.	Genius, imagination, intellect, knowledge.	Up in the clouds, inclined to disregard practical details or protocol.
Resource Investigator	RI	Extroverted, enthusiastic, curious, communicative.	A capacity for contacting people and exploring anything new. An ability to respond to challenge.	Liable to lose interest once the initial fascination has passed.
Monitor-Evaluator	ME	Sober, unemotional, prudent.	Judgement, discretion, hard-headedness.	Lacks inspiration or the ability to motivate others.
Team Worker	TW	Socially orientated, rather mild, sensitive.	An ability to respond to people and to situations, and to promote team spirit.	Indecisiveness at moments of crisis.
Completer-Finisher	CF	Painstaking, orderly, conscientious, anxious.	A capacity for follow-through. Perfectionism.	A tendency to worry about small things. A reluctance to 'let go'.

(Reprinted with permission from Belbin, R. M., *Management Teams: Why They Succeed or Fail*, Butterworth-Heinemann (1981) p. 78.)

change is the addition of a ninth role, that of 'Specialist'. This role was added because of the significance of the importance of a given form of professional expertise in much project work and its recurring importance as an issue in a career development. A description of the evolved nine team-roles is given in Table 7.3.

Table 7.3 Belbin's revised team roles

Roles and descriptions – team-role contribution		Allowable weaknesses
Plant:	Creative, imaginative, unorthodox. Solves difficult problems.	Ignores details. Too preoccupied to communicate effectively.
Resource Investigator:	Extrovert, enthusiastic, communicative. Explores opportunities. Develops contacts.	Overoptimistic. Loses interest once initial enthusiasm has passed.
Co-ordinator:	Mature, confident, a good chairperson. Clarifies goals, promotes decision-making. Delegates well.	Can be seen as manipulative. Delegates personal work.
Shaper:	Challenging, dynamic, thrives on pressure. Has the drive and courage to overcome obstacles.	Can provoke others. Hurts people's feelings.
Monitor-Evaluator:	Sober, strategic and and discerning. Sees all options. Judges accurately.	Lacks drive and ability to inspire others. Overly critical.
Team Worker:	Co-operative, mild, perceptive and diplomatic. Listens, builds, averts, friction, calms the waters.	Indecisive in crunch situations. Can be easily influenced.
Implementer:	Disciplined, reliable, conservative and efficient. Turns ideas into practical actions.	Somewhat inflexible. Slow to respond to new possibilities.
Completer:	Painstaking, conscientious, anxious. Searches out errors and omissions. Delivers on time.	Inclined to worry unduly. Reluctant to delegate. Can be a nit-picker.
Specialist:	Single-minded, self-sharing, dedicated. Provides knowledge and skills in rare supply.	Contributes on only a narrow front. Dwells on technicalities. Overlooks the 'big picture'.

Strength of contribution in any one of the roles is commonly associated with particular weaknesses. These are called allowable weaknesses. Executives are seldom strong in all nine team roles.

(Reprinted with permission from Belbin, R. M. *Team Roles at Work*, Butterworth-Heinemann (1993) p. 23.)

PATTERNS OF COMMUNICATION

The level of interaction among members of a group is influenced by the structuring of channels of communication. Laboratory research by *Bavelas*[4] and subsequent studies by other researchers such as *Leavitt*[5] have resulted in the design of a series of communication networks.

These networks were based on groups of five members engaged in a number of problem-solving tasks. Members were permitted to communicate with each other by written notes only, and not everyone was always free to communicate with everyone else.

Main communication networks

There are five main types of communication networks – Wheel, Circle, All-Channel, Y and Chains (*see* Fig 7.1).

- **The wheel,** also sometimes known as the star, is the most centralised network. This network is most efficient for simple tasks. Problems are solved more quickly with fewer mistakes and with fewer information flows. But as the problems of the group become more complex and demands on the link person increase, effectiveness suffers. The link person is at the centre of the network

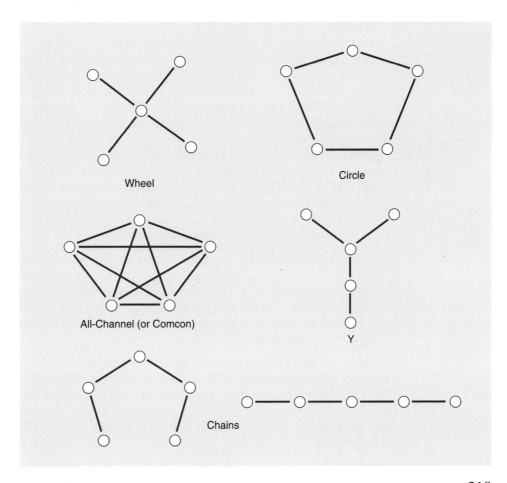

Wheel

Circle

All-Channel (or Comcon)

Y

Chains

Fig. 7.1
Communication
networks

and acts as the focus of activities and information flows, and the co-ordinator of group tasks. The central person is perceived as leader of the group and experiences a high level of satisfaction. However, for members on the periphery, the wheel is the least satisfying network.

- **The circle** is a more decentralised network. Overall it is less efficient. The group is unorganised, with low leadership predictability. Performance tends to be slow and erratic. However, the circle is quicker than the wheel in solving complex problems, and also copes with change or new tasks more efficiently. The circle network is most satisfying for all the members. Decision-making is likely to involve some degree of participation.

- **The all-channel (or comcon) network** is a decentralised network which involves full discussion and participation. This network appears to work best where a high level of interaction is required among all members of the group in order to solve complex problems. Leadership predictability is very low. There is a fairly high level of satisfaction for members. The all-channel network may not stand up well under pressure, in which case it will either disintegrate or reform into a wheel network.

- **A 'Y' or chain network** might be appropriate for more simple problem-solving tasks, requiring little interaction among members of the group. These networks are more centralised, with information flows along a predetermined channel. Leadership predictability is high to moderate. There is a low to moderate level of satisfaction for members.

Satisfaction of group members

Findings from these studies indicate that the greater the interconnectedness of the network, the higher the general level of satisfaction of members in the group. Groups allowed to establish their own communication networks, and who did so with the minimum of links, took less time to solve their tasks. Those groups who did not minimise the number of links in their network took more time to solve the tasks.[6]

From a review of studies in communication networks, *Shaw* confirmed that simple tasks were consistently undertaken most efficiently in more centralised networks such as the wheel. More complex tasks were performed more efficiently by decentralised networks such as the circle or the all-channel.[7] (*See* Fig. 7.2.) The characteristics of the different communication networks are determined by the extent of 'independence' and 'saturation'.

- **Independence** refers to the opportunities for group members to take action and to solve the problem without relying on the assistance of others.

- **Saturation** occurs when the task places an excessive information load or other demands upon a member of the network. This leads to inefficiency. The central person in a centralised network handling complex problems is more likely to experience saturation.

The individual's satisfaction with his or her position in the network relates to the degree of independence and the satisfaction of recognition and achievement needs. (*See* achievement motivation in Chapter 14.) A high level of dependence on other members may prevent the satisfaction of these needs, and if members of the network become frustrated they may not be so willing to share information with others.

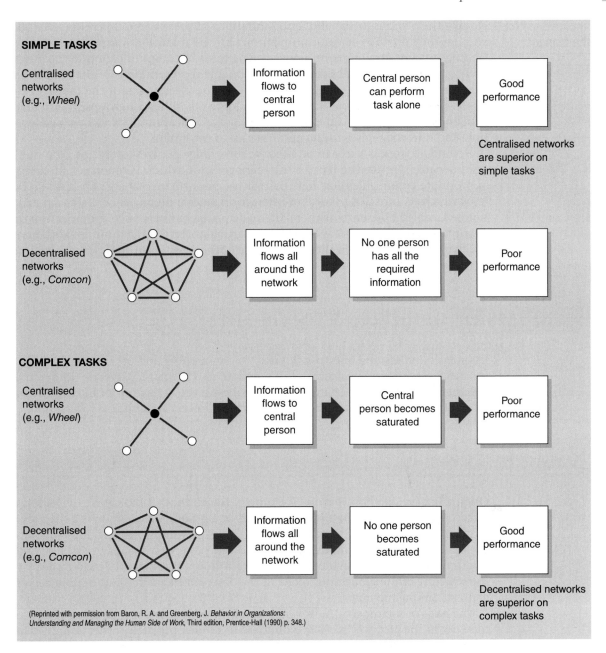

(Reprinted with permission from Baron, R. A. and Greenberg, J. *Behavior in Organizations: Understanding and Managing the Human Side of Work*, Third edition, Prentice-Hall (1990) p. 348.)

**Fig. 7.2
Communication
networks and
task complexity**

In the wheel network the central person has greater independence than the other members, but in the circle network all members have a moderate degree of dependence upon each other. Leadership is also important because this can influence the opportunity for independent action by the group members, and can also control the possibility of saturation.

Implications for the manager

Despite the obvious artificiality and limitations of these communication network studies, they do have certain implications for the manager. A knowledge of the findings may be applied to influence the patterns of communication in meetings and committees. They also provide a reasonable representation of the situations that might apply in large organisations. It will be interesting for the manager to observe the patterns of communication adopted by different groups in different situations. The manager can also note how communication networks change over time and how they relate to the performance of the group.

No one network is likely to be effective for a range of given problems. The studies draw attention to the part of the manager's job which is to ensure the most appropriate communication network for the performance of a given task. Problems which require a high level of interaction among members of the group may not be handled efficiently if there are inadequate channels of communication or sharing of information. The choice of a particular communication network may involve trade-offs between the performance of the work group and the satisfaction of its members.

ANALYSIS OF BEHAVIOUR IN GROUPS

In order to understand and to influence the functioning and operation of a group it is necessary to study patterns of interaction, and the parts played by individual members. Two of the main methods of analysing the behaviour of individuals in group situations are sociometry and interaction process analysis.

SOCIOMETRY

Originally developed by *Moreno*,[8] sociometry is a method of indicating the feelings of acceptance or rejection among members of a group. A sociogram is a diagrammatical illustration of the pattern of interpersonal relationships derived from sociometry. The sociogram depicts the choices, preferences, likes or dislikes, and interactions between individual members of a group. It can also be used to display the structure of the group and to record the observed frequency and/or duration of contacts among members.

The basis of sociometry, however, is usually 'buddy rating' or 'peer rating'. Each member in the group is asked to nominate or to rate, privately, other members in terms of some given context or characteristic, for example with whom they communicate, or how influential or how likeable they are. Questions may relate to either work or social activities, for example: who would you most prefer or least prefer as a workmate? or who would make a good leader of the group? or with whom would you choose and not choose to go on holiday?

Positive and negative choices may be recorded for each person, although sometimes positive choices only are required. The choices may be limited to a given number or they may be unlimited. Sometimes individuals may be asked to rank their choices.

Sociograms

Members' choices could be shown in tabular form. For example, Table 7.4 shows first and second choices for a group of final-year degree students. Members were asked to indicate, in confidence, those whom they would most prefer to talk to about: (i) a major work-related problem; and (ii) a difficult personal problem. Positive choices only were requested.

Table 7.4 Example of a 'tabulated' sociogram (positive choices only)

| Work-related problem | | | Personal problem | |
Second Choice	First Choice		First Choice	Second Choice
		A		III
		B	I	II
III	I	C	II	I
I		D	II	
		E	I	
		F	I	II
	I	G	II	
IIIII	II	H	II	
		J	I	I
	II	K		
IIII	IIIIIII	L		II
I	I	M	I	I
		N		II
I		O	I	
14	14		14	14

An advantage of the diagrammatical illustration however is that the sociogram provides a visual description of the sociometric structure of a group. It can indicate cliques and sub-groups, compatibility, and members who are popular, isolated or who act as links. Fig. 7.3 gives a simple illustration of a sociogram for a group of 15 members with single, positive choices only.

(i) G and M are popular (the stars) and most often chosen by members.
(ii) M is the link between two overlapping cliques, KML and MNO.
(iii) H and P are unpopular (isolated) and chosen least by members.

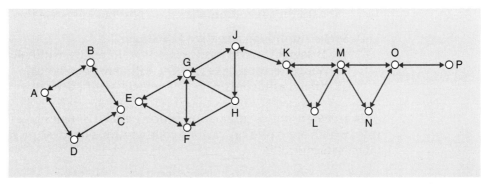

Fig. 7.3
A simple illustration of a sociogram

(iv) JKMO is a chain.

(v) ABCD is a sub-group and separated from the rest of the members.

It should be noted however that there are several methods of compiling and drawing sociograms, and a number of potential criticisms and limitations with the contribution of Moreno. Problems also arise over *how* to draw the sociogram and how to interpret the roles of individual members; 'the drawing of a sociogram is a highly arbitrary and time-consuming task'.[9] In the experience of the author less concern should be given to the concept of sociometry itself. It is better seen as a useful vehicle which, if handled sensitively, can serve to encourage meaningful discussions on patterns of social interactions, group behaviour and the perceptions of individual members towards one another.

INTERACTION ANALYSIS

The basic assumption behind interaction analysis is that behaviour in groups may be analysed from the viewpoint of its function. This approach has developed largely from the work of *Bales* on methods for the study of small groups. This aim is to provide ways of describing group process and indications of factors influencing the process.[10]

In Bales's 'Interaction Process Analysis' every act of behaviour is categorised, as it occurs, under twelve headings. These differentiate between 'task' functions and 'socio-emotional' functions. The categories apply to both verbal interaction and non-verbal interaction.

- **A. Socio-Emotional: Positive Reactions**
 1. **Shows solidarity**, raises others' status, gives help, reward.
 2. **Shows tension release**, jokes, laughs, shows satisfaction.
 3. **Agrees**, shows passive acceptance, understands, concurs, complies.

- **B. Task: Attempted Answers**
 4. **Gives suggestion**, direction, implying autonomy for others.
 5. **Gives opinion**, evaluation, analysis, expresses feeling, wish.
 6. **Gives orientation**, information, repeats, clarifies, confirms.

- **C. Task: Questions**
 7. **Asks for orientation**, information, repetition, confirmation.
 8. **Asks for opinion**, evaluation, analysis, expression of feeling.
 9. **Asks for suggestion**, direction, possible ways of action.

- **D. Socio-Emotional: Negative Reactions**
 10. **Disagrees**, shows passive rejection, formality, withholds help.
 11. **Shows tension**, asks for help, withdraws out of field.
 12. **Shows antagonism**, deflates others' status, defends or asserts self.

In an extension of interaction process analysis, Bales gives 27 typical group roles which are based on various combinations of these original main behavioural categories.[11]

Task and maintenance functions

If the group is to be effective, then, whatever its structure or the pattern of interrelationships among members, there are two main sets of functions or processes that must be undertaken – **task functions** and **maintenance functions.**

- **Task functions** are directed towards problem-solving, the accomplishment of the tasks of the group and the achievement of its goals. Most of the task-oriented behaviour will be concerned with 'production' activities, or the exchange and evaluation of ideas and information.
- **Maintenance functions** are concerned with the emotional life of the group and directed towards building and maintaining the group as an effective working unit. Most of the maintenance-oriented behaviour will be concerned with relationships among group members, giving encouragement and support, maintaining cohesiveness and the resolution of conflict.

Task and maintenance functions may be performed either by the group leader or by members. Ultimately it is the leader's responsibility to ensure that both sets of functions are carried out and the right balance is achieved between them. The appropriate combination of task-oriented behaviour and maintenance-oriented behaviour is essential to the success and continuity of the group.

In addition to these two types of behaviour members of a group may say or do something in attempting to satisfy some personal need or goal. The display of behaviour in this way is termed **self-oriented behaviour**. This gives a classification of three main types of functional behaviour which can be exhibited by individual members of a group: **task-oriented, maintenance-oriented** and **self-oriented.**

Classification of member roles

A popular system for the classification of member roles in the study of group behaviour is that devised originally by *Benne and Sheats*.[12] The description of member roles performed in well-functioning groups is classified into three broad headings: **group task roles, group maintenance roles** and **individual roles.**

Group task roles: these assume that the task of the group is to select, define and solve common problems. Any of the roles may be performed by the various members or the group leader.

(i) The **initiator-contributor**
(ii) The **information seeker**
(iii) The **opinion seeker**
(iv) The **information giver**
(v) The **opinion giver**
(vi) The **elaborator**
(vii) The **co-ordinator**
(viii) The **orienter**
(ix) The **evaluator-critic**
(x) The **energiser**
(xi) The **procedural technician**
(xii) The **recorder**

Group building and maintenance roles: the analysis of member-functions is oriented towards activities which build group-centred attitudes, or maintain group-centred behaviour. Contributions may involve a number of roles, and members or the leader may perform each of these roles.

(i) The **encourager**
(ii) The **harmoniser**
(iii) The **compromiser**
(iv) The **gatekeeper and expediter**
(v) The **standard-setter or ego ideal**
(vi) The **group observer and commentator**
(vii) The **follower**

Individual roles: these are directed towards the satisfaction of personal needs. Their purpose is not related either to group task or to the group functioning.

(i) The **aggressor**
(ii) The **blocker**
(iii) The **recognition-seeker**
(iv) The **self-confessor**
(v) The **playboy**
(vi) The **dominator**
(vii) The **help-seeker**
(viii) The **special interest pleader**

FRAMEWORKS OF BEHAVIOURAL ANALYSIS

Several frameworks have been designed for observers to categorise patterns of verbal and non-verbal behaviour of group members. Observers chart members' behaviour on specially designed forms. These forms may be used to focus on single individuals, or used to record the total group interaction with no indication of individual behaviour.

The system of categorisation may distinguish between different behaviours in terms of the functions they are performing. The completed observation forms can be used as a basis for discussion of individual or group performance in terms of the strengths/weaknesses of different functional behaviour.

In the following framework there are two observation sheets, one covering six types of leader–member **task-function behaviour** and the other covering six types of leader–member **group building and maintenance function behaviour**.

Task functions

1. **Initiating:** Proposing tasks or goals; defining a group problem, suggesting a procedure or ideas for solving a problem.
2. **Information or opinion seeking:** Requesting facts, seeking relevant information about a group concern, asking for suggestions and ideas.
3. **Information or opinion giving:** Offering facts, providing relevant information about group concern; stating a belief; giving suggestions or ideas.
4. **Clarifying or elaborating:** Interpreting or reflecting ideas and suggestions; clearing up confusions; indicating alternatives and issues before the group, giving examples.
5. **Summarising:** Pulling together related ideas, restating suggestions after group has discussed them; offering a decision or conclusion for the group to accept or reject.
6. **Consensus testing:** Sending up 'trial balloons' to see if group is nearing a conclusion; checking with group to see how much agreement has been reached.

> **Group building and maintenance functions**
>
> 1. **Encouraging:** Being friendly, warm and responsive to others, accepting others and their contributions, regarding others by giving them an opportunity for recognition.
> 2. **Expressing group feelings:** Sensing feeling, mood, relationships within the group, sharing one's own feelings with other members.
> 3. **Harmonising:** Attempting to reconcile disagreements, reducing tension through 'pouring oil on troubled waters', getting people to explore their differences.
> 4. **Compromising:** When own idea or status is involved in a conflict, offering to compromise own position, admitting error, disciplining oneself to maintain group cohesion.
> 5. **Gatekeeping:** Attempting to keep communication channels open, facilitating the participation of others; suggesting procedure for sharing opportunity to discuss group problems.
> 6. **Setting standards:** Expressing standards for group to achieve, applying standards in evaluating group functioning and production.

(Source: National Training Laboratory, Washington DC (1952).)

Use of different frameworks

Different frameworks use a different number of categories for studying behaviour in groups. The interaction analysis method can become complex, especially if non-verbal behaviour is included. Many of the categories in different frameworks may at first sight appear to be very similar.

It is important, therefore, to keep the framework simple, and easy to understand and complete. The observer's own personality, values and attitudes can influence the categorisation of behaviour. For these reasons it is preferable to use trained observers, and wherever possible and appropriate to use more than one observer for each group. The observers can then compare the level of consistency between their categorisations.

Observation sheets can be designed to suit the particular requirements of the group situation and the nature of the activity involved. An example of a reasonably simple, ten-point observation sheet used by the author is given in Fig. 7.4.

Completing the observation sheet

Where appropriate it may be helpful to note the initial seating, or standing, arrangements of the group. This will help in the identification of group members. Depending on the nature of the activity involved, it might also be possible to indicate main channels of interaction among individuals – for example to whom eye contact, hand movements, or ideas and questions are most frequently directed. A note could also be made of changes in arrangements during, and at the end of, the activity.

Headings on the observation sheet are not necessarily exclusive. For example, leadership could be included under Taking Initiative, or under Performing Group Roles. Similarly, the role of humorist could be included under Performing Group Roles, but might also appropriately be included under the heading of Harmonising.

Observers will tend to use their own methods for completing the sheet: for example, a simple stroke or tick for each contribution and perhaps a thick stroke for a particularly significant contribution. Some observers might use some other distinguishing mark to indicate non-verbal behaviour such as body movements, smiles or eye contact. The most important point, however, is that the charting should not become too complex. The observer should feel happy with the framework and be capable of explaining the entries in a meaningful way. Where more than one observer is present there should be some degree of consistency between them.

227

Nature of group						
Nature of activity						
Date Name of observer(s)						

Initial arrangement of group

	C D	
B		E
A		F

Name of group members (or reference letters)

	A	B	C	D	E	F
Taking initiative – e.g. attempted leadership, seeking suggestions, offering directions						
Brainstorming – e.g. offering ideas or suggestions, however valid						
Offering positive ideas – e.g. making helpful suggestions, attempting to problem-solve						
Drawing in others – e.g. encouraging contributions, seeking ideas and opinions						
Being responsive to others – e.g. giving encouragement and support, building on ideas						
Harmonising – e.g. acting as peacemaker, calming things down, compromising						
Challenging – e.g. seeking justification, showing disagreement in constructive way						
Being obstructive – e.g. criticising, putting others down, blocking contributions						
Clarifying/summarising – e.g. linking ideas, checking progress, clarifying objectives/proposals						
Performing group roles – e.g. spokesperson, recorder, time keeper, humorist						
Other comments						

Fig. 7.4
Observation sheet for behaviour in groups

GROUP PERFORMANCE AND EFFECTIVENESS

Groups are an essential feature in the life of the organisation. It is, however, difficult to draw any firm conclusions from a comparison between individual and group performance. An example of this can be seen from a consideration of decision-making. Certain groups, such as committees, may be concerned more specifically with decision-making, but all groups must make some decisions. Group decision-making can be costly and time-consuming, but would appear to offer a number of advantages.

- Groups can provide a pooling of resources, and can bring together a range of complementary knowledge and expertise.
- Interaction among members can have a 'snowball' effect and provoke future thoughts and ideas in the minds of others.
- Group discussion leads to the evaluation and correction of possible decisions.
- Provided full participation has been facilitated, decisions will have the acceptance of most members and they are more likely to be committed to decisions made and their implementation.

One might expect, therefore, a higher standard of decision-making to result from group discussion. However, on one hand there is the danger of compromise and decisions being made in line with the 'highest common view'; and on the other hand there is the phenomenon of the so-called risky-shift.

The risky-shift phenomenon

This suggests that instead of the group taking fewer risks and making safer or more conservative decisions, the reverse is often the case. There is a tendency for groups to make more risky decisions than would individual members of the group on their own. Studies suggest that people working in groups generally advocate more risky alternatives than if they were making an individual decision on the same problem.[13]

Presumably, this is because members do not feel the same sense of responsibility for group decisions or their outcomes. 'A decision which is everyone's is the responsibility of no one.' Other explanations offered for the risky-shift phenomenon include:

(i) people inclined to take risks are more influential in group discussions than more conservative people; and
(ii) risk-taking is regarded as a desirable cultural characteristic which is more likely to be expressed in a social situation such as group working.[14]

However, groups do appear to work well in the evaluation of ideas and to be more effective than individuals for problem-solving tasks requiring a range of knowledge and expertise. From a review of the research *Shaw* suggests that evidence supports the view that groups produce more solutions and better solutions to problems than do individuals.[15]

'Groupthink'

The effectiveness of group behaviour and performance can be adversely affected by the idea of 'groupthink'. From an examination of some well-known government policy-making groups, *Janis* concluded that decisions can be characterised by groupthink which he defines as: 'a deterioration of mental efficiency, reality testing, and moral judgment that results from in-group pressures'.[16] Groupthink

results in the propensity for the group to just drift along. For example, Britain's do-nothing policy prior to the Second World War, and in the USA the attack on Pearl Harbor, the Bay of Pigs invasion of Cuba and the escalation of the war in Vietnam were a result of groupthink.

The idea of groupthink is not, however, limited to government policy-making groups. Janis maintains that groupthink is a generalised feature and can be apparent in any organisational situation where groups are relied upon to make important decisions.

Janis identifies a number of specific symptoms of groupthink, including the following:

- There is a sense of invulnerability with excessive optimism and risk-taking. There is an unquestioned belief in the morality of the group.
- Pressures on individual members to conform and reach consensus mean that minority or unpopular ideas may be suppressed. Members who oppose the group are stereotyped as evil, weak or stupid.
- The search for group consensus can result in rationalisation by members to discount warnings and there is an illusion of unanimity. There is self-censorship of any deviation from group norms or apparent group consensus.

The effects of groupthink often occur in committees and working parties with a drifting along towards decisions which may be inappropriate or which are not questioned fully.[17]

BRAINSTORMING

A brainstorming approach involves the group adopting a 'freewheeling' attitude and generating as many ideas as possible, the more wild or apparently far-fetched the better.[18] As an illustrative exercise a group may be asked to generate as many and varied possible uses as they can for, for example, a house brick or a car fan belt.

There are a number of basic procedures for brainstorming.

- The initial emphasis is on the quantity of ideas generated, not the quality of ideas.
- No individual ideas are criticised or rejected at this stage, however wild or fanciful they may appear.
- Members are encouraged to elaborate or build on ideas expressed by others, and to bounce suggestions off one another.
- There is no comment on or evaluation of any particular idea until all ideas have been generated.

Brainstorming is based on encouraging members to suspend judgement and on the assumption that creative thinking is achieved best by encouraging the natural inclinations of group members and the free association of ideas. The quantity of ideas will lead to quality of ideas.

Effectiveness of brainstorming groups

One might reasonably expect that members of a brainstorming group would produce more creative problem-solving ideas than if the same members worked alone as individuals. Availability of time is an important factor. Over a longer period of

time the group may produce more ideas through brainstorming than individuals could.[19] Perhaps surprisingly, however, there appears to be doubt about the effectiveness of brainstorming groups over an individual working under the same conditions. Research findings suggest that brainstorming groups can inhibit creative thinking.

Taylor et al. compared 12 groups of four people who were participating together, with 12 'groups' of four people working separately. Performance was measured in terms of the number of alternative solutions to a series of given problems generated through 'brainstorming' over a given period of time. In each case the group with people working on their own produced more solutions and generally ones of a higher quality.[20]

In another study, by *Maginn and Harris*, 152 students were divided into groups of four and asked to brainstorm two problems. Some of the groups were informed that their ideas would be evaluated for originality and quality, and that they would be observed by judges, either from behind a one-way mirror or by tape recording. Other groups were told that although they would be listened to, their ideas would not be subject to evaluation.[21]

Although it was predicted that the groups facing evaluation would perform less well, the findings indicated that the performances of both sets of groups were similar. Maginn and Harris concluded that individual members put less effort into a task when responsibility for the outcome is shared with other members of the group. Unless this feeling of diminished responsibility can be overcome, individual brainstorming, although lonelier, is better.

The general tenor appears to be that research studies have not substantiated claims that brainstorming groups generate more and better ideas than the same number of individuals working on their own.[22]

Structured techniques for innovation

Despite the rather negative view of nominal group brainstorming, we should recognise the importance of innovation for successful organisational performance.[23] Any procedure which aids the process of creativity should be welcomed and there are a number of potential positive achievements in terms of related structural techniques for stimulating innovation. These include the Delphi technique and quality circles.

The **Delphi technique** is based on multiple, anonymous inputs from individual members of the group. Ideas and suggestions are recorded by a central manager and then recirculated to other members for their feedback. The central manager collates the responses and continues the circulation process again until consensus is reached. Although a time-consuming process the Delphi technique helps to overcome the limitations of face-to-face brainstorming and symptoms of groupthink.

Quality circles are discussed in Chapter 15.

VARIETY OF INTERRELATED FACTORS

Whatever the results of a comparison between individual and group performance, groups will always form part of the pattern of work organisation. It is a matter of judgement for the manager as to when, and how best, to use groups in the execution of work.

Any framework for viewing the performance and effectiveness of groups must take into account a variety of interrelated factors. These include:

- the composition, cohesiveness and maturity of the group;
- its structure, the clarification of role differentiation and channels of communication;
- patterns of interaction and group process, and attention to both task and maintenance functions;
- the work to be undertaken and the nature of the technology;
- management system and style of leadership;
- organisational processes and procedures;
- the social system of the group and the informal organisation; and
- the environment in which the group is operating.

These are the factors that the manager must attempt to influence in order to improve the effectiveness of the group. Ultimately, however, the performance of the group will be determined very largely by the characteristics and behaviour of its members. The nature of group personality means that what works well for one group may not work well for an apparently very similar group in the organisation.

GROUP DYNAMICS

Interest in the study of group process and behaviour has led to the development of group dynamics and a range of group training methods aimed at increasing group effectiveness through improving social interaction skills.

Group dynamics is the study of interactions and forces within small face-to-face groups. It is concerned with what happens when groups of people meet.

A central feature of group dynamics is **sensitivity training**, in which members of a group direct attention to the understanding of their own behaviour and to perceiving themselves as others see them. The objectives are usually stated as:

- to increase sensitivity (the ability to perceive accurately how others react to one-self);
- diagnostic ability (the skill of assessing behavioural relationships between others and reasons for such behaviour); and
- behavioural flexibility, or action skill (the ability to relate one's behaviour to the requirements of the situation).

T-GROUPS

A usual method of sensitivity training (which is increasingly used as a generic term) is the **T-group** (training group), sometimes called laboratory training.

A T-group has been defined as: 'an approach to human relations training which, broadly speaking, provides participants with an opportunity to learn more about themselves and their impact on others, and in particular to learn how to function more effectively in face-to-face situations'.[24]

The original form of a T-group is a small, leaderless, unstructured, face-to-face grouping. The group normally numbers between 8 and 12 members who may be strangers to each other or who may come from the same organisation (a family group). A deliberate attempt is made to minimise any status differentials among members. There is no agenda or planned activities. Trainers are present to help guide the group, but do not usually take an active role or act as formal leader. The agenda becomes the group's own behaviour in attempting to cope with the lack of structure or planned activities. Training is intended to concentrate on process rather than content, that is on the feeling level of communication rather than the informational value of communication.

Faced with confusion and lack of direction, individuals will act in characteristic ways. With the guidance of the trainers these patterns of behaviour become the focus of attention for the group. Participants are encouraged to examine their own self-concepts and to be more receptive to the feelings and behaviours of others. Feedback received by individuals from other members of the group is the main mechanism for learning.

This feedback creates a feeling of anxiety and tension, and the individual's own self-examination leads to consideration of new values, attitudes and behaviour. Typically, the group meets for a 1½-to-2-hour session each day for up to a fortnight. The sessions are supported by related lectures, study groups, case studies and other exercises.

The Johari window

A simple framework for looking at self-insight, which is used frequently to help individuals in the T-group process, is the 'Johari window' (Fig. 7.5). This classifies behaviour in matrix form between: what is known–unknown to self; and what is known–unknown to others.[25]

A central feature of the T-group is reduction of the individual's 'hidden' behaviour through self-disclosure and reduction of the 'blind' behaviour through feedback from others.

Hidden behaviour is that which the individual wishes to conceal from, or not to communicate to, other group members. It is part of the private self. An important role of the group is to establish whether members conceal too much, or too little, about themselves from other members.

The blind area includes mannerisms, gestures, and tone of voice, and represents behaviour of the impact of which on others the individual is unaware. This is sometimes referred to as the 'bad breath' area.

The group must establish an atmosphere of openness and trust in order that hidden and blind behaviours are reduced and the public behaviour enhanced.

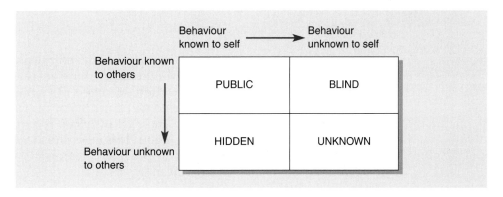

**Fig. 7.5
The Johari
window**

Value and effectiveness of T-groups

Reactions to the value and effectiveness of T-group training are very mixed. Specific benefits and changes in behaviour from T-group training are listed by *Mangham and Cooper* as:

Receiving Communications: more effort to understand, attentive listening
Relational Facility: co-operative, easier to deal with
Awareness of Human Behaviour: more analytic of others' actions, clear perceptions of people
Sensitivity to Group Behaviour: more conscious of group process
Sensitivity to Others' Feelings: sensitivity to the needs and feelings of others
Acceptance of Other People: more tolerant, considerate, patient
Tolerant of New Information: willing to accept suggestions, less dogmatic[26]

However, the experience can be very disturbing and unpleasant, at least for some members. For example, participants have described it as 'a bloodbath and a psychological nudist colony in which people are stripped bare to their attitudes'.[27]

Participants are required to lay bare their inner emotions and may feel an invasion of their privacy. The unstructured situation may permit trainers to impose their own perceptions and social viewpoints on members of the group.[28]

T-group training is difficult to evaluate objectively and there is still a main problem of the extent to which training is transferred 'back home' to practical work situations. However, a number of studies do suggest that participation as a member of a T-group does increase interpersonal skills, induce change, and lead to open communications and more flexible behaviour.[29]

T-groups probably do result in a change of behaviour but it is not always clear whether such change is positive or related to improved organisational performance.[30]

T-groups now take a number of different forms. Some place emphasis on the understanding of group processes, others place more emphasis on the development of the individual's self-awareness and feelings towards the behaviour of other people. They are now used frequently as a means of attempting to improve managerial development and organisational performance.

The *Blake and Mouton* managerial grid seminars, discussed in Chapter 13, can be seen as an applied, and refined, form of T-group. A number of different training packages have been designed, often under the broad heading of interpersonal skills, which are less confrontational and less disturbing for participants. The training often involves an analysis of group members' relationships with one another and the resolution of conflict.[31]

SYNOPSIS

■ Group performance and the satisfaction derived by individuals are influenced by the interactions among members of the group. If groups are to be successful there must be a spirit of unity and co-operation. Members of a group must work well together as a team. The level of interaction is influenced by the channels of communication (communication networks). There are five main types of communication networks – wheel, circle, all-channel, Y and chains. Despite the artificiality of communication network studies, they do provide a reasonable representation of situations that might apply in large organisations.

■ In order to understand and to influence the functioning and operation of a group, it is necessary to study the behaviour of individual members. Two main methods are (i) sociometry, and (ii) interaction analysis. Sociometry is usually based on 'buddy rating' or 'peer rating'. It is a method of indicating feelings of acceptance and/or rejection among members of a group. A sociogram gives a diagrammatical illustration of the pattern of interpersonal relationships derived from sociometry.

■ Interaction analysis is based on the assumption that behaviour in groups may be analysed from the viewpoint of its function or process. Two essential functions necessary for the success and continuity of a group are: (i) task-oriented behaviour; and (ii) maintenance-oriented behaviour. In addition, members of a group may display self-oriented behaviour. Several frameworks have been designed for observers to categorise patterns of verbal and non-verbal behaviour of group members. It is important, however, that the frameworks do not become too complex.

■ Groups are an essential feature in the life of the organisation. It is, however, difficult to draw firm conclusions from a comparison between individual and group performance. Group decision-making would appear to offer a number of advantages, but can be adversely affected by 'groupthink' and by the 'risky-shift' phenomenon. There also appears to be some doubt about the effectiveness of brainstorming groups over an individual working under the same conditions. Viewing the performance and effectiveness of groups must take into account a variety of interrelated factors, especially the characteristics and behaviour of their members.

■ Interest in the study of group process and behaviour has led to the development of group dynamics and a range of group training methods aimed at improving social interaction skills. A usual method is the T-group. This approach provides participants with an opportunity to learn more about themselves and their impact on others. Reactions to the value and effectiveness of T-group training is mixed. There are a number of potential benefits but some participants can find the experience disturbing and unpleasant.

? Review and discussion questions

1 Contrast different types of communication networks in small groups. Give examples of a situation in which each type of network is likely to be most appropriate.

2 What methods are available for analysing the behaviour of individuals in group situations? Assess the practical value to the manager of the analysis of group behaviour.

3 Explain what you understand by sociometry. How would you go about constructing a sociogram?

4 Distinguish between: (i) group task roles; (ii) group building and maintenance roles; and (iii) individual roles. Give examples of each of these types of group member roles.

5 Suggest a framework for the categorisation of patterns of behaviour in group situations. What considerations need to be kept in mind when using such frameworks?

6 Explain what is meant by: (i) 'groupthink'; (ii) the risky-shift phenomenon; and (iii) brainstorming. Assess the likely standard of individual, compared with group, problem-solving and decision-making.

7 Explain the meaning and purpose of sensitivity training. Give your views on the practical value of group dynamics as a means of increasing the effectiveness of work groups.

8 In what ways might a manager expect to benefit from an understanding of the behaviour of people in work groups? Give practical examples relating to your own experience.

 ## Assignment 1

Attempt, *preferably*, to observe a small group or project team at work; *alternatively*, next time you are involved in a small group discussion observe the members of your group.

(i) (a) Explain the nature of the **content** of the group's discussion and contrast this with the **process** of the discussion.
 (b) Complete the following grid by giving a tick in the appropriate box to denote the behaviour of individual members in terms of:
 • group task roles;
 • group building and maintenance roles;
 • individual roles.

Names of group members (or reference numbers)

								Totals
Group task roles								
Group building/ maintenance roles								
Individual roles								
Totals								

(ii) Explain the conclusions you draw concerning the conduct and apparent effectiveness of the group.

(iii) Depict the **communication network(s)** adopted by the group and comment on its apparent effectiveness.

 Assignment 2

A SELF-PERCEPTION INVENTORY

This inventory was developed from a number of earlier versions which had been designed to give Henley members a simple means of assessing their best team-roles. DIRECTIONS: For each section distribute a total of ten points among the sentences which you think best describe your behaviour. These points may be distributed among several sentences: in extreme cases they might be spread among all the sentences or ten points may be given to a single sentence. Enter the points in Table 1 on page 239.

I. What I believe I can contribute to a team:
 (a) I think I can quickly see and take advantage of new opportunities.
 (b) I can work well with a very wide range of people.
 (c) Producing ideas is one of my natural assets.
 (d) My ability rests in being able to draw people out whenever I detect they have something of value to contribute to group objectives.
 (e) My capacity to follow through has much to do with my personal effectiveness.
 (f) I am ready to face temporary unpopularity if it leads to worthwhile results in the end.
 (g) I can usually sense what is realistic and likely to work.
 (h) I can offer a reasoned case for alternative courses of action without introducing bias or prejudice.

II. If I have a possible shortcoming in teamwork, it could be that:
 (a) I am not at ease unless meetings are well-structured and controlled and generally well-conducted.
 (b) I am inclined to be too generous towards others who have a valid viewpoint that has not been given a proper airing.
 (c) I have a tendency to talk too much once the group gets on to new ideas.
 (d) My objective outlook makes it difficult for me to join in readily and enthusiastically with colleagues.
 (e) I am sometimes seen as forceful and authoritarian if there is a need to get something done.
 (f) I find it difficult to lead from the front, perhaps because I am overresponsive to group atmosphere.
 (g) I am apt to get too caught up in ideas that occur to me and so lose track of what is happening.
 (h) My colleagues tend to see me as worrying unnecessarily over detail and the possibility that things may go wrong.

III. When involved in a project with other people:
 (a) I have an aptitude for influencing people without pressurising them.
 (b) My general vigilance prevents careless mistakes and omissions being made.
 (c) I am ready to press for action to make sure that the meeting does not waste time or lose sight of the main objective.
 (d) I can be counted on to contribute something original.
 (e) I am always ready to back a good suggestion in the common interest.

(f) I am keen to look for the latest in new ideas and developments.

(g) I believe my capacity for judgement can help to bring about the right decisions.

(h) I can be relied upon to see that all essential work is organised.

IV. My characteristic approach to group work is that:

(a) I have a quiet interest in getting to know colleagues better.

(b) I am not reluctant to challenge the views of others or to hold a minority view myself.

(c) I can usually find a line of argument to refute unsound propositions.

(d) I think I have a talent for making things work once a plan has to be put into operation.

(e) I have a tendency to avoid the obvious and to come out with the unexpected.

(f) I bring a touch of perfectionism to any job I undertake.

(g) I am ready to make use of contacts outside the group itself.

(h) While I am interested in all views I have no hesitation in making up my mind once a decision has to be made.

V. I gain satisfaction in a job because:

(a) I enjoy analysing situations and weighing up all the possible choices.

(b) I am interested in finding practical solutions to problems.

(c) I like to feel I am fostering good working relationships.

(d) I can have a strong influence on decisions.

(e) I can meet people who may have something new to offer.

(f) I can get people to agree on a necessary course of action.

(g) I feel in my element where I can give a task my full attention.

(h) I like to find a field that stretches my imagination.

VI. If I am suddenly given a difficult task with limited time and unfamiliar people:

(a) I would feel like retiring to a corner to devise a way out of the impasse before developing a line.

(b) I would be ready to work with the person who showed the most positive approach.

(c) I would find some way of reducing the size of the task by establishing what different individuals might best contribute.

(d) My natural sense of urgency would help to ensure that we did not fall behind schedule.

(e) I believe I would keep cool and maintain my capacity to think straight.

(f) I would retain a steadiness of purpose in spite of the pressures.

(g) I would be prepared to take a positive lead if I felt the group was making no progress.

(h) I would open up discussions with a view to stimulating new thoughts and getting something moving.

VII. With reference to the problems to which I am subject in working in groups:

(a) I am apt to show my impatience with those who are obstructing progress.

(b) Others may criticise me for being too analytical and insufficiently intuitive.

(c) My desire to ensure that work is properly done can hold up proceedings.

(d) I tend to get bored rather easily and rely on one or two stimulating members to spark me off.

(e) I find it difficult to get started unless the goals are clear.

(f) I am sometimes poor at explaining and clarifying complex points that occur to me.

(g) I am conscious of demanding from others the things I cannot do myself.

(h) I hesitate to get my points across when I run up against real opposition.

Table 1 Points table for self-perception inventory

SECTION	ITEM a	b	c	d	e	f	g	h
I								
II								
III								
IV								
V								
VI								
VII								

To interpret the self-perception inventory you should look at the Analysis provided by your tutor.

(Reprinted with permission from Belbin, R. M., Management Teams: Why They Succeed or Fail, Butterworth-Heinemann (1981) pp. 153–6.)

 ## Assignment 3

WILDERNESS SURVIVAL: A CONSENSUS-SEEKING TASK

Here are 12 questions concerning personal survival in a wilderness situation. Your first task is *individually* to select the best of the three alternatives given under each item. Try to imagine yourself in the situation depicted. Assume that you are alone and have a minimum of equipment except where specified. The season is autumn. The days are warm and dry, but the nights are cold.

After you have completed this task individually, you will again consider each question as a member of a small group. Your group will have the task of deciding, *by consensus*, the best alternative for each question. Do not change your individual answers, even if you change your mind in the group discussion. Both the individual and group solutions will later be compared with the 'correct' answers provided by a group of naturalists who conduct classes in woodland survival.

	Your Answer	Your Group's Answer

1. You have strayed from your party in trackless timber. You have no special signalling equipment. The best way to attempt to contact your friends is to:
 a. call 'help' loudly but in a low register.
 b. yell or scream as loud as you can.
 c. whistle loudly and shrilly.

2. You are in 'snake country'. Your best action to avoid snakes is to:
 a. make a lot of noise with your feet.
 b. walk softly and quietly.
 c. travel at night.

3. You are hungry and lost in wild country. The best rule for determining which plants are safe to eat (those you do not recognise) is to:
 a. try anything you see the birds eat.
 b. eat anything except plants with bright red berries.
 c. put a bit of the plant on your lower lip for five minutes; if it seems all right, try a little.

4. The day becomes hot and dry. You have a full canteen of water (about one litre) with you. You should:
 a. ration it – about a cupful a day.
 b. not drink until you stop for the night, then drink what you think you need.
 c. drink as much as you think you need when you need it.

5. Your water is gone; you become very thirsty. You finally come to a dried-up watercourse. Your best chance of finding water is to:
 a. dig anywhere in the stream bed.
 b. dig up plant and tree roots near the bank.
 c. dig in the stream bed at the outside of a bend.

6. You decide to walk out of the wild country by following a series of ravines where a water supply is available. Night is coming on. The best place to make camp is:
 a. next to the water supply in the ravine.
 b. high on a ridge.
 c. midway up the slope.

7. Your flashlight glows dimly as you are about to make your way back to your campsite after a brief foraging trip. Darkness comes quickly in the woods and the surroundings seem unfamiliar. You should:
 a. head back at once, keeping the light on, hoping the light will glow enough for you to make out landmarks.
 b. put the batteries under your armpits to warm them, and then replace them in the flashlight.
 c. shine your torch for a few seconds, try to get the scene in mind, move out in the darkness, and repeat the process.

8. An early snow confines you to your small tent. You doze with your small stove going. There is danger if the flame is:
 a. yellow.
 b. blue.
 c. red.

9. You must ford a river that has a strong current, large rocks, and some white water. After carefully selecting your crossing spot, you should:
 a. leave your boots and pack on.
 b. take your boots and pack off.
 c. take off your pack, but leave your boots on.

10. In waist-deep water with a strong current, when crossing the stream, you should face:
 a. upstream.
 b. across the stream.
 c. downstream.

11. You find yourself rimrocked; your only route is up. The way is mossy, slippery rock. You should try it:
 a. barefoot.
 b. with boots on.
 c. in stocking feet.

12. Unarmed and unsuspecting, you surprise a large bear prowling around your campsite. As the bear rears up about ten metres from you, you should:
 a. run.
 b. climb the nearest tree.
 c. freeze, but be ready to back away slowly.

WILDERNESS SURVIVAL GROUP BRIEFING SHEET

Decision by consensus is a method of problem-solving and decision-making in groups in which all the parties involved actively discuss the issues surrounding the decision. The group thus pools the knowledge and experience of all its members. Any final decision must be supported by each member of the group. The ideas and feelings of all the members are integrated into a group decision, thus allowing several people to work together on a common problem, rather than producing a 'we–they' stand-off.

As you might imagine, decision by consensus is usually difficult to attain and will consume more time than other methods of deciding an issue. As the energies of the group become focused on the problem at hand (rather than on defending individual points of view), the quality of the decision tends to be enhanced. Research indicates, in fact, that this approach to problem-solving and decision-making results in a significantly higher-quality decision than other methods such as the use of majority power (voting), minority power (persuasion), and compromise.

In the decision-by-consensus process, each group member is asked to:

1. prepare his/her own position as well as possible prior to meeting with the group (but to realise that the task is incomplete and that the missing pieces are to be supplied by the other members of the group);
2. recognise an obligation to express his/her own opinion and explain it fully, so that the rest of the group has the benefit of all members' thinking;
3. recognise an obligation to listen to the opinions and feelings of all other group members and be ready to modify his/her own position on the basis of logic and understanding;
4. avoid conflict-reducing techniques such as voting, compromising, or giving in to keep the peace; to realise that differences of opinion are helpful; in exploring differences, the best course of action will make itself apparent.

You have just completed an individual solution to Wilderness Survival: A Consensus-Seeking Task. Now your small task group will decide on a group solution to the same dilemmas. Remember, decision by consensus is difficult to attain, and not every decision may meet with everyone's unqualified approval. There should be, however, a general feeling of support from all members before a group decision is made. Take the time you need to listen for understanding, consider *all* members' views, make your own view known, and be reasonable in arriving at a group decision.

Notes and references

1. See, for example: Allcorn, S. 'Understanding Groups at Work', *Personnel,* vol. 66, no. 8, August 1989, pp. 28–36.
2. Belbin, R. M. *Management Teams: Why They Succeed or Fail*, Butterworth–Heinemann (1981).
3. Belbin, R. M. *Team Roles at Work*, Butterworth-Heinemann (1993).
4. Bavelas, A. 'A Mathematical Model for Group Structures', *Applied Anthropology*, vol. 7, 1948, pp. 19–30, and Bavelas, A. 'Communication Patterns in Task-Oriented Groups', in Lasswell, H. N. and Lerner, D. (eds) *The Policy Sciences*, Stanford University Press (1951).
5. Leavitt, H. J. 'Some Effects of Certain Communication Patterns on Group Performance', *Journal of Abnormal and Social Psychology*, vol. 46, 1951, pp. 38–50. See also: Leavitt, H. J. *Managerial Psychology*, Fourth edition, University of Chicago Press (1978).
6. Guetzkow, H. and Dill, W. R. 'Factors in the Organizational Development of Task-Oriented Groups', *Sociometry,* vol. 20, 1957, pp. 175–204.
7. Shaw, M. E. 'Communication Networks', in Berkowitz, L. (ed.) *Advances in Experimental Social Psychology*, vol. 1, Academic Press (1964).
8. Moreno, J. L. *Who Shall Survive?* Beacon House (1953). See also: Moreno, J. L. and Jennings, H. H. *The Sociometry Reader*, Free Press of Glencoe (1960).
9. Rogers, E. M. and Kincaid, D. L. *Communication Networks: Towards a New Paradigm for Research*, The Free Press (1981) p. 92.
10. Bales, R. F. 'A Set of Categories for the Analysis of Small Group Interaction', *American Sociological Review*, vol. 15, April 1950, pp. 257–63.
11. Bales, R. F. *Personality and Interpersonal Behaviour*, Holt, Rinehart and Winston (1970).
12. Benne, K. D. and Sheats, P. 'Functional Roles of Group Members', *Journal of Social Issues*, vol. 4, 1948, pp. 41–9.
13. Kogan, N. and Wallach, M. A. 'Risk-Taking as a Function of the Situation, the Person and the Group', in Newcomb, T. M. (ed.) *New Directions in Psychology III*, Holt, Rinehart and Winston (1967).
14. For a comprehensive review of the 'risky-shift' phenomenon, see, for example: Clarke, R. D. 'Group Induced Shift Towards Risk: A Critical Appraisal', *Psychological Bulletin*, vol. 76, 1971, pp. 251–70.
15. Shaw, M. E. *Group Dynamics*, McGraw-Hill (1976).
16. Janis, J. L. *Victims of Groupthink*, Houghton Mifflin (1972) and Janis, J. L. *Groupthink*, Second edition, Houghton Mifflin (1982).
17. See, for example, Leana, C. R. 'A Partial Test of Janis' Groupthink Model: Effects of Group Cohesiveness and Leader Behavior on Defective Decision Making', *Journal of Management*, vol. 11, no. 1, 1985, pp. 5–17.
18. Osborn, A. F. *Applied Imagination Principles and Procedures of Creative Thinking*, Scribner's (1963).
19. Shaw, M. E. *Group Dynamics*, McGraw-Hill (1976).
20. Taylor, D. W., Berry, P. C. and Block, C. H. 'Does Group Participation when Using Brainstorming Facilitate or Inhibit Creative Thinking?' *Administrative Science Quarterly*, vol. 3, no. 1, June 1958, pp. 23–47. See also: Dunnette, M. D., Campbell, J. and Jaastad, K. 'The Effect of Group Participation on Brainstorming Effectiveness for Two Industrial Samples', *Journal of Applied Psychology*, vol. 47, 1963, pp. 30–7.
21. Maginn, B. K. and Harris, R. J. 'Effects of Anticipated Evaluation on Individual Brainstorming Performance', *Journal of Applied Psychology*, vol. 65, no. 2, 1980, pp. 219–25.
22. Diehl, M. and Strobe, W. 'Productivity Loss in Brainstorming Groups: Towards the Solution of the Riddle', *Journal of Personality and Social Psychology*, vol. 53, 1987, pp. 497–509.
23. See, for example: Waterman, R. *The Frontiers of Excellence*, Nicholas Brealey (1994).
24. Cooper, C. L. and Mangham, I. L. (eds) *T-Groups: A Survey of Research*, Wiley (1971) p. v.

25. Luft, J. *Group Processes: An Introduction to Group Dynamics*, Second edition, National Press (1970). (The term 'Johari Window' was derived from a combination of the first names of the original authors, Joseph Luft and Harry Ingham.)

26. Mangham, I. and Cooper, C. L. 'The Impact of T-Groups on Managerial Behaviour', *Journal of Management Studies*, February 1969, vol. 6, no. 1, p. 57.

27. Davis, K. *Human Behavior at Work*, Fifth edition, McGraw-Hill (1977) p. 183.

28. Davis, K. and Newstrom, J.W. *Human Behavior at Work: Organizational Behavior*, Eighth edition, McGraw-Hill (1989).

29. See, for example: Campbell, J. P. and Dunnette, M. D. 'Effectiveness of T-group Experiences in Managerial Training and Development', *Psychological Bulletin*, vol. 70, no. 2, 1968, pp. 73–103.

30. See, for example: McKenna, E. *Business Psychology and Organisational Behaviour*, Lawrence Erlbaum (1994).

31. For an overview of experimental small group methods and training needs, see, for example: Smith, P. B. *Group Processes and Personal Change*, Harper and Row (1980). See also: Brown, R. *Group Processes: Dynamics Within and Between Groups*, Basil Blackwell (1988).

8 THE NATURE OF LEADERSHIP

The organisation is made up of groups of people. An essential part of management is co-ordinating the activities of groups and directing the efforts of their members towards the goals and objectives of the organisation. This involves the process of leadership and the choice of an appropriate form of behaviour. The manager must understand the nature of leadership and factors which determine the effectiveness of the leadership relationship.[1]

 Learning objectives

To:

- Explain the meaning and importance of leadership in work organisations;

- Recognise the nature of the leadership relationship, and the exercise of power;

- Detail patterns of managerial leadership and main studies of leadership;

- Identify the functions and responsibilities of leadership;

- Examine leadership as an aspect of behaviour, and different styles of leadership;

- Assess contingency theories of leadership and situational factors which determine the characteristics of leadership;

- Appreciate the variables which determine effective managerial leadership.

Worth thinking about

Despite the vast amount of writing on the subject, it is extremely difficult to give a precise and agreed definition of leadership. Nor is there one best model or style of leadership. If leading writers cannot agree on the nature or essential characteristics of leadership how we can we ever be certain about what makes for an effective leader?

THE MEANING OF LEADERSHIP

There are many ways of looking at leadership and many interpretations of its meaning. Leadership might be interpreted in simple terms, such as 'getting others to follow' or 'getting people to do things willingly', or interpreted more specifically, for example as 'the use of authority in decision-making'. It may be exercised as an attribute of position, or because of personal knowledge or wisdom. Leadership might be based on a function of personality, or it can be seen as a behavioural category. It may also be viewed in terms of the role of the leaders and their ability to achieve effective performance from others. According to *Sir Peter Parker*, for example:

> Nothing in business circles brings such a rush of clichés to the head as leadership, one of those humpty-dumpty words which, as Alice said, mean whatever we want them to mean ... Leadership is one of those elusive priorities, an area in which there is no absolute, no guaranteed model. So it turns out to be not only vital but also fun to talk about what makes a leader.[2]

It is difficult, therefore, to generalise about leadership, but essentially it is **a relationship through which one person influences the behaviour or actions of other people**. This means that the process of leadership cannot be separated from the activities of groups and with effective teambuilding.

The importance of leadership

Leadership is related to motivation, interpersonal behaviour and the process of communication.[3] Good leadership also involves the effective process of delegation. The leadership relationship is not limited to leader behaviour resulting in subordinate behaviour. Leadership is a dynamic process. The leader–follower relationship is reciprocal and effective leadership is a two-way process which influences both individual and organisational performance.

Lord Sieff, for example, maintains that

> Leadership is vitally important at all levels within the company, from main board to the shopfloor. Leadership is the moral and intellectual ability to visualise and work for what is best for the company and its employees ... The most vital thing the leader does is to create team spirit around him and near him, not in a schoolboy sense, but in realistic terms of mature adults ... To be effective leadership has to be seen, and it is best seen in action.[4]

Good management leadership helps to develop teamwork and the integration of individual and group goals. It aids intrinsic motivation by emphasising the importance of the work that people do.[5]

The changing nature of business organisations, including flatter structures and recognition of the efficient use of human resources, coupled with advances in social democracy, have combined to place growing importance on leadership. The nature of management is moving away from an emphasis on getting results by the close control of the workforce and towards an environment of coaching, support and empowerment.[6]

LEADERSHIP AND MANAGEMENT

What is the relationship between leadership and management? Sometimes management and leadership are seen as synonymous. There is, however, a difference between the two and it does not follow that every leader is a manager.

Management is more usually viewed as getting things done through other people in order to achieve stated organisational objectives. The manager may react to specific situations and be more concerned with solving short-term problems. Management is regarded as relating to people working within a structured organisation and with prescribed roles. To people outside of the organisation the manager might not necessarily be seen in a leadership role.

The emphasis of leadership is on interpersonal behaviour in a broader context. It is often associated with the willing and enthusiastic behaviour of followers. **Leadership does not necessarily take place within the hierarchical structure of the organisation**. Many people operate as leaders without their role ever being clearly established or defined. A leader often has sufficient influence to bring about longer-term changes in people's attitudes and to make change more acceptable. Leadership can be seen primarily as an inspirational process.[7]

Differences in attitudes and relations with others

There are other differences between leadership and management. For example, *Zaleznik* explores difference in attitudes towards goals, conceptions of work, relations with others, self-perception and development.

- Managers tend to adopt impersonal or passive attitudes towards goals. Leaders adopt a more personal and active attitude towards goals.
- In order to get people to accept solutions, the manager needs continually to co-ordinate and balance in order to compromise conflicting values. The leader creates excitement in work and develops choices that give substance to images that excite people.
- In their relationships with other people, managers maintain a low level of emotional involvement. Leaders have empathy with other people and give attention to what events and actions mean.
- Managers see themselves more as conservators and regulators of the existing order of affairs with which they identify, and from which they gain rewards. Leaders work in, but do not belong to, the organisation. Their sense of identity does not depend upon membership or work roles and they search out opportunities for change.[8]

Management may arguably be viewed more in terms of planning, organising, directing and controlling the activities of subordinate staff. Leadership, however, is concerned more with attention to communicating with, motivating, encouraging and involving people.[9]

The 7-S organisational framework

The differences between leadership and management have been applied by *Watson* to the 7-S organisational framework of: strategy, structure, systems, style, staff, skills and superordinate (or shared) goals. Watson suggests that whereas managers tend towards reliance on

- strategy,
- structure, and
- systems,

leaders have an inherent inclination for utilisation of the 'soft' Ss of

- style,
- staff,
- skills, and
- shared goals.

Watson also suggests, although cautiously, that 7-S management could be seen as the province of leaders. Managers will not ordinarily be capable of achieving sufficient mastery of all seven factors to attain a consistently high level of organisational performance.[10]

MANAGERIAL LEADERSHIP

Despite the differences, there is a close relationship between leadership and management in work organisations, and it is not easy to separate them as distinct activities. Many methods of management training can also be used as a means of measuring leadership style. For example, the Leadership Grid (discussed in Chapter 13) was until recently known as the Managerial Grid.

To be an effective manager it is necessary to exercise the role of leadership. A common view is that the job of the manager requires the ability of leadership and that leadership is in effect a sub-set of management, although leadership is a special attribute which can be distinguished from other elements of management.

Being an effective manager involves the successful management of people. Chris Bonington, for example, suggests that the same basic skills of leadership which enabled his successful expedition to climb Everest can be learned and practised in business. There is a similarity between the leadership skills required on Everest and the same skills required by team leaders in management.[11]

Symbolic leadership

The movement away from managers relying solely on their positional power within a hierarchical structure of authority has placed greater emphasis on leadership and organisational culture, including attention to the symbols of leadership. In order to convey clearly the meaning intended, effective leadership involves managing through the skilful use of symbols – including, for example, form of communication and use of language, ceremonies, images and rituals, and physical environment.[12]

Symbolism is an important means by which managers communicate corporate intent and cultural messages. According to *Peters*, for example, in attempting to act out the vision of the organisation and to achieve their goals, managers deal in a number of different symbols.[13] *Brown* identifies the most interesting of these symbolic means as: how top executives spend their time; their use of language; their use of meetings, agendas and minutes; and their use of settings.[14]

THE LEADERSHIP RELATIONSHIP

A leader may be imposed, formally appointed or elected, chosen informally, or emerge naturally through the demands of the situation or the wishes of the group. Leadership may be attempted, successful or effective.[15]

- **Attempted leadership** is when any individual in the group attempts to exert influence over other members of the group.
- **Successful leadership** is when the influence brings about the behaviour and results that were intended by the leader.
- **Effective leadership** is when successful leadership results in functional behaviour and the achievement of group goals.

The leader may exercise authority as an attribute of position. In this case the manager is seen as a leader because of a stated position in the hierarchy. Leadership, however, is more than just adherence to a formal role prescription. It is more than eliciting mechanical behaviour which results from a superior–subordinate relationship in a hierarchical structure.

Remember that you can be appointed a manager but you are not a leader until your appointment is ratified in the hearts and minds of those who work for you.[16]

Sapiential authority or charisma

Leadership may be exercised on the basis of sapiential authority – that is, by wisdom, personal knowledge, reputation or expertise. A sapiential-type relationship places emphasis on a guiding and facilitating role and is often appropriate for people in creative, specialist or professional jobs where there may be particular resentment against a formal hierarchical style of managerial leadership.

Leadership may also be based on the personal qualities, or charisma, of the leader and the manner in which authority is exercised. This view of leadership gives rise to the question of 'born' or 'natural' leaders. Leadership may also focus on the role of the leader in terms of the relationship with followers and the adoption of a particular style of leadership.

A dynamic form of behaviour

Leadership is, therefore, a dynamic form of behaviour and there are a number of variables which affect the leadership relationship. Four major variables are identified by *McGregor* as:

- the characteristics of the leader;
- the attitude, needs and other personal characteristics of the followers;
- the nature of the organisation, such as its purpose, its structure, the tasks to be performed; and
- the social, economic and political environment.

McGregor concludes that 'leadership is not a property of the individual, but a complex relationship among these variables'.[17]

POWER AND LEADERSHIP INFLUENCE

Within an organisation, leadership influence will be dependent upon the type of power that the leader can exercise over the followers. The exercise of power is a social process which helps to explain how different people can influence the behaviour/actions of others. Five main sources of power upon which the influence of the leader is based have been identified by *French and Raven* as reward power, coercive power, legitimate power, referent power, and expert power.[18] We shall consider these in terms of the manager (as a leader) and subordinate relationship.

- **Reward power** is based on the subordinate's *perception* that the leader has the ability and resources to obtain rewards for those who comply with directives; for example, pay, promotion, praise, recognition, increased responsibilities, allocation and arrangement of work, granting of privileges.
- **Coercive power** is based on fear and the subordinate's *perception* that the leader has the ability to punish or to bring about undesirable outcomes for those who do not comply with directives; for example, withholding pay rises, promotion or privileges; allocation of undesirable duties or responsibilities; withdrawal of friendship or support; formal reprimands or possibly dismissal. This is in effect the opposite of reward power.
- **Legitimate power** is based on the subordinate's *perception* that the leader has a right to exercise influence because of the leader's role or position in the organisation. Legitimate power is based on authority, for example that of managers and supervisors within the hierarchical structure of an organisation. Legitimate power is therefore 'position' power because it is based on the role of the leader in the organisation, and not on the nature of the personal relationship with others.
- **Referent power** is based on the subordinate's *identification* with the leader. The leader exercises influence because of perceived attractiveness, personal characteristics, reputation or what is called 'charisma'. For example, a particular manager may not be in a position to reward or punish certain subordinates, but may still exercise power over the subordinates because the manager commands their respect or esteem.
- **Expert power** is based on the subordinate's *perception* of the leader as someone who is competent and who has some special knowledge or expertise in a given area. Expert power is based on credibility and clear evidence of knowledge or expertise; for example, the expert knowledge of 'functional' specialists such as the personnel manager, management accountant or systems analyst. The expert power is usually limited to narrow, well-defined areas or specialisms.

Subordinates' perception of influence

These sources of power are based on the subordinate's *perception* of the influence of the leader, whether it is real or not. For example, if a leader has the ability to control rewards and punishments but subordinates *do not believe this*, then in effect the leader has no reward or coercive power. Similarly, if subordinates in a line department *believe* a manager in a (different) staff department has executive authority over them then even if that manager has no such authority there is still a *perceived* legitimate power.

French and Raven point out that the five sources of power are interrelated and the use of one type of power (for example, coercive) may affect the ability to use another type of power (for example, referent). Also the same person may exercise different types of power, in particular circumstances and at different times.

> You have to look at leadership through the eyes of the followers and you have to live the message. What I have learned is that people become motivated when you guide them to the source of their own power and when you make heroes out of employees who personify what you want to see in the organization.
>
> *Anita Roddick*[19]

APPROACHES TO LEADERSHIP

Due to its complex and variable nature there are many ways of analysing leadership. It is helpful, therefore, to have some framework in which to consider different approaches to study of the subject.

One way is to examine managerial leadership in terms of:

- the qualities or traits approach;
- the functional or group approach, including action-centred leadership;
- leadership as a behavioural category;
- styles of leadership; and
- the situational approach and contingency models.

(*See* Fig. 8.1.)

THE QUALITIES OR TRAITS APPROACH

The first approach assumes that leaders are born and not made. Leadership consists of certain inherited characteristics, or personality traits, which distinguish leaders from their followers: the so-called 'Great Person' theory of leadership. The qualities approach focuses attention on the man or woman in the job and not on the job itself. It suggests that attention is given to the selection of leaders rather than to training for leadership.

For example, *Drucker* (writing originally in 1955) makes the point that:

> Leadership is of utmost importance. Indeed there is no substitute for it. But leadership cannot be created or promoted. It cannot be taught or learned.[20]

Search for common traits of leadership

There have been many research studies into the common traits of leadership. However, attempts at identifying common personality, or physical and mental, characteristics of different 'good' or 'successful' leaders have met with little success.

251

Fig. 8.1
A framework for the study of managerial leadership

For example, *Byrd*, in a study of trait theory research up to 1940, identified a long list of traits which studies had shown differentiated leaders and the led, but found that only 5 per cent of the traits were common to four or more of the studies.[21] Another study, by *Jennings*, concluded: 'Fifty years of study have failed to produce one personality trait or set of qualities that can be used to discriminate between leaders and non-leaders.'[22]

Later studies have identified some correlation between leadership and certain personality traits, for example a significant correlation between leadership effectiveness and the traits of intelligence, supervisory ability, initiative, self-assurance and individuality in the manner in which work was done.[23] *Stogdill* discovered that the average person occupying a position of leadership exceeded the average member of the group in characteristics such as intelligence, scholarship, dependability in exercising responsibility, originality, social participation and socio-economic status.[24]

It is noticeable that 'individuality' or 'originality' usually features in the list of traits. This itself suggests that there is little in common between specific personality traits of different leaders. It is perhaps possible therefore to identify general

characteristics of leadership ability, such as self-confidence, initiative, intelligence and belief in one's actions, but research into this area has revealed little more than this. Investigations have identified lists of traits which tend to be overlapping or contradictory and with little significant correlation for most factors.

Limitations of the traits approach

There are two further limitations with this approach.

- First, there is bound to be some subjective judgement in determining who is regarded as a 'good' or 'successful' leader.
- Second, the lists of possible traits tend to be very long and there is not always agreement on the most important.

Even if it were possible to identify an agreed list of more specific qualities, this would provide little explanation of the nature of leadership. It would do little to help in the development and training of future leaders. Although there is still some interest in the qualities, or traits, approach, attention has been directed more to other approaches to leadership.

The qualities or traits approach gives rise to the questions: **whether leaders are born or made**; and whether leadership is an art or a science. The important point, however, is that **these are not mutually exclusive alternatives**. Even if there are certain inborn qualities which make for a good leader, these natural talents need encouragement and development. Even if leadership is something of an art, it still requires the application of special skills and techniques.

THE FUNCTIONAL OR GROUP APPROACH

This approach to leadership focuses attention not on the personality of the leader, nor on the man or woman in the job, *per se*, but on the **functions of leadership**. Leadership is always present in any group engaged in a task. The functional approach views leadership in terms of how the leader's behaviour affects, and is affected by, the group of followers. This approach concentrates on the nature of the group, the followers or subordinates. It focuses on the content of leadership.

Greater attention can be given to the successful training of leaders and to the means of improving the leaders' performance by concentrating on the functions which will lead to effective performance by the work group.

The functional approach believes that the skills of leadership can be learnt, developed and perfected. In contrast to the view of *Drucker* (referred to above), *Kotter*, for example, makes the point that successful companies do not wait for leaders to come along.

They actively seek out people with leadership potential and expose them to career experiences designed to develop that potential. Indeed, with careful selection, nurturing and encouragement, dozens of people can play important leadership roles in a business organization.[25]

The advantages of the functional approach to leadership have been well expressed by *Miles*.

The functional approach does not get bogged down (as other theories tend to) on the issue of the appointed leader versus the emergent leader. Both the official

253

leader and the group member who happens to come up with the right function at the right time are doing the same thing: supplying functions needed by the group. The appointed leader who does not do so will become leader in name only, even though he may retain his authority until he retires twenty years hence. Most groups do have appointed leaders as a kind of 'safety net' or guarantee that someone will fill needed functions, but the approach taken here assumes that the appointed leader and members alike may exert leadership.[26]

Functions and responsibilities of leadership

To help understand the process of leadership it is necessary to analyse the role of the leader and the functions and responsibility of leadership. These functions require different emphasis in different situations according to the nature of the group. The same leadership position may also change over a period of time. It is possible, however, to list a range of general functions which are served by the leadership position. A useful summary is provided by *Krech et al.*, who identify 14 functions.[27]

- **The leader as executive** – top co-ordinator of the group activities and overseer of the execution of policies.
- **The leader as planner** – deciding the ways and means by which the group achieves its ends. This may involve both short-term and long-term planning.
- **The leader as policy-maker** – the establishment of group goals and policies.
- **The leader as expert** – a source of readily available information and skills, although there will be some reliance on technical expertise and advice from other members of the group.
- **The leader as external group representative** – the official spokesperson for the group, the representative of the group and the channel for both outgoing and incoming communications.
- **The leader as controller of internal relations** – determines specific aspects of the group structure.
- **The leader as purveyor of rewards and punishment** – control over group members by the power to provide rewards and apply punishments.
- **The leader as arbitrator and mediator** – controls interpersonal conflict within the group.
- **The leader as examplar** – a model of behaviour for members of the group, setting an example of what is expected.
- **The leader as symbol of the group** – enhancing group unity by providing some kind of cognitive focus and establishing the group as a distinct entity.
- **The leader as substitute for individual responsibility** – relieves the individual member of the group from the necessity of, and responsibility for, personal decision.
- **The leader as ideologist** – serving as the source of beliefs, values and standards of behaviour for individual members of the group.
- **The leader as father figure** – serving as focus for the positive emotional feelings of individual members and the object for identification and transference.
- **The leader as scapegoat** – serving as a target for aggression and hostility of the group, accepting blame in the case of failure.

These 14 functions could readily be consolidated into a shorter number of more general functions. But they help to illustrate the range of roles and responsibilities that the leader may be expected to fulfil, and the complexity of the nature of leadership.

It is important to note that **leadership resides in the functions and not in a particular person**. The various functions of leadership can be shared among members of the group. If a member provides a particular function which is relevant to the activities of the group, and accepted by group members, then in those circumstances this could become a leadership function.

ACTION-CENTRED LEADERSHIP

A general theory on the functional approach is associated with the work of *John Adair* and his ideas on action-centred leadership.[28] The effectiveness of the leader is dependent upon meeting three areas of need within the work group: the need to achieve the common **task**, the need for **team maintenance**, and the **individual needs** of group members. Adair symbolises these needs by three overlapping circles (*see* Fig. 8.2).

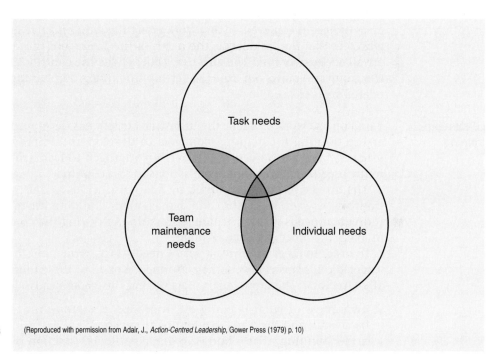

Fig. 8.2
Interaction of needs within the group

(Reproduced with permission from Adair, J., *Action-Centred Leadership*, Gower Press (1979) p. 10)

Task functions involve:

- achieving the objectives of the work group;
- defining group tasks;
- planning the work;
- allocation of resources;
- organisation of duties and responsibilities;
- controlling quality and checking performance;
- reviewing progress.

Team functions involve:

- maintaining morale and building team spirit;
- the cohesiveness of the group as a working unit;
- setting standards and maintaining discipline;
- systems of communication within the group;
- training the group;
- appointment of sub-leaders.

Individual functions involve:

- meeting the needs of the individual members of the group;
- attending to personal problems;
- giving praise and status;
- reconciling conflicts between group needs and needs of the individual;
- training the individual.

The action by the leader in any one area of need will affect one or both of the other areas of need. The ideal position is where complete integration of the three areas of need is achieved. In any work group the most effective leader is the person who sees that the task needs, the needs of the group and those of the individual are all adequately met. The effective leader elicits the contribution of members of the group and draws out other leadership from the group to satisfy the three inter-related areas of need.

Leadership training

Based on the work of Adair, the Industrial Society has developed a system of leadership training for helping managers to develop and improve their ability as leaders.[29] The action-centred leadership approach to leadership training is currently used by a number of organisations in this country.

The three-circle approach used by Adair also serves to illustrate the close relationship between leadership and management. Building the team and satisfying individual needs would include leadership. Achieving the common task clearly involves the process of management.

In order to meet the three areas of need – task, group and individual – certain leadership functions have to be performed. Not all of these functions are required all of the time. Therefore, Adair suggests that the leader needs:

- **awareness** of what is going on in groups, the group process or underlying behaviour, and the actual content of discussion;
- **understanding**, that is knowing that a particular function is required; and the **skill** to do it effectively, which can usually be judged by whether the group responds or changes course.[30]

LEADERSHIP AS A BEHAVIOURAL CATEGORY

This approach draws attention to the kinds of behaviour of people in leadership situations. One of the most extensive research studies on behavioural categories of leadership was the *Ohio State Leadership Studies* undertaken by the Bureau of Business

Research at Ohio State University. The focus was on the effects of leadership styles on group performance.

Questionnaires were designed which comprised a list of descriptive items each dealing with a specific aspect of leadership behaviour. The questionnaires were used repeatedly in different kinds of organisations and in a variety of leader–group member situations.

CONSIDERATION AND STRUCTURE

Results of the Ohio State studies indicated two major dimensions of leadership behaviour, labelled 'consideration' and 'initiating structure'.[31]

- **Consideration** reflects the extent to which the leader establishes trust, mutual respect and rapport with the group and shows concern, warmth, support and consideration for subordinates. This dimension is associated with two-way communication, participation and the human relations approach to leadership.
- **Structure** reflects the extent to which the leader defines and structures group interactions towards attainment of formal goals and organises group activities. This dimension is associated with efforts to achieve organisational goals.

Consideration and initiating structure can be seen as the same as maintenance function (building and maintaining the group as a working unit and relationships among group members) and task function (accomplishment of specific tasks of the groups and achievement of goals) discussed in the previous chapter.

Four types of leadership behaviour

Consideration and initiating structure were found to be uncorrelated and independent dimensions. They are separate behavioural categories and give rise to four types of leadership behaviour. Leaders may be:

- low on consideration and low on structure;
- low on consideration and high on structure;
- high on consideration and high on structure; or
- high on consideration and low on structure.

Leadership behaviour could, therefore, be shown on two separate axes instead of along a single continuum. As a result four quadrants were developed which illustrated the different combinations of 'consideration' and 'structure' (*see* Fig. 8.3).

Research into the effects of these four types of leadership behaviour suggest that some balance is needed between consideration and structure in order to satisfy both individual needs and organisational goals. A high consideration, high structure style appears to be generally more effective in terms of subordinate satisfaction and group performance, but the evidence is not conclusive and much seems to depend upon situational factors.

EMPLOYEE-CENTRED AND PRODUCTION-CENTRED SUPERVISORS

Another major research study was carried out at the *University of Michigan Institute for Social Research* at the same time as the Ohio State studies. Effective supervisors (measured along dimensions of group morale, productivity and cost reduction) appeared to display four common characteristics:

- delegation of authority and avoidance of close supervision;
- an interest and concern in their subordinates as individuals;
- participative problem-solving; and
- high standards of performance.

Likert, who has summarised the findings of the University of Michigan studies, used the terms **employee-centred** and **production-centred** supervisors.[32] These terms are similar to the dimensions of consideration and structure. The first three of these supervisory characteristics are examples of consideration. The fourth characteristic exemplifies structure. A contrast between employee-centred and job-centred supervision is given in Chapter 13.

The need for balance

Like consideration and structure, employee-centred and production-centred supervision need to be balanced. Likert concluded that employee-centred supervisors who get best results tend to recognise that one of their main responsibilities is production. Both the Ohio State studies and the University of Michigan studies appear to support the idea that there is no single behavioural category of leadership which is superior. There are many types of leadership behaviour and their effectiveness depends upon the variables in any given situation.

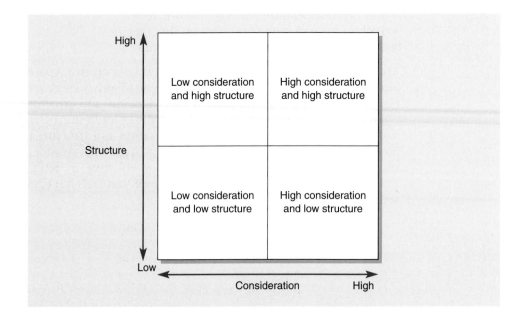

Fig. 8.3 The Ohio State quadrants of leadership behaviour

Major dimensions of managerial leadership

Despite the many types of actual leadership behaviour, we have seen that there appears to be general agreement on two major dimensions of managerial leadership. This can be extended to include the works of *McGregor* and of *Blake and McCanse* which are discussed as part of managerial behaviour in Chapter 13. (*See* Fig. 8.4.)

STYLES OF LEADERSHIP

Attention to leadership as a behavioural category has drawn attention to the importance of leadership style. In the work situation it has become increasingly clear that managers can no longer rely solely on the use of their position in the hierarchical structure as a means of exercising the functions of leadership. In order to get the best results from subordinates the manager must also have regard for the need to encourage high morale, a spirit of involvement and co-operation, and a willingness to work. This gives rise to consideration of the style of leadership and provides another heading under which to analyse leadership behaviour.

Leadership style is the way in which the functions of leadership are carried out, the way in which the manager typically behaves towards members of the group.

The development of behavioural science has drawn attention to the processes of interpersonal behaviour in the work situation and to the effects of leadership on those being led. The attention given to leadership style is based on the assumption that subordinates are more likely to work effectively for managers who adopt a certain style of leadership than they will for managers who adopt alternative styles.

Broad classification of leadership style

There are many dimensions to leadership and many possible ways of describing leadership style, such as, for example, dictatorial, unitary, bureaucratic, benevolent, charismatic, consultative, participative and abdicatorial.

The style of managerial leadership towards subordinate staff and the focus of power can be classified within a broad three-fold heading.

Group interaction analysis	Task functions	Maintenance functions
Ohio State leadership study	Initiating structure	Consideration
University of Michigan study	Production-centred supervision	Employee-centred supervision

McGregor, assumptions about people and work	Theory X	Theory Y
Blake and McCanse, Leadership Grid	Concern for production	Concern for people

Fig. 8.4
Two major dimensions of managerial leadership

259

- **The authoritarian (or autocratic) style** is where the focus of power is with the manager, and all interactions within the group move towards the manager. The manager alone exercises decision-making and authority for determining policy, procedures for achieving goals, work tasks and relationships, control of rewards or punishments.
- **The democratic style** is where the focus of power is more with the group as a whole and there is greater interaction within the group. The leadership functions are shared with members of the group and the manager is more part of a team. The group members have a greater say in decision-making, determination of policy, implementation of systems and procedures.
- **A genuine *laissez-faire* style** is where the manager observes that members of the group are working well on their own. The manager consciously makes a decision to pass the focus of power to members, to allow them freedom of action and not to interfere; but is readily available if help is needed. There is often confusion over this style of leadership behaviour. The word 'genuine' is emphasised because this is to be contrasted with the manager who could not care, who deliberately keeps away from the trouble spots and does not want to get involved. The manager just lets members of the group get on with the work in hand. Members are left to face decisions which rightly belong with the manager. This is more a non-style of leadership or it could perhaps be labelled as abdication.

Importance of participative approach

The importance of a more participative approach to leadership style and its effect on group performance was seen after publication of the research findings of the relay assembly test room experiment at the Hawthorne plant of the Western Electric Company of America. Later work by *Maslow*, who theorised that individuals possess a hierarchy of needs, resulted in greater research into the motivation and behaviour of individuals in the work situation.[33]

The subsequent attention given to theories of individual motivation gave rise to a more psychological approach to the study of work organisations. The main focus of concern was on the personal adjustment of the individual and the effects of group relationships and leadership styles. The style of leadership adopted is a function of the manager's attitude and assumptions about human nature and behaviour.

Work by such writers as *McGregor, Likert*, and *Blake and Mouton* (discussed in Chapter 13) appear to support the value of participative managerial leadership in improving organisational effectiveness.

Solo leader and team leader

Belbin distinguishes between two broad contrasting or diverging styles of leadership in industry: the solo leader and the team leader.[34] The solo leader enjoys free range, and rules as if absolutely. The leader takes no risks with other people, adopts a directive approach, prefers specific tasks and goals, expects compliance and acts as a model for others to follow. In times of crisis or urgency the talented solo leaders have been effective in overcoming departmental barriers and obstacles, and implementing decisions quickly. However, when the solo leaders fail, they are discarded.

By contrast, the team leader declines to rule as if absolutely, and deliberately limits his or her role. The leader creates a sense of mission, expresses greater respect for and trust in subordinates, recognises the skills and strengths of others, and is more inclined to delegate. Belbin suggests that solo leadership is familiar to most people because part of crowd psychology is to seek to be led and to have

faith in the leader. However, increasing uncertainty and continuous change together with societal pressure for the sharing of power has led to increasing attention to team leadership.

Attention to style of leadership

Attention to the manager's style of leadership has come about because of a greater understanding of the needs and expectations of people at work. It has also been influenced by such factors as:

- increasing business competitiveness and recognition of efficient use of human resources;
- changes in the value system of society;
- broader standards of education and training;
- advances in scientific and technical knowledge;
- the influence of trade unions;
- pressure for a greater social responsibility towards employees, for example through schemes of participation in decision-making and the quality of working life; and
- government legislation, for example in the areas of employment protection, and the influence of the European Union.

All of these factors have combined to create resistance against purely autocratic styles of leadership.

CONTINUUM OF LEADERSHIP BEHAVIOUR

One of the best known works on leadership style is that by *Tannenbaum and Schmidt* (Fig. 8.5).[35] They suggest a continuum of possible leadership behaviour available to a manager and along which various styles of leadership may be placed.

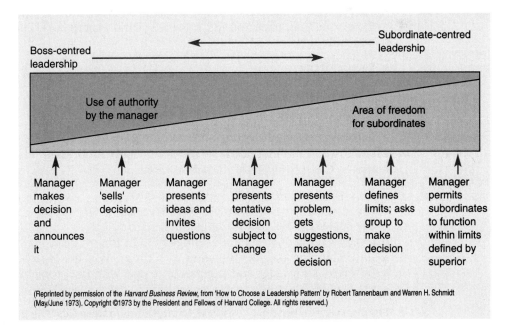

Fig. 8.5 Continuum of leadership behaviour

(Reprinted by permission of the *Harvard Business Review*, from 'How to Choose a Leadership Pattern' by Robert Tannenbaum and Warren H. Schmidt (May/June 1973). Copyright ©1973 by the President and Fellows of Harvard College. All rights reserved.)

At one extreme of the continuum is boss-centred leadership (authoritarian) and at the other extreme is subordinate-centred leadership (democratic).

The continuum presents a range of action related to the degree of authority used by the manager and to the area of freedom available to subordinates in arriving at decisions. The Tannenbaum and Schmidt continuum can be related to *McGregor's* supposition of Theory X and Theory Y. Boss-centred leadership is towards Theory X and subordinate-centred leadership is towards Theory Y.

Four main styles of leadership

Moving along the continuum, the manager may be characterised according to the degree of control that is maintained over subordinates. Neither extreme of the continuum is absolute as there is always some limitation on authority and on freedom. This approach can be seen as identifying four main styles of leadership by the manager: tells, sells, consults, joins.

- **Tells** – the manager identifies a problem, chooses a decision and announces this to subordinates, expecting them to implement it without an opportunity for participation.
- **Sells** – the manager still chooses a decision but recognises the possibility of some resistance from those faced with the decision and attempts to persuade subordinates to accept it.
- **Consults** – the manager identifies the problem but does not choose a decision until the problem is presented to the group, and the manager has listened to the advice and solutions suggested by subordinates.
- **Joins** – the manager defines the problem and the limits within which the decision must be chosen and then passes to the group, with the manager as a member, the right to make decisions.

Three main forces in deciding type of leadership

Tannenbaum and Schmidt suggest that there are three factors, or forces, of particular importance in deciding what types of leadership are practicable and desirable. These are: forces in the manager; forces in the subordinates; and forces in the situation.

Forces in the manager – the managers' behaviour will be influenced by their own personalities, backgrounds, knowledge and experiences. These internal forces will include:

- value systems;
- confidence in subordinates;
- leadership inclinations; and
- feelings of security in an uncertain situation.

Forces in the subordinate – subordinates are influenced by many personality variables and their individual set of expectations about their relationship with the manager. Characteristics of the subordinate are:

- the strength of the needs for independence;
- the readiness to assume responsibility for decision-making;
- the degree of tolerance for ambiguity;
- interest in the problem and feelings as to its importance;
- understanding and identification with the goals of the organisation;
- necessary knowledge and experience to deal with the problem; and
- the extent of learning to expect to share in decision-making.

The greater the positive response to these characteristics, the greater freedom of action can be allowed by the manager.

Forces in the situation – the manager's behaviour will be influenced by the general situation and environmental pressures. Characteristics in the situation include:

- type of organisation;
- group effectiveness;
- nature of the problem; and
- pressure of time.

Tannenbaum and Schmidt conclude that successful leaders are keenly aware of those forces which are most relevant to their behaviour at a particular time. They are able to behave appropriately in terms of their understanding of themselves, the individuals and the group, the organisation, and environmental influences. Successful managers are both perceptive and flexible.

Interdependency of forces

In the second publication of their work, which was originally written in 1958, Tannenbaum and Schmidt add a retrospective commentary in which they suggest how they would update their original ideas to reflect social developments and new concepts of management.[36] More attention would be given to the interdependency of the forces in the manager, in the subordinates and in the situation. (*See* Fig. 8.6.)

Forces lying outside the organisation would now also be included. Recognition is given to the possibility of the manager and/or subordinates taking initiative to

**Fig. 8.6
Continuum of
manager–non-
manager behaviour**

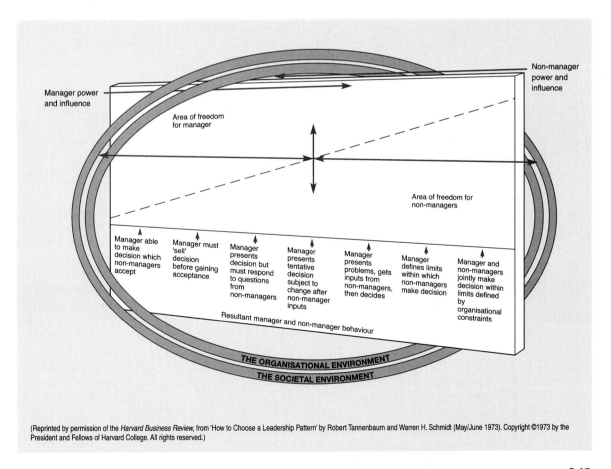

263

change the boundaries of the rectangle through interaction with external forces. Recognition is also given to the power available to all parties in the organisation (for example individual workers and trade unions) and to the factors which underlie decisions on the use of power by the manager.

The term 'non-manager' is now preferred to 'subordinate' as the terminological difference between 'manager' and 'non-manager' is functional rather than hierarchical. Tannenbaum and Schmidt suggest a new continuum of patterns of leadership behaviour in which the total area of freedom shared between managers and non-managers is redefined constantly by interactions between them and the forces in the environment.

THE SITUATIONAL APPROACH

The situational approach concentrates on the importance of the situation in the study of leadership. A variety of people with differing personalities and from different backgrounds have emerged as effective leaders in different situations. The person who becomes the leader of the work group is thought to be the person who knows best what to do and is seen by the group as the most suitable leader in the particular situation.

The continuum of leadership behaviour draws attention to forces in the situation as one of the main forces influencing the nature of managerial behaviour. The situational approach emphasises the situation as the dominant feature in considering the characteristics of effective leadership.

Obeying the law of the situation
It is interesting to note that the importance of the situation for managerial leadership was put forward over 50 years ago. *Mary Parker Follett* considered the way orders should be given in the manager–subordinate relationship. The problem is avoiding the two extremes of: (i) too great bossism in giving orders; and (ii) practically no orders given.

Follett's solution was what she called the 'depersonalising of orders and obeying the law of the situation'.

> My solution is to depersonalise the giving of orders, to unite all concerned in a study of the situation, to discover the law of the situation and obey that. Until we do this I do not think we shall have the most successful business administration ... This is, ideally what should take place between any head and subordinates. One **person** should not give orders to another **person** but both should agree to take their orders from the situation. If orders are simply part of the situation, the question of someone giving and someone receiving does not come up. Both accept the orders given by the situation.[37]

Limitations
There are, however, limitations to the situational approach. There are people who possess the appropriate knowledge and skills and appear to be the most suitable leaders in a given situation, but who do not emerge as effective leaders. Another limitation is that it does not explain fully the interpersonal behaviour or the different styles of leadership and their effect on members of the group. Finally, in the work organisation, it is not usually practicable to allow the situation continually to determine who should act as the leader.

CONTINGENCY THEORIES OF LEADERSHIP

Despite the limitations of the situational approach, situational factors are important in considering the characteristics of leadership. More recent studies focus on the interactions between the variables involved in a leadership situation and patterns of leadership behaviour, and provide another general approach to the study of leadership – contingency theory. Contingency theories are based on the belief that there is no single style of leadership appropriate to all situations. Major contingency models of leadership include:

Favourability of leadership situation – *Fiedler*
Quality and acceptance of leader's decision – *Vroom and Yetton*, and *Vroom and Jago*
Path–goal theory – *House*, and *House and Dessler*
Maturity of followers – *Hersey and Blanchard*, and *Nicholls*

FIEDLER'S CONTINGENCY MODEL

One of the first leader–situation models was developed by *Fiedler* in his contingency theory of leadership effectiveness.[38]

Fiedler's contingency model was based on studies of a wide range of group situations, and concentrated on the relationship between leadership and organisational performance. In order to measure the attitudes of the leader, Fiedler developed a 'least preferred co-worker' (LPC) scale. This measures the rating given by leaders about the person with whom they could work least well. The questionnaire contains up to 20 items. Examples of items in the LPC scale are pleasant/unpleasant, friendly/unfriendly, helpful/frustrating, distant/close, co-operative/uncooperative, boring/interesting, self-assured/ hesitant, open/guarded.

Each item is given a single ranking of between one and eight points, with eight points indicating the most favourable rating. For example:

Pleasant	:	:	:	:	:	:	:	:	Unpleasant
	8	7	6	5	4	3	2	1	

The LPC score is the sum of the numerical ratings on all the items for the 'least preferred co-worker'. The less critical the rating of the least preferred co-worker and the more favourably evaluated, the higher the leader's LPC score. The more critical the rating, the lower the LPC score.

The original interpretation of the LPC scale was that the leader with a high LPC score derived most satisfaction from interpersonal relationships and, when relationships with subordinates need to be improved, is motivated to act in a supportive, considerate manner.

The leader with a low LPC score derived most satisfaction from performance of the task and achieving objectives. Establishing good relationships with subordinates is a secondary motivation. It was thought that high LPC scores would be associated

with effective performance by the group. However, the interpretation of LPC has changed a number of times and there is still uncertainty about its actual meaning.

Favourability of leadership situation

Fiedler suggests that leadership behaviour is dependent upon the favourability of the leadership situation. There are three major variables which determine the favourability of the situation and which affect the leader's role and influence.

- **Leader–member relations** – the degree to which the leader is trusted and liked by group members, and their willingness to follow the leader's guidance.
- **The task structure** – the degree to which the task is clearly defined for the group and the extent to which it can be carried out by detailed instructions or standard procedures.
- **Position power** – the power of the leader by virtue of position in the organisation, and the degree to which the leader can exercise authority to influence (for example) rewards and punishments, or promotions and demotions.

Fig. 8.7
Correlations between leader's LPC scores and group effectiveness

From these three variables, Fiedler constructed eight combinations of group–task situations through which to relate leadership style (*see* Fig. 8.7).

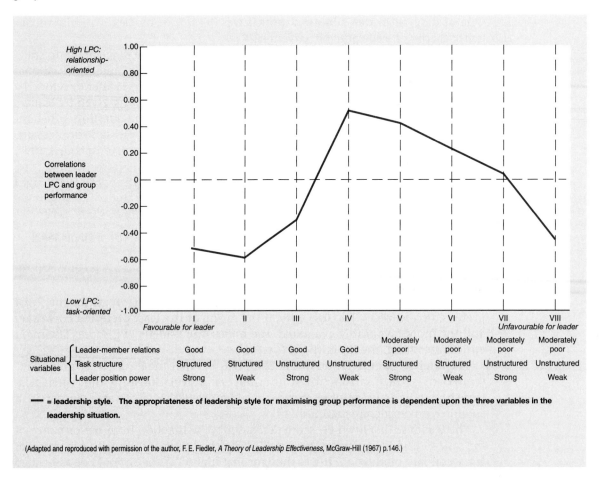

= leadership style. **The appropriateness of leadership style for maximising group performance is dependent upon the three variables in the leadership situation.**

(Adapted and reproduced with permission of the author, F. E. Fiedler, *A Theory of Leadership Effectiveness*, McGraw-Hill (1967) p.146.)

When the situation is

- **very favourable** (good leader–member relations, structured task, strong position power), or
- **very unfavourable** (poor leader–member relations, unstructured task, weak position power),

then a **task-oriented leader** (low LPC score) with a directive, controlling style will be more effective.

When the situation is

- **moderately favourable** and the variables are mixed,

then the leader with an interpersonal relationship orientation (high LPC score) and a **participative approach** will be more effective.

Fiedler is suggesting, therefore, that leadership style will vary as the favourability of the leadership situation varies.

Organisational variables

Fiedler's work has been subject to much criticism[39] but it does provide a further dimension to the study of leadership. It brings into consideration the organisational variables which affect leadership effectiveness and suggests that in given situations a task-oriented, or structured, style of leadership is most appropriate. The 'best' styles of leadership will be dependent upon the variable factors in the leadership situation.

Fiedler argues that leadership effectiveness may be improved by changing the leadership situation. Position power, task structure and leader–member relations can be changed to make the situation more compatible with the characteristics of the leader. Leaders with a low LPC score could be placed in a leadership situation which is very favourable or very unfavourable. Leaders with a high LPC score could be placed in a leadership situation which is of moderate favourability.

VROOM AND YETTON CONTINGENCY MODEL

Another contingency model of leadership is provided by *Vroom and Yetton*.[40] They base their analysis on two aspects of a leader's decision: its quality and its acceptance.

- **Decision quality**, or rationality, is the effect that the decision has on group performance.
- **Decision acceptance** refers to the motivation and commitment of group members in implementing the decision.

A third consideration is

- the amount of **time required** to make the decision.

The Vroom and Yetton model suggests five main management decision styles:

- **Autocratic**
 A.I: Leader solves the problem or makes the decision alone using information available at the time.
 A.II: Leader obtains information from subordinates but then decides on solution alone.

- **Consultative**

 C.I: The problem is shared with relevant subordinates, individually. The leader then makes the decision which may or may not reflect the influence of subordinates.

 C.II: The problem is shared with subordinates as a group. The leader then makes the decision which may or may not reflect the influence of subordinates.

- **Group**

 G.II: The problem is shared with subordinates as a group. The leader acts as chairperson, rather than an advocate. Together the leader and subordinates generate and evaluate alternatives and attempt to reach group consensus on a solution.

Decision rules

Vroom and Yetton suggest seven decision rules to help the manager discover the most appropriate leadership style in a given situation. The first three rules protect the **quality of decisions**.

(i) Is there a quality requirement such that one solution is likely to be more rational than another?

(ii) Is there sufficient information to make a high-quality decision?

(iii) Is the problem structured?

The last four rules protect the **acceptance of decisions**.

(iv) Is acceptance of the decision by subordinates critical to effective implementation?

(v) If you were to make the decision yourself, is it reasonably certain that it would be accepted by subordinates?

(vi) Do subordinates share the organisational goals to be obtained in solving the problem?

(vii) Is conflict among subordinates likely in preferred solutions?

These rules indicate decision styles that the manager should **avoid** in a given situation and indicate the use of others. Decision tree charts can be produced to help in the application of the rules and to relate the situation to the appropriate leadership style.

THE VROOM AND JAGO REVISED DECISION MODEL

In a revised version of the original model *Vroom and Jago* retain the five main decision-making styles but incorporate a larger number – 12 – of contingency variables.[41] The new model specifies that any of the five decision styles may be effective in given situations. The contingency variables relate to:

- quality requirement;
- commitment requirement;
- leader information;
- problem structure;
- commitment probability;
- goal congruence;
- subordinate conflict;

- subordinate information;
- time constraint;
- geographical dispersion;
- motivation-time; and
- motivation-development.

Unlike the Vroom and Yetton model which requires a definite yes/no answer, ten of these situational variables are answered on a five-point scale. For example, to the question 'How important is subordinate commitment to the decision?', the manager selects one of the following responses: no importance; low importance; average importance; high importance; critical importance.

Use of decision trees

Vroom and Jago developed four decision trees relating to a generic type of managerial problem:

- an individual-level problem with time constraints;
- an individual-level problem in which the manager wishes to develop an employee's decision-making ability;
- a group-level problem in which the manager wishes to develop employees' decision-making abilities; and
- a time-driven group problem.

The manager selects one of the trees and moves along the branches by answering the questions at each decision point. This leads to one of the five described decision-making styles.

PATH–GOAL THEORY

A third contingency model of leadership is the path–goal theory, the main work on which has been undertaken by *House*,[42] and by *House and Dessler*.[43] The model is based on the belief that the individual's motivation is dependent upon expectations that increased effort to achieve an improved level of performance will be successful, and expectations that improved performance will be instrumental in obtaining positive rewards and avoiding negative outcomes. This is the 'expectancy' theory of motivation, which is discussed in Chapter 14.

Four main types of leadership behaviour

The path–goal theory of leadership suggests that the performance of subordinates is affected by the extent to which the manager satisfies their expectations. Path–goal theory holds that subordinates will see leadership behaviour as a motivating influence to the extent that it means:

- satisfaction of their needs is dependent upon effective performance; and
- the necessary direction, guidance, training and support, which would otherwise be lacking, is provided.

House identifies four main types of leadership behaviour.

- **Directive leadership** involves letting subordinates know exactly what is expected of them and giving specific directions. Subordinates are expected to follow rules and regulations. This type of behaviour is similar to 'initiating structure' in the Ohio State Leadership Studies.

269

- **Supportive leadership** involves a friendly and approachable manner and displaying concern for the needs and welfare of subordinates. This type of behaviour is similar to 'consideration' in the Ohio State Leadership Studies.
- **Participative leadership** involves consulting with subordinates and the evaluation of their opinions and suggestions before the manager makes the decision.
- **Achievement-oriented leadership** involves setting challenging goals for subordinates, seeking improvement in their performance and showing confidence in subordinates' ability to perform well.

Path–goal theory suggests that the different types of behaviour can be practised by the same person at different times in varying situations. By using one of the four styles of leadership behaviour the manager attempts to influence subordinates' perceptions and motivation, and smooth the path to their goals. (*See* Fig. 8.8.)

Two main situational factors

Leadership behaviour is determined by two main situational factors: the personal characteristics of subordinates; and the nature of the task.

- **The personal characteristics of subordinates** determine how they will react to the manager's behaviour and the extent to which they see such behaviour as an immediate or potential source of need satisfaction.
- **The nature of the task** relates to the extent that it is routine and structured, or non-routine and unstructured.

For example, when a task is highly structured, the goals readily apparent and subordinates are confident, then attempts to further explain the job or to give directions are likely to be viewed as unacceptable behaviour. However, when a task is highly unstructured, the nature of the goals is not clear and subordinates lack experience, then a more directive style of leadership behaviour is likely to be welcomed by subordinates.

Effective leadership behaviour is based, therefore, on both the willingness of the manager to help subordinates and the needs of subordinates for help. Leadership behaviour will be motivational to the extent that it provides necessary direction, guidance and support, helps clarify path–goal relationships and removes any obstacles which hinder attainment of goals.

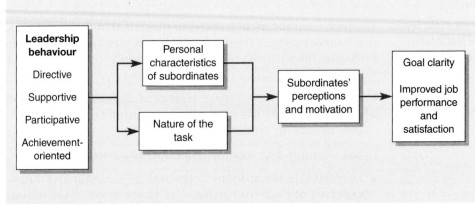

Fig. 8.8
Representation of the path–goal theory of leadership

READINESS OF THE FOLLOWERS OR GROUP

A major variable in the style of leadership adopted by the manager is the nature of subordinate staff. This view is developed by *Hersey and Blanchard* who present a form of situational leadership based on the 'readiness' level of the people the leader is attempting to influence. Readiness is the extent to which followers have the ability and willingness to accomplish a specific task. It is not a personal characteristic of the individual, but how ready the individual is to perform a particular task.[44]

Readiness (R) is divided into a continuum of four levels: R1 (low), R2 and R3 (moderate), and R4 (high).

- **R1 – low follower readiness** – refers to followers who are both *unable and unwilling*, and who lack commitment and motivation; or who are *unable and insecure*.
- **R2 – low to moderate follower readiness** – refers to followers who are *unable but willing*, and who lack ability but are motivated to make an effort; or who are *unable but confident*.
- **R3 – moderate to high follower readiness** – refers to followers who are *able but unwilling*, and who have the ability to perform but are unwilling to apply their ability; or who are *able but insecure*.
- **R4 – high follower readiness** – refers to followers who are both *able and willing*, and who have the ability and commitment to perform; or who are *able and confident*.

Task behaviour and relationship behaviour

For each of the four levels of maturity, the appropriate style of leadership is a combination of task behaviour and relationship behaviour.

- **Task behaviour** is the extent to which the leader provides directions for the actions of followers, sets goals for them, and defines their roles and how to undertake them.
- **Relationship behaviour** is the extent to which the leader engages in two-way communication with followers, listens to them, and provides support and encouragement.

From the combination of task behaviour and relationship behaviour derive four leadership styles (S): telling (S1), selling (S2), participating (S3) and delegating (S4). The appropriate leadership style corresponds with the readiness of the followers. (*See* Fig. 8.9.)

- **S1 – telling** – emphasises high amounts of guidance (task behaviour) but limited supportive (relationship) behaviour. This style is most appropriate for *low follower readiness* (R1).
- **S2 – selling** – emphasises high amounts of both directive (task) and relationship behaviours. This style is most appropriate for *low to moderate follower readiness* (R2).
- **S3 – participating** – emphasises a high amount of two-way communication and supportive (relationship) behaviour but low amounts of guidance (task behaviour). This style is most appropriate for *moderate to high follower readiness* (R3).
- **S4 – delegating** – emphasises little direction or support with low levels of both task and relationship behaviours. This style is most appropriate for *high follower readiness* (R4).

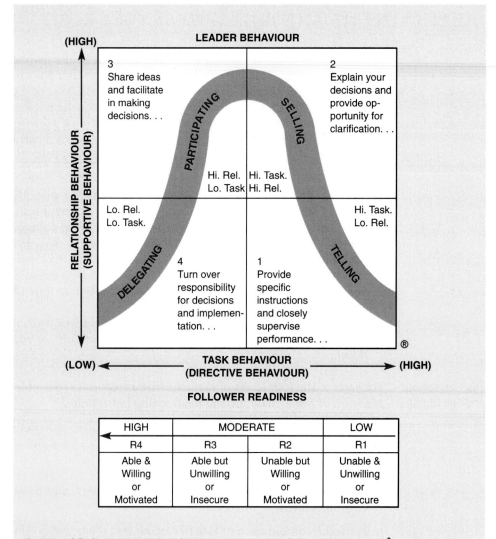

**Fig. 8.9
Situational
leadership model**

**Development of
subordinates**

Hersey and Blanchard suggest that the key to using situational leadership is that any leader behaviour may be more or less effective according to the readiness of the person the leader is attempting to influence. The model draws attention to the importance of developing the ability, confidence and commitment of subordinates. The manager should help subordinates to develop in readiness to the extent that they are able and willing to go. This development should take place by adjusting leadership behaviour through the four styles of telling, selling, participating and delegating.

REVISED MODEL OF SITUATIONAL LEADERSHIP

The validity of Hersey and Blanchard's basic model has been challenged by *Nicholls* who claims that the model violates three logical principles – consistency, continuity and conformity.

> It is inconsistent in the way it connects concern for task/relationships with ability/willingness. The development level continuum lacks continuity since it requires willingness to appear, disappear and reappear as the development level increases. Finally, it runs counter to conformity in that it does not start with a style of high task and high relationship for a group which is simultaneously unable and unwilling.[45]

Nicholls suggests a corrected model (Fig. 8.10) which no longer violates the principles of consistency, continuity and conformity, and which presents a completely new model for situational leadership.

Explanation Nicholls's situational leadership model can be explained as follows.

(i) For groups at low development level, that is both unable and unwilling, the leader acts in the same role as a **parent** who wishes to develop simultaneously the ability and the social skills of a child. As both ability and willingness increase, activity connected with both task and relationships can be reduced in a symmetrical way. This allows progression from 'tell', through 'consult' to the role of a **developer** (bottom left quadrant).

(ii) The developer role of leadership continues with a light touch to use 'participation' and 'delegation' in order to develop further the ability and willingness of the group.

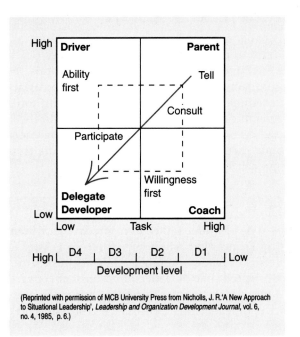

Fig. 8.10
New situational leadership model

(Reprinted with permission of MCB University Press from Nicholls, J. R.'A New Approach to Situational Leadership', *Leadership and Organization Development Journal*, vol. 6, no. 4, 1985, p. 6.)

(iii) However, if willingness develops more quickly than ability, the leader will have the opportunity to act more in the role of a **coach** who is anxious to improve ability.

(iv) If, however, ability develops more quickly than willingness, the leader may wish to revert to the role of **driver** in order to push the group to achieve results up to its potential and to prevent unwillingness causing a shortfall in performance.

(v) **Summary**: The model requires a smooth progression of the leader from parent, using a high task and high relationship leadership style; following the usual progression tell–sell/consult–participate–delegate; to the leader as developer and using a low task and low relationship leadership style.

But if ability and willingness do not develop in harmony, the leader may find it appropriate to act more like a coach to develop ability, or more like a driver to overcome unwillingness.

Response

In later editions of their work, *Hersey and Blanchard* appear to make reference to the points raised by *Nicholls*.

Some people have difficulty understanding the development of followers from R1 to R2 to R3. How can one go from being insecure to confident and then become insecure again? The important thing to remember is that at the lower levels of readiness, the leader is providing the direction – the what, where, when and how. Therefore, the decisions are *leader directed*. At the higher levels of readiness, followers become responsible for task direction, and the decisions are *follower-directed. This transition from leader-directed to self-directed may result in apprehension or insecurity.* As followers move from low levels of readiness to higher levels, the combinations of task and relationship behavior appropriate to the situation begin to change.[46]

NO ONE BEST STYLE OF LEADERSHIP

Research studies tend to indicate that democratic styles of leadership are more likely to produce effective performance from work groups. A human relations, people-oriented approach is more likely to lead to job satisfaction and to group cohesiveness. For example, *Likert and Likert* found that authoritative, task-centred systems of management can result in high productivity in the short term because of compliance based on fear. However, long-term improvements in high productivity and in labour turnover are more likely to result from a participative, group-oriented approach.[47]

Many forms of leadership

However, we have seen that there are many alternative forms of managerial leadership. It is not always the case that democratic styles are best. There are occasions when an autocratic style of leadership is more effective. For example, we have seen from the studies by *Fiedler* that when the situation is very favourable or very unfavourable in terms of leader–member relations, task structure and position power, then a task-oriented style of leadership is most effective. Some subordinates appear to prefer a more directive, task-oriented approach and respond better to more autocratic styles of leadership. (*See also* the discussion on managerial behaviour in Chapter 13.)

Contingency models demonstrate that there are many forms of leadership. Within an organisation different individuals may fulfil the functions of leadership and there are many different styles of leadership.

A potential danger with the contingency approach is that the manager may appear to lack consistency in leadership style. However, although subordinates may reasonably expect some degree of consistency from the manager in approaching the same type of problem with the same style, this is not to say that different types of problems should be approached in the same manner. Subordinates would ordinarily expect a different style of managerial leadership according to the contingencies of the situation.

Different styles at different stages of a business

Different types of leadership may also be most appropriate at different stages in the development of a business organisation. For example, *Clarke and Pratt* identify four different styles of managerial leadership required at different stages of business: champion, tank commander, housekeeper and lemon-squeezer.[48]

- **Champion** – as a new corporate venture develops into a business it needs a champion to fight for and defend the seedling business. The champion must be able to drive a small team to win orders, provide a wide range of management skills, and have the dash and energy to deal with a range of different matters.
- **Tank commander** – as the business enters its growth stage the manager must develop a strong, supportive team and have leadership qualities to be able to drive into readily exploitable parts of the market.
- **Housekeeper** – as the business runs up against boundaries erected by other growing businesses it enters the mature stage. The housekeeper has to ensure the efficient and economic management of the business. This involves skills in planning, cost control and the development of soundly based personnel policies.
- **Lemon-squeezer** – although the mature stage might last for many years, sometimes a business goes into premature decline. At this stage the need is for the kind of leader who can extract the maximum benefit from the situation. The lemon-squeezer needs to be both tough and innovative in order, for example, to cut costs, and improve productivity and staffing levels.

Finding and fitting the manager best suited to each stage of a business is a delicate task. Clarke and Pratt suggest that most managers are one type of leader or another. Although there are exceptions, few managers are flexible enough to switch between such different leadership roles.

The right leader for the right situation

The suggestion that different types of leaders are needed at different stages of the development of a company is supported by *Rodrigues*. Organisations functioning within a dynamic environment experience three stages of change: a problem-solving stage, an implementation-of-solution stage, and a stable stage. At each of these three organisational stages a leader with different traits, abilities, and behaviour is most effective.[49]

Rodrigues suggests that organisations which exist in a dynamic environment therefore generally require three types of leaders: the innovator(s); the implementor(s); and the pacifier(s).

- **The innovator** is characterised by the need for competition, the struggle to succeed, the search for new ideas, boldness, and the belief that the environment

can be controlled and manipulated. An innovator style of leadership is likely to be more effective at the problem-solving stage when an organisation needs renewing or at least some new ideas. Such a leader is best equipped to identify and 'sell' new ideas.

- **The implementor** is characterised by the need to control and influence situations, the ability to accomplish things through people, a systematic approach, and the ability to assume responsibility for decision-making. Once the innovator has sold the new ideas to the organisation, then an implementor style of leadership is likely to be most effective at the implementation stage.

- **The pacifier** is characterised by the need for a friendly atmosphere and social interaction, the capacity to decentralise decision-making and to pacify important individuals, and the desire to base decisions on feedback from earlier decisions. When the implementor has systematically brought the organisation to the stable stage, then a pacifier style of leadership is likely to be most effective. At this stage members usually feel more competent to perform the task in hand and will accept less direction from a leader.

Leadership and organisational culture

Leadership is not only an essential part of the process of management, it is also an integral part of the social structure and culture of the organisation. If the manager is to be successful in dealing with people and influencing their behaviour and action this requires a leadership style which helps to foster a supportive organisational culture.

Brown, for example, believes that

> Effective leadership and workable organization design and development programmes must be based on sensitivity to, and understanding of, culture. Excellent leaders are not merely aware of their organization's basic assumptions, they also know how to take action to mould and refine them. [50]

NATIONAL CULTURAL DIMENSIONS OF LEADERSHIP

Another major variable influencing choice of leadership style may be national culture. For example, *McGregor* concluded that the social, economic and political environment affected the leadership relationship, together with the attitudes and needs of 'followers'.[51] *Tannenbaum and Schmidt* identify leaders' own value systems as factors which influence their chosen style. They also highlight subordinates' – or non-managers' – needs for independence and tolerance of ambiguity as relevant variables in the choice of style.[52] These factors vary according to the cultural context in which the leadership relationship takes place.

Stereotyping the behaviour of leaders

One should be wary of stereotyping the behaviour of leaders or subordinates, and many myths appear to have grown around notions of 'orderly' German, 'undisciplined' Italian and even 'obstructive' British workers. However, there are reasons to suggest that there may indeed be national cultural differences which are relevant to an understanding of leadership. The work of *Hofstede* has already been referred to in Chapter 1. One dimension for classifying societies, power distance, is said to influence the extent to which subordinates accept inequality, which in turn may influence the extent to which leaders wield power.[53]

Thus one might expect a more autocratic style of leadership to be characteristic of organisations in countries as diverse as France, Spain, Hong Kong and Iran which all display a high level of power distance. In contrast, countries identified as low power distance societies included Britain, Italy, The Netherlands, the Scandinavian countries and the USA. Given the inclusion of the last country within this group, it is perhaps not surprising that so many American writers advocate adopting participative styles of leadership.

Constraints of legislation

It should also be noted that, whatever their preferred style of leadership, managers operating in particular countries will be constrained by the relevant legislative measures of those societies. Within the European Union, all member countries with the exception of the UK have been bound by the provisions of the Social Charter of 1989 and the Social Charter of the 1991 Maastricht Treaty. These agreements both refer to 'workers' rights to information, consultation and participation'. It is likely, therefore, that British managers in the early 1990s have had a significantly greater prerogative when managing people in the workplace.

In contrast, for most of the post-war period, German managers have had to work within the framework of a statutory policy of joint consultation with both works councils and worker representatives on boards of directors. *Lawrence*, for example, has described how West German personnel managers have been required to work together with employee representatives on matters relating to the recruitment, training and remuneration of staff.[54] Given this background, it is not surprising that *Hofstede* suggested that German organisations would be characterised by low power distance. (Industrial democracy in European countries, and the anticipated harmonisation of practice in the management of people, is discussed more fully in Chapter 18.)

VARIABLES AFFECTING LEADERSHIP EFFECTIVENESS

Clearly, there is no one 'best' style of leadership which will result in the maintenance of morale among group members and high work performance. Three main aspects to be considered in determining the most appropriate style of leadership are: the manager, the group and the work environment.

However, there are many variables which underlie the effectiveness of leadership in work organisations. More specifically, these include the following:

- the characteristics of the manager, personality, attitudes, abilities, value system; and the personal credibility of the manager;
- the type of power of the manager and the basis of the leadership relation;
- the characteristics of the subordinates; their needs and expectations; attitudes; knowledge, confidence and experience; and their motivation and commitment;
- the relationship between the manager and the group, and among members of the group;
- the type and nature of the organisation, and different stages in the development of the organisation;
- the nature of the tasks to be achieved, the extent to which structured or routine; the technology and methods of work organisation;

- organisation structure and systems of management;
- the type of problem and the nature of the manager's decisions;
- the nature and influence of the external environment;
- the social structure and culture of the organisation;
- the influence of national culture.

Education and training in management needs to emphasise not only interpersonal skills, but a flexibility of approach, diagnostic ability and the realisation that the most effective form of leadership behaviour is a product of the total leadership situation.

SYNOPSIS

■ There are many ways of looking at leadership, and many interpretations of its meaning, but essentially it is a relationship through which one person influences the behaviour or actions of other people. The leader–follower relationship is reciprocal and effective leadership is a two-way process. Leadership is related to motivation, the process of communication, the activities of groups and the process of delegation. The changing nature of business organisations has placed increasing importance on leadership.

■ There is a close relationship between leadership and management, especially in work organisations. However, there are differences between the two, and it does not follow that every leader is a manager. Leadership may be viewed in more general terms with emphasis on interpersonal behaviour in a broader context. Leadership is a dynamic form of behaviour and there are many variables which affect the nature of the leadership relationship.

■ Within an organisation, leadership influence will be dependent upon the type of power which the leader can exercise over other people. Leadership may be examined in terms of the qualities or traits approach; in terms of the functional or group approach; as a behavioural category; in terms of styles of leadership; and through the situational approach and contingency models. There is a wide range of general functions and responsibilities served by the leadership position. Leadership resides in the functions and not in a particular person. The various functions of leadership can be shared among members of the group.

■ Leadership style is the way in which the functions of leadership are carried out. Greater emphasis has been placed on more democratic styles of leadership. There is, however, a wide range of possible leadership behaviour available to the manager. Two major dimensions of leadership are consideration, concerned with relationships with the group; and structure, concerned with efforts to achieve organisational goals. Leadership style can be measured along a continuum between boss-centred (authoritarian) at one extreme and subordinate-centred (democratic) at the other extreme.

■ Contingency theories draw attention to the interactions between the variables involved in a leadership situation and patterns of leadership behaviour. The most appropriate form of leadership is dependent upon the variables in a particular leadership situation. Different contingency theories have concentrated on differ-

ent situational variables. These include: favourability of the leadership situation; decision acceptance and decision quality; path–goal theory; and the 'readiness' of followers.

■ Research studies tend to indicate that democratic styles of leadership are more likely to produce effective group performance. However, this is not always the case and there is no one 'best' style of leadership. Different types of leadership may also be needed at different stages of a business. National culture may also influence choice of leadership style. There are many variables which underlie the effectiveness of leadership in work organisations. The most effective form of leadership behaviour is a product of the total leadership situation.

Review and discussion questions

1 State clearly what you understand by the meaning of leadership. Distinguish leadership from management.

2 Discuss the main sources of power and leadership influence. Give a practical example of each of these main sources of power and influence within your own organisation.

3 Distinguish between different approaches to the study of leadership and discuss critically what you see as the relevance of each of these approaches.

4 Explain what is meant by leadership style. What are the major dimensions of leadership behaviour? Suggest why greater attention has been given to more participative styles of leadership.

5 Assume you are a departmental manager in an organisation. Using the Tannenbaum and Schmidt continuum identify, with reasons, your preferred style of leadership. Give an example of a situation in which you might need to adopt an alternative style of leadership.

6 What do you understand by leader–situation models of leadership? Assess the practical value to the manager of: (i) Fiedler's contingency model of leadership effectiveness; and (ii) Vroom and Yetton's contingency model of leadership.

7 Explain Hersey and Blanchard's model of situational leadership. Give your own views, with supporting reasons, on the validity of this model.

8 Discuss the main situational variables which are likely to influence the most appropriate form of managerial leadership behaviour. Detail three different work situations in which a different style of leadership is likely to be most effective.

9 If you were a consultant on leadership, what areas of needs would you include in designing a leadership training programme for managers in a large work organisation?

 Assignment 1

LEAST PREFERRED CO-WORKER (LPC) SCALE (Fig. A)

1 Think of the person with whom you can work least well. This person may be some-one you work with now or someone you knew in the past. The person does not have to be someone you like least.
2 Describe this person as he or she appears to you by completing the following scale. Place an 'X' in one of the eight spaces according to how well the adjective fits the person. Look at the words at both ends of the line before placing your 'X'.
3 There are no right or wrong answers. Work rapidly; your first answer is likely to be the best. Do not omit any items and mark each item only once.

Pleasant	8 7 6 5	4 3 2 1	Unpleasant
Friendly	8 7 6 5	4 3 2 1	Unfriendly
Rejecting	1 2 3 4	5 6 7 8	Accepting
Helpful	8 7 6 5	4 3 2 1	Frustrating
Unenthusiastic	1 2 3 4	5 6 7 8	Enthusiastic
Tense	1 2 3 4	5 6 7 8	Relaxed
Distant	1 2 3 4	5 6 7 8	Close
Cold	1 2 3 4	5 6 7 8	Warm
Co-operative	8 7 6 5	4 3 2 1	Uncooperative
Supportive	8 7 6 5	4 3 2 1	Hostile
Boring	1 2 3 4	5 6 7 8	Interesting
Quarrelsome	1 2 3 4	5 6 7 8	Harmonious
Self-assured	8 7 6 5	4 3 2 1	Hesitant
Efficient	8 7 6 5	4 3 2 1	Inefficient
Gloomy	1 2 3 4	5 6 7 8	Cheerful
Open	8 7 6 5	4 3 2 1	Guarded

Fig. A

Source: Least Preferred Co-worker (LPC Scale). (Reprinted with permission of F. E. Fiedler.)

After you have completed the scale compare your responses with those of your colleagues.

 Assignment 2

T-P LEADERSHIP QUESTIONNAIRE: AN ASSESSMENT OF STYLE

The following items describe aspects of leadership behaviour. Respond to each item according to the way you would most likely act if you were leader of a work group. Circle whether you would most likely behave in the described way: always (A); frequently (F); occasionally (O); seldom (S); or never (N).

1. I would most likely act as the spokesperson of the group.	A F O S N
2. I would encourage overtime work.	A F O S N
3. I would allow members complete freedom in their work.	A F O S N
4. I would encourage the use of uniform procedures.	A F O S N
5. I would permit the members to use their own judgement in solving problems.	A F O S N
6. I would stress being ahead of competing groups.	A F O S N
7. I would speak as a representative of the group.	A F O S N
8. I would needle members for greater effort.	A F O S N
9. I would try out my ideas in the group.	A F O S N
10. I would let the members do their work the way they think best.	A F O S N
11. I would be working hard for a promotion.	A F O S N
12. I would tolerate postponement and uncertainty.	A F O S N
13. I would speak for the group if there were visitors present.	A F O S N
14. I would keep the work moving at a rapid pace.	A F O S N
15. I would turn the members loose on a job and let them go to it.	A F O S N
16. I would settle conflicts when they occur in the group.	A F O S N
17. I would get swamped by details.	A F O S N
18. I would represent the group at outside meetings.	A F O S N
19. I would be reluctant to allow the members any freedom of action.	A F O S N
20. I would decide what should be done and how it should be done.	A F O S N
21. I would push for increased production.	A F O S N
22. I would let some members have authority which I could keep.	A F O S N
23. Things would usually turn out as I had predicted.	A F O S N
24. I would allow the group a high degree of initiative.	A F O S N
25. I would assign group members to particular tasks.	A F O S N
26. I would be willing to make changes.	A F O S N
27. I would ask the members to work harder.	A F O S N
28. I would trust the group members to exercise good judgement.	A F O S N
29. I would schedule the work to be done.	A F O S N
30. I would refuse to explain my actions.	A F O S N
31. I would persuade others that my ideas are to their advantage.	A F O S N
32. I would permit the group to set its own pace.	A F O S N
33. I would urge the group to beat its previous record.	A F O S N
34. I would act without consulting the group.	A F O S N
35. I would ask that group members follow standard rules and regulations.	A F O S N

T _____ P _____

Scoring

1. Circle the item number for items 8, 12, 17, 18, 19, 30, 34 and 35.
2. Write the number 1 in front of a *circled item number* if you responded S (seldom) or N (never) to that item.
3. Also write a number 1 in front of *item numbers not circled* if you responded A (always) or F (frequently).
4. Circle the number 1s which you have written in front of the following items: 3, 5, 8, 10, 15, 18, 19, 22, 24, 26, 28, 30, 32, 34 and 35.
5. *Count the circled number 1s.* This is your score for concern for people. Record the score in the blank following the letter P at the end of the questionnaire.
6. *Count the uncircled number 1s.* This is your score for concern for task. Record this number in the blank following the letter T.

After you have recorded your total scores compare your responses with those of your colleagues.

 Assignment 3

1. Think of:
 (a) one of the 'best' leaders, *and*
 (b) one of the 'worst' leaders
 that you have experienced, *preferably in a work situation.*

2. Identify and list those specific qualities, or lack of them, which were characteristic of *each* leader. Where possible, draw up your list under three broad headings of:
 (a) personal attributes – for example, intelligence, appearance;
 (b) social relationships – for example, approachability, interests;
 (c) task performance – for example, delegation, discipline.

3. Give a brief description of an actual situation which illustrates the behaviour/actions of *each* leader, and the results of such behaviour/action. Keep your answer balanced. Bear in mind that even the 'best' leader is likely to have some weak points; and even the 'worst' leader some good points. Try to be as objective as possible and avoid personal bias.

4. Draw up your *own* list, with brief supporting descriptions, of the main characteristics you would expect to be exhibited by a 'good' leader. Be prepared to justify your lists and descriptions in class discussion. See how your answers relate to your responses to Assignment 1 and Assignment 2 of this chapter.

C A S E S T U D Y

International Practice: British Petroleum

by Peter Phillips

British Petroleum (BP) is recreating itself as a radically different organization. In 1990 the company began a fundamental change of its culture, strategy and organization to position itself to face future challenges. As a result, the BP group now has three operating businesses and a small corporate centre (less than 200 staff). Decision making is pushed down to the lowest appropriate level. In general the company focuses on its core activities with the non-core being outsourced or bought in. There is a move towards sharing services between businesses and between regions.

For employees the changes have obviously been dramatic, BP was traditionally a cradle-to-grave organization. Downsizing and delayering, together with the constant process of change, have had a major impact on morale. Individuals have had to learn to adjust to new ways of working and develop new understandings of career and development. In effect there is a new employment partnership between BP and its employees.

Even though BP has emerged in good financial shape, more change is seen as inevitable and the pressure to reach new and higher levels of performance is intense.

Clearly the impact on leaders in the company has been dramatic. They are pivotal in the change process but have been no less affected by the changes in BP than other staff. In addition their roles have fundamentally changed. Prior to 1990 BP managers' roles were relatively clearly defined. There were rules and procedures covering most things, a vast guide to personnel policies, and a plethora of committees. Authorities were clearly delineated and controlled.

In an organization where all recruits were highly qualified, managers were selected on technical or professional excellence. Managers tended to solve the difficult problems and direct, check and control the work of their staff. Information was shared with those who needed to know and no further. Upward management – managing your boss – was a key skill, admitting weakness was frowned upon, the size of your empire was an indication of success, other groups were a source of competition.

These side effects of its long-established approach were offset by the fact that the company took care of its staff. There was a sense of being in an entitlement culture providing careers and jobs for life. With the onset of the major organizational and structural changes, the role of the company's managers became radically different. In the new cost conscious organization the competitive advantage was to come through the people. The leaders had to recognize and learn new skills to operate in the new world and build empowered teams to deliver the new agenda. A new set of 'OPEN' (Open Thinking, Personal Impact, Empowerment and Networking) behaviours was identified as essential for all employees in the new culture.

During 1990 and 1991, although the company as a whole arranged programmes to start and energize the change process, each leader had to help their team come to terms with and operate effectively in the new culture.

The primary focus at this stage in the organization was on achieving the radical new culture. The company's performance began to deteriorate – due principally

to the decline in oil price, economic recession and a high level of debt. Financial results were poor and major changes were made (including the then chairman resigning). These changes inevitably were focused on restoring the financial fortunes of the company. Costs needed to be cut, staff numbers were reduced in line with new priorities; a performance culture had to be quickly established to drive forward a leaner organization.

The impact on morale was serious as the company's declining fortunes were debated in the media. Leaders faced the challenge of achieving tough performance targets while rebuilding morale in an atmosphere of downsizing, outsourcing and cost cutting. In the performance culture the principles of the original culture change had been reaffirmed, but how the two cultures would gel had not entirely been explained. This tension needed to be managed by the company and its leaders.

The new balance of leadership

Leaders in the new organization must balance a number of tensions – such as between people and performance; the short and long-term; sustaining current performance and growing for the future. While cost-cutting skills are important, leaders need also to be able to spot and take new business opportunities. While keeping their eyes on the performance indicators, leaders have to encourage creativity, risk taking and challenge; skills for the future must be developed while delivering this year's targets. Performance has to be maintained and morale rebuilt and new understandings of the employment relationship established – living under the constant threat of more change.

To be successful BP has to be globally effective: its leaders have to be able to operate effectively in different cultures, to manage and relish cultural diversity. They have to be able to obtain both the benefits of localization and those from being part of a major corporation. They need to be able to work effectively in non-BP or part-BP cultures, such as alliance and joint ventures.

Leaders have to be flexible and adaptable to translate group strategy into different local environments, build the relationships, sell the message and build and sustain performance. Strong technical and professional skills are no longer sufficient. The ability to understand and influence people inside and outside the company is critical. In such an environment, an ability to develop and maintain strong personal networks becomes essential and in international assignments tends to require longer assignments than has traditionally been the case.

On international assignments there is comparitively little support and relatively few dictates from the business centres. The leaders have considerable independence within light frameworks to deliver the performance target, but have to be aware that they, in their local environment, represent BP. Often the senior leaders in countries are representing more than one business – yet, frequently while carrying this more general responsibility they are directly accountable for one particular business. This requires a knowledge and understanding of the strategy and goals of each business and a range of contacts not easily developed when development tends to be in one of the major businesses rather than through a more general approach.

For the most senior leaders of the group their role has also changed, though clearly the need to set the strategic direction and vision for the business is still key. They need to be able to inspire others and model the desired culture. The ability to lead change becomes critical, and organizational development skills – the ability to

create the organization to deliver the agenda – are essential. They have to become coaches to their own staff to provide the appropriate level of support and challenge both to sustain current performance and to grow for the future. They have to ensure that the whole organization is motivated and focused to reach its goals.

How leaders develop

Now, there is a premium on effective and relevant leadership development to help those who need to do so to learn new skills and prepare for the future. In the old organization there was a miasma of development committees, a paternalistic approach to staff development and expectation of progress. The principal tool of development was job movement, usually anticipated every one to two years.

BP has long had a fast-track scheme regarded by any as a model to benchmark against. The process identified high-fliers early in their careers – often in their late twenties – and ensured focused development through key assignments towards senior positions. This process was essential, partly to ensure a pool of high calibre successors for the group, also to ensure that, given the hierarchical structure of the group, people progressed fast enough. It also reflected the norm of promoting from within and reinforced the group culture.

The changes in the group since 1990 have dramatically altered this approach to development. The flatter smaller organization clearly had a major impact on opportunities, and business demands now call for longer periods in jobs. Responsibility for development shifted primarily to the individual, albeit in a partnership with the line manager. Personal development plans prepared by the individual and supported by the line are a key part of the performance culture.

A major contribution to the development of senior leaders in BP has been the Leadership Competency Model. This model which describes the key leadership behaviours required by tomorrow's leaders now underpins all group leadership activities. These competencies were developed with and owned by the businesses. The model provides the linking thread in BP's leadership development framework, which openly lays out the process for developing leaders at all levels. Rather than seeking to identify high-fliers early and predict and accelerate their development to their ultimate potential, the framework breaks the leadership pool into broad bands and outlines the key development processes and experiences in each pool. Attention is focused on development within the band and acquiring the qualities required for the next level – it is accepted that individuals will move through the band at their own pace, some of course will not move into the next. It is generally accepted that for most individuals development will occur primarily within one business. Movement into the group sphere (or fast-track scheme) occurs when individuals have established their technical base, demonstrated strong leadership and commercial skills and have a track record of delivering performance.

Development processes have been opened up to enable individuals to form a clear development plan (and career plan). The ground rules of the general employment relationship and personal development are being clarified so that both sides understand the requirements and expectations.

The competency model is being used to profile the strengths and weaknesses of the senior leaders of the group through 360 degree feedback and assessment processes. These enable the individual and line manager with other appraisal processes, to focus on the short and long-term development needs which are critical for both personal and organizational growth.

The model also informs and interacts with the succession planning process by making individual and job matching a more objective process. It also enables the company to focus on key roles such as associate presidents (the lead individuals in each country) and to identify particular skill requirements, develop succession plans and specific training programmes. etc.

Within the leadership development framework the group attempts to align all development processes so that they are part of the same jigsaw and closely associated with company performance. Given that individuals expect to spend longer in jobs, development now has to involve a much broader range of processes. Individuals have to find ways, with line support, to grow in their existing jobs and although training (internally or externally) has a role to play, other activities such as projects, short-term job swaps, external activities, coaching and computer-based and distance learning need also to be considered.

Within the parameters of the leadership development framework and the competency model, individuality, flexibility and scope for mavericks must be retained. The purpose of the development is to identify and develop the leaders who will deliver superior performance today and in the future. The aim is to let talent develop and flourish, not to clone leaders or apply a cultural straitjacket. The models must work globally and apply to all leaders irrespective of nationality, sex, etc. The organization needs to constantly review its models and processes in the light of strategic performance and environmental changes. This is vital for organizational renewal.

It is also accepted that competencies in themselves are not the complete picture. There are other factors involved. Personal attributes, such as moral integrity, sense of mission and will to win, are vital to really outstanding leadership. These must be monitored and developed in leaders. Accepting that these individual characteristics are important, it is essential that all managers demonstrate enthusiasm, commitment and curiosity.

Monitoring, measurement and reward are key parts of the process. They are essential to ensuring that the individual and the organization are developing in tandem. The vital role of the leader in shaping performance and coaching becomes fundamental to the organization's success.

The leader's role has changed and become more complex and, arguably, even more critical to the organization's success. They must:

- ensure that high performance levels are achieved and sustained:
- handle complexity and ambiguity; enjoy leading the change process;
- ensure that the organization, and its processes, are constantly developed to deliver the strategy and performance;
- ensure that the people within the company are motivated, developed and rewarded to produce outstanding results.

These are highly demanding tasks and skills. Developing leaders with the capacity to learn, adapt, coach, support and inspire others is a critical challenge for major companies. Meeting the challenge requires commitment, investment and creativity.

Peter Phillips is manager of Leadership Programmes at BP.

Reprinted with permission from *The Financial Times Handbook of Management,* Pitman Publishing,1995.

Notes and references

1. This chapter is based in parts on a development of the author's article: Mullins, L. J. 'Approaches to Leadership', *The British Journal of Administrative Management*, vol. 32, no. 8, November 1982, pp. 263–9.
2. Parker, P. 'The Shape of Leaders to Come', *Management Today*, July 1994, p. 5.
3. See, for example: Tack, A. *Motivational Leadership*, Gower (1984).
4. Sieff, M. (Lord Sieff of Brimpton), *Management the Marks & Spencer Way*, Fontana Collins (1991) p. 133.
5. Tustin, T. 'Follow My Leader', *Management Today*, December 1989. p. 5.
6. See, for example: Gretton, I. 'Taking the Lead in Leadership', *Professional Manager*, January 1995, pp. 20–2.
7. See, for example: Hunt, J. W. *Managing People at Work*, Third edition, McGraw-Hill (1992).
8. Zaleznik, A. 'Managers and Leaders: Are They Different?' *Harvard Business Review*, May–June 1977, pp. 67–78.
9. See, for example: Levine, S. and Crom, M. *The Leader in You*, Simon and Schuster (1994).
10. Watson, C. M. 'Leadership, Management and the Seven Keys', *Business Horizons*, March–April 1983, pp. 8–13.
11. Bonington, C. 'Leading to the Top: The Successful Management of People', *Office and Information Management International*, September 1988, pp. 8–9.
12. See, for example: Sims, D., Fineman, S. and Gabriel, Y. *Organizing and Organizations*, Sage Publications (1993).
13. Peters, T. J. 'Symbols, Patterns and Settings: An Optimistic Case For Getting Things Done', *Organizational Dynamics*, Autumn 1978, pp. 3–23.
14. Brown, A. D. *Organisational Culture*, Pitman (1995).
15. For example, see: Bass, B. M. *Leadership, Psychology and Organizational Behaviour*, Harper and Row (1960).
16. Adair, J. *Effective Teambuilding*, Gower (1986) p. 123.
17. McGregor, D. *The Human Side of Enterprise*, Penguin (1987) p. 182.
18. French, J. R. P. and Raven, B. 'The Bases of Social Power', in Cartwright, D. and Zander, A. F. (eds) *Group Dynamics: Research and Theory*, Third edition, Harper and Row (1968).
19. Roddick, A. *Body and Soul*, Ebury Press (1991) p. 214.
20. Drucker, P. F. *The Practice of Management*, Heinemann Professional (1989) p. 156.
21. Byrd, C. *Social Psychology*, Appleton-Century-Crofts (1940).
22. Jennings, E. E. 'The Anatomy of Leadership', *Management of Personnel Quarterly*, vol. 1, no. 1, Autumn 1961, p. 2.
23. Ghiselli, E. E. 'Management Talent', *American Psychologist*, vol, 18, October 1963, pp. 631–42.
24. Stogdill, R. M. *Handbook of Leadership*, Free Press (1974).
25. Kotter, J. P. 'What Leaders Really Do', *Harvard Business Review*, May–June 1990, p. 103.
26. Miles, M. B. *Learning to Work in Groups*, Columbia University (1959) p. 19.
27. Krech, D., Crutchfield, R. S. and Ballachey, E. L. *Individual in Society*, McGraw-Hill (1962).
28. Adair, J. *Action-Centred Leadership*, Gower (1979). See also: Adair, J. *The Skills of Leadership*, Gower (1984).
29. For a summary, see: Smith, E. P. *The Manager as a Leader* (Notes for Managers), The Industrial Society (June 1983).
30. Adair, J. *Effective Leadership*, Pan Books (1983).
31. Fleishman, E. A. 'Leadership Climate, Human Relations Training and Supervisory Behavior', in Fleishman, E. A. and Bass, A. R. *Studies in Personnel and Industrial Psychology*, Third edition, Dorsey (1974).

32. Likert, R. *New Patterns of Management*, McGraw-Hill (1961).
33. Maslow, A. H. 'A Theory of Human Motivation', *Psychological Review*, 50, July 1943, pp. 370–96, and Maslow, A. H. *Motivation and Personality*, Third edition, Harper and Row (1987).
34. Belbin, R. M. *Team Roles at Work*, Butterworth-Heinemann (1993).
35. Tannenbaum, R. and Schmidt, W. H. 'How to Choose a Leadership Pattern', *Harvard Business Review*, May–June 1973, pp. 162–75, 178–80.
36. *Ibid*. Retrospective commentary, pp. 166–8.
37. Follett, M. P. 'The Giving of Orders', in Metcalf, H. C. and Urwick, L. (eds) *Dynamic Administration*, Harper (1941). Reprinted in Pugh, D. S. (ed.) *Organization Theory*, Penguin (1971) pp. 154–5.
38. Fiedler, F. E. *A Theory of Leadership Effectiveness*, McGraw-Hill (1967).
39. For example, see: Filley, A. C., House, R. J. and Kerr, S. *Managerial Process and Organizational Behavior*, Second edition, Scott, Foresman (1976). They refer to the uncertainty of the interpretation of LPC and what aspects of leadership behaviour it actually represents.
40. Vroom, V. H. and Yetton, P. W. *Leadership and Decision-Making*, University of Pittsburgh Press (1973).
41. Vroom, V. H. and Jago, A. G. *The New Leadership: Managing Participation in Organizations*, Prentice-Hall (1988).
42. House, R. J. 'A Path–Goal Theory of Leadership Effectiveness', *Administrative Science Quarterly*, vol. 16, September 1971, pp. 321–38.
43. House, R. J. and Dessler, G. 'The Path–Goal Theory of Leadership', in Hunt, J. G. and Larson, L. L. (eds) *Contingency Approaches to Leadership*, Southern Illinois University Press (1974).
44. Hersey, P. and Blanchard, K. H. *Management of Organizational Behavior: Utilizing Human Resources*, Sixth edition, Prentice-Hall (1993).
45. Nicholls, J. R. 'A New Approach to Situational Leadership', *Leadership and Organization Development Journal*, vol. 6, no. 4, 1985, pp. 2–7.
46. Hersey, P. and Blanchard, K. H. *Management of Organizational Behavior: Utilizing Human Resources*, Sixth edition, Prentice-Hall (1993) p. 192.
47. Likert, R. and Likert, J. G. *New Ways of Managing Conflict*, McGraw-Hill (1976).
48. Clarke, C. and Pratt, S. 'Leadership's Four-Part Progress', *Management Today*, March 1985, pp. 84–6.
49. Rodrigues, C. A. 'Identifying the Right Leader for the Right Situation', *Personnel*, September 1988, pp. 43–6.
50. Brown, A. 'Organizational Culture: The Key to Effective Leadership and Organizational Development', *Leadership and Organization Development Journal*, vol. 13, no. 2, 1992, pp. 3–6.
51. McGregor, D, *The Human Side of Enterprise*, Penguin (1987).
52. Tannenbaum, R. and Schmidt, W. H. 'How to Choose a Leadership Pattern', *Harvard Business Review*, May–June 1973, pp. 162–75, 178–180.
53. Hofstede, G. *Culture's Consequences: International Differences in Work–Related Values*, Sage (1981).
54. Lawrence, P. 'The Personnel Function: An Anglo-German Comparison', in Brewster, C. and Tyson, S. (eds) *International Comparisons in Human Resource Management*, Pitman (1991).

Part 4

CONTEXT OF THE ORGANISATION

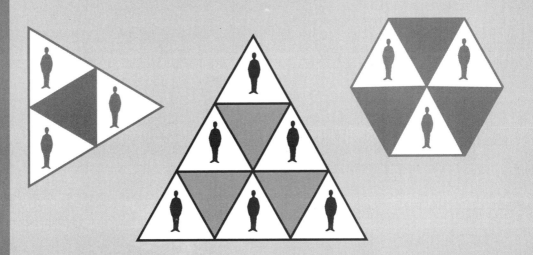

9 ORGANISATIONAL GOALS AND OBJECTIVES

The activities of a work organisation are directed towards an end, towards certain goals. Organisations pursue a variety of goals which are not mutually exclusive and which may conflict with each other. Goals are translated into objectives and policy in order to provide corporate guidelines for the operations and management of the organisation. Organisational goals, objectives and policy are therefore important features in the study of work organisations and their management.

 Learning objectives

To:

- Explain the nature of, and functions served by, organisational goals;

- Assess the importance of organisational ideologies and principles;

- Examine the need for objectives and policy, and the importance of the profit objective to business organisations;

- Assess the need for corporate strategy and explain the basis for decision-making and problem-solving;

- Examine the concept of social responsibilities of management;

- Explore approaches to the consideration of values and ethics in organisations;

- Recognise the importance of organisational goals, objectives and policy for the effective management of a work organisation.

Worth thinking about

A National Health Service trust chairman was heavily criticised for maintaining that the primary loyalty of doctors was owed to their employers, and that their duty to patients came a third priority after themselves. But when demands upon the health service are limitless and resources finite, why is the idea of owing first loyalty to the organisation you work in such a bad thing?

THE NATURE OF ORGANISATIONAL GOALS

All organisations have some function to perform, some contribution to make to the environment of which they are part. The function of the business organisation may be seen, for example, as the creation and/or supply of goods and services. This involves bringing together the factors of production in appropriate units of organisation, and their successful mix and direction, in order to create value added. Others might see the function of business organisations as, for example, providing a source of employment and of income.

In addition to performing some function, all organisations also have some incentive for their existence, and for their operations. The goals of an organisation are the reason for its existence. The activities of the organisation are directed to the attainment of its goals.

A goal is a future expectation, some desired future state. It is something the organisation is striving to accomplish. The meaning of a goal is, however, subject to a number of interpretations. It can be used in a very broad sense to refer to the overall purpose of an organisation, for example to produce television sets. A goal may also be used to refer to more specific desired accomplishments, for example to produce and sell a given number of a range of television sets within a given period of time.

The concept of organisational goals is more specific than that of the function of an organisation. The goals of an organisation will determine the nature of its inputs and outputs, the series of activities through which the outputs are achieved, and interactions with its external environment. The extent to which an organisation is successful in attaining its goals is a basis for the evaluation of organisational performance and effectiveness.

Goal model approach

The goal model approach concentrates on the study of organisational goals and the measurement of success against the realisation of goals. *Etzioni* suggests a potential disadvantage of this approach.[1] Goals are ideals and more attractive than actual achievement. Organisations are characterised by low effectiveness. They rarely achieve their goals with any degree of finality and can, therefore, almost always be reported as a failure. The goal model approach results in attention being focused on the organisation's lack of success in attaining goals at the expense of more meaningful forms of analysis. Instead of comparing organisations in terms of their stated goals, performance may be assessed relatively against different organisations.

The concept of organisational goals is ambiguous. Goals may be expressed very simply: in the case of business organisations, for example, to make a profit, or to increase productivity. Such broadly based goals might be taken for granted and they tell us little about the emphasis placed on the various activities of the organisation in meeting its goals. In any case, profit might more correctly be interpreted as a reward to the shareholders or providers of capital, and a means of ensuring the continued existence of the organisation and maintaining its growth and development.

Alternatives for decision-making

Goals have been defined by *Simon* as value premises which serve as inputs to decisions.[2] Goals at different levels within the organisation contribute to alternatives for decision-making. Simon compares goal-setting with the mathematical approach of linear programming and he sees goals more as sets of constraints which the organisation must satisfy – for example: profit for shareholders, or a minimum rate of return on investments; satisfying demands of consumers; complying with government legislation on safety standards; providing job satisfaction for staff; pacifying environmental groups such as Friends of the Earth. Goals limit the scope of actions and decision-making at lower levels of the organisation. Constraints may themselves be regarded as goals in that they represent objectives which management is trying to meet.

THE FUNCTIONS OF GOALS

Despite the problems associated with the goal model approach, the concept of organisational goals serves a number of important functions.[3]

- Goals provide a standard of performance. They focus attention on the activities of the organisation and the direction of the efforts of its members.
- Goals provide a basis for planning and management control related to the activities of the organisation.
- Goals provide guidelines for decision-making and justification for actions taken. They reduce uncertainty in decision-making and give a defence against possible criticism.
- Goals influence the structure of the organisation and help determine the nature of technology employed. The manner in which the organisation is structured will affect what it will attempt to achieve.
- Goals help to develop commitment of individuals and groups to the activities of the organisation. They focus attention on purposeful behaviour and provide a basis for motivation and reward systems.
- Goals give an indication of what the organisation is really like, its true nature and character, both for members and for people outside of the organisation.
- Goals serve as a basis for the evaluation of change and organisation development.
- Goals are the basis for objectives and policies of the organisation.

An important feature of work organisations

Goals are therefore an important feature of work organisations. To be effective goals should be emphasised, stated clearly and communicated to all members of the organisation. The movement towards greater delegation and empowerment down through the hierarchy means that staff at all levels must be aware of their key tasks

and actions, and exactly what is expected of them and their department/section. There must be clearly laid down organisational goals, objectives and strategy.[4]

The goal-setting process is of importance to all types of organisations and facilitates the attainment of objectives. In the public sector for example, organisations such as hospitals, local authorities and universities have complex, diverse and competing goals. The clarification of goals and objectives is the basis for corporate planning, and a planning, programming, budgeting systems (PPBS) approach to decision-making.

INTEGRATION OF GOALS

Strictly, organisations have no goals; only people do. Organisational goals are established by people, either individually, or, more usually, by a number of individuals co-operating together. For example, a group of senior managers may collectively agree on a particular desired course of action which may then come to be referred to as an organisational goal; but this is still the goal of those managers who initially determined it.

Success of the organisation is measured by the progress of people towards goals set by people. This gives rise to the questions:

- How far are the goals of management compatible with the goals of the organisation?
- To what extent do individual members obtain satisfaction of their own goals through the attainment of organisational goals?

Informal goals Members of the organisation have different, and often conflicting, goals. As a result, the goals which the organisation actually pursues (informal goals) may be

**Fig. 9.1
Compatibility of
goals within an
organisation**

distinguished from the officially stated goals (formal goals) which are set out in broad terms as the reasons for the purpose of the organisation. Informal goals may be inferred from the actual decisions made and actions taken within the organisation. Managers, and other members of the organisation, will have:

(i) their own perception of the goals of the organisation, for example to produce high-quality television sets which satisfy requirements of the customers; and

(ii) their personal goals, for example to earn high wages, to achieve promotion, to gain social satisfaction, to achieve status; which they expect to fulfil by participating in the activities of the organisation. (*See* Fig. 9.1.)

Compatibility of personal goals and organisational goals

If organisational goals and personal goals are pulling in different directions conflict will arise and performance is likely to suffer. An organisation will be more effective when personal goals are compatible with organisational goals. Organisational performance will depend ultimately on the extent to which individuals are provided with the opportunity to satisfy their own goals by contributing to the goals of the organisation.[5]

Management has a responsibility to clarify organisational goals and to attempt to integrate personal goals (including their own) with the overall objectives of the organisation. Only when organisational goals are shared by all members of the organisation will complete integration be achieved. In practice, this is unlikely. As *McGregor* points out:

> Perfect integration of organizational requirements and individual goals and needs is, of course, not a realistic objective. In adopting this principle, we seek that degree of integration in which the individual can achieve his goals *best* by directing his efforts towards the success of the organization.[6]

Management should endeavour, therefore, to structure the organisation so that people may realise their own (personal) goals by helping the organisation to satisfy its goals. One attempt at integrating organisational goals with the needs of the individual members of the organisation is provided by the approach of Management by Objectives. This is discussed in Chapter 13.

CLASSIFICATION OF ORGANISATIONAL GOALS

We have seen that goals are an important feature in the management of organisations. The goals of an organisation may be classified in a number of different ways.

The concept of compliance

Etzioni provides a classification which distinguishes three types of organisational goals in terms of their relationship with the concept of power and compliance.[7]

- **Order goals** are negative and attempt to place some kind of restraint upon members of the organisation and to prevent certain forms of behaviour.
- **Economic goals** are concerned with the production of goods and/or services for people outside of the organisation.
- **Cultural goals** are concerned with symbolic objects and with creating or maintaining value systems of society. Social goals, which serve the various needs of members of the organisation, are classified as a sub-type under cultural goals.

Most organisations would be expected to display one of three central combinations of organisational goals and compliance structure. Although there are other possibilities the three most usual combinations are:

- Organisations with order goals and a coercive compliance structure, for example closed prisons.
- Organisations with economic goals and a utilitarian compliance structure, for example business firms.
- Organisations with cultural goals and a normative compliance structure, for example professional bodies.

Organisations may, of course, serve more than one goal, and these goals may not necessarily fall into the same category. Usually, however, there is one main goal which maintains a relationship with compliance structure in keeping with one of the three central combinations.

The concept of power, involvement and compliance is discussed further in Chapter 17.

Goals as the outcome of bargaining

According to *Cyert and March*, goals result from the outcome of bargaining among members of sub-coalitions. They identify five organisational goals related specifically to a business firm.[8]

- **Production goal** – related to minimising variations in the range of production operations over a given period of time, and to the overall level of production.
- **Inventory goal** – aspirations related to levels of completed goods. The inventory goal acts as a buffer between production and sales.
- **Sales goal** – aspirations related to the level of sales, either in monetary terms, number of units, or both. The sales goal provides some general criteria of sales effectiveness.
- **Market share goal** – concerned with a measure of sales effectiveness or with comparative success. The market share goal can be used as an alternative to the sales goal, or both can be used.
- **Profit goal** – linked to accounting procedures for determining profit and loss. The profit goal may be an aspiration relating to amount of monetary profit, or profit share, or return on investment.

The five goals are not listed in any necessary order of importance, but all the goals must be satisfied. Cyert and March suggest that most of the time no order of importance is necessary, although there may be an implicit order of priority in different organisations.

A general model of organisational goals

A more general model of organisational goals is provided by *Gross* who gives a list appropriate to all types of organisations.[9]

- **Satisfaction of interests.** Organisations exist to satisfy multiple interests of various people, both members of the organisation and outsiders. These interests are hard to identify and overlapping. This category of purpose might be referred to as welfare, utility, benefit or payoff.
- **Output of services or goods:** the output of products, goods or services (tangible or intangible) which the organisation makes available to clients.
- **Efficiency or profitability:** the efficient use of available, scarce inputs relative to outputs. Inputs and outputs, and the relationship between them, may be cal-

culated in a number of ways. 'Profitability' is applicable when both outputs and inputs can be expressed in monetary terms.

● **Investment in organisational viability:** the diversion of inputs from the production of output to investment in physical, human and organisational assets in order to maintain survival and growth.

● **Mobilisation of resources.** The organisation must mobilise resources for inputs in order to produce goods or services or to invest in viability.

● **Observance of codes,** usually expressed in terms of acceptable margins of deviation. Codes include both formal and informal rules developed by the organisation and patterns of behaviour imposed by law, moral considerations and standards of professional ethics.

● **Rationality:** actions which are regarded as satisfactory in terms of desirability, feasibility and consistency. Rationality applies on both technical and administrative (managerial) considerations.

Organisational goals are not necessarily the same for any one group of people, for example top management. Rather they are representative of the organisation as a collection of individuals and groups, and define the characteristics and activities of the whole organisation as a system. All organisations have multiple goals. It is difficult to develop criteria of performance against such broadly based goals and they need to be translated into more specific goals capable of measurement in particular organisations.

A systems view of organistional goals

There are then a number of possible classifications. However, by adopting a systems view of organisations (as discussed in Chapter 3) we can distinguish four main types of organisational goals:

● **Consumer goals.** These relate to the nature of outputs in terms of the market to be served and consumer satisfaction: that is, the range and nature of goods and/or services produced or supplied in order to meet the needs of customers or clients. Examples are consumer products, educational services, or health care.

● **Product goals.** These relate to the nature and characteristics of the outputs themselves, that is, the goods and/or services provided. This is the main area in which organisations deliberately attempt to distinguish themselves from other organisations, for example in the range, design, quality and availability of their outputs.

● **Operational goals.** These relate to the series of activities involved in providing outputs, and to the operation and functioning of the organisation. Examples are the management of opportunities and risks, the choice of structure, the nature of technology, and management processes.

● **Secondary goals.** These relate to goals that are not the main aim of the organisation. They arise from the manner in which the organisation uses its power and influence in pursuit of its outputs, and in undertaking the series of activities to achieve these outputs. Political aims, aid to the community, the development of staff, and social responsibilities would come under this heading.

Alteration of goals

Survival of the organisation will depend upon its ability to adapt to change and to the demands of its external environment. In practice, however, organisations usually appear to alter their goals only on a gradual basis. Commitment to the objectives and policies of the organisation, people's cognitive limitations and their uncertainties and fears, may mean a reluctance to accept change. Organisations

may also find it difficult to make short-term, rapid changes in resource allocation. The very complexity of environmental influences may itself hinder rapid change. (*See also* the discussion on organisational change in Chapter 20.)

It is important, however, that the organisation does not restrict innovation but is ready to respond positively to changing circumstances and, increasingly, to anticipate future change. Management has to balance the need for adaptability in meeting the challenges and opportunities presented by change with, at the same time, preserving an atmosphere of stability and continuity in the interests of members of the organisation.

ORGANISATIONAL IDEOLOGIES AND PRINCIPLES

The goals of the organisation may be pursued in accordance with an underlying ideology, or philosophy, based on beliefs, values and attitudes. This ideology determines the 'culture' of the organisation and provides a set of principles which govern the overall conduct of the organisation's operations, codes of behaviour, the management of people and its dealings with other organisations.[10] These sets of principles may be recognised and implemented informally as 'accepted conventions' of the organisation or they may be stated formally in writing.

Lord Sieff, formerly Chairman and Chief Executive of Marks & Spencer, has set out what he considers the most important principles in business:

(i) Perhaps the most important of all is a policy of good human relations with all concerned in and with the operation – employees, customers and suppliers.
(ii) To offer customers goods and services which they want and which should be of a high quality and good value.
(iii) To work closely with suppliers and encourage them to use the most modern, efficient techniques of production and quality control dictated by the latest discoveries in science and technology.
(iv) To simplify operating procedures so that the business is carried out in an efficient manner.
(v) To ensure that those in management are not isolated or in watertight compartments and that, while an individual's responsibility (other than the chief executive's) may be limited to a particular area or areas, he or she should have general knowledge of the operation as a whole.
(vi) Never forget the importance of satisfying the customer.
(vii) To seek wherever possible a source in the United Kingdom.[11]

Another example is provided by the International Business Machines Corporation (IBM). The efforts of IBM towards becoming truly market-driven are guided by five basic goals.

- enhance customer partnership;
- be the product and services leader;
- grow with the industry;
- be the most efficient;
- sustain profitability.

To help meet the challenges from new types of customer in a fast moving and highly competitive market, IBM has defined four underlying principles:

- **Make the customer the final arbiter.** The customers alone decide the success of our efforts. A solution is not successful unless it satisfies our customers.
- **Understand the markets.** We must have a detailed understanding of our customers' businesses in order to provide them with the solutions they will want to buy.
- **Commit to leadership in the markets we choose to serve.** We must translate customers' needs and wants into products which are the very best of their kind in the sectors in which we operate.
- **Execute with excellence across the enterprise.** Each individual within IBM must take responsibility for performing every task with excellence.[12]

A further interesting example is provided by Anita Roddick, founder of The Body Shop.

> I think all business practices would improve immeasurably if they were guided by 'feminine' principles – qualities like love and care and intuition. Women, too, would understand the need for an ethical philosophy to guide international business.[13]

Guidelines for overall strategies

The Walt Disney Company has established corporate objectives as a set of guidelines that are used to focus individual and mutual efforts. These corporate objectives are:

- to sustain the Walt Disney Company as the world's finest entertainment company;
- to maximise stockholder wealth;
- to maintain the integrity of the Company name and its consumer franchise;
- to preserve basic Disney values.

These concepts help executives produce overall strategies that are used by management throughout the company as they operate the various business segments.[14]

Dominant aspect of an organisation's philosophy

Certain aspects of an organisation's philosophy may be so dominant that they become the 'hallmark' of that organisation and place constraints on other areas or forms of activities. An example is the high quality standard of Marks & Spencer's merchandise and their explicit policy of buying primarily from United Kingdom sources. In the case of the Walt Disney Company, quality service is embedded deeply within their corporate culture. The overriding byword of The Body Shop is honesty and this underlies their policy of: 'We WILL be the most honest cosmetic company.'[15] As another example, the highest-quality hallmark of Rolls-Royce cars would presumably prevent entry into the cheaper mass-production market.

Ethical and organisational foundation

The ideology of an organisation can be related to the idea of ethical foundation and organisational or operational foundation.[16]

- **Ethical foundation** embodies the basic principles which govern the external and internal relations of the organisation. External relations concern standards of fair trading and relations with, for example, customers, suppliers and the general public. Internal relations are concerned with fair standards of employment and relations with members of the organisation, including authorised union representatives.

- **Organisational or operational foundation** is concerned with the structure, operation, and conduct of the activities of the organisation. External aspects relate to, for example, methods of trading and channels of distribution. Internal aspects include methods of production, use of equipment and managerial practices relating to organisational performance, productivity and profitability.

OBJECTIVES AND POLICY

In accordance with its ideology or philosophy, the goals of the organisation are translated into objectives and policy. Terminology and use of the two terms varies but objectives are seen here as the 'what', and policy as the 'how', 'where' and 'when' – the means that follow the objectives.

- **Objectives** set out more specifically the goals of the organisation, the aims to be achieved and the desired end-results.
- **Policy** is developed within the framework of objectives. It provides the basis for decision-making and the course of action to follow in order to achieve objectives.

The relationship between the organisation, its objectives and management is illustrated by *Fayol* who stated that one of the managerial duties of an organisation is to: 'See that the human and material organization is consistent with the objective, resources and requirements of the concern'.[17] The establishment of objectives and policy is therefore an integral part of the process of management, and a necessary function in every organisation.

A systems view of goals and objectives

The objectives of an organisation are related to the input–conversion–output cycle. In order to achieve its objectives and satisfy its goals the organisation takes inputs from the environment, through a series of activities transforms or converts these inputs into outputs and returns them to the environment as inputs to other systems. The organisation operates within a dynamic setting and success in achieving its goals will be influenced by a multiplicity of interactions with the environment. (*See* Fig. 9.2.)

Whatever the type of organisation, there is need for lines of direction through the establishment of objectives and determination of policy. Objectives and policy form a basis for the process of management.

Objectives

The choice of objectives is an essential part of the decision-making process involving future courses of action. Objectives may be set out either in general terms or in more specific terms. General objectives are determined by top management. Specific objectives are formulated within the scope of general objectives and usually have more defined areas of application and time limits.

Objectives may be just implicit but the formal, explicit definition of objectives will help highlight the activities which the organisation needs to undertake and the comparative importance of its various functions. An explicit statement of objectives may assist communications and reduce misunderstandings, and provide more meaningful criteria for evaluating organisational performance. However,

**Fig. 9.2
A systems view of
organisational goals
and objectives**

objectives should not be stated in such a way that they detract from the recognition of possible new opportunities, potential danger areas, the initiative of staff or the need for innovation or change.

A policy is a guideline for organisational action and the implementation of goals and objectives. Policy is translated into rules, plans and procedures; it relates to all activities of the organisation, and to all levels of the organisation. Clearly stated policy can help reinforce the main functions of the organisation, make for consistency and reduce dependency on the actions of individual managers. Policy clarifies the roles and responsibilities of managers and other members of staff and provides guidelines for managerial behaviour. Securing agreement to a new or revised policy can help overcome reliance on outdated practices and aid the introduction of organisational change.[18]

Policy provides guiding principles for areas of decision-making and delegation. For example, specific decisions relating to personnel policy could include:

- to give priority to promotion from within the organisation;
- to enforce retirement at government pensionable age;
- whenever possible to employ only graduate or professionally qualified accountants;
- to permit line managers, in consultation with the personnel manager, to appoint staff up to a given salary/wage level.

Some policy decisions are directly influenced by external factors, for example government legislation on equal opportunities.

Distinction between objectives and policy

A distinction between objectives and policy is given by *O'Shaughnessy*.[19]

Objectives emphasize aims and are stated as expectations, but policies emphasize rules and are stated in the form of directives. For example:

Marketing	Objective:	complete market coverage
	Policy:	the Company *will* sell to every retail outlet that is credit-worthy, as decided by the Company Accountant.
Production	Objective:	low units costs from long production runs
	Policy:	the Company *will not* produce one-off jobs without the specific authority of the Board.
Finance	Objective:	to maintain adequate liquidity
	Policy:	accountant will draw up a cash budget and inform the Board if working capital is likely to fall below a specified limit.
Personnel	Objective:	good labour relations
	Policy:	set up and maintain schemes for: Joint Consultation, Job Evaluation, Wage Incentives.

Corporate guidelines

Objectives and policy together provide corporate guidelines for the operations and management of the organisation. The activities of the organisation derive their significance from the contribution they make to achieving objectives in the manner directed. The formulation of objectives and policy, and the allocation of resources, provide the basis for strategic planning which is the first stage in the planning and control processes of business organisations.[20]

THE PROFIT OBJECTIVE

In order to be successful the primary objectives of the business organisation may be seen as:

- to continue in existence, that is to **survive;**
- to maintain **growth and development;** and
- to make a **profit.**

All three objectives are inextricably linked and it is a matter of debate whether the organisation survives and develops in order to provide a profit, or makes a profit by which it can survive and develop.

If we accept survival as the ultimate objective of the business organisation, then this involves the need for a steady and continuous profit. Organisations must be prepared to accept the possibility of a reduction in short-term profitability in order to provide for future investments. The profit goal is achieved through the process of management and the combined efforts of members of the organisation. In times of economic recession the survival objective takes on particular importance, especially for small businesses. (*See* Fig. 9.3.)

**Fig. 9.3
Survival as the
ultimate objective**

> ## FORGET PROFIT: FIGHT TO SURVIVE
>
> **The Hampshire spokesperson for the National Federation of Self-Employed and Small Businesses predicted an avalanche of firms facing the threat of bankruptcies and redundancies. This is really the crunch for small businesses ... It's pure survival now. Profit has gone right out of the window. It's just a matter of whether you can pay the wages from week to week.**
>
> (*The News*, Portsmouth, 11 February 11 1991.)

Not a sufficient criterion for effective management

Although the objective of profit maximisation is undoubtedly of great importance, it is not, by itself, a sufficient criterion for the effective management of a business organisation.

In practice, there are many other considerations and motivations which affect the desire for the greatest profit or maximum economic efficiency and the accompanying assumptions which underlie the economic theory of the firm. (*See* Fig. 9.4.)

The meaning of 'profit maximisation' is not, by itself, very clear. Consideration has to be given to the range and quality of an organisation's products or services, to the costs of its operations and to environmental influences. Reducing attention to longer-term 'investments' such as quality and after-sales service, research and development, sales promotion, management development, satisfaction of staff and their employment conditions may increase profitability in the short term, but is likely to jeopardise future growth and development, and possibly even the ultimate survival of the organisation.

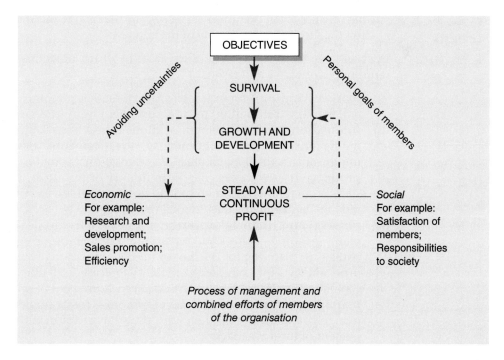

**Fig. 9.4
Objectives of a
business
organistion**

A business organisation has to provide some commodity or service by which it contributes to the economic and/or social needs of the community. It also has broader social responsibilities to society. (Social responsibilities are discussed later in this chapter.) Profit can be seen as the incentive for an organisation to carry out its activities effectively. Profit does at least provide some broad measure of effectiveness and highlights the difficulty in evaluating the effectiveness of not-for-profit organisations such as National Health Service hospitals, prisons or universities.

Avoiding uncertainties

Managers are more concerned with avoiding uncertainties than with prediction of uncertainties. Economic models of decision-making, based on the assumption of rational behaviour in choosing from known alternatives in order to maximise objectives, can be contrasted with behavioural models based not so much on maximising of objectives as on short-term expediency where a choice is made to avoid conflict and within limiting constraints.[21]

Also, as discussed earlier, members of the organisation will have their own personal goals and their own perception of the goals of the organisation.

FALLACY OF THE SINGLE OBJECTIVE

Drucker has referred to the fallacy of the single objective of a business. The search for the one, right objective is not only unlikely to be productive, but is certain to harm and misdirect the business enterprise.

> To emphasize only profit, for instance, misdirects managers to the point where they may endanger the survival of the business. To obtain profit today they tend to undermine the future...To manage a business is to balance a variety of needs and goals...the very nature of business enterprise requires multiple objectives which are needed in every area where performance and results directly and vitally affect the survival and prosperity of the business.[22]

Drucker goes on to suggest eight key areas in which objectives should be set in terms of performance and results:

(i) **market standing** – for example: share of market standing; range of products and markets; distribution; pricing; customer loyalty and satisfaction;

(ii) **innovation** – for example: innovations to reach marketing goals; developments arising from technological advancements; new processes and improvements in all major areas of organisational activity;

(iii) **productivity** – for example: optimum use of resources; use of techniques such as operational research to help decide alternative courses of action; the ratio of 'contributed value' to total revenue;

(iv) **physical and financial resources** – for example: physical facilities such as plant, machines, offices and replacement of facilities; supply of capital and budgeting; planning for the money needed; provision of supplies;

(v) **profitability** – for example: profitability forecasts and anticipated time scales; capital investment policy; yardsticks for measurement of profitability;

(vi) **manager performance and development** – for example: the direction of managers and setting up their jobs; the structure of management; the development of future managers;

(vii) **worker performance and attitude** – for example: union relations; the organisation of work; employee relations;

(viii) **public responsibility** – for example: demands made upon the organisation, such as by law or public opinion; responsibilities to society and the public interest.

Allocation of resources and decision-making

The organisation therefore must give attention to all those areas which are of direct and vital importance to its survival and prosperity. *Etzioni* makes the point that

> The systems model, however, leads one to conclude that just as there may be too little allocation of resources to meet the goals of the organization, so there may also be an over-allocation of these resources. The systems model explicitly recognizes that the organization solves certain problems other than those directly involved in the achievement of the goal, and that excessive concern with the latter may result in insufficient attention to other necessary organizational activities, and to a lack of coordination between the inflated goal activities and the de-emphasized non-goal activities.[23]

Individuals in the organisation are not necessarily guided at all times by the primary goal(s) of the organisation. *Simon* illustrates this in respect of the profit goal.

> Profit may not enter directly into the decision-making of most members of a business organisation. Again, this does not mean that it is improper or meaningless to regard profit as a principal goal of the business. It simply means that the decision-making mechanism is a loosely coupled system in which the profit constraint is only one among a number of constraints and enters into most sub-systems only in indirect ways.[24]

We have seen, then, that although the profit objective is clearly of importance, by itself it is not a sufficient criterion for the effective management of a business organisation. There are many other considerations and motivations which affect the desire for the greatest profit or maximum economic efficiency.

THE NEED FOR STRATEGY

Objectives and policy are formalised within the framework of a corporate strategy. *Tilles* has suggested that without an explicit statement of strategy it becomes more difficult for expanding organisations to reconcile co-ordinated action with entrepreneurial effort.[25] An explicit strategy for the business organisation is necessary for the following reasons. First, there is the need for people to co-operate together in order to achieve the benefits of mutual reinforcement. Second, there are the effects of changing environmental conditions.

The absence of an explicit concept of strategy may result in members of the organisation working at cross-purposes. The intentions of top management may not be communicated clearly to those at lower levels in the hierarchy who are expected to implement these intentions. Obsolete patterns of behaviour become very difficult to modify. Change comes about from either subjective or intuitive assessment, which become increasingly unreliable as the rate of change increases. Developing a statement of strategy demands a creative effort. If strategic planning is to be successful it requires different methods of behaviour and often fundamental change in the nature of interactions among managers.[26]

305

Appropriate mix of business

Tilles goes on to suggest that once objectives have been established, the appropriate mix of business engaged in can be evaluated against the following criteria.

Criteria related to individual performance

- **Probable contribution** – the estimated contribution of existing businesses to corporate performance given no major changes in competitive practice.
- **Minimum standards** – disengagement from unsatisfactory situations. Where standards of performance cannot be achieved with the existing mix of businesses, performance may frequently be improved by disinvestment of some businesses. As well as identifying attractive new opportunities, a well-managed company will have an active procedure for disengaging from unsatisfactory situations.
- **Trade-offs** – the requirement for trade-off decisions in establishing standards for unit performance, for example growth versus profitability, or short-term profitability versus long-term profitability.

Criteria related to the total mix

- **Risk level** – the degree of risk represented by the portfolio. Groups of businesses may be associated together within a single company because the risk inherent in the total is less than would be present if the businesses were separate.
- **Synergism** – the nature and extent of mutual reinforcement which individual businesses provide for the whole. This may be either operational reinforcement, where two businesses operated jointly improve the company's strategic advantage; or financial reinforcement because of the different patterns in funding or timing, or because of the appeal of the whole to the financial community.
- **Extrapolation** – the range of additional opportunities for which an appropriate mix of businesses provides a platform: where the company may go from its present position and what is required to do so. This may be expressed as the 'n + 1' situation. What should be the next business added to the existing portfolio?
- **Funds requirements** – the constraint of balancing the funds requirements and resources available in order to meet successfully the corporate strategy. If strategy is to be assessed rationally it must be translated into funds flow projections.

Managers' skills and competencies

Increased business competitiveness and the dynamic external environment have placed important emphasis on corporate strategy and the competencies of managers. For example, *Richardson and Thompson* argue that if organisations are to be effective in strategic terms they must be able to deal with the pressures and demands of change. Managers should be strategically aware and appreciate the origins and nature of change. They should possess a comprehensive set of skills and competencies and be able to deal effectively with the forces which represent opportunities and threats to the organisation. Effective strategic management creates a productive alliance between the nature and the demands of the environment, the organisation's culture and values, and the resources that the organisation has at its disposal.[27]

Corporate approach in local government

Some form of corporate strategy or planning is necessary for all organisations, particularly large organisations and including service organisations and those in the public sector. In local government, for example, the Bains Report urged local authorities to adopt a corporate approach to their affairs in order to ensure that their resources are deployed most effectively. The report makes the following comments:

Local government is not, in our view, limited to the narrow provision of a series of services to the local community, though we do not intend in any way to suggest that these services are not important. It has within its purview the overall economic, cultural and physical well-being of that community, and for this reason its decisions impinge with increasing frequency upon the individual lives of its citizens... This corporate approach should be displayed not only within the authority itself but also in its relations with other spheres of local government and with public bodies... We believe that the need for a corporate approach is beyond dispute if local government is to be efficient and effective.[28]

To give effect to this corporate approach, the Bains Report proposed the establishment of a central Policy and Resources Committee responsible for the formulation of the structure plan for a local authority county or district. The Policy and Resources Committee would aid the council in setting its objectives and priorities, and be instrumental in co-ordinating and controlling their implementation and in monitoring and reviewing the performance of the authority in the achievement of its defined objectives.

In the public sector, the establishment of objectives and policy requires clarification of the respective roles of both elected members and permanent officials. This dual nature of management requires harmonious relationships between the two parties and emphasises the need for a corporate approach.[29]

THE CONCEPT OF SYNERGY

An important aspect of corporate strategy and the growth and development of organisations is the concept of synergy which was developed in management applications by *Ansoff*.[30] Synergy results when the whole is greater than the sum of its component parts. It can be expressed, simply, in terms of the 2 + 2 = 5 effect.

Synergy is usually experienced in situations of expansion or where one organisation merges with another, such as an organisation responsible for the development and production of a product merging with an organisation which markets the product. An example could be a television manufacturer merging with a television rental organisation. The new organisation could benefit from the combined strengths and opportunities, skills and expertise, and from the streamlining and economy of its operations.

Another example could be the merger of a computer firm expert in the design and marketing of hardware, with a firm expert in software manufacture and systems design. An illustration of this is the merger of Nixdorf with Siemens. (*See* Fig. 9.5.)

It is possible, however, to experience negative synergy or the 2 + 2 = 3 situation. Such a situation might arise when a merger occurs between organisations operating in different fields, with different markets or with different methods, or where the new organisation becomes unwieldy or loses its cost-effectiveness. The original merger which resulted in the formation of British Leyland could, perhaps, be quoted as an example of negative synergy.

Synergy at work

Siemens and Nixdorf: It means Synergy at work.

Siemens Nixdorf is the fusion of two leading European IT companies. The marriage of two great sources of creative ideas and innovative solutions. The creation of a powerful international corporation, with the muscle to turn technological ideas into reality. The commitment to win market leadership – for itself and for its customers.

All our energies have been devoted to providing the widest range of information technology solutions, from the smallest notebook PC to the most powerful supercomputer, from stand-alone business systems to computer networks for multinational organisations.

Now the energies of Siemens and Nixdorf have come together, to form the largest European-based information technology company.

A company with a world view – and a presence in more than 50 countries.

A company that focuses on local support – half the 52,000-strong team work in sales and service.

A company that innovates – last year, it spent more than £500 million on research and development.

Today, the worldwide sales, customer service and support organisation is in place.

The technological and market sector expertise cannot be rivalled.

The reputation for software development and systems integration is established.

Working for – and with – its customers, the Siemens Nixdorf union of strengths is set to shape the future of computing.

Siemens Nixdorf Information Systems, Oldbury, Bracknell, Berks RG12 4FZ.

(*Source: Management Today*, November 1990, p. 83.)

Fig. 9.5
An example of the concept of synergy

SWOT ANALYSIS

Ansoff has also referred to the analysis of strengths and weaknesses of organisations following the formulation of objectives;[31] and to threats and opportunities in the process of strategic change.[32] This can be developed into what is known as SWOT analysis (sometimes also known as 'WOTS up'), which focuses on the Strengths, Weaknesses, Opportunities and Threats facing organisations.

The SWOT analysis provides convenient headings under which to study an organisation and may provide a basis for decision-making and problem-solving. You may therefore find the analysis helpful in tackling case studies.

- **Strengths** are those positive aspects or distinctive attributes or competencies which provide a significant market advantage or upon which the organisation can build, for example through the pursuit of diversification. These are characteristics of the organisation such as present market position, size, structure, managerial expertise, physical or financial resources, staffing, image or reputa-

tion. By searching out opportunities which match its strengths the organisation can optimise the effects of synergy.

- **Weaknesses** are those negative aspects or deficiencies in the present competencies or resources of the organisation, or its image or reputation, which limit its effectiveness and which need to be corrected or need action taken to minimise their effect. Examples of weaknesses could be operating within a particular narrow market, limited accommodation or outdated equipment, a high proportion of fixed costs, a bureaucratic structure, a high level of customer complaints or a shortage of key managerial staff.
- **Opportunities** are favourable conditions and usually arise from the nature of changes in the external environment. The organisation needs to be sensitive to the problems of business strategy and responsive to changes in, for example, new markets, technology advances, improved economic factors, or failure of competitors. Opportunities provide the potential for the organisation to offer new, or to develop existing, products, facilities or services.
- **Threats** are the converse of opportunities and refer to unfavourable situations which arise from external developments likely to endanger the operations and effectiveness of the organisation. Examples could include changes in legislation, the introduction of a radically new product by competitors, political or economic unrest, changing social conditions and the actions of pressure groups. Organisations need to be responsive to changes that have already occurred and to plan for anticipated significant changes in the environment and to be prepared to meet them.

THE MANAGEMENT OF OPPORTUNITIES AND RISKS

Every business needs to have a strategy and this strategy must be related to changing environmental conditions. In order to survive and maintain growth and expansion top management must protect the business from potentially harmful influences, and be ready to take maximum advantage of the challenges and opportunities presented. Whilst top management must always accept the need for innovation there is still the decision as to which opportunities it wishes to develop in relation to its resources, and those it chooses not to pursue. An effective business strategy depends upon the successful management of opportunities and risks.

Drucker suggests that strategy should be based on the priority of maximising opportunities, and that risks should be viewed not as grounds of action but as limitations on action.[33]

Drucker points out that while it is not possible to ensure that the right opportunities are chosen, it is certain that the right opportunities will not be selected unless:

(i) the focus is on maximising opportunities rather than on minimising risks;

(ii) major opportunities are scrutinised collectively and in respect of their characteristics rather than singly and in isolation;

(iii) opportunities and risks are understood in terms of the appropriateness of their fit to a particular business; and

(iv) a balance is struck between immediate and easy opportunities for improvement, and more difficult, long-range opportunities for innovation and changing the character of the business.

If the business is to be successful then its organisation structure must be related to its objectives and to its strategy. The structure must be designed so as to be appropriate to environmental influences, the continued development of the business, and the management of opportunities and risks. The nature of organisation structure is discussed in Chapter 10.

SOCIAL RESPONSIBILITIES OF MANAGEMENT

Organisations play a major and increasingly important role in the lives of us all, especially with the growth of large-scale business and the divorce of ownership from management.

The decisions and actions of management in organisations have an increasing impact on individuals, other organisations and the community. The power and influence which many business organisations now exercise should be tempered, therefore, by an attitude of responsibility by management.

In striving to satisfy its goals and achieve its objectives the organisation cannot operate in isolation from the environment of which it is part. The organisation requires the use of factors of production and other facilities of society. The economic efficiency of organisations is affected by governmental, social, technical and cultural variables. In return, society is in need of the goods and services created and supplied by organisations, including the creation and distribution of wealth. Organisations make a contribution to the quality of life and to the well-being of the community.

Organisational survival is dependent upon a series of exchanges between the organisation and its environment. These exchanges and the continual interaction with the environment give rise to a number of broader responsibilities to society in general. These broader responsibilities, which are both internal and external to the organisation, are usually referred to as social responsibilities. These social responsibilities arise from the interdependence of organisations, society and the environment.

The importance of social responsibilities

The importance of the exercise of social responsibility by business and by managers is emphasised by *Drucker*. This responsibility

> can no longer be based on the assumption that the self-interest of the owner of property will lead to the public good, or that self-interest and public good can be kept apart and considered to have nothing to do with each other. On the contrary, it requires of the manager that he assume responsibility for the public good, that he subordinate his actions to an ethical standard of conduct, and that he restrain his self-interest and his authority wherever their exercise would infringe upon the common weal and upon the freedom of the individual.[34]

The recognition of the importance of social responsibilities can be gauged in part by the extent of government action and legislation on such matters as, for example, employment protection, equal opportunities, companies acts, consumer law, product liability and safeguarding the environment. This has formalised certain areas of social responsibilities into a legal requirement. It is doubtful, however, if legislation alone is sufficient to make management, or other members of an organisation, behave in what might be regarded as a 'proper' manner.

Growing attention to social responsibilities

There has been a growing attention to the subject of social responsibilities and an increasing amount of literature on the subject. For example, a report by a (then) British Institute of Management working party sought to provide practical guidance relevant to both social and managerial needs.[35] Managers in BIM branches identified two prominent issues of social policy with which they were most concerned:

(i) assisting small businesses and enterprise agencies; and
(ii) the establishing of links with public bodies and the educational world.

As a general rule the key to the process of business social policy is seen widely as a partnership with national and local government and with not-for-profit organisations. The report gives guidance on what organisations and individual managers can do in relation to: assisting small enterprise and employment; links between industry and education; environmental enhancement; participating in political, civil and judicial activities; managing secondments; financial assistance and charitable donations.

In keeping with many recognised professional bodies, *The Institute of Management* has also published a *Code of Conduct* which is binding on all corporate members of the institute, together with supporting *Guides to Professional Management Practice*.[36] The guides supplement the code and set out the standards of conduct which members of the institute are expected to adhere to in pursuit of the objective of good management.

A number of business organisations also emphasise the importance of social responsibilities. For example, a Unilever educational publication sets out a commentary on social responsibility in terms of the manager's role, the company and society and the accountability of management. The report makes the point that 'social responsibility involves more than spending a little time and money on society's affairs. It is an attitude of mind which ought to be adopted by managers as a normal part of their professional outlook'.[37]

Another example is from Marks & Spencer.

Everybody who reads this book will have seen how much attention I attach to all management, from the top downwards, implementing a policy of good human relations at work and of business responsibility to the community.[38]

Finally, *Tam* poses the basic question, 'Can we live with an idea of "good" management which cannot be ultimately reconciled with what is good for society?' and maintains that 'the time has come for us to recognise that the only sustainable form of good management is that which takes into account the full range of responsibilities that underpin organisational success'.[39]

A matter of degree and balance

It should, however, be recognised that the distinction is blurred between (i) the exercise of a genuine social responsibility; and (ii) actions taken in pursuit of good business practice and the search for organisational efficiency. One approach is that attention to social responsibilities arises out of a moral or ethical motivation and the dictates of conscience, that is, out of genuine philanthropic objectives.

An alternative approach is that the motivation is through no more than enlightened self-interest and the belief that, in the long term, attention to social responsibilities is simply good business sense. In practice, it is a matter of degree and balance, of combining sound economic management with an appropriate concern for broader responsibilities to society.

311

As an example, Anita Roddick of The Body Shop has expressed the following beliefs:

> I am still looking for the modern-day equivalent of those Quakers who ran successful businesses, made money because they offered honest products and treated their people decently...

> The [cosmetic] industry seems to have absolutely no sense of social responsibility; and in its desperate need to chase profits in an area that has been experiencing, at best, sluggish growth for years, it is moving into territory where it should have no place.

> I am mystified by the fact that the business world is apparently proud to be seen as hard and uncaring and detached from human values. Why is altruism in business seen as alien to the point where anyone claiming to be motivated by it is considered suspect? I personally don't know how anybody can survive running a business in the nineties without caring. I don't know how they keep their role within the community.[40]

MAIN AREAS OF SOCIAL RESPONSIBILITY

Social responsibilities may be viewed in terms of **organisational stakeholders** – that is, those individuals or groups who have an interest in and/or are affected by the activities of the organisation or the behaviour of its members.[41] Stakeholders include a wide variety of interests but may be considered, for example, under six main headings of:

- employees;
- providers of finance;
- consumers;
- community and environment;
- government; and
- other organisations or groups.

Employees

People and organisations need each other. Social responsibilities to employees extend beyond terms and conditions of the formal contract of employment and give recognition to the worker as a human being. People today have wider expectations of the quality of working life, including: justice in treatment; democratic functioning of the organisation and opportunities for consultation and participation; training in new skills and technologies; effective personnel and industrial relations policies and practices; and provision of social and leisure facilities. Organisations should also, for example, give due consideration to the design of work organisation and job satisfaction, make every reasonable effort to give security of employment, and provide employment opportunities for minority groups.

It is in business organisations that the vast majority of people find their employment and spend a substantial part of their lives. A number of leading companies have taken steps to develop more ethical cultures and systems by involving individual employees in corporate affairs.[42] Many organisations also now choose to report details of their financial results and performance direct to all employees.

Providers of finance

Joint stock companies are in need of the collective investments of shareholders in order to finance their operations. Shareholders are drawn from a wide range of the population. The proportion of the adult population owning shares is around 22 per cent, and 18 per cent of the shareholding on the Stock Exchange is held, currently, by private individuals. Many people also subscribe indirectly as shareholders through pension funds and insurance companies, who between them account for 51 per cent of share ownership, and who act as trustees for the individual contributors.[43]

Shareholders expect a fair financial return as payment for risk bearing and the use of their capital. In addition, social responsibilities of management extend to include the safeguarding of investments, and the opportunity for shareholders to exercise their responsibility as owners of the company, to participate in policy decisions and to question top management on the affairs of the company. Management has a responsibility to declare personal interests, and to provide shareholders with full information presented in a readily understood form.

In the case of public sector organisations, finance may be provided by government grants/subsidies – which are funded 'compulsorily' by the public through taxation and rates – as well as loans, and charges for services provided. There is, therefore, a similar range of social responsibilities to the public as subscribers of capital.

Consumers

To many people, responsibilities to consumers may be seen as no more than a natural outcome of good business. There are, however, broader social responsibilities including:

- providing good value for money;
- the safety and durability of products/services;
- standard of after-sales service;
- prompt and courteous attention to queries and complaints;
- long-term satisfaction, for example serviceability, adequate supply of products/ services, and spare and replacement parts;
- fair standards of advertising and trading;
- full and unambiguous information to potential consumers.

Increasing concern for social responsibilities to consumers can be seen by the activities of such bodies as the Consumers' Association, and the number of television and radio programmes devoted to this subject. In the case of public corporations there are Users' National Councils or consumers' regulatory bodies which are independent and look after the interests of customers. In the case of local government there is a system of Commissioners for Local Administration (popularly referred to as 'Ombudsmen') designed to provide an independent investigation of citizens' complaints over alleged maladministration.

Community and environment

It is in the area of concern for the community at large that social responsibilities can be seen most clearly. Organisations have a responsibility not to misuse the scarce factors of production upon which the wealth of the country depends. Organisations have a responsibility to society, to respect environmental considerations and take care of amenities. Examples under this heading *include:*

- the effects and potential dangers of pollution, noise, disposal of waste;
- the siting and appearance of new buildings;

- transportation policies, such as the routing of heavy vehicles through narrow village roads; and
- avoidance of excessive packaging and more use of biodegradable materials.

A specific example is the protest against aerosol sprays containing chlorofluorocarbons. These have been blamed for damaging the ozone layer which protects the earth from harmful ultraviolet rays from the sun.

Government

Another important area of social responsibility could arguably be to the government. Organisations should, of course, respect and obey the law even where they regard it as not in their best interests. But what is debatable is the extent to which organisations should co-operate voluntarily with actions requested by the government. Some examples are: restraint from trading with certain overseas countries, and the acceptance of controls over imports or exports; actions designed to combat inflation, for example limits on the level of wage settlements; assisting in the control of potential social problems, for example advertising and sale of tobacco and the display of health warnings.

Other organisations or groups

The potential range of social responsibilities is numerous. Other organisations or groups to whom organisations might be regarded as having a social responsibility, or obligation, are **suppliers, business associates** and even **competitors.** Examples of social responsibilities might include: fair standards of trading; honouring terms and conditions of purchase or sale, and settlement dates, for example payment of accounts; assistance to smaller organisations; engagement only in fair competition; respect for copyright and patents.

Some organisations extend the range of social responsibilities even further by, for example: giving recognition to the needs of developing countries; limiting the extent of political involvement or campaigning; donations to, or sponsorship of, the arts, educational or research institutions, sporting organisations or charities.

SOCIAL REPORTS

The difficulties in reporting on an organisation's social responsibilities are well known. For example, how can one calculate the well-being created by, and the satisfaction with, its products or services, or the personal fulfilment of its members? The recognition of corporate social responsibilities does, however, imply a case for reporting on how such responsibilities have been discharged.

An increasing number of business organisations do attempt to produce some form of 'social' report. For example, IBM UK publish a Stakeholder Report summarising information under the following main headings:

- **employees** – population, earnings, graduates recruited, student employment, opinion survey comments, equal opportunity;
- **customers** – customer satisfaction, price/performance, customer training, customer visits to IBM centres;
- **suppliers** – amount of business, percentage of expenditure with British suppliers, investment in land and buildings, major construction projects;

- **the community** – secondments to community projects, support for enterprise agencies, schools and further education, contributions to charities, youth training, sponsorships, community projects.

PROFIT AND EFFECTIVE PERFORMANCE

Whatever the view of corporate social responsibility, management has as its priority the need to ensure the survival and effective performance of the organisation. As *Drucker* puts it:

> The first responsibility to society is to operate at a profit, and only slightly less important is the necessity for growth. The business is the wealth-creating and wealth-producing organ of our society. Management must maintain its wealth-producing resources intact by making adequate profits to offset the risk of economic activity. And it must besides increase the wealth-creating and wealth-producing capacity of these resources and with them the wealth of society.[44]

The attention given to social responsibilities must involve weighing the costs of meeting these responsibilities against the benefits derived. Provided the cost/benefit analysis is not detrimental to economic and/or competitive performance, management must then determine the extent to which, and the manner in which, the organisation will attempt to satisfy its social responsibilities. The recognition of social responsibilities should form an integral part of strategy and the establishment of objectives and policies of the organisation.

VALUES IN ORGANISATIONS

The idea of corporate social responsibility is however only one way in which to consider values in organisation. In the following section the shortcomings of the **social responsibility approach** will be examined, and two further approaches to the principles, standards and expected practices or judgements of 'good' or 'bad' behaviour made by individuals or groups of persons working in organisations will be explored. These approaches are

- **business ethics** and
- **corporate governance.**

The word 'values' is included in the above heading as a convenient concept for identifying common ground and differences between these three approaches.[45]

VALUES AND ETHICS

Questions about values, as the intrinsic worth or goodness of thought or actions, have been discussed in Europe since ethics was invented as a form of philosophical inquiry by the Ancient Greeks over 2500 years ago. The word 'ethics' is derived

315

from the Greek '*ethos*', meaning character or custom. Many Greek ideas began to spread across Europe with the rise of the Roman Empire, which explains why the words 'ethics' and 'morals' (from *mores*, the Latin for ethics) are often used interchangeably in modern English. For example, people may reach different 'moral' or 'ethical' judgements about Sunday trading, or may criticise the 'immoral' or 'unethical' behaviour of the media when it publishes the name of a National Lottery winner against the wishes of that individual. These examples aside, some writers on philosophy use the word 'morals' only to refer to the observable values and conduct of individuals or groups in society. They also restrict their use of the word 'ethics' to any logical discussion of our principles and values.

In the latter analytical sense, ethics is usually studied systematically as both a theoretical and practical discipline. The latter approach, known as applied ethics, makes an important contribution to both law and medicine in which legal ethics (jurisprudence) and medical ethics are well-establishment subjects. These examples are mentioned because the traditional approach to studying law and medicine made an important contribution to the emergence of Business Administration as an academic discipline, especially in the United States. For example, Harvard University adapted teaching models developed by its Law and Medical Schools in launching the Harvard Business School earlier this century.

Because the need for ethical behaviour in both the medical and legal professions is so obvious, it seemed only reasonable to some writers that attempts should be made to compare and contrast accepted values in business with those practised in the wider community.[46]

The legal basis for these views was presumed to be contained in a United States Supreme Court Ruling (1906) that 'The corporation is a creature of the state. It is presumed to be incorporated for the benefit of the public.'[47]

However, these early attempts to develop a new type of applied ethics for business were strongly opposed by those who regarded the role of people in business as fundamentally different from that practised within the 'closed professions' of medicine, law, engineering and accountancy.[48] That said, there is little to choose between the view that business is distinct from all other forms of human activity, however sophisticated the argument, and the Old American political battle-cry that 'The business of business is business'.[49]

CORPORATE SOCIAL RESPONSIBILITY

Nevertheless, concerns about the role of business in society persisted and led to the emergence of 'corporate social responsibility' in the early 1960s. Some writers attributed society's social ills to the rise of capitalism[50] and predicted that a number of fundamental values underlying the socio-economic system in the United States were in the process of being changed.[51] *Sharplin* argued that the complex relationship between business and society should be redefined within a new form of **Social Contract**, or 'set of written and unwritten rules and assumptions about behaviour patterns among the various elements in society'.[52]

This Social Contract includes the following obligations between the organisation and society (*see* also Fig. 9.6):

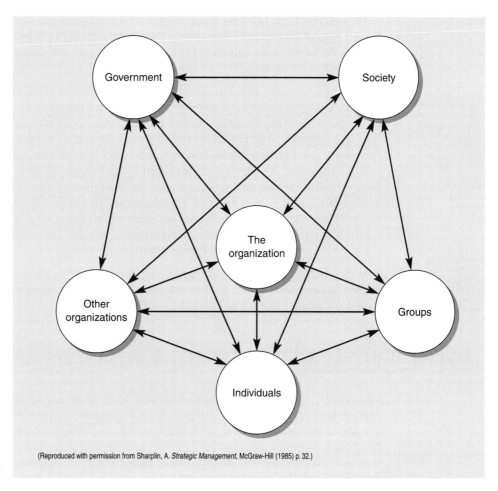

**Fig. 9.6
The Social Contract**

(Reproduced with permission from Sharplin, A. *Strategic Management*, McGraw-Hill (1985) p. 32.)

- **obligations to individuals:** including equitable wages, salaries and remuneration 'packages', and suitable working conditions, in return for the duties and responsibilities carried out by the employee;
- **obligations to groups and to organisations:** requiring organisations to complete with rivals on an 'honourable' basis by respecting the mutual rights and obligations of trading partners, groups, and other organisations;
- **obligations to government:** recognition that a mutually beneficial exchange exists between the organisation and government 'constituencies', requiring payment of taxes and implementation of health and safety standards, etc.;
- **obligations to society:** the expectation that organisations would automatically abide by both the letter and spirit of the law in dealing with consumer groups, etc.

The case against corporate social responsibility The corporate social responsibility development has always had its critics and perhaps the most eminent was the late Milton Friedman, American economist and Nobel Prize winner, who denounced it as a 'fundamentally subversive doctrine' that threatened the foundations of a free society in which:

317

there is one and only one social responsibility of business – to use its resources and engage in activities designed to increase its profits so long as it stays within the rules of the game, which is to say, engages in open and free competition without deception or fraud.[53]

It should be noted that Friedman's criticism was directed solely against the introduction of corporate social responsibility within profit-making business organisations in the private sector. He accepted that public sector organisations were different and that 'the imposition of taxes and the expenditure of tax proceeds are governmental functions ... as far as possible in accordance with the preferences and desires of the public'; however, his views were attacked by *Carr*[54] and others. No doubt this was because public sector organisations were less common in the United States than in Britain, prior to the great wave of 'privatisations' of public utility organisations that created such a sea change in the British economy in the early 1980s. Probably Friedman's best known critic is *Drucker,* who doubted whether private sector organisations could be relieved of their social responsibilities:

it can no longer be assumed that the self-interest of the owner of property will lead to the public good, or that self-interest and public good can be kept apart and considered to have nothing to do with each other.[55]

AGENCY VERSUS STAKEHOLDER THEORY

Friedman's views on the role of business in society are an example of agency theory, which recognises only one line of responsibility between the manager, as the agent of the shareholders, to the board of the directors, as shown in Fig. 9.7. His critics adopt a more complex perspective on corporate behaviour and contrast the traditional view of a hostile relationship between employers and employees with a model of management being involved in a network of relationships with the organisation's various stakeholders, as depicted in Fig. 9.8.[56]

Criticism of the stakeholder model

A reasonable criticism of the stakeholder model is that it fails to explain how managers are able to treat each stakeholder in an equitable manner. How are they to prioritise, or choose between them, when critical decisions must be taken which will result in a benefit to one at the expense of another? For example, if a loss occurs during a period of economic recession, who should suffer – the shareholders, through a cancelled dividend, or the employees, through a factory closure? This is no far-fetched example since there is considerable evidence in company reports that difficult decisions of this sort have had to be taken in the boardrooms of many British companies during recent years.

Clearly, a possible clash of values may arise between corporate responsibilities on the one hand and an individual's principles on the other. A distinction therefore needs to be made between corporate social responsibility issues, which should refer to the organisation's policies and activities, and the decisions and actions of individual managers, which should fall within the domain of business ethics.

**Fig. 9.7
Model of
relationship between
the manager and
shareholders**

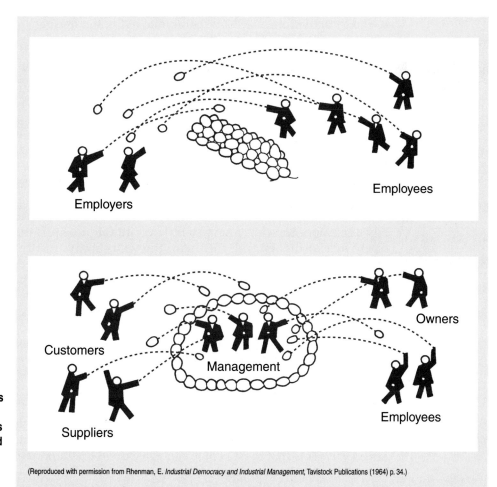

**Fig. 9.8
Contrasting models
of relationships
between employers
and employees and
management and
organisation's
stakeholders**

(Reproduced with permission from Rhenman, E. *Industrial Democracy and Industrial Management*, Tavistock Publications (1964) p. 34.)

BUSINESS ETHICS

Donaldson describes business ethics as 'the systematic study of moral (ethical) matters pertaining to business, industry or related activities, institutions or practices and beliefs'.[57]

The rise of business ethics is due to the changing nature of employment, as a result of the rapid spread of new technology, and the impact of various socio-economic and political factors on the structure, function and size of private and public sector organisations. The following represent some of the numerous subjects discussed by *De George*[58] and *Webley*[59] as falling within the domain of business ethics:

- personal ethics;
- workers' rights;
- consumer safety;
- discrimination;
- codes of conduct;
- accounting practices;
- energy utilisation;
- insider dealing;
- company 'perks';
- takeovers and mergers;
- global businesses;

- organisational responsibilities;
- workers' responsibilities;
- relations with trade unions;
- 'whistle-blowing' by staff;
- computer data and privacy
- environmental protection;
- animal rights and research;
- industrial espionage;
- corrupt practices;
- directors' remuneration;
- famine and Third World countries.

Three contrasting ethical standpoints

Members of organisations usually carry out different roles at work than, say, at home. At work, they may experience ethical dilemmas, or even disagree with others, because of doubts about how to proceed, or because of a clash of values. Some colleagues may be influenced more than others by principles or a sense of duty. Their views may be guided by religious beliefs or by other moral ideas. In ethics, values of this sort are said to be **deontological.**

Other colleagues may only be interested in the consequences or outcomes of any discussion. Some may have so little regard for principles that they are guided solely by expediency and, for them, the 'ends always justify the means'.[60] In ethics, values of this sort are said to be **teleological.**

Yet other colleagues may have noticed how values differ between countries and communities so that, for example, one society bans alcohol whereas another permits manufacturers to advertise it on sportsmen's shirts so that the name can be seen by millions of TV viewers. These colleagues may think that an act is right if it is approved by the social group to which a person belongs and wrong if it is not, and that otherwise moral beliefs should be regarded as the private concern of each individual. This view of moral values is referred to as **ethical or moral relativism.**

Virtue and moral character

The question arises of how one is to choose between these ethical standpoints. The short answer is that each individual has to make up his or her own mind. The longer answer is that most people can agree upon the importance of virtues such as honesty, truthfulness and integrity in the formation of what is accepted as 'good character', which essential if 'correct behaviour' is to be established between ourselves and those with whom we may even disagree. *Green* notes it is the 'ques-

tion of character – what it is that makes someone a morally good or bad person – [that] is the central and foremost one with which Ethics must deal. Hence, the major responsibility of managers is to choose subordinates whose moral integrity can be relied upon'.[61]

Webley argues that this process can be assisted by companies developing Codes of Business Ethics so that individual members of organisations may be provided with 'help in guiding day-to-day decisions'. Carefully drawn-up codes can also 'reassure customers, suppliers and even competitors of the integrity of the business'.[62]

Arguments against business ethics

Webley also notes that objections to business ethics fall into two categories. Firstly, some see the subject as a waste of time and energy because, since business is already regulated by law, codes of ethics are merely public relations exercises that fail to alter actual behaviour of people employed in business. Secondly, codes of ethics are 'a second best option' since the behaviour of individuals is formed by values acquired in childhood and introducing codes may undermine the person's right to make moral judgements within organisations.

A third related argument is that it is the board of directors that is most frequently found at the centre of the stakeholder model, not the individual manager as indicated in Fig. 9.8. In short, most decisions within organisations are taken collectively; this perspective on the responsibilities of directors is discussed below under the heading of corporate governance.

CORPORATE GOVERNANCE

The growing importance of corporate governance in organisations owes much to the impressive study of the changing structure of companies carried out by *Tricker*.[63] That said, recent developments were mainly influenced by the growth of corporate crime both in the United States and Britain.

The Harvard Compact

As a result of congressional hearings in the United States, the Harvard Business Review set up a Working Group on Corporate Governance in 1990. Matters investigated included investors' rights and management accountability, and the role of executive and non-executive directors in both monitoring management's performance and representing shareholders' interests.

The Working Group's findings were published as a New Compact for Owners and Directors which set out five recommendations each for directors and shareholders.[64] Directors were advised to evaluate the performance of the chief executive regularly against agreed goals and strategies. This evaluation should be performed by 'outside' non-executive directors, who should meet alone at least once a year, under a chairman. Qualifications for board members should also be set by the directors and communicated to the shareholders, and board candidates should be screened and recommended by 'outside' directors on the basis of the agreed qualifications.

Institutional shareholders were recommended to see themselves as owners, not just investors in a company, but should refrain from getting involved in the company's day-to-day activities. Shareholders should also evaluate the performance of directors regularly; they need to be properly informed about the company's activi-

ties in order to carry out this evaluation. Finally, shareholders should recognise and respect that their only common commitment is to the on-going prosperity of the company.

The Cadbury recommend- ations

The Harvard Compact is mentioned in some detail because of its considerable influence on the main recommendations of the Cadbury Report, *The Financial Aspects of Corporate Governance*, which were published in 1992, after the Committee, chaired by Sir Adrian Cadbury, had been set up one year earlier by the Financial Reporting Council, the Stock Exchange and the various chartered bodies of the accountancy profession.[65] The main recommendations appear in Table 9.1.

Table 9.1 **The main recommendations of the Cadbury Committee**

1. Boards should have separate audit and remuneration committees made up entirely of independent directors.

2. Audit committees should meet with the external auditors at least once a year and without executive directors.

3. The full remuneration package of all directors – including performance-related elements – should be disclosed in annual reports.

4. Directors' terms of office should run for no more than three years without shareholders' approval for reappointment.

5. Companies must make funds available to non-executive directors who wish to get independent professional advice.

6. The board must meet regularly.

7. The board should have a formal schedule of matters for decision.

8. Independent directors should be appointed for specified terms.

9. Independent directors should be appointed through a formal process.

10. Independent directors should have a standing outside the company which ensures that their views carry weight.

11. Independent directors should be fully independent and free from links with the company other than fees and shareholdings.

12. Fees for independent directors should reflect the time they spend on company business.

13. There should be an accepted division at the head of the company, which will ensure a balance of power and authority such that no one individual has unfettered powers of decision. Where the chairman is also chief executive, there should be a strong independent element on the board with an independent leader.

The case against the Cadbury Recommend- ations

The Cadbury Report received a cool reception from *The Times*, the *Independent* and the *Financial Times* in their editorial comments published on 28 May 1992. Comments ranged from viewing the Report as 'a timid step in the right direction' (the *Independent*) to dismissing it as 'A mouse roars'.[66]

Overall, the general opinion of informed commentators was that the Cadbury recommendations should have been more wide-ranging and should have included strategic, environmental and social responsibility matters as well as issues relating to accounting, auditing, remuneration, and the roles of executive and indepen-

dent directors. That said, the recommendations were opposed by the heads of some of Britain's largest businesses, although these were in a minority and an estimated 93 per cent of the leading UK companies have already implemented the Cadbury guidelines.

It is clear that far-reaching changes are restructuring the world economy, mainly due to the spread of 'free-market' economic policies and the rapid 'globalisation' of business following the introduction of information technology during the last 15 years. Regrettably, the decrease in government regulation coincided with an increase in business scandals and a growth in corporate crime. Some critics also blame 'free-market' economics for widening the gap between rich and poor and for the rise in unemployment in most industrialised countries. Others go further and argue that free-market economics is responsible for the increase in violent crime in many western societies. Whatever the truth of these assertions, there is undeniable concern about public standards in Britain and a general perception that politicians can no longer be trusted and that company directors are awarding themselves remuneration 'packages' out of all proportion to the modest average increase in prosperity of their companies.

The government has acknowledged these concerns by appointing two committees, one under Lord Nolan, to look into standards of public life, and the other under Sir Richard Greenbury, chairman of Marks & Spencer plc, to advise on the remuneration of company directors. Whatever their findings, it is already apparent that subjects like corporate social responsibility, business ethics and corporate governance have made a permanent impact on the relationship between society and those who run or work for organisations in the growing private and shrinking public sectors of the economy.

Conclusion

In conclusion, this section has attempted to describe the origins and development of three different, yet related, approaches to analysing the relationship between business organisations and society. Historically, corporate social responsibility came first and its concerns deal mainly with the organisation's role in reconciling what are often conflicting needs of its various stakeholders. Business ethics, on the other hand, seeks to address similar issues but mainly from the standpoint of the individuals who may experience difficulties in reconciling their personal values with those of the managers of the organisations where they work. Finally, corporate governance is an emerging discipline, accepted by most British and American medium to large-size companies, which seeks to address the consequences of changing patterns of ownership and points towards a redefinition of the relationship between the directors and, in particular, the increasingly powerful institutional shareholders.

SYNOPSIS

■ All organisations have some function to perform, and some incentive for their existence and for their operations. The goals of an organisation determine the nature of its outputs and the series of activities through which the outputs are achieved. The goal model approach concentrates on the study of organisational goals and the measurement of success against the realisation of these goals. There are potential disadvantages and limitations with this approach, but the concept of organisational goals serves a number of important functions.

■ Strictly, organisations have no goals, only people do. Members of an organisation have different and often conflicting goals. Management has a responsibility to clarify organisational goals and to attempt to integrate personal goals with the overall objectives of the organisation. Adopting a systems view of organisations, we can distinguish four main types of goals: consumer, product, operational and secondary. Organisational goals can, however, be classified in a number of different ways.

■ The goals of the organisation may be pursued in accordance with an underlying ideology or philosophy which determines the culture of the organisation and governs the overall conduct of its operations. Goals are translated into objectives and policy. Objectives set out the aims to be achieved, the desired end-results. The choice of objectives is an essential part of the decision-making process involving future courses of action. Policy is developed within the framework of objectives. It provides the basis for decision-making and the course of action to follow in order to achieve objectives.

■ Objectives and policy, together, provide corporate guidelines for the operation and management of the organisation. Although the objective of profit maximisation is undoubtedly important, it is not by itself a sufficient criterion for the effective management of a business organisation. In practice there are many other considerations and motivations which affect the desire for the greatest profit or maximum economic efficiency. Attention must be given to all those areas which are of direct and vital importance to the survival and prosperity of the organisation.

■ Objectives and policy are formalised within the framework of a corporate strategy. An explicit strategy is necessary in order that people may co-operate and because of the effects of changing environmental conditions. Once objectives have been set, the appropriate mix of business engaged in can be evaluated. A SWOT analysis may help the process of strategic change. An effective business strategy depends upon the successful management of opportunities and risks.

■ In striving to satisfy its goals and achieve its objectives, the organisation cannot operate in isolation from the environment of which it is part. Organisational survival is dependent upon a series of exchanges between the organisation and its environment. These exchanges and the continual interaction with the environment give rise to a number of broader responsibilities to society in general – the social responsibilities of management. There are however shortcomings with the social responsibility approach. Two further approaches to exploring values in organisations are business ethics and corporate governance.

Review and discussion questions

1 What are goals and what functions are served by organisational goals? Suggest a classification of organisational goals and relate this to your own organisation.

2 Illustrate the systems view of organisational goals and objectives. Give examples of how the goals of an organisation may change over time. Why is it that in practice organisational goals usually tend to be altered only on a gradual basis?

3 What do you see as the importance of organisational ideology or philosophy? Explain the extent to which there is a clear ideology and/or set of principles which govern the overall conduct of your own organisation.

4 Distinguish between objectives and policy. Identify examples of objectives and policy in your own organisation, and comment on how effectively you believe they have been implemented.

5 Discuss critically the extent to which profit maximisation is a sufficient criterion for the effective management of a business organisation. What other indicators might be applied in terms of organisational performance and results?

6 Explain the need for a corporate strategy and attempt to examine the corporate plan for your own or some other organisation. Suggest criteria for the evaluation of an appropriate mix of activities.

7 Assess the practical relevance of (i) the concept of synergy, and (ii) a SWOT analysis.

8 Discuss critically the extent to which you accept the concept of corporate social responsibilities. Explain the approaches of: (i) business ethics; and (ii) corporate governance to values in organisations.

Assignment

(i) Detail fully what you believe are the social responsibilities or obligations of your own, or some other work organisation of your choice.

(ii) Give specific examples of the ways in which the organisation has attempted to satisfy, and/or has failed to satisfy, these responsibilities or obligations.

(iii) Specify the extent to which attention has been given to values in the organisation, and to the principles, standards and expected practices or judgements of 'good' behaviour.

(iv) Compare your observations with those of your colleagues and summarise what conclusions you draw.

325

CASE STUDY

Square Deal plc

Square Deal plc is a newly formed subsidiary company of Square Deal International Inc. The intention is to use it to unify the efforts and improve the profitability of the hitherto separate UK subsidiaries of Arnold plc, Carlton plc and Foodrich plc. At present it has a managing director, an administrative/financial controller and a typist all sharing a large temporary office in central London.

Arnold plc has 69 food stores, all within a radius of 30 miles from London. Most of them contain either a small restaurant or a snack bar and occupy high street or suburban shopping centre locations. It owns one small bakery whose total production supplies ten stores with bread and cakes. Perishables for both re-sale and restaurant use are bought locally but all other products are bought centrally and distributed from one large warehouse. These products are charged to the stores at selling price on computer-printed internal invoices. Store managers are judged solely on revenue. Accounts for each store are produced on the batch computer system at head office which is an old building on the edge of a dockland redevelopment site in East London. The company owns the freehold, as it does of about half of its food stores.

Carlton plc has joint managing directors, one in charge of 21 restaurants and one in charge of property development. To date it has built four shopping centres and has plans for three more, all as part of schemes to regenerate old city centres in the north of England, around 150 miles from London. It leases out the shops with the exception of one per centre which it operates as a restaurant. Both MDs rigidly pursue a 15 per cent annual return on investment as their measure of achievement.

Foodrich plc was, until last year, a family firm which canned fruit and vegetables from its one factory situated about 100 miles from London, in the west of England. It was bought by Square Deal International Inc with the idea that it would supply 'own label' products to Arnold plc and large catering packs to both Arnold's and Carlton's restaurants. To do this, Foodrich was obliged to deny supplies to some of its regular customers and re-equip part of its plant to handle the large catering packs. The MD, son of the founder, has worked there for nearly 40 years and runs the company, making all decisions, both long-term and operational, using his experience and intuition. He is furious to learn that Arnold has not put all its 'own label' business in his direction and Carlton is still buying most catering packs from Foodrich's competitors while its new plant is grossly underused. Both Arnold's head buyer and the head chef at Carlton's claim they get the same quality cheaper from other companies. These recent changes at Foodrich have overwhelmed the MD and one result is that the financial year end accounts up until April will not be ready until some time in August. The accounts are the only defined measure of performance and are usually drawn up by the MD.

The MD of Square Deal plc has just spent a week touring parts of these three subsidiaries and has returned to the office with a variety of ideas and concerns about ways to unify efforts and improve profitability. To help crystallise some of these ideas he asks the administrator/controller to prepare written statements on various points. Assume you are this administrator/controller.

(a) Discuss the benefits and drawbacks of judging performance on a single criterion such as:
(i) revenue, in the case of the store managers,
(ii) return on investment, in the case of Carlton's MDs.

(b) Explain to what extent Arnold's head buyer and Carlton's head chef are justified in buying catering packs from other companies.

(c) Describe how further computerisation might help in this quest for unification and profit improvement.

(d) After you have finished this task, the MD tells you he is toying with the idea of regrouping the company under the name of Square Deal plc and dividing it into the following divisions, each operating as a profit centre:

<div align="center">Square Deal plc</div>

Restaurants division	Property division	Food retail division	Canning division	Bakery division

He is concerned about the effects of such a change on the morale of the managers and other employees so he asks you for a further statement. Discuss ideas that should maintain or improve morale if this regrouping were to take place.

(e) Highlight any other advantages or difficulties that you foresee in the regrouping idea.

Notes and references

1. Etzioni, A. *Modern Organizations*, Prentice-Hall (1964).
2. Simon, H. A. 'On the Concept of Organizational Goal', *Administrative Science Quarterly*, vol. 10, June 1964, pp. 1–22.
3. See, for example: Kast, F. E. and Rosenzweig, J. E. *Organization and Management: A Systems and Contingency Approach*, Fourth edition, McGraw-Hill (1985).
4. See, for example: Heller, R. 'The Manager's Dilemma', *Management Today*, January 1994, pp. 42–7.
5. A view expressed by a number of writers including, for example: Argyris, C. *Integrating the Individual and the Organization*, Wiley (1964).
6. McGregor, D. *The Human Side of Enterprise*, Penguin (1987) p. 55.
7. Etzioni, A. *A Comparative Analysis of Complex Organizations: On Power, Involvement and their Correlates*, Revised edition, Free Press (1975).
8. Cyert, R. and March, J. G. *A Behavioural Theory of the Firm*, Second edition, Blackwell (1992).
9. Gross, B. M. *Organizations and their Managing*, Free Press (1968).
10. See, for example: Brown, A. 'Organizational Culture: The Key to Effective Leadership and Organizational Development', *Leadership and Organization Development Journal*, vol. 13, no. 2, 1992, pp. 3–6.
11. Sieff, M. (Lord Sieff of Brimpton) *Management The Marks & Spencer Way*, Fontana Collins (1991) pp. 12–13.
12. Extracted from staff booklet 'Where you fit in' and with the kind permission of Sir Anthony Cleaver, Chairman, IBM United Kingdom Limited.
13. Roddick, A. *Body and Soul*, Ebury Press (1991) p. 17.
14. Walt Disney World *College Program* (January 1993).
15. Cowley, D. 'The Woman from the Body Shop', *Reader's Digest*, vol. 131, no. 785, September 1987, p. 41.
16. Brech, E. F. L. (ed.) *The Principles and Practice of Management*, Third edition, Longman (1975).
17. Fayol, H. *General and Industrial Management*, Pitman (1949) p. 53.
18. See, for example: Torrington, D., Weightman, J. and Johns, K. *Effective Management: People and Organisation*, Prentice-Hall (1989).
19. O'Shaughnessy, J. *Business Organization*, Allen and Unwin (1966) pp. 24–5.
20. For a fuller discussion of strategic management and planning see, for example: Asch, D. and Bowman, C. (eds) *Readings in Strategic Management*, Macmillan (1989).
21. Cyert, R. and March, J. G. *A Behavioural Theory of the Firm*, Second edition, Blackwell (1992).
22. Drucker, P. F. *The Practice of Management*, Heinemann Professional (1989) p. 59.
23. Etzioni, A. *Modern Organizations*, Prentice-Hall (1964) p. 17.
24. Simon, H. A. 'On the Concept of Organizational Goal', *Administrative Science Quarterly*, vol. 10, June 1964, p. 21.
25. Tilles, S. 'Making Strategy Explicit', in Ansoff, H. I. (ed.) *Business Strategy*, Penguin (1969).
26. For fuller details of strategic planning, see, for example: Johnson, G. and Scholes, K. *Exploring Corporate Strategy*, Third edition, Prentice-Hall (1993).
27. Richardson, B. and Thompson, J. 'Strategic Competency in the 1990s', *Administrator*, July 1994, pp. 2–6.
28. Department of the Environment, *The New Local Authorities: Management and Structure* (the Bains Report), HMSO (1972) pp. 6–7.
29. For an example, see: Rea, D. M. 'Strategy in Public Sector Organisations', in Jones, P. (ed.) *Management in Service Industries*, Pitman (1989).

30. Ansoff, H. I. (ed.) *Business Strategy*, Penguin (1969).
31. Ansoff, H. I. *Corporate Strategy*, Revised edition, Penguin (1987).
32. Ansoff, H. I. (ed.) *Business Strategy*, Penguin (1969).
33. Drucker, P. F. *Managing for Results*, Heinemann Professional (1989). See also: Drucker, P. F. *Managing in Turbulent Times*, Heinemann (1980).
34. Drucker, P. F. *The Practice of Management*, Heinemann Professional (1989) p. 376.
35. BIM Working Party 'Business Social Policy – What Is It?' British Institute of Management (March 1987).
36. *Code of Conduct* and *Guides to Professional Management Practice*, The Institute of Management, November 1992.
37. Kuin, P. 'Social Responsibility: There's More to Management', a Unilever Educational Publication, reprinted from *Unilever Magazine*, 1978, p. 3.
38. Sieff, M. (Lord Sieff of Brimpton), *Management the Marks & Spencer Way*, Fontana Collins (1991) p. 198.
39. Tam, H. 'Recognise Your Responsibilities', *Professional Manager*, March 1995, p. 16.
40. Roddick, A. *Body and Soul*, Ebury Press (1991) pp. 8, 9, 16.
41. See, for example: Worthington, I. and Britton, C. *The Business Environment*, Pitman (1994).
42. Winfield, M. *Minding Your Own Business*, Social Audit Ltd (1990).
43. Central Statistical Office, *Share Register Survey (end 1993)*, HMSO (1994).
44. Drucker, P. F. *The Practice of Management*, Heinemann Professional (1989) p. 380.
45. I am grateful to my colleague Tom McEwan, University of Portsmouth, for contributing the section from here to the end of this chapter.
46. Berle, A. A. and Means, G. C. *The Modern Corporation and Private Property*, Macmillan (1932); Dodd, M. 'Voluntary Standards and the Market Place', *Harvard Law Review*, Summer 1932; Whitehead, A. N. 'Universities and Their Function', in *The Aims of Education and Other Essays*, Ernest Benn and Co. (1928) Chapter VIII.
47. United States Supreme Court, *Hale v. Henkle*, 201, U.S.74 (1906).
48. Evers, S. Unpublished paper on Business Ethics, British Institute of Management, London (1992).
49. Attributed to Herbert Clark Hoover, American Presidential Election Campaign Speech, 1928.
50. Gurley, J. G. 'Economic Conversation and Beyond', *Industrial Management Review*, vol. 11, no. 3, 1970, pp. 17–25.
51. Cabot Lodge, G. C. 'Business and the Changing Society', *Harvard Business Review*, March–April 1974, pp. 59–72.
52. Sharplin, A. *Strategic Management*, McGraw-Hill (1985).
53. Friedman, M. 'The Social Responsibility of Business is to Increase its Profits', *The New York Times Magazine*, New York Times Corp., 13 September 1970, pp. 33, 122–6.
54. Carr, A. Z. 'Is Business Bluffing Ethical?', *Harvard Business Review*, January–February 1968.
55. Drucker, P. F. *The Practice of Management*, Heinemann Professional (1989) p. 376.
56. Rhenman, E. *Industrial Democracy and Industrial Management*, Tavistock Publications (1964) p. 34.
57. Donaldson, J. *Key Issues in Business Ethics*, Academic Press (1989).
58. De George, R. *Business Ethics*, Third edition, Macmillan (1989).
59. Webley, S. 'Codes of Business Ethics: Why Companies Should Develop Them – And How', *The Institute of Business Ethics*, 1993.
60. Machiavelli, N. *The Prince* (1532).
61. Green, R. M. *The Ethical Manager*, Prentice-Hall (1994) p. 55.
62. Webley, S. 'Codes of Business Ethics: Why Companies Should Develop Them – And How', *The Institute of Business Ethics*, 1993.
63. Tricker, R. *Corporate Governance*, Gower (1984).
64. Harvard Business Review Working Group on Corporate Governance, 'A New Compact for Owners and Directors', *Harvard Business Review*, July–August 1991, pp. 141–3.

65. The Cadbury Committee, *The Financial Aspects of Corporate Governance*, Stock Exchange Council, London (1992).
66. Sheridan, T. and Kendall, N. *Corporate Governance*, Financial Times/Pitman Publishing (1992) Chapter 7.

10 ORGANISATION STRUCTURE AND DESIGN

In order to achieve its goals and objectives the work of an organisation has to be divided among its members. Some structure is necessary to make possible the effective performance of key activities and to support the efforts of staff. Structure provides the framework of an organisation and its pattern of management. It is by means of structure that the purpose and work of the organisation is carried out. The manager needs to understand the importance and effects of organisation structure and design.

 Learning objectives

To:

- Explain the meaning and nature of organisation structure;

- Identify levels of organisation and dimensions of structure;

- Explain the importance of good structure and consequences of a deficient structure;

- Evaluate main factors to be considered in the design of organisation structure;

- Detail different methods for division of work and grouping together of activities;

- Assess the nature of the relationship between the structure of an organisation and the people who work within it;

- Recognise the importance of structure in influencing organisational performance.

Worth thinking about

Organisations are a form of social stratification. Advancement up the structure can reasonably be expected to be seen as a reward for hard work, an indication of achievement and obtained by reason of merit. But if so, does this mean that those people at lower levels of the structure do not work hard, have failed to achieve and lack merit?

THE MEANING AND NATURE OF ORGANISATION STRUCTURE

Structure is the pattern of relationships among positions in the organisation and among members of the organisation. The purpose of structure is the division of work among members of the organisation, and the co-ordination of their activities so they are directed towards achieving the goals and objectives of the organisation. The structure defines tasks and responsibilities, work roles and relationships, and channels of communication.

Structure makes possible the application of the process of management and creates a framework of order and command through which the activities of the organisation can be planned, organised, directed and controlled.

In the very small organisation there will be few, if any, problems of structure. The distribution of tasks, the definition of authority and responsibility, and the relationship between members of the organisation can be established on a personal and informal basis. But with increasing size there is greater need for a carefully designed and purposeful form of organisation. There is need for a formal structure. There is also need for a continual review of structure to ensure that it is the most appropriate form for the particular organisation, and in keeping with its growth and development.

Objectives of structure

The objectives of structure may be summarised as to provide for:

- the economic and efficient performance of the organisation and the level of resource utilisation;
- monitoring the activities of the organisation;
- accountability for areas of work undertaken by groups and individual members of the organisation;
- co-ordination of different parts of the organisation and different areas of work;
- flexibility in order to respond to future demands and developments, and to adapt to changing environmental influences; and
- the social satisfaction of members working in the organisation.[1]

These objectives provide the criteria for structural effectiveness. Structure, though, is not an end in itself but a means of improving organisational performance.

Drucker suggests that the organisation structure should satisfy three requirements.[2]

- **It must be organised for business performance.** The more direct and simple the structure the more efficient it is because there is less change needed in the individual activities directed to business performance and results. Structure should not rest on past achievements but be geared to future demands and growth of the organisation.
- **The structure should contain the least possible number of management levels.** The chain of command should be as short as possible. Every additional level makes for difficulties in direction and mutual understanding, distorts objectives, sets up additional stresses, creates inertia and slack, and increases the difficulties of the development of future managers moving up through the chain. The number of levels will tend to grow by themselves without the application of proper principles of organisation.
- **Organisation structure must make possible the training and testing of future top management.** In addition to their training, future managers should be tested before they reach the top. They should be given autonomy in positions of actual managerial responsibility while still young enough to benefit from the new experience. They should also have the opportunity of at least observing the operation of the business as a whole, and not be narrowed by too long an experience in the position of a functional specialist.

In order to satisfy these three requirements Drucker suggests that the organisation structure must be based preferably on the principle of federal decentralisation, with activities integrated into autonomous product businesses with their own product and market, and with responsibility for their profit and loss. If federal decentralisation is not possible then the organisation structure should be based on the principle of functional decentralisation with integrated units having the maximum responsibility for major and distinct stages of the business process.

LEVELS OF ORGANISATION

Organisations are layered. The determination of policy and decision-making, the execution of work, and the exercise of authority and responsibility are carried out by different people at varying levels of seniority throughout the organisation structure. It is possible to look at organisations in terms of interrelated levels in the hierarchical structure, for example, the technical level, the managerial level and the community level.[3]

The technical level

The technical level is concerned with specific operations and discrete tasks, with the actual job or tasks to be done, and with performance of the technical function. Examples are: the physical production of goods in a manufacturing firm; administrative processes giving direct service to the public in government departments; the actual process of teaching in an educational establishment.

The managerial level

The technical level interrelates with **the managerial level**, or organisational level, which is concerned with the co-ordination and integration of work at the technical level. Decisions at the managerial level relate to the resources necessary for performance of the technical function, and to the beneficiaries of the products or services provided. Decisions will be concerned with: (i) mediating between the organisation and its external environment, such as the users of the organisation's products or services, and the procurement of resources; and (ii) the 'administration' of the internal affairs of the organisation including the control of the operations of the technical function.

The community level

In turn, the managerial level interrelates with **the community level** or institutional level, concerned with broad objectives and the work of the organisation as a whole. Decisions at the community level will be concerned with the selection of operations, and the development of the organisation in relation to external agencies and the wider social environment. Examples of the community level within organisations are: the board of directors of joint stock companies; governing bodies of educational establishments which include external representatives; and trustees of non-profit organisations. Such bodies provide a mediating link between the managerial organisation and co-ordination of work of the technical organisation, and the wider community interests. Control at the institutional level of the organisation may be exercised, for example, by legislation, codes of standards or good practice, trade or professional associations, political or governmental action, and public interest.

Interrelationship of levels

In practice there is not a clear division between determination of policy and decision-making, co-ordination of activities and the actual execution of work. Most decisions are taken with reference to the execution of wider decisions, and most execution of work involves decision. Decisions taken at the institutional level determine objectives for the managerial level, and decisions at the manager-

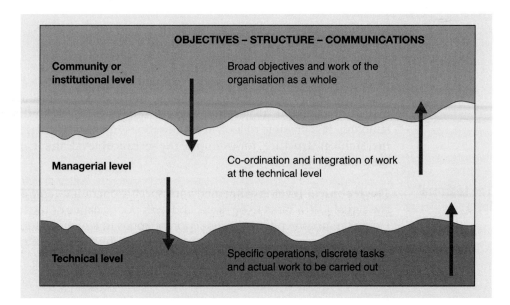

Fig. 10.1 Interrelated levels of organisation

ial level set objectives for the technical level. **Therefore if the organisation as a whole is to perform effectively there must be clear objectives; a soundly designed structure; and good communications, both upwards and downwards, among the different levels of the organisation.** (*See* Fig. 10.1.)

The managerial level, for example, would be unable to plan and supervise the execution of work of the technical function without the knowledge, expertise, practical know-how and enthusiasm of people who are closest to the actual tasks to be undertaken. People operating at the technical level should, therefore, make known to higher levels the practical difficulties and operational problems concerning their work. It is the duty of the managerial level to take appropriate action on this information, and to consult with people at the community or institutional level.

Not all activities concerned with the management of an organisation can be considered, necessarily, in terms of these three levels of work. There will be certain activities which are analysed more meaningfully in terms of a greater, or possibly a smaller, number of levels. However, the three broad levels provide a basis for an analysis of the interrelated activities of the organisation.

The management process in local government

An example of the interrelationship between the different levels of an organisation can be seen from the comments in the Bains Report on management in local government.[4] The report recognises that elected members remain responsible for ultimate direction and control of the authority, key decisions on objectives and plans to attain them, and reviewing progress and performance of services. However, the report also refers to the dual nature of management and to the changing relationship between permanent officers and elected members at the different stages of the management process.

The report concludes:

> We doubt whether it is possible to divide the total management process into two separate halves, one for members and the other for officers . . . That process itself can be seen as a scale, with the setting of objectives and allocation of major resources at one end, moving through the designing of programmes and plans, to the execution of those plans at the other end. As one moves through that management scale, the balance between the two elements changes from member control with officer advice at the 'objective' end to officer control with member advice at the 'execution' end.[5]

DIMENSIONS OF STRUCTURE

The variables which determine the dimensions of organisation structure can be identified in a number of ways but are usually taken to include the grouping of activities, the responsibilities of individuals, levels of hierarchical authority (the scalar chain), span of control and formal organisational relationships. The dimensions of structure can, however, be identified in a number of ways.[6]

Child, for example, suggests six major dimensions as components of an organisation structure:

● allocation of individual tasks and responsibilities, job specialisation and definition;
● formal reporting relationships, levels of authority and spans of control;

- grouping together of sections, departments, divisions and larger units;
- systems for communication of information, integration of effort and participation;
- delegation of authority and procedures for monitoring and evaluating the use of discretion;
- motivation of employees through systems for appraisal of performance and reward.[7]

Essential design parameters

Another approach to the identification of dimensions of structure is suggested by *Mintzberg* who gives a set of nine essential design parameters which form the basic components of organisation structure.

- How many tasks should a given position in the organisation contain and how specialised should each task be?
- To what extent should the work content of each position be standardised?
- What skills and knowledge should be required for each position?
- On what basis should positions be grouped into units and units into larger units?
- How large should each unit be; how many individuals should report to a given manager?
- To what extent should the output of each position or unit be standardised?
- What mechanisms should be established to facilitate mutual adjustment among positions and units?
- How much decision-making power should be delegated to the managers of line units down the chain of authority?
- How much decision-making power should pass from the line managers to the staff specialists and operators?[8]

These nine design parameters can be grouped under four broad headings: design of position; design of superstructure; design of lateral linkages; and design of decision-making systems.

Information technology

An additional dimension of structural design is **information technology**. The importance of information technology was discussed in Chapter 3. Computer-based information and decision-support systems influence choices in design of production or service activities, hierarchical structures and organisation of support staffs. Information technology may influence the centralisation/decentralisation of decision-making and control systems.[9]

A minister of state for industry and information technology has referred to the immense potential of information technology, and how the speed in development is changing the nature and organisation of work.

> This move towards an information-based economy is having a profound effect upon the nature and organisation of work. There will be fewer people in factories making things and more people in smaller units: processing, storing, creating and handling information. Administrators and managers in these smaller units will have to develop new and more agile skills in organization. The winners will be those who are mobile and flexible, and the losers will be the over-centralized bureaucratic hierarchies.[10]

The impact of information technology will have significant effects on the structure, management and functioning of most organisations. The introduction of

new technology will demand new patterns of work organisation. It will affect individual jobs, the formation and structure of groups, the nature of supervision and managerial roles. Information technology results in changes to lines of command and authority, and influences the need for restructuring the organisation and attention to job design.[11]

New technology has typically resulted in a 'flatter' organisational pyramid with fewer levels of management required. In the case of new office technology it allows the potential for staff at clerical/operator level to carry out a wider range of functions and to check their own work. The result is a change in the traditional supervisory function and a demand for fewer supervisors.

THE IMPORTANCE OF GOOD STRUCTURE

The structure of an organisation affects not only productivity and economic efficiency but also the morale and job satisfaction of the workforce. Structure should be designed, therefore, so as to encourage the willing participation of members of the organisation and effective organisational performance.

According to *Drucker* it is the correct design of structure which is of most significance in determining organisational performance.

> Good organization structure does not by itself produce good performance. But a poor organization structure makes good performance impossible, no matter how good the individual managers may be. To improve organization structure . . . will therefore always improve performance.[12]

The importance of good structure is also emphasised by *Child*.

> The allocation of responsibilities, the grouping of functions, decision-making, co-ordination, control and reward – all these are fundamental requirements for the continued operation of an organization. The quality of an organization's structure will affect how well these requirements are met.[13]

The functions of the formal structure, and the activities and defined relationships within it, exist independently of the members of the organisation who carry out the work. However, personalities are an important part of the working of the organisation. In practice, the actual operation of the organisation and success in meeting its objectives will depend upon the behaviour of people who work within the structure and who give shape and personality to the framework.

Lord Forte, for example, has drawn attention to the importance of the human element in organisation structure:

> the human aspect in a business is vital: you can keep drawing squares and lines, but within these squares you must have people and they must be deeply involved with the business. If this does not happen, then the lines and squares and the diagrams mean nothing.[14]

The human element

The overall effectiveness of the organisation will be affected both by sound structural design and by the individuals filling the various positions within the structure. Management will need to acknowledge the existence of the informal organisation (discussed in Chapter 3) which arises from the interactions of people

working in the organisation. The organisation is a social system and people who work within it will establish their own norms of behaviour, and social groupings and relationships, irrespective of those defined in the formal structure.

The human relations writers are critical of the emphasis on the formal organisation. They favour a structure in which there is increased participation from people at all levels of the organisation, greater freedom for the individual, and more meaningful work organisation and relationships. One of the strongest critics of the formal organisation is *Argyris*.[15] He claims that the formal, bureaucratic organisation restricts individual growth and self-fulfilment and, in the psychologically healthy person, causes a feeling of failure, frustration and conflict. Argyris argues that the organisation should provide a more 'authentic' relationship for its members.

The view of the human relations writers represents more of an attitude towards organisation than specific proposals, but it reminds us of the importance of the human element in the design of structure. Managers need to consider how structural design and methods of work organisation influence the behaviour and performance of members of the organisation.

Relationship between people and organisation

The operation of the organisation and actual working arrangements will be influenced by the style of management, the personalities of members and the informal organisation. These factors may lead to differences between the formal structure of the organisation and what happens in practice. *Stewart*, for example, found the relationship between people and organisation to be reciprocal.

> People modify the working of the formal organization, but their behaviour is also influenced by it. The method of work organization can determine how people relate to one another, which may affect both their productivity and morale. Managers, therefore, need to be conscious of the ways in which methods of work organization may influence people's attitudes and action.[16]

Building an organisation involves more than concern for structure, methods of work and technical efficiency. The hallmark of many successful business organisations is the attention given to the human element; to the development of a culture which helps to create a feeling of belonging, commitment and satisfaction.[17]

Structure must be designed, therefore, so as to maintain the balance of the socio-technical system and the effectiveness of the organisation as a whole. Attention must be given to the interactions between both the structural and technological requirements of the organisation; and social factors and the needs and demands of the human part of the organisation.

THE DESIGN OF ORGANISATION STRUCTURE

There is, however, in the final analysis, an underlying need to establish a framework of order and system of command by which the work to be undertaken is accomplished successfully. This demands that attention be given to certain basic principles and considerations in the design of organisation structure, or in reviewing the effectiveness of an existing structure. (*See* Fig. 10.2.)

These principles and considerations present management with a series of important decision points. There are many situational variables (contingency

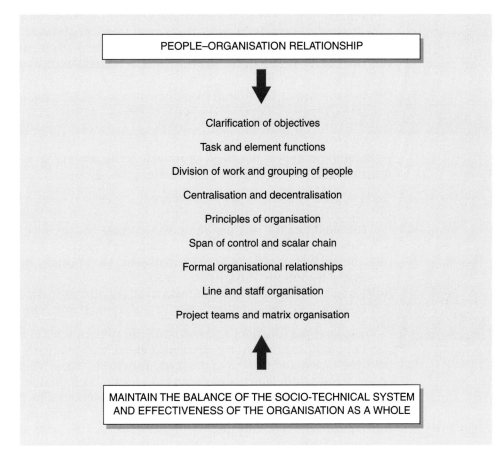

**Fig. 10.2
Basic
considerations in
the design of
organisation
structure**

factors) which influence decisions on the most appropriate structure. These situational variables are examined in the next chapter.

Structure provides the framework for the activities of the organisation and must harmonise with its goals and objectives. The first step, therefore, is to examine the objectives of the organisation. Only when objectives have been clearly defined can alternative forms of structure be analysed and compared.

CLARIFICATION OF OBJECTIVES

A clear definition of objectives is necessary in order to provide a basis for the division of work and grouping of duties into sub-units. The objectives for these sub-units must be related to the objectives of the organisation as a whole in order that an appropriate pattern of structure can be established.

Clearly stated and agreed objectives will provide a framework for the design of structure, and a suitable pattern of organisation to achieve those objectives. The nature of the organisation and its strategy will indicate the most appropriate organisational levels for different functions and activities, and the formal relationships between them. Clearly defined objectives will help facilitate systems of

communication between different parts of the organisation and the extent of decentralisation and delegation. The formal structure should help make possible the attainment of objectives. It should assist in the performance of the essential functions of the organisation and the major activities which it needs to undertake.

TASK AND ELEMENT FUNCTIONS

In order to produce some good, or provide some service, there are four essential functions that the organisation must perform.

(i) The good or service must be developed.
(ii) Something of value must be created. In the case of the business organisation this might be the production or manufacture of a product; in the case of the public sector organisation the provision of a service.
(iii) The product or services must be marketed. They must be distributed or made available to those who are to use them.
(iv) Finance is needed in order to make available the resources used in the development, creation and distribution of the products or services provided.

These essential functions of developing the good or service, manufacturing the good or providing the service, marketing them, and financing the organisation, are what *Woodward* refers to as the **'task' functions**. These are the basic activities of the organisation which are related to the actual completion of the productive process and directed towards specific and definable end-results. To ensure the efficient achievement of overall objectives of the organisation the results of the task functions must be co-ordinated.[18]

Other activities of the organisation are not directed towards specific and definable ends but are supportive of the task functions and an intrinsic part of the management process. These are referred to as **'element' functions** and include, for example, personnel, planning, management services, public relations, quality control and maintenance. In other organisations, noticeably in service industries, personnel can be seen as closely associated with a task function.[19] But in the majority of organisations the personnel function does not normally have any direct accountability for the performance of a specific end-task.

Implications for organisation structure

The two kinds of functions, task and element, differ in a number of ways and these differences have important implications for organisation. Failure to distinguish between the two types of functions can lead to confusion in the planning of structure and in the relationship between members of the organisation.

For example, in her study of the management organisation of firms in this country, *Woodward* comments on the bad relationships between accountants and other managers referred to during the study. One reason for this hostility was the bringing together of two quite separate financial functions essential to the efficient operation of a business.

> People concerned with works accounting tended to assume responsibility for end results that was not properly theirs; they saw their role as a controlling and sanctioning one rather than as a servicing and supportive one. Line managers resented this attitude and retaliated by becoming aggressive and obstructive.[20]

According to Woodward, activities concerned with raising funds for the business, keeping accounts and determination of financial policy are task functions. But management accounting, concerned with prediction and control of production administration, is an element function, and is primarily a servicing and supportive one. Relationships between the accountants and other managers seemed better when the two functions were organisationally separate. This was noticeable especially in divisionalised organisation when each product division had its own accounting staff providing line managers with the necessary information to control their own departments. In these cases the task function of finance was completely divorced from the element function of management accounting in which the servicing and supportive role is of most importance.

THE DIVISION OF WORK

Within the formal structure of an organisation work has to be divided among its members and different jobs related to each other. The division of work and the grouping together of people should, wherever possible, be organised by reference to some common characteristic which forms a logical link between the activities involved. It is necessary to maintain a balance between an emphasis on subject matter or function at higher levels of the organisation, and specialisation and concern for staff at the operational level.

Work can be divided, and activities linked together, in a variety of different ways.

Major purpose or function

The most commonly used basis for grouping activities is according to specialisation, the use of the same set of resources, or the shared expertise of members of staff. It is a matter for decision in each organisation as to which activities are important enough to be organised into separate functions, departments or sections. Work may be departmentalised and based, for example, on differentiation between task and element functions, discussed above. (*See* Fig. 10.3.)

Product or service

In division by product or service, the contributions of different specialists are integrated into separate, semi-autonomous units with collective responsibility for a major part of the business process or for a complete cycle of work. This form of grouping is more common in the larger diversified organisations and may be used as a means of sub-dividing departments into sections. An example is the bringing together of all activities concerned with a particular production line, product or service. (*See* Fig. 10.4.) Another example is a hospital where medical and support staff are grouped together in different units dealing with particular treatments such as accidents and emergency, medical or surgery. With grouping by product or service there is a danger that the divisions may attempt to become too autonomous, presenting management with a problem of co-ordination and control.

Location

In division by location, different services are provided by area or geographical boundaries according to particular needs or demands, the convenience of consumers, or for ease of administration. (*See* Fig. 10.5.) Examples are the provision of local authority services for people living in a particular locality; the siting of hospitals or post offices; the provision of technical or agricultural further education in

341

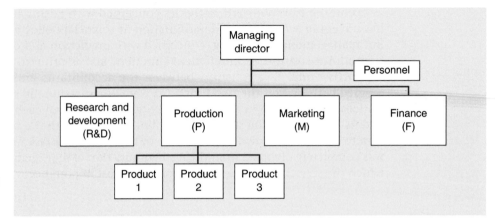

Fig. 10.3
Division of work by major purpose or function

Fig. 10.4
Division of work by product or service

*In the case of division of work by product or service, or by geographical location, it is possible that certain aspects of support services, such as personnel management, may also be assigned to individual units of the organisation. However, the main responsibility of the personnel manager, as a separate entity, is to provide a specialist advisory service to all unit managers and to ensure implementation of personnel policy throughout the organisation as a whole. Responsibility for the main aspects of the personnel function is likely to remain, therefore, in a direct line of authority from top management.

Fig. 10.5
Division of work by location

industrial or rural areas; sales territories for business firms; or the grouping of a number of retail shops under an area manager. Another example is provided by organisations with multi-site working and the grouping of a range of similar activities or functions located together on one site.

A problem with grouping by location is the definition of the geographical boundaries and the most appropriate size for a given area. The improvement in communications, particularly telecommunications, tends, however, to reduce the importance of location. For example, administrative staff may no longer need to be located within the main production unit.

Nature of the work performed

Division may be according to the nature of the work performed where there is some special common feature of the work such as the need for speedy decisions, accuracy, confidentiality/security, or where local conditions require first-hand knowledge not immediately available elsewhere. Another example may be the grouping together of equipment or machinery which is noisy or which produces dust, fumes or unpleasant odours.

Common time scales

Division may be according to time scales, for example, shift working and the extent to which different tasks should be undertaken by different shifts. In a further education college there may be separate departments or groupings to deal with the different needs of full-time day students and part-time evening students. Another example of activities grouped according to time is in a hotel. Activities in the kitchen tend to be short term, especially when guests in the restaurant are waiting to be served, and a range of different tasks have to be co-ordinated very quickly. Other activities, for example market research and forecasting future room occupancy, are longer-term decisions, and subject to different organisational requirements.

Common processes

When common processes are used in a range of different activities, this may be used as the basis of division. This method of grouping is similar to the division by nature of the work, but includes, for example, the decision whether to establish a centralised resource centre for all departments of the organisation, or to allow each department to have its own service. With manufacturing industries a range of products may pass through a common production facility or configuration of machines which may be grouped together in a single unit: for example, a batch production engineering firm having departments based on like skills or methods of operation. Services using expensive equipment such as mainframe computers may need to be grouped together in this way for reasons of efficiency and economy.

Staff employed

The allocation of duties and responsibilities may be according to experience, or where a particular technical skill or special qualification is required: for example, the division of work between surgeons, doctors and nurses; or between barristers, solicitors and legal executives. Another example is the sharing of routine work processes among members of a supervised group. In smaller organisations the allocation of work may be on an *ad hoc*, personal basis according to the knowledge and skills contributed by individuals. Work may also be planned deliberately to give a variety of tasks and responsibilities to provide improved job satisfaction or to assist in the training of staff.

Customer or people to be served

Separate groups may be established to deal with different consumer requirements: for example, the division between trade or retail customers, or between home or export sales. In hospitals there are different groupings dealing with, for example, patients in the gynaecology, geriatric and children's wards. In large clothes shops

343

there may be separate departments for men's, women's and children's clothing. Government departments are often grouped by this method and work is divided according to for whom the services are provided; for example, the unemployed, low-pay families, students, young people or senior citizens. A further example is the provision of canteen services which may be grouped by customer demand according to price; range or standard of meals available, speed of service; or type of customer; this gives rise to separate facilities such as the directors' dining room, or for staff and students in educational establishments.

Combination of groupings

These different ways of dividing work can be combined in various forms and most organisations will contain examples of alternative combinations for grouping activities. Some activities might be grouped according to one method and other activities according to a different method. Decisions on the methods of grouping will include considerations of:

- the need for co-ordination;
- the identification of clearly defined divisions of work;
- economy;
- the process of managing the activities;
- avoiding conflict; and
- the design of work organisation which takes account of the nature of staff employed, their interests and job satisfaction.

Management must decide upon the most significant factors which will determine the methods for division of work and linking of activities appropriate to the changing circumstances within the particular organisation.

CENTRALISATION AND DECENTRALISATION

One particular problem which arises from division of work and grouping of activities is the extent of centralisation or decentralisation. Most organisations necessarily involve a degree of decentralisation arising from such features as an increase in size, the geographical separation of different parts of the organisation, or the need to extend activities or services to remote areas. Our main concern is with decentralisation in terms of specific delegation to sub-units or groups within the organisation such that they enjoy a measure of autonomy or independence.

Advantages of centralisation

The advantages often claimed for centralisation tend to relate to economic and administrative considerations and include:

- the easier implementation of a common policy for the organisation as a whole;
- preventing sub-units becoming too independent;
- making for easier co-ordination and management control;
- improved economies of scale and a reduction in overhead costs;
- greater use of specialisation, including better facilities and equipment;
- improved decision-making which might otherwise be slower and a result of compromise because of diffused authority.

Arguments against centralisation

However, such advantages frequently are not realised fully, and do not lead to an actual improvement in service. There are a number of contrary arguments against centralisation, including the criticism that it creates a more mechanistic structure and may result in lengthening the scalar chain. There are also positive arguments, which tend to relate more to behavioural considerations, in favour of decentralisation:

- it enables decisions to be made closer to the operational level of work;
- support services, such as administration, are more likely to be effective if provided as close as possible to the activities they are intended to serve;
- it provides opportunities for training in management;
- usually, it has an encouraging effect on the motivation and morale of staff.

The advisability of decentralisation must be considered in terms of: the nature of the product or service provided; policy-making; the day-to-day management of the organisation; and the need for standardisation of procedures, or conditions or terms of employment of staff.

Decentralisation generally tends to be easier to implement in private sector organisations than in the public sector organisations where there is a greater demand for the accountability of their operations, regularity of procedures and uniformity of treatment.

PRINCIPLES OF ORGANISATION

The classical writers placed emphasis on the definition of structure in terms of division of work, chain of command, span of control and reporting relationships. Attention was focused on the requirements of the formal organisation and the search for a common set of principles applicable to all circumstances. Probably the leading authority in the country was *Lyndall Urwick*, who originally specified eight principles of organisation, but revised these to ten in his later writing.[21]

(i) **The principle of the objective**
'Every organisation and every part of the organisation must be an expression of the purpose of the undertaking concerned, or it is meaningless and therefore redundant.'

(ii) **The principle of specialisation**
'The activities of every member of any organised group should be confined, as far as possible, to the performance of a single function.'

(iii) **The principle of co-ordination**
'The purpose of organising *per se*, as distinguished from the purpose of the undertaking, is to facilitate co-ordination: unity of effort.'

(iv) **The principle of authority**
'In every organised group the supreme authority must rest somewhere. There should be a clear line of authority to every individual in the group.'

(v) **The principle of responsibility**
'The responsibility of the superior for the acts of the subordinate is absolute.'

(vi) **The principle of definition**
'The content of each position, both the duties involved, the authority and responsibility contemplated and the relationships with other positions should be clearly defined in writing and published to all concerned.'

(vii) **The principle of correspondence**
'In every position, the responsibility and the authority should correspond.'

(viii) **The principle of span of control**
'No person should supervise more than five, or at the most, six direct subordinates whose work interlocks.'

(ix) **The principle of balance**
'It is essential that the various units of an organisation should be kept in balance.'

(x) **The principle of continuity**
'Re-organisation is a continuous process: in every undertaking specific provision should be made for it.'

Relevance of principles

As we mentioned in Chapter 2, the idea of common sets of principles on organisation and management has been subject to much criticism. Many of the principles are bland statements expressed in non-operation terms and give little basis for specific managerial action, and they tend to view people as a given rather than a variable in the system. However, the principles do provide general guidance on the structuring of organisations and much of the more recent writing on the subject appears to be based on the original statements.

The basic concept can be of value to the practical manager **if modified to suit the demands of the particular situation**, including the nature of staffing in the organisation. The proper application of these principles is likely to help improve organisational performance. Two of the more specific principles of general interest in the structuring of organisations are (i) the span of control and (ii) the scalar chain.

SPAN OF CONTROL

The span of control arises in line authority and refers to the **number of subordinates who report directly** to a given manager or supervisor. It does not refer to the total of subordinate operating staff, that is those staff who report first to another person. Hence the term 'span of responsibility' or 'span of supervision' is sometimes considered to be more appropriate.

The classical writers tended to suggest a definite figure for the span of control. *Brech,* for example, suggested that it should be limited to a reasonable number of interrelated executive or supervisory subordinates, but for only the most exceptional person would this number exceed single figures.[22] *V. A. Graicunas* developed a mathematical formula for the span of control.[23] The limitation of the number of subordinates who can effectively be supervised is based on the total of direct and cross relationships,

$$R = n \left(\frac{2^n}{2} + n - 1 \right)$$

where n is the number of subordinates, and R is the number of interrelationships.

For example, with 5 subordinates the total number of interrelationships requiring the attention of the manager is 100; with 6 subordinates the number of interrelationships is 222. *Urwick* supports the idea of Graicunas and, as we have seen from his list of principles, states that the span of control should not exceed five, or at the most six direct subordinates whose work interlocks. At lower levels

of the organisation, however, where there is less interlocking, or where responsibility is concerned more with the performance of specific tasks, the span of control may be larger.

Factors influencing span of control

Practical studies of span of control, however, show that it varies widely in different organisations and that the average span is larger than suggested by Graicunas and Urwick. For example, in *Woodward*'s study of 100 manufacturing firms in southeast Essex (discussed in the following chapter) she found that the size of span of control varied directly with technology and type of production system.[24]

In addition to the type of production system there are a number of other factors that will influence the limit of span of control. These include:

- the nature of the organisation, the complexity of the work and the similarity of functions, and the range of responsibilities;
- the ability and personal qualities of the manager including the capacity to cope with interruptions;
- the amount of time the manager has available from other activities to spend with subordinates;
- the ability and training of subordinate staff, and the extent of direction and guidance needed;
- the effectiveness of co-ordination and the nature of communication and control systems;
- the physical location or geographical spread of subordinates;
- the length of the scalar chain, which is discussed in the following section.

Importance of span of control

If the span of control is **too wide** it becomes difficult to supervise subordinates effectively and this places more stress on the manager. With larger groupings, informal leaders and sub-groups or cliques are more likely to develop, and these may operate contrary to the policy of management. There may be lack of time to carry out all activities properly. Planning and development, training, inspection and control may suffer in particular, leading to poor job performance. A wide span of control may limit opportunities for promotion. Too wide a span of control may also result in a slowness to adapt to change or to the introduction of new methods or procedures.

If the span of control is **too narrow** this may present a problem of co-ordination and consistency in decision-making, and hinder effective communications across the organisation structure. Morale and initiative of subordinates may suffer as a result of too close a level of supervision. Narrow spans of control increase administrative costs and can prevent the best use being made of the limited resource of managerial talent. They can lead to additional levels of authority in the organisation creating an unnecessarily long scalar chain.

THE SCALAR CHAIN

This refers to the number of different levels in the structure of the organisation, the chain of hierarchical command. The scalar chain establishes the vertical graduation of authority and responsibility, and the framework for superior–subordinate relationships *(see* Fig. 10.6). Every person must know his or her position within the structure of the organisation. The very act of organising introduces the concept of

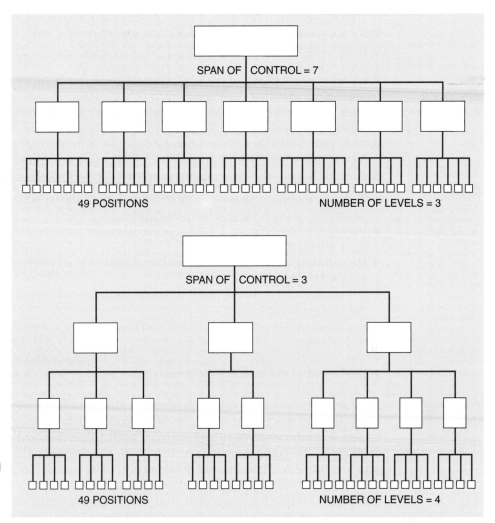

**Fig. 10.6
How span of control
and scalar chain
affect organisation
structure**

the scalar chain. Most organisation charts demonstrate that this principle is used widely as a basis for organisational design. A clear line of authority and responsibility is necessary for the effective operation of the organisation.

It seems to be generally accepted, however, that for reasons of morale and to help decision-making and communications there should be as few levels as possible in the scalar chain. There is the danger of adding to the structure in such a way that it results in increased hierarchical authority and control, leads to the risk of empire building and the creation of unnecessary work in justification of the new position. But if efforts are made to reduce the number of levels this may bring about an increase in the span of control with the resulting difficulties already discussed. The design of structure necessitates, therefore, maintaining an appropriate balance between span of control and scalar chain.

**Need for a
balanced
structure**

The combination of span of control and scalar chain determines the overall pyramid shape of the organisation and whether the hierarchical structure is 'flat' or 'tall'. (*See* Fig. 10.7.) The pyramid represents the structure of authority. Broader

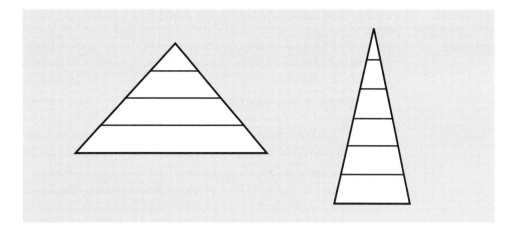

Fig. 10.7
'Flat' and 'tall'
hierarchical
structures

spans of control and few levels of authority result in a flat hierarchical structure as tends to be found, for example, in universities. Narrower spans of control and more levels of authority result in a taller hierarchical structure as tends to be found, for example, in the civil service or the armed forces.

Although there is no one, ideal combination of span of control and scalar chain, which depends upon the particular situation for each organisation (*see* the discussion of contingency theory in the next chapter), it is important to provide an appropriate, balanced structure.

Inverted hierarchical structure

Greater awareness of the importance of service, total quality management and the continual search for competitive advantage has resulted in the concept of an inversion of the traditional hierarchical structure with customers at the summit and top management at the base. This will be accompanied by the devolution of power and delegation to the empowered, self-managing workers near the top of the inverted pyramid.[25]

'FLATTER' ORGANISATION STRUCTURES

The need for improved efficiency and competitiveness, the demand for more participative styles of management and greater involvement of staff, and developments in information technology have all contributed to a general movement towards 'downsizing' or flatter organisation structures.[26] Claims for flatter structures include savings on managerial costs, improved communications and a reduction in the length of the scalar chain with fewer levels between the top and the base of the hierarchical pyramid.

The movement towards flatter structures also raises the question of the extent to which downsizing should go at the centre and the importance of aligning head office structure to corporate strategy. Downsizing can result in increased decentralisation with more functions performed closer to the action.[27] The flat structure is arguably in keeping with the Quality of Working Life culture and helps to tap the knowledge and expertise necessary for fast, effective decision-making at appropriate levels of the organisation.[28]

349

Difficulties with the flatter structure

Flatter structures are likely to be achieved by reducing the number of layers of middle managers and supervisors. Remaining managers are forced to assume responsibility for a much greater span of control. Despite the advantages claimed for a flatter structure it may also give rise to a number of particular difficulties. For example, it might:

- inhibit the flow of effective communications between top management and the workforce;
- reduce the opportunities for promotion, achievement or enhanced status; and
- limit opportunities for the training and development of future managers.[29]

The process of de-layering can also have contrary outcomes. According to *Gretton*, for example, it can lead to a climate of low morale, distrust of management and sometimes a deterioration in productivity. Managers face an increased workload and responsibilities, and many managers may also move among organisations on a short-term contract with little loyalty to their employers.[30]

FORMAL ORGANISATIONAL RELATIONSHIPS

In any organisation structure certain formal relationships between individual positions will arise from the defined pattern of responsibilities. There is often confusion over the meaning of different terms and their implications for organisational structure, but these **individual authority relationships** may be identified as line, functional, staff or lateral. (*See* Fig. 10.8.) The design of organisation structure in terms of the principle of line, functional, staff or lateral, determines the pattern of role relationships and interactions with other roles, discussed in Chapter 6.

Line relationships

In **line relationships**, authority flows vertically down through the structure, for example from the managing director to managers, section leaders, supervisors and other staff. There is a direct relationship between superior and subordinate, with each subordinate responsible to only one person. Line relationships are associated with functional or departmental division of work and organisational control. Line managers have authority and responsibility for all matters and activities within their own department.

Functional relationships

Functional relationships apply to the relationship between people in specialist or advisory positions, and line managers and their subordinates. The specialist offers a common service throughout all departments of the organisation, but has no direct authority over those who make use of the service. There is only an indirect relationship. For example, the personnel manager has no authority over staff in other departments – this is the responsibility of the line manager. But, as the position and role of the personnel manager would have been sanctioned by top management, other staff might be expected to accept the advice which is given. The personnel manager, however, could be assigned some direct, executive authority for certain specified responsibilities such as, for example, health and safety matters throughout the whole organisation. Note, however, that specialists in a functional relationship with other managers still have a line relationship with both their own superior and their own departmental subordinate staff.

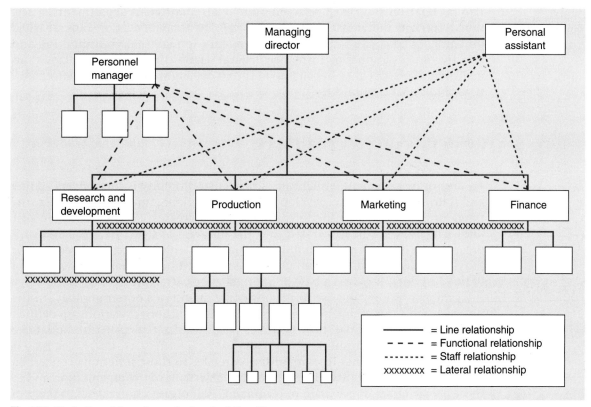

Fig. 10.8 Illustration of formal organisational relationships

Staff relationships

Staff relationships arise from the appointment of personal assistants to senior members of staff. Persons in a staff position normally have little or no direct authority in their own right but act as an extension of their superior and exercise only 'representative' authority. They often act in a 'gatekeeper' role. There is no direct relationship between the personal assistant and other staff except where delegated authority and responsibility have been given for some specific activity. In practice, however, personal assistants often do have some influence over other staff, especially those in the same department or grouping. This may be partially because of the close relationship between the personal assistant and the superior, and partially dependent upon the knowledge and experience of the assistant, and the strength of the assistant's own personality.

> In businesses and governmental agencies, from doctors' offices to licensing and regulatory boards, one may come face to face with people who have established themselves as gatekeeper to the boss. Gatekeepers aspire to and are rewarded with various titles, like administrative assistant, office manager or special assistant to such-and-such. But the essential role is usually that of secretary to the boss . . . Aspiring gatekeepers typically evoke polarised reactions among the office staff . . . Peers, unlike the boss, quickly recognise the individual's lack of integrity and willingness to step on all toes en route to the position of guardian of the gate.[31]

Lateral relationships

Lateral relationships exist between individuals in different departments or sections, especially individuals on the same level. These lateral relationships are based on contact and consultation and are necessary to maintain co-ordination and effective organisational performance. Lateral relationships may be specified formally but in practice they depend upon the co-operation of staff and in effect are a type of informal relationship.

LINE AND STAFF ORGANISATION

An area of management which causes particular difficulty is the concept of line and staff. As organisations develop in size and work becomes more complex, the range of activities and functions undertaken increases. People with specialist knowledge have to be integrated into the managerial structure. Line and staff organisation is concerned with different functions which are to be undertaken. It provides a means of making full use of specialists while maintaining the concept of line authority. It creates a type of informal matrix structure (*see* Fig. 10.9).

Again, confusion can arise from conflicting definitions of terminology. In the line and staff form of organisation, the individual authority relationship defined previously as 'functional' now becomes part of the actual structure under the heading of staff relationships.

One viewpoint is that line organisation relates to those functions concerned with specific responsibility for achieving the objectives of the organisation and to those people in the direct chain of command. Staff organisation relates to the provision of specialist and support functions for the line organisation and creates an advisory relationship. This is in keeping with the idea of task and element functions discussed earlier.

Difficulties with line and staff relations

The concept of line and staff relations presents a number of difficulties. With the increasing complexity of organisations and the rise of specialist services it becomes harder to distinguish clearly between what is directly essential to the operation of the organisation, and what might be regarded only as an auxiliary function. The distinction between a line manager and a staff manager is not absolute. There may be a fine division between offering professional advice and the giving of instructions.

Friction inevitably seems to occur between line and staff managers. Neither side may fully understand nor appreciate the purpose and role of the other. Staff managers are often criticised for unnecessary interference in the work of the line manager and for being out of touch with practical realities. Line managers may feel that the staff managers have an easier and less demanding job because they have no direct responsibility for producing a product or providing a service for the customer, and are free from day-to-day operational problems.

Staff managers may feel that their own difficulties and work problems are not appreciated fully by the line manager. Staff managers often complain about resistance to their attempts to provide assistance and co-ordination, and the unnecessary demands for departmental independence by line managers. A major source of difficulty is to persuade line managers to accept, and act upon, the advice and recommendations which are offered.

352

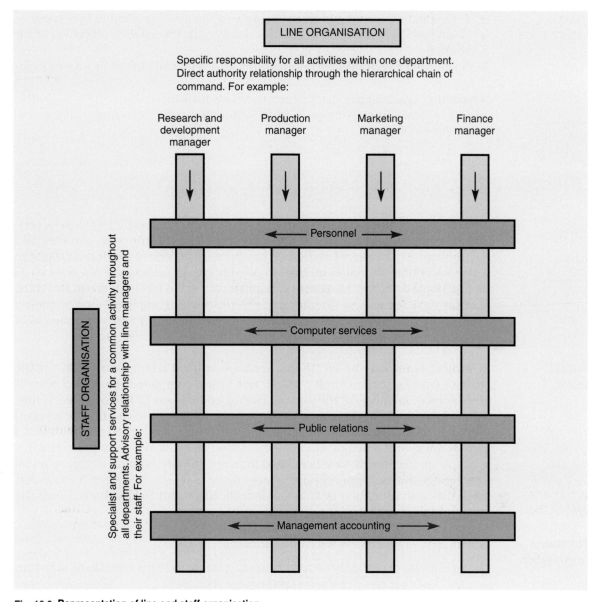

Fig. 10.9 **Representation of line and staff organisation**

The line and staff relationship can also give rise to problems of 'role incongruence' discussed in Chapter 6.

Internal marketing of staff departments

Clutterbuck suggests that a common feature of commercial life is staff departments such as personnel and information technology that have poor reputations with line managers. Even where line managers are clear what they want staff departments to do, they are rarely credited with initiative or much relevance to business objectives. In order to raise their profile, their perceived value and their contribution to the organisation there are a number of critical activities in the internal marketing of staff departments:

- understanding and responding effectively to the needs of internal customers;
- linking all the department's activities closely with the strategic objectives of the business;
- developing excellent communications and relationships with internal customers;
- ensuring internal customers' expectations are realistic; and
- continuously improving professionalism and capability in line with internal customers' needs.[32]

PROJECT TEAMS AND MATRIX ORGANISATION

The division of work and methods of grouping described earlier tend to be relatively permanent forms of structure. With the growth in newer, complex and technologically advanced systems it has become necessary for organisations to adapt traditional structures in order to provide greater integration of a wide range of functional activities. In recent years greater attention has been given, therefore, to more flexible forms of structure and the creation of groupings based on project teams and matrix organisation. Members of staff from different departments or sections are assigned to the team for the duration of a particular project.

Project teams

A **project team** may be set up as a separate unit on a temporary basis for the attainment of a particular task. When this task is completed the project team is disbanded or members of the unit are reassigned to a new task. Project teams may be used for people working together on a common task or to co-ordinate work on a specific project such as the design and development, production and testing of a new product; or the design and implementation of a new system or procedure. For example, project teams have been used in many military systems, aeronautics and space programmes. A project team is more likely to be effective when it has a clear objective, a well-defined task, and a definite end-result to be achieved, and the composition of the team is chosen with care.

The matrix organisation

The matrix organisation is a combination of:

(i) functional departments which provide a stable base for specialised activities and a permanent location for members of staff; and

(ii) units that integrate various activities of different functional departments on a project team, product, programme, geographical or systems basis. As an example, ICI is organised on matrix lines, by territory, function and business.

A matrix structure might be adopted in a university or college with grouping both by common subject specialism, and by association with particular courses or programmes of study.

The matrix organisation therefore establishes a grid, or matrix, with a two-way flow of authority and responsibility (*see* Fig. 10.10). Within the functional departments authority and responsibility flow vertically down the line, but the authority and responsibility of the project manager flow horizontally across the organisation structure.

Fig. 10.10
Outline of matrix structure

———— *line authority* exercised over departmental staff through direct chain of command.
– – – – *project authority* exercised over selected staff assigned from departments as appropriate.

A matrix design might be adopted where there is:

(i) **more than one critical orientation to the operations of the organisation,** for example an insurance company that has to respond simultaneously to both functional differentiation such as life, fire, marine, motor, and to different geographical areas;

(ii) **a need to process simultaneously large amounts of information,** for example a local authority social services department seeking help for an individual will need to know where to go for help from outside agencies such as police, priest, community relations officer; and at the same time whom to contact from internal resources within the organisation such as the appropriate social worker, health visitor or housing officer;

(iii) **the need for sharing of resources** which could only be justified on a total organisational basis such as the occasional or part-time use by individual departments of specialist staff or services.

Developing an effective matrix organisation, however, takes time, and a willingness to learn new roles and behaviour which means that matrix structures are often difficult for management to implement effectively.[33]

Difficulties with matrix structures Matrix organisation offers the advantages of flexibility; greater security and control of project information; and opportunities for staff development. There are, however, a number of potential difficulties and problem areas.

- There may be a limited number of staff reporting directly to the project manager with extra staff assigned as required by departmental managers. This may result in a feeling of ambiguity. Staff may be reluctant to accept constant change and prefer the organisational stability from membership of their own functional grouping.
- Matrix organisation can result in a more complex structure. By using two methods of grouping it sacrifices the unity of command and can cause problems of co-ordination.
- There may be a problem of defining the extent of the project manager's authority over staff from other departments and of gaining the support of other functional managers.
- Functional groups may tend to neglect their normal duties and responsibilities.

According to *Bartlett and Ghoshal*, matrix structures have proved all but unmanageable. Dual reporting leads to conflict and confusion; the proliferation of channels of communication creates informational log-jams; and overlapping responsibilities result in a loss of accountability.[34]

EFFECTS OF A DEFICIENT ORGANISATION STRUCTURE

It is not easy to describe, in a positive manner, what constitutes a 'good' or an effective organisation structure although, clearly, attention should be given to the design principles discussed above. However, the negative effects of a poorly designed structure can be identified more easily. In his discussion on the principles of organisation and co-ordination, *Urwick* suggests that 'Lack of design is Illogical, Cruel, Wasteful and Inefficient'.[35]

- **It is illogical** because in good social practice, as in good engineering practice, design should come first. No member of the organisation should be appointed to a senior position without identification of the responsibilities and relationships attached to that position and its role within the social pattern of the organisation.
- **It is cruel** because it is the individual members of the organisation who suffer most from lack of design. If members are appointed to the organisation without a clear definition of their duties or the qualifications required to perform those duties, it is these members who are likely to be blamed for poor results which do not match the vague ideas of what was expected of them.
- **It is wasteful** because if jobs are not put together along the lines of functional specialisation then new members of the organisation cannot be training effectively to take over these jobs. If jobs have to be fitted **to members** of the organisation, rather than members of the organisation **to jobs**, then every new member has to be trained in such a way so as to aim to replace the special, personal experience of the previous job incumbent. Where both the requirements of the job and the member of the organisation are unknown quantities this is likely to lead to indecision and much time wasted in ineffective discussion.

- **It is inefficient** because if the organisation is not founded on principles, managers are forced to fall back on personalities. Unless there are clearly established principles, which are understood by everyone in the organisation, managers will start 'playing politics' in matters of promotion and similar issues.

Urwick lays emphasis on the technical planning of the organisation and determining and laying out structure before giving any thought to the individual members of the organisation. Although Urwick acknowledges that the personal touch is important, and part of the obvious duty of the manager, it is not a substitute for the need for definite planning of the structure. 'In short, a very large proportion of the friction and confusion in current society, with its manifest consequences in human suffering, may be traced back directly to faulty organisation in the structural sense.'[36]

Consequences of badly designed structure

Urwick's emphasis on the logical design of organisation structure rather than the development around the personalities of its members is typical of the classical approach to organisation and management. Despite this rather narrow view, more recent writers have drawn similar conclusions as to the consequences of badly designed structure.

For example, *Child* points out that:

> There are a number of problems which so often mark the struggling organization and which even at the best of times are dangers that have to be looked for. These are low motivation and morale, late and inappropriate decisions, conflict and lack of co-ordination, rising costs and a generally poor response to new opportunities and external change. Structural deficiencies can play a part in exacerbating all these problems.[37]

Child then goes on to explain the consequences of structural deficiencies.

- **Low motivation and morale** may result from apparently inconsistent and arbitrary decisions; insufficient delegation of decision-making; lack of clarity in job definition and assessment of performance; competing pressures from different parts of the organisation; and managers and supervisors overloaded through inadequate support systems.
- **Late and inappropriate decisions** may result from: lack of relevant, timely information to the right people; poor co-ordination of decision-makers in different units; overloading of decision-makers due to insufficient delegation; and inadequate procedures for revaluation of past decisions.
- **Conflict and lack of co-ordination** may result from: conflicting goals and people working at cross-purposes because of lack of clarity on objectives and priorities; failure to bring people together into teams or through lack of liaison; and breakdown between planning and actual operational work.
- **Poor response to new opportunities and external change** may result from: failure to establish specialist jobs concerned with forecasting environmental change; failure to give adequate attention to innovation and planning of change as main management activities; inadequate co-ordination between identification of market changes and research into possible technological solutions.
- **Rising costs** may result from: a long hierarchy of authority with a high proportion of senior positions; an excess of administrative work at the expense of productive work; and the presence of some, or all, of the other organisational problems.

ATTENTION TO HUMAN PART OF THE ORGANISATION

It is clear, then, that it is essential to give full attention to the structure of an organisation. **In analysing the effectiveness of structure, consideration should be given to both the formal and technological requirements and principles of design; and to social factors, and the needs and demands of the human part of the organisation. Structure should be designed so as to maintain the balance of the socio-technical system, and to encourage the willing participation of members and effective organisational performance.**

An organisation can be separated into two parts or structures which can then be examined. One section is a definable structure that will be present in every company, the other is the structure caused by human intervention. The latter provides the company with its distinctive appearance, and may be regarded as the manager's particular response to the design requirements of organised behaviour. Essentially the effectiveness of an organisation depends on how accurately human design matches the structure of organised behaviour.[38]

ORGANISATION CHARTS

The structure of an organisation is usually depicted in the form of an organisation chart. This will show, at a given moment in time, how work is divided and the grouping together of activities, the levels of authority and formal organisational relationships. The organisation chart provides a pictorial representation of the structural framework of an organisation. Some charts are very sketchy and give only a minimum amount of information. Other charts give varying amounts of additional detail such as an indication of the broad nature of duties and responsibilities of the various units. Some charts give the names of postholders and even photographs; and some may even give the salary gradings for individual positions.

Charts are usually displayed in a traditional, vertical form such as those already depicted in Figs 10.6 and 10.8 above. They can, however, be displayed either horizontally with the information reading from left to right, or concentrically with top management at the centre. The main advantage of both the horizontal and the concentric organisation charts is that they tend to reduce the indication of superior or subordinate status. They also offer the practical advantage of more space on the outer margin. In addition, the concentric chart may help to depict the organisation more as a unified whole.

Organisation charts are useful in explaining the outline structure of an organisation. They may be used as a basis for the analysis and review of structure, for training and management succession, and for formulating changes. The chart may indicate **apparent weaknesses** in structure such as, for example:

- too wide a span of control;
- overlapping areas of authority;
- lack of unity of command;
- too long a scalar chain;
- unclear reporting relationships and/or lines of communication;
- unstaffed functions.

Limitations of organisation charts

There are, however, a number of limitations with traditional organisation charts. They depict only a static view of the organisation, and show how it looks and what the structure should be. Charts do not show the comparative authority and responsibility of positions on the same level, or lateral contacts and informal relations. Neither do charts show the extent of personal delegation from superior to subordinates, or the precise relationships between line and staff positions. Organisation charts can become out of date quickly and are often slow to be amended to reflect changes in the actual structure.

Charts do not describe how the organisation actually works or the behaviour of people represented on the chart. *Gray and Starke* give a humorous but perhaps realistic illustration of how an organisation actually works[39] (*see* Fig. 10.11).

Whilst acknowledging that organisation charts have some uses, *Townsend* likens them to 'rigor mortis' and advises that they should be drawn in pencil.

> Never formalize, print and circulate them. Good organizations are living bodies that grow new muscles to meet challenges. A chart demoralizes people. Nobody thinks of himself as *below* other people. And in a good company he isn't. Yet on paper there it is . . . In the best organizations people see themselves working in a circle as if around one table.[40]

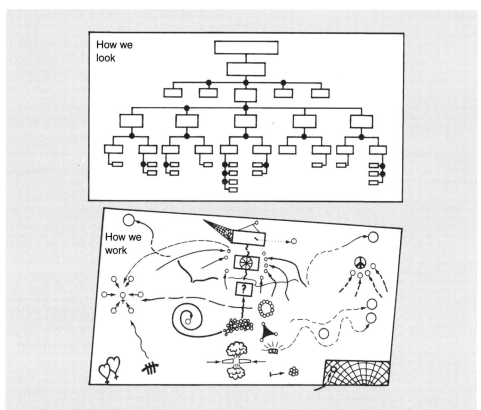

Fig. 10.11
How the organisation should be compared with how it actually works

(Reprinted with permission from Gray, J. L., and Starke, F A. *Organizational Behavior: Concepts and Applications,* Fourth edition, Merrill Publishing Company, an imprint of Macmillan Publishing Company (1988) p. 431.)

Comprehensible form of organisation chart

Despite these limitations, the organisation chart is a valuable and convenient way of illustrating the framework of structure – **provided the chart is drawn up in a comprehensible form.** There is always the question of what the chart does not show and what the observer interprets from it. Some charts add a rider, for example: 'position of boxes does not necessarily indicate importance of status or level of authority', or 'the chart indicates lines of communication and not necessarily lines of authority'. Such comments may only serve to add to the doubts, and it is quite possible that the chart really does indicate what the rider attempts to disclaim.

There are a number of conventions in drawing up organisation charts. It is not the purpose here to go into specific details, but it is important to remember that the chart should always give:

- the date when it was drawn up;
- the name of the organisation, branch or department (as appropriate) to which it refers;
- whether it is an existing or proposed structure;
- the extent of coverage, for example if it refers to the management structure only, or if it excludes servicing departments;
- a reference to identify the person who drew up the chart.

SYNOPSIS

- Structure provides the framework of an organisation and makes possible the application of the process of management. Some structure is necessary to make possible the effective performance of key activities and to support the efforts of staff. Organisations are layered and within the hierarchical structure there are three broad, interrelated levels: technical, managerial and community. The dimensions of structure can be identified in a number of ways but are usually taken to include the groupings of activities, responsibilities of individuals, levels of hierarchical authority, span of control and formal organisational relationships. An additional, important dimension of structure is the impact of information technology.

- The structure of an organisation affects not only productivity and economic efficiency but also the morale and job satisfaction of its members. The overall effectiveness of the organisation will be influenced both by sound structural design, and by the behaviour of people who work within the structure. Attention must be given to maintaining the socio-technical system and to integrating the structural and technological requirements of the organisation, and the needs and demands of the human part of the organisation.

- There is an underlying need to establish a framework of order and system of command through which the activities of the organisation can be planned, organised, directed and controlled. This demands attention to certain basic considerations in the design of organisation structure, and presents management with a series of decision points. There is a general movement towards 'flatter' organisation structures but this can give rise to particular difficulties.

- The essence of structure is the division of work among members of the organisation and the co-ordination of their activities. Work can be divided and activities

linked in a number of ways. Most organisations will contain examples of alternative combinations for grouping activities and relating different jobs to each other. A particular form of structure which can cause difficulty is the line and staff organisation. With the growth in newer, complex and technologically advanced systems, and the need to provide integration of a wide range of functional activities, greater attention has been given to more flexible forms of structure, such as matrix organisation.

■ A badly designed structure can have a number of negative effects and is likely to give rise to inefficiency, low motivation and morale, late and inappropriate decisions, conflict, rising costs and lack of development. The structure of an organisation is depicted usually in the form of an organisation chart which may be used as a basis for the analysis and review of structure, and may indicate apparent weaknesses. There are, however, limitations with traditional organisation charts. There are also a number of conventions in drawing up the charts.

Review and discussion questions

1 What are the objectives of organising? Distinguish different levels in the hierarchical structure of an organisation.

2 Summarise the major dimensions of organisation structure and give examples from your own organisation.

3 What is the importance of good structure? How does structure relate to the overall effectiveness of an organisation?

4 How might the work of a large organisation be divided among its members? Give examples where each method might be most appropriate. Examine the means for division of work in your own organisation and comment upon their effectiveness.

5 Explain the main factors to be considered in the design of organisation structure. Debate critically the value of 'principles' of organisation.

6 Distinguish clearly between 'span of control' and 'scalar chain'. Discuss the practical implications of span of control and scalar chain for the structure and effective operation of an organisation.

7 To what extent would you agree with the contention that a logical structure for organisation is better for efficiency and morale than a structure allowed to develop around personalities? What are the likely consequences of a poorly designed structure?

8 Prepare diagrams to help explain (i) line and staff organisation, and (ii) a matrix form of organisation structure. What are the reasons for adopting each of these forms of structure and what problem areas might arise?

 Assignment

Examine closely arrangements for the division of work and linking together of activities in your own or some other organisation of your choice.

(i) Investigate and make notes on the variety of ways in which work is divided and combinations for grouping of activities within the organisation.

(ii) Comment critically on the apparent effectiveness of different methods adopted for the division of work among members of the organisation.

(iii) Give reasons, and where possible practical examples, in support of your comments.

(iv) Explain any changes you would recommend in order to help improve organisational performance. Where appropriate prepare a revised, or a new, organisation chart.

CASE STUDY

Part one

The personal assistant to the commercial director of a large manufacturing group is at present looking into the costing systems of the metal furniture division employing some 500 people, 30 of whom are in the general offices at the works.

The division manufactures metal furniture in the Home Counties for industrial and business use, selling catalogue lines from stock mainly to retailers.

The works takes in raw material and parts at the receiving bay, then machines batches of components, assembles, finishes and dispatches orders to customers in the firm's transport or by carrier from the warehouse at the other end of the works.

The office manager is responsible for all the clerical and commercial functions except the sales and general ledgers which are kept at Head Office. The sales manager is at the London showrooms, but all customers' orders are handled by office staff at the works.

One afternoon, the secretary to the commercial director's personal assistant comes into the office and says that her friend Cynthia is in tears. Mr Smith, the personal assistant, protests that it is not his concern but is persuaded to listen. In due course he discovers that Cynthia is the senior computer operator in the general office and that she is upset because she is worried about her work.

Mr L. O. Kate, the senior cost clerk, complains that the period overhead rates have not been calculated: Mr T. Clarke says his jobs should have been done first; Mr I. Payem insists that the bonus figures and tax computations for the wages which are due for payment the very next day must be ready by lunchtime. The buyers want the batches of incoming invoices checked; the sales statistics clerk is looking for percentages and cumulative figures.

Cynthia does not really get on with most of the other staff in the general office, who resent the fact that she is paid more. Mr Jones, the office manager, does not seem to notice that she exists and his secretary, who has been around longer than anyone else, orders Cynthia and everyone else about.

Mr Smith, trying to be tactful, has a quiet word with Mr Jones. Mr Jones says that Mr Smith is quite right to come to him about the matter. He is also always ready to make his 30 years' experience available to 'you smart young people'. He adds that he is sure there is nothing for Mr Smith to worry about – all his staff report directly to him and he would not have it any other way. He will, however, have a word with Tom, his chief clerk, and ask him to keep an eye on her. Tom is rather busy with a small buying problem, and with balancing the wages, and one or two other things at the moment – but he will tell him about the girl.

Still a trifle concerned, Mr Smith has a word with the local personnel assistant, who reminds him that the division's personnel department deals only with shop-floor people. On his next visit to Head Office, he has a look in the office staff files, but can find no sign that job descriptions or charts of an organisation were ever compiled for the office staff at the division.

(a) Comment on the apparent nature of the relationship among people in the office.
(b) Suggest a preferred organisation structure which might help to resolve some of the problems involved.

Part two

Mr Smith, the personal assistant to the commercial director, has now been appointed office manager of the division after the early retirement of Mr Jones. The appointment as office manager took place some time after the events outlined in part one of the case study and the office staff had just moved into a large open-plan office instead of being spread in several rooms around the building.

It is assumed that the preferred organisation you designed after the incidents described in part one of the case study is slowly being introduced as it becomes possible to persuade the staff to change their attitudes and methods of working.

One day early in February, the commercial director's secretary telephones to ask about the monthly return of packing and carriage for December. The office manager explains that he is not aware of any delay but will inquire and ring back. He sends for the chief clerk, who is rather vague about the return, and who asks permission to work overtime in the buying section that evening. The office manager agrees, with some reservations, and takes his inquiries further.

He finds from a few moments' conversation in the office that the clerk who deals with incoming invoices is clear and to the point. He has the whole month's charges for packing materials neatly summarised, the internal debit note from the garage cost centre, and the haulage contractors' accounts okayed by the dispatch supervisor. So total costs are ready; and that leaves the income side, the amounts 'recovered' from each of the customers' orders for the month.

The office manager finds that this is dealt with by Ms B., who takes each copy invoice for the month and evaluates notional percentages incorporated in the price to cover packing and carriage which varies according to the sales area zone. These details are then summarised in a very large book which, it turns out, no one else in the office understands at all.

Ms B. has not finished the December figures yet because she is busy with some special data the sales manager in London has asked her to provide. She also mentions that the packing and carriage return for January is due at Head Office at the end of next week – and if she had been asked, she would have said.

Mr Smith, the office manager, considers that the procedure she has just outlined is a long-winded way of getting a general indication that recovery matches expense during the year. Still a bit put out by the chief clerk's lack of interest, he rashly tells her that the procedure is poor.

Ms B. stiffens and says she has always tried very hard at her job and done what she was told to do, and it was always satisfactory in the past. If Mr Smith cared he could ask Mr Jones – but things aren't the same any more, she adds.

Mr Smith mumbles reassurances and asks if she could possibly clear up the December figures by Friday. Ms B. agrees reluctantly – but what shall she do about finishing off the sales manager's request? Then, almost as an afterthought, she reminds him that it has already been agreed that she shall take next week off as special leave.

Later that afternoon the chief clerk puts his head round the door and drops his small bomb – Ms B. has given a month's notice.

Mr Smith rings Head Office to ask the chief accountant if he can tell him anything more about the packing and carriage return. The chief accountant promises to send Mr Smith a photocopy of an old file note he has unearthed.

But relief is short-lived for the chief accountant goes on to darken the day still more by asking if Mr Smith has heard the managing director's latest? An official

announcement will be made shortly: 'In view of anticipated trading difficulties, overtime working will now be strictly limited, no new staff may be recruited, and replacements will be restricted to works direct labour only. Capital expenditure will be halted and all managers are required to exercise the strictest economy.'

(a) What do you see as the main issues or problem areas?
(b) Suggest what actions you recommend be taken to help resolve the present situation and overcome future difficulties.

Notes and references

1. Adapted from Knight, K. (ed.) *Matrix Management: A Cross-functional Approach to Organization*, Gower (1977) pp. 114–15.
2. Drucker, P. F. *The Practice of Management*, Heinemann Professional (1989).
3. Parsons, T. 'Some Ingredients of a General Theory of Formal Organization', in Litterer, J. A. *Organizations: Structure and Behaviour*, Third edition, Wiley (1980).
4. Department of the Environment, *The New Local Authorities: Management and Structure* (The Bains Report), HMSO (1972).
5. *Ibid.*, pp. 10–11.
6. For a summary of empirical literature on the determination of structural dimensions see: Blackburn, R. S. 'Dimensions of Structure: A Review and Reappraisal', *Academy of Management Review*, vol. 7, no. 1, January 1982, pp. 59–66.
7. Child, J. *Organization: A Guide to Problems and Practice*, Second edition, Paul Chapman (1988).
8. Mintzberg, H. *The Structuring of Organizations*, Prentice-Hall (1979).
9. See, for example: Robey, D. *Designing Organizations*, Third edition, Irwin (1991).
10. Baker, K. 'What I.T. is all about', *The British Journal of Administrative Management*, vol. 32, no. 9/10, December 1982/January 1983, pp. 293–4.
11. See, for example: Atkinson, P. 'The Impact of Information Technology and Office Automation on Administrative Managment', *British Journal of Administrative Management*, vol. 35, no. 3, June 1985, pp. 100–5. See also: Stewart, R. *Managing Today and Tomorrow*, Macmillan (1991).
12. Drucker, P. F. *The Practice of Management*, Heinemann Professional (1989) p. 223.
13. Child, J. *Organization: A Guide to Problems and Practice*, Second edition, Paul Chapman (1988) p. 4.
14. Forte, C. (Lord Forte) *Forte: The Autobiography of Charles Forte*, Sidgwick and Jackson (1986) p. 122.
15. Argyris, C. *Integrating the Individual and the Organization*, Wiley (1964).
16. Stewart, R. *The Reality of Management*, Second edition, Pan Books (1986) p. 127.
17. For a fuller discussion, see: Sadler, P. *Designing Organisations: The Foundation for Excellence*, Mercury (1991).
18. Woodward, J. *Industrial Organization: Theory and Practice*, Second edition, Oxford University Press (1980).
19. See, for example: Mullins, L. J. *Hospitality Management: A Human Resources Approach*, Second edition, Pitman (1995).
20. Woodward, J. *Industrial Organization: Theory and Practice*, Second edition, Oxford University Press (1980) p. 113.
21. Urwick, L. *Notes on the Theory of Organisation*, American Management Association (1952).
22. Brech, E. F. L. *Organisation: The Framework of Management*, Second edition, Longman (1965).
23. Graicunas, V. A. 'Relationship in Organization', in *Papers on the Science of Administration*, University of Columbia (1937).
24. Woodward, J. *Industrial Organization: Theory and Practice*, Second edition, Oxford University Press (1980).
25. Heller, R. 'The Manager's Dilemma', *Management Today*, January 1994, pp. 42–7.
26. See, for example: Benton, P. 'Turbulent Times', *Management Today*, January 1991, p. 5.
27. Foster, G. 'The Central Question', *Management Today*, April 1994, pp. 56–61.
28. James, G. *Quality of Working Life and Total Quality Management*, Occasional Paper No. 5, ACAS Work Research Unit, November 1991.

29. See, for example: Armitage, K. 'The Problems Raised by "Flatter" Management', *The British Journal of Administrative Management*, vol. 4, February 1991, pp. 28–9.

30. Gretton, I. 'Striving to Succeed in a Changing Environment', *Professional Manager*, July 1993, pp. 15–17.

31. Learner, P. M. 'Beware the Gatekeeper', *Amtrak Express*, July/August 1994, pp. 14–17.

32. Clutterbuck, D. 'Marketing the Staff Departments', *Professional Manager*, January 1994, pp. 7–9.

33. Adapted from Kolondy, H. F. 'Managing in a Matrix', *Business Horizons*, March/April 1981, pp. 17–24.

34. Bartlett, A. and Ghoshal, S. 'Matrix Management: Not a Structure, a Frame of Mind', *Harvard Business Review*, July–August 1990, pp. 138–45.

35. Urwick, L. *The Elements of Administration*, Second edition, Pitman (1947) p. 38.

36. *Ibid.*, p. 39.

37. Child, J. *Organisation: A Guide to Problems and Practice*, Second edition, Paul Chapman (1988) pp. 5–6.

38. Dunderdale, P. 'Analysing Effective Organisations', *Professional Manager*, September 1994, pp. 23–4.

39. Gray, J. L. and Starke, F. A. *Organizational Behaviour: Concepts and Applications*, Fourth edition, Merrill Publishing Company, an imprint of Macmillan Publishing Company (1988).

40. Townsend, R. *Further Up the Organisation*, Coronet Books (1985) p. 159.

11 CONTINGENCY APPROACH TO ORGANISATION AND MANAGEMENT

There are many variables which influence the most appropriate organisation structure and system of management. The contingency approach rejects earlier views based on one best form of structure. Instead, it attempts to analyse structure in terms of relationships among its components and the environment of the organisation, and emphasises flexibility. The 'fit' between structure, systems of management, and the behaviour of people, will depend upon (be *contingent* upon) situational variables for each particular organisation.

 Learning objectives

To:

- Explain the meaning and nature of the contingency approach, and contrast with earlier approaches to organisation and management;

- Recognise the importance of situational variables for organisational design;

- Examine main contingency models and assess their implication for management;

- Analyse structure in terms of relationships among its components and the environment of the organisation;

- Evaluate the relevance and practical value of the contingency approach;

- Recognise the importance of alternative forms of structure and the demand for flexibility;

- Appreciate the importance of human nature and what may happen in practice in organisations.

Worth thinking about

'We trained very hard, but it seemed that every time we were beginning to form up into teams we would be reorganised. I was to learn later in life that we tend to meet any new situation by reorganising and a wonderful method it can be for creating the illusion of progress while producing confusion, inefficiency and demoralisation.'
Gaius Petronius (AD 66)

To what extent has anything changed in the past 1930 years?

THE MEANING AND NATURE OF THE CONTINGENCY APPROACH

In the last chapter we examined a number of basic principles and considerations which underlie the design of organisation structure. These principles and considerations suggest a prescriptive stance towards improving organisational effectiveness.

By contrast, the contingency approach takes the view that there is no one best, universal structure. There are a large number of variables, or situational factors, which influence organisational design and performance. The contingency approach emphasises the need for flexibility.

Earlier approaches to organisation and management

Both the classical and human relations approaches to organisation and management believed in one best form of structure and tended to concentrate on limited aspects of organisation. Both approaches also tended to study the organisation in isolation from its environment.

The **classical approach** focused attention on the formal structure, technical requirements of the organisation and general sets of principles. There was an assumption of rational and logical behaviour. The identification of general objectives and the clarification of purposes and responsibilities at all levels of the organisation would lead to the most effective structure. Bureaucracy, as a sub-group of the classical approach, views the structure of the organisation in terms of specialisation, hierarchy of authority, system of rules and impersonality.

The **human relations approach** focused attention on the informal organisation, and on the psychological and social needs of people at work. The neo-human relations writers concentrated on the personal adjustment of individuals within the structure of the organisation. Members were assumed to be committed to achieving the goals of the organisation. Attention was given to design of a structure which removed alienating aspects of work and restrictions on effective performance.

The **systems view** of organisation and management placed emphasis on the socio-technical approach, the interrelationships of sub-systems and multiple channels of interaction, and recognised the importance of the external environment.

The concept of contingency

The **contingency approach** can be seen as a development of the systems approach and goes a stage further in relating the environment, and other vari-

ables, to specific structures of organisation. *Hunt* explains the concept of contingency as follows:

> The concept of contingency also implies that there is no one, absolute 'best' design; rather, there is a multitude of possibilities and the best or preferred choice will be contingent on the situation being analysed. Universal models designed to suit all situations are therefore rejected. This is consistent with the fact that most organizations are networks of a variety of bits of design rather than conforming, as one entity, to a particular model. So we might find units of bureaucracy, units of matrix structures, units with project teams, units with extremely loose, almost *ad hoc* structures – and all these within, say, the same oil company. In this sense, the contingency theorists merely reflected the findings of hundreds of researchers. There are common elements in the hierarchies of different organizations but there are also very many differences peculiar to the local situation.[1]

The most appropriate structure is dependent, therefore, upon the contingencies of the situation for each individual organisation. These situational factors account for variations in the structure of different organisations.

An 'if–then' relationship

The contingency approach can be seen as a form of 'if–then' matrix relationship.[2] If certain situational factors exist, **then** certain variables in organisation structure and systems of management are most appropriate. A simplified illustration of contingency relationships is given in Fig. 11.1.

Situational factors may be identified in a number of ways. The more obvious bases for comparison include the type of organisation and its purpose (which was discussed in Chapter 3); power and control; history; and the characteristics of the

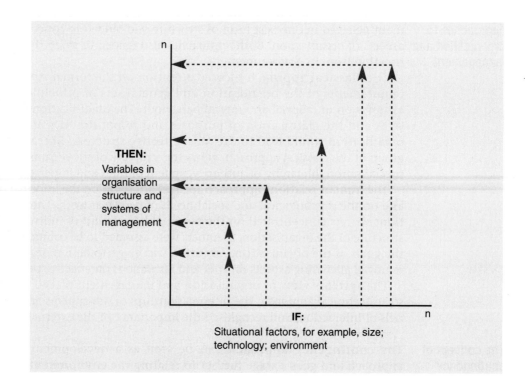

Fig. 11.1
The 'if–then' contingency relationship

members of the organisation such as their abilities, skills and experience and their needs and motivations. The choice of structure can also be influenced by the preferences of top management.[3] It is also debatable whether national culture is a contingent factor (*see* discussion later in this chapter).

Contingency models

Other important variables are size, technology and environment. A number of studies have been carried out into the extent to which these contingency factors influence organisational design and effectiveness. Among the most significant contingency 'models' are those shown in Fig. 11.2.

Fig. 11.2 Examples of contingency models

SIZE OF ORGANISATION

The size of an organisation has obvious implications for the design of its structure. In the very small organisations there is little need for a formal structure. But with increasing size, and the associated problems of the execution of work and management of staff, organisations may be divided into departments, or semi-autonomous sub-units, or, in large business organisations, distinct fields or industries. In larger organisations there are likely to be more formalised relationships and greater use of rules and standardised procedures. Studies such as those undertaken by the University of Aston[4] suggest that size has important implications for organisational design. Size explains best many of the characteristics of organisation structure, for example the importance of standardisation through rules and procedures as a mechanism for co-ordination in larger organisations.

Size, however, is not a simple variable. It can be defined and measured in different ways, although the most common indication of size is the number of persons employed by the organisation. There is the problem of distinguishing the effects of size from other organisational variables. And there is conflicting evidence on the relationship of size to the structure and operation of the organisation.

Relationship between size and behaviour

Summarising the results of a number of studies on the relationship between the size of organisational sub-units and individual attitude and behaviour, *Porter et al.* found that in the larger sub-units there appeared to be a clear, negative relationship to job satisfaction, absenteeism and staff turnover, subject to three qualifications:

- accident rates and productivity were equivocal;
- most studies involved rank and file employees; and
- there was a problem of distinguishing among types of sub-units.

Porter *et al.* concluded that: 'The weight of evidence would seem to make a strong indictment against large-sized subunits, both from the individual's point of view and from the organization's standpoint.'[5]

Size and economic performance

In a study of the effects of size on the rate of growth and economic performance, *Child* acknowledges the tendency for increased size to be associated with increased bureaucracy. He argues that the more bureaucratised, larger organisations perform better than the less bureaucratised, larger organisations (*see* Fig. 11.3). Child found that:

> Much as critics may decry bureaucracy . . . the more profitable and faster growing companies, in the larger size category of 2,000 employees and above, were those that had developed this type of organization. The larger the company, the greater the association between more bureaucracy and superior performance. At the other end of the scale, among small firms of only a hundred or so employees, the better performers generally managed with very little formal organization.[6]

TECHNOLOGY

Two major studies concerning technology are by:

- *Woodward* – patterns of organisation, production technology and business success; and
- *Perrow* – main dimensions of technology and organisation structure.

THE WOODWARD STUDY

A major study of the effects of technology on organisation structure was carried out by *Joan Woodward*.[7] Her pioneering work presents the results of empirical study of 100 manufacturing firms in south-east Essex and the relationships between the application of principles of organisation and business success. The main thesis was 'that industrial organizations which design their formal organizational structures to fit the type of production technology they employ are likely to be commercially successful'.[8]

Information was obtained from each of the firms under the four headings of:

(i) history, background and objectives;
(ii) manufacturing processes and methods;
(iii) forms and routines used in the organisation and operation of the firm;
(iv) information relating to an assessment of commercial success.

Fig. 11.3
Size of organisation,
bureaucracy and
performance

(Reproduced with permission from Child, J. *Organization: A Guide to Problems and Practice*, Second edition, Paul Chapman (1988) p. 222.)

The researchers then studied differences in the structure, management, organisation and operation of the firms, and their efficiency and business success. The assessment of business success was made through an examination of profits made and capital investment in expansion programmes, together with other considerations such as rate of development in personnel and plant, fluctuation of shares on the Stock Exchange, level of salaries to senior management, reputation of the firm and staff turnover. Firms were classified into three broad groups: 'average', 'above average' and 'below average'.

Types of production systems

The firms were divided into different types of production systems, from least to most technological complexity, with three main groupings of:

● **Unit and small batch production**

 (i) production of units to customer's requirements;
 (ii) production of prototypes;
 (iii) fabrication of large equipment in stages;
 (iv) production of small batches to customer's orders.

● **Large batch and mass production**

 (v) production of large batches;
 (vi) production of large batches on assembly lines;
 (vii) mass production.

● **process production**

 (viii) intermittent production of chemicals in multi-purpose plant;
 (ix) continuous flow production of liquids, gases and crystalline substances.

373

The research showed that the firms varied considerably in their organisation structure and that many of the variations appeared to be linked closely with differences in manufacturing techniques.

Types of organisation structure

The researchers examined the organisation structure of the firms under three main types:

35 firms had essentially a **line** type of organisation.

2 firms were organised **functionally** (as suggested by F. W. Taylor).

59 firms had varying degrees of **line staff** organisation.

(4 firms were unclassified.)

There was a trend for the line staff type of organisation to be developed highly in the middle ranges of the scale. The two firms with a functional type of organisation and fifteen of the firms with a predominantly line organisation were in the process production grouping. The other firms with line organisations were in the unit production grouping.

Eight firms which had a simple organisation structure based on line specialisation of basic task functions only were all in the 'average' or 'above average' success classification. Three of these firms employed less than 500 people, four employed between 500 and 1000 people, and one employed more than 1000 people. All firms were in either the unit production or process production groupings. No successful firms with large batch or mass production had this simple form of organisation structure.

Patterns of organisation and technology

Organisational patterns were found to be related more to similarity of objectives and production techniques than to size, type of industry, or the business success of the firm. Among the organisational characteristics showing a direct relationship to technology were span of control and scalar chain (discussed in Chapter 10), percentage of total turnover allocated to wages and salaries, ratio of managers to total personnel, and ratio of clerical and administrative staff to manual workers. The number of distinct levels of management between the board and operators could be anything from 2 to 12, and varied with the type of production system. The more advanced the technology the longer the length of the line. Details of levels of management and span of control are summarised in Table 11.1.

Woodward acknowledges that technology is not the only variable which affects organisation but is one that could be isolated more easily for study. She does, however, draw attention to the importance of technology, organisation and business success.

The figures relating to the span of control of the chief executive, the number of levels in the line of command, labour costs, and the various labour ratios showed a similar trend. The fact that organizational characteristics, technology and success were linked together in this way suggested that not only was the system of production an important variable in the determination of organizational structure, but also that one particular form of organization was most appropriate to each system of production. In unit production, for example, not only did short and relatively broad based pyramids predominate, but they also appeared to ensure success. Process production, on the other hand, would seem to require the taller and more narrowly based pyramid.[9]

Table 11.1 Summary of levels of management and span of control

Number of levels of management authority			
Number of firms	*Type of production*	*Range of levels*	*Median*
24	Unit and small batch	2 to 4	3
31	Large batch and mass production	3 to 8 or more	4
25	Process production	4 to 8 or more	6
Average span of control of first line supervisor			
Number of firms	*Type of production*	*Range of span*	*Median*
24	Unit and small batch	Less than 10 to 51–60	23
31	Large batch and mass production	11–20 to 81–90	49
25	Process production	Less than 10 to 31–40	13

(Adapted from Woodward, J. *Industrial Organization: Theory and Practice*, Second edition, Oxford University Press (1980) pp. 52 and 69.)

Principles of organisation and business success

There appeared to be no direct link between principles of organisation and business success. As far as organisation was concerned, the 20 outstandingly successful firms had little in common.

The classical approach appeared to fail in providing a direct and simple basis for relating organisational structure and business success. **There was, however, a stronger relationship between organisation structure and success within each of the three main groupings of production systems.**

Twenty firms were placed in the 'above average' classification of business success – five unit production, five mass production, six process production – and the remainder with combined systems.

Seventeen firms were classified as 'below average' – five unit production, six mass production, four process production, and two with combined systems.

It was found that within each production grouping the successful firms had common organisational characteristics which tended to be clustered round the medians for the grouping as a whole. Figures for those firms classified as 'below average' tended to be at the extremes of the range. It was also found that in terms of the *Burns and Stalker* analysis (discussed below), successful firms in the large batch production range tended to have a mechanistic management system, while successful firms outside of this range tended to have organic management systems.

Relationship between development, production and marketing

Another important finding of *Woodward*'s study was the nature of the actual cycle of manufacturing and the relationship between three key 'task' functions of development, production and marketing. The most critical of these functions varied according to the type of production system. (*See* Fig. 11.4.)

- **Unit and small batch:** production was based on firm orders only with marketing the first activity. Greater stress was laid on technical expertise, and the quality and efficiency of the product. Research and development were the second, and most critical, activities. Because of the need for flexibility, close integration of functions and frequent personal contacts, an organic structure was required.

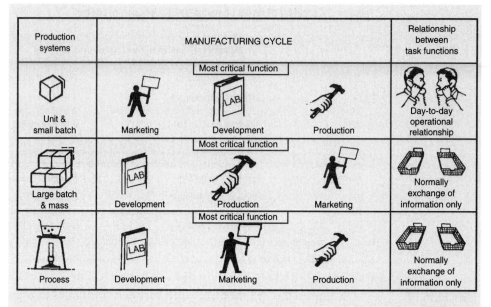

**Fig. 11.4
Characteristics of
production systems**

(Reproduced with permission from Woodward, J. *Industrial Organization: Theory and Practice*, Second edition, Oxford University Press (1980) p. 128.)

- **Large batch and mass:** production schedules were not dependent directly on firm orders. The first phase of manufacturing was product development, followed by production which was the most important function, and then third, marketing. The three functions were more independent and did not rely so much on close operational relationships among people responsible for development, production and sales.
- **Process:** the importance of securing a market meant that marketing was the central and critical activity. Products were either impossible or difficult to store, or capacity for storage was very limited. The flow of production was directly determined, therefore, by the market situation. Emphasis of technical knowledge was more on how products could be used than on how they could be made.

Subsequent studies

A subsequent study by *Zwerman* supported, very largely, the findings of Woodward. Zwerman's study involved a slightly different sample of organisations and was carried out in Minneapolis in the USA.[10] In other respects, however, the study attempted to replicate Woodward's work. Zwerman reached a similar conclusion, that the type of production technology was related closely to variations in organisation structure.

However, a further study by *Collins and Hull* of 95 American manufacturing firms questioned the extent to which span of control is a by-product of main types of production technology. Variations in the span of control of production operations were attributed to the underlying effects of size, task complexity and automation. Collins and Hull suggest that the technology versus size debate has moved beyond an 'either–or' proposition to a 'both–and' proposition.[11]

MAJOR DIMENSIONS OF TECHNOLOGY: THE WORK OF PERROW

The work by Woodward was extended by *Perrow* who drew attention to two major dimensions of technology:

- the extent to which the work task is predictable or variable; and
- the extent to which technology can be analysed.[12]

Variability refers to the number of exceptional or unpredictable cases and the extent to which problems are familiar. For example, a mass production factory is likely to have only a few exceptions but the manufacture of a designer range of clothing would have many exceptional and unpredictable cases.

The analysis of technology refers to the extent to which the task functions are broken down and highly specified, and the extent to which problems can be solved in recognised ways or by the use of routine procedures.

Combining the two dimensions provides a continuum of technology from Routine → Non-routine. With non-routine technology there are a large number of exceptional cases involving difficult and varied problem-solving.

The two dimensions of variability and the analysis of problems can also be represented as a matrix. (*See* Fig. 11.5.)

Technology and structure

The classification of each type of technology relates to a particular organisation structure. *Perrow* suggests that by classifying organisations according to their technology and predictability of work tasks, we should be able to predict the most effective form of structure.

Variables such as the discretion and power of sub-groups, the basis of co-ordination and the interdependence of groups result from the use of different technologies.

In the **routine type of organisation** there is minimum discretion at both the technical and supervisory levels, but the power of the middle management level is high; co-ordination is based on planning; and there is likely to be low interdependence between the two groups. This arrangement approaches a bureaucratic structure.

	FEW EXCEPTIONS	MANY EXCEPTIONS
PROBLEMS CANNOT BE ANALYSED	*Craft technology* Making a whole product probably in the same way each time, e.g. fine glassware	*Non-routine technology* e.g. psychiatric care in a mental hospital; manufacture of nuclear fuel systems
PROBLEMS CAN BE ANALYSED	*Routine technology* Manufacture of standard products; highly mechanised mass production	*Engineering technology* e.g. made-to-order machines such as electrical components; research consultancy

Fig. 11.5 Matrix of technology variables

(Adapted from Perrow, C. *Organizational Analysis: A Sociological View*, Tavistock Publications (1970) p. 78, and Mitchell, T. R. *People in Organizations*, Second edition, McGraw-Hill (1982) p. 32.)

In the **non-routine type of organisation** there is a high level of discretion and power at both the technical and supervisory levels; co-ordination is through feedback; and there is high group interdependence. This model resembles an organic structure.

ENVIRONMENT

Two important studies which focused not just on technology but on the effects of uncertainty and a changing external environment on the organisation, and its management and structure, are those by:

● *Burns and Stalker* – divergent systems of management practice, 'mechanistic' and 'organic'; and
● *Lawrence and Lorsch* – the organisation of specific departments, and the extent of 'differentiation' and 'integration'.

BURNS AND STALKER STUDY

The study by *Burns and Stalker* was an analysis of 20 industrial firms in the United Kingdom and the effects of the external environment on their pattern of management and economic performance.[13] The firms were drawn from a number of different industries: a rayon manufacturer; a large engineering company; Scottish firms attempting to enter the electronics field; and English firms operating in varying sectors of the electronics industry.

Mechanistic and organic systems
From an examination of the settings in which the firms operated, Burns and Stalker distinguished five different kinds of environments ranging from 'stable' to 'least predictable'. They also identified two divergent systems of management practice and structure – the **'mechanistic' system** and the **'organic' system.** These represented the polar extremes of the form which such systems could take when adapted to technical and commercial change. Burns and Stalker suggested that both types of system represented a 'rational' form of organisation which could be created and maintained explicitly and deliberately to make full use of the human resources in the most efficient manner according to the circumstances of the organisation.

The mechanistic system is a more rigid structure and more appropriate to stable conditions. The characteristics of a mechanistic management system are similar to those of bureaucracy. It is characterised by:

● the specialisation of tasks;
● closely defined duties, responsibilities and technical methods;
● a clear hierarchical structure;
● knowledge centred at the top of the hierarchy;
● the tendency for vertical interaction between superior and subordinate;
● the use of instructions and decisions by superiors on methods of operation and working behaviour; and
● insistence on loyalty to the organisation and obedience to superiors.

The organic system is a more fluid structure appropriate to changing conditions. It appears to be required when new problems and unforeseen circumstances arise constantly and require actions outside defined roles in the hierarchical structure. The organic system is characterised by:

- the contribution of special knowledge and experience to the tasks of the organisation:
- the adjustment and continual redefinition of tasks;
- a network structure of control, authority and communication;
- technical or commercial knowledge located throughout the organisation, not just at the top;
- superior knowledge not coinciding necessarily with positional authority;
- a lateral direction of communication, and communication based more on information and advice than instructions and decisions;
- commitment to the common task of the organisation; and
- the importance and prestige attached to individual contribution.

A summary of the characteristics of mechanistic and organic organisations is provided by Litterer.[14] (*See* Fig. 11.6.)

MECHANISTIC		ORGANIC
High, many and sharp differentiations	SPECIALISATION	Low, no hard boundaries, relatively few different jobs
High, methods spelled out	STANDARDISATION	Low, individuals decide own methods
Means	ORIENTATION OF MEMBERS	Goals
By superior	CONFLICT RESOLUTION	Interaction
Hierarchical, based on implied contractual relation	PATTERN OF AUTHORITY CONTROL AND COMMUNICATION	Wide net based upon common commitment
At top of organisation	LOCUS OF SUPERIOR COMPETENCE	Wherever there is skill and competence
Vertical	INTERACTION	Lateral
Directions, orders	COMMUNICATION CONTENT	Advice, information
To organisation	LOYALTY	To project and group
From organisational position	PRESTIGE	From personal contribution

Fig. 11.6 Characteristics of mechanistic and organic organisations

(Reprinted with the permission of the author from Litterer, J. A. *The Analysis of Organizations*, Second edition, Wiley (1973) p. 339.)

Location of authority

Although the organic system is not hierarchical in the same sense as the mechanistic system, Burns and Stalker emphasise that it is still stratified, with positions differentiated according to seniority and greater expertise. The location of authority, however, is by consensus and the lead is taken by the 'best authority', that is the person who is seen to be most informed and capable. Commitment to the goals of the organisation is greater in the organic system, and it becomes more difficult to distinguish the formal and informal organisation. The development of shared beliefs in the values and goals of the organisation in the organic system runs counter to the co-operation and monitoring of performance achieved through the chain of hierarchical command in the mechanistic system.

Burns and Stalker point out that there are intermediate stages between the two extreme systems which represent not a dichotomy but a polarity. The relationship between the mechanistic and organic systems is not rigid. An organisation moving between a relatively stable and a relatively changing environment may also move between the two systems.

'MIXED' FORMS OF ORGANISATION STRUCTURE

Many organisations will be hybrid – that is a mix of both mechanistic and organic structures. And often this is an uneasy mix which can lead to tension and conflict! For example, a group of people engaged on a set of broad functional activities may prefer, and perform best in, an organic structure; whilst another group tend to prefer a mechanistic structure and to work within established rules, systems and procedures.

The different perceptions of appropriate organisational styles and working methods present a particular challenge to management. There is need for a senior member of staff, in an appropriate position in the hierarchy and who has the respect of both groups, to act in a bridging role and to help establish harmony between them.[15]

A typical example of a hybrid organisation could be a university with differences in perception between the academic staff and the non-teaching staff. The non-teaching staff have an important function in helping to keep the organisation operational and working effectively, and may fail to understand why academics appear to find it difficult, or resent, working within prescribed administrative systems and procedures. The academic staff may well feel that they can only work effectively within an organic structure, and tend to see non-teaching staff as bureaucratic and resistant to novel or different ideas.

Universities may also tend to be more mechanistic at top management level with an apparent proliferation of committees and sub-committees, because of their dealings with, for example, government bodies.

The distinction between mechanistic and organic structures is often most pronounced between 'production' and 'service' functions of an organisation. An example of a hybrid organisation from the private sector could be a large hotel. Here the work tasks and operations of the kitchen (the production element) suggest that a more mechanistic structure might be appropriate. Other departments, more concerned with a service element, such as front office reception, may work better with a more organic structure.[16]

Matching structures, systems and styles of management

The design of an organisation is an exercise in matching structures, systems and style of management, and the people employed, to the various activities of the organisation. If there is a mismatch, then problems can arise. *Parris* gives an example from the television programme 'M * A * S * H' (Mobile Army Surgical Hospital):

> Activities that are concerned with keeping things going but work in unstable conditions is an area where mismatching can occur as they contain elements of work that could be made systematic and simplified but as a consequence of their need to react quickly to changes to systematisation could make them less flexible. *However* since they are often dealing with complex problems a degree of systematisation is necessary. An example of this would be the 4077th MASH where to meet the demands of treating emergencies in battle they need to react quickly. But to treat complex injuries with complex technology and maintain records etc. for the future treatment and other associated administration, a certain level of routine is necessary. Similarly when the unit is overloaded and necessary medical supplies are not available, considerable 'negotiation' and 'dealing' with other units etc. is undertaken. The organisation that has evolved is a sort of Task Culture where everyone works as a team to process the work with easy working relationships etc., but it does have role elements in the efficiency with which paperwork is processed. It has power culture elements for . . . [the Company Clerk] to negotiate and bargain with other units and the unit commander has to use personal intervention to keep the unit going and protect it from the rest of the organisation in which it exists.
>
> The problems of imposing an inappropriate organisational design exists in the shape of [those who] represent the dominant role organisation in which the unit exists. Their attempts to impose military rules and procedures and impose the formal rank in the unit are seen as highly inappropriate, often farcical.[17]

LAWRENCE AND LORSCH STUDY

Lawrence and Lorsch undertook a study of six firms in the plastics industry followed by a further study of two firms in the container industry and two firms in the consumer food industry.[18] They attempted to extend the work of Burns and Stalker and examined not only the overall structure, but also the way in which specific departments were organised to meet different aspects of the firm's external environment.

Lawrence and Lorsch sought to answer the following questions:

(i) What are the differences in the environmental demands facing various organisations, and how do these demands relate to the internal functioning of effective organisations?

(ii) Do organisations operating in a stable environment make greater use of the formal hierarchy to achieve integration, and if so, why? Is it because less integration is required, or because decisions can be made more effectively at higher levels of the organisation or by fewer people?

(iii) Is the same degree of differentiation in orientation and departmental structure found in organisations in different industrial environments?

(iv) If greater integration is required among functional departments in different industries, does this influence problems of integrating different parts of the organisation and the methods of achieving integration?

Differentiation and integration	The word 'functional' was used to indicate major aspects or departments of the organisation such as research, production and marketing. The first stage of the study was an investigation of six firms in the plastics industry which were operating in relatively comparable, dynamic environments. The internal structures of the firms were analysed in terms of **'differentiation'** and **'integration'**.

Differentiation describes 'the difference in cognitive and emotional orientation among managers in different functional departments' with respect to:

- the goal orientation of managers, for example the extent to which attention was focused on particular goals of the department;
- the time orientation of managers and relation to aspects of the environment with which they are concerned, for example longer-term horizons, or short-term horizons and problems requiring immediate solutions;
- the interpersonal relations of managers to other members, for example a managerial style based on concern for the task, or on concern for people relationships; and
- the formality of structure, for example the extent of mechanistic or organic design.

Integration describes 'the quality of the state of collaboration that exists among departments that are required to achieve unity of effort by the demands of the environment'. It is the degree of co-ordination and co-operation between different departments with interdependent tasks.

Lawrence and Lorsch's view of integration was not the minimising of differences between departments and the provision of a common outlook. It was the recognition that different departments could have their own distinctive form of structure according to the nature of their task, and the use of mediating devices to co-ordinate the different outlooks of departments.

Different structures for individual departments	Given the possibility that different demands of the environment are characterised by different levels of uncertainty, then it follows that individual departments may develop different structures. The study of the firms in the plastics industry supported this hypothesis and Lawrence and Lorsch found a clear differentiation between the major departments of research, production and sales, for example:

- **Research** was more concerned with the long-run view and was confronted with pressures for new ideas and product innovation. The department operated in a dynamic, scientific environment and had the least bureaucratic structure.
- **Production** was more concerned with the here and now, short-term problems such as quality control and meeting delivery dates. The department operated in a fairly stable, technical environment and had the most bureaucratic structure.
- **Sales** was in the middle between research and production. The department was concerned with chasing production and had a moderately stable market environment.

The two most successful firms were those with the highest degree of integration and were also among the most highly differentiated.

Organisation structure and different environments

This view of differentiation and integration was confirmed in the subsequent study of firms in the container and consumer food industries. In this part of the study a comparison was made of both high and low performance firms operating in different environments. The aim was to discover what forms of organisation structure were required for different environments.

It was concluded that the extent of differentiation and integration in effective organisations will vary according to the demands of the particular environment.

- The more diverse and dynamic the environment, the more the effective organisation will be differentiated and highly integrated.
- In more stable environments, less differentiation will be required but a high degree of integration is still required. Differences in the environment will require different methods of achieving integration.

Integrating mechanisms

The mechanisms used to achieve integration depend on the amount of integration required and the difficulty in achieving it.

- In mechanistic structures, integration may be attempted through the use of policies, rules and procedures.
- In organic structures, integration may be attempted through teamwork and mutual co-operation.
- As the requirements for the amount of integration increase, additional means may be adopted, such as formal lateral relations, committees and project teams.
- When there is a high degree of differentiation, the use of assigned 'integrators' or possibly a separate unit with a number of integrators were suggested. Because they are not dominated by any particular perspective these integrators can help resolve problems of co-ordination and work programming between different departments.

It is important, however, to achieve the right balance of integration. Too great a level of integration may involve costs which are likely to exceed possible benefits. Too little a level of integration is likely to result in departments 'doing their own thing', lower quality decisions and failure to make the best use of resources.[19]

Patterns of organisation and management

Lawrence and Lorsch do not see the classical and human relations approaches as being out of date but as part of a continuum of patterns of organisation and management related to the environment in which they operate. The work of Lawrence and Lorsch is an extension of this continuum and their case for 'a contingency theory of organisations' has provided a further insight into the relationship between organisation structure and the demands of the environment.

EVALUATION OF THE CONTINGENCY APPROACH

The contingency approach draws attention to the situational factors which account for variations in the structure of organisations. It is more concerned with differences among organisations than with similarities. It rejects a number of assumptions of the classical and human relations approaches, and the idea of one best form of structure. For its part, however, the contingency approach tends to assume that organisational performance is dependent upon the degree to which the structure of the organisation matches the prevailing contingencies.

**Criticisms/
limitations**

As with other approaches to organisation and management, contingency theory has been subject to a number of criticisms or doubts about its practical value to management. Among the writers who have assessed the contribution and relevance of the contingency approach are *Child*,[20] *Dawson*[21] and *Mintzberg*.[22]

The criticisms, difficulties and limitations of the contingency approach usually revolve around seven main issues.

(i) **Causal relationship**
The nature of the causal relationship between organisation and performance is open to question. Most contingency models imply a causal relationship between structure, as an intervening variable, and performance as a dependent variable. It is probable, however, that certain factors such as the personal characteristics of management and staff, and changes in product markets and market conditions, influence performance independently of structure. These factors cannot be coped with just by changes in structure. In addition to the possible effects organisation has on performance, it is also possible that organisational performance is an influence on structural design. Managers may be stimulated to make changes to structure as a result of feedback of information on performance.

Poor performance may result in less organisational slack and opportunities to make use of expensive integrating devices. Child suggests that it is possible that the poor performance firms identified by Lawrence and Lorsch as not having solved the problem of integration were unable to do so because of lack of resources, existing conditions of poor performance, and the tendency to centralise decision-making and increase control.

(ii) **Organisational performance**
Implicit in contingency theory is the notion that the fit among components of the organisation and situation variables is related to maximising organisational performance. However, organisational performance is multi-faceted and the measurement of performance applied in many of the contingency studies has not been precise. It is impossible to derive a single criterion for the appropriateness of the fit among various features of organisation and improved performance. (Recall, for example, the discussion on the fallacy of the single objective and the eight key areas of performance and results, in Chapter 9.)

(iii) **Independent variables**
The supposed status of the independent 'contingent' variables as the 'given' and beyond the control of members of the organisation is open to question. Large organisations may be in a position to exercise control over certain aspects of their environment. For example, an organisation may be in a monopoly position or have its own protected niche in the environment. Organisations may also be able to influence their environment through, for example, advertising or political pressure groups. Some organisations, therefore, may be less dependent upon their environment and in a more secure position compared with other organisations. Any mismatch in contingency factors is likely to have less severe consequences for survival and level of performance.

(iv) **Multiple contingencies**
Different patterns of contingency factors have distinctive implications for organisational design. Organisations face multiple contingencies and there is potential for multi-way relationships among the range of organisational variables. Different contingencies may result in the need for different patterns of

structure (as with a hybrid form of organisation discussed above); for example, a department operating within a dynamic environment and demanding a more organic structure, within an organisation where other departments function within a more bureaucratic structure.

(v) **Planned change**

Contingency models of organisation fail to give sufficient emphasis to unanticipated consequences of planned change; for example, the effects of the introduction of new technology on the internal working of the organisation or on the social interactions among groups of people engaged in certain activities.

(vi) **Power factors**

Organisation structure is not necessarily determined only by impersonal contingency conditions, but also by what are referred to as 'power' factors. The pressure of external control – such as government control of public sector organisations; the political context; the power needs of various members and managerial preferences; the culture of the organisation and the power of social norms – also enters into the design of structure.

(vii) **Timing of organisational change**

Most organisations operate under conditions of constant change, and this raises the question of the frequency and timing of organisational change. Developing organisations cannot, without difficulty, change their formal structure at too frequent an interval. There must be a significant change in contingency factors before an organisation will respond. Changes in structure tend to lag behind situational change. There is, therefore, a degree of luck about whether at any moment in time there is a good fit between structure and prevailing contingency factors.

CONTRIBUTION OF CONTINGENCY THEORY

Despite the criticisms and limitations of contingency theory it has provided a further insight into our understanding of relationships among factors influencing the structure, management and operations of work organisations. An appropriate form of organisation will help prevent problems caused by unsuitable structures. The contingency approach has relevance in terms of, for example, division of work and co-ordination of activities; hierarchy and definition of responsibilities; methods of work; motivation and commitment of staff; and style and systems of management.

The basic concepts of the contingency approach help managers to develop a more thorough understanding of complex situations and to take appropriate action.[23] It also draws attention to the difficulties with mixed forms of organisation, and to the importance of different structures for different activities and situations – as illustrated in the example of 'M * A * S * H' given above.

Not every situation is unique

According to *Robey,* modern contingency theory provides an increasing amount of empirical research, it defines variables ignored in earlier work, and it directs the attention of the manager to the contingencies to be considered in the design of organisation structure. However, the contingency approach runs the risk of concluding that 'it all depends on everything', and the greatest danger is the over-emphasis on differences between organisations and the exclusion of similarities.

If the contingency approach is to be useful in guiding organisation design it should not treat every situation as being unique. 'Rather it must strike a balance between universal prescriptions and the statement that all situations are different (which is really no theory at all). Thus, modern theory uses a limited number of contingencies to help explain structural differences between organizations.'[24]

IS CULTURE A CONTINGENT FACTOR?

Several writers have sought to examine whether the principles of contingency theory hold true in different national contexts. *Hickson et al.* investigated 70 manufacturing units in Britain, the United States of America and Canada. They discovered that while there were differences in organisational arrangements, these could not be attributed to cultural effects.[25] The relationship between variables such as size, and the degree of specialisation and formality was found to be constant in all three countries, and the researchers suggested this would 'hold for work organisations in all societies'.

Contrasting perspectives

Maurice, Sorge and Warner, however, concluded that 'matched' organisations in different societies grow in contrasting ways, which may be the result of distinctive patterns in the wider society.[26] For example, their research showed that British organisations appeared to grow laterally, that is to develop large numbers of specialised managers. This may be a reflection of the comparatively specialised nature of British education and the influential role played by the professions. In contrast, the smaller number of categories of workers found in the German organisations studied may be traced back to the notion of the company apprenticeship prevalent in that country. In this way culture can itself be seen as a contingent factor.

An alternative perspective is provided by *Child and Kieser*. Their study of British and (West) German organisations revealed a consistent link between factors such as size and specialisation in both countries.[27] However, working arrangements differed in that managers held different views of their roles and authority. Child and Kieser suggest that within the framework of a contingency model, culturally derived preferences and philosophies may influence the actions of managers in the workplace.

RESTRUCTURING AND THE DEMAND FOR FLEXIBILITY

Whatever the criticisms or limitations of contingency models, the application of modern contingency theory can help contribute to more successful organisation. The movement towards tighter and leaner organisations has drawn attention to the importance of alternative forms of structure and placed increased emphasis on the demand for flexibility. For example, *Morgan* argues that we are leaving the age of organised structures and moving into an era where self-organisation will become a key competence. Looser organisations and different forms of control will entail a close examination of such issues as growth and size, teamwork, decentralisation, franchising and sub-contracting.[28]

Economic pressures and rapid developments in information technology have highlighted the need for review of structural design. Organisations have reduced the size of their workforce, especially full-time staff, and have flatter structures with fewer levels of authority. According to a recent Institute of Management survey restructuring and the use of flexible working patterns have become imperative for large employers. The core and complementary model of employment is now firmly established as an integral part of employers' human resource strategies.[29]

THE SHAMROCK ORGANISATION

One particular approach to flexible structural design and the core and complementary model of employment is *Handy*'s concept of the 'shamrock' organisation.[30] The three leaves to each stem of the shamrock are symbolic of the organisation which is seen as made up of three distinct groups of people who are managed, organised and paid differently, and with different expectations: the professional core; the contractual fringe; and the flexible labour force. (*See* Fig. 11.7.)

- **The professional core** comprises qualified professionals, technicians and managers essential to the existence and effective performance of the organisation. Collectively these people own the knowledge which distinguishes the organisation. They get most of their identity and purpose from their work and are likely to be committed to it and dependent on it. The professional core are expensive and the tendency has been for organisations to restructure in order to reduce their numbers.
- **The contractual fringe** comprises those people, or other organisations, outside of the organisation who provide specialist services and undertake all non-essential work which can be done by somebody else, and in theory are able to do it better for less. The organisational principle is that the contractual fringe are paid for results not for time, in fees and not wages. It is wise for the shamrock

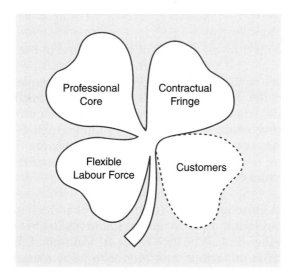

Fig. 11.7
Representation of Handy's shamrock organisation

387

organisation to put boring and repetitive work out to contract, specifying the results expected and paying the fee.

● **The flexible labour force** represents all those part-time and temporary workers who make up the fastest growing group in the pattern of employment. It provides for flexibility in human resourcing. People are brought in as occasional extra part-time labour or temporary staff as changing work situations demand. Their commitment will be to a job and work group rather than to a career or organisation. Part-time or temporary work may be a matter of choice, not just a necessity.

Three significant workforces

According to Handy, organisations now have three significant workforces, each with a different kind of comitment to the organisation and a different set of expectations, and each workforce needs to be managed in different ways. The concept of the shamrock organisation can encourage managers to question the operations of their organisations. It gives rise to important decisions concerning what activities, and which people, should belong to the core; and concerning the management and control of sub-contracting, and of the flexible workforce.

Managers could use the concept of the shamrock organisation and how this might best be adapted and utilised in a review of structure to suit the particular circumstances of the nature and operations of their own organisation.

Managing the flexible labour force

The increase in the flexible labour force is particularly noticeable with the growth of service industries. Services are created and consumed simultaneously. Unlike manufacturing, services are time-perishable and cannot be stored. The flexible labour force has increasingly been used as a cheaper and more convenient means of dealing with the peaks and troughs of demands, and as a means of adjusting the level of service to match changing customer requirements.

Although casual and part-time staff are unlikely to have the same degree of commitment or ambition as the core it is important that they are taken seriously and regarded as a valuable part of the organisation. If treated as casual labour such people respond casually. The flexible workforce should be treated with respect, given fair and equitable treatment, adequate training and status, and decent pay and conditions. If casual and part-time staff are to respond in a positive way and provide a high standard of service then they have to be managed in a considerate and effective manner.

Customers as the fourth leaf?

Handy also refers to the growing practice of saving labour in the core by introducing another, informal, and unpaid, form of sub-contracting – that of getting customers to do some of the work of the organisation. Examples include the collection rather than the delivery of goods, self-assembly furniture, automated banking facilities, and self-serve petrol. In the hospitality industry there are many examples of this 'serve yourself' philosophy. Examples include the provision of shoe-cleaning equipment or machines; hotel guests making their own tea and coffee in their rooms; restaurant self-service breakfast and buffet meals; the provision of vending machines for snacks and beverages.

Challenges of the shamrock

Handy suggests that although on the face of it the shamrock is logical these are not easy organisations to run. Each leaf of the shamrock has to be managed differently yet as part of the whole. The core is the critical hub of the organisational network and this raises important questions as to what activities belong in the

core; and which people belong in the core, and for how long. Fixed-term contracts will be an increasing feature. Fewer people mean the need for better people, and pressure for alertness and quality will place greater demands on the core people.

ORGANISATIONAL PRACTICES

To conclude our discussion on the contingency approach to organisation it is convenient, here, to consider two sets of observations on the nature of human behaviour and what may actually happen, in practice, in organisations. Although these observations on organisational practice are presented in a satirical manner, they nevertheless make a serious and significant point about the structure, management and functioning of organisations, and the study of hierarchies.

PARKINSON'S LAW

A major feature of Parkinson's Law is that of the 'Rising Pyramid', that is: **'Work expands so as to fill the time available for its completion.'**[31] General recognition of this is illustrated in the proverb, 'It is the busiest person who has time to spare.' There is little, if any, relationship between the quantity of work to be done and the size of the staff doing it. Underlying this general tendency are two almost axiomatic statements:

(i) an official wants to multiply subordinates, not rivals; and
(ii) officials make work for each other.

Parkinson goes on to give the following example. If a civil servant, A, believes he is overworked there are three possible remedies: (i) resignation; (ii) ask to halve the work by having it shared with a colleague, B; or (iii) seek the assistance of two subordinates, C and D. The first two options are unlikely. Resignation would involve loss of pension rights, and sharing work with a colleague on the same level would only bring in a rival for promotion. So A would prefer the appointment of two junior members of staff, C and D. This would increase A's status. There must be at least two subordinates, so that by dividing work between C and D, A will be the only person to understand the work of them both. Also, each subordinate is kept in order by fear of the other's promotion.

When, in turn, C complains of overwork, A, with the agreement of C, will advise the appointment of two assistants, E and F. But as D's position is much the same and to avoid internal friction, two assistants, G and H, will also be recommended to help D. There are now seven people, A, C, D, E, F, G, H, doing what one person did before, and the promotion of A is almost certain.

People making work for each other

With the seven people now employed, the second stage comes into operation. The seven people make so much work for each other that they are all fully occupied and A is actually working harder than ever. For example, an incoming document comes before each of them in turn. E decides it is F's concern; F places a draft reply for C, who makes drastic amendments before consulting with D, who asks G to action it.

But then G goes on leave and hands the file to H, who drafts a minute signed by D and returned to C, who revises the first draft and puts the new version before A.

What does A do? A could find many excuses for signing C's draft unread. But being a conscientious person, and although beset with problems created by subordinates both for A and for themselves, A reads through the draft carefully, deletes the fussy paragraphs added by C and H, and restores it to the format presented in the first instance by F.

To illustrate his point about the size of an organisation and the relative size of the administrative staff component, Parkinson gives the case of admiralty statistics relating to the Royal Navy between 1914 and 1928. During these years the capital ships in commission decreased by 68 per cent, and officers and other ranks in the Royal Navy by 31 per cent. But over the same period, the number of dockyard workers increased by 9 per cent, dockyard officials and clerks by 40 per cent and admiralty officials by 78 per cent.

Other features of organisational practice

Among other features of organisational practice that Parkinson discusses are: principles of personnel selection; the nature of committees; personality screen; high finance – and the 'Law of Triviality' which means in a committee that the time spent on any agenda item will be in inverse proportion to the sum involved; layout of the organisation's administration block; and 'injelitis' – the disease of induced inferiority.

Relevance of observations

Despite the light vein of Parkinson's writing, the relevance of his observations can be gauged from comments in the Introduction by H.R.H. The Duke of Edinburgh. 'The most important point about this book for serious students of management and administration is that it illustrates the gulf that exists between the rational/intellectual approach to human organization and the frequent irrational facts of human nature' and

> The law should be compulsory reading at all business schools and for all management consultants. Management structures solve nothing if they do not take the facts of human nature into proper consideration, and one of the most important facts is that no one really likes having to make decisions. Consequently structures may generate a lot of activity but little or no useful work.[32]

THE PETER PRINCIPLE

This is concerned with the study of occupational incompetence and the study of hierarchies. The analysis of hundreds of cases of occupational incompetence led to the formulation of the 'Peter Principle', which is: **'In a hierarchy every employee tends to rise to their level of incompetence.'**[33]

Employees competent in their position are promoted and competence in each new position qualifies for promotion to the next higher position until a position of incompetence is reached. The principle is based on perceived incompetence at all levels of every hierarchy – political, legal, educational and industrial – and ways in which employees move upwards through a hierarchy, and what happens to them after promotion.

Among the many examples quoted by Peter are those from the teaching occupation.

A is a competent and conforming college student who becomes a teacher following the textbook, curriculum guide and timetable schedule, and who works well except when there is no rule or precedent available. A never breaks a rule or disobeys an order but will not gain promotion because, although competent as a student, A has reached a level of incompetence as a classroom teacher.

B, a competent student and inspiring teacher, although not good with paperwork, is promoted to head of the science department because of success as a teacher. The head of science is responsible for ordering all science supplies and keeping extensive records and B's incompetence becomes evident.

C, a competent student, teacher and head of department is promoted to assistant principal, and being intellectually competent is further promoted to principal. C is now required to work directly with higher officials. But by working so hard at running the school, C misses important meetings with superiors and has no energy to become involved with community organisations. C thus becomes regarded as an incompetent principal.

Means of promotion

Peter suggests two main means by which a person can affect promotion rate: 'Pull' and 'Push'.

Pull is an employee's relationship – by blood, marriage or acquaintance – with a person above the employee in the hierarchy.

Push is sometimes manifested by an abnormal interest in study, vocational training and self-improvement.

In small hierarchies, push may have a marginal effect in accelerating promotion; in larger hierarchies the effect is minimal. Pull is, therefore, likely to be more effective than Push. 'Never stand when you can sit; never walk when you can ride; never Push when you can Pull.'[34]

SYNOPSIS

■ Earlier approaches to organisation and management believed in one best form of structure and tended to concentrate on limited aspects of organisation. The contingency approach, however, emphasises the need for flexibility and takes the view that there is no one best structure or system of management. There are a large number of variables, or situational factors, which influence organisational design and performance.

■ The most appropriate structure is dependent upon the contingencies of the situation for each individual organisation. The contingency approach can be seen as a form of 'if–then' matrix relationship. **If** certain situational factors exist, **then** certain variables in organisation structure and systems of management are most appropriate.

■ Situational factors may be identified in a number of ways and a number of studies have been carried out into the extent to which these contingency factors influence organisational design and effectiveness. Among the most significant contingency models are those by Porter and Child (size of organisations); Woodward and Perrow (technology); and Burns and Stalker, and Lawrence and Lorsch (environment).

■ As with other approaches to organisation and management, the contingency approach has been subject to a number of criticisms or doubts about its practical value to management. However, despite the criticisms and limitations of contingency theory it has provided a further insight into our understanding of relationships among factors influencing the structure, management and operations of organisations. The contingency approach also draws attention to the importance of different structures for different activities of the organisation.

■ The application of modern contingency theory can contribute to more successful organisation. The movement towards tighter and leaner organisations has drawn attention to the importance of alternative forms of structure and places increased emphasis on the demand for flexibility. Economic pressures and rapid developments in information technology have highlighted the need for review of structural design. One particular approach to flexible structural design, and the core and complementary model of employment, is the concept of the 'shamrock' organisation.

■ It is also necessary to consider the nature of human behaviour and what may actually happen, in practice, in organisations. One example of organisational practice is Parkinson's Law: 'Work expands so as to fill the time available for its completion.' Another example is the Peter Principle: 'In a hierarchy every employee tends to rise to their level of incompetence.' These observations make a serious point about the structure, management and functioning of organisations.

 ## Review and discussion questions

1 Explain what is meant by the contingency approach to organisation. How does the contingency approach differ from other approaches to organisation and management?

2 Discuss ways in which different types of production technology have implications for the design of organisation structure. Give examples relating to the 'production' system of your own organisation compared with that of some other organisation.

3 Contrast 'mechanistic' and 'organic' systems of management practice and structure. What is the significance of this distinction? Suggest ways in which your own organisation tends towards one type of system or the other.

4 What do you understand by a 'hybrid' or mixed form of organisation structure? What particular problems might arise with this form of structure? Where possible support your answer with practical examples.

5 Explain what is meant by 'differentiation' and 'integration' of the internal structure of an organisation. What are the implications of differentiation and integration, and what mechanisms might be adopted to achieve integration?

6 Summarise the main criticisms, difficulties and limitations which could be claimed of contingency theory.

7 Assess the positive value and contribution of contingency theory to the structure, management and operation of work organisations. Give your own examples of situational factors which are likely to account for variations in the structure and management of different organisations.

8 Explain your understanding of (i) Parkinson's Law and (ii) the Peter Principle as observations on the nature of human behaviour. What are the implications of these observations for organisational practice?

 ## Assignment

In self-selecting groups of three or four, visit a work organisation of your choice.

(i) Investigate and make notes about:
 (a) the nature and main purpose of the organisation;
 (b) its size;
 (c) the nature of technology/'production' systems;
 (d) characteristics of the staff employed:
 (e) main environmental influences; and
 (f) any other relevant factors.

(ii) Obtain, or prepare, a chart depicting the structural design of the organisation.

(iii) Using your knowledge of the **contingency** approach, comment on the apparent effectiveness of the structure of the organisation and/or particular departments of the organisation. Identify what you believe to be good and bad examples of structure.

(iv) Explain, with supporting reasons, what changes to structure you would recommend in order to help improve organisational performance.

(v) Where appropriate, prepare a revised organisation chart.

Notes and references

1. Hunt, J. W. *Managing People at Work: A Manager's Guide to Behaviour in Organisations*, Third edition, McGraw-Hill (1992) p. 170.
2. See, for example: Luthans, F. *Organizational Behaviour*, Fourth edition, McGraw-Hill (1985).
3. Miller, D. and Droge, C. 'Psychological and Traditional Determinants of Structure', *Administrative Science Quarterly*, 31 December 1986, pp. 539–60.
4. Pugh, D. S., Hickson, D. J., Hinings, C. R. and Turner, C. 'The Context of Organization Structure', *Administrative Science Quarterly*, 14 March 1969, pp. 91–113.
5. Porter, L. W., Lawler, E. E. and Hackman, J. R. *Behaviour in Organizations*, McGraw-Hill (1975) p. 250.
6. Child, J. *Organization: A Guide to Problems and Practice*, Second edition, Paul Chapman (1988) p. 221.

7. Woodward, J. *Industrial Organization: Theory and Practice*, Second edition, Oxford University Press (1980).
8. Dawson, S. and Wedderburn, D., 'Introduction' to Woodward, J. *Industrial Organization: Theory and Practice*, Second edition, Oxford University Press (1980) p. xiii.
9. Woodward, J. *Industrial Organization: Theory and Practice*, Second edition, Oxford University Press (1980) pp. 69, 71.
10. Zwerman, W. L. *New Perspectives on Organization Theory*, Greenwood (1970).
11. Collins, P. D. and Hull, F. 'Technology and Span of Control: Woodward Revisited', *Journal of Management Studies*, 23(2), March 1986, pp. 143–64.
12. Perrow, C. *Organizational Analysis: A Sociological View*, Tavistock Publications (1970).
13. Burns, T. and Stalker, G. M. *The Management of Innovation*, Tavistock Publications (1966).
14. Litterer, J. A. *The Analysis of Organizations*, Second edition, Wiley (1973).
15. Wilkins, R. 'The Management Challenge of Hybrid Organisations', *Administrator*, vol. 7, no. 8, September 1987, p. 3.
16. Mullins, L. J. *Hospitality Management: A Human Resources Approach*, Second edition, Pitman (1995).
17. Parris, J. 'Designing your Organisation', *Management Services*, vol. 23, no. 10, October 1979, p. 14.
18. Lawrence, P. R. and Lorsch, J. W. *Organization and Environment*, Irwin (1969).
19. Boschken, H. L. 'Strategy and Structure: Reconceiving the Relationship', *Journal of Management*, 16(1), March 1990, pp. 135–50.
20. Child, J. *Organization: A Guide to Problems and Practice*, Second edition, Paul Chapman (1988).
21. Dawson, S. 'Organisational Analysis and the Study of Policy Formulation and Implementation', *Public Administration Bulletin*, 31, December 1979, pp. 52–68.
22. Mintzberg, H. *The Structuring of Organizations*, Prentice-Hall (1979).
23. See, for example: Fincham, R. and Rhodes, P. S. *The Individual, Work and Organization*, Second edition, Weidenfeld and Nicolson (1992).
24. Robey, D. *Designing Organizations*, Irwin (1982) p. 59.
25. Hickson, D., Hinings, C., McMillan, C. and Schwitter, J. 'The Culture Free Context of Organisation Structure: A Tri National Comparison', *Sociology*, 8, 1974, pp. 59–80.
26. Maurice, M., Sorge, A. and Warner, M. 'Societal Differences in Organising Manufacturing Units: A Comparison of France, West Germany and Britain', *Organisation Studies*, vol. 1, no. 1, 1980, pp. 59–86.
27. Child, J. and Kieser, A. 'Organisation and Managerial Roles in Britain and West German Companies: An Examination of the Culture-Free Thesis', in Lammers, C. and Hickson, D. (eds) *Organisations Alike and Unlike*, Routledge and Kegan Paul (1979).
28. Morgan, G. *Imaginization: The Art of Creative Management*, Sage Publications (1993).
29. *Survey of Long Term Employment Strategies*, The Institute of Management and Manpower PLC, September 1994.
30. Handy, C. B. *The Age of Unreason*, Business Books (1989).
31. Parkinson, C. N. *Parkinson's Law*, Penguin (1986) p. 14.
32. H.R.H. The Duke of Edinburgh, 'Introduction' to Parkinson, C. N. *Parkinson's Law*, Penguin (1986) pp. 9, 10.
33. Peter, L. J. and Hull, R. *The Peter Principle*, Pan Books (1970) p. 22.
34. *Ibid.* p. 56.

Part 5

MANAGEMENT AS AN INTEGRATING ACTIVITY

12 THE NATURE OF MANAGEMENT

Organisations can only achieve their goals and objectives by the co-ordinated efforts of their members and it is the task of management to get work done through other people. It is by the process of management and execution of work that the activities of the organisation are carried out. Management is an integral part of the people–organisation relationship. It is essentially an integrating activity which permeates every facet of the operations of an organisation. Management is fundamental to the effective operation of work organisations.

 Learning objectives

To:

- Explain the meaning of management;

- Examine main activities, or functions, of management;

- Analyse the essential nature of managerial work;

- Contrast management in service and production industries and in private and public sector organisations;

- Detail the attributes and qualities of a successful manager;

- Review the work of a manager and outline empirical studies on the nature of managerial behaviour;

- Recognise the importance of management to the effective performance of work organisations.

Worth thinking about

According to Peter Drucker, management is a practice rather than a science or a profession so there are no precise solutions, and the ultimate test of management is achievement and business performance. To what extent, then, does this suggest that in the effective management of business organisations the ends justify the means?

THE MEANING OF MANAGEMENT

Management is a generic term and subject to many interpretations. A number of different ideas are attributed to the meaning of management and to the work of a manager. In certain respects everyone could be regarded as a manager to some extent. Everyone has some choice whether or not to do something, and some control, however slight, over the planning and organisation of their work. But we are concerned with management as involving people looking beyond themselves and exercising formal authority over the activities and performance of other people.

For our purposes we can, therefore, regard management as:

- taking place within a structured organisational setting and with prescribed roles;
- directed towards the attainment of aims and objectives;
- achieved through the efforts of other people; and
- using systems and procedures.

Drucker sees management as denoting a function as well as the people who discharge it, a social position and authority, and also a discipline and field of study. 'Management is tasks. Management is a discipline. But management is also people. Every achievement of management is the achievement of a manager. Every failure is a failure of a manager.'[1]

Other writers, however, take the view that management is not a separate discipline. The problem is identifying a single discipline which encompasses the work of a manager, or agreeing the disciplines that a manager needs in order effectively to carry out this work.

Manager as a job title

Even within a work organisation you cannot identify, necessarily, a manager by what a person is called or by his or her job title. In some organisations there is a liberal use of the title 'manager' in an apparent attempt to enhance the status and morale of staff. As a result there are a number of people whose job title includes the term manager but who, in reality, are not performing the full activities of a manager.

On the other hand, there are many people whose job title does not include the term manager (for example group accountant, head chef, chief inspector, captain, headteacher, production controller, district nursing officer, company secretary), but who, in terms of the activities they undertake and the authority and responsibility they exercise, may be very much a manager.

Managers born or made? Management an art or science?

There is frequent debate about whether managers are born or made; or whether management is an art or a science. Briefly, the important point is that neither of these is a mutually exclusive alternative. The answer to either question is surely a combination of both. Even if there are certain innate qualities which make for a potentially good manager, these natural talents must be encouraged and developed through proper guidance, education and training, and planned experience.

Clearly, management must always be something of an art, especially in so far as it involves personal judgement and dealing with people. However, it still requires knowledge of the fundamentals of management, and competence in the application of specific skills and techniques – as illustrated, for example, with developments in information technology.

MANAGEMENT AND ADMINISTRATION

There is often confusion over different interpretations of the two terms 'management' and 'administration'. One of the main reasons for this confusion would seem to result from the translation of *Fayol*'s book *Administration industrielle et générale* from the French into English. In the original (1929) English edition there was a direct translation of 'administration', but in the wider republication of the book in 1949 the term 'management' replaced 'administration' in the title. In the introduction to the revised edition *Urwick* indicates regret at this change.[2] He refers to Fayol's use of the word administration as indicating a specific function which enters all tasks involving supervision of the work of others. It is not concerned with the status of those who exercise this function.

Urwick also expresses concern at the possible division between management being seen to apply only to business organisations, and (public) administration as applying to the same functions in public service organisations.

Dictionary definitions tend to see the two words as synonymous. Management is sometimes referred to as 'administration of business concerns' and administration as 'management of public affairs'. There is clearly an overlap between the two terms and they tend to be used, therefore, in accordance with the convenience of individual writers. This confirms the feeling that although most people perceive a difference between the two terms this difference is not easy to describe.

The use of the term administration has traditionally been associated with public sector organisations, but the term management is now used increasingly. This can be seen, for example, in local government from 1972 following publication of the Bains Report of the study group appointed to 'examine management principles and structures in local government at both elected member and officer levels'. The report includes frequent reference to corporate management, the management process, and the management team, and gave rise to the term 'Town Hall Limited'.[3] There is also an increasing number of books which examine management in the public sector.[4] (A comparison of management in private enterprise and public sector organisations is to be found later in this chapter.)

Administration part of management

There appears, therefore, to be growing acceptance of the term management as the general descriptive label and administration as relating to the more specific function of the operation of procedures used by management. Administration can be

seen as taking place in accordance with some sort of rules or procedures, whereas management implies a greater degree of discretion.

For our purposes administration is interpreted as part of the management process, and concerned with the design and implementation of systems and procedures to help meet stated objectives.

THE PROCESS OF MANAGEMENT

The nature of management is variable. Management relates to all activities of the organisation and is undertaken at all levels of the organisation. Management is not a separate, discrete function. It cannot be departmentalised or centralised. An organisation cannot have a department of management in the same way as it can have a department for other functions, such as production, marketing, accounting, or personnel.

Management is seen best, therefore, as a process common to all other functions carried out within the organisation. Management is essentially an integrating activity.

The overall responsibility of management can be seen as the attainment of the given objectives of the organisation. Objectives are the desired end-results the organisation is striving to achieve. Within the framework of objectives, policy provides the guidelines for the operations and activities of the organisation.

Policy determines the manner in which the affairs of the organisation are to be conducted. The establishment of objectives and the formulation of policy rest with the board of directors (or their equivalent) and it is part of their responsibility for determining the direction of the organisation as a whole and for its survival, development and profitability. Clarification of objectives and policy is a prerequisite if the process of management is to be effective. But what does the process of management actually involve, and what activities does it encompass?

Management is a complex and discursive subject. Despite the widespread use of the term and the large amount written about the subject, it is not easy to find agreement on a simple yet comprehensive definition of management or of a manager. Moreover, **'management' is not homogeneous. It takes place in different ways and at different levels of the organisation.** One approach, especially favoured by classical writers, is to analyse the nature of management and to search for common activities (or functions, or elements) applicable to managers in all organisations.

Common activities of management

One of the first, and most widely quoted, analyses is that given by *Henri Fayol*, who analysed the activities of industrial undertakings into six groups: technical (production, manufacture and adaptation); commercial (buying, selling, exchange and market information); financial (obtaining capital and making optimum use of available funds); security (safeguarding property and persons); accounting (information on the economic position, stocktaking, balance sheet, costs, statistics); and managerial. (The term 'management' is a translation of the French term 'administration'.)[5]

The managerial activity is divided into five elements of management, which are defined as: 'to forecast and plan, to organise, to command, to co-ordinate and to control'. Fayol describes these elements as:

- **Planning** (translated from the French *prevoyance* = to foresee, and taken to include forecasting) – examining the future, deciding what needs to be achieved and developing a plan of action.
- **Organising** – providing the material and human resources and building the structure to carry out the activities of the organisation.
- **Command** – maintaining activity among personnel, getting the optimum return from all employees in the interests of the whole organisation.
- **Co-ordination** – unifying and harmonising all activities and effort of the organisation to facilitate its working and success.
- **Control** – verifying that everything occurs in accordance with plans, instructions, established principles and expressed command.

Principles of management

Fayol also suggests that a set of well-established principles would help concentrate general discussion on management theory. But he emphasises that these principles must be flexible and adaptable to changing circumstances. Fayol recognised that there was no limit to the principles of management but in his writing advocated 14.

(i) **Division of work** – the object is to produce more and better work from the same effort, and the advantages of specialisation. However, there are limits to division of work which experience and a sense of proportion tell us should not be exceeded.

(ii) **Authority and responsibility** – responsibility is the corollary of authority. Wherever authority is exercised, responsibility arises. The application of sanctions is essential to good management, and is needed to encourage useful actions and to discourage their opposite. The best safeguard against abuse of authority is the personal integrity of the manager.

(iii) **Discipline** is essential for the efficient operation of the organisation. Discipline is in essence the outward mark of respect for agreements between the organisation and its members. The manager must decide on the most appropriate form of sanction in cases of offences against discipline.

(iv) **Unity of command** – in any action an employee should receive orders from one superior only; if not, authority is undermined and discipline, order and stability threatened. Dual command is a perpetual source of conflicts.

(v) **Unity of direction** – in order to provide for unity of action, co-ordination and focusing of effort, there should be one head and one plan for any group of activities with the same objective.

(vi) **Subordination of individual interest to general interest** – the interest of the organisation should dominate individual or group interests.

(vii) **Remuneration of personnel** – remuneration should as far as possible satisfy both employee and employer. Methods of payment can influence organisational performance and the method should be fair and should encourage keenness by rewarding well-directed effort, but not lead to overpayment.

(viii) **Centralisation** is always present to some extent in any organisation. The degree of centralisation is a question of proportion and will vary in particular organisations.

(ix) **Scalar chain** – the chain of superiors from the ultimate authority to the lowest ranks. Respect for line authority must be reconciled with activities which require urgent action, and with the need to provide for some measure of initiative at all levels of authority.

(x) **Order** – includes material order and social order. The object of material order is avoidance of loss. There should be an appointed place for each thing, and each thing in its appointed place. Social order involves an appointed place for each employee, and each employee in his or her appointed place. Social order requires good organisation and good selection.

(xi) **Equity** – the desire for equity and for equality of treatment are aspirations to be taken into account in dealing with employees throughout all levels of the scalar chain.

(xii) **Stability of tenure of personnel** – generally, prosperous organisations have a stable managerial personnel. But changes of personnel are inevitable and stability of tenure is a question of proportion.

(xiii) **Initiative** – represents a source of strength for the organisation and should be encouraged and developed. Tact and integrity are required to promote initiative and to retain respect for authority and discipline.

(xiv) **Esprit de corps** should be fostered, as harmony and unity among members of the organisation is a great strength in the organisation. The principle of unity of command should be observed. It is necessary to avoid the dangers of divide and rule of one's own team, and the abuse of written communication. Wherever possible verbal contacts should be used.

A number of these principles relate directly to, or are influenced by, the organisation structure in which the process of management takes place. Fayol's set of principles can be compared therefore with those given by Urwick and discussed in Chapter 10.

MANAGEMENT AS A SOCIAL PROCESS

Another well-known analysis is given by *Brech* who defines management as:

A social process entailing responsibility for the effective and economical planning and regulation of the operations of an enterprise, in fulfilment of given purposes or tasks, such responsibility involving:
(a) judgment and decision in determining plans and in using data to control performance and progress against plans;
(b) the guidance, integration, motivation and supervision of the personnel composing the enterprise and carrying out its operations.[6]

Brech identifies four main elements of management:

- **Planning** – determining the broad lines for carrying out operations, preparing methods by which they are carried out and setting standards of performance.
- **Control** – checking actual performance against standards to ensure satisfactory progress and performance, and recording as a guide to possible future operations.
- **Co-ordination** – balancing and maintaining the team by ensuring a suitable division of work and seeing that tasks are performed in harmony.
- **Motivation** – or inspiring morale. Getting members of the team to work effectively, to give loyalty to the group and to the task, to carry out their tasks properly, and to play an effective part in the activities of the organisation. With this general inspiration is a process of supervision or leadership to ensure the teams are carrying out their activities properly.

OTHER ANALYSES

Many other writers have provided an analysis of the elements of management. At first sight these analyses may appear to differ in certain aspects, but on closer study they show a basic similarity. Debate on the inclusion or exclusion of a particular element of management tends to revolve round the use and interpretation of different terms, and the emphasis which is placed upon them.

For example, what *Fayol* calls **command** – maintaining activity among personnel and getting optimum return from employees – might be taken to mean what *Brech* refers to as **motivation** – getting members of the team to work effectively and to carry out properly the activities allocated to them. Brech does not use the term **organising** but this appears to be covered under the headings of **planning** and **co-ordination**.

Authority over subordinate staff

Based on his experience as chief executive of the Glacier Metal Company, *Wilfred (Lord) Brown* defines the concept of a 'manager' in terms of someone who has more work than he or she can perform personally, who arranges for some of this work to be carried out by others, and who is accountable to a higher authority for the manner in which all of this work is carried out. Brown gives a boundary definition of a managerial role as:

> a role from which some work has to be delegated to subordinate roles. The occupant of the managerial role is accountable for his subordinates' work and must at least have authority to veto the appointment of persons to the subordinate roles, to insist that they be removed from these roles if they are unsatisfactory, and to determine which portions of his own work shall be carried out by each subordinate.[7]

This is a very demanding definition. Strict adherence to these requirements, and in particular the authority to veto the appointment of subordinates and to insist that they be removed if unsatisfactory, would rule out the majority of people who actually carry the title of manager in modern organisations. **The definition does, however, remind us of the changing nature of management and the extent of the manager's individual authority over subordinate staff.**

THE TASKS AND CONTRIBUTION OF A MANAGER

Another approach to describing management is given by *Drucker* who identifies three tasks, equally important, but essentially different, that have to be performed:

- fulfilling the specific purpose and mission of the institution, whether business enterprise, hospital, or university;
- making work productive and the worker achieving;
- managing social impacts and social responsibilities.[8]

Drucker then goes on to identify five basic operations in the work of the manager:

- **Sets objectives** – determines objectives and the goals for each area of objectives, and describes what needs to be done to achieve these objectives.

- **Organises** – analyses the activities, decisions and relations required, classifies and divides work, creates organisation structure, and selects staff.
- **Motivates and communicates** – creates a team out of people responsible for various jobs.
- **Measures** – establishes targets and measurements of performance which focus on both the individual and the organisation as a whole.
- **Develops people** – directs, encourages and trains. How well subordinates develop themselves depends on the way a manager manages.

These categories require a combination of analytical ability, synthesising ability, integrity, human perception and insight, and social skill.

Responsibility for the work of other people

Drucker argues that the traditional definition of management based on the responsibility for the work of other people is unsatisfactory and too narrow, and emphasises a secondary rather than a primary characteristic. There are people, often in responsible positions, who are clearly 'management' but who do not have responsibility for the work of other people.

A person's function and contribution may be unaffected by the number of subordinate staff. A 'manager' is someone who performs the tasks of management whether or not he or she has power over others.

> Who is a manager can be defined only by that person's function and by the contribution he or she is expected to make. And the function that distinguishes the manager above all others is the function no one but the manager can perform. The one contribution a manager is uniquely expected to make is to give others vision and ability to perform. It is vision and moral responsibility that, in the last analysis, define the manager.[9]

PARTICULAR APPROACHES TO MANAGEMENT

There are numerous other definitions of management. Many of these definitions reflect the influence of a particular approach to management thinking. *Simon*, for example, sees management as synonymous with decision-making.[10] Other examples include such definitions as 'management is delegation', or 'the task of management is to create teams out of individuals'.

There are other definitions such as 'the responsibility of management is to achieve results', or 'management is the ordering and co-ordination of functions to achieve a given purpose', which tell us little about the actual process of management. These definitions may all be correct as far as they go, but on their own are too narrow or too vague to provide an adequate description of management.

ESSENTIAL NATURE OF MANAGERIAL WORK

The essential nature of managerial work is not easy to describe, therefore, as aspects which are common in many applications escape us in others.[11]

However, if we look at how people at work actually spend their time we should

be able to distinguish between those whose main occupation is the carrying out of discrete tasks and the actual doing of work themselves; and those who spend proportionally more of their time in determining the nature of work to be undertaken by other people, the planning and organising of their work, issuing them with instructions and giving advice, and checking on their performance.

'Managing' and 'doing'

By distinguishing 'managing' from 'doing' in this way we can see management as clarifying objectives and the planning of work, organising the distribution of activities and tasks to other people, direction of subordinate staff and controlling the performance of other people's work. This provides us with a convenient description and summary of managerial work as: **clarification** of objectives, **planning**, **organising**, **directing** and **controlling**. (*See* Fig. 12.1.)

The degree of emphasis given to these different activities may vary widely, however, from one manager to another. Some managers are likely to spend more time on certain activities than other managers. The application of these activities reflects a wide range of management practice and managerial style.

Clarification of objectives

The setting of objectives and formulation of policy takes place at different levels in the organisation, but as part of the same process. The board of directors, or similar body, establishes objectives and formulates policy (direction) for the organisation as a whole. Management is responsible for the implementation of policy decisions

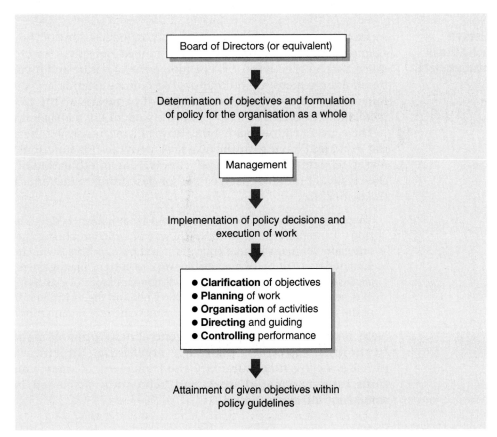

Fig. 12.1
Summary of essential nature of managerial work

and the execution of work designed to meet these objectives. However, as mentioned in the discussion on levels of organisation in Chapter 10, it is not easy to distinguish between policy and its execution.

In the same way that the board of directors is concerned with planning, organisation and control as part of the responsibility for the operations of the organisation as a whole, so the execution of policy will involve the manager in decision-making and the clarification of objectives for subordinate staff. This will entail answers to such questions as: Exactly what is required? What activities are involved? What are the available resources? What are the time scales? What standards are required and how is performance to be measured? What restrictions or limitations apply? Clarification of objectives provides the basis for the planning and organisation of work, and the activities of staff.

Direction and motivation

Having already identified direction (of the organisation as a whole) as a responsibility of the board of directors it is tempting to use the term 'motivating' instead of 'directing' in our definition of the activities of management. This would avoid possible confusion over terminology: and motivation is perhaps a less emotive word. But is motivating an adequate description? It is certainly part of the manager's job to motivate staff but it involves more than this. Subordinate staff also need development and guidance. They need to be motivated **to perform well in the right areas**. The manager has a responsibility to see that subordinate staff are effective as well as efficient. Their efforts must be **directed** towards the achievement of given objectives in accordance with stated policy.

General activities of management

As we have seen, 'co-ordination' is often included as one of the activities of management. But the harmonising of effort to meet objectives (co-ordination) is not so much a separate activity; it is of a more general nature and involves all the activities of management. Co-ordination, like communication and decision-making, is inherent in the process of management. It permeates all the activities of management and is descriptive more of how the work of the manager is carried out.

There are, of course, many other ways of conceptualising the nature of managerial work, and relying on the 'classical' activities (or functions) of management might, to some, appear outdated. However, in an evaluation of the usefulness of the classical functions perspective for describing managerial work, *Carroll and Gillen* conclude:

> There seems to be some confusion about what managers do... The classical functions still represent the most useful way of conceptualizing the manager's job, especially for management education, and perhaps this is why it is still the most favoured description of managerial work in current management textbooks. The classical functions provide clear and discrete methods of classifying the thousands of different activities that managers carry out and the techniques they use in terms of the functions they perform for the achievement of organisational goals.[12]

Note, however, that although the general description of management as clarification of objectives, planning, organising, directing and controlling provides a convenient summary and framework of study, empirical investigations into managerial work and behaviour, discussed below, present a somewhat different picture.

THE EFFORTS OF OTHER PEOPLE

Despite the view expressed by *Drucker* on the tasks and contribution of a manager, one of the most popular ways of defining management is that it involves getting work done second-hand, that is **through the efforts of other people. Managers are judged not just on their own performance but on the results achieved by subordinate staff.** There are, then, many ways of looking at the meaning of management. The basic criteria must be a compromise between the ideas of some of the more lucid writers on the subject.

Stewart attempts to integrate the various definitions of management and summarises the manager's job, broadly defined as:

> deciding what should be done and then getting other people to do it. A longer definition would be concerned with how these tasks are to be accomplished. The first task comprises setting objectives, planning (including decision-making), and setting up formal organization. The second consists of motivation, communication, control (including measurement), and the development of people.[13]

The definition of management as 'getting work done through the efforts of other people' may not perhaps meet all criteria, or satisfy everyone's perception of the nature of managerial work. It does, however, have the advantage of simplicity and focuses on what in reality is at the heart of effective management.

> Managing means leading, making things happen through people: for me that is relevant to all levels of management, not just the top management.
>
> *Sir Peter Parker*[14]

The role of supervisors

An important and integral part of the process of management is the role of supervisors. Too often however supervisors may be regarded primarily as 'doers' rather than managers. But they are usually very much in the front line of management and have a prime responsibility for seeing that work gets done by others. Supervisors are required to act in a fair and sensitive manner and to provide a pivotal role as both the link and buffer between the expectations of senior management and operatives.[15]

Supervisors can be seen as having a particular concern with the directing and guiding, and controlling performance activities of management. They need to have the required training and skills to deal promptly and first-hand with problems of production or service, handle difficulties or complaints diplomatically, and perhaps discipline staff. The general movement towards flatter organisation structures and fewer levels of management has highlighted the importance of the role of supervisors.

The importance of management

Whatever the essential nature of managerial work is said to be, the importance and responsibility of management are widely, and rightly, recognised.

> The responsibility of management in our society is decisive not only for the enterprise itself but for management's public standing, its success and status, for the very future of our economic and social system and the survival of the enterprise as an autonomous institution.[16]

MANAGEMENT IN SERVICE INDUSTRIES

Compared with 'production' industries, services tend to display a number of characteristic features, including the following.

- The consumer is a participant in the service process. This requires particular attention to the surroundings and characteristics of the service operations.
- Services cannot be stored, they are time perishable and if they are not used they are likely to be wasted. For example, the income lost from a hotel room unsold on one day is lost forever.
- Unlike physical products, services are less tangible and more difficult to explain or communicate. Benefits derived from services tend to be associated with feelings and emotions.
- In service operations work activities are people-oriented and the characteristics of the workforce are particularly important in determining organisational effectiveness.
- Measurement of output is difficult and there is unlikely to be a single, important criterion by which to measure effective performance.[17]

The same general problems of management

To what extent then are service industries any different from other industries? According to *Levitt*, for example, it is only in a matter of degree.

> Purveyors of service, for their part, think that they and their problems are fundamentally different from other businesses and their problems. They feel that service is people-intensive, while the rest of the economy is capital-intensive. But these distinctions are largely spurious. There are no such things as service industries. There are only industries whose service components are greater or less than those of other industries. Everybody is in service.[18]

In addressing the question 'what is the nature of management in service industries?' *Jones* suggests that implicit in the question is the fundamental assumption that managers of services face different problems and act differently from other managers. However, Jones acknowledges that this assumption is contentious. And even where there is agreement that services are in some way different, there is no agreement on the cause or importance of this difference.[19]

In order to operate effectively service industries need management in the same way as any other industry. Both require attention to the same general problems of management. (*See* the discussion on management in public and private sector organisations in the following section.) Increasing attention is being given to the applications of general management theory within the service industry and to the links between management in service and other industries.[20]

The systems approach and contingency theory, discussed in earlier chapters, also serve to illustrate both differences and common features in the nature of management in work organisations.

MANAGEMENT IN PRIVATE ENTERPRISE AND PUBLIC SECTOR ORGANISATIONS

There are differences between management in the private and public sectors. These differences arise from particular features of public sector organisations, such as:

- aims concerned with providing a service for, and for the well-being of, the community rather than just of a commercial nature;
- the scale, variety and complexity of their operations;
- the tendency for them to be subject more to press reports on their activities;
- the political environment in which they operate, and in the case of local government, for example, the relationship between elected members and permanent officers;
- the generally high level of trade union involvement;
- the difficulties in measuring standards of performance of services provided compared with profitability;
- the demand for uniformity of treatment and public accountability for their operations; and
- the tendency towards more rigid personnel policies, for example specific limitations on levels of authority and responsibility, fixed salary gradings based on general pay scales, long-term career structures and set promotion procedures.

A number of these features frequently combine to result in increased bureaucracy within public sector organisations.

The same general problems of management

Both private enterprise and public sector organisations, however, face the same general problems of management. Both are concerned with, for example:

- the efficiency and effectiveness of their operations;
- the clarification of aims and objectives;
- the design of a suitable structure; and
- carrying out essential administrative functions.

Basic principles of management apply in any series of activities in any organisation. The common activities of management apply to a greater or lesser extent in both private enterprise and public sector organisations.

> It is a truism that the public sector manager faces a very different set of challenges from that of his or her private sector counterpart... However, the last decade has seen more and more recognition of the similarities, rather than the differences, between the public and private sector. Management tools familiar to the private sector are now seen as equally relevant in the public sector – even in government departments.[21]

Set of interrelated activities

Based on an analysis of management development in central and local government, *Bourn* suggests management as a set of interrelated activities:

(i) forecasting, setting objectives and planning;
(ii) the definition of problems that need to be solved to achieve these objectives;

(iii) the search for various solutions that might be offered to these problems;

(iv) the determination of the best or most acceptable solutions;

(v) the securing of agreement that such solutions should be implemented;

(vi) the preparation and issue of instructions for carrying out the agreed solutions;

(vii) the execution of the solutions;

(viii) the devising of an auditing process for checking whether such solutions are properly carried out and, if they are, that they do in fact solve the problems for which they were devised;

(ix) the design, introduction and maintenance of the organisational structures which are most appropriate for these activities;

(x) the selection, training, development and management of the appropriate staff.[22]

Clearly, this set of activities is of equal relevance to management in business organisations, and can be seen as an extension of the generalised definition of clarification of objectives, planning, organising, directing and controlling suggested above. Although greater emphasis might be placed on certain activities this analysis helps demonstrate the degree of commonality between the basic process of management in both private and public sector organisations.

> There has been much discussion in the UK and other countries about the adoption of private-sector business techniques in the public sector. There is genuine concern over whether they are appropriate. Do they need adaption? Is the public sector uniquely different? The challenge therefore for top management in the public sector is to find ways of addressing and overcoming these concerns . . . To put the Department [of Social Security] into perspective in business terms, it is equivalent to a company that handles more money each year than the annual turnover of BP, ICI and BT put together, and operates a money transfer system larger than any of the clearing banks. More importantly, through National Insurance, pensions and other benefits it provides, almost every man, woman and child is a customer of the organisation . . .
>
> There are at first sight unique differences between the public and private sector. Further examination, however, of what characterises these differences leads me to the view that individually they are not in fact unique but they mirror the wide range of businesses that can be found outside the public sector. However there are some factors at the extremes of the range of variabilities which will influence how we operate. What is unique is finding them all under one umbrella – that of national government . . . The environment in which we operate is in many ways more challenging than that of the private sector . . . And government departments don't have the international profit/loss account or return on assets to act as an overall measure of efficiency.
>
> *Sir Michael Partridge, Permanent Secretary,*
> *Department of Social Security*[23]

Management in local government

As discussed in Chapter 3, there is an increasing movement towards the 'privatisation' of public sector operations. The Local Government Act 1988 and the Environmental Protection Act 1990 provide for a wide range of local authority services to be put out to compulsory competitive tendering (CCT). There is also growing recognition that the duties and responsibilities of local government staff may satisfy the definition of a manager. One example is the recent change in job title of Home Help Organiser to Home Care Manager.[24] The changing structure of local government and the proposed creation of larger, all-purpose bodies will further enhance the corporate importance of managers.[25]

> Those who do not immediately associate local government with high quality services and effective management may be forgiven. After all, for nearly two decades central government, ably assisted by the popular press, has characterised local government as profligate and inefficient. It is time for that image to be challenged . . . Five years ago, my own authority, Berkshire County Council, saw the need to replace administration with vigorous management . . . We have effectively bought better management for our staff and better value and quality for the council tax payer.
>
> *Tony Allen, Chief Executive, Berkshire County Council*[26]

THE ATTRIBUTES AND QUALITIES OF A MANAGER

In order to carry out the process of management and the execution of work, the manager requires a combination of technical competence, social and human skills, and conceptual ability. Social and human skills reflect the ability to get along with other people, and are important attributes at all levels of management. The degree of technical competence or conceptual ability required will vary according to the level of the organisation at which the manager is working. Recall, for example, the discussion on the distinction between direction and the role of company directors and management earlier in this chapter.

As the manager advances up the organisational hierarchy, greater emphasis is likely to be placed on conceptual ability, and proportionately less on technical competence. This can be illustrated by reference to the levels of organisation discussed in Chapter 10. (*See* Fig. 12.2.)

Technical competence relates to the application of specific knowledge, methods and skills to discrete tasks. Technical competence is likely to be required more at the supervisory level and for the training of subordinate staff, and with day-to-day operations concerned in the actual production of goods or services.

Social and human skills refer to interpersonal relationships in working with and through other people, and the exercise of judgement. A distinctive feature of management is the ability to secure the effective use of the human resources of the organisation. This involves effective teamwork and the direction and leadership of staff to achieve co-ordinated effort. Under this heading can be included sensitivity to particular situations, and flexibility in adopting the most appropriate style of management.[27]

411

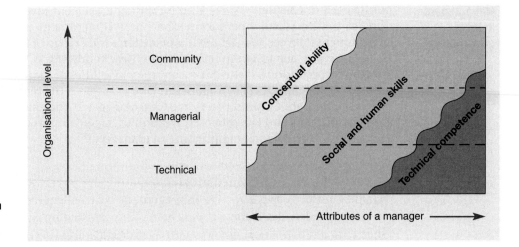

Fig. 12.2
The combination
of attributes of
a manager

Conceptual ability is required in order to view the complexities of the operations of the organisation as a whole, including environmental influences. It also involves decision-making skills. The manager's personal contribution should be related to the overall objectives of the organisation and to its strategic planning.

Although a simplistic approach, this framework provides a useful basis from which to examine the combination and balance of the attributes of an effective manager.

Qualities of a
successful
manager

A more detailed list of attributes is provided by *Pedler, Burgoyne and Boydell*. From their experience of the nature of management work and a research project, they identify 11 qualities which were possessed by successful managers and not possessed by less successful managers.[28]

The qualities are grouped into three different levels but many of the attributes are interconnected and possession of one contributes to possession of another. (*See* Fig. 12.3.)

Basic knowledge and information is needed by the manager in making decisions and taking action. This is the foundation level.

The **specific skills and attributes** directly affect behaviour and performance. The skill or quality of continuing sensitivity to events allows managers to acquire basic knowledge and information.

The **'meta-qualities'** allow managers to develop and deploy skills and resources, and to develop the situation-specific skills needed in particular circumstances.

Managerial
competencies

Following the establishment, in 1988, of the Management Charter Initiative (MCI) attention has been focused on the relevant knowledge, skills and attributes required of managers to actually do their jobs. MCI champions the competence-based approach to management training and development. Managers are assessed against national standards covering the key management functions. These standards are then broken down into greater detail to specify the actual activities that managers undertake in their day-to-day work.[29]

Management development, including the Management Charter Initiative, is discussed further in Chapter 21.

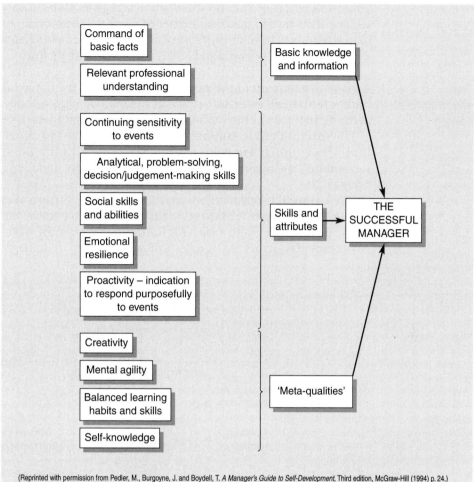

Fig. 12.3
Eleven qualities of a successful manager

(Reprinted with permission from Pedler, M., Burgoyne, J. and Boydell, T. *A Manager's Guide to Self-Development*, Third edition, McGraw-Hill (1994) p. 24.)

THE WORK OF A MANAGER

Despite similarities in the general activities of management, the jobs of individual managers will differ widely. The work of the manager is varied and fragmented. In practice it will be influenced by such factors as:

- the nature of the organisation, its philosophy, objectives and size;
- the type of structure;
- activities and tasks involved;
- technology and methods of performing work;
- the nature of people employed; and
- the level in the organisation at which the manager is working.

These differences do not just exist between organisations in the private and public sectors; they are often more a matter of degree. For example, many large business organisations may have more in common in their management and operations with public sector organisations than with small private firms.

The environmental setting

A major determinant of the work of the manager is the nature of the environment, both internal and external, in which the manager is working. Managers have to perform their jobs in the situation in which they find themselves. (*See* Fig. 12.4.)

The internal environment relates to the culture and climate of the organisation – 'how things are done around here' – and to the prevailing atmosphere surrounding the organisation. Organisational culture and climate are discussed in Chapter 20.

The external environment relates to the organisation as an open system, as discussed in Chapter 3. Managers must be responsive to the changing opportunities and challenges, and risks and limitations facing the organisation. External environmental factors are largely outside the control of management.

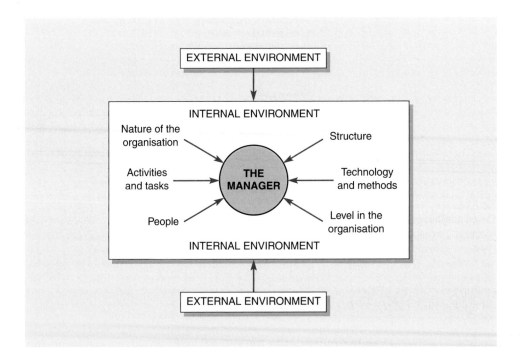

Fig. 12.4
The work of a manager – the environmental setting

The diversity of management

More recent studies on the nature of management have been based on wider observation and research, and have concentrated on the diversity of management and differences in the jobs of managers. Among the best-known empirical studies on the nature of managers' jobs, and how managers actually spend their time, are those by *Mintzberg, Kotter,* and *Stewart*.

MANAGERIAL ROLES

Based on the study of the work of five chief executives of medium to large organisations, *Mintzberg* classifies the activities which constitute the essential functions of a top manager's job.[30] What managers do cannot be related to the classical view of the activities of management. The manager's job can be described more meaningfully in terms of various 'roles' or organised sets of behaviour associated with a position.[31] Mintzberg recognises that people who 'manage' have formal authority over the unit they command, and this leads to a special position of status in the organisation.

As a result of this formal authority and status, managerial activities can be seen as a set of ten roles which may be divided into three groups: (i) interpersonal roles; (ii) informational roles; and (iii) decisional roles (*see* Fig. 12.5).

Interpersonal roles

The interpersonal roles are relations with other people arising from the manager's status and authority.

(i) **Figurehead role** is the most basic and simple of managerial roles. The manager is a symbol and represents the organisation in matters of formality. The manager is involved in matters of a ceremonial nature, such as the signing of documents, participation as a social necessity, and being available for people who insist on access to the 'top'.

(ii) **Leader role** is among the most significant of roles and it permeates all activities of a manager. By virtue of the authority vested in the manager there is a responsibility for staffing, and for the motivation and guidance of subordinates.

(iii) **Liaison role** involves the manager in horizontal relationships with individuals and groups outside their own unit, or outside the organisation. An important part of the manager's job is the linking between the organisation and the environment.

(Reprinted by permission of the *Harvard Business Review* from 'The Manager's Job: Folklore and Fact', by Henry Mintzberg, *HBR Classic*, March–April 1990, p.169. Copyright © 1990 by the President and Fellows of Harvard College. All rights reserved.)

Fig. 12.5
The manager's roles

Informational roles

The **informational roles** relate to the sources and communication of information arising from the manager's interpersonal roles.

(iv) **Monitor role** identifies the manager in seeking and receiving information. This information enables the manager to develop an understanding of the working of the organisation and its environment. Information may be received from internal or external sources, and may be formal or informal.

(v) **Disseminator role** involves the manager in transmitting external information through the liaison role into the organisation, and internal information through leader role between the subordinates. The information may be largely factual or may contain value judgements. The manager is the nerve centre of information. If the manager feels unable, or chooses not, to pass on information this can present difficulties for delegation.

(vi) **Spokesperson role** involves the manager as formal authority in transmitting information to people outside the unit, such as the board of directors or other superiors, and the general public such as suppliers, customers, government departments and the press.

Decisional roles

The **decisional roles** involve the making of strategic organisational decisions on the basis of the manager's status and authority, and access to information.

(vii) **Entrepreneurial role** is the manager's function to initiate and plan controlled (that is, voluntary) change through exploiting opportunities or solving problems, and taking action to improve the existing situation. The manager may play a major part, personally, in seeking improvement, or may delegate responsibility to subordinates.

(viii) **Disturbance handler role** involves the manager in reacting to involuntary situations and unpredictable events. When an unexpected disturbance occurs the manager must take action to correct the situation.

(ix) **Resource allocator role** involves the manager in using formal authority to decide where effort will be expended, and making choices on the allocation of resources such as money, time, materials and staff. The manager decides the programming of work and maintains control by authorising important decisions before implementation.

(x) **Negotiator role** is participation in negotiation activity with other individuals or organisations, for example a new agreement with a trade union. Because of the manager's authority, credibility, access to information, and responsibility for resource allocation, negotiation is an important part of the job.

Arbitrary division of activities

Mintzberg emphasises that this set of ten roles is a somewhat arbitrary division of the manager's activities. It presents one of many possible ways of categorising the view of managerial roles. The ten roles are not easily isolated in practice but form an integrated whole. If any role is removed this affects the effectiveness of the manager's overall performance.

The ten roles suggest that the manager is in fact a specialist required to perform a particular set of specialised roles. Mintzberg argues that empirical evidence supports the contention that this set of roles is common to the work of all managers. An example of this is provided by *Wolf* who analysed the work of the audit manager and assigned critical task requirements to the ten managerial

roles identified by Mintzberg.[32] Another example is the study by *Shortt* who undertook a Mintzbergian analysis of 62 general managers of inns in Northern Island.[33]

Mintzberg's model of managerial roles is a positive attempt to provide a realistic approach to classifying the actual activities of management. There are, however, criticisms that the roles lack specificity and that a number of items under each role are related not to a single factor but to several factors. For example, *McCall and Segrist* found that activities involved in figurehead, disseminator, disturbance handler and negotiator were not separate roles but overlapped too much with activities under the six other roles.[34]

Why organisations need managers

As a result of describing the nature of managerial work in terms of a set of ten roles, *Mintzberg* suggests six basic purposes of the manager, or reasons why organisations need managers:

- to ensure the organisation serves its basic purpose, the efficient production of goods or services;
- to design and maintain the stability of the operations of the organisation;
- to take charge of strategy-making and adapt the organisation in a controlled way to changes in its environment;
- to ensure the organisation serves the ends of those people who control it;
- to serve as the key informational link between the organisation and the environment; and
- as formal authority to operate the organisation's status system.

BEHAVIOUR PATTERN OF GENERAL MANAGERS

From a detailed study of 15 successful American general managers involved in a broad range of industries, *Kotter* found that although their jobs differed and the managers undertook their jobs in a different manner they all had two significant activities in common: **agenda-setting** and **network-building**.[35]

- **Agenda-setting** is a constant activity of managers. This is a set of items, or series of agendas involving aims and objectives, plans, strategies, ideas, decisions to be made and priorities of action in order to bring about desired end-results. For example, the University of Portsmouth strategic plan sets 'the target of moving into the top third of universities in Britain over the next ten years'. This requires individual managers responsible for achieving this target to have a continual and changing series of agendas to help bring this intention into reality.
- **Network-building** involves the managers interacting with other people and establishing a network of co-operative relations. These networks are outside of the formal structure. They have often included a very large number of people, many of whom were in addition to their boss or direct subordinates, and also included individuals and groups outside the organisation. Meetings provided exchanges of information over a wide range of topics in a short period of time. A major feature of network-building was to establish and maintain contacts that could assist in the successful achievement of agenda items.

On the basis of interviews, observations, questionnaires and relevant documents, Kotter found the following features of a typical pattern of daily behaviour for a general manager (GM).[36]

(i) They spent most of their time with others.
(ii) The people they spent time with included many in addition to their superior and direct subordinates.
(iii) The breadth of topics covered in discussions was very wide.
(iv) In these conversations, GMs typically asked a lot of questions.
(v) During these conversations GMs rarely seemed to make 'big' decisions.
(vi) Discussions usually contained a considerable amount of joking, kidding, and non-work-related issues.
(vii) In not a small number of these encounters, the substantive issue discussed was relatively unimportant to the business or organisation.
(viii) In such encounters, the GMs rarely gave 'orders' in a traditional sense.
(ix) Nevertheless, GMs frequently attempted to influence others.
(x) In allocation of time with other people, GMs often reacted to the initiatives of others.
(xi) Most of their time with others was spent in short, disjointed conversations.
(xii) They worked long hours. (The average GM studied worked just under 60 hours per week. Although some work was done at home, and whilst commuting or travelling, they spent most of their time at work.)

PATTERNS OF MANAGERIAL WORK AND BEHAVIOUR

Based on earlier studies of managerial jobs,[37] *Stewart* has developed a model for understanding managerial work and behaviour.[38] The model directs attention to the generalisations that can be made about managerial work, and differences which exist among managerial jobs. It acknowledges the wide variety, found from previous studies, among different managers in similar jobs in terms of how they view their jobs and the work they do.

Demands, constraints and choices

The three main categories of the model are **demands**, **constraints** and **choices**. These identify the flexibility in a managerial job.

- **Demands** are what anyone in the job *has* to do. They are not what the manager ought to do, but only what must be done: for example, meeting minimum criteria of performance, work which requires personal involvement, complying with bureaucratic procedures which cannot be avoided, meetings that must be attended.
- **Constraints** are internal or external factors which limit what the manager can do: for example, resource limitations, legal or trade union constraints, the nature of technology, physical location, organisational constraints, attitudes of other people.
- **Choices** are the activities that the manager is free to do, but does not have to do. They are opportunities for one job-holder to undertake different work from another, or to do the work in a different way: for example, what work is done within a defined area, to change the area of work, the sharing of work, participation in organisational or public activities.

The flexibility of managerial jobs

Stewart suggests that the model provides a framework for thinking about the nature of managerial jobs, and about the manner in which managers undertake them. To understand what managerial jobs are really like it is necessary to understand the nature of their flexibility. Account should be taken of variations in behaviour and differences in jobs before attempting to generalise about managerial work. Study of managers in similar jobs indicates that their focus of attention differs. Opportunities for individual managers to do what they believe to be most important exist to a greater or lesser extent in all managerial jobs. Stewart also concludes that the model has implications for organisational design, job design, management effectiveness, selection, education and training, and career decisions.[39]

How managers really behave

From a review of research into managerial behaviour, Stewart concludes that the picture built up gives a very different impression from the traditional description of a manager as one who plans, organises, co-ordinates, motivates, and controls in a logical, ordered process. Management is very much a human activity.

> The picture that emerges from studies of what managers do is of someone who lives in a whirl of activity, in which attention must be switched every few minutes from one subject, problem, and person to another; of an uncertain world where relevant information includes gossip and speculation about how other people are thinking and what they are likely to do; and where it is necessary, particularly in senior posts, to develop a network of people who can fill one in on what is going on and what is likely to happen. It is a picture, too, not of a manager who sits quietly controlling but who is dependent upon many people, other than subordinates, with whom reciprocating relationships should be created; who needs to learn how to trade, bargain, and compromise; and a picture of managers who, increasingly as they ascend the management ladder, live in a political world where they must learn how to influence people other than subordinates, how to manoeuvre, and how to enlist support for what they want to do. In short, it is a much more human activity than that commonly suggested in management textbooks.[40]

SYNOPSIS

■ Management' is a generic term and subject to many interpretations. Our concern is with management as involving the exercise of formal authority over the work of other people. For our purposes we can regard management as being: within a structured organisational setting; directed towards aims and objectives; achieved through the efforts of other people; and using systems and procedures.

■ Management is both an art and a science; and it is a combination of both innate qualities, and education and training. The nature of management is variable. It relates to all activities of the organisation and is undertaken at all levels. Management is essentially an integrating activity which permeates all other aspects of the organisation.

■ It is not easy to find agreement on the definition of management, or of a manager. Management is not homogeneous but takes place in different ways. One approach is to analyse the nature of management and to identify common activi-

ties and principles. By distinguishing 'managing' from 'doing' we can summarise the nature of managerial work as clarification of objectives, planning, organising, directing and controlling. The degree of emphasis given to these different activities may vary widely, however, from one manager to another. There are, however, many other approaches to the analysis of management.

■ There are important differences between service and production industries, and in management in the private enterprise and public sectors. However, all organisations face the same general problems of management. Increasing attention is being given to applications of general management theory within service industries and to the adoption of business techniques in the public sector.

■ In order to carry out the process of management and execution of work, the manager requires a combination of technical competence, social and human skills, and conceptual ability. The qualities of a successful manager can also be grouped under three different levels: basic knowledge and information; specific skills and attributes; and 'meta-qualities'. Increasing importance is attached to managerial competencies.

■ The jobs of individual managers differ widely. Empirical studies have concentrated on the diversity of management and differences in the nature of managerial work. These studies have drawn attention to such features as: managerial roles; agenda-setting and network-building; demands, constraints and choices in a managerial job; behaviour patterns and how managers actually spend their time. Studies have also illustrated the flexibility of a managerial job.

Review and discussion questions

1 Explain what you understand by the term 'management'. Distinguish management from administration and from supervision.

2 How would you summarise the essential nature of managerial work? In what ways does the job of a manager differ from any other job in a work organisation?

3 From your own experience, identify with examples main activities of management. What do you see as the main attribute(s) or qualities required of a manager in undertaking each of these activities?

4 To what extent is it possible to establish rules or principles of good management? Assess critically the practical applications of these rules or principles.

5 Contrast the nature of management in (i) service and production industries; and (ii) private enterprise and public sector organisations.

6 Explain managerial activities as a set of interrelated roles. Give examples of each of these roles from your own organisation.

7 Why do organisations need managers? Suggest how the flexibility in managerial jobs might be identified, and compare and contrast any two different managerial jobs.

8 Discuss critically the suggestion that management is a much more human activity than that commonly suggested in management textbooks. Support your discussion with practical examples.

 ## Assignment

Select a particular managerial job and observe the manager in action, preferably over an extended period of time.

(i) Make notes, with supporting examples, of the proportion of the manager's work and time which is spent on:
 (a) the carrying out of discrete tasks and the actual 'doing' of work personally; and
 (b) deciding what work is to be done and planning, organising, directing or controlling the work of other people.

(ii) Analyse particular ways in which features of the internal and external environment influence the work of the manager.

(iii) Suggest, with supporting reasons, the **particular** attributes or qualities which appear to be necessary for successful performance of the manager's job.

(iv) Analyse the job in terms of the activities of: (a) agenda-setting; and (b) network-building.

(v) Identify clearly those factors which determine the demands, constraints and choices of the job. Comment critically on how these factors determine the flexibility in the manager's job.

(vi) State clearly the conclusions you draw from your observations and compare with those of your colleagues.

CASE STUDY

What is management?

A thing may look specious in theory, and yet be ruinous in practice;
a thing may look evil in theory, and yet be in practice excellent.

EDMUND BURKE

Adam Smith sat at his desk and reflected that it was now exactly twelve months since he had been appointed general assistant to Charles Gaynor, Managing Director of Gaynor Hotels. During this time he had been used as adviser, counsellor, internal consultant and therapist. He had investigated problems, developed concepts, established principles and generally contributed to the decision-taking process which took place in the mind of his employer, Gaynor.

His attention had been attracted by an article he had been reading, which said:

> In order to maintain its internal dynamic which is essential to progress, a company needs the existence of a rebel group which is primarily concerned with challenging company policy; a group which regards as its main function the generation of sceptical attitudes towards the company's methods of operation, organization and policies. Such a group should adopt as a working principle the slogan, 'if it works it's obsolescent'. In other words the mere fact that a system is working satisfactorily should in itself be sufficient reason for its re-examination.*

Adam ruminated on this and considered that with Carson, his assistant, they really had created a two-man management services activity since they had concentrated on looking at, and solving, old problems in new ways. A pocket of rational thought in a wilderness of emotionalism – if only that were really true, thought Adam!

He felt depressed; although he realised that some progress had been made, it seemed infinitesimal when one looked at the company as a whole. Where is the real answer to the achievement of progress, thought Adam, if only one could put one's finger on it. Particular aspects, methods, solutions and so on were looked at which all seemed part of the answer, but where was the whole answer? Charles Gaynor, although a man inculcated at an early age with the attitudes and ways of traditional hotelkeeping, was most receptive to new ideas; indeed, he could generate them himself and boasted of his preparedness to accept necessary change. But nothing much seemed to have changed in these twelve months; Gaynor Hotels was still making a profit, its managers were still 'managing' but problems continued to abound and there seemed just as many unanswered questions.

Adam leaned forward on his desk with his head in his hands. He wondered if the company was really progressing, if things were any better, and whether he was just deceiving himself. Perhaps the problem was that the company was just 'managing', that it was just getting by, just keeping its head above water. Is it really geared to grow and develop and prosper, is it really looking ahead and ready to exploit the changing circumstances of a changing world? That's the central question, thought Adam, and I wish I could answer it confidently.

*Ward, T. R., *Management Services – The Way Ahead*, National O & M Conference, 1964; published as an Anbar Monograph, Anbar Publications, 1965.

Management! It is all in the management, a handful of men cannot carry a company – it is in the strength and depth of *all* the people who form the firm. His thoughts were interrupted by the door opening and Gaynor appearing with a benevolent smile, and a friendly 'Good afternoon, Adam.'

Gaynor: I thought I would let you know it looks as though I will have to fire a manager, or to put it euphemistically, to ask him to resign.

Adam: Who is it, sir?

Gaynor: Hedges, at the Zephyr. Nasty business and the sort of scandal I deplore. I had a letter from a Mr Coloniki; his wife is secretary to Hedges who, he asserted, has been sleeping with her. I thought there couldn't be anything in it and I referred it to our Mr Hedges never expecting anything other than a denial. Well the damn fool confirmed it as being true, he *has* been sleeping with his secretary. Doesn't leave me much alternative, does it? I can't compromise my principles and I will not have my hotel executives entering into this sort of relationship with their staff. My goodness! What sort of an example is it? Oh, the stupid man, and he was doing quite a good job for us.

Adam: Well, sir, there's an old Hungarian proverb which says that when a man's fancy is titillated his brain goes to water.

Gaynor: How very true! But a little control, a little sense of responsibility, a little maturity, that's all I ask. It isn't even as if he was serious about her; as he told me, it was just his 'little indiscretion' and he hoped that I wouldn't find out. By the way, you didn't already know about it, did you?

Adam: No, certainly not, sir. I haven't heard the slightest suggestion.

Gaynor: Well, back to the old problem of finding a new manager; as if good managers grew on trees! They are such rare animals, they take such a great deal of finding, such a great deal of raising.

Adam: How about his assistant, Gripple, do you think that he might be ready to take over?

Gaynor: He might... I don't know, even if we knew what job we were really picking him for; I mean, what *is* management, what is it *really*? What are we looking for?

Adam: Well, quite honestly, sir, I do not think that he's ready. I think he could develop into a manager, but he needs more time.

Gaynor: All right, we will have to find somebody. I'll tell you what we can do: you take over as manager of the Zephyr for the next month or so. During that time I will find a new manager. This *has* caught us unawares, I can't think of anybody suitable in the company at present.

Adam: But I've never actually managed a hotel!

Gaynor: Well, it will be an excellent experience for you. Anyway, I have no doubt about *your* management abilities. But you still didn't answer my question just now. What actually *is* management – do you know what it is?

Adam: Strange you should ask me that this afternoon, I think that I was just about to ask myself the same question as you walked in.

Gaynor: Fine, but can you answer it?

Adam: Well, it's obviously to do with concern for profits and it's equally to do with concern for people and creating a climate where they can grow and develop.

Gaynor: That's rather vague.

Adam: Well, let me go on, sir. If it's to do with concern for profits then it is also to do with knowledge of modern management methods and techniques and how to use them. If it's to do with concern for people, then it's also to do with knowledge of human behaviour and its applications.

Gaynor: You're struggling, Adam. I remember we talked about the purpose of business and it must lead on from there. We agreed that this was the satisfaction of the needs, wants and desires of those who control the business and generally, but not always, this involved a certain level of profitability. Now purpose must define or set the aims and objectives. Subsequently the policy indicates the means as to how to accomplish these. Policy acts then as the firm guide in all decision-making at an operational level. Management, therefore, is the implementation of policy to achieve company aims and objectives. Yes, I rather like that – I must remember to use it again.

Adam: I know you won't mind Mr Gaynor, but I can't agree with you.

Gaynor: Go on then, I am not very busy at the moment.

Adam: I don't disagree with what you say, but really I am concerned with the assumptions which are being made. Indeed, the business purpose sets aims or objectives but this implies that the business purpose has been established, is commonly perceived and is accepted. You next assume that policy is rationally formulated and promulgated, that managers are aware of it, and take their decisions within its limitations.

Gaynor: Perhaps that describes the ideal situation, but I would still maintain that what I said – what was it – management is the implementation of policy to achieve company aims and objectives, is a good description.

Adam: May I ask what policy Mr Hedges offended?

Gaynor: Ah well now, there are several. First it is unethical; second, if it became known it would damage our image and create havoc in staff relationships, and there are more besides.

Adam: But Mr Hedges took a decision, presumably with a knowledge of the policies you mention, whose effects could militate against our aims and objectives as well as damage his career.

Gaynor: And a damn fool he was, too!

Adam: Were it a less serious affair, and something which was only a minor departure from company policy, I can't help wondering how he or we would know that a departure had occurred. For example, if a manager gave 11 per cent commission to travel agents during the winter to obtain some preference from them, would this be stopped if you became aware of it?

Gaynor: I hope that he would have discussed this with me first, but I can appreciate the point. After all we must be flexible enough to deal with special situations.

Adam: Doesn't this, then, highlight the problem of what we mean by policy? Earlier you said that policy acts as a firm guide, but payment of commission is pretty well fixed at 10 per cent although you would be prepared to consider exceptions. I hope I am not splitting hairs if I suggest that our policy is to pay commissions, a procedure has been established which fixes this at 10 per cent.

Gaynor: I think, in this case, you are tending to split hairs but I see what you are getting at; a confusion exists between policy and procedures. I must admit that I have confused these at times, yes I see the point – policy should act as a guide. But formulating policy in this way must make it so general that it cannot provide much of a guide, a paradox in fact. Another thought that occurs to me is that if the policy is to be an effective guide it should be written out and available for the manager to consult. I must say that this would be an unenviable task!

Adam: Reading textbooks about management I have found the exhortation to have a written policy a common theme. I have never actually seen one so far for a hotel and one can appreciate why this is so. At the same time I would think it comparatively easy to spell out some policies; in the financial areas, for example, this would seem a fairly straightforward exercise.

Gaynor: Yes, and I think it could be done in the operating area too. I must admit, though, that I am not sure that I would like to have an exhaustive written policy document. I feel it would be a restriction on me.

Adam: I believe this is a fairly common feeling among senior executives; Glacier Metal Company introduced a written policy and their experience was that flexibility *increased* since when a change had to be made, everybody could be informed and a written amendment incorporated. This makes sense to me, but I have always had a sneaking feeling that they wrote a procedure manual rather than a policy handbook.

Gaynor: So you are back to your distinction between policy and procedures! Am I to take it, then, that you are advocating that we should try to produce a policy document for the company?

Adam: No, sir, I may tend to overstate the case, but I would think that the existence of such a document represents a failure of management. At a unit level, and indeed at company level, it is essential to have *procedure* manuals since these provide a means of establishing and maintaining standards as well as a basis for training. I would also say that it is essential for a company to spend a lot of time clarifying its objectives and aims at the top level. The real problem is that many so-called policy documents are little more than a public relations handout. If a company is clear about what it wants to be, surely it should make every effort for everybody to understand and accept these aims and behave in a supportive way towards them.

Gaynor: I would have thought that having a written policy would help to do this, since people could see just what the aims are and act accordingly.

Adam: I am sure that this is partly true, but what I am trying to say is that if, starting at the top, members of an organisation demonstrate by their behaviour what the policy is, this will be reflected downwards. If the senior executives behave as though they believed the customer was important, then other employees will adopt similar behaviour.

Gaynor: In other words, people will learn by example; I am rather intrigued that you should have such a charming old-fashioned idea!

Adam: By example, yes. But it is a little more than this. Put into the jargon, I would say that it is minimising corporate discrepancy. That is, reducing the difference between what a company as a collection of people say, and what in fact they do.

Gaynor: Very well, I agree with what you say but I must say there are some grave dangers of misinterpretation. If the conclusion without the supporting argument is adopted it can become an excuse for avoiding the necessary analytical thinking at the top level. We seem to have strayed a long way from my attempt to define management; taking into account all you have said we still have a good description.

Adam: I agree, but the whole problem of vocabulary in management continues to be a stumbling-block. I always remember a lecturer at college who said at his first lecture to us that he had to devise a vocabulary to talk to us which we would automatically adopt, but never to attempt to use it outside. Since there is no generally accepted or defined vocabulary he had to fashion his own to communicate with us. We all forgot, of course, and it took some time to stop using our private language when we went into industry.

Gaynor: You still forget sometimes!

Adam: Sorry! If we do understand that policy and company aims and objectives are in some way related to individual interpretation, depending on the perceptions of the people involved, then I think it is a good *des*cription. But shouldn't a definition of this sort be a *pre*scription? By saying what it is, it gives some indication of how to do it?

Gaynor: Description, prescription, you're chopping words again. I will accept, although I think you are trying to find a philosopher's stone if a definition can tell a manager how to do his job!

Adam: To come back to the definition, sir, suppose the policy is wrong or the aims and objectives are wrong. Is it true to say that an individual is managing if he keeps things going to achieve these and doesn't have the wit or the insight to besiege his superiors for a change of direction?

Gaynor: Ah! Now you are introducing value judgements about 'good' management and 'bad' management!

Adam: No Mr Gaynor. You will accuse me of sophistry again, but I would say that a person who is a manager is managing effectively. If he is ineffective, then he is not a manager.

Gaynor: Save me from quibblers! But do go on.

Adam: When I was in America I was given an assignment to collect together as many definitions of management as I could find. It really was a fascinating exercise but eventually I found myself in such a muddle that I could hardly think straight. The things that people have to say about this process, which hundreds of thousands of people go about for five days a week, year in and year out is amazing. The one that I remember, and considered the most banal of a very sad bunch, was 'Management is getting things done through people.'

Gaynor: Oh! I always considered that a truism.

Adam: Well, yes. But it doesn't advance our understanding. Bus conductors, waitresses and supervisors get things done through people – but they are not managers.

Gaynor: Very interesting; so you don't think supervisors are managers?

Adam: No. Managers are tacticians; that is they are the people who are once-removed from the actual operators who serve the food or make the beds. Managers

are concerned with the deployment of resources. A manager *says* what has to be done, a supervisor frequently *shows* people what has to be done. The supervisor is a technician, the manager is a tactician. In this sense he is *always* 'getting things done through other people' and the other people are his supervisors.

Gaynor: Well then why does this 'getting things done through other people' grate on you so much?

Adam: Chiefly because of its lack of prescription. Would you say that a person is an effective manager who spends all his time with his supervisors, guiding, instructing, directing and giving decisions?

Gaynor: No, certainly not. I would expect him to set the guidelines – policy, if you like – and by his selection and development of the supervisors, reach a stage where they got on with the work and left him time to think.

Adam: Exactly. I think it has been sufficiently demonstrated from studies of managers' and supervisors' behaviour that these are very different roles. We must be careful, however, about actual titles that go with a job.

Gaynor: Yes indeed. It was always a source of amusement to me, when I had the title of General Manager, to sit next to people, with the same designation, at conferences who ran a hotel with twenty bedrooms. I would be the first to insist that we belonged to the same industry, but our needs and problems were vastly different! Do we have any common ground, I wonder? The other thing that concerns me is the entrepreneurial aspect. The owner of a twenty-bedroom hotel is an entrepreneur, whereas Kimble at the Diana is a manager employed by the company. Yet he is responsible for about twenty times the turnover of this entrepreneur!

Adam: I have often pondered about this. In many ways it is a very personal thing. Occasionally I meet people who ask me why I work for Gaynor Hotels when I could be my own boss running a small hotel in the Cotswolds and probably able to take each afternoon off for golf. But it really depends on what you mean by being one's own boss. I am sure there is great satisfaction in being personally involved with the customer in the small business, but the real boss is then the bank manager and there is a very real dependence on suppliers. I think that one can over-emphasise the differences between the entrepreneur and the manager. Probably the owner of a small hotel spends about 5 per cent of his time on entrepreneurial decisions and the rest of the time he is a manager. So Kimble and the proprietor have 95 per cent of common activity if they are running similar establishments.

Gaynor: I suppose I am the professional entrepreneur of this company, but I have never been able to find any courses which deal with this topic! But we are still groping about. You have the advantage of your research on definitions of management, what are your conclusions? After all, people like me that just manage, what time do we have for all this introspection?

Adam: Now I am in difficulties! On the one hand I am asked to offer my conclusions against your experience, and on the other hand I am asked to sit in judgement on the multitude of writers on management!

Gaynor: I thought this is what you did anyway, but please! You know that I want to know about your ideas and that I shall use my experience to challenge you where I think you are wrong. I know that you will produce research findings, that I have never heard of, like rabbits from a hat. But I am still interested in your ideas.

Adam: Sorry, Mr Gaynor, but I just realised the enormity of what you asked me to do. It is one thing to make comments about a definition that somebody proposes; it is quite another thing to be asked, from limited experience, to fly in the face of the savants!

Gaynor: I quite understand, but go ahead.

Adam: Well, the early writers about management became heavily involved in trying to define management but I think because they were engineers or technologists, they wanted it cut and dried. They saw the world in mechanical terms and placed all the emphasis on what should be done to create orderliness and an organisation which works like a smoothly oiled machine.

Gaynor: Then the social scientists came along and started to demonstrate that most of the problems were centred round people who did not behave like machines. In fact they were unpredictable.

Adam: Yes, but I think that the success of techniques in advertising show that there are quite a lot of predictable elements in people's behaviour. But the effect of the behavioural scientists' findings tended to tip the balance with a lot of managers from concern for production to concern for people. In fact I sometimes think this still persists today to a large extent; from the way some people talk, one would think that the Hawthorne experiments were the only studies which have been conducted in this field.

Gaynor: You mean that a manager should be involved in maintaining a balance between his concern for people and for production?

Adam: Yes. This means that management is a process which involves achieving business goals while at the same time providing a means of satisfaction for the individual needs or goals of employees. Now I think that the real danger to maintaining this balance might be described as the return on invested time. A comparatively short time spent in replanning a layout of a kitchen, or the desirability of installing a room state indicator, can quickly produce economies. We can see that more meals can be produced or customers allocated rooms speedily. But to increase people's effectiveness requires a much greater investment in time to establish what goals they are seeking to achieve.

Gaynor: I think most managers would agree with you and that they appreciate the need for developing people, but there is always the pressure of other things to be done and the consequent shortage of time. And what about decision-taking, I would think that this is a basic and fundamental part of managing?

Adam: The problem of time is something I would like to come back to. I must admit that I feel slightly nervous when decision-taking is regarded as some prerogative of managers. After all, everybody is involved in taking decisions every day. A housewife faces a major problem in a supermarket when she has to decide between paying xp for a family-sized pack of detergent or a few pence more for a special large size accompanied by a free plastic flower!

Gaynor: I see what you mean, but surely we cannot divorce this business of making decisions from a process of management? I keep reading that use of computers is likely to remove a lot of decision-taking from middle management in the future. But I don't think this will come for a long time and I certainly think that in running hotels there will continue to be a lot of decisions which would defy any

computer. We will still need the reception manager who can fit an unexpected regular customer into the hotel which the computer says is full.

Adam: Yes indeed, we cannot ignore that decisions have to be taken in business organisations and it needs some careful thinking to distinguish between normal human decision-taking and the special characteristics of those in business.

Gaynor: That should not be too difficult. I am sometimes very conscious of spending time collecting information in order to make a decision. In a similar way, you or the chief accountant sometimes spend time preparing briefs about the possible alternatives available and the likely results. A lot of this involves figures and projections and so on. With no disrespect to you, most of this could be done better on a computer, but I will still have to make the decision about which line to follow. I would also think that the unit managers will have to continue making similar decisions; perhaps these are less important in that a wrong one will be unlikely to damage the company, whereas mine might! In these decisions, at both levels, we have to use experience and our personal judgement.

Adam: If most of the operating decisions at unit level are to be made by computers in the future, the manager's role becomes one of a human relations mechanic.

Gaynor: I don't see it that way. I hope that they will use information from the computer in reaching operating decisions; I suppose I am agreeing with your balance between people and production. My concern, however, is that this is the only method I can see for developing executives. As you know, we are a fairly decentralised company and I want my managers to feel that they are more than what you call 'human relations mechanics'. This really goes back to what I was thinking earlier when I used the word 'policy'. One would like to feel, as a company, that decisions are made in accordance with the policy and this is the paradox you saw. I am reluctant to start writing everything down, but I do want decisions made which support what we are trying to be as a company. Perhaps it would be a better way of describing this to say that I would like to create an ethos or spirit that ensures this.

Adam: I would say that creating this environment or ethos is a very important part of the management process. It can probably be compared to the training we have as children; having confidence in social situations because we have a good idea of what is the 'right thing to do' like not putting our elbows on the table.

Gaynor: I thought only great-aunts worried about that nowadays! But I think you have something. Tell me, where does problem-solving come into all this? I certainly seem to spend a significant part of my time dealing with problems and I am sure it is the same with all managers.

Adam: Just before you came in I was thinking about this; after a year I am still involved in solving problems and I find this rather disappointing.

Gaynor: This is what I mean. Surely you can't expect problems to stop requiring solving, I would think that this is almost the core of what management is about.

Adam: This makes me feel uncomfortable. Identifying problems and solving them certainly is a significant part of managing. But I can't help feeling that this is catching hold of the wrong end of the stick. Surely if we concentrated on identifying the *causes* of problems and removing those we could be much more effective?

Gaynor: I am not sure I understand you.

Adam: Perhaps I can illustrate it with the problem we had at the Apollo. Rather, I should say, problems; no potential managers were being produced, there was a high labour turnover and so on. We could have attempted to solve these by introducing different methods of selection, higher pay and various other means. These might have had some effect but in the long run we hadn't identified and remedied the cause. That was Whitstone, whose autocratic behaviour as a manager was the cause of the problems.

Gaynor: Yes, I see what you mean. It is like worrying about the problem of high labour costs at Head Office when the cause is people wanting to have things in writing as a protection.

Adam: Exactly. But having said that, I am not sure just how this fits in with the management process. Undoubtedly managers are involved in solving problems and now it sounds as though I am saying they shouldn't be.

Gaynor: From what you say, and it is certainly a new slant for me, I would see this as part of the ethos. It involves analysing the cause of problems rather than saying 'we have a problem'. This reminds me of one of the British Institute of Management's luncheons when Peter Drucker spoke. It was very impressive to me when he said something like 'We are concerned with effective management rather than efficient management, because a manager can be very efficient at doing something that does not need to be done'. I remember that I was disturbed for several days afterwards!

Adam: This really typifies how one can see a whole new dimension to the task of managing by taking a step sideways and looking at the words we use. I sometimes think that words and clichés are like old slippers, they are comfortable until you notice the holes in them.

Gaynor: Comfortable, but not presentable! What about communication? I recall that we have said something about this before. It must come in somewhere.

Adam: I think on that occasion you quoted Thoreau and said, 'How can I hear what you say, when what you are keeps drumming in my ears'.

Gaynor: Ah yes! A favourite quote of mine.

Adam: Well, the way I see it is that if your ethos exists, then communication will occur. Most people in talking about communication generally emphasise the skills of writing, speaking and reading. Sometimes they also include the skill of listening. These are, of course, important, but I would think that the emotional and social context are important. Which is just what Thoreau was saying.

Gaynor: So you don't consider communication is a part of managing.

Adam: Oh, I think it is, but if we mix Drucker with Thoreau and add a dash of your observation on the ethos of the enterprise, we can see that communication is a function of the internal environment. If trust exists and people appreciate the objectives, then communication will occur. If not, then no communication.

Gaynor: In some ways I would describe it as 'good' and 'poor' communication, but I am a little worried that you might take me to task on these words! Look, I have a lunch appointment and must go in a few minutes. This has been a very interesting discussion, what shall I do, sum up what we have been saying or leave it to you to prepare a memo?

Adam: I would rather you summarised, Mr Gaynor. After all, I don't want to land myself with solving a problem of overloaded Head Office typists!

Gaynor: Your motives are suspect, but let me see. The Management Process seems to be concerned with creating an environment in which a balance between concern for production and concern for people is maintained as well as providing a guide to decision-taking. It is directed towards an analysis of the causes from which problems arise and seeks to provide for achievement of organisational objectives whilst satisfying individual needs. Is that adequate?

Adam: It really is a concise statement of what we have been talking about.

Gaynor: Does it satisfy your demands for prescription?

Adam: I think it does because it stresses the things that a manager must do. Creating the environment, for example. But I wonder how long this takes to achieve.

Gaynor: You have a chance to find out, Adam. Tell me about it when you come back from the Zephyr! Goodbye for now, and enjoy yourself.

Notes and references

1. Drucker, P. F. *Management*, Pan Books (1979) p. 14.
2. Fayol, H. *General and Industrial Management*, Pitman (1949). See also: Gray, I. *Henri Fayol's General and Industrial Management*, Pitman (1988).
3. Department of the Environment *The New Local Authorities: Management and Structure* (the Bains Report), HMSO (1972).
4. See, for example: Lawton, A. and Rose, A. *Organisation and Management in the Public Sector*, Second edition, Pitman (1994).
5. Fayol, H. *General and Industrial Management*, Pitman (1949).
6. Brech, E. F. L. *Principles and Practice of Management*, Third edition, Longman (1975) p. 19.
7. Brown, W. *Organization*, Penguin (1974) p. 45.
8. Drucker, P. F. *People and Performance*, Heinemann (1977) p. 28.
9. *Ibid.* p. 59.
10. Simon, H. A. *The New Science of Management Decision*, Revised edition, Prentice-Hall (1977).
11. For a summary, see: Mullins, L. J. 'The Essential Nature of Managerial Work', *Industrial Management & Data Systems*, May/June 1987, pp. 15–17.
12. Carroll, S. J. and Gillen, D. J. 'Are the Classical Management Functions Useful in Describing Managerial Work?' *Academy of Management Review*, vol. 12, no. 1, 1987, p. 48.
13. Stewart, R. *The Reality of Management*, Second edition, Pan Books (1986) p. 12.
14. Parker, P. 'The Shape of Leaders to Come', *Management Today*, July 1994, p. 5.
15. See, for example: Wentworth, F. 'It's Time We Took Supervisors Seriously', *Professional Manager*, January 1993, pp. 15–17.
16. Drucker, P. F. *The Practice of Management*, Heinemann Professional (1989) p. 377.
17. Fitzsimmons, J. A. and Sullivan, R. S. *Service Operations Management*, McGraw-Hill (1982).
18. Levitt, T. 'Production-Line Approach to Service', *Harvard Business Review*, September–October 1972, p. 41.
19. Jones, P. (ed.) *Management in Service Industries*, Pitman (1989).
20. See, for example: Mullins, L. J. *Hospitality Management: A Human Resources Approach*, Second edition, Pitman (1995).
21. Fell, D. 'Public Relations', *Management Today*, October 1990, p. 50.
22. Bourn, J. *Management in Central and Local Government*, Pitman (1979) pp.17–18.
23. Partridge, M. 'Private Lessons for Public Service', *Management Today*, November 1994, p. 5.
24. Mullins, L. J. 'From Home Help Organiser to Home Care Manager', *Local Government Administrator*, pp. vii–xvi, Supplement to *Administrator*, December 1989.
25. See, for example: Harrison, A. 'The Rise of the Super-Administrator', *Administrator*, June 1994, pp. 4–6.
26. Allen, T. 'Hands Off Local Government', *Management Today*, September 1993, p. 5.
27. See, for example: Clarke, K. 'Survival Skills For a New Breed', *Management Today*, December 1993, p. 5.
28. Pedler, M., Burgoyne, J. and Boydell, T. *A Manager's Guide to Self-Development*, Third edition, McGraw-Hill (1994).
29. For example, see: Summers, A. 'Setting Standards of Competence for Management Training', *The British Journal of Administrative Management*, October/November 1994, pp. 18–19.
30. Mintzberg, H. *The Nature of Managerial Work*, Harper and Row (1973).
31. Mintzberg, H. 'The Manager's Job: Folklore and Fact', *Harvard Business Review Classic*, March–April 1990, pp. 163–76.
32. Wolf, F. M. 'The Nature of Managerial Work: An Investigation of the Work of the Audit Manager', *Accounting Review*, vol. LVI, no. 4, October 1981, pp. 861–81.

33. Shortt, G. 'Work Activities of Hotel Managers in Northern Island: A Mintzbergian Analysis', *International Journal of Hospitality Management*, vol. 8. no. 2, 1989, pp. 121–30.
34. McCall, M. W. and Segrist, C. A. *In Pursuit of the Manager's Job: Building on Mintzberg*, Centre for Creative Learning, Greenboro, NC (1980).
35. Kottler, J. P. *The General Managers*, The Free Press (1982).
36 Kotter, J. P. 'What Effective General Managers Really Do', *Harvard Business Review*, vol. 60, no. 6, November–December 1982, pp. 156–67.
37. Stewart, R. *Contrasts in Management*, McGraw-Hill (1976).
38. Stewart, R. *Choices for the Manager*, McGraw-Hill (1982).
39. See also: Stewart, R. *Managing Today and Tomorrow*, Macmillan (1991).
40. Stewart, R. 'Managerial Behaviour: How Research Has Changed the Traditional Picture', in Earl, M. J. (ed.) *Perspectives on Management: A Multidisciplinary Analysis*, Oxford University Press (1983) pp. 96–7.

13 MANAGERIAL BEHAVIOUR AND EFFECTIVENESS

It is the responsibility of managers to manage and to achieve results through the efforts of other people. This involves the effective utilisation of human resources. The way in which managers exercise their responsibilities and duties is important. Consideration must be given to the management of people. Managers are only likely to be effective if they adopt an appropriate style of behaviour.

 Learning objectives

To:

- Contrast different attitudes and assumptions of managers about human nature and behaviour at work;

- Examine managerial styles in terms of concern for production and concern for people;

- Assess different systems of management and relate these systems to organisational characteristics;

- Evaluate Management by Objectives as a means of improving organisational performance;

- Appreciate the importance of adopting a caring and positive approach to the management of people;

- Analyse managerial effectiveness and suggest criteria for evaluating the effectiveness of managers;

- Recognise the importance of adopting an appropriate style of managerial behaviour.

Worth thinking about

A first step in the effective management of other people is confidence in your own ability, and awareness of your own strengths and weaknesses. Why is it then that many managers find it difficult to admit their mistakes, to say sorry or to laugh at themselves? 'Mea culpa' should be part of the philosophy and language of every manager.

MANAGERIAL BEHAVIOUR

The behaviour of managers and their style of management will influence the effort expended and level of performance achieved by subordinate staff.

To repeat the point made in Chapter 1 – in the belief of the author, the majority of people come to work with the **original attitude** of being eager to do a good job, and desirous of performing well and to the best of their abilities. Where actual performance fails to match the ideal this is largely a result of how staff perceive they are treated by management. There is, therefore, a heavy responsibility on managers and on the styles and systems of management adopted.

Management style can be as important as management competence. The general movement towards flatter organisation structures, flexible working and greater employee involvement places greater emphasis on an integrating rather than a traditional controlling style of management.

The way in which managers approach the performance of their jobs and the behaviour they display towards subordinate staff is likely to be conditioned by predispositions about people, and human nature and work.

MANAGERS' ATTITUDES TOWARDS PEOPLE

Drawing on *Maslow*'s hierarchy of needs model (which is discussed in Chapter 14), *McGregor* put forward two suppositions about human nature and behaviour at work. He argues that the style of management adopted is a function of the manager's attitudes towards people and assumptions about human nature and behaviour. The two suppositions are called Theory X and Theory Y, and are based on polar assumptions about people and work.[1]

Theory X assumptions about human nature

Theory X represents the assumptions on which traditional organisations are based, and was widely accepted and practised before the development of the human relations approach. Its assumptions are that:

- the average person is lazy and has an inherent dislike of work;
- most people must be coerced, controlled, directed and threatened with punishment if the organisation is to achieve its objectives;

435

- the average person avoids responsibility, prefers to be directed, lacks ambition and values security most of all; and
- motivation occurs only at the physiological and security levels.

The central principle of Theory X is direction and control through a centralised system of organisation and the exercise of authority. McGregor questions whether the Theory X approach to human nature is correct, and the relevance today of management practices which are based upon it.

Assumptions based on a Theory X approach, and the traditional use of rewards and sanctions exercised by the nature of the manager's position and authority, are likely to result in an exploitative or authoritarian style of management.

Theory Y assumptions about human nature

At the other extreme to Theory X is Theory Y which represents the assumptions consistent with current research knowledge. **The central principle of Theory Y is the integration of individual and organisational goals.** Its assumptions are:

- for most people work is as natural as play or rest;
- people will exercise self-direction and self-control in the service of objectives to which they are committed;
- commitment to objectives is a function of rewards associated with their achievement;
- given the right conditions, the average worker can learn to accept and to seek responsibility;
- the capacity for creativity in solving organisational problems is distributed widely in the population;
- the intellectual potential of the average person is only partially utilised; and
- motivation occurs at the affiliation, esteem and self-actualisation levels as well as the physiological and security levels.

McGregor implies that a Theory Y approach is the best way to elicit co-operation from members of an organisation. It is the task of management to create the conditions in which individuals may satisfy their motivational needs, and in which they achieve their own goals through meeting the goals of the organisation.

McGregor develops an analysis of the implications of accepting Theory Y in regard to performance appraisal, administration of salaries and promotions, participation, staff–line relationships, leadership, management development and the managerial team.

Managerial strategies

Although Theory X and Theory Y are based on polar extremes and are an oversimplification, they do represent identifiable philosophies which influence managerial behaviour and strategies. For example, as *Lord Sieff* comments:

> Now and again it is necessary to criticize people, but rather than tick them off, provided you can leave them in no doubt as to what the issue is, I am sure it pays to avoid being censorious but try instead to appeal to the innate capacity for self-criticism. Whatever you do, avoid making a mountain out of a molehill.[2]

Most people have the potential to be self-motivating. They can best achieve their personal goals through self-direction of their efforts towards meeting the goals of the organisation. Broadening educational standards and changing social values mean that people today have wider expectations of the quality of working

life, including opportunities for consultation and participation in decisions which affect them. Managers should develop practices based more on an accurate understanding of human behaviour and motivation.

The Theory Y approach, however, is not a 'soft' option. In practice it is often difficult to achieve successfully. It can be frustrating and time-consuming, and mistakes will occur.

> Since 1952 I've been stumbling around buildings and running primitive Theory Y departments, divisions, and finally one whole Theory Y company: Avis.
>
> In 1962, after thirteen years, Avis had never made a profit (except one year when they jiggled their depreciation rates). Three years later the company had grown internationally (not by acquisitions) from $30 million in sales to $75 million in sales, and had made successive annual profits of $1 million, $3 million, and $5 million. If I had anything to do with this, I ascribe it all to my application of Theory Y. And a faltering, stumbling, groping, mistake-ridden application it was.
>
> *Robert Townsend*[3]

Demands of the situation

The two views of Theory X and Theory Y tend to represent extremes of the natural inclination of managers towards a particular style of behaviour. In practice, however, the actual style of management behaviour adopted will be influenced by the demands of the situation.[4]

Where the job offers a high degree of intrinsic satisfaction or involves a variety of tasks, an element of problem-solving and the exercise of initiative, or where output is difficult to measure in quantitative terms, an informal, participative approach would seem to be more effective. It is more likely to lead to a higher level of staff morale. In many cases this would apply to work of a scientific, technical or professional nature. Where commitment to the goals of the organisation is almost a prerequisite of membership, such as in certain voluntary or charity organisations, for example, then a Theory Y approach would clearly seem to be most appropriate.

Use of a Theory X approach

However, even if a manager has a basic belief in Theory Y assumptions there may be occasions when it is necessary, or more appropriate, to adopt a Theory X approach. When the nature of the job itself offers little intrinsic reward or limited opportunities to satisfy higher-level needs, a more dictatorial style of management might work best. Some jobs are designed narrowly, with highly predictable tasks, and output measured precisely. This is the case, for example, with many complex production processes in manufacturing firms. With these types of jobs a Theory X approach may be needed if an adequate level of performance is to be maintained.

A Theory X approach is also indicated in emergency situations, or where shortage of time or other overriding factors demand the use of authority in directing actions to the tasks in hand. For example, in the hustle, heat and noise of a busy hotel kitchen preparing fresh meals for a large banquet, with many tasks to be co-ordinated over very short time scales, it seems to be recognised that a Theory X

style of management is most appropriate. In such circumstances this style of management appears to be accepted by the kitchen staff.

If subordinates match the Theory Y assumptions of the manager, then this style of management may well be effective. However, there are many staff who, whatever the nature of their job, do not wish to accept responsibility at work. They seem to prefer, and respond better to, a more directed and controlled style of management. There are times, therefore, when the manager may be justified in adopting Theory X assumptions about staff.

Behavioural implications of management accounting

As part of a study of behavioural implications of management accounting and working theories held by accountants, *Caplan* provided a questionnaire on information about the use of standard costs and variance analysis.[5] The questionnaire was given to 20 accountants and a total of 20 production and general managers in different organisations. A series of questions were asked under three broad headings of:

(i) Organisation goals;
(ii) Management accounting goals; and
(iii) The standard cost system.

Although based on a small sample, responses to the questionnaire suggest a widely held belief by accountants in Theory X assumptions.

JAPANESE 'THEORY Z' ENVIRONMENT

A comparison of management style and practice in different cultural settings is provided by *Ouchi*. In contrast to the traditional, more bureaucratic American organisational environment, Ouchi recommends a Japanese style 'Theory Z' environment.

> The problem of productivity in the United States will not be solved with monetary policy nor through more investment in research and development. It will only be remedied when we learn how to manage people in such a way that they can work together more effectively. Theory Z offers several such ways.[6]

The characteristics of a Theory Z organisation are described by Ouchi as:

- long-term employment, often for a lifetime;
- relatively slow process of evaluation and promotion;
- development of company-specific skills, and moderately specialised career path;
- implicit, informal control mechanisms supported by explicit, formal measures;
- participative decision-making by consensus;
- collective decision-making but individual ultimate responsibility;
- broad concern for the welfare of subordinates and co-workers as a natural part of a working relationship, and informal relationships among people.

In Britain, the operations of the successful Marks & Spencer organisation have been likened to a manner that approaches the typical Japanese company, and with close similarities to the characteristics of Theory Z organisation.[7]

THE MANAGERIAL/LEADERSHIP GRID®

One means of describing and evaluating different styles of management is the *Blake and Mouton* Managerial Grid®. First published as the Managerial Grid in 1964, restated in 1978 and 1985[8] and republished in 1991 as the Leadership Grid,[9] the Grid provides a basis for comparison of managerial styles in terms of two principal dimensions:

(i) concern for production; and
(ii) concern for people.

Concern for production is the amount of emphasis which the manager places on accomplishing the tasks in hand, achieving a high level of production and getting results or profits. This is represented along the horizontal axis of the Grid.

Concern for people is the amount of emphasis which the manager gives to subordinates and colleagues as individuals and to their needs and expectations. This is represented along the vertical axis of the Grid.

Each axis is on a scale of 1–9 indicating varying degrees of concern that the manager has for either production or for people. The manner in which these two concerns are linked together depends upon the use of the hierarchy, the 'boss aspect', and assumptions that the manager makes about how to achieve production with and through people, and the use of power.

Five basic combinations

'Concern for' is not how much concern, but indicates the character and strength of assumptions which underlie the manager's own basic attitudes and style of management. The significant point is 'how' the manager expresses concern about production or about people. The four corners and the centre of the Grid provide five basic combinations of degree of concern for production coupled with degree of concern for people (*see* Fig. 13.1):

* **the impoverished manager** (1,1 rating), low concern for production and low concern for people;
* **the authority-compliance manager** (9,1 rating), high concern for production and low concern for people;
* **the country club manager** (1,9 rating), low concern for production and high concern for people;
* **the middle-of-the-road manager** (5,5 rating), moderate concern for production and moderate concern for people; and
* **the team manager** (9,9 rating), high concern for production and high concern for people.

Managers with a 1,1 rating tend to be remote from their subordinates and believe in the minimum movement from their present position. They do as little as they can with production or with people. Too much attention to production will cause difficulties with staff and too much attention to the needs of staff will cause problems with production.

Managers with a 9,1 rating are autocratic. They tend to rely on a centralised system and the use of authority. Staff are regarded as a means of production and motivation is based on competition between people in order to get work done. If staff challenge an instruction or standard procedure they are likely to be viewed as uncooperative.

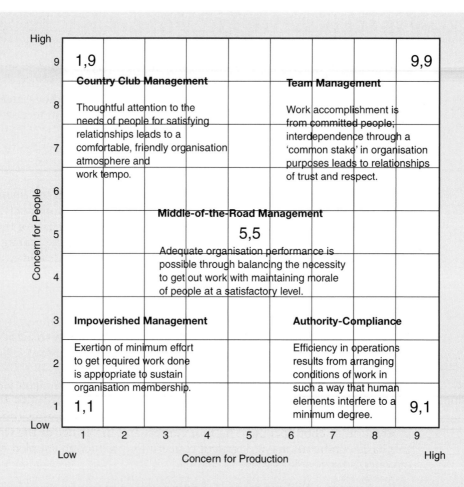

The following is the text content from the figure:

High

9 1,9 9,9

Country Club Management Team Management

8 Thoughtful attention to the Work accomplishment is
 needs of people for satisfying from committed people;
 relationships leads to a interdependence through a
7 comfortable, friendly organisation 'common stake' in organisation
 atmosphere and purposes leads to relationships
 work tempo. of trust and respect.

6

 Middle-of-the-Road Management

5 5,5

 Adequate organisation performance is
 possible through balancing the necessity
4 to get out work with maintaining morale
 of people at a satisfactory level.

3 Impoverished Management Authority-Compliance

 Exertion of minimum effort Efficiency in operations
2 to get required work done results from arranging
 is appropriate to sustain conditions of work in
 organisation membership. such a way that human
 elements interfere to a
1 1,1 minimum degree. 9,1

Low

 1 2 3 4 5 6 7 8 9

 Low Concern for Production High

Concern for People (vertical axis label)

(Reproduced with permission from: The Leadership Grid ® figure from *Leadership Dilemmas – Grid Solutions* by Robert R. Blake and Anne Adams McCanse, Houston: Gulf Publishing Company, p. 29. Copyright© 1991, by Scientific Methods, Inc. Reproduced by permission of the owners.)

**Fig. 13.1
The Leadership
Grid®**

The 1,9 rating managers believe that a contented staff will undertake what is required of them and achieve a reasonable level of output. Production is secondary to the avoidance of conflict and maintenance of harmony among the staff. Managers will seek to find compromises between staff and solutions acceptable to everyone. Although innovation may be encouraged, they tend to reject good ideas if likely to cause difficulties among the staff.

The 5,5 rating is the middle-of-the-road management with the approach of 'live and let live' and a tendency to avoid the real issues. This style of management is the 'dampened pendulum' with managers swinging between concern for production and concern for people. Under pressure, this style of management tends to become task management (9,1). But where this strains relations and causes resentment from staff, pressure is eased and managers adopt a compromise approach. If there is a swing too much the other way (towards 1,9) managers are likely to take a tighter and more hardened approach.

Managers with a 9,9 rating believe in the integrating of the task needs and concern for people. They believe in creating a situation whereby people can satisfy their own needs by commitment to the objectives of the organisation. Managers will discuss problems with the staff, seek their ideas and give them freedom of action. Difficulties in working relationships will be handled by confronting staff directly and attempting to work out solutions with them.

These five styles of management represent the extremes of the Grid. With a nine point scale on each axis there is a total of 81 different 'mixtures' of concern for production and concern for people. Most people would come up with a score somewhere in an intermediary position on the Grid.

Two additional grid styles

The 1991 edition of the Grid also covers two additional styles: 9+9 paternalism, and opportunism.

- In **9+9 paternalistic management**, reward and approval are granted to people in return for loyalty and obedience; and punishment is threatened for failure to comply.
- In **opportunistic management**, organisational performance occurs according to a system of exchanges, whereby effort is given only for an equivalent measure of the same. People adapt to the situation to gain maximum advantage of it.

A summary of the seven basic combinations of the Grid is given in Fig. 13.2.

Framework for patterns of behaviour

The Managerial Grid provides a framework in which managers can identify, study and review their patterns of behaviour. Instead of viewing management styles as a dichotomy of 'either/or', *Blake and Mouton* claim that the Managerial Grid illustrates that the manager can gain the benefits of maximising, simultaneously, methods which are both production-oriented and people-oriented. The 9,9 position, although an ideal, is worth working for.

Based on their experience of using the original Grid, Blake and Mouton give three reasons why it is important to consider which style of management is used to achieve production through people.

- The 9,9 style of management correlates positively with bottom line productivity.
- 9,9 oriented managers enjoy maximum career success.
- There is now greater knowledge about the correlation between extreme grid styles of management, and mental and physical health.

Blake and Mouton provide a self-assessment questionnaire in two parts. First, there are five different descriptions of managerial behaviour which are to be ranked 5 to 1 as most to least typical. Second, there is a series of five statements relating to the different descriptions, under each of six headings: (1) decisions, (2) convictions, (3) conflict, (4) temper, (5) humour and (6) effort. From each heading is selected the one statement which describes best the person's behaviour. Results obtained from the questionnaire give an indication of the person's likely dominant style of management. Responses to the questionnaire can be compared with those of typical managers who are generally successful.

Dominant style of management

From their research, Blake and Mouton emphasise that managers may switch from one style to another or combine elements of different styles. However, they also found that managers tend to have one dominant style of management which they

1,1 **Impoverished management**, often referred to as *laissez-faire* leadership. Leaders in this position have little concern for people or productivity, avoid taking sides, and stay out of conflicts. They do just enough to get by.

1,9 **Country club management**. Managers in this position have great concern for people and little concern for production. They try to avoid conflicts and concentrate on being well liked. To them the task is less important than good interpersonal relations. Their goal is to keep people happy. (This is a soft Theory X approach and not a sound human relations approach.)

9,1 **Authority-obedience**. Managers in this position have great concern for production and little concern for people. They desire tight control in order to get tasks done efficiently. They consider creativity and human relations to be unnecessary.

5,5 **Organisation Man management**, often termed middle-of-the-road leadership. Leaders in this position have medium concern for people and production. They attempt to balance their concern for both people and production, but are not committed to either.

9+9 **Paternalistic 'father knows best' management**, a style in which reward is promised for compliance and punishment threatened for non-compliance.

Opp **Opportunistic 'what's in it for me' management**, in which the style utilised depends on which style the leader feels will return him or her the greatest self-benefit.

9,9 **Team management**. This style of leadership is considered to be ideal. Such managers have great concern for both people and production. They work to motivate employees to reach their highest levels of accomplishment. They are flexible and responsive to change, and they understand the need to change.

(*Source*: Robert R. Blake and Jane S. Mouton, *The Managerial Grid III* (Houston: Gulf Publishing Company, copyright © 1985), Chapters 1–7 as modified here. Reproduced by permission of the owners.)

Fig. 13.2
Seven combinations of the Grid

use more often than any other. They found also that many managers have a 'back-up' style which they adopt if their dominant style does not work in a particular situation.

The dominant style of management is influenced in any particular situation by any of four conditions.

- **Organisation** – the nature of the organisation in which the manager is employed, and the extent to which there are rigid rules and regulations.
- **Values** – the personal values, beliefs or ideals which the manager holds concerning how to treat people or to manage results.
- **Personal history** – the deep-rooted personal history of the manager may be an important factor, and lead to a preference for a particular approach because that style may have been experienced frequently in the past.
- **Chance** – the manager may not have been confronted with, or had personal experience of, alternative sets of assumptions about how to manage. 'Chance' has not provided the manager with an opportunity to learn.

Organisation development programme

Blake and Mouton have designed an organisation development programme based on group dynamics which is aimed at bringing about a style of management with a 9,9 concern for production and concern for people. The programme consists of six phases divided into two parts. Part one involves management development through: (i) laboratory-seminar training and introduction to the concepts of the Grid; and (ii) teambuilding. Part two involves helping managers work towards organisation development through: (iii) inter-group development; (iv) designing organisational strategy; (v) implementing development; and (vi) consolidation, and stabilising progress made during the earlier phases. (*See also* Chapter 20.)

From a review of the Managerial Grid programme, *Lester* believes it undoubtedly lends itself supremely well to training programmes. Although its relevance to real-life issues is less sure, in presenting a sophisticated learning package the Grid provides many potential applications for those who wish to study organisation development.[10]

MANAGEMENT SYSTEMS

Work by *McGregor,* and by *Blake and Mouton,* suggests that an organisation is more likely to harness its staffing resources effectively if there is a participative style of management. This view is supported by the work of *Likert.* On the basis of a questionnaire to managers in over 200 organisations and research into the performance characteristics of different types of organisations, Likert identifies a four-fold model of management systems.[11] These systems are designated by number:

System 1 (Exploitive authoritative);
System 2 (Benevolent authoritative);
System 3 (Consultative); and
System 4 (Participative group).

System 1 – Exploitive authoritative – decisions are imposed on subordinates, motivation is based on threats, there is very little teamwork or communication; responsibility is centred at the top of the organisational hierarchy.

System 2 – Benevolent authoritative – there is a condescending form of leadership, motivation is based on a system of rewards, there is only limited teamwork or communication; there is responsibility at managerial levels but not at lower levels of the organisational hierarchy.

System 3 – Consultative – leadership involves some trust in subordinates, motivation is based on rewards but also some involvement, there is a fair degree of teamwork, and communication takes place vertically and horizontally; responsibility for achieving the goals of the organisation is spread more widely throughout the hierarchy.

System 4 – Participative group – leadership involves trust and confidence in subordinates, motivation is based on rewards for achievement of agreed goals, there is participation and a high degree of teamwork and communication; responsibility for achieving the goals of the organisation is widespread throughout all levels of the hierarchy.

Profile of organisational characteristics

Likert has also established a 'profile of organisational characteristics' describing the nature of the four different management systems. The profile compares the four systems in terms of a table of organisational variables under the headings of:

(i) leadership processes;
(ii) motivational forces;
(iii) communication process;
(iv) interaction–influence process;
(v) decision-making process;
(vi) goal setting or ordering; and
(vii) control processes.

Using this table, Likert undertook a survey of several hundred managers comprising different groups from a wide range of experience, and in both line and staff positions. His studies confirmed that least productive departments or units tended to employ management practices within Systems 1 and 2, and the most productive departments or units employed management practices within Systems 3 and 4.

A shorter and simpler form of the profile of organisational characteristics is provided by Likert and Likert (Fig. 13.3).[12]

Effects of different systems

Systems 1 and 2 can be related to *McGregor's* Theory X. System 4 provides the basic assumptions and approaches of Theory Y, and is based on involvement, supportive relationships and participation. Organisational decisions are improved as they are based on more accurate information and there is greater motivation to implement the decisions. *Likert* found, for example, that: 'In Systems 1 and 2 organizations . . . high performance goals by superiors, coupled with high-pressure supervision using tight budgets and controls, yield high productivity initially because of compliance based on fear.'[13]

However, because of unfavourable attitudes, poor communication, lack of co-operative motivation and restriction of output, the long-term result is high absence and labour turnover, and low productivity and earnings. Likert suggests that the nearer the behavioural characteristics of an organisation approach System 4 the more likely this will lead to long-term improvement in labour turnover and high productivity, low scrap, low costs and high earnings.

SYSTEM 4 MANAGEMENT

Likert sets out three fundamental concepts of System 4 management. These are the use of:

- the principle of supportive relationships among members of the organisation and in particular between superior and subordinate;
- group decision-making and group methods of organisation and supervision; and
- high performance aspirations for all members of the organisation.

Supportive relationships

Supportive relationships are intended to enhance self-esteem and ego building, contribute to subordinates' sense of personal worth and importance, and maintain their sense of significance and dignity. The superior's behaviour is regarded as supportive when this entails:

	Organisational variables	System 1	System 2	System 3	System 4	Item no.
		Exploitive Authoritative	Benevolent Authoritative	Consultative	Participative Group	
Leadership	How much confidence and trust is shown in subordinates?	Virtually none	Some	Substantial amount	A great deal	1
	How free do they feel to talk to superiors about job?	Not very free	Somewhat free	Quite free	Very free	2
	How often are subordinates' ideas sought and used constructively?	Seldom	Sometimes	Often	Very frequently	3
Motivation	Is predominant use made of 1 fear, 2 threats, 3 punishment, 4 rewards, 5 involvement?	1,2,3 occasionally 4	4, some 3	4, some 3 and 5	5,4 based on group set goals	4
	Where is responsibility felt for achieving organisation's goals?	Mostly at top	Top and middle	Fairly general	At all levels	5
	How much co-operative teamwork exists?	Very little	Relatively little	Moderate amount	Great deal	6
Communication	What is the usual direction of information flow?	Downward	Mostly downward	Down and up	Down, up and sideways	7
	How is downward communication accepted?	With suspicion	Possibly with suspicion	With caution	With a receptive mind	8
	How accurate is upward communication?	Usually inaccurate	Often inaccurate	Often accurate	Almost always accurate	9
	How well do superiors know problems faced by subordinates?	Not very well	Rather well	Quite well	Very well	10
Decisions	At what level are decisions made?	Mostly at top	Policy at top, some delegation	Broad policy at top, more delegation	Throughout but well integrated	11
	Are subordinates involved in decisions related to thier work?	Almost never	Occasionally consulted	Generally consulted	Fully involved	12
	What does decision-making process contribute to motivation?	Not very much	Relatively little	Some contribution	Substantial contribution	13
Goals	How are organisational goals established?	Orders issued	Orders, some comments invited	After discussion by orders	By group action (except in crisis)	14
	How much covert resistance to goals is present?	Strong resistance	Moderate resistance	Some resistance at times	Little or none	15
Control	How concentrated are review and control functions?	Very highly at top	Quite highly at top	Moderate delegation to lower levels	Widely shared	16
	Is there an informal organisation resisting the formal one?	Yes	Usually	Sometimes	No...same goals as formal	17
	What are cost, productivity and other control data used for?	Policing, punishment	Reward, punishment	Reward, some self-guidance	Self-guidance, problem-solving	18

(Adapted and reproduced with permission from Likert, R. and Likert, J. G., *New Ways of Managing Conflict*, McGraw-Hill (1976) p. 75.)

Fig. 13.3 Short form profile of organisational characteristics

- mutual confidence and trust;
- help to maintain a good income;
- understanding of work problems and help in doing the job;
- genuine interest in personal problems;
- help with training to assist promotion;
- sharing of information;
- seeking opinions about work problems;
- being friendly and approachable; and
- giving credit and recognition where due.

Group decision-making

Group decision-making and supervision use an overlapping form of structure. Individuals known as 'linking-pins' are members not only of their own group but also of the next superior group and, where appropriate, of peer groups. This enables each work group to be linked to the rest of the organisation. (The 'linking-pin' process was discussed in Chapter 6.)

In System 4 management interaction and decision-making rely heavily on group processes, and discussions focus on the decisions to be made. Likert emphasises that group methods of decision-making should not be confused with the use of committees. With the group method of decision-making the superior is held responsible for the quality and implementation of decisions. The superior is responsible for developing subordinates into an effective group.

In considering high performance aspirations, Likert refers to studies which suggest that employees generally want stable employment and job security, opportunities for promotion, and satisfactory compensation. They want, also, to feel proud of their organisation, and its performance and accomplishments. In System 4 management, superiors should therefore have high performance aspirations, but so also should every member of the organisation. To be effective, these high performance goals should not be imposed but set by a participative mechanism involving group decision-making and a multiple overlapping group structure. The mechanism should enable employees to be involved in setting high performance goals which help to satisfy their own needs.

Causal, intervening and end-result variables

Likert also refers to three broad classes of variables relating to the firm's human organisation and its operations: (i) causal, (ii) intervening and (iii) end-result.

- **Causal variables** are independent variables which can be amended by the organisation and its management, for example management policies, the structure of an organisation, and leadership strategies. Causal variables determine development of an organisation and the results it achieves.
- **Intervening variables** indicate the internal health of the organisation, for example the loyalties, attitudes, motivations and performance of members and their collective capacity for interaction, communication and decision-making.
- **End-result variables** indicate the final outcome and reflect the influences of intervening variables. The end-result variables reflect the achievement of the organisation, for example productivity, costs, scrap, earnings.

Attempts to improve the intervening variables are likely to be more successful through changing the causal variables, rather than changing directly the intervening variables. End-result variables are most likely to be improved by changing the causal variables, rather than the intervening variables.

In Fig. 13.4 Likert gives a simplified example of the interrelationships between causal, intervening and end-result variables in the System 1 or 2, and System 4 management. The arrows indicate the pattern of relationships between the three classes of variables.

The presence of these variables yields these variables which, in turn, lead to these variables

(Reproduced with permission from Likert, R., *The Human Organization*, McGraw-Hill (1967) p. 137.)

Fig. 13.4 Simplified diagram of relationships among variables for System 1 or 2 and System 4 operation

MANAGEMENT BY OBJECTIVES (MBO)

One particular participative approach to the activities involved in planning, organisation, direction and control, and to the execution of work, is Management by Objectives (MBO). MBO is a phrase used to describe a style or system of management which attempts to relate organisational goals to individual performance and development through the involvement of all levels of management. The underlying basis of a system of MBO is:

● the setting of objectives and targets;
● participation by individual managers in agreeing unit objectives and criteria of performance; and
● the continual review and appraisal of results.

The phrase Management by Objectives appears to have been introduced by *Drucker* in 1954.[14] The approach was taken up by *McGregor* who advocated its use as a preferred means of goal-setting, appraisal of managerial performance and self-assessment. The system of MBO has been adopted in a wide range of organisational settings, in the public as well as the private sector.

Odiorne describes Management by Objectives as:

> a process whereby the superior and subordinate managers of an organization jointly identify its common goals, define each individual's major areas of responsibility in terms of the results expected of him, and use these measures as guides for operating the unit and assessing the contribution of each of its members.[15]

Humble refers to the importance of **key results analysis.** This will identify clearly the main purpose of the job, and the key tasks to be achieved in those areas of work related directly to achieving objectives, and which performance has a significant effect on the effectiveness of the organisation. There should be a related process of guidance, training and development for the subordinates.[16]

The cycle of MBO activities

MBO involves a continuous cycle of interrelated activities. (*See* Fig. 13.5.)

- The clarification of organisational goals and objectives. These should be communicated clearly to, and understood fully by, all members of staff.
- Review of organisational structure. The need is for a flexible structure and systems of management which make for effective communications, quick decision-making and timely feedback information.
- Participation with subordinates in order to gain their willing acceptance of objectives and targets, key result areas, and standards and measurements of performance.
- Agreement on performance improvement plans which will enable subordinates to make the optimum contribution to: (i) meeting their own objectives and targets; and (ii) improved organisational performance.
- Establishment of an effective monitoring and review system for appraisal of progress and performance, including self-checking and evaluation.
- Undertaking any necessary revisions to, or restatement of, subordinates' objectives and targets.
- Review of organisational performance against stated goals and objectives.

To be fully effective, MBO also needs to be linked with a meaningful system of rewards and career progression which recognises the subordinate's level of contribution and performance.

Participation and freedom of action

A system of MBO means that instead of subordinates being told exactly how to do their work, they are given definite tasks and results to be achieved. The central feature of MBO is that objectives and targets are not imposed but established and agreed through participation of subordinates with superiors. Within agreed limits and the policies of the organisation, the subordinates are given freedom of action to decide how best to achieve these results. Measurement of performance is in terms of the subordinates' degree of accomplishment rather than the ability to follow detailed instructions on how to undertake their work. **A system of Management by Objectives can be contrasted, therefore, with a style of management based on direction and control, and the adherence to rules.**

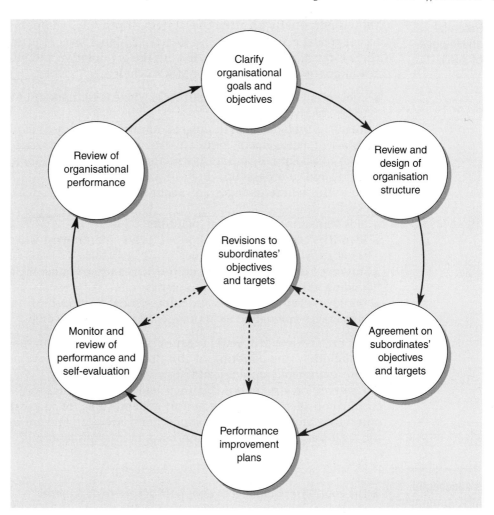

Fig. 13.5
The cycle of MBO
activities

APPLICATIONS OF MBO

MBO is sometimes regarded as applying to subordinate managers and to the clarification of objectives for the units under their control. However, **there is no reason why the principles of MBO cannot be applied to staff throughout all levels of an organisation.** The introduction of MBO for managers may result in them adopting a more participative style of management with their subordinate staff.

MBO draws attention to the objectives for individual members of the organisation and how these objectives relate to the objectives for the organisation as a whole. MBO can be integrated into a system of corporate planning and top level management decisions on long-term objectives for the organisation as a whole. In public sector organisations, such as local government, MBO can be integrated into a planning, programming, budgeting system and decisions on the allocation of resources.

MBO can take a number of different forms in different organisations and is more correctly described as *a style or system of management.*

Potential advantages of MBO

MBO is potentially an attractive system. It provides an opportunity for staff to accept greater responsibility and to make a higher level of personal contribution. There is much to recommend it to both the organisation and individual managers. Advantages generally claimed for MBO include:

- concentrates attention on main areas where it is important for the organisation to be effective;
- identifies problem areas in progress towards achievement of objectives;
- improves management control information and performance standards;
- leads to a sound organisation structure, clarifies responsibilities, and aids delegation and co-ordination;
- identifies where changes are needed and seeks continual improvement in results;
- aids management succession planning;
- identifies training needs, and provides an environment which encourages personal growth and self-discipline;
- improves appraisal systems, and provides a more equitable procedure for determining rewards and promotion plans;
- improves communications and interpersonal relationships; and
- encourages motivation to improve individual performance.

Based on a review of specific organisational MBO programmes, *Carroll and Tosi* conclude that 'the adoption of this approach can improve managerial performance, managerial attitudes, and organizational planning'.

However, they point out that their research also indicates that 'MBO programs require considerable time and effort expenditures for successful adoption, and unless they are given adequate support and attention and are well integrated into the organization, they will fail or not live up to expectations'.[17]

Requirements of a successful MBO programme

If an MBO programme is to be successful it requires:

- the commitment and active support of top management;
- specialist advice on implementation of the system and a thorough understanding by all the staff concerned;
- careful attention to the setting of key tasks, target figures and performance standards;
- objectives which are profitable to the organisation, clearly defined, realistically attainable, and capable of measurement;
- genuine participation by staff in agreeing objectives and targets;
- the right spirit and interest from staff concerned and effective teamwork;
- avoidance of excessive paperwork and forms which lead to a mechanistic approach; and
- maintaining the impetus of the system.

CRITICISMS AND LIMITATIONS OF MBO

MBO, however, is not a panacea and it is subject to a number of criticisms and potential limitations. MBO has been likened to a modern form of scientific management. It is also subject to the same possible criticisms of too great an emphasis

on individual job definitions together with a management authority structure, and the assumption of no conflict between individual and organisational goals. MBO should not be applied simply as a pressure device by which management apply increasingly demanding targets which staff are expected to achieve.[18]

It is not always easy to set specific targets or figures for certain more senior jobs, or where the work involves a high degree of self-established role prescriptions (discussed in Chapter 6). The same might apply to jobs which require a high level of interpersonal relationships, especially where this involves confidential matters, for example counselling. There is a potential danger that where objectives and targets are more difficult to specify and measure in precise terms these are neglected, and greater emphasis is placed on objectives which are more easily monitored.

MBO appears to have suffered some decline in popularity. However, reviews and surveys suggest that although there are numerous arguments on the pros and cons, and questions still remain, basically MBO can be an effective system.[19]

MBO-based appraisal schemes

Conflicts can arise between individual and organisational objectives. The system of MBO is usually associated with a sophisticated performance appraisal scheme and rating scales. But this approach may cause people to lose sight of the underlying principles and to regard the system as a substitute for the successful management of people.[20] (Performance appraisal is discussed in Chapter 18.)

The practical effectiveness of MBO appears to be a matter of debate and many of the criticisms or limitations are related to the formulation of appraisal schemes. *Kane and Freeman* explain a number of common problems which are inherent flaws in any MBO-based appraisal scheme.

(i) **The rate-setting phenomenon.** When rewards are based on performance appraisals employees can be expected to adopt an economic rationality orientation towards their objectives, and to attempt to set and maintain objectives at the lowest level possible to maximise the probability of attaining them.

(ii) **Lack of comparability in performance standards.** It is impossible to set standards for attaining each rating level which are comparable in difficulty. To the extent that members of staff participate in setting their own objectives their difficulty is determined more by relative bargaining skills than by concern for equity.

(iii) **Basing performance appraisal on MBO results in the forcing of objectives to fit the boundaries of individual jobs** rather than work groups or organisational sub-divisions.

(iv) **Excessive emphasis on short-term accomplishment.** When appraisal results are used for personnel decisions (such as pay, merit awards, promotion or retention) such decisions are usually made within an annual period. The organisation must, therefore, set objectives related to short-term perspectives.

(v) **Substitution of supervisory discretion for measurement.** A performance appraisal scheme must satisfy the requirements of a measurement system. If cases occur that are not covered by any of the assignment rules, the measurement process falls under the control of the subjective whims of the measurers.

(vi) **Lost flexibility.** Most organisations go through periods of change and uncertainty when it is necessary for the nature or emphasis of activities to shift. Staff are bound to perceive that it is risky to respond to contingencies at their own discretion and sacrifice progress towards their objectives.

(vii) **Distortion of accountability.** The philosophy of MBO has been that objectives should refer to the expected output levels of a manager's work unit rather than to the expected effectiveness of the manager's performance. A highly effective manager can receive low appraisal ratings when the work unit fails to achieve its objectives for reasons outside the control of the manager. An ineffective manager can still receive high ratings when the work unit achieves its objective despite the incompetence of the manager.

(viii) **Uselessness as a predictor for promotion decisions.** Performance in a lower-level job can predict performance in a higher-level job only if the two jobs share common functions. Performance measurements on specific functions cannot be isolated when an MBO-based appraisal scheme is used.

(ix) **The bottle-neck syndrome.** Objectives must be set for every work unit at the onset of the organisation's annual period of operation, and all 'come due' at the same time. This creates a tremendous administrative bottle-neck for managers and supervisors.[21]

MANAGING PEOPLE

There are many aspects to management but the one essential ingredient of any successful manager is the ability to handle people effectively. The work of *Likert*, for example, has drawn attention to the importance of System 4 management and a people-centred approach to managing people within a work organisation.

Popular books on management and the nature of organisational effectiveness appear to take a positive view of human nature and support an approach which gives encouragement for people to work willingly and to perform to the best of their ability.[22]

However, as many of us will have witnessed for ourselves, an understanding, people-centred approach to management seems often to be lacking in practice. Too many managers appear to attempt to manage through the use of rules, systems, procedures and paperwork, rather than **with and through people.**

It is important that managers have a highly developed sense of **people perception**, and understand the feelings of staff, and their needs and expectations. It is people who are being managed and people should be considered in human terms. A genuine concern for people and for their welfare goes a long way in encouraging them to perform well.

The culture of management

The culture of management is important. For example, *Freemantle* suggests that a festering deficiency in management culture is that managers are not really concerned about people until they become a problem. As a result: 'management thinking has become corrupted by two major obsessions: (1) an obsession with developing sophisticated systems for managing people more successfully (paper panaceas); (2) an obsession with trade union power (union paranoia)'.[23]

According to Freemantle, the perception of 'people as costs' leads to relatively little weight being given to people management and leadership skills when appointing managers. Many companies tend to appoint technical specialists to managerial positions, neglecting the vital task of managing people. Chief executives and personnel managers have allowed middle managers to opt out of the key task of leading

their people in favour of filling in even more forms (the paper panacea). However, Freemantle does point out exceptions such as Mars, IBM, and Marks & Spencer, who in pursuit of excellence devote a high priority to people management and considerable time, energy and effort to the vital process of managing people.

In order to eliminate the corruption of management thinking, it is important to remove the paper panaceas and divert attention from paranoia about trade unions. Freemantle believes that managers must get back to the basics and concentrate their minds on five essential principles (which are very much in line with the views of the author):

- the successful management of people based on honesty, trust, openness, mutual respect, co-operation and support;
- developing a perception of employees as an essential asset to be invested in, rather than a variable cost to be minimised;
- ensuring managers have a clearly established set of principles (such as the above) which they can apply on a minute-by-minute basis in their daily management task;
- fundamentals of leadership (as opposed to leadership systems) relating to vision, charisma and ability to gain team commitment and co-operation;
- the establishment of basic but essential practices, such as: clarity about their accountabilities; knowing how to care for people; knowing how to command respect; knowing the difference between a leader and a manager; knowing how to set high standards and achieve them; knowing how to manage people successfully and to achieve individual managerial excellence.

BASIC MANAGERIAL PHILOSOPHIES

A positive policy of investment in people and an interpersonal relationship approach to management is, in the longer term, worth the effort. For example, the government-sponsored initiative 'Investors in People' is based on a commitment to the benefits organisations can gain from a rigorous approach to the development of human resources.[24]

It is the belief of the author that there are a number of basic, underlying philosophies which are likely to make for the successful management of people *and* lead to improved work performance.[25]

Consideration, respect and trust People generally respond according to the way they are treated. If you give a little you will invariably get a lot back. Make people feel important and give them a sense of personal worth. The majority of staff will respond constructively if treated with consideration and respect, and as responsible individuals who wish to serve the organisation well.

For example, in discussing productivity through people, *Peters and Waterman* make the following comment:

> Treat people as adults. Treat them as partners; treat them with dignity; treat them with respect. Treat *them* – not capital spending and automation – as the primary source of productivity gains. These are fundamental lessons from the excellent companies' research. In other words, if you want productivity and the financial reward that goes with it, you must treat your workers as your most important asset.[26]

453

Recognition and credit	People can be praised to success. Give full recognition and credit when it is due and let people know you appreciate them. Too often managers are unresponsive to good performance, which may occur the vast majority of the time, and appear to take this for granted; but are quick to criticise on the few occasions when performance falls below expectations. Positive feedback on good performance is a strong motivator, *and* staff are then more likely to accept and respond to constructive criticism. If staff are to take a pride in their work they need to know when they are performing well and to receive appropriate recognition for their efforts.
Involvement and availability	Involve yourself with the work of the staff, and make sure you fully understand the difficulties and distastes of their duties and responsibilities. Ensure an open flow of communications, and encourage participation and feedback. Take an active interest in the work of staff but without excessive supervision or inhibiting their freedom of action. Wherever possible be available to staff as a priority, rather than to administration, and remember the importance of giving time to listen to the feelings and problems of staff.
Fair and equitable treatment	Treat people fairly but according to merit. Ensure justice in treatment, equitable systems of motivation and rewards, clear personnel policies and procedures, avoidance of discrimination, and full observance of all laws or codes of conduct relating to employment. People expect certain outcomes in exchange for certain contributions or inputs. A feeling of inequality causes tension and motivates the person to indulge in certain forms of behaviour in order to remove or to reduce the perceived inequity.[27]
Positive action on an individual basis	Treat members of staff as individuals. Deal with individual situations on an individual basis and avoid the 'blanket' approach. For example, it has come to the manager's attention that a couple of members of staff have failed to provide some urgently requested information on time. The manager's reaction is to send a circular to *all* members of the department reminding them of the need for, and importance of, meeting deadlines. This may appear to be an easy way out to the manager. But what is likely to be the reactions of staff?

The two members concerned might shield behind the generality of the circular and persuade themselves that it doesn't apply particularly to them. They might even choose to believe that the manager must be referring to other members of staff, perhaps in a different section, and take little notice of the circular. In contrast, the majority of staff in the department who do have a good record of providing requested information on time may well be annoyed or upset by the circular.

There could be some staff who despite pressing personal difficulties have taken great pride in their work and made a special effort to maintain an excellent record of co-operation – quite possibly without any previous positive recognition from management. **It would be understandable if the reaction of these staff was one of resentment and disillusionment, and with a possible adverse effect on their future attitude to work.** The manager has more to lose than to gain from adopting a 'blanket' approach to a particular problem and by the failure to take selective, positive action on an individual basis.

Emphasis on end-results	The manager should place emphasis on end-results and levels of actual performance and achievement, rather than on compliance with detailed instructions, rules or regulations. For example, where set attendance times are *clearly* seen as a

necessary requirement of the job, it is right that managers should ensure that time-keeping is adhered to and enforced as appropriate. But in many cases rigid times of attendance are not an essential requirement for effective performance.

Who makes the greatest contribution to the work of the organisation? Person A who is always on time, keeps to the exact lunch break and never leaves early – or late; but spends much of the day in idle conversation and gossip, shuffling papers and looking at the work, and achieves only adequate performance; or person B who may 'not be seen about the place so much', but always gives maximum effort, makes full use of time and is never idle, is flexible, delivers whatever is expected on time, and achieves a consistently high level of performance?

Good time-keeping can be an important part of the job. But if 'always being there' is not a requirement, *per se*, for effective performance, what is to be gained by insisting on rigid times of attendance? Such a requirement is likely to be perceived by person-B-type staff as an unwarranted bureaucratic style of management. And it could turn a person B into a person A – with an adverse effect on the level of effective performance.

The increasing movement to flexible working patterns and teleworking coupled with demands to boost productivity are placing growing emphasis on what staff actually achieve rather than the time spent at work. The important criteria are the level and quality of performance.

Staff and customer satisfaction

The starting point for customer, or consumer, satisfaction is good manager–subordinate relationships. Supportive and harmonious working relationships are more likely to create a working environment which results in high levels of both staff *and* consumer satisfaction. Managers need to adopt a positive attitude towards staff and to develop a spirit of mutual co-operation. Staff should feel that they are working *with* the manager rather than *for* the manager.

From a further examination of several well-performing firms in America, *Waterman* draws attention to organisational arrangements as the key, achieved from a humanist rather than a 'business process re-engineering' viewpoint. Successful firms are organised to meet the needs of their people so that they attract better people, who are more motivated to do a superior job and better organised to satisfy the needs of their customers. Firms need to manage the intricate interplay between people, strategy, organisational arrangements and customers. The conclusion is 'people first'. Treat your own people and your customers well and good results will follow.[28]

CHOICE OF MANAGERIAL STYLE

Some might argue that these philosophies are too idealistic and that given the harsh realities of the working environment managers need to adopt a more dominant stance. But **it is not suggested that managers should in any way give up the right to manage: it is a question of *how* they manage and how they use their authority:** for example, a 'Theory X' style with emphasis on direction and control, and the use of rewards and sanctions exercised by nature of the manager's position and authority; or a 'Theory Y' style in which individuals may satisfy their motivational needs through integration with meeting the goals of the organisation.

Golden rule management

One example of an interesting and enlightened people approach is put forward by Mary Kay Ash, founder of the huge, multi-million-dollar company Mary Kay Cosmetics in the USA.[29]

Ash writes about the intentional development of a management concept that allows fairness to flourish in business, the belief that people will shine if given a chance, and methods that are applicable to any organisation. Her concept of the management of people is based on the Golden Rule 'Do unto others as you would have them do unto you', with emphasis on being a 'people company'. (Again, this is a philosophy very much in line with the views of the author.)

> People come first at Mary Kay Cosmetics – our beauty consultants, sales directors and employees, our customers, and our suppliers. We pride ourselves as a 'company known for the people it keeps.' Our belief in caring for people, however, does not conflict with our need as a corporation to generate a profit.[30]

The philosophy of 'Golden Rule Management' is applied in such ways as, for example:

- **Treat people fairly but according to merit.** In order to balance responsibilities to the company, the employee, and all other employees, every manager must be able to say 'no'. But employees should be encouraged to turn a 'no' into the motivation to accomplish more.
- However busy you are, **make the other person feel important**, and let people know you appreciate them.
- **Motivate people through giving praise.** A good manager must understand the value of praising people to success.
- **Encourage feedback** and don't undervalue the ability to listen.
- **Sandwich every bit of criticism between two layers of heavy praise.**
- **An open-door philosophy.**
- **Help other people get what they want** – and you will get what you want. Good managers' success is reflected in the success of their people.
- **Never hide behind policy or pomposity.**

Beauty consultants who follow the guiding rules of Mary Kay Cosmetics are rewarded by the incentive of expensive gifts.

A caring and positive approach

There are, of course, many successful organisations that do adopt a caring and positive approach to the management of people. Examples include the underlying policy of good human relations adopted by Marks & Spencer, and the beliefs and philosophies of Anita Roddick and The Body Shop, both of which were referred to in Chapter 9. (The Marks & Spencer policy of good human relations at work is discussed further in Chapter 18.)

> We accepted that it was our inherent responsibility to motivate and involve our staff and franchise holders, to try and make the working week a pleasure instead of a living death. How could we do that? In all kinds of ways. By education. By stretching their abilities and their imaginations. By involving them in issues of greater significance than selling a pot of cream.
>
> *Anita Roddick*[31]

No single best choice of style

It has to be recognised, however, that no single choice of managerial style is likely to appeal to, or be welcomed by, all members of staff. For example the open letter of introduction to all staff by Liz Forgan when she took over as managing director of BBC Radio, reported in the *Daily Mail*, evoked mixed reactions.

Dear Network Radio,

Why does everyone I know in telly now creep out of the woodwork and confess that secretly it's radio they really love?

Why does every letter from a listener start, 'Hands off . . .' and enclose 10,000 signatures?

What kind of a medium is this that strikes so deep into the human psyche?

I reckon my first job is to start understanding the answers to the above and I hope that you, who know them, will help me do so.

We are all in an exciting frenzy of change and reorganisation and we've got a mammoth job to do to present ourselves to the world lean, fit and sparkling as befits those asking for Royal Charters and billion-pound licence fees.

It will be bumpy now and then. All change carries with it some grief and some breakages along the road. But the trick is going to be to keep our eyes on the prize all the way through the process, however many pages of management babble I churn out, however many sacred cows seem to be heading for the abattoir, however endless the Reviews and the Projects and the Plans may seem.

And the prize is of course the freedom to go on offering our listeners the incredible range and quality of programming which the BBC has offered them over the years. And for me that means Bon Jovi to Buxtehude, Terry Wogan to Test Match Special, Wittgenstein to Woman's Hour (whatever Hour that may turn out to be).

I've been listening like crazy for the past few weeks and I am simply knocked out by the treasure house of interest, revelation and pleasure you are putting out.

David [*predecessor David Hatch*] is handing me a tremendous legacy of talent and commitment in the teams he has built up and nurtured. I am enormously grateful to him for his generosity and help and I don't care what he says about not being a voice for Radio for his new job, I have no intention of letting him mean it.

Please treat my office like Waterloo Station. I'll try to see that the refreshment facilities are better but stop in on your way to places and talk to me about what you think.

My new phrase from Bill Clinton's campaign is that I don't want to be an 'in box' manager.

See you Monday. Liz.

Liz Forgan, Managing Director, BBC Radio[32]

THE HUMAN COST OF POOR MANAGEMENT

The style of managerial behaviour has an obvious and direct effect both on the well-being of staff and on their level of work performance. Managers decide the manner in which work duties and responsibilities are to be undertaken. Different styles of management may be appropriate in managing different people in different circumstances. And a more autocratic management may not *necessarily* be a bad thing.

However, the environment of the work organisation and the nature of the manager–subordinate relationship can cause tension and stress. Increasing attention is being given to the number of health problems that are classified as stress-related and affected by working conditions. It is important to remember both the effects on organisational performance *and* the potentially high human cost of inappropriate management.[33]

MANAGERIAL EFFECTIVENESS

The overall responsibility of management can be seen as the attainment of the given objectives of the organisation. Upon the attainment of its aims and objectives will rest the success and ultimate survival of the organisation. There is therefore a clear and important need for effective management. And this need is just as strong in public sector organisations as in private enterprise organisations. Indeed, it could be argued that in local government, for example, the accountability of public servants to elected members for their actions means that professional standards of management of the highest order are even more essential.[34] But whether in private or public sector organisations, managerial effectiveness is a difficult concept both to define and to measure.

Efficiency and effectiveness

Managerial efficiency can be distinguished from managerial effectiveness.

Efficiency is concerned with 'doing things right', and relates to inputs and what the manager does.

Effectiveness is concerned with 'doing the right things', and relates to outputs of the job and what the manager actually achieves.[35]

To be **efficient** the manager must attend therefore to the **input requirements of the job** – to clarification of objectives, planning, organisation, direction and control. But in order to be **effective**, the manager must give attention to **outputs of the job** – to performance in terms of such factors as obtaining best possible results in the important areas of the organisation, optimising use of resources, increasing profitability, and attainment of the aims and objectives of the organisation.

Effectiveness must be related to the achievement of some purpose, objective or task – to the performance of the process of management and the execution of work. Criteria for assessing the effectiveness of a manager should be considered in terms of measuring the results that the manager is intended to achieve. But **what is also important is the manner in which the manager achieves results and the effects on other people.** This may well influence effectiveness in the longer term. Managerial effectiveness results from a combination of personal attributes and dimensions of the manager's job in meeting the demands of the situation, and satisfying the requirements of the organisation.

MEASURES OF EFFECTIVENESS

Management involves getting work done through the co-ordinated efforts of other people. **Managers are most likely to be judged, not just on their own performance, but also on the results achieved by subordinate staff.** The manager's effectiveness may be assessed *in part*, therefore, by such factors as:

- the strength of motivation and morale of staff;
- the success of their training and development; and
- the creation of an organisational environment in which staff work willingly and effectively.

The difficulty is determining objective measurement of such factors. Some possible indication might be given by, for example:

- the level of staff turnover;
- the incidence of sickness;
- absenteeism;
- poor time-keeping; and
- accidents at work.

However, such figures are likely to be influenced also by broader organisational or environmental considerations, for example poor job security due to the economic climate, which are outside the direct control of the individual manager. In any case, there is the general question of the extent to which such figures bear a direct relationship to the actual performance of subordinate staff.

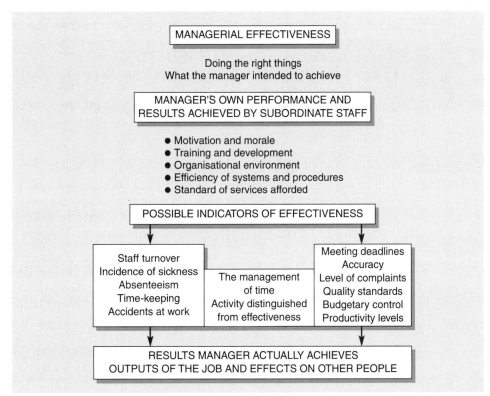

**Fig. 13.6
Possible indicators
of managerial
effectiveness**

Other criteria of effectiveness

Other criteria which may give some indication of managerial effectiveness include the efficiency of systems and procedures, and the standard of services afforded to other departments. Again, however, there is the question of how to determine objective measurement of such criteria.

For some management jobs it might be possible to identify more quantitative factors which *may* give an indication of managerial effectiveness, including:

- meeting important deadlines;
- accuracy of work carried out by the department, perhaps measured by the number of recorded errors;
- level of complaints received from superiors, other departments, customers or clients, suppliers, the public;
- adherence to quality standards, for example, the amount of scrap or waste material;
- keeping within agreed cost or budgetary control limits; and
- productivity. (*See* Fig. 13.6.)

THE MANAGEMENT OF TIME

Whatever the attributes or qualities of a successful manager, or the quality of sub-ordinate staff, one essential underlying criterion is the effective use of time. With many managers who complain that they do not have sufficient time it may be more a case that they have failed to organise themselves or their work properly. The most important members of staff to be managed are themselves.

Although it is currently a popular topic of attention, the importance of time management has long been recognised as an inherent feature of management. For example, *Drucker* (writing originally in 1955) refers to the importance of the time dimension through the concern of management with decisions for actions.[36] Drucker also refers to time as the limiting factor for effective executives. Time is a unique resource – you cannot rent, hire, buy or otherwise obtain more time. The supply of time is totally inelastic; time is totally irreplaceable and everything requires time.[37]

Effectiveness and activity

For many managers appearing always to be busy, a cluttered desk and a continual flurry of activity are outward signs of their effectiveness. The trouble is that such managers may be too busy 'doing' rather than **thinking about what they, and their staff, should be doing and how they should be doing it.** It is important therefore to distinguish effectiveness from activity. *Rees*, for example, suggests that:

> Activity-centred behaviour is in any case much more likely to spring from incompetence and/or insecurity rather than adroit political behaviour. This type of behaviour is likely to aggravate the position of the manager in the long run rather than ameliorate it.[38]

There are a number of suggested procedures and techniques for managing time[39] but the essential requirements of good time management are:

- clear objectives;
- careful forward planning;
- the definition of priorities and action; and
- the ability to delegate successfully.

An example of a 'mind map' for the management of time is presented in Fig. 13.7 on page 462.[40]

The need for balance

Despite growing interest in time management it should not be viewed in isolation from related activities of management such as leadership and delegation. For example, as we discussed in Chapter 8, a key aspect of managerial leadership is visibility. Time management needs to be balanced against potential benefits from maintaining an open-door policy or the 'MBWA' approach – Management By Walking About.[41] When making a conscious effort to find more time for themselves, managers need to take account of their availability for consultation with subordinates, superiors or colleagues; and ensuring effective processes of communication.

Manager's checklist

Stewart suggests that it is often salutary for managers to compare what they think they do against what happens in practice. Answers to the following questions will help managers decide what, if anything, they should check, and to review their effective management of time.[42]

1. Am I giving adequate attention to current activities, to reviewing the past and to planning for the future? In particular, am I giving enough thought to the future?
2. Am I dividing my time correctly between different aspects of my job? Is there, perhaps, one part of my job on which I spend too much of my time?
3. Have I changed what I am trying to do, and how I work to allow for the effects of changes in my work?
4. Am I certain that I am not doing any work that I ought to have delegated?
5. Who are the people that I ought to be seeing? Am I spending too much or too little time with any of them?
6. Do I organise my working day and week, as far as possible, according to priorities, or do I tend to deal with each problem as it turns up, or even as I think of it, without stopping to think whether there is something more important that I should be working on?
7. Am I able to complete a task, or am I constantly interrupted? If the latter, are all these interruptions an essential part of my work?

There are three questions that managers should ask of each of their activities.

- Should it be done at all?
- If so, when should it be done?
- Should it be delegated?

(The nature of delegation is discussed in Chapter 16.)

An example

An example of time management and encouragement for managers to improve their self-management is given in the following case study (starting on page 463).[43]

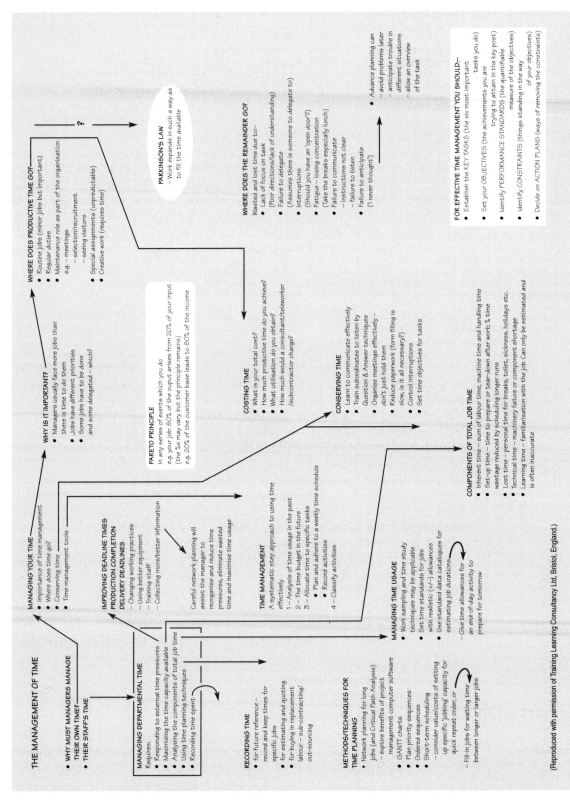

Fig. 13.7 Summary outline of the management of time

(Reproduced with permission of Training Learning Consultancy Ltd, Bristol, England.)

CASE STUDY

Chemical company

When, in the mid 1980s, Mike joined the Group as training manager, his aim was to establish a culture that would focus on serving the customer and encouraging employees to solve their own problems, and also help them to make their own decisions within their areas of work responsibility.

He remembers that operators at the company's process plants 'used to be expected to put their brains on the coat hanger when they came to work. Virtually, you couldn't close a pump without the work manager's approval.'

Supervisors, he recalls, were too ready to divert from their own priority work to do jobs that operators ought to be doing. The superintendents would spend time on problems well within the capabilities of the supervisors to solve, and would turn to the plant manager for help with their own problems.

There was a constant spiralling down, Mike says. This was tolerable if everyone reverted to their original positions and responsibilities when a crisis ended. But some plants were constantly in crisis. 'Everyone was looking after other people's jobs rather than their own.'

So, Mike, now the group's human resources manager, turned for help to the concept of time management. Importantly, he considered it as the warp and weft of the group's much larger training effort.

'I saw time management as an enabling technique,' he says, 'one that would interface with other courses such as assertiveness training while encouraging people to make the time to step back and think more clearly about their jobs.'

In the last two years the group has run 15 of Time/system's two-day courses at its headquarters for some 300 employees at home and abroad. Participants have ranged from plant managers to first line supervisors, and from scientists in the 400-strong technical division to technicians and administrative personnel.

Mike believes that linking the concept of time management to other elements of company training has proved highly successful, pointing to the results at a large plant near Hartlepool engaged in experimenting with a special process, to replace the existing process, currently accounting for 90 per cent of the company's production worldwide. The new process will radically reduce environmentally damaging effluent.

Mike confirms that there has been an improvement in work culture and practice at the plant.

At another location about 50 of the plant's 520 staff, at first-line supervisor level and above, have been on the time management course. Mike asserts that because supervisors now sit down to prioritise their time, they aren't so ready with reflex responses to operators' inessential requests for help. In effect, through their 'A' Time training, they have reassessed their own priorities.

When it comes to time management, extensive use is made of Time/system's planning books. David, plant manager, who carries his wherever he goes, uses the lunch hour to remind himself of his schedule for the rest of the day and to plan the following day's activities. Early each morning he convenes a meeting of his superintendents and supervisors, to review what has happened in the plant in the previous 24 hours.

He says that because so many people at supervisor level and above use a common format for their notes and planning, there is less chance of anything important being overlooked. And because there is not much need to refer back to files, the daily review and planning meetings are speeded up.

The job of John, at the central laboratory, is to provide mathematical and statistical support to the work of the technical division. 'I was astounded to discover,' he says, 'that it was possible to decide my own priorities, structure them into my forward planning and organise my work week around them.'

The course made him realise that much of his overwork was of his own making.

'I couldn't say "no" to requests for assistance from other departments. I imagined that if I turned people down they were going to be so aggrieved that they would never come back with another problem, and eventually I wouldn't have a reason for my existence.'

His own priority work focused on reaching a decision whether to build some computer software in-house for use in the plant in Malaysia, or whether to rely entirely on bought-in software packages. It was a decision which had to be made by the end of January.

To reduce interruptions to his 'A' Time he began saying 'no' – 'it wasn't as difficult as I had thought'. He even told one internal customer that he couldn't help him solve his problem for another three months.

Time management training has helped him to be more assertive, he insists. 'And because I couldn't turn every customer down, I also had to learn more effective delegation.'

Another 'backroom boy' who looked afresh at his working day, and became more assertive as a result, is David, who has been with the company more than 30 years.

He attended the training without high expectations. But it prompted him to analyse his job and he found that up to 40 per cent of his time was being spent talking with customers and responding to their needs. The other 60 per cent was devoted to long-term aims of improving the service his department offers, keeping up with new techniques and developing new methods.

That was satisfactory, he decided, so long as the ratio remained around 60/40. 'To keep it like that I began to query the difference between "urgent" and "important" when requests for attention came in. Every customer says his problem is important. But is it genuinely urgent?'

In a service department, as David points out, you have to respond to requests for service with a smile. 'But that doesn't mean abandoning your critical faculties, and failing to set priorities.'

'Time management training taught me that many of our problems were self-generated. Rather than devoting so much time reacting to the problems thrown up by the new computer system, we should have spent more time ensuring smooth administration.'

It comes down, as Mike suggests, to taking the time to think more clearly about the job, analyse it and set priorities. Time management is about making time, but also filling it productively.

(Reprinted with the permission of The Institute of Administrative Management.)

3-D MODEL OF MANAGERIAL BEHAVIOUR

However effectiveness is measured, managers are only likely to be effective if they adopt the most appropriate style of behaviour.

A development of the *Blake and Mouton* Managerial Grid, discussed earlier, is the three-dimensional (3-D) model of managerial behaviour suggested by *Reddin*.[44] By adding a third dimension of managerial effectiveness to task orientation and relationship orientation, the 3-D model identifies eight possible styles of managerial behaviour.

Task orientation (TO) is the extent to which the manager directs both personal and subordinates' efforts through planning, organisation and control.

Relationship orientation (RO) is dependent upon the manager's personal job relationships. This is characterised by consideration for subordinates' feelings, mutual trust and encouragement.

The combination of TO and RO determines the manager's basic style of behaviour. The four possible basic styles (*see* Fig. 13.8) are similar to those identified by Blake and Mouton in the Managerial Grid.

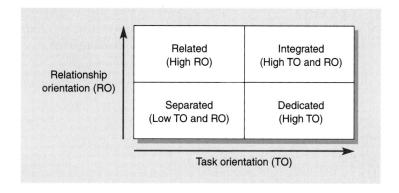

**Fig. 13.8
The four basic styles of managerial behaviour**

Apparent effectiveness and personal effectiveness

Each of these four basic styles of management can be effective or ineffective depending on the situation in which they are applied. **Effectiveness** is defined by Reddin as 'the extent to which a manager achieves the output requirements of his position . . . Managerial effectiveness has to be defined in terms of output rather than input, by what a manager achieves rather than by what he does'.

Reddin distinguishes managerial effectiveness from (i) apparent effectiveness, and (ii) personal effectiveness.

Apparent effectiveness is the extent to which the behaviour of the manager – for example punctuality, giving prompt answers, tidiness, making quick decisions and good public relations – gives the appearance of effectiveness. Such qualities may or may not be relevant to effectiveness.

Personal effectiveness is the extent to which the manager achieves personal objectives – for example power and prestige – rather than the objectives of the organisation.

Eight styles of managerial behaviour

Applying the third dimension of managerial effectiveness provides eight styles of managerial behaviour – four effective styles, which achieve output requirements, and four ineffective styles (*see* Fig. 13.9). For each of the basic styles – separated, dedicated, related or integrated – there is a more effective or less effective version. Effectiveness results from the appropriateness of a particular style of management to the demands of the situation in which it is applied. When one of the basic styles (for example 'separated') is adopted in an appropriate situation, a more effective style ('bureaucrat') results. When the basic style is adopted in an inappropriate situation, the result is a less effective style ('deserter').

The eight styles of management may be described briefly as follows.

More effective styles

(i) **Bureaucrat** – a low concern for both task and relationships. The manager adopting this style is seen as being interested mainly in rules and procedures to control the situation, and as conscientious.

(ii) **Benevolent autocrat** – a high concern for task and a low concern for relationships. Managers adopting this style know what they want and how to achieve it without causing resentment.

(iii) **Developer** – a high concern for relationships and a low concern for task. The manager adopting this style is seen as having implicit trust in people and concerned mainly with developing them as individuals.

(iv) **Executive** – a high concern for both task and relationships. The manager adopting this style is seen as a good motivator, sets high standards, treats people as individuals, and favours team management.

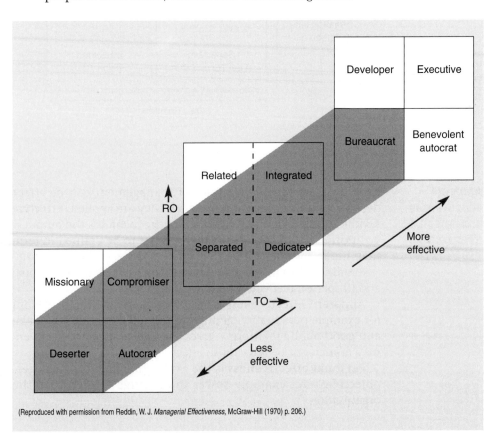

Fig. 13.9
The 3-D model of managerial effectiveness

(Reproduced with permission from Reddin, W. J. *Managerial Effectiveness*, McGraw-Hill (1970) p. 206.)

Less effective styles

(v) **Deserter** – low concern for both task and relationships in a situation where such behaviour is inappropriate. The manager lacks involvement and is passive or negative.

(vi) **Autocrat** – a high concern for task and a low concern for relationships in a situation where such behaviour is not appropriate. The manager is seen as lacking confidence in others, unpleasant, and interested only in the task in hand.

(vii) **Missionary** – a high concern for relationships and a low concern for task where such behaviour is inappropriate. The manager is seen as interested mainly in preserving harmony.

(viii) **Compromiser** – a high concern for both task and relationships in a situation requiring high concern for neither, or for only one orientation. The manager is seen as a poor decision-maker, too easily influenced by the pressures of the situation, and as avoiding immediate pressures and problems at the expense of maximising long-term output.

Appropriate style of behaviour

According to *Reddin's* 3-D theory, managerial effectiveness cannot be measured simply in terms of achieving production or relationships with other people. The manager must also be adaptable in adopting the appropriate style of behaviour which will determine effectiveness in achieving the output requirements of the job. Reddin has developed a 'management-style-diagnosis' test to identify styles of management and of organisations. The test comprises 64 paired statements which compare one style of management with another. From each pair of statements is selected the one statement which describes best the manager's behaviour in his or her present job. Analysis of the answers can help the manager to evaluate his or her own perceived style of management.

GENERAL CRITERIA OF MANAGERIAL EFFECTIVENESS

From a review of the work of a number of writers, *Langford* identifies four broad groups of criteria of managerial effectiveness, and a single overall criterion of effectiveness.[45]

- **The manager's work** – decision-making, problem-solving, innovation, management of time and handling information.
- **The manager himself/herself** – motivation, role perception, coping with stress/ambiguity, seniority, and average salary grade for age.
- **The manager's relationships with other people** – subordinates, superiors, peers and clients; handling conflict and leadership/power.
- **The manager as part of the organisation** – maintenance of the organisation, and technical and financial control.
- **Criterion of general effectiveness** – allocation of resources, achieving purpose, goal attainment, planning, organising, co-ordinating, controlling.

Langford found that the most frequently mentioned criterion was overall effectiveness, followed by relationships with subordinates. Next in order of importance were the criteria of decision-making, problem-solving, self-development of the manager and maintenance of the organisation. Coping with ambiguity and the handling of conflict were seen as relatively unimportant criteria, although Langford suggests this might be related to the circumstances at the time when the various works were written.

SYNOPSIS

■ It is the responsibility of managers to manage and to achieve results through the efforts of other people. This involves the effective management of human resources. The way in which managers exercise their authority and carry out their responsibilities is important. The style of management adopted, and the behaviour displayed towards subordinate staff, is likely to be conditioned by predispositions about people, human nature and work.

■ One means of describing different styles of management is the Managerial Grid, now republished as the Leadership Grid®, and the combination of concern for production and concern for people. The four corners and the centre of the Grid, together with two additional styles, provide seven basic combinations. Managers tend to have one dominant style of management, and many managers also have a 'back-up' style. A four-fold model of management systems is exploitive authoritative, benevolent authoritative, consultative, and participative group. These systems can be related to a profile of organisational characteristics.

■ Work by leading writers suggests that a participative style of management is more likely to harness effectively the human resources of an organisation. One particular style or system of management is Management by Objectives (MBO). Participation is inherent if MBO is to work well, and there is an assumption that most people will work willingly if given freedom of action to decide how best to achieve agreed objectives. MBO is potentially an attractive and rewarding style of management. However, there are a number of limitations and possible shortcomings.

■ There are many aspects to management but one essential ingredient of any successful manager is the ability to handle people effectively. It is important that managers have a highly developed sense of 'people perception' and understand the feelings of staff, and their needs and expectations. It is people who are being managed, and people should be considered in human terms. There are a number of basic, underlying philosophies which are likely to make for the successful management of people and lead to improved work performance.

■ There is a clear and important need for managerial effectiveness, which can be distinguished from managerial efficiency. Effectiveness is concerned with doing the right things and relates to outputs of the job and to what the manager actually achieves. The concept of managerial effectiveness, however, is difficult both to define and to measure. One essential underlying criterion is the effective use of time and distinguishing between activity and effectiveness.

■ The combination of task orientation and relationship orientation results in four basic styles of behaviour. Each of these styles can be effective or ineffective depending on the situation in which it is applied. Broad groupings of criteria of managerial effectiveness are: the manager's work, the manager himself/herself, relationships with other people; the manager as part of the organisation; together with an overall criterion of general effectiveness.

Review and discussion questions

1 Distinguish between different sets of attitudes and assumptions about people at work that might be held by managers. Give examples, preferably from your own experience, of how these different attitudes and assumptions might influence actual managerial behaviour.

2 Discuss the extent to which you believe the characteristics of a Theory Z environment could successfully be applied to work organisations in this country.

3 Using the Blake and Mouton Managerial Grid (now the Leadership Grid), identify your likely dominant style of behaviour in dealing with subordinate staff. In what situations might you need to adopt a back-up style of behaviour and what style is that likely to be?

4 Critically assess the value of Management by Objectives (MBO) as a means of improving organisational performance. In what ways might MBO be applied (or has MBO been applied) to your own organisation? What difficulties/problems might arise (or have arisen) from the introduction of MBO?

5 From your own experience, explain fully a situation which you believe demonstrates an effective way of dealing with subordinate staff. To what extent can you relate this situation to the application of theories or principles of management?

6 Discuss what you see as the most important considerations in adopting a people-centred approach to management. What do you understand by the culture of management?

7 How would you attempt to distinguish between an effective and an ineffective manager? Give specific examples of the criteria you would apply to assess the effectiveness of a particular managerial job of your choice.

8 Explain Reddin's 3-D model of managerial behaviour. Give a practical example of situations which demonstrate (i) a more effective style, and (ii) a less effective style.

Assignment 1

PRINCIPLE OF SUPPORTIVE RELATIONSHIPS QUESTIONNAIRE

To test whether a superior's (and the organisation's) behaviour is supportive, consider the following questions.

1 How much confidence and trust do you feel your superior has in you? How much do you have in your superior?

2 To what extent does your boss convey to you a feeling of confidence that you can do your job successfully? Does your boss expect the 'impossible' and fully believe you can and will do it?

3 To what extent is your superior interested in helping you to achieve and maintain a good income?

4 To what extent does your superior try to understand your problems and do something about them?

5 How much is your superior really interested in helping you with your personal and family problems?

6 How much help do you get from your superior in doing your work?
 (a) How much interest in training you and helping you learn better ways of doing your work?
 (b) How much help for you to solve your problems constructively – not telling you the answer but helping you think through your problems?
 (c) To what extent does your superior see that you get the supplies, budget, equipment, etc., you need to do your job well?

7 To what extent is your superior interested in helping you get the training which will assist you in being promoted?

8 To what extent does your superior try to keep you informed about matters related to your job?

9 How fully does your superior share information with you about the company, its financial condition, earnings, etc., or keep such information to himself/herself?

10 Does your superior ask your opinion when a problem comes up which involves your work? Does your superior value your ideas and seek them and endeavour to use them?

11 Is your superior friendly and easily approached?

12 To what extent is your superior generous in the credit and recognition given to others for the accomplishments and contributions rather than seeking to claim all the credit personally?

 ## Assignment 2

In self-selecting groups of three or four visit a work organisation of your choice, preferably one that is well known to at least one member of your group.

(i) Using **Likert's short form of profile of organisational characteristics**, investigate the organisational variables and circle what you believe to be the most accurate answer for each of the 18 questions.

(ii) Make clear any necessary assumptions, and where possible give brief supporting reasons for your choice of answers.

(iii) Summarise the extent to which your answers suggest a clear inclination towards one particular model of management system.

(iv) Explain the conclusions you draw from your investigation and the pattern of your answers.

 Assignment 3

(i) Give your views on Liz Forgan's open letter of introduction to BBC Radio staff (page 457). What would be your reaction to such a letter from a new managing director (or similar position) in your own organisation?

(ii) Meet in small groups to share and discuss your views. What conclusions do you draw?

 C A S E S T U D Y 1

The library in Labworth Street is located in an inner city area of the local authority. Whilst small and in rather old premises, it has been popular over the years with residents of the local community, who have looked to it as a community focal point. The library is also well thought of by local authority officials.

The staff has consisted of the Chief Librarian, four qualified Librarians and three Library Assistants, all of whom have worked well together with a high degree of mutual co-operation by, for example, voluntarily exchanging shifts to accommodate the domestic situations of a colleague. The staff have often curtailed their breaks when the needs of library clients have required it. The library has been open on Monday and Friday from 9:00 to 12:00 and 2:00 to 6:00. When closed, time has been spent on staff training, administrative investigations and book restocking. Regular returns have also had to be made to the local authority as part of the latter's information gathering and performance monitoring role.

That was the situation up to six months ago, when a new person, Rita Jones, was appointed in charge of the library. She is determined to make the library service even more efficient, believing that such a strategy is absolutely necessary in a climate of debate over the library service being considered for transfer to the private sector.

At the outset she felt that the methods by which the staff operated had to be changed. She instructed staff that the informal switching of shifts had to cease and that any change in rosters had to be approved by her in advance. She had noticed that staff used to spend a considerable amount of time talking to the public socially, rather than just on matters concerned with the library service, and instructions were issued that this had to cease: 'Time could not be wasted on informal discussion.' More effort also had to be given to improving the information flow to the local authority, to provide evidence of the library's efficiency.

Over a relatively short period of time, the atmosphere within the library changed. The staff seemed to lose some of their enthusiasm, manifested in late arrival for work. On some occasions the library did not open on time because of confusion over shift patterns. The incidence of days off sick increased, and relations between staff deteriorated as they worked purely in accordance with their job descriptions. The overall attitude of the staff impacted on the quality of service to customers, who began complaining to local councillors of poor service from library staff – such as long queues at the desk, abrupt service at the inquiry point, books not being on the correct shelves, and inefficient operation of the book reservation system. The reputation of the library and the use of services was clearly in decline.

In response to concerns expressed by officials, Rita Jones explained that she was endeavouring to improve the system in the library and that inevitably there were some short-term problems. She believed that, in the long run, the situation would improve. She recognised that, in spite of financial constraints, the budget for stock and staffing costs was adequate.

In order to assist Rita Jones in tackling the problems arising in her organisation, prepare for her a memorandum of advice clearly setting out the management issues you see arising from the case, and the related alternative actions she might take to resolve these matters.

CASE STUDY 2

Tony Jackson was first employed in a busy branch office of a building society on a Youth Training Scheme but left after two years because there was no permanent position available at that time. However, nine months later and following a period of continual rapid growth in business a new position was established in the branch. Jackson applied and got the job. After speaking on the telephone to the personnel department at head office, Mary Rogers the branch manager told her staff that she had always got on well with Tony Jackson. He seemed very bright, did everything asked of him and never caused her any trouble.

Jane Taylor had been employed with the branch for the past four years, since leaving sixth form college. Her main duties were those of a cashier and assisting with mortgage advance accounts. Two weeks before Jackson was due to start work Mary Rogers asked to see her.

'From now on, Jane, I would like you to act as senior branch assistant. I need someone to take some of the weight off my shoulders. Your main task will be to be responsible for the quality and accuracy of the work of the staff and to look after things when I'm not here.'

'Well...er...thank you, Miss Rogers. This is unexpected. It sounds exciting, but I wonder if....'

'Oh, I know you can manage, Jane,' continued Mary Rogers. 'You know I tend to rely on you already. Anyway I've arranged for you to attend a refresher course at head office the week after next. It's all about our systems and procedures, and new ideas on automated technology, I think they called it. I am sure you will cope. And I know the extra money for the job will be helpful, won't it?'

'Yes, that's true enough – the money will certainly be helpful – but ...'

'Good, that's fine then. I'm glad we got that settled. Now you must excuse me,' said Mary Rogers standing up. 'I have to attend to these returns due at head office by the end of next week. Then I have some new ideas for introducing even more business and providing a detailed analysis schedule of advances that I am working on. And I am due to see Pat Gray at the solicitors some time. Always plenty to do, Jane. We must have another chat sometime.'

As Jane left the manager's office she reflected upon the extra money. With the new house and a large mortgage it would by very welcome.

Approximately two months later

Jane Taylor is speaking with Mary Rogers in her office.

'I am sorry to trouble you, Miss Rogers, but it seems that Tony Jackson and I may have a clash of personalities.'

'What do you mean, Jane?' asked Mary Rogers.

'Putting my own feelings to one side, I made a conscious effort not to let it affect my work or responsibilities. But he does not accept jobs I give him without a fuss and tries to pass his work onto the YTS. He also tries to embarrass other members of staff when they are serving customers,' explained Jane.

'How do you mean he embarrasses you?'

'Among other things, he shouts to other assistant at the far end of the office and refers to customers by nicknames to try and make us laugh.'

'Oh dear, well we can't have that, can we now, Jane? What have you done about it?'

'I did try to tell him about it and told him not to be so stupid and childish, but it didn't seem to do any good.'

'All right, Jane, you had better leave it to me,' sighed Mary Rogers. 'I suppose I had better see what I can do. In the meanwhile I think you should try to learn to exercise your authority more.'

Lunchtime, three weeks later

Jane Taylor is with a friend in a local public house.

'What's the matter, Jane? You seem a bit down lately. You're not still annoyed about that assistant, are you?' asked the friend.

'It's not just that, but, oh I don't know...but, yes it does upset me,' replied Jane. 'You remember I told you about me seeing the branch manager; well, afterwards I had another go at Jackson. I told him to concentrate on his own work, but this is often below standard and when I showed him his mistakes he just said, "What do you expect, I'm only human." '

'But you didn't just leave it like that?' inquired the friend.

'No, a couple of days later to try and overcome the problem I took him to the staff kitchen. I told him we all had to work together and as assistant manager I had a responsibility to keep the office running smoothly, and that an effort should be made for all of us to get on with each other. If not, I would take the matter further and report it to Miss Rogers. He just shrugged his shoulders and said, "Yeah, all right, let's go and see Mary."'

'So then what happened?' asked the friend expectantly.

'His reaction was unexpected. It threw me a bit. I think I said something like "when I'm ready" and walked away. Mind you, his work did seem to improve for a time. But then last week I told him I needed his help with this urgent job and he got all huffy with me. When I told him it was about time he grew up and stopped behaving like that he just said, "If you treat me like a piece of dirt, I'll behave like a piece of dirt" or words to that effect.'

'So did you go to see Miss Rogers, then?' the friend asked.

'I was going to. But, no, not yet. I know I really should go and see her again sometime before too long,' replied Jane. 'Anyhow, sorry, must dash now. We are still so busy at work – business seems to be growing all the time. See you again sometime.'

Later that same week

Mary Rogers is on the telephone to head office.

'...By the way, I have a member of staff we appointed who I think would benefit from a reminder about the importance of good supervision. I see you are running a course on Human Relations next month. Can you do your usual perfect organisation and fit her in? At least we can suggest she might like to attend. She can be a bit prickly at times but I am sure with all your experience you will know how to use the best words when you write to her.'

Ten days later

Jane Taylor meets her friend in the public house again.

'I'm glad to see you, Veronica. I was hoping I might find you here,' Jane said to her friend.

'What's up, work still troubling you?' asked Veronica. 'I seem to remember you were going to sort things out with the manager. What did she do about that assistant of yours?'

'Yes, I was thinking of going to see her, but then Miss Rogers called me in to see her. She said that she had spoken with Tony Jackson and explained that as senior assistant I had more experience and authority than Tony, and that he should do as he was asked from now on.'

'Good! Quite right too. That's the way it should be,' said Veronica. 'So what's the matter now?'

'Well his concentration and work had appeared to improve again but his attitude got even worse. Then this last week Miss Rogers has been off sick and I am temporarily in charge of the office once again. I usually distribute the work equally in the morning and then carry out the branch manager's duties. Sometimes work comes in during the day and I distribute that straight away. When I leave work in Jackson's tray he usually "tuts" or makes some sort of sarcastic comment as I am returning to the manager's office. It is so unsettling and you can sense an unpleasant atmosphere in the whole office. And it looks like another assistant, Graham Wilkins, is thinking of leaving. That would be a pity. He is so good at his job. I don't know what to do next. Oh, and I have also been told about a course on management skills in a couple of weeks at head office. I suppose I shall have to go.'

(i) Discuss the various issues of managerial behaviour and related matters raised by this case study.

(ii) Explain what actions you think should be taken in order to help improve the situation. Give supporting reasons.

Notes and references

1. McGregor, D. *The Human Side of Enterprise*, Penguin (1987).
2. Sieff, M. (Lord Sieff of Brimpton) *Management The Marks & Spencer Way*, Fontana Collins (1991) pp. 144–5.
3. Townsend, R. *Further Up the Organisation*, Coronet Books (1985) pp. 168–9.
4. See, for example: Mullins, L. J. 'Management and Managerial Behaviour', *International Journal of Hospitality Management*, vol. 4, no. 1, 1985, pp. 39–41.
5. Caplan, E. H. *Management Accounting and Behavioral Science*, Addison-Wesley (1971).
6. Ouchi, W. G. *Theory Z: How American Business Can Meet the Japanese Challenge*, Addison-Wesley (1981) p. 4.
7. Tse, K. K. *Marks & Spencer*, Pergamon Press (1985).
8. Blake, R. R. and Mouton, J. S. *The Managerial Grid III*, Gulf Publishing Company (1985).
9. Blake, R. R. and McCanse, A. A. *Leadership Dilemmas – Grid Solutions*, Gulf Publishing Company (1991).
10. Lester, T. 'Taking Guard on the Grid', *Management Today*, March 1991, pp. 93–6.
11. Likert, R. *New Patterns of Management*, McGraw-Hill (1961).
12. Likert, R. and Likert, J. G. *New Ways of Managing Conflict*, McGraw-Hill (1976).
13. Likert, R. *The Human Organization*, McGraw-Hill (1967) p. 138.
14. Drucker, P. F. *The Practice of Management*, Heinemann Professional (1989).
15. Odiorne, G. S. *Management by Objectives*, Pitman (1965) pp. 55–6. See also: Odiorne, G. S. *MBO II: A System of Managerial Leadership for the 80's*, Second edition, Pitman (1979).
16. Humble, J. W. *Management by Objectives*, Management Publications Limited for the British Institute of Management (1972).
17. Carroll, S. J. and Tosi, H. L. *Management by Objectives: Applications and Research*, Macmillan (1973) p. 16.
18. For a discussion on the way managers react to MBO, see: Jamieson, B. D. 'Behavioral Problems with Management by Objectives', in Huseman, B. D. and Carroll, A. B. *Readings in Organizational Behavior*, Allyn and Bacon (1979).
19. Kondrasuk, J. N. 'Studies in MBO Effectiveness', *Academy of Management Review*, vol. 6, no. 3, 1981, pp. 419–30.
20. Freemantle, D. 'The People Factor', *Management Today*, December 1985, pp. 68–71.
21. Kane, J. S. and Freeman, K. A. 'MBO and Performance Appraisal: A Mixture That's Not a Solution', *Personnel*, vol. 63, no. 12, December 1986, pp. 26–36.
22. See, for example: Blanchard, K. and Johnson, S. *The One Minute Manager*, Willow Books (1983).
23. Freemantle, D. 'The People Factor', *Management Today*, December 1985, p. 68.
24. See, for example: Goss, D. 'Investing in People: Human Resource Development and Organisational Change', in Adam-Smith, D. and Peacock, A. *Cases in Organisational Behaviour*, Pitman (1994) pp. 288–94.
25. Mullins, L. J. 'Managing With and Through People', *Transactions*, Portsmouth Business School, vol. 2, no. 2, Summer 1991, pp. 1–18.
26. Peters, T. J. and Waterman, R. H. *In Search of Excellence*, Harper and Row (1982) p. 238.
27. Adams, J. S. 'Injustice in Social Exchange' abridged in Steers, R. M. and Porter, L. W. *Motivation and Work Behavior*, Second edition, McGraw-Hill (1979) pp. 107–24.
28. Waterman, R. *The Frontiers of Excellence*, Nicholas Brealey (1994).
29. Ash, M. K. *On People Management*, Macdonald & Co. (1985).
30. *Ibid.* p. xix.
31. Roddick, A. *Body and Soul*, Ebury Press (1991) p. 109.
32. *Daily Mail*, 2 February 1993.
33. See, for example: Rockledge, S. 'The Human Cost of Bad Management', *Administrator*, vol. 7, no. 1, January 1987, p. 13.

34. Charsley, W. F. 'Effective Management – So You Think You've got it Right?' *British Journal of Administrative Management*, vol. 1, November 1986, pp. 11–12. See also: Allen, T. 'Hands Off Local Government', *Management Today*, September 1993, p. 5.

35. See, for example: Drucker, P. F. *People and Performance*, Heinemann (1977).

36. Drucker, P. F. *The Practice of Management*, Heinemann Professional (1989).

37. Drucker, P. F. *The Effective Executive*, Heinemann Professional (1988).

38. Rees, W. D. *The Skills of Management*, Third edition, Routledge (1991) p. 25.

39. For example, see: Johns, T. *Perfect Time Management*, Century Business (1993).

40. Training Learning Consultancy Ltd., Bristol, England.

41. Coates, J. 'It is Legitimate to be Unavailable', *Industrial and Commercial Training*, vol. 22, no. 5, 1990, pp. 8–11; for a fuller account of 'MBWA', see: Peters, T. J. and Austin, N. K. *A Passion for Excellence*, William Collins (1985).

42. Stewart, R. *Managers and Their Jobs*, Second edition, Macmillan (1988) p. 123.

43. Butcher, D. 'Personal Productivity is a Matter of Timing', *The British Journal of Administrative Management*, October 1991, pp. 19–20.

44. Reddin, W. J. *Managerial Effectiveness*, McGraw-Hill (1970).

45. Langford, V. 'Managerial Effectiveness: A Review of the Literature', in Brodie, M. and Bennett, R. (eds) *Perspectives of Managerial Effectiveness*, Thames Valley Regional Management Centre (1979).

Part 6

ORGANISATIONAL PROCESSES

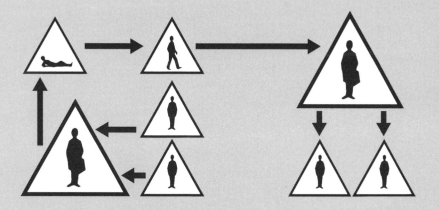

14 THE NATURE OF WORK MOTIVATION

The relationship between the organisation and its members is governed by what motivates them to work and the fulfilment they derive from it. The manager needs to understand how to elicit the co-operation of staff and direct their performance to achieving the goals and objectives of the organisation. The manager must know how best to motivate staff so that they work willingly and effectively.

Learning objectives

To:

- Explain the meaning and underlying concept of motivation;

- Identify main types of needs and expectations of people at work;

- Explain possible reactions to frustration at work;

- Outline different approaches to work motivation;

- Explain the nature of different theories of motivation;

- Examine main theories of motivation and evaluate their relevance to particular work situations;

- Appreciate the complex nature of work motivation.

Worth thinking about

'Why all this fuss over motivation? Motivating people is easy – I was taught that if you are not motivated you are dead.' . . . 'Yes, but motivating people to work to the best of their abilities and directing their efforts to the goals of the organisation is the real issue – and this is certainly not always easy.'

THE MEANING OF MOTIVATION

The study of motivation is concerned, basically, with why people behave in a certain way. In general terms, motivation can be described as the direction and persistence of action. It is concerned with why people choose a particular course of action in preference to others, and why they continue with a chosen action, often over a long period, and in the face of difficulties and problems.[1]

From a review of motivation theory, *Mitchell* identifies four common characteristics which underlie the definition of motivation.[2]

- **Motivation is typified as an individual phenomenon.** Every person is unique and all the major theories of motivation allow for this uniqueness to be demonstrated in one way or another.
- **Motivation is described, usually, as intentional.** Motivation is assumed to be under the worker's control, and behaviours that are influenced by motivation, such as effort expended, are seen as choices of action.
- **Motivation is multifaceted.** The two factors of greatest importance are: (i) what gets people activated (arousal); and (ii) the force of an individual to engage in desired behaviour (direction or choice of behaviour).
- **The purpose of motivational theories is to predict behaviour.** Motivation is not the behaviour itself, and it is not performance. Motivation concerns action, and the internal and external forces which influence a person's choice of action.

On the basis of these characteristics, Mitchell defines motivation as 'the degree to which an individual wants and chooses to engage in certain specified behaviours'.

Underlying concept of motivation

The underlying concept of motivation is some driving force within individuals by which they attempt to achieve some goal in order to fulfil some need or expectation. This concept gives rise to the basic motivational model, which is illustrated in Fig. 14.1.

People's behaviour is determined by what motivates them. Their performance is a product of both ability level and motivation.

Performance = function (ability × motivation)

Therefore, if the manager is to improve the work of the organisation, attention must be given to the level of motivation of its members. The manager must also encourage staff to direct their efforts (their driving force) towards the successful attainment of the goals and objectives of the organisation.

**Fig. 14.1
A simplified
illustration of the
basic motivational
model**

But what is this driving force? What are people's needs and expectations, and how do they influence behaviour and performance at work? Motivation is a complex subject, it is a very personal thing, and it is influenced by many variables. Individuals have a variety of changing, and often conflicting, needs and expectations which they attempt to satisfy in a number of different ways.

NEEDS AND EXPECTATIONS AT WORK

These various needs and expectations can be categorised in a number of ways, for example the simple divisions into physiological and social motives, or into intrinsic and extrinsic motivation.

Extrinsic motivation is related to 'tangible' rewards such as salary and fringe benefits, security, promotion, contract of service, the work environment and conditions of work. Such tangible rewards are often determined at the organisational level and may be largely outside the control of individual managers.

Intrinsic motivation is related to 'psychological' rewards such as the opportunity to use one's ability, a sense of challenge and achievement, receiving appreciation, positive recognition, and being treated in a caring and considerate manner. The psychological rewards are those that can usually be determined by the actions and behaviour of individual managers.[3]

Broad classification for motivation to work

As a starting point, the following is a useful, broad, three-fold classification for the motivation to work[4] (*see* Fig. 14.2):

- **Economic rewards** – such as pay, fringe benefits, pension rights, material goods and security. This is an **instrumental** orientation to work and concerned with 'other things'.
- **Intrinsic satisfaction** – which is derived from the nature of the work itself, interest in the job, and personal growth and development. This is a **personal** orientation to work and concerned with 'oneself'.
- **Social relationships** – such as friendships, group working, and the desire for affiliation, status and dependency. This is a **relational** orientation to work and concerned with 'other people'.

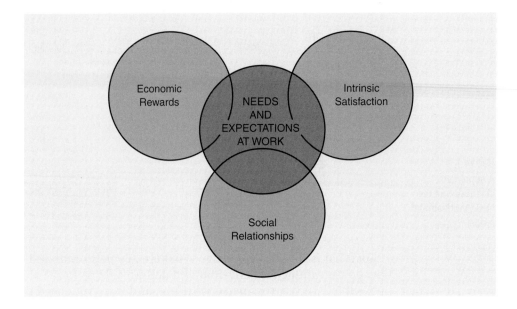

Fig. 14.2
Needs and
expectations of
people at work

A person's motivation, job satisfaction and work performance will be determined by the comparative strength of these sets of needs and expectations, and the extent to which they are fulfilled. For example, some people may make a deliberate choice to forgo intrinsic satisfaction and social relationships (particularly in the short term or in the earlier years of their working life) in return for high economic rewards. Other people are happy to accept comparatively lower economic rewards in favour of a job which has high intrinsic satisfaction and/or social relationships.

The
psychological
contract

In addition to the above categories, the motivation to work is also influenced by the concept of the 'psychological contract', which was discussed in Chapter 1. The psychological contract involves a series of expectations between the individual member and the organisation. These expectations are not defined formally, and although the individual member and the organisation may not be consciously aware of the expectations, their relationship is still affected by these expectations.

FRUSTRATION-INDUCED BEHAVIOUR

If a person's motivational driving force is blocked before reaching a desired goal, there are two possible sets of outcomes: constructive behaviour or frustration. (*See* Fig. 14.3.)

Constructive
behaviour

Constructive behaviour is a positive reaction to the blockage of a desired goal and can take two main forms: problem-solving or restructuring.

- **Problem-solving** is the removal of the barrier; for example, repairing a damaged machine, or by-passing an uncooperative superior.
- **Restructuring**, or compromise, is the substitution of an alternative goal, although such a goal may be of a lower order; for example, taking an additional part-time job because of failure to be promoted to a higher grading.

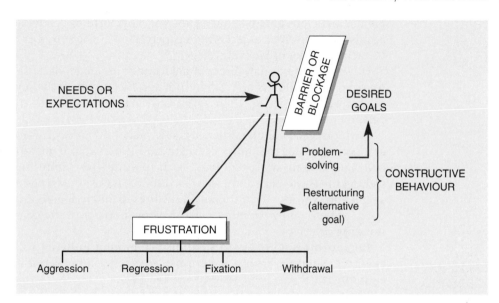

**Fig. 14.3
A basic model
of frustration**

Note: Even if a person engages in constructive behaviour in response to a barrier or blockage it could be said that the person was 'frustrated', if only mildly or in the short term, in an attempt to satisfy a desired goal. However, the term frustration is usually interpreted as applying to **negative responses** to a barrier or blockage which prevents satisfaction of a desired goal.

**Frustration
(negative
responses)**

**Fig. 14.4
An example
of displaced
aggression!**

Frustration is a negative response to the blockage of a desired goal and results in a defensive form of behaviour. There are many possible reactions to frustration caused by the failure to achieve a desired goal. These can be summarised under four broad headings: aggression; regression; fixation; withdrawal.[5] However, these categories are not mutually exclusive. Most forms of frustration-induced behaviour at work are a combination of aggression, regression and fixation.

Aggression is a physical or verbal attack on some person or object; for example, striking a supervisor, rage or abusive language, destruction of equipment or docu-

(Cartoon by Annie Tempest reproduced with the permission of Solo Syndication Limited from the *Daily Mail*, 26 February 1988. Copyright © Mail Newspapers plc.)

483

ments, malicious gossip about a superior. This form of behaviour may be directed against the person or object which is perceived as the source of frustration, that is the actual barrier or blocking agent.

However, where such direct attack cannot be made, because, for example, the source of frustration is not clear or not specific, or where the source is feared, such as a powerful superior, then aggression may be displaced towards some other person or object.

With **displaced aggression** the person may find an easier, safer person or object as a scapegoat for the outlet of frustration; for example, picking arguments with colleagues, being short-tempered with subordinates, shouting at the cleaners or kicking the waste-paper bin. (*See* Fig. 14.4.) A more constructive form of displaced aggression is working off frustrated feelings through demanding physical work or sport, or perhaps by shouting/cursing when alone or in the company of an understanding colleague.

Regression is reverting to a childish or more primitive form of behaviour; for example, sulking, crying, tantrums, or kicking a broken machine or piece of equipment.

Fixation is persisting in a form of behaviour which has no adaptive value and continuing to repeat actions which have no positive results; for example, the inability to accept change or new ideas, repeatedly trying a machine which clearly will not work, insisting on applying for promotion even though not qualified for the job.

Withdrawal is apathy, giving up or resignation; for example, arriving at work late and leaving early, sickness and absenteeism, refusal to accept responsibility, avoiding decision-making, passing work over to colleagues, or leaving the job altogether.

Factors influencing frustration

Among the factors which determine an individual's reaction to frustration are:

- the level and potency of need (*see*, for example, Maslow's theory of motivation, discussed below);
- the degree of attachment to the desired goal;
- the strength of motivation;
- the perceived nature of the barrier or blocking agent; and
- the personality characteristics of the individual.

It is important that managers attempt to reduce potential frustration through, for example:

- effective recruitment, selection and socialisation;
- training and development;
- job design and work organisation;
- equitable personnel policies;
- recognition and rewards;
- effective communications;
- participative styles of management;
- attempting to understand the individual's perception of the situation.

APPROACHES TO MOTIVATION AT WORK

The development of different approaches to organisation and management has highlighted the changing concept of motivation at work.[6]

Economic needs motivation

Earlier writers, such as *F. W. Taylor*, believed in economic needs motivation. Workers would be motivated by obtaining the highest possible wages through working in the most efficient and productive way. Performance was limited by physiological fatigue. For Taylor, motivation was a comparatively simple issue – what the workers wanted from their employers more than anything else was high wages.[7] This approach is **the rational–economic concept of motivation.**

Social concept of motivation

The **human relations** writers, however, demonstrated that people go to work to satisfy a range of different needs, and not simply for monetary reward. They emphasised the importance of the social needs of individuals, and gave recognition to the work organisation as a social organisation. This was illustrated, for example, in the Hawthorne experiments. The human relations approach to organisation and management led to **the social concept of motivation.**

The **systems approach** also supports the social concept of motivation. The socio-technical system is concerned with the interactions between both the psychological and social factors, and the needs and demands of people; and the structural and technical requirements of the organisation. The longwall coal-mining study, for example, demonstrated the importance of redesigning work in a manner which provides opportunities for teamwork and social interaction.

Self-actualisation

The findings of the Hawthorne experiments, and the subsequent attention to the social organisation and theories of individual motivation, gave rise to the work of the neo-human relations writers. These writers adopted a more psychological orientation to motivation. Greater attention was focused on the content and meaning of the task, and attempts to make work more intrinsically satisfying. The major focus of concern was the personal adjustment of the individual within the work situation. This approach is **the self-actualisation concept of motivation.**

Complex-person concept of motivation

The **contingency approach** to organisation and management takes the view that there are a large number of variables, or situational factors, which influence organisational performance. Contingency theory is concerned more with differences between organisations than with similarities. Managers must be adaptable, and vary their behaviour according to the particular situation, and the different needs and motivations of staff. The varying situational factors together with the complicated nature of human behaviour lead to **the complex-person concept of motivation.**

Why the mystery of motivation?

An interesting, if somewhat cynical, viewpoint on approaches to motivation is put forward by *Ritti*, who suggests that managers do act on what they know.

> Truth to tell, we know a good deal about human motivation. And most of what we know is probably correct. Then why the mystery of motivation? The answer is simply that we don't act on what we know. Frederick Winslow Taylor put his finger squarely on the problem at the turn of the century. Taylor said that if management would only show workers how to do the job better, and then share the

return of a better job with them, there would be no problem. Still, he lamented, management will never do that, for fear of driving wages up. And for the most part, he was right. So it is that the most popular schemes for raising levels of motivation all promise you can get something for nothing, a kind a motivational perpetual motion. Stress the intrinsic motivators (these don't include money, naturally), enrich the job, allow participation in decisions. In short, do everything but what Taylor recommended.[8]

INFLUENCES ON MOTIVATION

A major determinant of behaviour is the particular situation in which individual workers find themselves. Motivation varies over time and according to circumstances. It is often most acute for people at a mid-career position, and especially for those who find opportunities for further advancement or promotion are blocked.

The complex nature of motivation is supported by the work of *Vroom*. Citing more than 500 research investigations he concludes that there is no all-embracing theory of motivation to work.[9] Differences in patterns of motivation are illustrated by *Hunt*, who has developed average 'goal profiles' showing the relative importance of different categories of needs for people in different occupations, and changes in profiles at different stages for an average manager.[10]

Differences among cultures

In the same way that age and the type of job influence a person's motivation, Hunt also draws attention to how differences among cultures affect the way people prioritise their goals. Managers in nine countries were asked to rank six goal categories in terms of their importance to them now (*see* Fig. 14.5). The goal categories were:

- **comfort** (including primary needs and drives, and a comfortable lifestyle);
- **structure** (including financial security and certainty);
- **relationships** (including love, warmth and friendships);
- **recognition** (including status and praise);
- **power** (including control and authority); and
- **autonomy/creativity/growth** (including self-actualisation or self-fulfilment).

The results indicate clear differences among the samples, although Hunt acknowledges that it is less clear whether these are national culture differences, differences in the use of language, and/or corporate culture influences. Cross-cultural differences are often subtle and impressionistic rather than obvious.

THEORIES OF MOTIVATION

There are many competing theories which attempt to explain the nature of motivation. These theories are all at least partially true, and all help to explain the behaviour of certain people at certain times. However, **the search for a generalised theory of motivation at work appears a vain quest.** Nevertheless, any theory or study which aids an understanding of how best to motivate people at work must be useful.

	High mean ranking	Low mean ranking
Comfort	1. Spain 2. UK/US 3. France	1. Belgium 2. Sweden 3. Netherlands
Structure	1. UK 2. France 3. Switzerland	1. Netherlands 2. US 3. Sweden
Relationships	1. Sweden 2. Netherlands 3. Germany/Spain	1. UK 2. US 3. Italy
Recognition	1. Italy 2. US 3. UK	1. Sweden 2. Netherlands 3. Spain
Power	1. Germany 2. US 3. France	1. Spain 2. Sweden 3. Netherlands
Autonomy/creativity/growth	1. Sweden 2. US/UK 3. Netherlands	1. Spain 2. Italy 3. France

**Fig. 14.5
Cross-cultural
goal differences**

N = 5500 managers

(Reproduced with permission from Hunt, J. W. *Managing People at Work: A Manager's Guide to Behaviour in Organisations*, Third edition, McGraw-Hill (1992) p. 37.)

All managers have a duty to motivate their teams. Motivated people take more pride in their jobs and work better. But many managers don't know how to motivate their staff.[11]

It is because of the complexity of motivation, and the fact that there is no single answer to what motivates people to work well, that the different theories are important to the manager. They show there are many motives which influence people's behaviour and performance. Collectively, the different theories provide a framework within which to direct attention to the problem of how best to motivate staff to work willingly and effectively.

It is important to emphasise, however, that these various theories are not conclusive. They all have their critics (this is particularly true of the content theories of motivation), or have been subject to alternative findings which purport to contradict the original ideas. Many of these theories were not intended, originally, to have the significance that some writers have subsequently placed upon them. It is always easy to quote an example which appears to contradict any generalised observation on what motivates people to work. However, these different theories provide a basis for study and discussion, and for review of the most effective motivational style. (*See* Fig. 14.6.)

The manager, therefore, must judge the relevance of these different theories, how best to draw upon them, and how they might effectively be applied in particular work situations. The manager should be aware of at least the main theories of motivation.

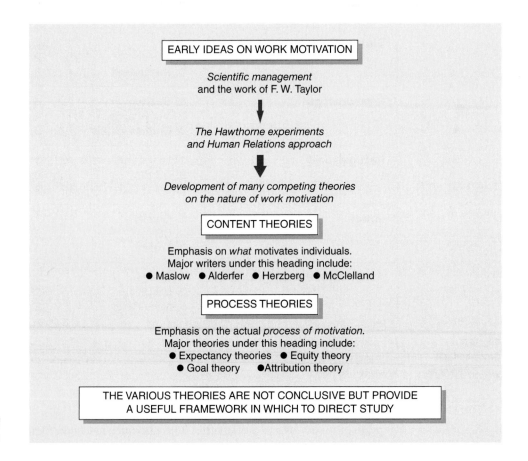

Fig. 14.6
An overview of main theories of work motivation

Content theories and process theories

The usual approach to the study of motivation is through an understanding of internal cognitive processes – that is, what people feel and how they think. This understanding should help the manager to predict likely behaviour of staff in given situations. These different cognitive theories of motivation are usually divided into two contrasting approaches: content theories and process theories.

Content theories attempt to explain those specific things which actually motivate the individual at work. These theories are concerned with identifying people's needs and their relative strengths, and the goals they pursue in order to satisfy these needs. Content theories place emphasis on **what motivates.**

Process theories attempt to identify the relationship among the dynamic variables which make up motivation. These theories are concerned more with **how** behaviour is initiated, directed and sustained. Process theories place emphasis on the **actual process of motivation.** These theories are discussed later in this chapter.

CONTENT THEORIES OF MOTIVATION

Major content theories of motivation include:

- *Maslow's* hierarchy of needs model;
- *Alderfer's* modified need hierarchy model;
- *Herzberg's* two-factor theory; and
- *McClelland's* achievement motivation theory.

MASLOW'S HIERARCHY OF NEEDS THEORY

A useful starting point is the work of *Maslow*, and his theory of individual development and motivation, published originally in 1943.[12] Maslow's basic proposition is that people are wanting beings, they always want more, and what they want depends on what they already have. He suggests that human needs are arranged in a series of levels, a hierarchy of importance.

The hierarchy ranges through five levels, from, at the lowest level, physiological needs, through safely needs, love needs, and esteem needs, to the need for self-actualisation at the highest level. The hierarchy may be shown as a series of steps, but is usually displayed in the form of a pyramid (Fig. 14.7). This is an appropriate form of illustration as it implies a thinning out of needs as people progress up the hierarchy.

- **Physiological needs.** These include homeostasis (the body's automatic efforts to retain normal functioning) such as satisfaction of hunger and thirst, the need for oxygen and to maintain temperature regulation. Also sleep, sensory pleasures, activity, maternal behaviour, and arguably sexual desire.
- **Safety needs.** These include safety and security, freedom from pain or threat of physical attack, protection from danger or deprivation, the need for predictability and orderliness.

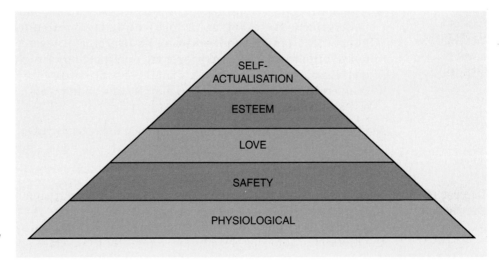

**Fig. 14.7
Maslow's hierarchy
of needs model**

- **Love needs** (often referred to as social needs). These include affection, sense of belonging, social activities, friendships, and both the giving and receiving of love.
- **Esteem needs** (sometimes referred to as ego needs). These include both self-respect and the esteem of others. Self-respect involves the desire for confidence, strength, independence and freedom, and achievement. Esteem of others involves reputation or prestige, status, recognition, attention and appreciation.
- **Self-actualisation needs.** This is the development and realisation of one's full potential. Maslow sees this as: 'What humans can be, they must be', or 'becoming everything that one is capable of becoming'. Self-actualisation needs are not necessarily a creative urge, and may take many forms which vary widely from one individual to another.

Once a lower need has been satisfied it no longer acts as a strong motivator. The needs of the next higher level in the hierarchy demand satisfaction and become the motivating influence. Only unsatisfied needs motivate a person. Thus Maslow asserts that '*a satisfied need is no longer a motivator*'.

Not necessarily a fixed order

Although Maslow suggests that most people have these basic needs in about the order indicated, he also makes it clear that **the hierarchy is not necessarily a fixed order.** There will be a number of exceptions to the order indicated. For some people there will be a reversal of the hierarchy, for example:

- Self-esteem may seem to be more important than love to some people. This is the most common reversal of the hierarchy. It is often based on the belief that the person most loved is strong, confident or inspires respect. People seeking love try to put on a show of aggressive, confident behaviour. They are not really seeking self-esteem as an end in itself but for the sake of love needs.
- For some innately creative people the drive for creativity and self-actualisation may arise despite lack of satisfaction of more basic needs.
- Higher-level needs may be lost in some people who will continue to be satisfied at lower levels only: for example, a person who has experienced chronic unemployment.
- Some people who have been deprived of love in early childhood may experience the permanent loss of love needs.
- A need which has continued to be satisfied over a long period of time may be undervalued. For example, people who have never suffered from chronic hunger may tend to underestimate its effects, and regard food as rather an unimportant thing. Where people are dominated by a higher-level need this may assume greater importance than more basic needs.
- People with high ideals or values may become martyrs and give up everything else for the sake of their beliefs.

Maslow claims that the hierarchy is relatively universal between different cultures, but he recognises that there are differences in an individual's motivational content in a particular culture.

Degrees of satisfaction

Maslow points out that a false impression may be given that a need must be satisfied fully before a subsequent need arises. **He suggests that a more realistic description is in terms of decreasing percentages of satisfaction along levels of the hierarchy.** For example, arbitrary figures for the average person may be: satis-

fied 85 per cent in physiological needs; 70 per cent in safety needs; 50 per cent in love needs; 40 per cent in esteem needs; and 10 per cent in self-actualisation needs. There is a gradual emergence of a higher-level need as lower-level needs become more satisfied. The relative importance of these needs changes during the psychological development of the individual.

Maslow subsequently modified his views by noting that satisfaction of self-actualisation needs by growth-motivated individuals can actually enhance these needs rather than reduce them. Also, he accepted that some higher-level needs may still emerge after long deprivation of lower-level needs, rather than only after their satisfaction.

EVALUATION OF MASLOW'S THEORY

Based on Maslow's theory, once lower-level needs have been satisfied (say at the physiological and safety levels) giving more of the same does not provide motivation. Individuals advance up the hierarchy as each lower-level need becomes satisfied. Therefore, to provide motivation for a change in behaviour, the manager must direct attention to the next higher level of needs (in this case, love or social needs) that seek satisfaction.

Applications to the work situation

However, there are a number of problems in relating Maslow's theory to the work situation. These include the following:

- People do not necessarily satisfy their needs, especially higher-level needs, just through the work situation. They satisfy them through other areas of their life as well. Therefore the manager would need to have a complete understanding of people's private and social life, not just their behaviour at work.
- There is doubt about the time which elapses between the satisfaction of a lower-level need and the emergence of a higher-level need.
- Individual differences mean that people place different values on the same need. For example, some people prefer what they might see as the comparative safety of working in a bureaucratic organisation to a more highly paid and higher status position, but with less job security, in a different organisation.
- Some rewards or outcomes at work satisfy more than one need. Higher salary or promotion, for example, can be applied to all levels of the hierarchy.
- Even for people within the same level of the hierarchy, the motivating factors will not be the same. There are many different ways in which people may seek satisfaction of, for example, their esteem needs.
- Maslow viewed satisfaction as the main motivational outcome of behaviour. But job satisfaction does not necessarily lead to improved work performance.

Studies of Maslow's theory

An examination of Maslow's need hierarchy theory in an organisational setting was undertaken by *Hall and Nougaim*.[13] This was a longitudinal study, over a five-year period, of 49 young managers in the American Telephone and Telegraph Company. The top four levels of Maslow's hierarchy were used, with physiological needs excluded. An attempt was made to test the developmental change aspect of Maslow's theory. Researchers conducted lengthy interviews, each year, with the managers. Part of the study involved an analysis, for each year, of a comparison

between the satisfaction score for one need with the strength score for the next higher level need. The comparison was undertaken by independent coders.

Although a positive relationship was found between need strength and need satisfaction, there was only a low statistical significance. Hall and Nougaim suggest the results indicate needs changed more because of developing career concern than the strength of need satisfaction. This study appears to provide only very limited support for the developmental theory of Maslow.

A somewhat similar study on 187 managers in two organisations was undertaken by *Lawler and Suttle*.[14] They used different samples and somewhat different methods of analysis from Hall and Nougaim. But, again, although some positive relationship to Maslow's theory was found, there were few findings of statistical significance.

Maslow's theory is difficult to test empirically and has been subject to various interpretations by different writers. Reviews of the need hierarchy model suggest little clear or consistent support for the theory and raise doubts about the validity of the classification of basic human needs.[15]

However, it is important to stress that Maslow himself recognised the limitations of his theory and did not imply that it should command widespread, empirical support. He suggested only that the theory should be considered as a framework for future research and points out: 'It is easier to perceive and to criticise the aspects in motivation theory than to remedy them.'

A useful basis for evaluation

Although Maslow did not originally intend that the need hierarchy should necessarily be applied to the work situation, it still remains popular as a theory of motivation at work. Despite criticisms and doubts about its limitations, the theory has had a significant impact on management approaches to motivation and the design of organisations to meet individual needs. It is a convenient framework for viewing the different needs and expectations that people have, where they are in the hierarchy, and the different motivators that might be applied to people at different levels.

The work of Maslow has drawn attention to a number of different motivators and stimulated study and research. The need hierarchy model provides a useful base for the evaluation of motivation at work. For example, *Steers and Porter* suggest a list of general rewards and organisational factors used to satisfy different needs (*see* Fig. 14.8).[16]

ALDERFER'S MODIFIED NEED HIERARCHY MODEL

A modified need hierarchy model has been presented by *Alderfer*.[17] This model condenses *Maslow's* five levels of need into only three levels based on the core needs of existence, relatedness and growth (ERG theory). (*See* Fig. 14.9.)

- **Existence needs** are concerned with sustaining human existence and survival, and cover physiological and safety needs of a material nature.
- **Relatedness needs** are concerned with relationships to the social environment, and cover love or belonging, affiliation, and meaningful interpersonal relationships of a safety or esteem nature.
- **Growth needs** are concerned with the development of potential, and cover self-esteem and self-actualisation.

Needs levels	General rewards	Organisational factors
1 Physiological	Food, water, sex sleep	**a** Pay **b** Pleasant working conditions **c** Cafeteria
2 Safety	Safety, security, stability, protection	**a** Safe working conditions **b** Company benefits **c** Job security
3 Social	Love, affection, belongingness	**a** Cohesive work group **b** Friendly supervision **c** Professional associations
4 Esteem	Self-esteem, self-respect, prestige, status	**a** Social recognition **b** Job title **c** High status job **d** Feedback from the job itself
5 Self-actualisation	Growth, advancement, creativity	**a** Challenging job **b** Opportunities for creativity **c** Achievement in work **d** Advancement in the organisation

Fig. 14.8
Applying Maslow's
need hierarchy

(Reproduced with permission from Steers, R. M. and Porter, L. W. *Motivation and Work Behavior*, Fifth edition, McGraw-Hill (1991) p. 35.)

A continuum of needs

Like Maslow, Alderfer suggests that individuals progress through the hierarchy from existence needs, to relatedness needs, to growth needs, as the lower-level needs become satisfied. However, Alderfer suggests these needs are more a continuum than hierarchical levels. More than one need may be activated at the same time. Individuals may also progress down the hierarchy. There is a frustration–regression process. For example, if an individual is continually frustrated in attempting to satisfy growth needs, relatedness needs may reassume most importance. The lower-level needs become the main focus of the individual's efforts.

Alderfer proposed a number of basic propositions relating to the three need relationships. Some of these propositions followed Maslow's theory, some were the reverse of the theory. A number of studies were undertaken to test these propositions across different samples of people in different types of organisations.

Results from the studies were mixed. For example, the proposition that the less existence needs are satisfied the more they will be desired received constant support from all six samples. However, the proposition that satisfaction of existence needs activates desire for relatedness needs was not supported in any of the six samples.

Satisfaction of needs

Unlike Maslow's theory, the results of Alderfer's work suggest that lower-level needs do not have to be satisfied before a higher-level need emerges as a motivating influence. The results, however, do support the idea that lower-level needs decrease in strength as they become satisfied.

ERG theory states that an individual is motivated to satisfy one or more basic sets of needs. Therefore if a person's needs at a particular level are blocked then

493

Maslow's hierarchy of needs	Alderfer's ERG theory	Herzberg's two-factor theory
PHYSIOLOGICAL	EXISTENCE	HYGIENE FACTORS
SAFETY		
LOVE	RELATEDNESS	
ESTEEM	GROWTH	MOTIVATORS
SELF-ACTUALISATION		

Fig. 14.9 Relationships among Maslow's, Alderfer's and Herzberg's theories of motivation

attention should be focused on the satisfaction of needs at the other levels. For example, if a subordinate's growth needs are blocked because the job does not allow sufficient opportunity for personal development, then the manager should attempt to provide greater opportunities for the subordinate to satisfy existence and relatedness needs.

HERZBERG'S MOTIVATION–HYGIENE THEORY

Herzberg's original study consisted of interviews with 203 accountants and engineers, chosen because of their growing importance in the business world, from different industries in the Pittsburgh area of America.[18] He used the critical incident method. Subjects were asked to relate times when they felt exceptionally good or exceptionally bad about their present job or any previous job. They were asked to give reasons and a description of the sequence of events giving rise to that feeling. Responses to the interviews were generally consistent, and revealed that there were two different sets of factors affecting motivation and work. This led to the two-factor theory of motivation and job satisfaction.

Hygiene and motivating factors

One set of factors are those which, if absent, cause dissatisfaction. These factors are related to job context, they are concerned with job environment and extrinsic to the job itself. **These factors are the 'hygiene' factors** (analogous to the medical term meaning preventive and environmental) or 'maintenance' factors. They serve to prevent dissatisfaction.

The other set of factors are those which, if present, serve to motivate the individual to superior effort and performance. These factors are related to job content of the work itself. **They are the 'motivators' or growth factors.** The strength of these factors will affect feelings of satisfaction or no satisfaction, but not dissatisfaction (*see* Fig. 14.10).

The hygiene factors can be related roughly to Maslow's lower-level needs and the motivators to Maslow's higher-level needs. (See Fig. 14.9.) Proper attention to the hygiene factors will tend to prevent dissatisfaction, but does not by itself create a positive attitude or motivation to work. It brings motivation up to a zero

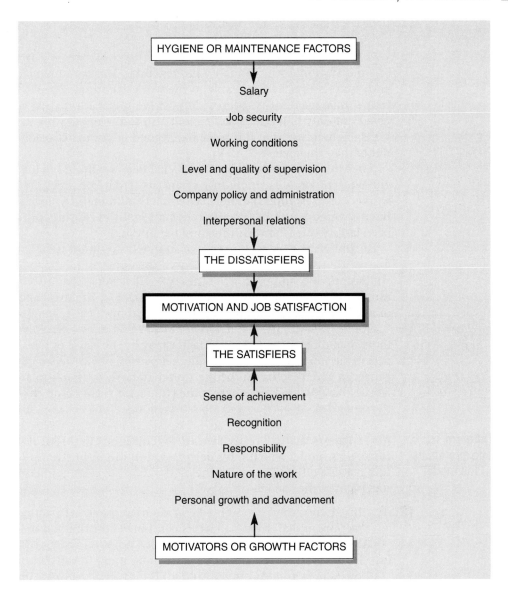

**Fig. 14.10
Representation of
Herzberg's
two-factor theory**

state. **The opposite of dissatisfaction is not satisfaction but, simply, no dissatisfaction.** To motivate workers to give of their best the manager must give proper attention to the motivators or growth factors.

Herzberg emphasises that hygiene factors are not a 'second class citizen system'. They are as important as the motivators, but for different reasons. Hygiene factors are necessary to avoid unpleasantness at work and to deny unfair treatment. 'Management should never deny people proper treatment at work.' The motivators relate to what people are allowed to do at work. They are the variables which actually motivate people.

EVALUATION OF HERZBERG'S WORK

The motivation–hygiene theory has extended *Maslow*'s hierarchy of need theory and is more directly applicable to the work situation. *Herzberg*'s theory suggests that if management is to provide positive motivation then attention must be given not only to hygiene factors, but also to the motivating factors. The work of Herzberg indicates that it is more likely good performance leads to job satisfaction rather than the reverse.

Since the original study the theory had been replicated many times with different types of workers, including scientists, engineers, technicians, professional workers, nurses, food handlers, assemblers, and maintenance staff. The samples have covered a number of different nationalities. Results of these studies have been largely consistent with the original findings.[19]

Herzberg's theory is, however, a source of frequent debate. There have been many other studies to test the theory. The conclusions have been mixed. Some studies provide support for the theory.[20] However, it has also been attacked by a number of writers. For example, *Vroom* claims that the two-factor theory was only one of many conclusions that could be drawn from the research.[21]

From a review of the research *House and Wigdor* draw attention to the influence of individual differences.[22] A given factor may be the cause of job satisfaction for one person but job dissatisfaction for another person, or vice versa. Within the sample of people, a given factor can be the source of both satisfaction and dissatisfaction. House and Wigdor conclude that the two-factor theory is an over-simplification of the sources of satisfaction and job satisfaction.

Different interpretations of the model

King suggests that there are at least five different theoretical interpretations of Herzberg's model which have been tested in different studies.[23] Each interpretation places a different slant on the model. This suggests doubts about the clarity of statement of the theory.

(i) Do all motivators combined contribute more to satisfaction than to dissatisfaction, and all hygiene factors combined contribute more to dissatisfaction than to satisfaction?

(ii) Do all motivators combined contribute more to satisfaction than do all the hygiene factors combined, and all the hygiene factors combined contribute more to dissatisfaction than all motivators combined?

(iii) Does each motivator contribute more to satisfaction than to dissatisfaction, and each hygiene factor contribute more to dissatisfaction than to satisfaction?

(iv) Does each principal motivator contribute more to satisfaction than does any hygiene factor, and does each principal hygiene factor contribute more to dissatisfaction than does any motivator?

(v) Is it only motivators which determine satisfaction and only hygiene factors which determine dissatisfaction?

King concludes that theories (i) and (ii) are subject to the defensive bias of the respondents, and have not been tested adequately. Theories (iii), (iv) and (v) appear to be supported by other studies but are invalid because they reflect bias in the research.

There are two common general criticisms of Herzberg's theory. One criticism is that the theory has only limited application to 'manual' workers. The other criticism is that the theory is 'methodologically bound'.

Applications to manual workers

It is often claimed that the theory applies least to people with largely unskilled jobs or whose work is uninteresting, repetitive and monotonous, and limited in scope. Yet these are the people who often present management with the biggest problem of motivation. Some workers do not seem greatly interested in the job content of their work, or with the motivators or growth factors.

For example, in *Goldthorpe*'s study of manual workers on assembly line and other factory work, he found a group of workers who adopted an 'instrumental orientation' to their job.[24] The workers' primary concern was with economic interests – pay and security – rather than with the nature of the work or the satisfaction of social needs. Their earnings were well in excess of the average manual wage at the time, that is, they were 'affluent' workers. Work was seen as a means to an end, a means of earning money through which to satisfy outside demands and interests.

As another example, *Weaver* contends that such theories of motivation have little meaning for hourly workers in the hotel and restaurant industry. The work of, for example, cooks, dishwashers, waiting or housekeeping staff does not change much among different companies so such staff feel little attachment to a particular company. Where there is little pleasure in the work itself or the job offers little opportunity for career advancement, personal challenge or growth, people are working for their pay cheque and are best motivated by direct cash rewards for above-average productivity.[25]

However, work by *Blackburn and Mann* suggests that not all manual workers share an instrumental orientation to work. From a sample of 1000 workers in relatively low-skilled jobs, they found a variety of work orientations. These included primary concerns for outdoor work or indoor work, autonomy, intrinsic aspects, worthwhileness of the job, work colleagues, working conditions, hours of work, and promotion, as well as economic rewards.[26]

Criticism of methodolgy

A second, general criticism concerns methodology. It is claimed that the critical incident method, and the description of events giving rise to good or bad feelings, influences the results. People are more likely to attribute satisfying incidents at work, that is the motivators, as a favourable reflection on their own performance. The dissatisfying incidents, that is the hygiene factors, are more likely to be attributed to external influences, and the efforts of other people. Descriptions from the respondents had to be interpreted by the interviewers. This gives rise to the difficulty of distinguishing clearly between the different dimensions, and to the risk of possible interviewer bias. When studies have been conducted without the use of the critical incident method, results generally are different from those predicted by the two-factor theory.[27]

Importance of job design

Whatever the validity of the two-factor theory much of the criticism is with the value of hindsight, and *Herzberg* did at least attempt an empirical approach to the study of motivation at work. Also, his work has drawn attention to the importance of job design in order to bring about job enrichment. Herzberg has emphasised the importance of the 'quality of work life'. He advocates the restructuring of jobs to give greater emphasis to the motivating factors at work, to make jobs more interesting and to satisfy higher level needs. Job design and job enrichment are discussed in the following chapter.

McCLELLAND'S ACHIEVEMENT MOTIVATION THEORY

McClelland's work originated from investigations into the relationship between hunger needs and the extent to which imagery of food dominated thought processes. From subsequent research McClelland identified four main arousal-based, and socially developed, motives:

- the Achievement motive;
- the Power motive;
- the Affiliative motives; and
- the Avoidance motives.[28]

The first three motives correspond, roughly, to *Maslow*'s self-actualisation, esteem and love needs.

The relative intensity of these motives varies between individuals. It also tends to vary between different occupations. Managers appear to be higher in achievement motivation than in affiliation motivation. McClelland saw the achievement need (n-Ach) as the most critical for the country's economic growth and success. The need to achieve is linked to entrepreneurial spirit and the development of available resources.

Use of projective tests

Research studies by *McClelland* use a series of projective 'tests'. For example, individuals are shown a number of pictures in which some activity is depicted. Respondents are asked to look briefly (10–15 seconds) at the pictures, and then to describe what they think is happening, what the people in the picture are thinking and what events have led to the situation depicted. An example of a picture used in a projective test is given in Assignment 3 at the end of this chapter. The descriptions are used as a basis for analysing the strength of the individual's motives.

People with high achievement needs

Despite the apparent subjective nature of the judgements, McClelland has, over years of empirical research, identified four characteristics of people with a strong achievement need (n-Ach): a preference for moderate task difficulty; personal responsibility for performance; the need for feedback; and innovativeness.

- They prefer **moderate task difficulty** and goals as an achievement incentive. This provides the best opportunity of proving they can do better. If the task is too difficult or too risky, it would reduce the chances of success and of gaining need satisfaction. If the course of action is too easy or too safe, there is little challenge in accomplishing the task and little satisfaction from success.
- They prefer **personal responsibility for performance**. They like to attain success through the focus of their own abilities and efforts rather than by teamwork or chance factors outside their control. Personal satisfaction is derived from the accomplishment of the task, and recognition need not come from other people.
- They have the need for **clear and unambiguous feedback** on how well they are performing. A knowledge of results within a reasonable time is necessary for self-evaluation. Feedback enables them to determine success or failure in the accomplishment of their goals, and to derive satisfaction from their activities.
- They are **more innovative**. As they always seek moderately challenging tasks they tend always to be moving on to something a little more challenging. In seeking short cuts they are more likely to cheat. There is a constant search for variety and for information to find new ways of doing things. They are more restless and avoid routine, and also tend to travel more.

Extent of achievement motivation

The extent of achievement motivation varies between individuals. Some people think about achievement a lot more than others. Some people rate very highly in achievement motivation. They are challenged by opportunities and work hard to achieve a goal. Other people rate very low in achievement motivation. They do not care much and have little urge to achieve.

For people with a high achievement motivation, money is not an incentive but may serve as a means of giving feedback on performance. High achievers seem unlikely to remain long with an organisation that does not pay them well for good performance. Money may seem to be important to high achievers, but they value it more as symbolising successful task performance and goal achievement. For people with low achievement motivation money may serve more as a direct incentive for performance.

McClelland's research has attempted to understand the characteristics of high achievers. He suggests that n-Ach is not hereditary but results from environmental influences, and he has investigated the possibility of training people to develop a greater motivation to achieve.[29] McClelland suggests four steps in attempting to develop achievement drive:

- Striving to attain feedback on performance. Reinforcement of success serves to strengthen the desire to attain higher performance.
- Developing models of achievement by seeking to emulate people who have performed well.
- Attempting to modify their self-image and to see themselves as needing challenges and success.
- Controlling day-dreaming and thinking about themselves in more positive terms.

McClelland was concerned with economic growth in underdeveloped countries. He has designed training programmes intended to increase the achievement motivation and entrepreneurial activity of managers.

The need for power

McClelland has also suggested that the effective manager should possess a high need for power.[30] However, the effective manager also scores high on inhibition. Power is directed more towards the organisation and concern for group goals, and is exercised on behalf of other people. This is 'socialised' power. It is distinguished from 'personalised' power which is characterised by satisfaction from exercising dominance over other people, and personal aggrandisement.

PROCESS THEORIES OF MOTIVATION

Process theories attempt to identify the relationships among the dynamic variables which make up motivation. They provide a further contribution to our understanding of the complex nature of work motivation. Many of the process theories cannot be linked to a single writer, but major approaches and leading writers under this heading include:

- Expectancy-based models – *Vroom*, and *Porter and Lawler*
- Equity theory – *Adams*
- Goal theory – *Locke*
- Attribution theory – *Heider*, and *Kelley* (this was discussed in Chapter 5).

Expectancy theories of motivation

The underlying basis of expectancy theory is that people are influenced by the expected results of their actions. Motivation is a function of the relationship between:

(1) effort expended and perceived level of performance; and
(2) the expectation that rewards (desired outcomes) will be related to performance.

There must also be

(3) the expectation that rewards (desired outcomes) are available.

These relationships determine the strength of the 'motivational link'. (*See* Fig. 14.11.)

**Fig. 14.11
Expectancy theory:
the motivational link**

Performance therefore depends upon the perceived expectation regarding effort expended and achieving the desired outcome. For example, the desire for promotion will result in high performance only if the person believes there is a strong expectation that this will lead to promotion. If, however, the person believes promotion to be based solely on age and length of service there is no motivation to achieve high performance. A person's behaviour reflects a conscious choice between the comparative evaluation of alternative behaviours. **The choice of behaviour is based on the expectancy of the most favourable consequences.**

Expectancy theory cannot be linked to a single individual writer. There are a number of different versions and some of the models are rather complex. More recent approaches to expectancy theory have been associated with the work of *Vroom* and of *Porter and Lawler*.

VROOM'S EXPECTANCY THEORY

Vroom was the first person to propose an expectancy theory aimed specifically at work motivation.[31] His model is based on three key variables: **valence, instrumentality and expectancy** (VIE theory or expectancy/valence theory). The theory is founded on the idea that people prefer certain outcomes from their behaviour over others. They anticipate feelings of satisfaction should the preferred outcome be achieved.

Valence

The feeling about specific outcomes is termed **valence. This is the attractiveness of, or preference for, a particular outcome to the individual.** *Vroom* distinguishes valence from value. A person may desire an object but then gain little satisfaction from obtaining it. Alternatively, a person may strive to avoid an object but finds, subsequently, that it provides satisfaction. **Valence is the anticipated satisfaction from an outcome.** This may differ substantially from value, which is the actual satisfaction provided by an outcome.

The valence of certain outcomes may be derived in their own right, but more usually they are derived from the other outcomes to which they are expected to lead. An obvious example is money. Some people may see money as having an intrinsic worth and derive satisfaction from the actual accumulation of wealth. Most people, however, see money in terms of the many satisfying outcomes to which it can lead.

Instrumentality

The valence of outcomes derive, therefore, from their **instrumentality.** This leads to a distinction between first-level outcomes and second-level outcomes.

The first-level outcomes are performance-related. They refer to the quantity of output or to the comparative level of performance. Some people may seek to perform well 'for its own sake' and without thought to expected consequences of their actions. Usually, however, performance outcomes acquire valence because of the expectation that they will lead to other outcomes as an anticipated source of satisfaction – second-level outcomes.

The second-level outcomes are need-related. They are derived through achievement of first-level outcomes, that is through achieving high performance. Many need-related outcomes are dependent upon actual performance rather than effort expended. People generally receive rewards for what they have achieved, rather than for effort alone or through trying hard.

On the basis of *Vroom's* expectancy theory it is possible to depict a general model of behaviour. (*See* Fig. 14.12.)

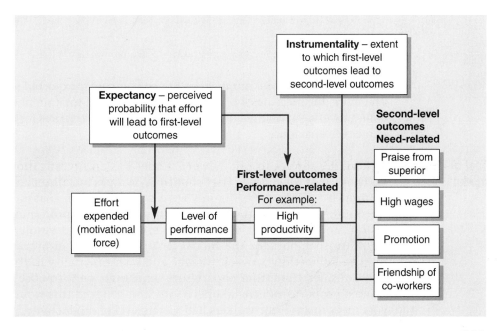

**Fig. 14.12
Basic model of expectancy theory**

The strength of the valence of an outcome is dependent upon the extent to which the outcome serves as a means to other outcomes. An outcome with a high valence is likely to be one that is perceived to be instrumental in leading to the achievement of a large number of need-related outcomes. Instrumentality is the association between first-level outcomes and second-level outcomes, measured on a range between +1.0 and –1.0. For example, if it is believed that good work performance (a first-level outcome) always results in a pay increase (a second-level outcome) instrumentality will be constant at +1.0. If the person believes a pay increase is certain to be obtained without good performance, or impossible even with it, instrumentality will be –1.0.

Expectancy

When a person chooses between alternative behaviours which have uncertain outcomes, the choice is affected not only by the preference for a particular outcome, but also by the probability that such an outcome will be achieved. People develop a **perception** of the degree of probability that the choice of a particular action will actually lead to the desired outcome. This is **expectancy.** It is the relationship between a chosen course of action and its predicted outcome. Expectancy relates effort expended to the achievement of first-level outcomes. Its value ranges between 0, indicating zero probability that an action will be followed by the outcome, and 1, indicating certainty that an action will result in the outcome.

Motivational force

The combination of valence and expectancy determines the person's motivation for a given form of behaviour. This is the **motivational force.** The force of an action is unaffected by outcomes which have no valence, or by outcomes that are regarded as unlikely to result from a course of action. Expressed as an equation, motivation (M) is the sum of the products of the valences of all outcomes (V), times the strength of expectancies that action will result in achieving these outcomes (E). Therefore, if either, or both, valence or expectancy is zero, then motivation is zero. The choice between alternative behaviours is indicated by the highest attractiveness score.

$$M = \sum^{n} E \cdot V$$

There are likely to be a number of different outcomes expected for a given action. Therefore, the measure of $E \cdot V$ is summed across the total number of possible outcomes to arrive at a single figure indicating the attractiveness for the contemplated choice of behaviour.

Test of Vroom's model

Among the studies to test *Vroom's* model was an investigation undertaken by *Galbraith and Cummings.*[32] They studied 32 workers in a firm manufacturing heavy equipment. Productivity figures were compared with measures of job-related (second-level) outcomes such as pay, fringe benefits, promotion, style of supervision, and popularity with co-workers. The overall results suggested little significant support for the model as a whole. They did, however, indicate a marked interaction between valence and instrumentality in the case of support and consideration from supervisors, and high performance. Where workers wanted support from their supervisors, and believed this would be achieved by good performance, the workers had a high level of productivity.

THE PORTER AND LAWLER EXPECTANCY MODEL

Vroom's expectancy/valence theory has been developed by *Porter and Lawler*.[33] Their model goes beyond motivational force and considers performance as a whole. They point out that effort expended (motivational force) does not lead directly to performance. It is mediated by individual abilities and traits, and by the person's role perceptions. They also introduce rewards as an intervening variable. Porter and Lawler see motivation, satisfaction and performance as separate variables, and attempt to explain the complex relationships among them.

Explanation of relationships

These relationships are expressed diagrammatically (Fig. 14.13) rather than mathematically. In contrast to the human relations approach which tended to assume that job satisfaction leads to improved performance, Porter and Lawler suggest that satisfaction is an effect rather than a cause of performance. It is performance that leads to job satisfaction.

Value of reward (Box 1) is similar to valence in Vroom's model. People desire various outcomes (rewards) which they hope to achieve from work. The value placed on a reward depends on the strength of its desirability.

Perceived effort–reward probability (Box 2) is similar to expectancy. It refers to a person's expectation that certain outcomes (rewards) are dependent upon a given amount of effort.

Effort (Box 3) is how hard the person tries, the amount of energy a person exerts on a given activity. It does not relate to how successful a person is in carrying out an activity. The amount of energy exerted is dependent upon the interaction of the input variables of value of reward, and perception of the effort–reward relationship.

**Fig. 14.13
The Porter and Lawler motivation model**

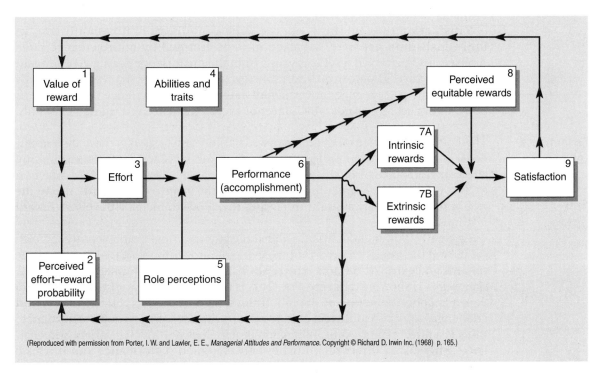

(Reproduced with permission from Porter, I. W. and Lawler, E. E., *Managerial Attitudes and Performance*. Copyright © Richard D. Irwin Inc. (1968) p. 165.)

Abilities and traits (Box 4): Porter and Lawler suggest that effort does not lead directly to performance, but is influenced by individual characteristics. Factors such as intelligence, skills, knowledge, training and personality affect the ability to perform a given activity.

Role perceptions (Box 5) refer to the way in which individuals view their work and the role they should adopt. This influences the type of effort exerted. Role perceptions will influence the direction and level of action which is believed to be necessary for effective performance.

Performance (Box 6) depends not only on the amount of effort exerted but also on the intervening influences of the person's abilities and traits, and their role perceptions. If the person lacks the right ability or personality, or has an inaccurate role perception of what is required, then the exertion of a large amount of energy may still result in a low level of performance, or task accomplishment.

Rewards (Boxes 7A and 7B) are desirable outcomes. Intrinsic rewards derive from the individuals themselves and include a sense of achievement, a feeling of responsibility and recognition (for example Herzberg's motivators). Extrinsic rewards derive from the organisation and the actions of others, and include salary, working conditions and supervision (for example Herzberg's hygiene factors). The proportion of intrinsic and extrinsic rewards will vary among individuals and in different work situations, but there must be a minimum of both. Porter and Lawler see both intrinsic and extrinsic rewards to be important and desirable outcomes. They suggest, however, that intrinsic rewards are more likely to produce job satisfaction related to performance than are extrinsic rewards.

Perceived equitable rewards (Box 8): this is the level of rewards people feel they should fairly receive for a given standard of performance. Most people have an implicit perception about the level of rewards they should receive commensurate with the requirements and demands of the job, and the contribution expected of them.

Satisfaction (Box 9): this is not the same as motivation. It is an attitude, an individual's internal state. Satisfaction is determined by both actual rewards received, and perceived level of rewards from the organisation for a given standard of performance. If perceived equitable rewards are greater than actual rewards received, the person experiences dissatisfaction. The experience of satisfaction derives from actual rewards which meet or exceed the perceived equitable rewards.

Performance and rewards

The Porter and Lawler model recognises that job satisfaction is more dependent upon performance than performance is upon job satisfaction. Satisfaction only affects performance through a feedback loop to value of reward. When satisfaction follows receipt of a reward it tends to influence the value of the reward. Also to the extent that performance results in reward, this tends to increase the effort–reward relationship.

Originally, Porter and Lawler included rewards as a single variable. After empirical testing the model was redrawn to divide rewards into two variables – intrinsic rewards and extrinsic rewards. The relationship between performance and intrinsic rewards is shown as a jagged line. This is because the extent of the relationship depends upon the nature of the job. If the design of the job permits variety and challenge, so that people feel able to reward themselves for good performance, there is a direct relationship. Where job design does not involve variety and challenge, there is no direct relationship between good performance and intrinsic

rewards. The wavy line between performance and extrinsic rewards indicates that such rewards do not often provide a direct link to performance.

A second revision to the original model involved drawing a link between performance and perceived equitable rewards. Self-rating of performance links directly with the perceived equitable reward variable. Higher levels of self-rated performance are associated with higher levels of expected equitable rewards. The heavily arrowed line indicates a relationship from the self-rated part of performance to perceived equitable rewards.

Investigations of the model

Porter and Lawler conducted an investigation of their own model. This study involved 563 questionnaires from managers in seven different industrial and government organisations. The main focus of the study was on pay as an outcome. The questionnaires obtained measures from the managers for a number of variables such as value of reward, effort–reward probability, role perceptions, perceived equitable rewards, and satisfaction. Information on the managers' effort and performance was obtained from their superiors. The results indicated that where pay is concerned, value of reward and perceived effort–reward probability do combine to influence effort.

Those managers who believed pay to be closely related to performance outcome received a higher effort and performance rating from their superiors. Those managers who perceived little relationship between pay and performance had lower ratings for effort and performance. The study by Porter and Lawler also demonstrated the interaction of effort and role perceptions to produce a high level of performance. Their study suggested, also, that the relationship between performance and satisfaction with their pay held good only for those managers whose performance was related directly to their actual pay.

A study by *Graen*, into the factors contributing to job satisfaction and performance, provided results which were generally supportive of expectancy theory.[34] A total of 169 women were engaged in part-time, temporary clerical tasks in a simulated work organisation. One group of workers received verbal recognition directly related to their prior performance. A second group received a pay increase in the hope that they would do much better. The third group received no special treatment. Questionnaires were used to obtain measures of the different variables of the theory, and details of job satisfaction and performance. In general, intrinsic rewards were found to contribute substantially more to job satisfaction and performance than did the extrinsic rewards.

LAWLER'S REVISED EXPECTANCY MODEL

Following the original Porter and Lawler model, further work was undertaken by *Lawler* (*see* Fig. 14.14).[35] He suggests that in deciding on the attractiveness of alternative behaviours, there are two types of expectancies to be considered: effort–performance expectancies ($E \rightarrow P$); and performance–outcome expectancies ($P \rightarrow O$).

The first expectancy ($E \rightarrow P$) is the person's perception of the probability that a given amount of effort will result in achieving an intended level of performance. It is measured on a scale between 0 and 1. The closer the perceived relationship between effort and performance, the higher the $E \rightarrow P$ expectancy score.

Fig. 14.14
An illustration of the Lawler expectancy model

The second expectancy (**P → O**) is the person's perception of the probability that a given level of performance will actually lead to particular need-related outcomes. This is measured also on a scale between 0 and 1. The closer the perceived relationship between performance and outcome, the higher the P → O expectancy score.

Motivational force to perform

The multiplicative combination of the two types of expectancies, E → P and the sum of the products P → O, determines expectancy. The motivational force to perform (effort expended) is determined by multiplying E → P and P → O by the strength of outcome valence (V).

$$E(Effort) = (E \rightarrow P) \times \sum[(P \rightarrow O) \times V]$$

The distinction between the two types of expectancies arises because they are determined by different conditions. E → P expectancy is determined in part by the person's ability and self-confidence, past experience, and the difficulty of the task. P → O expectancy is determined by the attractiveness of the outcomes and the belief about who controls the outcomes, the person him/ herself or other people.

IMPLICATIONS FOR MANAGERS OF EXPECTANCY THEORIES

There are a number of different versions of expectancy theory. The main elements tend to be very similar, however, and this suggests the development of a generally accepted approach. Numerous research studies aimed at testing expectancy models

appear to suggest general support for the theory, but they also highlight difficulties with some of the concepts involved and with methodology. Expectancy models are not always easy to understand, or to apply. There are many variables which affect behaviour at work. A problem can arise in attempting to include a large number of variables or in identifying those variables which are most appropriate in particular situations.

Expectancy theory does, however, draw attention to the complexities of work motivation. It provides further information in helping to explain the nature of behaviour and motivation in the work situation, and helps to identify problems in performance. Expectancy theory indicates that managers should give attention to a number of factors, including the following:

- Use rewards appropriate in terms of individual performance. Outcomes with high valence should be used as an incentive for improved performance.
- Attempt to establish clear relationships between effort–performance and rewards, as perceived by the individual.
- Establish clear procedures for the evaluation of individual levels of performance.
- Pay attention to intervening variables such as abilities and traits, role perceptions, organisational procedures, and support facilities, which, although not necessarily direct motivational factors, may still affect performance.
- Minimise undesirable outcomes which may be perceived to result from a high level of performance, such as industrial accidents or sanctions from co-workers; or to result despite a high level of performance, such as short-time working or layoffs.

Just a model

Porter and Lawler emphasise that the expectancy theory model applies only to behaviours which are under the voluntary control of the individual. The two general types of choices over which individuals have voluntary control of work performance in organisations are:

(i) the amount of effort and energy expended; and
(ii) the manner in which they go about performing their work.

Porter and Lawler also emphasise that the expectancy model is just a model.

People rarely actually sit down and list their expected outcomes for a contemplated behaviour, estimate expectancies and valences, multiply, and add up the total unless, of course, they are asked to do so by a researcher. Yet people *do* consider the likely outcomes of their actions, do weigh and evaluate the attractiveness of various alternatives, and do use these estimates in coming to a decision about what they will do. The expectancy model provides an analytic tool for mirroring that process and for predicting its outcome, but it does not purport to reflect the actual decision-making steps taken by an individual.[36]

The motivation of knowledge workers

Recent advantages in telecommunications and in scientific and technological knowledge have led to greater emphasis on the knowledge and expertise of staff. *Tampoe* suggests that at the core of the new industrial trend are the 'knowledge-workers' – those employees who apply their theoretical and practical understanding of a specific area of knowledge to produce outcomes of a commercial, social or personal value. The performance of knowledge workers should be judged on both the cleverness of ideas and the utility and commercial value of their applied knowledge. Creativity is necessary and needs to be encouraged but should be bounded by

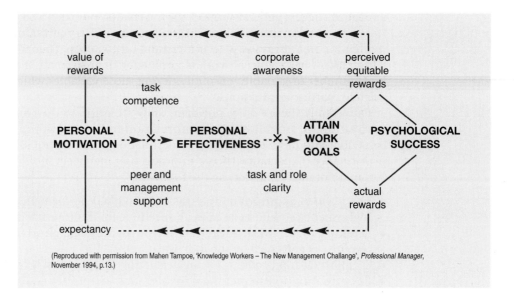

(Reproduced with permission from Mahen Tampoe, 'Knowledge Workers – The New Management Challange', *Professional Manager*, November 1994, p.13.)

**Fig. 14.15
Motivating
knowledge
workers**

commercial realism. This presents management with a new challenge of how to motivate the knowledge workers.[37]

Tampoe suggests that the personal motivation of knowledge workers is based on the value they place on the rewards they expect to earn at work. In addition to the individual's own motivation, the performance of knowledge workers is dependent upon four key characteristics (*see* Fig. 14.15):

- task competence;
- peer and management support;
- task and role clarity; and
- corporate awareness.

The challenge to management is to ensure the effectiveness of the four key variables and to recognise the need for staff to supervise and manage themselves and the wider rewards expected by knowledge workers.

EQUITY THEORY OF MOTIVATION

One of the major variables of satisfaction in the Porter and Lawler expectancy model is perceived equitable rewards. This leads to consideration of another process theory of motivation – equity theory. Applied to the work situation, equity theory is usually associated with the work of *Adams*.[38]

Equity theory focuses on people's feelings of how fairly they have been treated in comparison with the treatment received by others. It is based on exchange theory. People evaluate their social relationships in the same way as buying or selling an item. People expect certain outcomes in exchange for certain contributions, or inputs.

Social relationships involve an exchange process. For example, a person may expect promotion as an outcome of a high level of contribution (input) in helping

to achieve an important organisational objective. People also compare their own position with that of others. They determine the perceived equity of their own position. Their feelings about the equity of the exchange are affected by the treatment they receive when compared with what happens to other people.

Most exchanges involve a number of inputs and outcomes. According to equity theory, people place a weighting on these various inputs and outcomes according to how they perceive their importance. When the ratio of a person's total outcomes to total inputs equals the *perceived* ratio of other people's total outcomes to total inputs there is **equity**.

When there is an unequal comparison of ratios the person experiences a sense of **inequity**. The feeling of inequity might arise when an individual's ratio of outcomes to inputs is either less than, or greater than, that of other people. For example, Adams suggests that workers prefer equitable pay to overpayment. Workers on piece-rate incentive payment schemes who feel they are overpaid will reduce their level of productivity in order to restore equity.

Behaviour as consequence of inequity

A feeling of inequity causes tension, which is an unpleasant experience. The presence of inequity therefore motivates the person to remove or to reduce the level of tension and the perceived inequity. The magnitude of perceived inequity determines the level of tension. The level of tension created determines the strength of motivation. *Adams* identifies six broad types of possible behaviour as consequences of inequity (*see* Fig. 14.16).

**Fig. 14.16
An illustration of
Adams's equity
theory of motivation**

- **Changes to inputs** – a person may increase or decrease the level of his or her inputs, for example through the amount or quality of work, absenteeism, or working additional hours without pay.

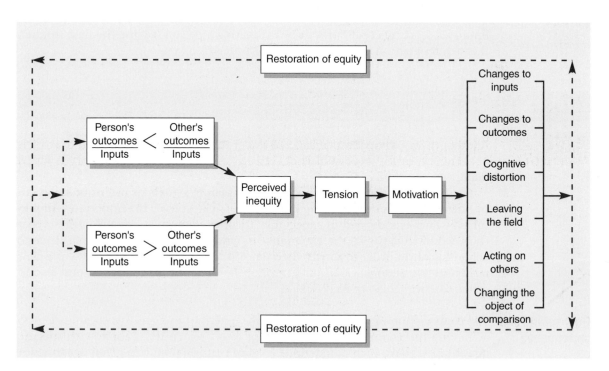

- **Changes to outcomes** – a person may attempt to change outcomes such as pay, working conditions, status and recognition, without changes to inputs.
- **Cognitive distortion of inputs and outcomes** – in contrast to actual changes, people may distort, cognitively, their inputs or outcomes to achieve the same results. Adams suggests that although it is difficult for people to distort facts about themselves, it is possible, within limits, to distort the utility of those facts: for example, the belief about how hard they are really working, the relevance of a particular qualification, or what they can or cannot obtain with a given level of pay.
- **Leaving the field** – a person may try to find a new situation with a more favourable balance, for example, by absenteeism, request for a transfer, resigning from a job or from the organisation altogether.
- **Acting on others** – a person may attempt to bring about changes in others, for example to lower their inputs or accept greater outcomes. Or the person may cognitively distort the inputs and outcomes of others. Alternatively, a person may try to force others to leave the field.
- **Changing the object of comparison** – this involves changing the reference group with whom comparison is made. For example, where another person with a previously similar outcome–input ratio receives greater outcomes without any apparent increase in contribution, that other person may be perceived as now belonging to a different level in the organisation structure. The comparison need not necessarily be made with people who have the same inputs and outcomes. The important thing is a similar ratio of outcomes to inputs.

Under the control of the manager

The manager may seek to remove or reduce tension and perceived inequity among staff by influencing these types of behaviour, for example by attempting to change a person's inputs or encouraging a different object of comparison. However, there are likely to be only two courses of action under the direct control of the manager. Outcomes can be changed by for example increased pay, additional perks or improved working conditions; or by instigating a person leaving the field through transfer, resignation or, as an extreme measure, dismissal.

GOAL THEORY

Another theory sometimes considered under the heading of motivation to work is goal theory, or the theory of goal-setting (*see* Fig. 14.17). This theory is based mainly on the work of *Locke*.[39]

The basic premise of goal theory is that people's goals or intentions play an important part in determining behaviour. Locke accepts the importance of perceived value, as indicated in expectancy theories of motivation, and suggests that these values give rise to the experience of emotions and desires. People strive to achieve goals in order to satisfy their emotions and desires. Goals guide people's responses and actions. Goals direct work behaviour and performance, and lead to certain consequences or feedback.

Goal-setting and performance

The combination of goal difficulty and the extent of the person's commitment to achieving the goal regulates the level of effort expended. People with specific quantitative goals, such as a defined level of performance, or a given deadline for

**Fig. 14.17
An illustration of
Locke's theory of
goal-setting**

completion of a task, will perform better than people with no set goal or only a vague goal such as 'do the best you can'. People who have difficult goals will perform better than people with easier goals.

A number of research studies have attempted to examine the relationship between goal-setting and performance. Although, almost inevitably, there are some contrary findings, the majority of evidence suggests strong support for the theory, and its effects on motivation.[40] Locke subsequently pointed out that 'goal-setting is more appropriately viewed as a motivational technique rather than as a formal theory of motivation'.[41] But, however it is viewed, the theory of goal-setting provides a useful approach to work motivation and performance.

Practical implications for the manager

Goal theory has a number of practical implications for the manager.

- Specific performance goals should systematically be identified and set in order to direct behaviour and maintain motivation.
- Goals should be set at a challenging but realistic level. Difficult goals lead to higher performance. However, if goals are set at too high a level, or are regarded as impossible to achieve, performance will suffer, especially over a longer period.
- Complete, accurate and timely feedback and knowledge of results is usually associated with high performance. Feedback provides a means of checking progress on goal attainment and forms the basis for any revision of goals.
- Goals can be determined either by a superior or by individuals themselves. Goals set by other people are more likely to be accepted when there is participation. Employee participation in the setting of goals may lead to higher performance.[42]

Much of the theory of goal-setting can be related to the system of Management by Objectives (discussed in Chapter 13). MBO is often viewed as an application of goal-setting, although MBO was devised originally before the development of goal-setting theory.

ATTRIBUTION THEORY

A more recent approach to the study of motivation is attribution theory. Attribution is the process by which people interpret the perceived causes of behaviour. Attribution theory has been discussed in Chapter 5. *p 154 - 156*

511

SYNOPSIS

- The underlying concept of motivation is some driving force within individuals by which they attempt to achieve some goal in order to fulfil some need or expectation. Individuals have a variety of changing, and often competing, needs and expectations which they attempt to satisfy in a number of different ways. One useful three-fold classification of individual needs and expectations at work is economic, intrinsic and social. If a person's motivational driving force is blocked before reaching a desired goal, this can result in frustration-induced behaviour. Main reactions to frustration are aggression, regression, fixation and withdrawal.

- The development of different approaches to organisation and management has highlighted the changing concept of motivation at work. These different approaches have led through the rational–economic concept of motivation, the social concept of motivation, the self-actualisation concept of motivation, to the complex-person concept of motivation.

- There are many competing theories which attempt to explain motivation at work. These theories are not conclusive and all have their critics or have been subject to alternative findings, particularly the content theories. However, it is because of the complexity of motivation that these different theories are important to the manager. They show that there are many motives which influence people's behaviour at work. They provide a framework within which to direct attention to the problem of how best to motivate staff to work willingly and effectively.

- The different theories of motivation may be divided into two contrasting groups: content theories and process theories. Content theories place emphasis on what motivates and are concerned with identifying people's needs and their relative strengths, and the goals they pursue in order to satisfy these needs. Main content theories include: Maslow's hierarchy of needs model; Alderfer's modified need hierarchy model; Herzberg's two-factor theory; and McClelland's achievement motivation theory.

- Process theories place emphasis on the actual process of motivation. These theories are concerned with the relationships among the dynamic variables which make up motivation, and with how behaviour is initiated, directed and sustained. Many of the process theories cannot be linked to a single writer, but major approaches under this heading include: expectancy-based models; equity theory; goal theory; and also attribution theory.

- It is always easy to quote an example which appears to contradict any generalised observation on what motivates people to work. However, these different theories provide a basis for study and discussion, and for review of the most effective motivational style. The manager must judge the relevance of these different theories and how best to apply them to particular work situations.

512

Review and discussion questions

1 Explain what you understand by motivation and the underlying concept of motivation. Summarise the main needs and expectations to be taken into account in considering the motivation of people at work.

2 What do you understand by frustrated-induced behaviour? Give a practical example, preferably from your own work experience, of the main forms of this behaviour.

3 Why is the study of the different theories of motivation important to the manager? Distinguish between content and process theories of motivation.

4 Critically assess the practical value of Maslow's hierarchy of needs model to improving the motivation of people at work. Give examples of the extent to which the theory could meaningfully be applied to staff in your own organisation.

5 Discuss critically the validity of the contention that the motivation for staff to work well depends on more than a high salary and good working conditions.

6 Explain your understanding of expectancy-based theories of motivation. Use a simple diagram to help explain an expectancy theory of your choice. What implications do expectancy theories of motivation have for the manager?

7 Give practical examples of situations in which each of the following theories of motivation might be appropriate: (i) achievement motivation; (ii) equity theory; (iii) goal theory.

8 Explain fully and with supporting reasons which *one* theory of motivation you believe is likely to be *most* appropriate in a particular work situation of your choice.

Assignment 1

1 List, as far as possible in rank order, the specific needs and expectations which are most important to you as an individual. (Do *not* include *basic* physiological needs such as to satisfy thirst or hunger, or a *minimal* standard of accommodation.)

2 Explain, briefly, to what extent these needs and expectations are met currently from your present work situation; and/or to what extent you anticipate they will be met from your future career ambitions.

3 Think of any work experience which you have had – even a short-term, vacation or part-time job. Briefly describe:
 (a) those aspects of the job and/or experiences which motivated you to work well; and
 (b) those which had a demotivating influence on your behaviour/actions.

4 Be prepared to share your feelings and comments as part of a class discussion.

 Assignment 2

MOTIVATION: A FEEDBACK EXERCISE

The following questions have seven possible responses:

1 Please mark one of the seven responses by circling the number that corresponds to the response that fits your opinion. For example, if you 'strongly agree', circle the number '+3'.

2 Complete every item. You have about ten minutes to do so.

	Strongly agree	Agree	Slightly agree	Don't know	Slightly disagree	Disagree	Strongly disagree
	+3	+2	+1	0	−1	−2	−3
1. Special wage increases should be given to employees who do their jobs very well.	+3	+2	+1	0	−1	−2	−3
2. Better job descriptions would be helpful so that employees will know exactly what is expected of them.	+3	+2	+1	0	−1	−2	−3
3. Employees need to be reminded that their jobs are dependent on the company's ability to compete effectively.	+3	+2	+1	0	−1	−2	−3
4. Supervisors should give a good deal of attention to the physical working conditions of their employees.	+3	+2	+1	0	−1	−2	−3
5. Supervisors ought to work hard to develop a friendly working atmosphere among their people.	+3	+2	+1	0	−1	−2	−3
6. Individual recognition for above-standard performance means a lot to employees.	+3	+2	+1	0	−1	−2	−3
7. Indifferent supervision can often bruise feelings.	+3	+2	+1	0	−1	−2	−3

	Strongly agree	Agree	Slightly agree	Don't know	Slightly disagree	Disagree	Strongly disagree
	+3	+2	+1	0	−1	−2	−3
8. Employees want to feel that their real skills and capacities are put to use in their jobs.	+3	+2	+1	0	−1	−2	−3
9. The company retirement benefits and share programmes are important factors in keeping employees in their jobs.	+3	+2	+1	0	−1	−2	−3
10. Almost every job can be made more stimulating and challenging.	+3	+2	+1	0	−1	−2	−3
11. Many employees want to give their best in everything they do.	+3	+2	+1	0	−1	−2	−3
12. Management could show more interest in the employees by sponsoring social events after hours.	+3	+2	+1	0	−1	−2	−3
13. Pride in one's work is actually an important reward.	+3	+2	+1	0	−1	−2	−3
14. Employees want to be able to think of themselves as 'the best' at their own jobs.	+3	+2	+1	0	−1	−2	−3
15. The quality of the relationships in the informal work group is quite important.	+3	+2	+1	0	−1	−2	−3
16. Individual incentive bonuses would improve the performance of employees.	+3	+2	+1	0	−1	−2	−3
17. Visibility with upper management is important to employees.	+3	+2	+1	0	−1	−2	−3
18. Employees generally like to schedule their own work and to make job-related decisions with a minimum of supervision.	+3	+2	+1	0	−1	−2	−3

	Strongly agree	Agree	Slightly agree	Don't know	Slightly disagree	Disagree	Strongly disagree
	+3	+2	+1	0	−1	−2	−3
19. Job security is important to employees.	+3	+2	+1	0	−1	−2	−3
20. Having good equipment to work with is important to employees.	+3	+2	+1	0	−1	−2	−3

After you have circled one number for each of the twenty questions, compare your responses with those of your colleagues.

 ## Assignment 3

1 Study the picture below for 10–15 seconds.

2 What is going on in this picture?
What is the person thinking?
What has led up to this situation?

3 Write your own short story about the picture.

After you have written your story, compare your response with those of your colleagues.

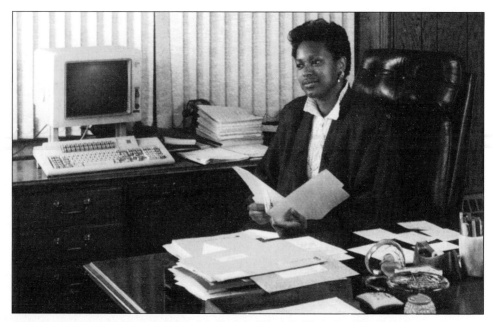

Sample picture in a projective test

(Reprinted by permission from p. 213 of *Organizational Behavior*, Sixth edition, by Don Hellriegel, John W Stocum, Jr. and Richard W. Woodman; Copyright © 1992 by West Publishing Company. All rights reserved.)

Notes and references

1. Krech, D., Crutchfield, R. S. and Ballachey, E. L. *Individual in Society*, McGraw-Hill (1962).
2. Mitchell, T. R. 'Motivation: New Directions for Theory, Research, and Practice', *Academy of Management Review*, vol. 7, no. 1, January 1982, pp. 80–8.
3. See, for example: Rudolph, P. A. and Kleiner, B. H. 'The Art of Motivating Employees', *Journal of Managerial Psychology*, 4 (5), 1989, pp. i–iv.
4. See, for example: Bennett, R. *Managing Personnel and Performance*, Business Books (1981).
5. For example, see: Brown, J. A. C. *The Social Psychology of Industry*, Penguin (1954 and 1986).
6. For a development of this approach, see: Schein, E. H. *Organizational Psychology*, Third edition, Prentice-Hall (1988).
7. Taylor, F. W. *Scientific Management*, Harper and Row (1947).
8. Ritti, R. R. *The Ropes to Skip and the Ropes to Know*, Fourth edition, Wiley (1994) p. 72.
9. Vroom, V. H. *Work and Motivation*, Wiley (1964). (Also published by Krieger (1982).)
10. Hunt, J. W. *Managing People at Work: A Manager's Guide to Behaviour in Organisations*, Third edition, McGraw-Hill (1992).
11. *Management News*, the newspaper of the British Institute of Management, No. 64, February 1990, p. 6.
12. Maslow, A. H. 'A Theory of Human Motivation', *Psychological Review*, 50, July 1943, pp. 370–96 and Maslow, A. H. *Motivation and Personality*, Third edition, Harper and Row (1987).
13. Hall. D. T. and Nougaim, K. E. 'An Examination of Maslow's Need Hierarchy in an Organizational Setting', *Organizational Behavior and Human Performance*, vol. 3, February 1968, pp. 12–35.
14. Lawler, E. E. and Suttle, J. L. 'A Causal Correlational Test of the Need Hierarchy Concept', *Organizational Behaviour and Human Performance*, vol. 7, 1972, pp. 265–87.
15. Wahba, M. A. and Bridwell, L. G. 'Maslow Reconsidered: A Review of Research on the Need Hierarchy Theory', *Organizational Behavior and Human Performance*, vol. 15, 1976, pp. 212–40.
16. Steers, R. M. and Porter, L. W. *Motivation and Work Behaviour*, Fifth edition, McGraw-Hill (1991).
17. Alderfer, C. P. *Existence, Relatedness and Growth*, Collier Macmillan (1972).
18. Herzberg, F., Mausner, B. and Synderman, B. B. *The Motivation to Work*, Second edition, Chapman and Hall (1959).
19. Herzberg, F. *Work and the Nature of Man*, Granada Publishing Ltd (1974).
20. For examples, see: (i) Bockman, V. M. 'The Herzberg Controversy', *Personnel Psychology*, vol. 24, Summer 1971, pp. 155–89, which analyses existing evidence from a wide variety of studies; (ii) Filley, A. C., House, R. J. and Kerr, S. *Managerial Process and Organizational Behavior*, Second edition, Scott Foresman (1976). A number of different sets of interviews found a high level of validity for the theoretical prediction.
21. Vroom, V. H. *Work and Motivation*, Wiley (1964). (Also published by Krieger (1982).)
22. House, R. J. and Wigdor, L. A. 'Herzberg's Dual-Factor Theory of Job Satisfaction and Motivation: A Review of the Evidence and a Criticism', *Personnel Psychology*, vol. 20, Winter 1967, pp. 369–90.
23. King, N. 'A Clarification and Evaluation of the Two-Factor Theory of Job Satisfaction', *Psychological Bulletin*, vol. 74, July 1970, pp. 18–31.
24. Goldthorpe, J. *et al. The Affluent Worker*, Cambridge University Press (1968).
25. Weaver, T. 'Theory M: Motivating with Money', *Cornell HRA Quarterly*, vol. 29 no. 3, November 1988, pp. 40–5.
26. Blackburn, R. M. and Mann, M. *The Working Class in the Labour Market*, Macmillan (1979).

27. See, for example: Hulin, C. L. and Smith, P. A. 'An Empirical Investigation of Two Implications of the Two-Factor Theory of Job Satisfaction', *Journal of Applied Psychology*, vol. 51, October 1967, pp. 396–402.

28. McClelland, D. C. *Human Motivation*, Cambridge University Press (1988).

29. McClelland, D. C. 'Business Drive and National Achievement', *Harvard Business Review*, vol. 40, July–August 1962, pp. 99–112.

30. McClelland, D. C. and Burnham, D. H. 'Power is the Great Motivation', *Harvard Business Review*, vol. 54, March–April 1976, pp. 100–10.

31. Vroom, V. H. *Work and Motivation*, Wiley (1964). (Also published by Krieger (1982).)

32. Galbraith, J. and Cummings, L. L. 'An Empirical Investigation of the Motivational Determinants of Task Performance', *Organizational Behavior and Human Performance*, vol. 2, 1967, pp. 237–57.

33. Porter, L. W. and Lawler, E. E. *Managerial Attitudes and Performance*, Irwin (1968).

34. Graen, G. 'Instrumentality Theory of Work Motivation', *Journal of Applied Psychology Monographs*, vol. 53, no. 2, 1969, part 2.

35. Lawler, E. E. *Motivation in Work Organizations*, Brooks/Cole (1973).

36. Porter, L. W., Lawler, E. E. and Hackman, J. R. *Behavior in Organizations*, McGraw-Hill (1975), pp. 57–8.

37. Tampoe, M. 'Knowledge Workers – The New Management Challenge', *Professional Manager*, November 1994, pp. 12–13.

38. Adams, J. S. 'Injustice in Social Exchange', in Berkowitz, L. (ed.) *Advances in Experimental Social Psychology*, Academic Press (1965). Abridged in Steers, R. M. and Porter, L. W. *Motivation and Work Behavior*, Second edition, McGraw-Hill (1979), pp. 107–24.

39. Locke, E. A. 'Towards a Theory of Task Motivation and Incentives', *Organizational Behavior and Human Performance*, vol. 3, 1968, pp. 157–89.

40. For examples, see: (i) Latham, G. P. and Yukl, G. A. 'A Review of the Research on the Applications of Goal Setting in Organizations', *Academy of Management Journal*, vol. 18, 1975, pp. 824–45; (ii) Latham, G. P. and Locke, E. A. 'Goal Setting: A Motivational Technique that Works', *Organizational Dynamics*, Autumn 1979, pp. 28-80.

41. Locke, E. A. 'Personal Attitudes and Motivation', *Annual Review of Psychology*, vol. 26, 1975, pp. 457–80.

42. For a summary of research supporting these conclusions, see: Miner, J. B. *Theories of Organizational Behavior*, Holt, Rinehart and Winston (1980).

518

15 JOB SATISFACTION AND WORK PERFORMANCE

To make the best use of people as a valuable resource of the organisation, attention must be given to the relationship between staff and the nature and content of their jobs. The work organisation and the design of jobs can have a significant effect on staff. Attention needs to be given to the quality of working life. The manager needs to understand how best to make work more satisfying for staff and to overcome obstacles to effective performance.

 Learning objectives

To:

- Explain the meaning and nature of job satisfaction;

- Detail dimensions of job satisfaction;

- Explain the nature of technology, work and psychological well-being;

- Examine sources of stress at work;

- Detail main approaches to improving job design and work organisation;

- Assess broader organisational approaches to improved job design;

- Evaluate the relationships between job satisfaction and effective work performance.

Worth thinking about

'I read recently a major study that says although people may not wish to admit it openly the greatest influence on job satisfaction is how much they are paid and how this compares with other people.' . . . 'Well I read recently quotes from celebrity CEOs that what is more important to people and their performance at work is not money but genuine recognition and praise.'

THE MEANING AND NATURE OF JOB SATISFACTION

Motivation to work well is usually related to job satisfaction, but the nature of this relationship is not clear. One view is that the motivation required for a person to achieve a high level of performance is satisfaction with the job. However, although the level of job satisfaction may well affect the strength of motivation, this is not always the case.

Attempting to understand the nature of job satisfaction is not easy. It is a complex concept which can mean a variety of things for different people. Satisfaction is not the same as motivation. **Job satisfaction is more of an attitude, an internal state. It could, for example, be associated with a personal feeling of achievement, either quantitative or qualitative.** Motivation is a process which *may* lead to job satisfaction.

Motivation and job satisfaction

The content theories of motivation (discussed in Chapter 14) are related more to job satisfaction. In particular, *Herzberg*'s two-factor theory is essentially a theory of job satisfaction. His belief is that job enrichment should give people the opportunity to use their talents and abilities, and to exercise more self-control over the job. Inherent in the job should be a learning and growth experience.[1] Building on from the two-factor theory, Herzberg has identified a number of factors as part of an approach to job design and job enrichment.[2]

The content theories of motivation also assume a direct relationship between job satisfaction and improved performance. The expectancy theories of motivation, however, recognise the complexity of work motivation and consider in more detail the relationship between motivation, satisfaction and performance.

In recent years attention to job satisfaction has become more closely associated with broader organisational approaches to improved job design and the quality of working life movement.

JOB SATISFACTION AND WORK PERFORMANCE

Job satisfaction does not necessarily lead to improved work performance. For example, from the results of twenty studies, *Vroom* found no simple relationship, and only a low median correlation (0.14), between job satisfaction and job performance.[3]

Argyle suggests a probable relationship between satisfaction and productivity for highly skilled workers, or for those workers involved deeply with their work. However, individual differences cloud the position. There may well be workers who work hard when contented. But some workers are happiest when they can take things easy. Other workers may work hard to forget their troubles.

Argyle also examined the relationship between job satisfaction and absenteeism, and labour turnover. Both are affected by factors other than job satisfaction, but it is concluded that there is a lower level of voluntary absenteeism, and of labour turnover, when there is a high level of job satisfaction.[4]

No clear relationship

The relationship between job satisfaction and performance is an issue of continuing debate and controversy. One view, associated with the early human relations approach, is that satisfaction leads to performance. An alternative view is that performance leads to satisfaction. *Luthans*, however, suggests that: 'Although most people assume a positive relationship, the preponderance of research evidence indicates that there is no strong linkage between satisfaction and productivity.'[5]

Bassett also suggests that research studies have found only a limited relationship between satisfaction and work output and offer scant comfort to those seeking to confirm that a satisfied worker is a productive worker. Labour turnover and absenteeism are commonly associated with dissatisfaction but although there may be some correlation there are many other possible factors. There appear to be no universal generalisations about worker dissatisfaction that offer easy management solutions to problems of turnover and absenteeism. Bassett suggests that it is primarily in the realm of job design that opportunity for constructive improvement of worker satisfaction appears to be high.[6] (Job design is discussed later in this chapter.)

DIMENSIONS OF JOB SATISFACTION

Job satisfaction is itself a complex concept and difficult to measure objectively. The level of job satisfaction is affected by a wide range of variables relating to individual, social, cultural, organisational and environmental factors.

- **Individual factors** include: personality, education, intelligence and abilities, age, marital status, orientation to work.
- **Social factors** include: relationships with co-workers, group working and norms, opportunities for interaction, informal organisation.
- **Cultural factors** include: underlying attitudes, beliefs and values.
- **Organisational factors** include: nature and size, formal structure, personnel policies and procedures, employee relations, nature of the work, technology and work organisation, supervision and styles of leadership, management systems, working conditions.
- **Environmental factors** include: economic, social, technical and governmental influences.

These different factors all affect job satisfaction of certain individuals in a given set of circumstances but not necessarily in others. The various studies of job satisfaction all have some validity.

Many factors influencing job satisfaction

There is some doubt whether job satisfaction consists of a single dimension or a number of separate dimensions. Some workers may be satisfied with certain aspects of their work and dissatisfied with other aspects. There does, however, appear to be a positive correlation between satisfaction in different areas of work. This suggests a single overall factor of job satisfaction. However, it seems that there is no one, general, comprehensive theory which explains job satisfaction.[7]

There is also a wide range of factors which influence job satisfaction including, for example, Herzberg's hygiene and motivating factors. This means that there are many possible approaches in which to view the subject area. (One possible framework is given in Fig. 15.1.)

Some of the major factors which have a particular influence on job satisfaction include:

- frustration and alienation;
- the nature of technology;
- meaningful work and the nature of supervision;
- work and psychological well-being;
- stress at work.

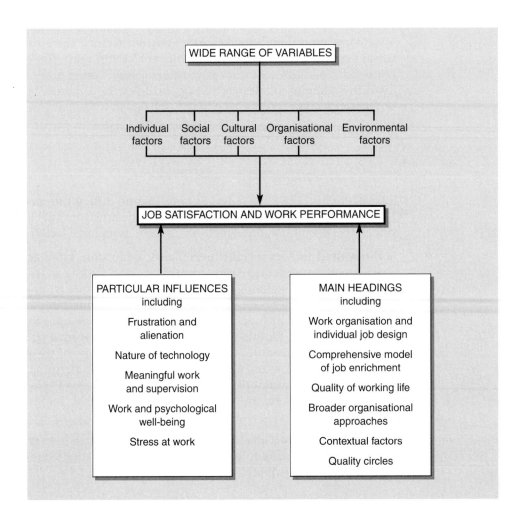

**Fig. 15.1
A framework for the study of job satisfaction**

Other main headings under which to view job satisfaction include:

● work organisation and individual job design;
● comprehensive model of job enrichment;
● quality of working life;
● broader organisational approaches;
● contextual factors;
● quality circles.

ALIENATION AT WORK

One approach to job satisfaction is in terms of frustration and alienation at work. Alienation refers to the detachment of the person from his or her work role. The concept of alienation at work is associated originally with the views of *Marx*.[8] He saw the division of labour in pursuit of profit, and exploitation by employers, as a denial of the workers' need for self-expression. Workers become estranged from the product of their work. Work no longer provided a satisfying experience in itself, but represented a means of satisfying other external demands.

The concept of alienation has been extended by *Blauner*.[9] He describes alienation in terms of four dimensions: powerlessness, meaninglessness, isolation and self-estrangement.

● **Powerlessness** denotes the workers' lack of control over management policy, immediate work processes, or conditions of employment.
● **Meaninglessness** stems from standardisation and division of labour. It denotes the inability to see the purpose of work done, or to identify with the total production process or finished product.
● **Isolation** is not belonging to an integrated work group or to the social work organisation, and not being guided by group norms of behaviour.
● **Self-estrangement** is the failure to see work as an end in itself or as a central life issue. Workers experience a depersonalised detachment, and work is seen solely as a means to an end.

Analysis of different technologies

Blauner examined these dimensions in a comparative analysis of four different technologies: craft, machine minding, assembly line and automated process. He suggested that all modern bureaucratic organisations have inherent alienating tendencies and found most manual workers were alienated to some degree. The extent of alienation experienced is likely to be a function of the nature of technology. Assembly line technology was found to be most alienating. Machine minding and automated process were in the middle. Craft technology was the least alienating.

There is, of course, no reason to suggest that the experience of alienation at work is limited, necessarily, to manual workers. Marx emphasised that the social organisation of production in pursuit of profit led to alienation for all persons involved irrespective of their position in the organisation. *Weber* linked the growth of bureaucratic organisations, generally, with an increase in alienation at work.[10]

THE NATURE OF TECHNOLOGY

The work of Blauner has drawn attention to the nature of technology as a major influence on job satisfaction. Technology relates to both the physical aspects of machines, equipment, processes and work layout; and the actual methods, systems and procedures involved in the carrying out of work. Technology is therefore a major influence on the general climate of the organisation and the behaviour of people at work.[11]

In a study in a new American car assembly plant, *Walker and Guest* examined the effects of mass production, assembly line work on employee behaviour.[12] They describe the characteristics of assembly line work as: repetitious and machine paced; involving a minimum of skill; using predetermined techniques with no choice of tools or methods; and closely defined divisions of the production process. The workers were able to perform their jobs with only 'surface mental attention'.

The nature of the job, the technological layout and the high level of noise restricted the amount of social interaction and contacts that workers could have with each other. The opportunities for interpersonal relationships were important, and when these opportunities were missing the workers felt deprived. The workers' main contact with authority was through the supervisors and this was an important factor in job satisfaction. There was little contact with the managers and as a result relationships with management were of little importance.

Workers in jobs involving a high degree of the characteristics of mass production disliked those aspects of their jobs. They also had a higher rate of absenteeism than workers in jobs with fewer of the characteristics of mass production.

Mass production work and stress

From an analysis of the results of two surveys of employee attitudes conducted by the University of Michigan and the Swedish Institute for Social Research, *Karasek* examined the relationship between mass production work and stress.[13] It was suggested that stress was related to two main job characteristics: (i) workload; and (ii) discretion in how to do the work. The most stressful jobs were those that combined high workload with low discretion.

Both the American and Swedish surveys supported this argument. High-stress jobs in America included: assembly line workers; garment stitchers; goods and material handling; nurses' aides and orderlies; and telephone operators. Karasek suggests that the use of mental ability, exercising judgement and making decisions is not usually stressful. Stress can be reduced, therefore, if workers are given greater discretion in how their work is performed. As discretion can be increased without changing workloads, mental health could be improved without affecting productivity.

Information technology

The impact of information technology (discussed in Chapter 3) can also have a significant influence on job satisfaction. Information technology will demand new patterns of work. It will affect the nature and content of individual jobs; the function and structure of work groups; changes in the nature of supervision; the hierarchical structure of jobs and responsibilities; and the management task.[14]

MEANINGFUL WORK

From an extension of earlier studies at Texas Instruments, *Myers* examined the nature of meaningful work. An example of how the meaningfulness of a job can be determined is through a series of questions: (i) in terms of the supervisor's insight into the scope of meaningful work; and (ii) an analysis of work by the job incumbents themselves.[15] (*See* Fig. 15.2.)

From discussions on the emerging role of the supervisor it was concluded that an effective supervisor is one who 'provides a climate in which people have a sense of working for themselves'. In terms of day-to-day relationships the primary role of the supervisor was 'staying out of the way to let people manage their work'.[16]

Nature and level of supervision

We can see, then, that the nature and level of supervision is another factor which can influence the satisfaction people derive from their work. Supervision involves technical knowledge, human relations skills and co-ordination of work activities, Effective supervision is necessary for job satisfaction and for high levels of work performance.[17] Kindly and thoughtful leader behaviour is likely to generate high worker satisfaction. Supervisors who adopt a considerate manner towards their workers tend to have the more highly satisfied work groups.[18]

Sample Items from Supervisor Worksheet for Analysing Meaningfulness of Work

Planning. Can the individual or group –
- Name customers and state delivery dates for products or services?
- State the product quality and quantity commitments?
- Organise their work layout and influence personnel assignments?
- Set goals and standards based on customer needs and fix priorities?
- State the sources of their materials and problems in obtaining them?
- List direct and overhead costs, selling price and other profit and loss information?

Doing. Does the job –
- Utilise people's talents and require their attention?
- Enable people to see the relationship of their work to other operations?

- Provide access to all the information they need to do their work?
- Have a satisfactory work cycle – neither too long nor too short?
- Give people feedback on how well they are doing?
- Enable them to see how they contribute to the usefulness of the product for the customer?

Controlling. Can the individual or group –
- State customer quality requirements and reasons for these standards?
- Keep their own records of quality and quantity?
- Check quality and quantity of work and revise procedures?
- Evaluate and modify work layout on their own initiative?
- Identify and correct unsafe working conditions?
- Obtain information from people outside the group as a means of evaluating performance?

Sample Items from Job Incumbent Checklist for Describing Meaningfulness of Work

	No	Sometimes	Yes
Planning			
● Does my job allow me to set my own performance goals?	()	()	()
● Is setting my own goals essential to good job performance?	()	()	()
● Do I want more opportunity to set my own performance goals?	()	()	()
Doing			
● Does my job provide variety?	()	()	()
● Is variety in my job essential to good job performance?	()	()	()
● Do I want more variety in my work?	()	()	()
Controlling			
● Does my job allow me to measure my work performance?	()	()	()
● Is opportunity to evaluate my own work essential?	()	()	()
● Do I want more opportunity to measure my own job performance?	()	()	()

Fig. 15.2 Questions to determine the meaningfulness of a job

WORK AND PSYCHOLOGICAL WELL-BEING

As part of a study of the psychological importance of work undertaken by the Social and Applied Psychology Unit at the University of Sheffield, *Warr* has examined variations among jobs, and aspects and types of work which enhance or impair psychological well-being.[19] Controlled experiments are carried out to change the content of jobs in a direction predicted to increase employee well-being.

One example of the study set out to examine consequences of increasing the control which lower-level production workers have over their work tasks and interrelationships. Jobs were redesigned to shift responsibilities from supervisors to teams of shop-floor workers. The workers were given greater control over the pacing of their work, distribution of tasks among themselves, and general organisation of their time and effort.

These changes increased the scope of workers' decision-making, and introduced wider opportunities for skill use, work variety and constructive interpersonal contacts. Information on employee attitudes, well-being and performance was gathered before the changes, and then 6 and 18 months later. Results indicated that employee well-being increased substantially. Overall job satisfaction was significantly greater and psychological distress declined significantly.

Psychologically 'good' and 'bad' jobs

The Social and Applied Psychology Unit contains a psychological clinic which receives workers referred by their medical practitioners as suffering from neurotic problems linked to their jobs. From studies of people in the clinic, and in jobs, Warr has derived a perspective on features of paid work which are psychologically 'good' or 'bad'. (*See* Fig 15.3.) Many of these features are desirable only up to a point. For example: most people want a reasonable, but not excessive, degree of interpersonal contact; and some psychological threat is inherent in the development of skills and pursuit of challenging goals. Warr points out that one of the tasks of occupational research is to determine the optimum level of these variables.

		'Good' jobs have	*'Bad' jobs have*
1	Money	more	less
2	Variety	more	less
3	Goals, traction	more	less
4	Decision latitude	more	less
5	Skill use/development	more	less
6	Psychological threat	less	more
7	Security	more	less
8	Interpersonal contact	more	less
9	Valued social position	more	less

Fig. 15.3 Characteristics of psychologically 'good' and 'bad' jobs

(Reprinted with permission from Peter Warr, 'Work, Jobs and Unemployment', *Bulletin of the British Psychological Society*, vol. 36, 1983, p. 309.)

STRESS AT WORK

There appears little doubt that one of the major adverse influences on job satisfaction, work performance and productivity, and absenteeism and turnover is the incidence of stress at work.[20] Stress is a complex and dynamic concept. It is a source of tension and frustration, and can arise through a number of interrelated influences on behaviour, including the individual, group, organisational and environmental factors discussed in Chapter 1.

According to *McKenna*, for example:

> In human terms any situation that is seen as burdensome, threatening, ambiguous or boring is likely to induce stress. This is the type of situation that would normally strike the individual as deserving immediate attention or concern and is viewed as unfortunate or annoying. There tends to be the feeling that the situation should not exist, but because of it the person feels disappointed or annoyed and eventually is prone to anxiety, depression, anger, hostility, inadequacy, and low frustration tolerance.[21]

Role relationships and conflict

One potential major source of work stress arises from role incongruence and role conflict (discussed in Chapter 6). It was suggested that although a certain amount of stress may *arguably* be seen as a good thing and helps to promote a high level of performance, it is also potentially very harmful. Role stress can lead to difficulties in communication and interpersonal relationships and can have an adverse affect on morale, performance and effectiveness at work, and health.

Demands for improved business competitiveness and lower operating costs have frequently led to restructuring of organisations and reductions in staffing levels. This has placed greater pressures on remaining staff and resulted in a growing number of work-related health problems, work stress and a less efficient workforce.[22]

Handy suggests five organisational situations that are likely to create role problems and therefore stress for the individual:

- **Responsibility for the work of others** – reconciling overlapping or conflicting objectives of groups and organisations, of groups and individuals, of self and superiors.
- **Innovative functions** – conflicting priorities and different psychological demands between the routine and administrative aspects of the job and the creative side.
- **Integrative or boundary functions** – the particularly stressful role to the co-ordinator, link person or outside contact, perhaps due to the lack of control over their demands or resources.
- **Relationship problems** – difficulties with a boss, subordinates or colleagues. For some people, particularly those with a technical orientation, the need to work with other people is a worrying complication.
- **Career uncertainty** – if future career prospects become doubtful the uncertainty can quickly become stressful and spread to affect the whole of a person's work. [23]

Managerial stress

The Institute of Management and Personal Performance Consultants UK Limited conducted a wide-ranging survey into the state of managerial morale. The survey of almost a thousand managers who are members of the Institute of Management aimed to establish whether the combined effects of recession and organisational restructuring were leading to increased stress among managers; and to identify the key causes and effects of management stress.[24]

Among the findings of the survey were that, although for over 80 per cent of managers work is a source of satisfaction, it is also a source of stress for seven in ten managers and a source of worry for over half. The main causes of anxiety are employment prospects and the demands of work on time and relationships. The impact of stress is far-reaching. Three-quarters say it has some impact on their morale, on their effectiveness at work and on their relationship with their partner. Seven in ten believe their overall health is affected. (*See* Fig. 15.4a.)

Within work hours, managers viewed the major source of stress as the incompetence of their superiors. Other major sources of stress were poor internal communications, office politics, time pressures and deadlines, unrealistic business objectives, constant interruptions, and securing access to the right information. (*See* Fig. 15.4b.)

Base: 989 respondents	Strongly agree %	Agree %	Not sure %	Disagree %	Strongly disagree %
My work is a source of satisfaction	29	53	8	9	1
My work is a source of worry	7	49	10	28	6
My work is a source of stress	16	55	14	13	2
My work is a source of pleasure	14	52	17	14	2
I am suffering from too much work	9	31	22	34	4
I have a good balance between home and work	7	36	18	33	6
I have lost interest in work	3	10	11	43	33
I look forward to going to work	12	48	21	16	4
I sometimes feel unable to cope at work	2	22	11	47	17

Extent to which work-related anxiety affects work and home life				
Base: all respondents	Not at all %	To some extent %	Quite a lot %	Very much %
---	---	---	---	---
Morale at work	23	40	23	14
Effectiveness at work	24	43	22	10
Relationship with partner	25	43	22	10
Relationship with family	32	39	20	9
Health	28	44	19	10

Fig. 15.4a Attitudes to work and effects of work-related anxiety

Base: as for Fig. 15.4a, but excluding non-applicable responses	Very stressful %	A little stressful %	Not at all stressful %
Work/home issues			
Number of hours worked	15	62	23
Travel during work	7	43	50
Journey to work	10	36	54
Weekend working	12	58	30
Arranging childcare	6	23	71
Arranging care for elderly/disabled relatives	10	29	61
Finding time to spend with children	14	57	29
Finding time to spend with partner	17	62	21
Finding time to relax	24	56	20
Organisation of work			
Unrealistic business objectives	21	60	19
Poor internal communications	30	58	12
Securing access to the right information	20	62	18
Lack of power and influence	19	53	28
Time pressures and deadlines	23	63	14
Office politics	29	49	22
Attending too many meetings	19	56	25
Inadequately trained staff	18	58	24
Incompetent senior management	35	45	20
Insufficient work	11	26	63
Constant interruptions	20	63	17
Relationships with colleagues	6	44	50
Relationships with superiors	13	49	38
Managing junior staff	3	37	60
Managing staff problems	4	48	48
Using existing technology	3	37	60
Keeping up with new technology	7	53	40
Handling constant change	10	55	35

Fig. 15.4b
Work, home and organisational issues as sources of stress

Note: percentages may not total 100 due to rounding.

(Reproduced with permission from *Managers Under Stress: A Survey of Management Morale in the '90s*, The Institute of Management, December 1993.)

WORK ORGANISATION AND JOB DESIGN

The application of motivational theories, and greater understanding of dimensions of job satisfaction and work performance, have led to increasing interest in job design. The nature of the work organisation and the design of jobs can have a significant effect on the job satisfaction of staff and on the level of organisational performance.

Job design is concerned with the relationship between workers and the nature and content of jobs, and their task functions. It attempts to meet people's personal and social needs at work through reorganisation or restructuring of work. There are two major reasons for attention to job design:

- to enhance the personal satisfaction that people derive from their work; and
- to make the best use of people as a valuable resource of the organisation and to help overcome obstacles to their effective performance.

(See also the discussion on quality of working life later in this chapter.)

INDIVIDUAL JOB REDESIGN

Earlier approaches to job design concentrated on the restructuring of individual jobs and the application of three main methods: (i) job rotation; (ii) job enlargement; and (iii) job enrichment. (*See* Fig. 15.5.)

Job rotation

Job rotation is the most basic form of individual job design. Job rotation involves moving a person from one job or task to another. It attempts to add some variety and to help remove boredom, at least in the short term. However, if the tasks involved are all very similar and routine, then once the person is familiar with the new task the work may quickly prove boring again.

Job rotation may lead to the acquisition of additional skills but does not necessarily develop the level of skills. Strictly, job rotation is not really job design because neither the nature of the task nor the method of working is restructured. However, job rotation may help the person identify more with the completed product or service. It can also be used as a form of training.

Job enlargement

Job enlargement involves increasing the scope of the job and the range of tasks that the person carries out. It is usually achieved by combining a number of

**Fig. 15.5
Main methods
of individual
job redesign**

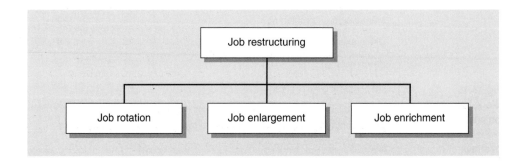

related operations at the same level. **Job enlargement is horizontal job design; it makes a job structurally bigger.** It lengthens the time cycle of operations and may give the person greater variety.

Job enlargement, however, is not always very popular and may often be resisted by workers. Although it may give the person more to do, it does little to improve intrinsic satisfaction or a sense of achievement. Workers may see job enlargement as simply increasing the number of routine, boring tasks they have to perform. Some workers seem to prefer simple, routine tasks which they can undertake almost automatically, and with little thought or concentration. This enables them to day-dream and to socialise with colleagues without affecting their performance.

Job enrichment **Job enrichment** is an extension of the more basic job rotation and job enlargement methods of job design. Job enrichment arose out of *Herzberg*'s two-factor theory. It attempts to enrich the job by incorporating motivating or growth factors such as increased responsibility and involvement, opportunities for advancement and the sense of achievement.

Job enrichment involves vertical job enlargement. It aims to give the person greater autonomy and authority over the planning, execution and control of their own work. It focuses attention on intrinsic satisfaction. Job enrichment increases the complexity of the work and should provide the person with a more meaningful and challenging job. It provides greater opportunities for psychological growth.

Main methods of achieving job enrichment include the following:

- permitting workers greater freedom and control over the scheduling and pacing of their work as opposed to machine pacing;
- allowing workers to undertake a full task cycle, build or assemble a complete product or component, or deliver a complete service;
- providing workers with tasks or jobs which challenge their abilities and make fuller use of their training, expertise and skills;
- giving workers greater freedom to work in self-managing teams with greater responsibility for monitoring their own performance and the minimum of direct supervision; and
- providing workers with the opportunity to have greater direct contact with clients, consumers or users of the product or service.

A COMPREHENSIVE MODEL OF JOB ENRICHMENT

Attempts to improve intrinsic motivation must not only include considerations of job characteristics but also take account of individual differences and attributes, and people's orientation to work. A popular and comprehensive model of job enrichment has been developed by *Hackman and Oldham* (Fig. 15.6).[25] The model views job enrichment in terms of increasing five core job dimensions: skill variety, task identity, task significance, autonomy and feedback. These core job characteristics create three psychological states:

- experienced meaningfulness of the work;
- experienced responsibility for the outcomes of the work; and
- knowledge of the actual results of the work activities.

**Fig. 15.6
A job characteristics
model of work
motivation**

(Reproduced with permission from Hackman, J. R. and Oldham, G. R. *Work Redesign*, p. 90, © 1980 by Addison-Wesley Publishing Company, Inc. Reprinted with permission of the publishers.)

**Five core
dimensions**

The five core job dimensions can be summarised as follows:

- **skill variety** – the extent to which a job entails different activities and involves a range of different skills and talents;
- **task identity** – the extent to which a job involves completion of a whole piece of work with a visible outcome;
- **task significance** – the extent to which a job has a meaningful impact on other people, either inside or outside the organisation;
- **autonomy** – the extent to which a job provides freedom, independence and discretion in planning the work and determining how to undertake it;
- **feedback** – the extent to which work activities result in direct and clear information on the effectiveness of job performance.

An example of a job with little enrichment could be that of a mass production assembly line worker, or a copy typist, where all five core characteristics are likely to score low. An example of an enriched job could be that of a parish priest who draws upon a wide range of social skills and talents, who can usually identify with the whole task, and whose job has clear and important meaning and significance. There is a very high level of autonomy, and likely to be direct and clear feedback.

**Motivating
potential score**

From these five core job dimensions Hackman and Oldham have developed an equation which gives a single index of a person's job profile. By answering a questionnaire – the Job Diagnostic Survey (JDS) – and by giving a score (between 1 and 7) to each job dimension, the person can calculate an overall measure of job enrichment, called the motivating potential score (MPS).

Examples of questions from the JDS are:

- How much variety is there in your job?
- To what extent does your job involve doing a whole and identifiable piece of work?
- In general, how significant or important is your job?
- How much autonomy is there in your job?
- To what extent does doing the job itself provide you with information about your work performance?

$$\text{MPS} = \left\{ \frac{\underset{\text{variety}}{\text{Skill}} + \underset{\text{identity}}{\text{Task}} + \underset{\text{significance}}{\text{Task}}}{3} \right\} \times \text{Autonomy} \times \text{Feedback}$$

The first three job dimensions of skill variety, task identity and task significance are averaged, since it is the combination of these dimensions which contributes to experienced meaningfulness of work. The remaining two job dimensions, autonomy and feedback, stand on their own. Since scores for skill variety, task identity and task significance are additive, this means that the absence of one dimension can be partially offset by the presence of the other dimensions. However, if either autonomy or feedback is absent then, because of the multiplicative relationship, the MPS would be zero. The job would offer no potential to motivate the person.

Empirical support

Empirical support for the model is mixed. From their own studies Hackman and Oldham claim that people with enriched jobs, and high score levels on the Job Diagnostic Survey, experienced more satisfaction and internal motivation. The core job dimensions of skill variety, task identity and task significance combined to predict the level of experienced meaningfulness of the work.

The core dimensions of autonomy and feedback did not relate so clearly to experienced responsibility and knowledge of results. Some of the other dimensions were as good, or better, in predicting these psychological conditions. In general, however, the results of their studies showed that jobs which scored high on the core dimensions were associated with high levels of personal and work outcomes.

Although the core job dimensions do appear to influence personal and work outcomes, there is some doubt as to the validity of the causal relationships – that is, the extent to which the job characteristics influence critical psychological states, and the psychological states then influence outcomes.[26] There is also some doubt as to the extent to which high correlations might be expected on the basis of people's desire for consistency in their approach, rather than as a result of any other links among the measures involved.[27]

JOB ENRICHMENT AND JOB SATISFACTION

In general, there appears little doubt that restructuring the nature of work itself, and providing job enrichment by making it more interesting and challenging, does increase job satisfaction.[28] However, it also appears that interest in job design

and job satisfaction is consistently lower with those at the lower rungs of the hierarchical ladder and that satisfaction rises as a function of the level of organisation.[29]

From a review of developments in the field, and case study evidence, *Taylor* concludes that theories of job enrichment and employee motivation do work.[30] From the case studies, Taylor appears to support Herzberg's motivation–hygiene theory (discussed in Chapter 14). The factors which affect motivation to work are job content factors and job context factors.

The situations people find most satisfying and rewarding are invariably those which provide the opportunity to satisfy **job content**: a sense of achievement; some act of recognition and appraisal; authority and responsibility; growth, advancement and self-development; and the nature of the work itself – variety, creativity and a challenge.

Job context factors are those relating to: company policy and administration–organisation; interpersonal relationships; security and effect on personal life; status; work conditions; salary; and competent supervision. If any of the job context factors are allowed to deteriorate in any way a climate of dissatisfaction and tension, frustration and friction will prevail and people will not perform at their best.

From the case studies, Taylor found that the situations people find most satisfying and rewarding are invariably those which provide the opportunities to satisfy job content. If any of the job context factors are allowed to deteriorate in any way, a climate of dissatisfaction and tension, frustration and friction will prevail and people will not perform at their best.

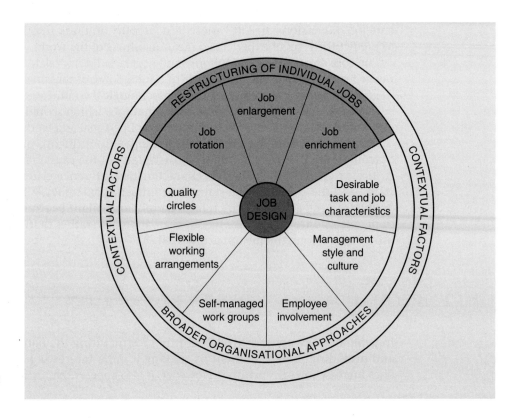

Fig. 15.7
Main approaches to job design

It is however important to remember that not all workers are necessarily seeking an enriched, more demanding or more challenging job. There will always be some workers who do not wish to accept greater responsibility or autonomy. They appear to prefer simple and routine work, and to accept a high level of direction and control by management.

BROADER ORGANISATIONAL APPROACHES TO IMPROVED JOB DESIGN

Approaches to improved job design now take on a broader perspective. For example, in the context of technological change the focus of attention has spread from manipulating the tasks of individual jobs to the wider organisational context. Attention needs to be given to improving the effectiveness of the organisation in achieving its goals and objectives; and helping the development of skills and resources to manage successfully changes in the way the organisation functions. (*See* Fig. 15.7.)

THE QUALITY OF WORKING LIFE

Increased interest in job design has been associated with the development of a broader social concern for the quality of working life (QWL). In 1973 a Department of Employment report, *On the Quality of Working Life*, summarised case studies of people's experiences of work and descriptions of experiments in improving work systems in four countries, including the UK.[31] It made recommendations for future government initiatives. The report dealt with five main themes:

- efficiency at work;
- satisfaction at work;
- the link between satisfaction and efficiency;
- the influence of environmental factors and particularly work technology; and
- developments of thought in social science and people's expectations from work.

Reasons for attention to QWL
It is not always easy to determine the extent to which attention to QWL is based on the exercise of a genuine social responsibility (discussed in Chapter 9) or based on the pursuit of increased economic efficiency. In practice the distinction is blurred and attention to QWL is likely to be motivated by a combination of concern with two related issues:

- a moral or ethical motivation based on the recognition of broader educational standards, changing social values and wider expectations of the quality of working life, including the satisfaction that people derive from their work, and the functioning and management of organisations; and
- motivation through good business practice and enlightened self-interest, the need for cost competitiveness, and attempts to overcome high levels of absenteeism, staff turnover and dissatisfaction, and other obstacles to the search for improved organisational performance.

In considering workers' experience of work, the Department of Employment report drew attention to an American survey, whose authors concluded:

> If one believes that our economic system exists to serve the people rather than that the people exist to serve the system, it follows that increased attention should be directed towards two basic human problems in the workplace: (1) satisfaction of people with the economic and tangible returns from their efforts; and (2) self-fulfilment of individuals through their work. Although considerable progress has been made in solving the first problem, the importance of the second has barely begun to be recognized. The health of the economy is still measured solely in terms of the efficiency with which it can produce large quantities of consumer goods. A second measure – and concern – is needed: one which considers the contribution work is making to the quality of life and to the growth and happiness of the worker.[32]

The essential culture of QWL

Since the publication of the Department of Employment report in 1973, increasing emphasis is being given to the importance of a QWL culture. Such a culture can be seen as a necessary foundation for a successful strategy of Total Quality Management.

In order to translate the concept of QWL into practice it is best understood if it is seen as a goal, as a process for achieving that goal and as a philosophy setting out the way people should be managed.

- **QWL as a goal** – improving organisational performance through the creation of more challenging, satisfying and effective jobs and work environments for people at all levels of the organisation.
- **QWL as a process** – calling for efforts to realise this goal through the active involvement and participation of people throughout the organisation. Through their involvement people can make more meaningful contributions to the business and experience greater feelings of satisfaction, pride in accomplishment and personal growth.
- **QWL as a philosophy** – viewing people as 'assets' to be 'released' and developed, and capable of contributing knowledge, skills, experience and commitment, rather than as 'costs' that are merely extensions of the production and to be controlled.[33]

DESIRABLE TASK AND JOB CHARACTERISTICS

ACAS has summarised evidence about desirable task characteristics and job characteristics as follows.

Tasks should:
- combine to form a coherent whole job, either independently or with related jobs, whose performance makes a significant contribution which is visible to the job-holder;
- provide some variety of pace, method, location and skill;
- provide feedback on performance both directly and through other people;
- provide some degree of discretion and control in the timing, sequence and pace of work effort;
- include some degree of responsibility for outcomes.

Some needs are, in the short run, easily satisfied. In fact, it is feasible to have *too much* variety, which is experienced as unpredictability or incompatibility.

Jobs should:

- provide opportunity for learning and problem-solving within the individual's competence;
- be seen as leading towards some sort of desirable future;
- provide opportunity for development in ways that are relevant to the individual;
- enable people to contribute to decisions affecting their jobs and their objectives;
- ensure that the goals and other people's expectations are clear and provide a degree of challenge;
- provide adequate resources (training, information, equipment, materials);
- provide adequate support from the contact with others.

Again, it is possible, temporarily at any rate, to be faced with too much challenge, too many new problems to solve, which are experienced as stress resulting from overload or conflicting objectives.

As an essential background and context to the design of tasks and jobs:

- industrial relations policies and procedures should be agreed and understood and issues handled in accordance with these arrangements;
- payment systems should be seen as fair and reflect the full contribution of individuals and groups;
- other personnel policies and practices should be fair and adequate; and physical surroundings, health and safety provisions should be satisfactory.[34]

These are general statements which need to be translated in practice, taking account of how people perceive their present tasks and what they regard as improvements, and involving them in changes which affect them and their jobs.

MANAGEMENT STYLE AND CULTURE

The potential benefits of improved job design are unlikely to be realised if attention is focused on the content of jobs alone. Equal, if not more important, is the *process* by which redesign is carried out. This has led to recognition of the importance of management style and, increasingly, of organisation culture. Central to improving the quality of working life is a participative, open style of management involving employees in decisions that affect them, including the design or choice of the technology itself. Personnel policies, including, for example, those relating to pay and benefits, should facilitate and help new concepts of improved job design. Management should attempt to develop a relationship of trust among all members and sections of the organisation, and a confident partnership approach to trade unions.

At the same time, the increasing pace of technological and structural change has made it imperative to address the issues of managing change in ways that would ensure the best outcomes for organisations and for the people in them. An important issue is still the jobs which people are asked to do. When change is being planned, particularly if new technology is to be introduced, a 'window of

opportunity' exists to think about the work that people will do and the design of their jobs. The aim is to ensure that the quality of working life is enhanced rather than undermined.

Views about people at work

Improving job design needs to take account of how people perceive their present tasks, and involving them in changes which affect them and their jobs. It involves the ways of thinking about people at work set out in Fig. 15.8.

Concern for the quality of working life has also been supported by government legislation, for example in the areas of employment protection, employee involvement, and health and safety at work. Such legislation directs management attention to the importance of the work environment and the context in which work is carried out, which in turn can have a direct effect on job satisfaction.

An example of participative work redesign from the metal-can industry in the northern Netherlands is given in Appendix 1 to this chapter.

EMPLOYEE INVOLVEMENT AND EMPOWERMENT

The general movement away from mass production and towards customer-driven niche markets, the downsizing of organisations, and advances in scientific and technological knowledge have emphasised the demand for a highly skilled, trained and motivated workforce. Recognition of the efficient use of human resources for business success together with advances in social democracy have highlighted the increasing importance of employee involvement and industrial partnership including the role played by trade unions.[35]

Increasing business competitiveness demands that organisations have to offer the best quality products or services for the best price. This requires that organisations develop and harness the talents and commitment of all their employees. Getting the best out of people and attempting to improve job satisfaction demand a spirit of teamwork and co-operation, and allowing people a greater say in decisions that affect them at work. In order to improve business performance managers will need to relinquish close control in favour of greater empowerment of employees.

From a discussion of the benefits and problems of empowerment and a review of its operation in a number of companies, *Pickard* concludes that empowerment does appear to be having a radical effect on the way people work. As an example, Pickard describes improved job satisfaction and the changing attitude of staff arising from the introduction of empowerment at Harvester restaurants. Within a framework handed down from head office, staff work in teams which are responsible for making decisions on the running of individual restaurants.[36]

Benefits of employee involvement

A recent Department of Employment publication draws attention to how technological and structural changes have increased the importance of the contribution of the individual and the need for employers to involve their employees. It describes with the aid of real examples of good practice the variety and diversity of successful employee involvement schemes operated by UK employers.[37]

No organisation can perform at its best unless each employee is committed to the corporate objectives and works as an effective team member. Many organisations

ALTERNATIVE VIEWS OF PEOPLE AT WORK	
Derived and developed from presentations made at 'QWL in the 80s' Conference, Toronto, 30 August 1981	
PEOPLE AS 'OBJECTS'	**PEOPLE AS 'AGENTS'**
Workers	
The worker is an extension of his machine	The machine complements the workers by extending the effects of his or her skills
and	*and*
a dispensable spare part	the worker is a unique resource to be developed
which implies	*which suggests*
work should be broken down into single tasks requiring narrow skills	tasks should be grouped and require multiple, broad skills
therefore	*therefore*
design jobs to the lowest common denominator to enhance control	design jobs to take account of people's needs as well as technical requirements
because	*with*
workers require and like laid-down rules and external controls, for example supervisors, specialist staffs and procedures	a degree of self-determination individually or in groups which will be more creative, flexible and effective
and so	*taking into account that whilst*
rewards suitable for workers are wages, benefits and security	economic rewards remain the major concern, there are other factors; the individuals' and the community's needs require to be met
as	*because*
workers cannot and do not want to think about their work, they like repetitive tasks and they do not want responsibility	people have a wide range of talents which if work structures are right they can and will use
because	*and*
workers work, managers think.	the ideas of everyone there can be applied to improve the enterprise.
Managers	
Management's sources of power are its prerogative and status	A manager's authority is earned through competence
which requires	*entailing*
autocratic management with many layers of authority	flat organisation charts and a participative style
because	*so that*
the organisation's objectives are paramount	members' and the community's goals count
and	*and*
financial management is more important than human resource management, because without profits there is no enterprise.	both financial performance *and* human asset management can be measured and both contribute to the survival of the enterprise.
Unions	
A union's job is to improve the terms and conditions of employment of its members	The union's job is not only to improve the terms and conditions of workers in real terms, but to enhance the quality of working life in every respect
thus	*and*
the 'adversarial' stance is the only suitable one for a union	it is appropriate for unions to encourage and take part in participation at many levels on many subjects as well as to bargain
attitudes and behaviour which lead to:	
organisation competitiveness and gamesmanship	co-operative collaboration
with	*towards*
alienation and combat.	commitment and effectiveness.

An important task for the Work Research Unit is and will continue to be to make the ideas associated here with 'people as agents' operational.
(Crown copyright. Reproduced with permission of the Controller of Her Majesty's Stationery Office.)

Fig. 15.8 Extract from the *1981 Report of the Tripartite Steering Group on Job Satisfaction to the Secretary of State for Employment (1982)*

have already discovered benefits of effective employee involvement, including:

- improved performance and productivity;
- improved quality and customer care;
- a more co-operative atmosphere in the workforce;
- reduced staff turnover;
- reduced lost time through absenteeism and disputes; and
- added value through drawing on the skills and knowledge of all employees.

The culture of the organisation

Successful employee involvement can take a number of different forms including:

- effective communication, sharing information and consultation;
- financial participation;
- involving staff in problem-solving, and a commitment to quality management; and
- training and developing the individual.

The report concludes by emphasising that employee involvement is good for organisations and their employees. But successful employee involvement depends on mutual trust and it may be necessary to change the culture of the organisation. In order for an organisation to benefit fully from employee involvement initiatives they must become part and parcel of that organisation's management culture and business plans.

An account of employee involvement through job redesign at Lloyds Bank is given in Appendix 2 to this chapter.

SELF-MANAGED WORK GROUPS

An important development in work redesign and job enrichment is a form of work organisation based on self-managed work groups and team working. This involves a socio-technical approach with technological processes, production methods and the way in which work is carried out integrated with the social system of the organisation, including the informal group structure. Although the effectiveness of self-managed groups does not appear to be all positive, individual members of the group do have higher levels of job satisfaction.[38]

The group assumes greater autonomy and responsibility for the effective performance of the work. Key features of the self-managed work group include the following:

- specific goals are set for the group but members decide the best means by which these goals are to be achieved;
- group members have greater freedom and choice, and wider discretion over the planning, execution and control of their own work;
- collectively members of the group have the necessary variety of expertise and skills to successfully undertake the tasks of the group;
- the level of external supervision is reduced and the role of supervisor becomes more one of giving advice and support to the group;
- feedback and evaluation is related to the performance of the group as a whole.

Popularity and applications

In the USA, self-managed teams are widespread and increasing in popularity.[39] By contrast, in the UK their use to date appears to have only limited applications. However, increasing pressures to demonstrate cost competitiveness may result in autonomous work groups being incorporated into a package of changes associated with the requirements for high-performance work design.[40]

It also seems likely that greater concern for the quality of working life, current trends in restructuring and increasing demands for work flexibility are likely to promote a greater interest in self-managed teams.

According to ACAS, the use of autonomous working groups 'remains one of a variety of work forms for companies to consider in searches for enhanced productivity, flexibility, employee involvement and work satisfaction'.[41]

The introduction of self-managed work groups can also result in a marked reduction in stress.[42]

Autonomy and control

A strong supporter of the idea of the autonomous work group is *Waterman*. In order to build spirit, morale and commitment in any organisation Waterman believes that people should be in control of at least some part of their lives and that they should be given some influence over things that affect them. The quintessence of this belief is the self-managing team – groups of three to ten people who work without any direct supervision. Employees should be organised into teams that cut across old boundaries, trained and placed in jobs that challenge their abilities, given the information they need, informed of what they need to accomplish, and then turned loose.[43]

FLEXIBLE WORKING ARRANGEMENTS

One popular example of giving people greater freedom and control over the scheduling of their work is flexible working hours or flexitime. Within certain limits ('core' times) staff are free to vary arrival, lunch and departure times at work to suit their own individual needs and preferences. However, recent advances in computerisation and telecommunications have had a dramatic and significant effect on the opportunities for flexible working.

Developments in information technology mean that people can now work from almost any geographical location: from head office, a satellite office, a shared access telecentre; or from their home, hotel room or car. An increasingly popular means of teleworking is telecommuting where staff work from home with a computer network, fax and telephone.[44]

A survey by the Institute of Management and Manpower plc found that the key factors affecting employment decisions and the shape and size of the workforce are the need to cut costs, and the related requirements to boost productivity and increase flexibility. Flexible working is now essential and the rule for Britain's largest employers. The core/complementary model of employment is now firmly established as an integral part of employers' human resource strategies and companies are addressing the management implications of their new style workforce.[45]

CONTEXTUAL FACTORS IN JOB DESIGN

The different methods of job design are not necessarily separate approaches. They are interrelated and there is some overlapping among them. For example, goal-setting, which was discussed in Chapter 14, is sometimes viewed as another approach to job design. Goal setting involves building goals, feedback and incentives into the structure of the job. In addition, there are many other associated (contextual) factors which affect job design, including, for example: organisational culture; organisation structure; the system of management and style of leadership; trade unions; personnel policies and procedures; communications; group norms; ergonomics; and the working environment.

Job design: a continuous movement

Whatever form job design takes, it should be augmented by:

- developmental design; and
- organisational supports.[46]

Job design should be a continuous and progressive movement in order to satisfy people's needs for growth and learning. It should be seen as a cumulative process which does not end until individuals have reached, but not exceeded, their growth capacity.

Organisational supports are also necessary to maintain and aid the development of job design. This involves management commitment and support for the idea of job design. It also involves structural support such as the availability of accurate information for decision-making. Attention must be given to 'hygiene' factors, such as pay and working conditions, and to the removal of the causes of dissatisfaction, in order to provide the right environment for job design.

Job satisfaction and personnel management

Theories of work motivation and job satisfaction have influenced management systems and styles of leadership, and developments in personnel policies and procedures. The personnel management function is centred on people's needs while working in an organisation, and ways in which their work promotes or frustrates the fulfilment of these needs.[47] The practice of modern personnel management is directed towards providing conditions under which people work willingly and effectively, and contribute to the success of the organisation. This involves concern for employee motivation and job satisfaction.

QUALITY CIRCLES

One particular feature increasingly associated as a part of the quality of working life movement is the concept of quality circles. **A quality circle is a group of people within an organisation who meet together on a regular basis to identify, analyse and solve problems relating to quality, productivity or other**

aspects of day-to-day working arrangements using problem-solving techniques. Quality circles are broadly compatible with the quality of working life in that they provide an opportunity for people at work to become more involved in matters which have a bearing on the jobs that they do.[48]

Although quality circles actually originated in America they were exported to Japan and are more usually associated with their wide applications (since 1962) in Japanese manufacturing industries, as well as in some white-collar operations. Since the refinement of the quality circle process in Japan there has been increasing interest in their use in America and Britain as well as in many other countries. In America, quality circles appear to have been first implemented in 1974.[49]

The essential features of a quality circle group include the following:

- membership is voluntary;
- the group usually numbers between five and ten members;
- membership is normally drawn from people undertaking similar work or from the same work station;
- the group select the problems to be tackled and the methods of operation;
- a leader can be chosen from within the group but is usually the immediate supervisor;
- the group members receive training in communication and problem-solving skills, quality control techniques and group processes;
- the group recommend solutions to management and where possible have authority to implement agreed solutions.

The introduction of quality circles The development of effective quality circle groups requires consideration of a number of important criteria:

- commitment and support of top management;
- full consultation with staff;
- a participative approach by management, and appropriate systems and style of managerial behaviour;
- delegation of decision-making;
- trust and goodwill on all sides;
- an effective support structure of consultation and negotiation;
- support of trade unions and/or staff representatives;
- an effective training programme including development of quantitative skills;
- continuous monitoring and review of results.[50]

In assessing the potential for introducing quality circles into an organisation, *Collard* suggests four broad areas for consideration:

(i) the existing management style of the organisation;
(ii) the industrial relations climate;
(iii) the current state of the organisation; and
(iv) the scope for reducing non-productive time.

These should be considered first at the organisational level, and second at the individual department level. It is then necessary to have an action plan, and a pilot study which allows the evaluation of quality circles.[51]

Top Management	Middle Management	First-line Management
Difficulties in distinguishing circles from techniques such as task forces, committee structure, management–employee 'rap' sessions, departmental meetings	Fear that circles will show up their own shortcomings as work organisers	Workers taken off the job to solve problems are not really working – time-wasting potential
Superficial and a gimmick	Fear of some loss of control	Existing workload
Threat to the established pattern of organisation hierarchy and to management prerogative	Scepticism about the concept being a 'vogue' management technique	Part of some management ploy
	Encroach on areas of traditional authority and responsibility	They do not know how circles operate
Introduction of circles would be an admission of bad management	Threat to their respective patterns of power	Quality circles would be used by employees for knocking other people and getting their own back
The company is sufficiently well organised to cope promptly with situations at management and shop-floor levels	They were expected to solve problems the circles had 'dumped' on them	Fear of being exposed as a poor leader
	Circles cause us extra problems because they do not know the ripple effect their actions cause in other parts of the organisation	Merely an extension of the company's existing suggestion scheme
It is not the right time	Threat to legitimacy and authority	Conflict with suggestion scheme
Changes required in management style	Fear the increased knowledge of circle members through circle training – unfamiliar with the circle analysis techniques	Fear the increased knowledge of circle members through circle training
Introduction of circles might disturb the present good relations with the unions	We don't need circles attitude	Fear of redundancies
Alien culture argument	Unnecessary powers being given to the circles	
Anticipated resistance from middle management	Increased data available to members and potentially through them to the rest of the workforce	
Because it is a personnel department initiative	Circles do not follow prescribed organisational channels	
Fear of interference from the union	The facilitator goes around me	

Fig. 15.9 Reasons given for management resistance to quality circles

(Reproduced with permission of MCB University Press from Dale, Barrie and Barlow, Eric, 'Quality Circles: The View From Within', *Management Decision*, vol. 25, no. 4 (1987). p. 7.)

There are a number of potential limitations on the effectiveness of quality circles.

- Any attempt at solving organisational problems cannot be considered as a single dimension. The promotion of quality circles needs to be approached in terms of possible effects on related sub-systems of the organisation, for example personnel management and industrial relations procedures.
- Quality circles can rely too heavily on intrinsic motivation and the assumption that involvement and recognition are sufficient rewards in themselves. This reflects a major difference between the operation of quality circles in the west and in Japan. Workers in Japan appear, for example, to accept that financial gains will go to the organisation.[52]
- The greater involvement of members in problem-solving and decision-making may be resented by some groups, for example quality control departments, or by managers or trade union officials who may be suspicious of possible challenges to their traditional authority.

Applications of quality circles

Quality circles do not always succeed, however, and there is frequent opposition from top management and first-line management, but most particularly from middle management. Because the basic concept of quality circles is so deceptively simple, not enough thought is always given to their formation. Many quality circles have malfunctioned because of insufficient preparation and management support, or because of union opposition or a range of other difficulties.[53] (*See* Fig. 15.9.)

The application of quality circles does appear simple and straightforward, but early experience must be viewed in the context of Japanese culture and management systems. However, quality circles offer a number of potential benefits. They provide problem-solving at a more local level and the participation of employees in work-related decisions which concern them. They help supervisors keep control of the shop/office floor and encourage the use of supervisors as communicators.[54] Quality circles do work and are used successfully by a number of British organisations including Rolls-Royce (the UK pioneer in 1978), IBM, Duracell, British Telecom and Wedgwood. Quality circles have also been introduced successfully by Scott's Hotels Limited, the master franchise holder for Marriott and Courtyard hotels in the UK.[55]

There are some doubts as to the extent to which the hopes for, or potential benefits of, quality circles are realised fully in organisations.[56] In appropriate applications, quality circles can be part of a broad, long-term strategy for organisational change aimed both at improved economic performance and the quality of working life.

One of the leading exponents of quality circles in Britain is the Wedgwood pottery group. They have more than 100 circles of up to ten workers each.[57] The following extract outlines the company's approach.

Quality Circles at Wedgwood

About two years ago we were in the state that I think many companies are today, we had heard something about Quality Circles, we were wondering whether it would help us if we introduced them at Wedgwood, but we had not decided one way or the other. So what I want to do is to describe why and how we did so, and the enjoyment and the benefits all the participants have since derived from them.

Why did we eventually decide to go ahead? And the reason, the real reason, was for the survival of our company. About three years ago the company had about 8,000 employees; now that has now gone down to under 5,000. They are divided among 12 factories, all within a five mile radius. Now those may not sound very large numbers compared with some firms, but we felt that with what for us seemed a quite large factory, management, the senior management, was losing touch with shop floor operatives and also with middle management and supervision. And the person who started us on the road to Quality Circles was the man at the very top – the Chairman of the company.

Total commitment

I believe the fact that Quality Circles have been successful at Wedgwood – and they have been remarkably successful – is basically for one reason and one reason only: that there has been absolute and total commitment from the very beginning, from the top and right down to the bottom. And that, I believe, is absolutely essential for any company that is considering Quality Circles – total commitment. If you start off at half-cock, your Circles will go off at half-cock, and one failing Circle can do more damage than 20 good ones can achieve.

Involving the people who do the jobs

Why did the Board decide to go ahead? As I have already mentioned, there was the feeling that senior management was losing touch with the shop floor. In much of British industry we are stuck with a 'we and they' attitude that somehow has to be stopped – and Quality Circles is one way

of getting round it, because for the first time ever, Quality Circles enable the people who are doing a regular job in the factory – in our case, such as making plates or decorating cups – to play a very important part in the running of the factory, and to know that they are doing so. It is, after all, the people who have spent much of their lives sticking handles on cups, who know more about that job, and its problems and possibilities for improvement, than anyone else, often even than their managers. Managers, certainly in our industry, are basically administrators, and we tend to change them around from one job to another, so that often they have no real down to earth knowledge of the jobs their people are actually doing – and they are often very tricky jobs requiring a great deal of skill and practice. So through Quality Circles, we believed that we might find out from the people who are actually doing the job, what are the problems associated with it, and how they can be solved – and this has proved to be the case: we are now getting answers to many of the problems that we had never been able to solve before.

Voluntary participation

We wanted eight to ten members of each Circle and they were to be entirely voluntary. So the Circle leaders went around the members of their work-group saying something like: 'Look, Mary, I think you are the sort of person who might enjoy this'. And the response might be: 'Well, I'll come if Bill and his wife will come too', and so on. But it was made absolutely clear to everyone that it was entirely voluntary; if they came and didn't like it, they could leave at any time; or they could even leave half way through a project and come back three months later.

So we got the nucleus of the first six Circles, and we started to train them as to what it was all about, with me sitting in the whole time. And then the second six Circles on the same basis. All the time we emphasised not only that it was voluntary, but that it was a thing to enjoy. It shouldn't be looked upon as hard work. It is enjoyment. And it is of interest that, of all Circles we started with, the original members are all still with us – so they are still enjoying it.

Extending the programme

Then we did a repeat of the whole thing, choosing another 12 leaders, training them and getting two more successive groups of six Circles started. Now we are up to 104 Circles altogether, which is a large number for this country, but not large compared with America where the Circle movement originally started, and minuscule compared with some com-panies in Japan.

Circle presentations to senior management

Once the Circles have chosen their own problems that they want to tackle, and have analysed the causes, they come up with a solution and make their presentation to senior management – and this is a very important part of the programme. The presentation may be made to the Company Chairman if the Circle thinks it is important enough; a lot of them are made to other Board members or General Managers. So far there have been 297 such individual presentations. The average time between presentations – i.e. the time it takes a Circle to identify, analyse and solve a problem – is five weeks. Some have been as short as three weeks – but in one case as long as nine months. That was a problem that involved a lot of hard work and a great deal of data gathering.

Problems solved by Circles at Wedgwood

Now to convert that picture of a Quality Circle into our factories at Wedgwood, to show the kinds of problems that have been solved, but without going into technical details that probably only other pottery people could follow.

One problem that has been common to the whole pottery industry throughout its history, is that when you make top quality bone china plates, you can only make 40 plates from each mould, and you have always had to throw the first three away because they were no good. And nobody had ever come up with a solution. But the mould makers' Quality Circle in one of our factories decided to tackle this problem, and they came up with something that was absolutely novel, that no-one had ever even thought of before – and now we don't throw those first three plates away any more.

Nor do any of the other factories in our Wedgwood group – and of course it didn't take long before it got to our competitors as well, but I am quite pleased about that, because it all helps the industry as a whole – and we are a very close-knit community. But this is just one of the things that would never have happened except for the people who have actually been making the moulds all their lives, getting together and putting their minds to the problem.

Eliminating spoilt plates

Another problem which was tackled by one of our earliest Circles was the identification marks on the back of plates. It is perhaps a rather strange thing that every hand-painted plate has an identification mark on its back to show who painted it. Now these marks, which were chosen by each individual for herself, vary greatly in complexity and therefore in the time it took to make them, but they also had a nasty habit of sometimes partly flaking off or falling off during firing, and therefore ruining the plate below. The Circle came up with these solutions – a simple dot rather than a complicated mark, with the positioning of the dot in relation to the back-stamp as the individual identifying device.

The same Circle then tackled another problem – the elimination of colour specks and 'crawl' that ruined so many plates, the cause of which had been absolutely unknown previously. And with some of the larger plates that sell at £100 or so each, the saving here was quite extraordinary.

Another Circle designed a new trolley for moving the unfired pottery to the kiln, that greatly reduced the risk of pieces of pottery knocking together and being broken.

Working with manufacturers to improve quality of material

Another designed a quite different and much more effectively shaped brush for painting plates. This they did in co-operation with the brush manufacturer, by going to visit his factory in London and explaining their problems with the traditional type of brush. This was a wonderful experience both for the manufacturer and for our

Circle members – the people who actually used the product discussing with the people who made it, what their real problems and needs were. And as a result of this experience, most of our suppliers now have to work with the Circles that use their materials – and there is no better judge of the quality of materials coming into the factory than the people who have actually got to use them!

One Circle has even tackled the question of the factory bus service, and the loading and unloading points – and in conjunction with the bus company, significantly improved the service and facilities for the very many of our employees who depend on it to get to and from work.

What are the pitfalls?

With over 100 Circles now operating I could give innumerable examples of Quality Circle achievements. But perhaps I should mention also what the pitfalls are, because it is also important to know what these may be, in order to steer clear of them. In fact, we have not had any really serious problems. We have had some people who drop out of a Circle because someone else is in it, or perhaps because they have not agreed with the solution the Circle put forward. Often it only needs the facilitator to keep his ear to the ground and know what is going on, to smooth out that sort of difficulty before it gets serious.

Management inadequacies revealed

I think the only genuine trouble we have had is with some of our junior managers who have tended to feel pilloried when they have taken on the role of Circle leader. This we have found par-

ticularly with some of the older people who are perhaps not quite as good as they like to think they are; and in many cases they have been superseded by up and coming operatives who have shown remarkable signs of being just the right people to run the Circle. This has undoubtedly caused a certain amount of aggro.

But the really good people among our junior managers and supervisors have derived great benefit from the Circles, and the improvement in personal relations, and the fact that people now feel very much a part of the factory, is what is so very encouraging.

Improvements from Circles at Wedgwood

Wedgwood is not just a factory full of people painting flowers on the sides of cups. It is a very tightly controlled factory – that is why it is so successful. Even in the days when we were having so many cutbacks, our turnover and profit figures have been maintained.

The introduction of Quality Circles has been accepted as one of the main reasons why our quality and our productivity have improved. In addition our industrial relations have improved out of all measure – because people now once again, even though we have grown so big, feel they are back in a smaller unit where they can speak directly to people they couldn't speak to before. Quality Circles have certainly done something for all our Circle members at Wedgwood, that otherwise I believe could never have happened.

(Extracted with permission of the Involvement and Participation Association from: Dick Fletcher 'Quality Circles at Wedgwood', *Industrial Participation*, no. 578, Summer 1982, pp. 2–9.)

THE HAPPY/PRODUCTIVE WORKER

Despite many theories and studies of the relationship between job satisfaction and work performance there are still doubts as to how to manage an organisation so that staff have both high job satisfaction and productivity. *Staw* suggests that it is difficult to bring about changes in both satisfaction and performance and that it is necessary to lower expectations in the pursuit of the 'happy/productive worker'.[58]

Instead of the alternating practice of fanfare and despair, Staw puts forward three approaches that may make for sustained slow progress in overcoming forces for stability in both job attitudes and performance.

- **The individually oriented system.** This is based on traditional good management and would emphasise, for example: extrinsic rewards linked to performance; realistic and challenging goals; accurate employee performance; equitable promotions policy; training and skills development; job enlargement and job enrichment.

 The major principle underlying such features is to structure work and/or reward systems so that high performance is either intrinsically or extrinsically rewarding to the individual, and to create a situation in which high performance contributes to job satisfaction. However, to be effective the individually oriented system needs to be implemented correctly, and into a well-run organisation with an efficient structure and motivational system.

- **The group-oriented system.** This is where satisfaction and performance are derived from group participation. This would include methods such as: work organised around intact groups; resources distributed on a group basis; greater group autonomy for selection, training and reward systems; the use of the group to enforce norms of behaviour; and encouraging inter-group rivalry to build within-group solidarity.

 Group-oriented systems may be difficult to control but they can be very powerful. Because individuals will work to achieve group praise and loyalty, an effectively managed group-oriented system can make a potential contribution to high job satisfaction and performance.

- **The organisationally oriented system.** This is where working conditions are organised so that individuals gain satisfaction from contribution to the welfare of the organisation as a whole, for example, through applying the principles of Theory Z organisation. If individuals can identify closely with the organisation as a whole, then organisational performance will be intrinsically rewarding to the individual.

 This system would include common features such as: effective socialisation into the organisation; job rotation in different units; long training periods with the development of skills specific to the organisation; long-term or protected employment; decentralised operations; few status distinctions; education and sharing of information about the organisation; linking individual rewards to organisational performance through profit sharing, bonuses and share options.

SYNOPSIS

■ Motivation to work well is usually related to job satisfaction, but the nature of this relationship is not clear. Although the level of job satisfaction may well affect the strength of motivation this is not always the case. Job satisfaction is more of an internal state and could, for example, be associated with a feeling of personal achievement. The relationship between job satisfaction and effective work performance is an issue of continuing debate and controversy.

■ Job satisfaction is a complex concept and difficult to measure objectively. The level of job satisfaction is affected by a wide range of individual, social, organisational and cultural variables. Dimensions of job satisfaction include consideration of: alienation at work; the nature of technology; meaningful work and supervision; psychological well-being and stress at work. The application of motivational theories and a greater understanding of dimensions of job satisfaction has led to increasing interest in improving job design.

■ Earlier approaches to job design concentrated on the restructuring of individual jobs and application of job rotation, job enlargement and job enrichment. Approaches to improving job design now take a broader perspective, and in the context of technological change, for example, focus attention on the wider organisational issues. Whatever form job design takes it must take account of contextual factors and should be a continuous and progressive movement augmented by (i) developmental design and (ii) organisational supports.

■ Increased interest in job design has been associated with the development of a broader social concern for the quality of working life, including consideration of workers' experience of work. This includes consideration of desirable task and job characteristics; management style and organisation culture; employee involvement; self-managed work groups; and flexible working arrangements.

■ One particular feature associated as a part of the quality of working life movement is the concept of quality circles. These are groups within an organisation who meet together to identify, analyse and solve problems relating to quality, productivity or other aspects of day-to-day working arrangements using problem-solving techniques. There are a number of important considerations relating to the effective introduction of quality circles, but they do appear to work. Quality circles can be part of a broad strategy for organisational change aimed at improving both economic performance and the quality of working life.

■ Despite many theories and studies there are still doubts as to how to manage an organisation so that staff have both high job satisfaction and productivity. It may be necessary to lower expectations in the pursuit of the 'happy/productive worker' and to make for sustained, slow progress in overcoming forces for stability in both job attitudes and performance. Three possible approaches are: the individually oriented system, the group oriented system and the organisationally oriented system.

APPENDIX 1

Participative work redesign:
a case study from the metal-can industry

Nico Terra

The quality of working life changes as a consequence of the accommodation of organisations to a rapidly changing or 'turbulent' environment. Moreover, the quality of working life and the development of new forms of work organisation tend to become a strategic issue in tailoring production to customer demands (quality, just-in-time delivery, flexibility) and to employee demands (healthy and interesting jobs with opportunities for learning and development). Generally speaking, management is well aware of the necessity to adapt to customers' demands but the role of employees in these processes of change is still too small. A tradition of participation has not yet emerged, but it is very necessary if one takes into account the desired design criteria for the future organisation: flexibility, decentralisation of control and (thus) more room in the production process for the competencies of the employee. Successful implementation of a participative work organisation can be attained only by means of a participative change process. Experiments with employee involvement in this field show positive effects. Crucial for success is, among other things, the equipment of the employees: the availability of the necessary means and the development of their expertise to play their role in the redesign of jobs.

The case

A plant from the metal-can industry in the north of the Netherlands has successfully changed its organisation and way of working as a reaction to external and internal developments. It has done so by redesigning and reorganising the traditional functional production organisation and assembly line structure with fragmented and restricted jobs into a product-oriented organisation, operated by self-managing production teams with rewarding jobs.

In this process blue-collar workers have played an active role in diagnosing and redesigning these jobs. Both management and groups of employees have applied a methodology to assess and redesign jobs from the perspective of integrating both the well-being of the employee and the effectiveness of the organisation. This methodology, called WEBA (acronym of 'well-being at work' in Dutch), has functioned effectively as a common framework for improving jobs and working conditions and for negotiating contrasting points of view.

'The quality of most jobs in the production departments has improved and now meets high standards concerning health and well-being at the workplace. This assessment has been confirmed by various different independent measurements.'

Situation at the start

At the start of the project in 1989, the plant was a production site for a Dutch corporation, specialising in metal-can production. The plant had a workforce of 430 employees. It operated a three-shift system and was highly unionised. Production volume was around 110 million cans a year. The organisation of production could be characterised as functional and Tayloristic: many specialised staff and production departments, many hierarchical levels and an assembly line type of work. The division of labour was excessive and the conditions and content of most

production jobs were of low quality. The sickness and absenteeism rate was high: between 20 per cent and 25 per cent absenteeism in the production departments was no exception.

There were several impulses for change in this situation, where the company just had to reorganise. It subsequently laid off workers in different plants, and it transformed its production plants into business units with specific product–market combinations and more opportunities for local policy. A new general manager was also appointed.

The low quality of most of the production jobs and the high rate of sickness and absenteeism were a serious hindrance for the development and implementation of new strategies, including quality management and technological and organisational innovation.

The change process

The main goals of the desired change process were defined as:

- improvement of the quality of the organisation, of the production jobs and of the product; and
- creating better structural opportunities for the competencies of the employees.

The process of achieving these goals was divided up into stages:

1. diagnosis
2. redesign of:
 - the production structure at organisational level
 - the task structure at job level
 - physical and ergonomic conditions
3. implementation
4. evaluation.

Management, works council and unions agreed upon the following prerequisites for the implementation of change:

- no compulsory lay-offs at the plant
- employee participation
- a training programme for employees
- re-evaluation of the pay structure, following reorganisation.

Employee participation

At all stages of the project, employees and their representatives (works council and unions) have played an important role.

Groups of blue-collar workers actively participated in the analysis and redesign of their jobs, particularly during stages 1 and 2.

Meanwhile, in every production department a group of employees, representing all the different jobs in the department, had been formed. Each group consisted of about six employees and was equipped with a design-oriented checklist (WEBA) and training and professional support to describe and analyse existing labour processes and job contents and to create (if possible) different scenarios for their redesign. The groups met about eight times during work time in a period of six months.

All groups produced a report on their activities, each containing the profiles of 15 different production jobs and proposals for improvements. These reports were discussed in the departments and then presented to the management team.

The transformation

The functional organisation has been transformed into a product-oriented organisation with three parallel product flows. Each production flow consists of three lines. As a direct result of the activities of the work groups, production lines in each flow have been rearranged into a new layout where possible, new production machines have been installed and the physical working conditions improved.

Every flow is operated by a production team of about 20 multi-skilled workers who share a team mentor. Teams are responsible for the production of a complete product (components and cans), including detailed planning, quality, transport, maintenance and training. The number of different job titles has been cut drastically – from 15 mostly specialised and narrow job titles to between five and seven multi-skilled ones in every new production department. This new structure of work organisation was implemented over a period of three years and was accompanied by an extensive training programme.

Effects

The results are positive for both management and employees. The quality of most jobs in the production departments has improved and now meets high standards concerning health and well-being at the workplace. This assessment has been confirmed by various different independent measurements.

- The average wage has risen.
- Sickness and absenteeism have structurally decreased with a 50 per cent saving, amounting to around one million guilders a year at direct controlling costs.
- Flexibility has improved, creating better opportunities to meet smaller and more specialised orders following adoption of a policy to cultivate a 'niche position' in the market for aerosols.
- Productivity has risen significantly without the imple- mentation of any fundamental technology innovation. Overall productivity has gone up from 0.26 to 0.43 million cans per worker a year. This rise to 66 per cent can be attributed to mechanisation (especially packing), the new line layout and the new work organisation.
- Employees are better qualified, informed and motivated.
- The plant was recently awarded a certificate by the International Organisation for Standardisation for quality assurance (ISO 9000) which was largely the result of this project.

Evaluation

Active, direct participation of the employees has played an important role in this change process in two respects:

1. Strategically: it created an important **basis** for the re- design proposals among all employees.
2. Qualitatively: it created detailed **solutions** for problems in the existing work environment and effective proposals for its improvement. The new management philosophy and the application of the job design methodology were significant factors in this success.

(Reprinted from *P+ European Participation Monitor*, no. 8, 1994, pp. 11–13, with permission of the European Foundation for the Improvement of Living and Working Conditions.)

APPENDIX 2

Employee involvement through job redesign at Lloyds Bank

Lloyds Bank believes that the most significant threat to an organisation's competitive advantage may lie as much within the organisation as outside, since low levels of employee morale and motivation can lead to low productivity, increased absence rates, resistance to change and a failure to capture the benefits of investment in new technology. We examine a pilot programme conducted by Lloyds Bank in South Wales and Severnside, which set out to establish whether and how the high employee involvement needed to remedy such a situation could be achieved.

The culture of the clearing banks has historically been the very opposite of a 'high involvement culture', involving high levels of direction and control with the accompanying large managerial structures, according to Lloyds Bank. The bank's view, however, is that business success around the world has been achieved by successful companies through 'high involvement' strategies, which have pushed responsibility, accountability and ownership down to all layers in the business.

Pilot programme

Lloyds Bank management decided to embark on a programme of involving employees in redesigning their own jobs, with a view to obtaining a range of economic and behavioural benefits. The company set up a pilot programme in one of its regions – South Wales and Severnside – in 1992 in order to identify whether job redesign could succeed in the bank, and to formulate practical implementation techniques.

The pilot was managed jointly by the region and the bank's personnel department, under the guidance of an external consultant.

The directors of two areas within the region – Swansea and Cardiff – were invited to partici-

pate in the programme. They in turn nominated two branches each.

Employee numbers at the four branches ranged from 22 to 128. The branch managers were invited to take part in the programme, and once they had accepted, presentations were made to branch staff who were invited to participate and to volunteer to join the job design team set up in each of the four branches. The process was voluntary at each stage.

Cross-functional teams in the branches worked on different assignments over different time periods. The external consultant trained the teams in job design principles and techniques and facilitated the early stages of the process. By the end of 1992 all four teams had begun to implement some or all of their own recommendations. An evaluation has been carried out of the economic and behavioural benefits accruing during the first six months of the new ways of working, although the main benefits are expected to accrue over a much longer time scale.

The process

A systematic, seven-stage, process for job design was adopted, although this was customised to some extent to meet the different requirements of each branch.

The role of the trade unions

Lloyds Bank recognises two unions: the banking and finance union BIFU and the Lloyds Group Union, previously a staff association but now a recognised trade union. The bank consulted both unions nationally before it embarked on the job design pilot, and says that both unions were in favour of the initiative. The bank did not formally consult local union representatives, although the individuals concerned were consulted as members of staff of the branches in question, took an active part in the pilots, and were, the bank says, very helpful and supportive.

The process is as follows:

Stage 1. Develop terms of reference, identify constraints, decide on the communications process and establish a relationship with the management team.

Stage 2. Define the scope of the project and the priorities within it.

Stage 3. Select and develop appropriate methodology to carry out the project. This may involve providing the job design team with training in job design tools or techniques, or helping the team to develop their own problem-solving methods.

Stage 4. Collect existing data or identify ways to collect additional data. Map out existing work flows and patterns.

Stage 5. Analyse the data, identifying problems and opportunities, and share this with the rest of the branch. Avoid intuitive assumptions, which tend to fail.

Stage 6. Select and evaluate options, decide on nature of job redesign, and ensure that the chosen solutions are integrated into the other branch activities. This will involve communicating with colleagues and obtaining their approval of the job redesign proposals.

Stage 7. Implement the redesign for a trial period, probably six months, and measure its

outcomes against the 'key success criteria' (set out in the document extract on p. 558).

What happened in the branches?

The Swansea branch, which has 128 staff, was recently formed through an amalgamation of two city-centre branches. It has a number of retail outlets. The merger posed challenges unlikely to be faced by many other branches, in particular the fact that there had, in the past, been significant competition between the two main branches, which militated against teamwork.

The job design team was established in February 1992 to identify ways of successfully amalgamating the two branches into one, restructured, branch.

The team consisted of eight volunteers from the main functions across both sites, and met for half a day each week. Cover was provided from within the branch. The team decided, as a result of feedback from the staff about what they wanted from job design and in view of the merger, that it was appropriate to look at the whole operation including the use of each site, the organisation of staff and their key tasks.

The team collected data on workflows and tasks and activities across all sites, and met for several months. It made a number of recommen-

Executive summary

When Lloyds Bank, in the early 1990s, reviewed its strategies for becoming more competitive, an important assumption was that it was not taking full advantage of the abilities of its non-managerial employees, and that these were being under-utilised by existing methods of work organisation. The company therefore decided to explore ways of encouraging staff to put forward and implement solutions to problems such as improving customer service and introducing more flexible working practices.

The method of employee involvement chosen for a pilot study was 'job design', defined by the company as 'a structured, systematic and managed process in which people in the workplace are required to analyse and redesign work in a way which meets the needs of customers, processes (including equipment and premises) and staff'.

The company set up the pilot project on job design in four branches in one region. Participation at every level was voluntary. The job design teams were set different objectives, depending on the issues faced by the individual branches.

These included amalgamating the working and service delivery methods of two previously competing branches, making more staff available for customer service, improving the sales and marketing effort, and setting up multi-skilled teams. Each team worked on its initial tasks for about six months, implementing both small and large changes to work organisation.

The project revealed an under-utilisation of staff, some inappropriate procedures and poorly designed jobs. Lloyds Bank believes many organisations would find that they have similar problems if they embarked on such an exercise.

Overall, the company is very pleased with the outcome of the pilot programme, which has contributed to improved productivity, sales, customer service and the quality of working life, and now intends to examine how the principles of high involvement can be incorporated into the overall change processes planned for the medium- and long-term future.

dations ranging from minor procedural changes which were implemented 'along the way', to major structural changes which were held up until a major refurbishment programme was carried out. The objective of the design team – to design the complete branch work structure – was accomplished in late 1992 and implemented in January 1993. The changes included the development of multi-skilled teams, the reallocation of tasks to logical flows, and the creation of a one-stop telephone banking team. The team is continuing its work on identifying further opportunities for improvement.

Because the merger created a certain amount of turmoil in 1992, the bank says that some of the improvements that occurred in 1993 would have taken place in any case. However, the bank believes that the job redesign process has played a significant part in the improvements in sales, and reductions in error rates, customer complaints, overtime and absenteeism. In addition, productivity has increased, together with levels of job satisfaction, employee morale and motivation.

Overall, branch managers believe that job design has helped them to achieve improvements and bring about 'hassle-free' change as well as developing the skills of a number of individuals.

Improving customer services at Port Talbot

The Port Talbot job design team, established in March 1992, was set the task of redesigning work to provide a greater number of people for customer service. The branch has 43 staff, and is located in a town suffering from economic depression brought about by the decline of the steel works. The team of four people analysed a number of processes and procedures including job quality, workflows and the number and nature of telephone calls, to try to identify opportunities for work improvement through work redesign. The team also developed measurements of customer satisfaction.

Recommendations were presented in September 1992 and involved restructuring work tasks and flows, moving away from individual duties to group activities, the relocation of some staff (within the branch) and the rotation of some supervisory tasks.

The results of the changes were monitored. This presented some difficulties since high levels of customer satisfaction existed before the changes. However, the initial task of providing more people for the 'customer interface' was achieved, and sales for the first three months of the new arrangements were at the highest level ever achieved by the branch.

The second phase of the work of the job design team at Port Talbot concentrated on particular areas of business activity. The team was reconstructed to reflect this, and the tasks and activities carried out in these areas were analysed carefully in addition to the workflow and physical layout. The changes suggested by the job design team, and subsequently implemented, included multi-skilled teams, and the reallocation of certain activities to other areas of the branch. The revised working is still at an early stage but improvements in the form of increased sales and greater efficiency have already begun to materialise.

The benefits to the Port Talbot branch have been viewed as improvements to customer service and quality of work life; reduction in error rates; enhanced flexibility and cover between staff, enabling additional unexpected workload to be absorbed; and greatly increased sales.

Concentrating on sales

The job design team at Church Village, a branch with 22 staff, was established in June 1992 to identify how the sales and marketing effort could be improved. The team consisted of five people nominally meeting for half a day each week, although workload pressures, particularly when other staff were absent, reduced the actual frequency of the meetings.

The team concentrated on gathering market intelligence, necessitating the acquisition of a PC to analyse the data. The previous way of working had been that jobs were rotated so that staff undertook a variety of tasks, and sales were regarded as a team effort, for which everyone in the branch was responsible.

The conclusions of the job design team were that there needed to be a move away from this full multi-skilling. Some staff were found to be considerably better at selling than others, so the job design team redesigned roles to create several full-time sales jobs, together with more specialised teams to concentrate on particular areas of expertise.

Branch staff agreed unanimously to the recommendations, which were implemented in January 1993. In the subsequent three months, there was a significant increase in sales and fewer errors. Behavioural benefits were exemplified by the willingness of colleagues to cover for each other when staffing was tight, high levels of morale and motivation, and openness to change.

This last attribute was particularly useful, since the branch was absorbed into a 'cluster' based on Pontypridd and its staffing reduced by two-thirds in April 1993. The difference in morale between Church Village and the other branches in the cluster was so noticeable to the new management team that they immediately adopted job design for the cluster, and re-formed the team to cover it. The benefits of involvement were equally clear to the staff in other outlets in the cluster, the bank says.

Multi-skilled flexible teams

At Queen Street, a city centre branch with 68 staff in Cardiff, a job design team was formed in September 1992 to determine how the branch could be organised using multi-skilled teams focused on different areas of activity. The team was asked to advise on the number of teams, and the roles to be performed by each team, with the longer-term follow-on objective of establishing optimum working practices for each team.

The job design team examined overall workflows, the viewpoint of customers and the physical layout of the branch. It recommended the creation of seven multi-skilled flexible teams, each team being responsible for a complete activity, such as customer services, secretarial, and machine room. The layout of the branch was redesigned to gain maximum benefit from the new flexible teams.

The first reactions from customers and staff have been extremely favourable, although the main benefits are expected to come on stream as each team is subjected to detailed design.

Project findings

An examination by the bank of the outcomes of the pilot programme revealed the following:

- **staff were not properly utilised:** although understandably under pressure and working hard, the quality of contributions could be improved, since staff were clearly capable of grasping business issues and making practical, logical recommendations;
- **processes and premises were key issues:** seemingly minor variations in branch layout and location play a significant part in the local implementation of standard procedures. Processes had developed on a piecemeal basis over time, although the benefits of a major business re-engineering programme were in the pipeline at the time of the pilot;
- **poorly designed existing jobs were demotivating staff:** employee loyalty and resilience ensured that levels of efficiency were maintained, but redesigning jobs to improve the quality of work life is a significant untapped source of performance improvement;
- **the concepts underlying job design are difficult to understand:** staff used to an environment where status and obedience have been more important than participation and initiative will need 'hands on' support if they are to grasp what is now required of them. This is particularly important given the very high level of synergy of job design with other initiatives, such as total quality;
- **more high-level strategic thinking and direction is required:** staff involving themselves with questions over the future direction of the business want the centre to focus on communicating the strategic direction and major processes;
- **staff have become committed to change:** the local nature of decision-making in job design has meant that the speed of change has been rapid and that peer pressure has reduced resistance to change.

Implementation

Translating the findings of the pilot projects into a programme for wider implementation requires the bank to make decisions in a number of key areas:

- **cultural fit:** significant work has been undertaken developing a new culture, and moving towards a total quality environment. The

Key principles of job design at Lloyds Bank

A structured, systematic and managed process in which people in the workplace are required to analyse and redesign work in a way which meets the needs of customers, processes (including equipment and premises) and staff. A team of volunteers from across all functions in the branch meet at agreed intervals (usually a half day each week) to analyse in detail the specific issues which they have agreed to resolve. The management team and the job design team agree the issue to be tackled and the success criteria against which the recommendations will be assessed. The job design team will involve all colleagues through discussions, written briefings, data gathering, etc., and will be required to manage the implementation of the changes under the direction of the management team. The scale of the issue being addressed will dictate the scale of the proposals [which] could be a comprehensive review of the entire branch structure or identifying small problems of machine location. The primary focus is always on the way jobs are designed, to ensure that the full contribution of people is unlocked.

Direction

It isn't a brainstorming session with ideas being floated. As with any other successful development it's 95% perspiration and 5% inspiration, with a great deal of data analysis not only of the process but also of customers and employees. It isn't a free-for-all in which all rules and procedures are abandoned; everything is challenged but there is a close and continuous relationship between the management team and the job design team. Terms of reference are drawn up to show the constraints and requirements. Additionally, help is sought from operational support, inspectors, architects etc. to ensure that implications are fully considered before proposals are formulated. By examining the processes, people better understand why improvements are needed and are better equipped to recognise and welcome improvements to processes and procedures which come along.

It isn't an opportunity to increase staffing: although some resources are diverted to job design, the 'everyday work' is still performed by the same overall number of people. It isn't a 'quick fix' or a permanent solution; it takes time to gather data, analyse, consult and fully manage implementation. There will be 'quick hits' along the way but those are bonuses. Since the process is about adapting to change it is recognised that ongoing

review is natural, and that today's solutions may be overtaken by new processes, procedures or circumstances in the future. The process of job design brings about a willingness to welcome continuing change and improvements.

Holistic

The process must aim to improve all aspects of the business, not improvement in one area at the expense of another. The key success criteria are established as:

- improvement to profitability (measured by the cost/income ratio);
- improvement to service quality;
- increase to sales;
- protecting asset quality (particularly where improvement to sales is achieved); and
- improving the quality of work life.

Inevitably, the branches will place emphasis on those elements which are holding back the branch or causing concern. A shared understanding between the management team and the job design team on the priorities is usually achieved immediately.

People-focused

The bank is not alone in having a significant number of jobs which are boring or frustrating. It is often the case that work is designed with little research/analysis into the impact on the people performing the work. The approach in South Wales and Severnside used the socio-technical system method, which diagnoses the areas of work which are either under-utilising skills or causing too great a constraint or ambiguity/uncertainty, and which therefore:

- generate lethargy and cause people to work at sub-optimum performance;
- generate mild stress which leads to difficult behaviour, such as resistance to change, lateness or absence.

By redesigning the work in a way which removes the barriers to performance, the same number of people can generate greater output with less effort and greater fulfilment. This inevitably leads to improved service and reduced errors, which begins a virtuous circle of improvement. The theory 'that people are capable of far more than they are asked' has been fully proven in practice.

(*Source:* Lloyds Bank.)

bank has recognised that this is a slow process which needs to be fully and carefully engaged in at senior levels before being gradually cascaded down throughout the organisation;

- **integration:** major changes have been put in place, including a widespread business re-engineering programme aimed at improving the quality of customer service through improvements to operational efficiency. Being able to balance the need for uniform processes and corporate identity with local involvement and the responsible use of initiatives requires careful preparation and communication; and

- **time scale:** the biggest drawback to high-involvement programmes such as the job design pilot is that it is a slow process and necessitates a great deal of groundwork and patience for the benefits to mature. It needs, says the bank, 'cooking time' to ensure that

all levels of management and staff are really engaged with the process.

Senior executives in the bank are now reviewing the way forward to determine how the benefits of a high-involvement strategy can be applied to a large distributed workforce in a way which enhances the benefits gained from the business re-engineering programme and achieves the desired cultural change. In the meantime, the bank is piloting limited further implementation in order to develop a resource/tool kit and identify the extent to which back-up support is needed.

The bank believes that the job design programme has played a part in contributing to the success of the pilot branches and is a jigsaw piece in the complete picture of business improvement. Work now needs to be taken to fit all the pieces of the jigsaw together, to make a coherent plan.

(Reproduced with permission from IRS Employment Trends 550, *Industrial Relations Review and Report*, December 1993, pp. 13–16.)

 Review and discussion questions

1 What exactly do you understand by job satisfaction? What are the main dimensions of job satisfaction? Give specific examples of causes of job dissatisfaction in your own organisation.

2 What factors are likely to influence job design and what factors might affect its potential success? Contrast different approaches to job design and give examples of situations in which these approaches might be appropriate, and acceptable, to the staff concerned.

3 Discuss the extent to which you believe theories of job enrichment lead to improved job satisfaction. Where possible, give practical examples in support of your answer.

4 Why do you think that increasing attention is being given to the quality of working life? As a manager, detail the main areas in which you could take action in order to improve the quality of working life of staff.

5 Detail fully what you believe are the main desirable task characteristics and job characteristics, and give examples from your own experience.

6 Outline the core dimensions of a job. Estimate the approximate Motivating Potential Score (MPS) for any job that you have held and/or attempt to establish the likely MPS for a job that you hope to have in the future.

7 Explain the essential features of a quality circle group. What are some of the main reasons for management resistance to quality circles?

8 Evaluate critically the relationship between job satisfaction and effective work performance. Give reasons in support of your views.

CASE STUDY 1

The wide open spaces

Rio Cosmetics Ltd.

Rio Cosmetics have chosen to concentrate their effort on what they regard as the most lucrative section of the market. As their Marketing Manager says, 'We've gone for short-term profit maximisation – rather than for diversification.' Their production is therefore concentrated on a single tube of deodorant marketed under the brand name 'Freche'. The product is heavily advertised on TV and Rio have made considerable profits over the past 5 years. However, a substantial competitor has now entered the market, and Rio's share of the market has dropped to 18%, its lowest level in three years.

The Board are now looking for explanations. They have asked for reports from the Sales and Production Departments. They have also asked the Personnel Department to report on some disturbing statistics regarding the workforce. In particular:

1. There has been a dramatic increase in absenteeism over the last year.
2. Although the number of line workers has remained fairly stable (at around 2115 during the last four or five years), weekly average output has fallen from 312,000 to 287,000 units.
3. During the last year 21% of the line workers have been late at least once a week, in spite of the fact that they lose a quarter of an hour's pay when this happens. (Before this year the figure was fairly constant at around 10%.)

In addition:

Within the past four months, the number of consumers complaining direct to the company have doubled according to the information supplied by the Quality Control Department, who keep a record of the number of letters received each week. They advise that the majority of these complaints have been traced back to what they describe as 'human errors' on the production line. Furthermore, three serious cases of pilfering have been notified by the Security Section within the past week.

Other information available

The rate of pay is approximately 10% higher than could be obtained by the line workers elsewhere.

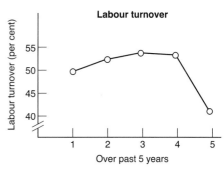

Older workers are not discouraged, but the average age of the workforce is only 19 years. It is increasingly difficult to find acceptable line supervisors.

Production starts at 8 a.m. and finishes at 5 p.m. – 5 days a week – with an hour lunch break and two 20-minute tea breaks.

The graphs shown have been prepared covering labour turnover and absenteeism over the past five years.

What explanations and recommendations would you offer the Board of Directors?

CASE STUDY 2

You are a management consultant called in to advise an organisation which has undergone significant change, involving both voluntary and compulsory redundancies, in the last two years. Employee members have reduced by 60% whilst the workload has remained unchanged for the organisation as a whole. Employees, including managers and supervisors, now work under significantly increased work pressure. Senior management are concerned about the low morale and commitment to the organisation which they now perceive amongst the remaining workforce. Six months ago the senior management team decided to introduce a major exercise to improve communication within the organisation. They wished employees at all levels to understand better the problems of the organisation, the management strategy adopted to deal with these problems, and the senior management team's growing confidence that the situation was now improving significantly. Productivity and cost effectiveness had improved substantially. Moreover major programmes of technical improvement and investment were now under way.

One important element of this programme was a training course in interactive skills for first-line supervisors. The personnel manager has told you that this programme has failed.

Personnel Manager: 'We wanted to build up the supervisors' role with their own people. Therefore we wished the supervisor to talk with his people about our plans and to get their ideas and views. We put them through a one week course in interactive skills and human relations skills. But it failed. They enjoyed the course. They all said they gained a lot from it. But when we asked them to communicate to their people about plans for this year, they said they did not feel confident enough.'

Consultant: 'Do they understand the plans? Do you feel that the plans have been presented to them in a clear enough way? Are their own managers communicating effectively with the supervisors? Do their managers provide support and encouragement to the supervisors?'

Personnel Manager: 'I'm not sure, possibly not. We give them copies of our detailed plans. They see everything. In any case I think they are afraid of being criticised by their staff. They don't want arguments with them and they don't feel sure enough about the plans. They wonder about job losses in the future.'

The role of first-line supervisors had been changed with the introduction of a professional Personnel Function. Supervisors no longer fully understood the terms and conditions of employment, bonus schemes, job evaluation systems and employment legislation relevant to the organisation. Moreover the manpower reductions had meant that supervisors were increasingly taking on tasks once carried out by their subordinates. Thus the role of the supervisor had come to be solely a technical, and no longer a managerial role.

(a) Assess the effectiveness of the training programme, identifying the problems experienced.
(b) Identify the main issues you feel will need attention if communications within this organisation are to be improved.
(c) State what advice you will offer to the organisation about how to proceed from the current situation.

Notes and references

1. Herzberg. F. 'One More Time: How do you Motivate Employees?' *Harvard Business Review*, vol. 46, 1968, pp. 53–62.
2. Herzberg, F. 'Orthodox Job Enrichment'. *Defense Management Journal*, vol. 13, April 1977, pp. 21–7. Abridged in Davis, L. E. and Taylor, J. C. (eds) *Design of Jobs*, Second edition, Goodyear (1979).
3. Vroom, V. H. *Work and Motivation*, Wiley (1964). (Also published by Krieger (1982).)
4. Argyle, M. *The Social Psychology of Work*, Second edition, Penguin (1989).
5. Luthans, F. *Organizational Behaviour*, Sixth edition, McGraw-Hill (1992) p. 123.
6. Bassett, G. 'The Case Against Job Satisfaction', *Business Horizons*, vol. 37, no. 3, May–June 1994, pp. 61–8.
7. Grunberg, M. M. *Understanding Job Satisfaction*, Macmillan (1979).
8. Marx, K. 'The Notion of Alienation', in Coser, L. A. and Rosenburg, B. *Sociological Theory*, Collier Macmillan (1969) pp. 505–10.
9. Blauner, R. *Alienation and Freedom*, University of Chicago Press (1964).
10. See: Gerth, H. H. and Wright, M. C. 'Marx and Weber', in *From Max Weber: Essays in Sociology*, Routledge and Kegan Paul (1970), pp. 46–50.
11. See, for example: Huczynski, A. A. and Buchanan, D. A. *Organizational Behaviour: An Introductory Text*, Second edition, Prentice-Hall (1991).
12. Walker, C. R. and Guest, R. H. *The Man on the Assembly Line*, Harvard University Press (1952).
13. Karasek, R. A. 'Job Demands, Job Decision Latitude and Mental Strain: Implications for Job Redesign', *Administrative Science Quarterly*, vol. 24, no. 2, 1979, pp. 285–308.
14. See, for example: Thompson, L. *New Office Technology*, Work Research Unit Occasional Paper, no. 34, Department of Employment, April 1985.
15. Myers, M. S. 'Every Employee a Manager', *California Management Review*, vol. 10, no. 3, Spring 1968, pp. 9–20.
16. *Ibid.* p. 17.
17. Scarpello, V. and Vandenberg, R. J. 'The Satisfaction with My Supervisor Scale: Its Utility for Research and Practical Applications', *Journal of Management*, vol. 13, no. 3, 1987, pp. 447–66.
18. Bassett, G. 'The Case Against Job Satisfaction', *Business Horizons*, vol. 37, no. 3, May–June 1994, pp. 61–8.
19. Warr, P. 'Work, Jobs and Unemployment', *Bulletin of the British Psychological Society*, 36, 1983, pp. 305–11.
20. See, for example: Robbins, S. P. *Organizational Behavior*, Sixth edition, Prentice-Hall (1993).
21. McKenna, E. *Business Psychology and Organisational Behavior*, Lawrence Erlbaum (1994) p. 585.
22. See, for example: Ridd, J. 'Hidden Costs of Work Stress', *The British Journal of Administrative Management*, October/November 1994, pp. 14–15.
23. Handy, C. B. *Understanding Organizations*, Fourth edition, Penguin (1993).
24. *Managers Under Stress: A Survey of Management Morale in the '90s*, The Institute of Management, December 1993.
25. Hackman, J. R. and Oldham, G. R. *Work Redesign*, Addison-Wesley (1980).
26. Wall, T. D., Clegg, C. W. and Jackson, P. R. 'An Evaluation of the Job Characteristics Model', *Journal of Occupational Psychology*, vol. 51, no. 2, 1978, pp. 183–96.
27. Algera, J. A. 'Objective and Perceived Task Characteristics as a Determinant of Reactions by Task Performers', *Journal of Occupational Psychology*, vol. 56, no. 2, 1983, pp. 95–107.

28. Grunberg, M. M. *Understanding Job Satisfaction*, Macmillan (1979).

29. Bassett, G. 'The Case Against Job Satisfaction', *Business Horizons*, vol. 37, no. 3, May–June 1994, pp. 61–8.

30. Taylor, L. K. *Not for Bread Alone: An Appreciation of Job Enrichment*, Third edition, Business Books (1980).

31. Wilson, N. A. B. *On the Quality of Working Life*: report prepared for the Department of Employment, Manpower Paper no. 7, HMSO (1973).

32. Herrick, N. Q. and Quinn, R. P. 'The Working Conditions Survey as a Source of Social Indicators', *Monthly Labor Review*, US Department of Labor, April 1971.

33. *Effective Organisations: The People Factor*, Advisory Booklet Number 16, ACAS, September 1991, and James, G. *Quality of Working Life and Total Quality Management*, ACAS Work Research Unit, Occasional Paper, no. 50, November 1991.

34. White, G. *Effective and Satisfactory Work Systems*, ACAS Work Research Unit, Occasional Paper, no. 27 (December 1983).

35. See, for example: Coupar, W. 'Employee Involvement and Performance: UK Experience', *European Participation Monitor*, no. 9, 1994, pp. 45–50.

36. Pickard, J. 'The Real Meaning of Empowerment', *Personnel Management*, vol. 25, no. 11, November 1993, pp. 28–33.

37. *The Competitive Edge: Employee Involvement in Britain*, Department of Employment, September 1994.

38. Cordery, J. L., Mueller, W. S. and Smith, L. M. 'Attitudinal and Behavioral Effects of Autonomous Group Working', *Academy of Management Journal*, June 1991, pp. 464–76.

39. See, for example: Robbins, S. P. *Organizational Behaviour*, Sixth edition, Prentice-Hall (1993).

40. See, for example: Buchanan, D. 'Job Enrichment is Dead: Long Live High-Performance Work Design!', *Personnel Management*, vol. 19, no. 5, May 1987, pp. 40–3.

41. Grayson, D. *Self-Regulating Work Groups – An Aspect of Organisational Change*, ACAS Work Research Unit, Occasional Paper, no. 46, July 1990, Preface.

42. Hall, K. and Savery, L. K. 'Stress Management', *Management Decision*, vol. 25, no. 6, 1987, pp. 29–35.

43. Waterman, R. *The Frontiers of Excellence*, Nicholas Brealey (1994).

44. For example, see: Kinsman, F. 'The Virtual Office and the Flexible Organisation', *Administrator*, April 1994, pp. 31–2.

45. *Survey of Long Term Employment Strategies*, The Institute of Management and Manpower PLC, September 1994.

46. Cooper, R. *Job Motivation and Job Design*, Institute of Personnel Management (1974).

47. See, for example: Cuming, M. W. *The Theory and Practice of Personnel Management*, Seventh edition, Heinemann (1993).

48. Russell, S. *Quality Circles in Perspective*, ACAS Work Research Unit, Occasional Paper, no. 24, (February 1983).

49. Meyer, G. W. and Scott, R. G. 'Quality Circles: Panacea or Pandora's Box', *Organizational Dynamics*, Spring 1985, pp. 34–50.

50. For further information on the introduction of quality circles see, for example: Robson, M. *Quality Circles: A Practical Guide*, Second edition, Gower (1988).

51. Collard, R. 'The Practical Applications of Quality Circles', *Management Review and Digest*, vol. 8, no. 4, January 1982, pp. 3–5.

52. Jones, W. G. 'Quality's Vicious Circles', *Management Today*, March 1983, pp. 97–8, 100, 102.

53. Dale, B. and Barlow, E. 'Quality Circles: The View From Within', *Management Decision*, vol. 25, no. 4, 1987, pp. 5–9.

54. Middleton, R. 'Team Briefing and Quality Circles Prove Their Value', *British Journal of Administrative Management*, vol. 34, no. 7, November 1984, pp. 255–7.

55. Simmons, P. and Teare, R. 'Evolving a Total Quality Culture', *International Journal of Contemporary Hospitality Management*, vol. 5, no. 3, 1993, pp. v–viii.

56. See, for example: Hill, S. 'Why Quality Circles Failed But Total Quality Management Might Succeed', *British Journal of Industrial Relations*, vol. 29, no. 4, 1991, pp. 541–68.

57. Fletcher, D. 'Quality Circles at Wedgwood', *Industrial Participation*, no. 578, Summer 1982, pp. 2–9.

58. Staw, B. M. 'Organizational Psychology and the Pursuit of the Happy/Productive Worker', *California Management Review*, vol. 28, no. 4, Summer 1986, pp. 40–53.

16

THE NATURE OF DELEGATION

A particular feature of work organisations is the need for delegation. The various activities of the organisation have to be distributed among its members. Management involves getting work done through the efforts of other people. This entails the process of delegation and the creation of a special manager–subordinate relationship. In order to ensure the effective execution of work the manager needs to understand how best to implement the process of delegation.

 Learning objectives

To:

- Explain dimensions of, and approaches to, delegation;

- Examine the process of delegation and the nature of the manager–subordinate relationship;

- Identify the benefits of delegation to the manager and to subordinate staff;

- Assess why managers may fail to delegate and other factors influencing opportunities for delegation;

- Explain the need for a balance between delegation and management control;

- Detail a planned and systematic approach to delegation, and justify delegation as a social skill;

- Appreciate the importance of successful delegation to the effective performance of the organisation.

Worth thinking about

A young, junior manager: 'That training session on delegation was useful. I really must remember that the higher up the ladder I go the less I should have to do myself.' An older, senior manger: 'That sounds fine in theory but why do so many of us believe in the truth in the old saying that if you want a job done properly do it yourself?'

DIMENSIONS OF DELEGATION

In order to manage it is necessary to manage the work of other people. This involves the process of delegation. In the case of the very small organisation where one person does everything alone, the question of delegation does not arise. But as soon as additional members of staff are employed it is necessary to plan, organise, direct and control their activities. It is a fundamental principle of management that for organisational effectiveness there must be delegation.[1]

Delegation is a necessary function of management, and although it is clearly related to other concepts such as leadership and managerial style it is significant enough to be treated as a specific aspect of management and organisational behaviour.[2]

Delegation can be seen as taking place either at the organisational level or at the individual level.

The organisational level

The structure of the organisation (as depicted in organisation charts, for example) is itself a result of delegation. If there is no delegation, then there is no structure. As organisations grow in size, so the extent of delegation increases. Delegation is therefore a function of size. It relates to the location of decision-making within the organisation. Delegation involves the passing on of authority and responsibility to various levels throughout the organisation.

At the organisational level, delegation involves consideration of centralisation/decentralisation, and divisionalisation or departmentalisation. Decentralisation may be federal or functional.[3] **Federal decentralisation** is the establishment of autonomous units operating in their own market with self-control and with the main responsibility of contributing profit to the parent body. **Functional decentralisation** is based on individual processes or products.

Divisions or departments may be established on the basis of 'task' or 'element' functions of the organisation (discussed in Chapter 10). The extent of decentralisation and divisionalisation provides the basic structural pattern of the formal organisation.

The individual level

The nature of organisation structure has already been discussed in earlier chapters. In this chapter we are concerned with delegation at the individual, or personal, level and with the nature of the manager–subordinate relationship.

Within the structure of the organisation the various activities that have to be undertaken must be distributed among individual members of the workforce.

At the individual (or personal) level, delegation is the process of entrusting authority and responsibility to others.

Delegation is not just the arbitrary shedding of work. It is not just the issuing and following of orders or carrying out specified duties in accordance with detailed instructions

APPROACHES TO DELEGATION

The concept of delegation may appear to be straightforward. But anyone with experience of a work situation is likely to be aware of the importance of delegation and the consequences of badly managed delegation. Successful delegation is a social skill. (See also the discussion on the art of delegation, later in this chapter.) Where managers lack this skill, or do not have a sufficient awareness of people-perception, there are two extreme forms of behaviour which can result.

- At one extreme is the almost total lack of meaningful delegation. Subordinate staff are only permitted to operate within closely defined and often routine areas of work, with detailed supervision. Staff are treated as if they are incapable of thinking for themselves and given little or no opportunity to exercise initiative or responsibility.
- At the other extreme there can be an excessive zeal for so-called 'delegation' when a manager leaves subordinates to their own resources, often with only minimal guidance or training, and expects them to take the consequences for their own actions or decisions. These 'super-delegators' tend to misuse the practice of delegation and are often like the Artful Dodger. Somehow, such managers often contrive not to be around when difficult situations arise. Such a form of behaviour is not delegation, it is an abdication of the manager's responsibility.

Either of these two extreme forms of behaviour can be frustrating and potentially stressful for subordinate staff, and unlikely to lead to improved organisational effectiveness. The nature of delegation can have a significant effect on the morale, motivation and work performance of staff. In all but the smallest organisation the only way to get work done effectively is through delegation, but even such an important practice as delegation can be misused or over-applied.

A manager's approach to delegation is, therefore, of considerable importance and should not be underestimated. But what does the process of delegation actually involve? And how can it be carried out successfully?

THE PROCESS OF DELEGATION

It is arguably possible to have delegation upwards, for example when a manager temporarily takes over the work of a subordinate who is absent through illness or holiday. It is also possible to delegate laterally to another manager on the same level. However, delegation is usually interpreted as a movement down the organisation. It is the authorisation to undertake activities that would otherwise be carried out by someone in a more senior position.

Delegation means the conferring of a specified authority by a higher authority. In its essence it involves a dual responsibility. The one to whom authority is delegated becomes responsible to the superior for doing the job, but the superior remains responsible for getting the job done. This principle of delegation is the centre of all processes in formal organization.[4]

THE MANAGER–SUBORDINATE RELATIONSHIP

Delegation creates a special manager–subordinate relationship. It is founded on the concepts of:

- authority;
- responsibility; and
- accountability (ultimate responsibility).

Authority and responsibility

Authority is the right to take action or make decisions that the manager would otherwise have done. It involves more than just carrying out specified duties according to detailed instructions. Authority legitimises the exercise of power within the structure and rules of the organisation. It enables the subordinate to issue valid instructions for others to follow.

Responsibility involves an obligation by the subordinate to perform certain duties or make certain decisions and having to accept possible reprimand from the manager for unsatisfactory performance.

Authority and responsibility are at the basis of the manager–subordinate relationship and recognised as 'rules' or principles of management. Responsibility is a corollary of authority. Wherever authority is exercised, responsibility arises. Sanctions are needed to encourage useful actions and to discourage others.[5]

Almost inevitably there is debate on the interpretation and meaning of different terms, and on the actual process of delegation itself.[6] Some writers argue that responsibility cannot be delegated, but this is too simple a view. Authority without responsibility gives rise to a possible abuse of delegation. For example, if a manager gives a subordinate authority to incur expenditure on certain items up to the value of £100 without prior reference, the subordinate should be held responsible to the manager for incurring such expenditure. The subordinate is obligated to exercise due care and attention to actions taken and decisions made.

Authority commensurate with responsibility

Most textbooks appear to support writers of the classical approach to management and the principle that authority should be commensurate with responsibility. In his revised list of management principles, *Urwick*, for example, makes the point that responsibility and authority should correspond in every position.[7]

Delegation, therefore, embraces both authority and responsibility. It is not practical to delegate one without the other.

Responsibility must be supported by authority, and by the power to influence the areas of performance for which the subordinate is to be held responsible. Authority can be delegated readily, but many problems of delegation stem from failure to provide the necessary information and resources in order to achieve expected results, or from failure to delegate sufficient authority to enable subordinates to fulfil their responsibilities.

570

For example, if a section head is held responsible to a departmental manager for the performance of junior staff but does not have the power (authority) to influence their selection and appointment, their motivation, the allocation of their duties, their training and development, or their sanctions and rewards, then the section leader can hardly be held responsible for unsatisfactory performance of the junior staff.

To hold subordinates responsible for certain areas of performance without also conferring on them the necessary authority to take action and make decisions within the limits of that responsibility is an abuse of delegation.

- There should be sufficient responsibility to match the authority which is delegated.
- Responsibility should be sufficient to give the subordinate freedom of action within agreed terms of reference and to avoid excessive supervision.
- Part of the manager's job is the development of subordinates. Subordinates need the feeling of responsibility to help in the performance of their tasks, and in dealing with other staff.
- Delegated duties are sometimes delegated further down the line.

Accountability (ultimate responsibility)

The meaning of the term 'responsibility' is, however, subject to possible confusion: although delegation embraces both authority *and* responsibility, effective delegation is not abdication of responsibility.

Ultimate responsibility cannot be delegated. Managers have to accept 'responsibility' for the control of their staff, for the performance of all duties allocated to their department/section within the structure of the organisation, and for the standard of results achieved. That is 'the buck stops here'.

The manager is in turn responsible to higher management. This is the essence of the nature of the 'dual responsibility' of delegation. The manager is answerable to a superior and cannot shift responsibility back to subordinates. The responsibility of the superior for the acts of subordinates is absolute.[8]

Fig. 16.1
The basis of delegation

In order to help clarify the position of 'dual responsibility' in delegation, it might be better expressed as 'The subordinate is **responsible** to the manager for doing the job, while the manager is responsible for seeing that the job gets done. The manager is **accountable** to a superior for the actions of subordinates.' **Accountability is interpreted as meaning ultimate responsibility**. The use of these two terms helps to explain the basis of the process of delegation. (*See* Fig. 16.1.)

If a manager delegates some task to a subordinate member of staff who does a bad job, then the manager must accept ultimate responsibility for the subordinate's actions. It is the manager who is answerable to a superior. It is not for the manager to say: 'Don't blame me boss, you don't expect me to do everything myself. You knew I would have to ask a member of my staff to do the work, I can't help it if "x" did a bad job.' The manager should accept the blame as the person who was obligated to the boss for the performance of the department/section, and **accountable** to see that the task was completed satisfactorily.

Managers should protect and support subordinate staff and accept, personally, any reprimand for unsatisfactory performance. It is then up to managers to sort out things in their own department/section, to counsel members of staff concerned and to review their system of delegation.

BENEFITS OF DELEGATION

Delegation is not an easy task. It involves behavioural as well as organisational and economic considerations, and it is subject to a number of possible abuses. But, properly handled, delegation offers many potential benefits to both the manager and subordinates. Delegation should lead to the optimum use of human resources and improved organisational performance. Studies of successful organisations lend support to the advantages to be gained from effective delegation.[9]

Best use of time

You may recall that in Chapter 13 we discussed the importance of the effective management of time. Time is one of the most valuable, but limited, resources and it is important that the manager utilises time to the maximum advantage.[10] By delegating those activities which can be done just as well by subordinate staff the manager is using to advantage the human resources of the organisation. Managers are also giving themselves more time in which to manage.

Successful delegation will help to overcome Gresham's Law of Planning which states that programmed activity tends to drive out non-programmed activity. Programmed activity involves decisions which are repetitive and routine; non-programmed activity involves decisions which are novel and unstructured.[11]

Successful delegation frees managers from day-to-day routine duties and enables them to concentrate more of their time on non-programmed activities. This simple, but important, point was made many years ago by *Sir Ian Hamilton* in a study of the organisation of military units:

the higher up the ladder you climb the less you have to do; provided (1) you have some courage; (2) you have some trust; (3) you have your office so organised that you don't have to deal with more than three or four responsible heads. If big men are overwhelmed with detail it is always their own fault.[12]

Delegation leaves the manager free to make profitable use of time, to concentrate on the more important tasks and to spend more time in managing and less in doing. This should lead to a more even flow of work and a reduction of bottlenecks. It should make the manager more accessible for consultation with subordinates, superiors or other managers. This should also improve the process of communications.

A means of training and development

Delegation provides a means of training and development, and of testing the subordinate's suitability for promotion. It can be used as a means of assessing the likely performance of a subordinate at a higher level of authority and responsibility. Delegation thereby helps to avoid the 'Peter Principle' – that is: 'In a hierarchy every employee tends to rise to his level of incompetence.'[13]

If managers have trained, competent subordinates capable of taking their place this will not only aid organisational progress but should also enhance their own prospects for further advancement. **Managers should therefore be encouraged to delegate in order to make themselves dispensable.**[14]

Specialist knowledge and skills

As organisations become more complex there is an increasing need for staff with specialist knowledge and skills. This need is reinforced, for example, by the rate of change in environmental influences (technical, economic, social and governmental) which give rise to areas of specialist interest and knowledge. Delegation can encourage the development of specialist expertise and enables specific aspects of management to be brought within the province of a number of specialist staff for greater efficiency. This is likely to enhance the quality of decision-making.

Geographical location

Another reason for delegation is the geographical separation of departments or sections of the organisation. For example, where a branch office is located some distance away from the head office the branch manager will need an adequate level of delegation in order to maintain the day-to-day operational efficiency of the office.

Sound economics

Successful delegation benefits both the manager and the subordinate and enables them both to play their respective roles in improving organisational effectiveness. It is a principle of delegation that decisions should be made at the lowest level in the organisation compatible with efficiency. It is a question of opportunity cost. If decisions are made at a higher level than necessary they are being made at greater cost than necessary. Delegation is therefore a matter of sound economics as well as good organisation.

Strength of the workforce

Delegation should lead to an improvement in the strength of the workforce. It should give subordinates greater scope for action and opportunities to develop their aptitudes and abilities, and increase their commitment to the goals of the organisation.[15] Delegation can lead to improved morale by increasing motivation and job satisfaction. It can help satisfy the employee's higher-level needs.

Delegation focuses attention on 'motivators' or 'growth' factors and creates a climate in which subordinates can become more involved in the planning and decision-making processes of the organisation. Delegation is a form of participation. Where subordinates are brought to accept and welcome delegation this will encourage a positive attitude to their work and a willingness to discharge their authority and responsibilities.

In previous chapters we have discussed how the changing nature of business organisations has emphasised the requirement for management to harness and develop the talents and commitment of all employees. The need for the most efficient use of human resources has placed increasing importance on employee involvement and empowerment, self-managed teams and flexible working arrangements. This in turn has highlighted both the need for, and benefits of, effective systems of delegation.

REASONS FOR LACK OF DELEGATION

With so many good reasons for delegation, why is it that managers often fail to delegate or do not delegate successfully? There are many factors which affect the amount of delegation, and its effectiveness. Delegation is influenced by the manager's perception of subordinate staff. It is also influenced by the subordinate's perception of the manager's reasons for delegation. **Failure to delegate often results from the manager's fear**.

- The manager may fear that the subordinate is not capable of doing a sufficiently good job. Also, the manager may fear being blamed for the subordinate's mistakes.
- Conversely, the manager may fear that the subordinate will do too good a job and show the manager in a bad light.

The manager should, of course, remember that the task of management is to get work done through the efforts of other people. If the subordinate does a particularly good job this should reflect favourably on the manager.

Dependence upon other people

As *Stewart* points out, managers who think about what can be done only in terms of what they can do, cannot be effective. Managing is not a solo activity.

Managers must learn to accept their dependence upon people. A key part of being a good manager is managing that dependence. Managers who say that they cannot delegate because they have poor subordinates may genuinely be unfortunate in the calibre of the subordinates that they have inherited or been given. More often this view is a criticism of themselves: a criticism either of their unwillingness to delegate when they could and should do so, or a criticism of their selection, training and development of their subordinates.[16]

Lack of training

Managers may not have been 'trained' themselves in the skills and art of delegation. They may lack an awareness of the need for, and importance of, effective delegation, or what it entails. Another reason for a reluctance to delegate may, in part, be due to the fact that throughout childhood and in college life delegation is usually discouraged. There are few opportunities to learn how to delegate. Hence when people first become managers they tend to display poor delegation skills.[17]

Obstacles to delegation

Newman has identified some of the main obstacles to effective delegation in terms of the attitudes of the manager, and reasons why the subordinate shrinks from accepting new responsibilities. Reasons for reluctance to delegate are:

(i) the 'I can do it better myself' fallacy;
(ii) lack of ability to direct;

(iii) lack of confidence in subordinates;

(iv) absence of selective controls which give warning of impending difficulties; and

(v) a temperamental aversion to taking a chance.

Subordinates avoid responsibility because:

(i) they find it easier to ask the boss to make decisions;

(ii) they fear criticism for mistakes;

(iii) they believe they lack the necessary information and resources to do a good job;

(iv) the subordinates may already have more work than they can do;

(v) they lack self-confidence; and

(vi) positive incentives may be inadequate.[18]

Assumptions about human nature and behaviour

A reluctance to delegate might arise from the manager's belief in, and set of assumptions about, human nature and behaviour.[19] The Theory X manager believes that people have an inherent dislike of work, wish to avoid responsibility, and must be coerced, controlled, directed, and threatened with punishment in order to achieve results. Such a manager is likely, therefore, to be interested in only limited schemes of delegation, within clearly defined limits and with an easy system of reward and punishment.

On the other hand, the Theory Y manager believes that people find work a natural and rewarding activity, they learn to accept and to seek responsibility, and they will respond positively to opportunities for personal growth and to sympathetic leadership. Such a manager is more likely to be interested in wider schemes of delegation based on consultation with subordinates, and with responsibility willingly accepted out of personal commitment.

OTHER FACTORS INFLUENCING DELEGATION

Apart from the manager's own possible reluctance to delegate, there are a number of other organisational factors which may influence the opportunities for effective delegation.

Management system

The type of management system will influence the likely extent and nature of delegation. For example, *Likert* identified four types of management systems: System 1 (exploitive authoritative); System 2 (benevolent authoritative); System 3 (consultative) and System 4 (participative group).

System 4 is based on involvement, group decision-making, supportive relationships and participation.[20] Real delegation is therefore likely to be greater under System 4 management.

Design of organisation structure

Opportunities for personal delegation will also be affected by the actual design of the organisation structure: for example, the degree of centralisation and the nature of divisionalisation, the extent to which role prescriptions are defined formally, the span of control of individual managers and the scalar chain (the number of levels of authority within the structure).

In practice, however, people rarely act in the manner which is officially expected. Within the formal organisation structure there will always be an informal structure which arises from the social interaction of people working in the organisation and the development of groups with their own relationships and norms of behaviour, irrespective of those defined within the formal structure. Delegation will therefore also be affected by the informal organisation.

Nature of organisation structure

Another factor affecting the amount of delegation is the nature of the organisation structure, for example in terms of whether the organisation is 'mechanistic' or 'organic'.[21] **The mechanistic system** is a more rigid structure and is characterised by specialisation, a clear hierarchical structure, closely defined duties and responsibilities, and formal downward flow of information.

The organic system is a more fluid structure and is characterised by a network structure of control, authority and communication, the continual adjustment and redefinition of jobs, and communication based on information and advice rather than instructions. New problems constantly arise and require actions which cannot be allocated among defined roles in the hierarchical structure. The nature of the organic system suggests both a greater opportunity for delegation, and a greater willingness to delegate.

The characteristics of a mechanistic system are similar to those of a bureaucratic structure. Large-scale organisations are almost certain to exhibit many of the characteristics of bureaucracy and this is most noticeable within the public sector. In the case of public sector organisations there is a particular demand for uniformity of treatment, regularity of procedures and accountability for their operations. It might be seen therefore that opportunities for personal delegation will be greater in small organisations, especially within the private sector.

Flexibility of job descriptions/ gradings

Where detailed job descriptions are adopted and applied rigidly as part of the philosophy of the organisation, then this can inhibit personal delegation. Staff may be reluctant to accept additional responsibilities which appear to fall outside the scope of their job description. Grading standards may also be an important factor and it may be expected that work is seen to be done at the 'proper' level. An example is the Civil Service where, to some extent, the decision as to who does what is bound by the grading of duties.

Individual characteristics

Notwithstanding any other consideration the extent and nature of delegation will ultimately be affected by the nature of individual characteristics. The ages, ability, training, attitude, motivation and character of the subordinates concerned will, in practice, be major determinants of delegation.

An example is where a strong and forceful personality overcomes the lack of formal delegation. Or where an inadequate manager is supported by a more competent subordinate who effectively acts as the manager. Failure to delegate successfully to a more knowledgeable subordinate may mean that the subordinate emerges as an informal leader and this could have possible adverse consequences for the manager, and for the organisation. Another example, and potential difficulty, is when a manager is persuaded to delegate increased responsibility to persons in a staff relationship who may have little authority in their own right but are anxious to enhance their power within the organisation. [22]

THE NEED FOR CONTROL

The concept of ultimate responsibility gives rise to the need for effective management control over the actions and decisions of subordinate staff. Whatever the extent of their delegated authority and responsibility, subordinates remain accountable to the manager who should, and hopefully would, wish to be kept informed of their actions and decisions. Subordinates must account to the manager for the discharge of the responsibilities which they have been given. The manager will therefore need to keep open the lines of delegation and to have an upward flow of communication. The manager will need to be kept informed of the relevance and quality of decisions made by subordinates.

The concept of accountability is therefore an important principle of management. The manager remains accountable to a superior not just for the work carried out personally but for the total operation of the department/section. This is essential in order to maintain effective co-ordination and control, and to maintain the chain of command. Successful delegation involves 'letting go without losing control'. [23]

A question of balance

Authority, responsibility and accountability must be kept in parity throughout the organisation. The manager must remain in control. The manager must be on the lookout for subordinates who are more concerned with personal empire building than with meeting stated organisational objectives. The manager must prevent a strong personality exceeding the limits of formal delegation.

We have said that delegation creates a special manager–subordinate relationship. This involves both the giving of trust and the retention of control.

> The essence of the delegation problem lies in the trust–control dilemma. The dilemma is that in any one managerial situation, the sum of trust + control is always constant. The trust is the trust that the subordinate feels that the manager has in him. The control is the control that the manager has over the work of the subordinate.[24]

Control is, therefore, an integral part of the system of delegation. But control should not be so close as to inhibit the effective operation or benefits of delegation. **It is a question of balance**. (*See* Fig. 16.2.) The nature of management control is discussed in the following chapter.

A SYSTEMATIC APPROACH TO DELEGATION

In order to overcome the lack of delegation and to realise the full benefits without loss of control it is necessary to adopt a planned and systematic approach. Setting up a successful system of delegation involves the manager examining four basic questions.

- What tasks could be performed better by subordinate staff?
- What opportunities are there for subordinate staff to learn and develop by undertaking delegated tasks and responsibilities?
- How should the increased responsibilities be implemented and to whom should they be given?

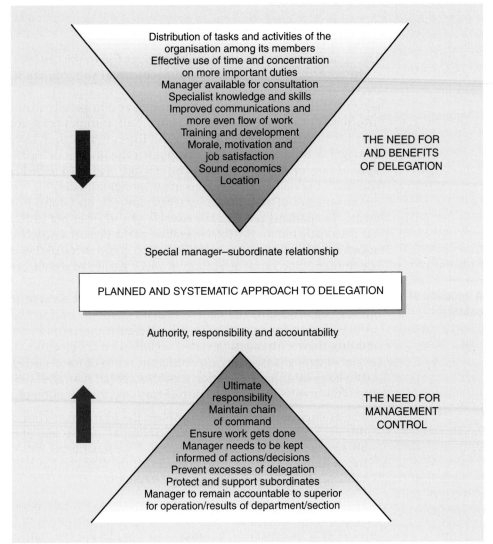

Distribution of tasks and activities of the
organisation among its members
Effective use of time and concentration
on more important duties
Manager available for consultation
Specialist knowledge and skills
Improved communications and
more even flow of work
Training and development
Morale, motivation and
job satisfaction
Sound economics
Location

THE NEED FOR
AND BENEFITS
OF DELEGATION

Special manager–subordinate relationship

PLANNED AND SYSTEMATIC APPROACH TO DELEGATION

Authority, responsibility and accountability

Ultimate
responsibility
Maintain chain
of command
Ensure work gets done
Manager needs to be kept
informed of actions/decisions
Prevent excesses of delegation
Protect and support subordinates
Manager to remain accountable to superior
for operation/results of department/section

THE NEED FOR
MANAGEMENT
CONTROL

Fig. 16.2
**The balance
between delegation
and control**

- What forms of monitoring control system would be most appropriate?

In order to set up an effective system of delegation subordinates should know exactly what is expected of them, what has to be achieved, the boundaries within which they have freedom of action, and how far they can exercise independent decision-making. It is possible to identify five main stages in a planned and systematic approach to delegation (*see* Fig. 16.3):

- clarification of objectives, and suitable patterns of organisation;
- agreement on terms of reference, and acceptance of authority and responsibility;
- guidance, support and training, and patterns of communication;
- effective monitoring and review procedures; and
- freedom of action within agreed terms of reference.

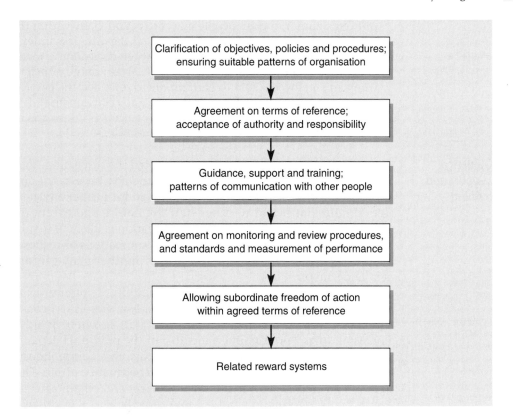

**Fig. 16.3
Main stages in
the process of
delegation**

Clarification of objectives, policies and procedures; ensuring suitable patterns of organisation

Agreement on terms of reference; acceptance of authority and responsibility

Guidance, support and training; patterns of communication with other people

Agreement on monitoring and review procedures, and standards and measurement of performance

Allowing subordinate freedom of action within agreed terms of reference

Related reward systems

**Clarification of
objectives and
organisation**

The first stage in a planned and systematic approach to delegation is the clarification of objectives and the design of suitable patterns of organisation to achieve these objectives. Policies and procedures must be established and defined in order to provide a framework for the exercise of authority and the acceptance of responsibility. Managers must be clear about their own role, and the opportunities and limitations of their own jobs. There must be a clear chain of command with effective communications and co-ordination between the various levels of authority (scalar chain) within the organisation structure.

**Agreement
on terms of
reference**

The manager can then negotiate and agree the subordinate's role prescription and terms of reference. Those areas of work in which the subordinate is responsible for achieving results should be identified clearly. Emphasis should generally be placed on end-results rather than a set of detailed instructions. When, however, the manner in which delegated activities are to be carried out is of particular importance, this should be discussed fully with the subordinate who should understand the reasons for, and nature of, any limitations of discretion or restrictions imposed. The division of activities and responsibilities between the manager and subordinate should be established and agreed.

It is important to **make sure that subordinates accept the extent of, and any restrictions on, the authority and responsibility delegated to them**. Subordinates should feel a sense of commitment to their new tasks or assignments and free to discuss any doubts or concerns. Delegation involves the acceptance theory of authority. *Davis* explains this as follows:

Although authority gives people power to act officially within the scope of their delegation, this power becomes somewhat meaningless unless those affected accept it and respond to it. In most cases when delegation is made, a subordinate is left free to choose a response within a certain range of behaviour. But even when an employee is told to perform one certain act, the employee still has the choice of doing it or not doing it and taking the consequences. It is, therefore, the subordinate who controls the response to authority. Managers cannot afford to overlook this human fact when they use authority.[25]

Guidance, support and training

When subordinates have agreed and accepted the delegation, they should be properly briefed, given guidance and support and any necessary training. They should be advised where, and to whom, they can go for further advice or help. The manager should make clear to other staff the nature and extent of delegation, and obtain their co-operation. Where the delegation is likely to involve contact or consultation with people in other departments or sections or requests for information, the manager should also communicate with other managers and seek their consent and support.

The simple process of smoothing the pattern of communications should ordinarily require little effort by the manager. Not only is it a courtesy but it can do much to enlist the co-operation of other staff and help avoid any possible misunderstandings. For example, a member of the personnel department, X, has been delegated by the personnel manager to draw up a comprehensive staffing report which requires certain information from the finance office. The personnel manager should consult with the finance manager and obtain agreement for X to have access to this information and to speak directly with Y in the finance office; hopefully Y will then be informed of the situation by the finance manager.

Not only should this pattern of communication enable Y to understand why X is seeking information, it should also help to make for an easier working relationship between them. The finance manager will also now understand what is going on if X and Y are seen going through finance office files.

Monitoring and review procedures

The manager should agree time limits for delegation (such as a target date for completion of a specific task or a specified time period). It is necessary to agree the level and nature of supervision, and to establish a system to monitor progress and provide feedback. It is also important to agree response deadlines, check points and specific times to meet, and the review of performance within the agreed terms of reference: for example, to discuss progress with the manager at the end of each week, or to discuss the first draft of a report before it progresses further, and by an agreed date.

Delegation is not an irrevocable act; it can always be withdrawn.

It is also important to make clear expected levels of achievement and agree on performance standards (wherever practically possible in quantitative terms), and how performance in each area is to be measured and evaluated.

Freedom of action

The subordinate should then be left alone to get on with the job. One of the most frustrating aspects of delegation is the manager who passes on authority but stays close behind the subordinates' shoulders keeping a constant watch over their actions. This is contrary to the nature of delegation. **The true nature of successful delegation means that the subordinate is given freedom of action within the boundaries established and agreed in the previous stages.**

A planned and systematic approach means that effective delegation can be achieved without loss of control. Modern methods of management can also assist the effectiveness of delegation. Procedures such as management by exception and staff appraisal are useful means of helping to maintain control without inhibiting the growth of delegation. Delegation can be increased under a system of Management by Objectives which allows staff to accept greater responsibility and to make a greater personal contribution.

Related reward systems

Wherever possible, the process of delegation should be related to some form of associated 'reward' system. Examples could include bonus payments, improved job satisfaction, reduction of work stress, and enhanced opportunities for promotion or personal development, including further delegation.

THE ART OF DELEGATION

The art of delegation is to agree clear terms of reference with subordinates, to give them the necessary authority and responsibility and then to monitor their performance without undue interference or the continual checking of their work. Effective delegation is a social skill. It requires a clear understanding of people-perception, reliance on other people, confidence and trust, and courage.

Reliance on other people

Delegation entails reliance on other people. It is important that the manager chooses the right subordinates to whom to delegate authority and responsibility. The manager must know what to delegate, when and to whom. Matters of policy and disciplinary power, for example, usually rest with the manager and cannot legitimately be delegated. Delegation is a matter of judgement and involves the question of discretion.

Confidence and trust

Delegation is also a matter of confidence and trust – both in subordinates and in the manager's own performance and system of delegation. **In allowing freedom of action to subordinates within agreed terms of reference and the limits of authority, managers must accept that subordinates may undertake delegated activities in a different manner from themselves.** This can be one of the most difficult aspects of successful delegation. It involves the manager adopting an approach along the following lines of thought and action.

'There are a number of alternative, but equally acceptable, ways in which this task could be undertaken. After discussions with C to whom the task has been delegated, C has chosen that particular way. It would not have been the way I would have done it. However if C undertakes the task satisfactorily within our agreed terms of reference and performance criteria, then this is fine and credit should be given to C. If, however, things go wrong, then in effect C's way has become my way. I must be supportive of C, accept ultimate responsibility and any possible criticism from my superior.'

This is at the basis of the true nature of delegation. But learning to put trust in other people is one of the most difficult lessons for many managers, and some never learn it.[26]

Training and learning experience

Delegation is also a matter of courage. If a subordinate comes to a manager with a problem the manager should insist on a recommendation from the subordinate. Delegation involves subordinates making decisions and managers should avoid 'reverse delegation' and subordinates pushing control and decisions back upward to the manager.[27]

Mistakes will inevitably occur and the subordinate will need to be supported by the manager, and protected against unwarranted criticism. The acceptance of ultimate responsibility highlights the educational aspect of the manager's job. The manager should view mistakes as part of the subordinate's training and learning experience, and an opportunity for further development. Lord Forte, for example, advocates the following philosophy in dealing with subordinate staff:

> 'I am sorry I have made a mistake.'
> 'No, you have not made a mistake,' I replied. 'We have made a mistake.'[28]

By the same token managers should openly admit their own mistakes.

> Admit your own mistakes openly, maybe even joyfully. Encourage your associates to do likewise by commiserating with them. Never castigate. Babies learn to walk by falling down. If you beat a baby every time he falls down, he'll never care much for walking . . . Beware the boss who walks on water and never makes a mistake. Save yourself a lot of grief and seek employment elsewhere.[29]

DELEGATION AND WORK STRESS

Not only does poor delegation fail to take advantage of the potential benefits to both the individual and the organisation, but it can also be a potential source of work stress. The downsizing or organisations, reduction in staffing levels and increased business competitiveness have placed greater pressures on managers. This can lead to enforced or inadequate systems of delegation resulting in role conflict, health problems and work stress.

Research into managers in various types of organisations in Western Australia showed that delegation of responsibility to middle managers required great skill, which was too seldom present. Replies from 532 managers in 36 organisations indicated a clear correlation between lack of autonomy and stress at work.[30]

Stress was often caused by the hierarchical structure of the organisation not permitting sufficient autonomy. As a result, projects were frequently delayed and also managers' authority within their own departments was undermined.

SYNOPSIS

- It is a fundamental principle of management that for organisational effectiveness there must be delegation. At the organisational level, delegation involves consideration of centralisation/decentralisation and divisionalisation or departmentalisation. At the individual, or personal, level delegation is the process of entrusting authority and responsibility to others. It is possible to have delegation upwards, and also laterally. However, delegation is usually interpreted as a movement down the organisation. It is the authorisation to undertake activities that would otherwise be carried out by someone in a more senior position.

- Delegation creates a special manager–subordinate relationship. A manager's approach to delegation is important and should not be underestimated. Authority is the right to take actions or make decisions that the manager would otherwise have done. Responsibility involves an obligation by the subordinate to perform certain activities and having to accept possible reprimand from the manager for unsatisfactory performance. Delegation embraces both authority and responsibility. Accountability (ultimate responsibility), however, cannot be delegated.

- Managers remain accountable to a superior for the actions of subordinates and the performance of all duties allocated to their department/section.

- Delegation is not an easy task. It involves behavioural as well as organisational and economic considerations, and it is subject to a number of possible abuses. But if delegation is properly planned and implemented it offers a number of potential benefits both to the manager and to subordinate staff, and should lead to improved organisational performance.

- Managers often fail to delegate or to delegate successfully. There are many factors which affect the extent and effectiveness of delegation. Some of the main obstacles to delegation are the attitudes of managers, and subordinates who shrink from accepting new responsibilities. Delegation is also affected by the style of leadership and system of management, the organisation structure, the informal organisation, and the personalities of the people concerned. Individual characteristics are a major determinant of delegation.

- Control is an integral part of the system of delegation. But control should not be so close as to inhibit the effective operation of delegation. It is a question of balance. Authority, responsibility and accountability must be kept in parity throughout the organisation. Delegation must be properly planned and approached in a systematic manner. Subordinates must know exactly what is expected of them, what has to be achieved, and the boundaries within which they have freedom of action.

- The art of delegation is to agree clear terms of reference with subordinates, give them the necessary authority and responsibility, and then monitor their performance without undue interference or the continual checking of their work. A planned and systematic approach means that the full benefits of delegation can be achieved without loss of control. Delegation entails the reliance on other people. It is also a matter of confidence and trust, and should be seen as a training and learning experience.

Review and discussion questions

1 What do you understand by the dimensions of, and approaches to, delegation in work organisations?

2 How would you explain the relationship between a manager and subordinate staff that is created by the process of delegation?

3 Discuss the extent to which you accept the contention that lack of delegation results in management at too low a level. Support your answer with examples from your own or some other organisation.

4 What are the reasons for delegation in work organisations? What benefits would you expect to result, for both the manager and subordinate staff, from successful delegation?

5 Explain what you believe are the qualities required of an effective delegator. What is meant by the art of delegation?

6 Explain why you think it is that delegation, whilst often advocated, is not always practised fully.

7 As a departmental manager, explain fully how you would attempt to realise the full advantages of delegation without loss of control over subordinate staff.

8 Give practical examples of the factors which are likely to influence the extent of delegation in a particular work organisation/work situation of your choice.

Assignment

Examine a process of delegation in your own or some other organisation.

(i) Note the extent to which the four basic questions concerning the setting up of a successful system of delegation appear to have been considered.

(ii) Examine the extent to which the five main stages in a planned and systematic approach to delegation appear to have been followed. In particular, explain:
 (a) the nature of the guidance, support and training given to the subordinate(s); and
 (b) the nature of the monitoring and review procedures for delegation.

(iii) Inquire of (a) the manager undertaking the delegation and (b) the member(s) of staff concerned what benefits they have each gained from the delegation and any difficulties experienced.

(iv) Explain ways in which you believe the process of delegation appears to be successful, or not. Where appropriate, suggest ways in which you think the process of delegation could be made more effective.

CASE STUDY

The enthusiastic delegator

When Charles Turner was told, on his fortieth birthday, that he was to be pro-
moted manager of the Electrical Insulation Materials Sales Department of the big
Climax Fibre and Textile Company Limited, his gratification was strongly tem-
pered by doubts about his own personal adequacy for the job.

Climax had only started to market its 'Highohm' range of electrical insulation
materials two years previously. Though the Highohm products were not easy to sell
– their small but definite technical advantages over competing products were more
or less cancelled out by higher prices – their entry to the market had been spectacu-
larly successful. Existing production capacity was already almost fully sold, and a
big new plant, which would more than double capacity, was under construction
and expected to start up in six to nine months' time. Turner was left in no doubt by
his sales director that, as manager, he would be expected, through his small sales
force, to ensure that sales of Highohm products continued to increase and that
most of the extra capacity of the new plant was sold within no more than a year of
production commencing. In addition, he was expected personally to service the
'house accounts' – five very large customers who between them were responsible
for over 25 per cent of all Highohm purchases. The biggest of them, Bucks Electrical
Cables, was reputed to be extremely awkward to deal with, and one of Turner's
immediate worries in his new appointment was that he would lose this account
and 10 per cent of his sales in one dreadful moment of catastrophe.

This was not his only worry. He wondered how Jim Ferris, who managed the
Northern and Scottish Area, would react to his appointment. Turner did not know
Ferris very well, though his predecessor as sales manager, Frank Spofforth, had
often spoken of him in glowing terms. He was a self-confident man in his late
twenties, reputedly very dynamic, highly intelligent, and a brilliant salesman of
industrial products. He had achieved remarkable success in running the Northern
and Scottish Area: 44 per cent of all Highohm sales were made there, as against
only 28 per cent from the South and Midlands Area, which Turner had managed
prior to his promotion. (Remaining sales came from the 'house accounts' and from
exports.) Turner, in fact, wondered why he, and not Ferris, had been promoted.

A further worry for Turner was the new plant. He had always felt that it was
much too big and he was extremely dubious that more than a small part of the
extra capacity it provided could be rapidly taken up in increased sales.

Most of all, however, Turner doubted his own abilities. He knew that he was
thorough, methodical, painstaking and cautious, but these were hardly the quali-
ties essential for managing a sales operation. His caution tended to make him slow
and hesitant. He rarely produced new ideas and he disliked making decisions
unless he had all the facts and had gone over them several times. He thought he
was by nature fitted to keep an existing successful operation going, but he gravely
doubted his ability as a leader of a dynamic pioneering effort.

Turner had hoped that he would have a long period of changeover working
alongside his predecessor, Spofforth. In fact, Spofforth was urgently wanted in the
new post to which he had been promoted, and Turner, within a few days of being

told of his new appointment, found himself in sole command. The organisation which he inherited was as follows:

SALES MANAGER
(C. T. B. Turner)

LONDON OFFICE MANCHESTER OFFICE

SOUTH & MIDLANDS NORTHERN &
AREA MANAGER SCOTTISH AREA
(vacant) MANAGER
(J. J. Ferris)

EXPORT REPRESENTATIVE
(selling through
overseas agents)

3 representatives 3 representatives

One of his immediate problems was to fill the South and Midlands Area manager vacancy. There were others, however; the plant had developed an intermittent defect which slowed production and meant that many deliveries were late. Several customers, notably Bucks Electrical Cables, were protesting vigorously. Furthermore, the sales director wanted two major reports. Each, Turner thought, would take at least a week of his time and severely tax his ability to produce new ideas and constructive proposals as well as his ability to write lucidly and elegantly. Yet he could not delay their production, or make anything less than a first-rate job of them, for fear of beginning his new appointment by disappointing the sales director.

Turner decided that he would ask Ferris to come to London for a few days. Apart from enabling him to obtain Ferris's views on the problems he faced, it would give him the opportunity to try to smooth out any resentment at his promotion.

Much to Turner's gratification, Ferris was extremely helpful. He made short work of Turner's reports. He was an abundant producer of ideas, and soon sketched out what seemed to Turner an eminently satisfactory set of proposals for both reports. He then offered to draft the reports for Turner, and dictated both during one afternoon. Turner, who normally made several laborious pencil drafts before attempting to finalise a report, was astonished at Ferris's facility. The drafts seemed to him quite perfect, and he signed them and sent them to the sales director.

Ferris next offered to go to 'pacify' Bucks Electrical Cables. Turner demurred saying it was his duty to deal personally with this problem, but Ferris insisted that Turner was too busy with managerial problems to spare the time. Turner was secretly relieved at not having to deal with these awkward customers. Ferris later telephoned to say that he had just taken three Bucks Electrical directors to lunch and they had all parted the best of friends.

Finally Ferris put forward an idea about the area manager vacancy. He, Ferris, would take over the South and Midlands Area and his senior representative in the north, Palmer, could be promoted Northern and Scottish Area manager. Turner was strongly attracted by the prospect of having Ferris's services 'on tap' in London, and readily agreed to this proposal.

Ferris tackled his new job as South and Midlands Area manager with characteristic vigour and sales were soon moving upwards – indeed, the production people had to make Herculean efforts to squeeze out the additional product needed to cope with the increased orders. He found time, however, to give substantial personal help to Turner, and Turner came increasingly to rely on him. Whenever he had a problem to solve, a decision to make, or a report to write, he consulted Ferris. Normally it was Ferris who supplied the solution, suggested the decision to be adopted, or wrote the report.

Turner often felt guilty about the extent to which he relied on Ferris and sometimes apologised to him for 'leaning' so much on him. Ferris, however, had a soothing answer. This, he explained, was the normal process of delegation. It would be quite wrong for Turner to be continually involved in detail problems; his function was to formulate the problems and leave his subordinates to solve them. Gradually, Turner came to accept the idea that his relationship with Ferris was no more than sound management; he even began to boast to his manager friends about the 'delegation' that he practised and the trouble-free life he led.

The new plant and the reorganisation

Thus, as the start-up of the new plant became imminent, Turner had a plan ready – Ferris's plan. Several new representatives had been recruited and Britain was to be divided into four sales areas – South, Midlands, North and Scotland. Ferris would continue to look after the South and Palmer the North; a nominee of Ferris, Murdoch, would manage Scotland; the Midlands Area was to be managed by Blackham, who was an older, senior representative recently transferred to Electrical Insulation Sales from another department. A new two-man technical service section was to be formed at the London office to service customers throughout Britain; and an additional export representative was to be engaged to participate in a drive for more overseas sales.

Ferris took on a wide range of new responsibilities through the reorganisation. Apart from managing the southern area and continuing to give personal assistance to Turner, he had persuaded Turner that he should in future service the 'house accounts'. He would also 'keep an eye on exports', and would accompany the export representatives on flying visits overseas when agents needed gingering up. It had been Ferris's idea that a technical service section should be formed and it was natural that he should direct its work. To free him from too much detailed work in managing the southern area, he was given an extra senior representative. The new organisation was therefore in practice as follows:

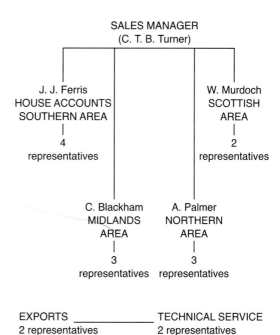

SALES MANAGER
(C. T. B. Turner)

J. J. Ferris
HOUSE ACCOUNTS
SOUTHERN AREA
4 representatives

W. Murdoch
SCOTTISH
AREA
2 representatives

C. Blackham
MIDLANDS
AREA
3 representatives

A. Palmer
NORTHERN
AREA
3 representatives

EXPORTS
2 representatives

TECHNICAL SERVICE
2 representatives

This organisation was not shown on the published charts, since both Turner and Ferris agreed that it would look better if exports and technical service were shown as formally responsible to Turner.

The first few months for the new organisation were difficult. The new plant came into production, but sales hardly rose at all. Ferris visited all the areas to coach representatives and accompany them on calls to major potential customers. He sent the technical service representatives out to scour the country, making contact with the development staffs of possible users of Highohm materials. He made numerous trips to European and Commonwealth countries to exhort the overseas agents to greater endeavour.

At length, sales began to increase – at first slowly, but then in a steep curve that took the new plant up to 80 per cent of capacity. Exports were responsible for the biggest part of the increase, but all the UK areas showed good growth, with the Midlands slightly ahead of the others.

Turner, who had only been saved from utter despondency during the months of difficulty by Ferris's unvarying confidence and optimism, now began to regain his serenity. He was congratulated by the board on the achievement of his department in selling the output of the new plant, and was given a substantial increase in salary. He became rather more self-confident, though he would still take no decision of importance without reference to Ferris.

Strains in the organisation

The area managers soon discerned something of the extent to which Turner depended on Ferris. Palmer and Murdoch, who were both protégés of Ferris, regarded it as natural. Blackham, the Midlands Area manager, however, began to make it clear that he strongly disapproved of what he called the 'imbalance of power' in the department. He pressed for more responsibility to be delegated to him. In particular he asked to take over the two 'house accounts' in the Midlands Area. He also asked that all the area managers should be consulted before important decisions were taken.

On Ferris's advice, Turner told Blackham that he had enough to do already in developing sales in the Midlands without taking over the 'house accounts'. In any case, these important customers were best served by someone they knew and trusted. Turner and Ferris agreed, however, that more consultation with the area managers was desirable and monthly 'area manager meetings' were instituted.

These did little to decrease Blackham's dissatisfaction. Though Turner nominally took the chair, it was Ferris who really conducted the meetings. Blackham resented this, but what riled him still more was that it was usually obvious that, irrespective of what the other managers said, Turner was going to make his decisions according to whatever advice Ferris gave him. Often, indeed, it was clear that Turner and Ferris had already discussed and decided issues before the meeting.

Blackham showed his dissatisfaction with the meetings by taunting Ferris and Turner with ironic asides and frequent sardonic laughter. This did not appear to worry Ferris, but it upset Turner.

Accordingly, while Ferris was away on a trip abroad, Turner sent for Blackham and appealed to him to co-operate with himself and Ferris. Blackham bitterly attacked Ferris, saying that he had deliberately taken advantage of Turner's good nature to build up his own personal 'empire' within the department. Turner protested that this was not the case; it was just that he believed in delegation and since Ferris was exceptionally able, experienced, vigorous and willing to accept responsibility, it was

natural that considerable responsibility should be delegated to him.

Blackham laughed sardonically. Turner did not delegate responsibility, he said, he abdicated it. Ferris did not just accept responsibility, he made a series of takeover bids for it.

Turner defended the system. At least it worked, he said. The department had great successes to its credit.

Blackham insisted that he was just as able and willing to accept responsibility as Ferris. It was unfair of Turner to delegate only to Ferris. The other area managers should be given the chance to show what they could do.

The meeting ended inconclusively, but Turner, who prided himself on being fair-minded, was half-persuaded that Blackham and the other area managers should be given more responsibility. As soon as Ferris returned, he consulted him on what changes in organisation might be made.

Ferris strongly opposed giving any further responsibility to the area managers, especially to Blackham, whose recent behaviour, he said, must make his judgement and temperament strongly suspect. What was wrong in the department was that the particular responsibilities he himself carried were not accompanied by appropriate formal authority. Ferris therefore proposed that he should be appointed deputy manager of the department. He was not seeking extra salary and would be quite content with only a status promotion, but he felt the time had come for it to be made clear that he was senior to Blackham and the other area managers.

This idea appealed to Turner. He felt it was only just that Ferris should be given some form of promotion. He also believed that promotion for Ferris might silence some of Blackham's criticisms.

He therefore went to ask the sales director for permission to create the new position of deputy manager, and for Ferris to be promoted to it. The sales director demurred. He said he felt that Turner's department was too small to warrant the appointment of a full-time deputy manager, and, in any case, Ferris was rather young to be promoted to such a post over the heads of older men such as Blackham. Turner pressed his case by outlining the range of duties undertaken by Ferris. The sales director questioned him closely upon this, and Turner was forced to reveal a great deal about the organisation of the department, and of his relationship with Ferris. He also mentioned his troubles with Blackham.

The sales director was obviously not at all pleased with what he had discovered. He said, 'I have always assumed that since your department has produced good results, its organisation, staffing and personal relationships have been satisfactory. Now I must consider whether or not I should intervene and impose changes.'

(a) When an inadequate manager is supported by a more able subordinate, is it likely that the subordinate will become the effective manager of the unit? Is it desirable? If not, what steps (apart from replacement of the manager) could be taken to prevent it?

(b) Where are the boundaries between proper delegation of authority and abdication of responsibility? Was Turner, in fact, guilty of the latter?

(c) Where does willingness to accept responsibility end and personal 'empire building' begin? Was Ferris an 'empire builder'? If so, with what motives?

(d) How far can a theoretically undesirable system be justified on the ground that 'it works'?

(e) Should the sales director intervene in Turner's organisational and personal relations problems? If so, what should he do?

Notes and references

1. Mullins, L. J. 'Delegation and Management', *British Journal of Administrative Management*, vol. 31, no. 7, October 1981, pp. 218–24.
2. See, for example: Leana, C. R. 'Predictors and Consequences of Delegation', *Academy of Management Journal*, vol. 29, 1986, pp. 754–74.
3. Drucker, P. F. *The Practice of Management*, Heinemann Professional (1989).
4. Mooney, J. D. *The Principles of Organisation*, Revised edition, Harper and Row (1947) p. 17.
5. Gray, I. *Henri Fayol's General and Industrial Management*, Pitman (1988).
6. See, for example: Haire, M. (ed.) *Organization Theory in Industrial Practice*, Wiley (1962).
7. Urwick, L. F. *Notes on the Theory of Organization*, American Management Association (1952).
8. *Ibid.*
9. For example: Peters, T. J. and Austin, N. *A Passion for Excellence: The Leadership Difference*, Random House (1985); and Waterman, R. H. *The Frontiers of Excellence*, Nicholas Brealey (1994).
10. See, for example: Drucker, P. F. *The Practice of Management*, Heinemann Professional (1988).
11. Simon, H. A. *The New Science of Management Decision*, Revised edition, Prentice-Hall (1977).
12. Hamilton, Sir Ian *The Soul and Body of an Army*, Arnold (1921) p. 236.
13. Peter, L. J. and Hull, R. *The Peter Principle*, Pan Books (1970) p. 22.
14. See, for example: Coates, J. 'It is Legitimate to be Unavailable', *Industrial and Commercial Training*, vol. 22, no. 5, 1990, pp. 8–11.
15. See, for example: Vinton, D. 'Delegation for Employee Development', *Training and Development Journal*, vol. 41, no. 1, January 1987, pp. 65–7.
16. Stewart, R. *The Reality of Management*, Second edition, Pan Books (1986) p. 190.
17. Hunt, J. W. *Managing People at Work: A Manager's Guide to Behaviour in Organisations*, Third edition, McGraw-Hill (1992).
18. Newman, W. H. 'Overcoming Obstacles to Effective Delegation', *Management Review*, January 1956, pp. 36–41.
19. McGregor, D. *The Human Side of Enterprise*, Penguin (1987).
20. Likert, R. and Likert, J. G. *New Ways of Managing Conflict*, McGraw-Hill (1976).
21. Burns, T. and Stalker, G. M. *The Management of Innovation*, Tavistock Publications (1966).
22. See, for example: Lerner, P. M. 'Beware the Gatekeeper', *Amtrak Expresss*, July/August 1994, pp.14–17.
23. Payne, J. and Payne, S. *Letting Go Without Losing Control*, The Institute of Management/Pitman (1994).
24. Handy, C. B. *Understanding Organizations*, Fourth edition, Penguin (1993) p. 283.
25. Davis, K. and Newstrom, J. W. *Human Behaviour at Work*, Eighth edition, McGraw-Hill (1989) pp. 336–7.
26. Stewart, R. *The Reality of Management*, Second edition, Pan Books (1986).
27. See, for example: Robbins, S. P. *Training in Inter-Personal Skills: Tips for Managing People at Work*, Prentice-Hall (1989).
28. Forte, Charles (Lord) *Forte: The Autobiography of Charles Forte*, Sidgwick and Jackson (1986) p. 24.
29. Townsend, R. *Further Up the Organisation*, Coronet Books (1985) p. 141.
30. Hall, K. and Savery, L. K. 'Stress Management', *Management Decision*, vol. 25, no. 6, 1987, pp. 29–35.

17

THE NATURE OF ORGANISATIONAL CONTROL

An important feature of the people–organisation relationship is the need for control. Control systems exist in all spheres of the operations of the organisation and are a necessary part of the process of management. Control is concerned with gauging the measure of success in achieving the goals and objectives of the organisation. The manager needs to understand the nature of power and control in order to improve organisational performance.[1]

 Learning objectives

To:

- Explain the meaning of control and different approaches to organisational control;

- Identify the essential elements in a management control system, and different forms of control;

- Detail characteristics of an effective control system, and examine the importance of behavioural factors;

- Explain the nature of power, involvement and control;

- Examine perspectives of organisational power;

- Assess the nature of financial and accounting systems of control;

- Appreciate the effects of control and power on individual behaviour and organisational performance.

Worth thinking about

'As I am responsible for the performance of subordinate staff then it is only right that I exercise control and power over them.' . . . *'But surely if you help people to accept a feeling of responsibility for their own actions and behaviour they are more likely to exercise self-control. And this must be better for them and for you.'*

THE MEANING OF CONTROL

The word control may be interpreted in a number of different ways with varying connotations. *Tannenbaum*, for example, sees control as an inherent characteristic of the nature of organisations. The process of control is at the centre of the exchange between the benefits that the individual derives from membership of an organisation and the costs of such benefits.

> Organization implies control. A social organization is an ordered arrangement of individual human interactions. Control processes help circumscribe idiosyncratic behaviors and keep them conformant to the rational plan of the organization. Organizations require a certain amount of conformity as well as the integration of diverse activities. It is the function of control to bring about conformance to organizational requirements and achievement of the ultimate purposes of the organization.[2]

Control often has an emotive connotation and is interpreted in a negative manner to suggest direction or command by the giving of orders. By their very nature, control systems are concerned with the regulation of behaviour. People may be suspicious of control systems and see them as emphasising punishment, an indication of authoritarian management, and a means of exerting pressure and maintaining discipline. Some writers seem to take this view, and even to suggest that organisational control is exploitation of employees.[3]

This is too narrow an interpretation, however. There is far more to control than simply a means of restricting behaviour or the exercise of authority over others. Control is not only a function of the formal organisation and a hierarchical structure of authority. It is also a function of interpersonal influence.[4] **Control is a general concept which is applied to both individual behaviour and organisational performance.**

Individual behaviour

Control can stand for reliability, order and stability. Whenever a person inquires 'I would like to know how well I am doing', this in effect can be seen as asking for control. Members of staff want to know what is expected of them and how well they are performing. This places emphasis on the exchange of information, and feedback and comparison of actual results against planned targets. Control is a basis for training needs, the motivation to achieve standards and for the development of individuals.[5]

Most people show an ambivalence towards control. While they may not wish to have them applied to their own performance they recognise the need for, and usefulness of, control systems. Under certain conditions, however, people may actually desire control. *Lawler*, for example, gives three reasons why employees might want to be subject to a control system:

- to give feedback about task performance;
- to provide some degree of structure of tasks, definition of how the tasks are to be carried out, and how performance will be measured; and
- where reward systems, for example pay, are based on performance.[6]

Organisational performance

At the organisational level, management need to exercise 'control' over the behaviour and actions of staff in order to ensure a satisfactory level of performance. Managerial control systems are a means of checking progress to determine whether the objectives of the organisation are being achieved. Control completes the cycle of managerial activities. It involves the planning and organisation of work functions, and guiding and regulating the activities of staff. Control provides a check on the execution of work and on the success or failure of the operations of the organisation. The whole purpose of management control is the improvement in performance at both the individual and organisational level. (*See* Fig. 17.1.)

The controversial nature of control

The concern for the regulation of behaviour and improvement in performance raises questions as to the ethical nature of control. For example, in discussing the goals of organisational behaviour (OB) *Robbins* makes the following observation:

> The most controversial goal is using OB knowledge to control behavior. When a manager asks, for instance: 'What can I do to make Dave put more effort on his job?' that manager is concerned with control. Why is control controversial? A democratic society is built upon the concept of personal freedom. Therefore, the idea that one person should attempt to get others to behave in some premeditated

**Fig. 17.1
The nature of
management control**

way, when the subjects of that control may be unaware that their behavior is being manipulated, has been viewed in some circles as unethical and/or repugnant . . . However, you should be aware that the control objective is frequently seen by managers as the most valuable contribution that OB makes towards their effectiveness on the job.[7]

APPROACHES TO ORGANISATIONAL CONTROL

Different approaches to organisation and management have illustrated different approaches to the nature of control.

Classical writers

The classical writers placed emphasis on structure and formal organisation, sets of principles to guide managerial actions, standardised procedures, and the assumption of rational and logical behaviour. Writers who place emphasis on the technical requirements of the organisation tend to support a high level of control as necessary for efficiency. For example, *Fayol* describes control as follows:

> In an undertaking, control consists in verifying whether everything occurs in conformity with the plan adopted, the instructions issued and principles established. It has for object to point out weaknesses and errors in order to rectify them and prevent recurrence. It operates on everything, things, people, actions.[8]

It may also be recalled that the ideas of 'Taylorism' and scientific management (discussed in Chapter 2) can be seen as representing a form of management control over the workers and the actual process of work. A distinctive feature of *Taylor*'s thought was that workers should be controlled not only by the giving of orders and maintenance of discipline, but also by removing from them any decisions about the manner in which their work was to be carried out.[9]

Human relations approach

The definition given by *Fayol* illustrates the far-reaching nature of control and the technical requirements of a management control system. But it tends to ignore the behavioural implications. This raises the question of how much control over people and actions, that is over behaviour, is necessary and in what form in order to help improve organisational effectiveness.

The human relations approach placed emphasis on the social organisation, and on the importance of groups and informal relationships. Those writers who place emphasis on the social needs of individuals within the work organisation see a high level of control as self-defeating. It produces a negative response, increases internal conflict or results only in short-term improvement in performance.[10] Control should not be seen, therefore, only in the sense that it suggests close and constant supervision or as an organisational constraint on freedom of action by the individual.

Open-systems model

In terms of the open systems model of the organisation, control relates to both end-results – the outputs and measurement of achieving organisational goals in terms of desired aims and objectives – and to the means – inputs and series of activities by which these inputs are transformed to outputs. Control emphasises the interrelationships among inputs, outputs and the series of activities which lead to the outputs.

Control can be seen as a mediator between the input and output processes. It helps to maintain the working of the organisational system. For example, budgetary control is a mediator relating to financial resources. Inventory control and production control relate to material resources. Staff appraisal is a control mediator in the area of human resources.[11] The organisation as an open system is subject to changes in its environment. The operation of management control systems will need, therefore, to be responsive to external influences.

Contingency approach

The contingency approach takes the view that there is no one, best structure. The most appropriate organisation structure and system of management, including methods of control, depend upon contingencies of the situation. Recall the discussion on the organisational setting (Chapter 3) and consider likely variations in the extent and form of management control among such diverse organisations as, for example, a prison, a local government department, a hotel, a mass production factory, a bank, or a university.

The nature of management control is an organisational variable. It may even be that control systems provide a better means of predicting certain facets of organisational behaviour than the classification of technology; (*see* the discussion on classification of control systems later in this chapter).

ELEMENTS OF AN ORGANISATIONAL CONTROL SYSTEM

Whatever the nature of control there are five essential elements in an organisational control system (*see* Fig. 17.2.):

- planning what is desired;
- establishing standards of performance;
- monitoring actual performance;
- comparing actual achievement against the planned target; and
- rectifying and taking corrective action.

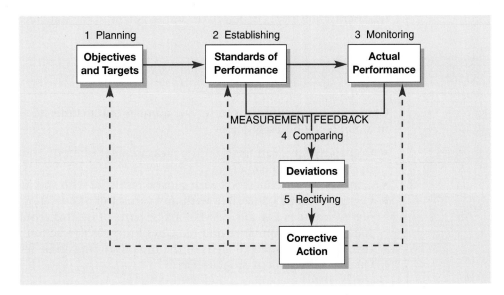

**Fig. 17.2
The five essential stages of organisational control**

Planning what is desired

Planning what is desired involves clarification of the aims to be achieved. It is important that people understand exactly what is required of them. This requires that objectives and targets are specified clearly, and given some measurable attribute. Planning provides the framework against which the process of control takes place.

Defined standards of performance

Related to planning is the establishment of defined standards of performance against which the level of success can be determined. This requires realistic measurements by which the degree and quality of goal achievement can be determined. Whenever possible these measurements should be stated in quantitative terms. Planning and measurement are prerequisites of control. Without them there can be no control. Objectives and targets, and standards of performance, should be stated clearly and communicated to those concerned, and to those who are subject to the operation of the control system.

Monitoring and comparing performance

The third aspect of control is the need for a means of monitoring actual performance. This requires feedback and a system of reporting information which is accurate, relevant and timely, and in a form that enables management to highlight deviations from the planned standard of performance. Feedback also provides the basis for decisions to adjust the control system, for example the need to revise the original plan. Feedback should relate to both the desired end-results and the means designed to achieve them.

Next, it is necessary **to compare actual performance against planned targets**. This requires a means of interpreting and evaluating information in order to give details of progress, reveal deviations, and identify probable causes. This information should be fed back to those concerned to let them know how well they are getting on.

Corrective action

The final element of a management control system is the taking of corrective action to rectify the situation which has led to the failure to achieve objectives or targets, or other forms of deviations identified. This requires consideration of what can be done to improve performance. It requires the authority to take appropriate action to correct the situation, to review the operation of the control system and to make any necessary adjustments to objectives and targets or to the standards of performance.

FORMS OF CONTROL

Control is far-reaching, it can serve a number of functions and can be manifested in a number of different forms.

- Control systems can focus on the measurement of inputs, outputs, processes or the behaviour of people.
- Controls can be concerned with general results or with specific actions.
- Controls can be concerned with an evaluation of overall performance of the organisation as a whole or with major parts of it. This requires broadly based standards of performance and remedies for corrective action. Total quality control, concerned with all areas of the organisation, can be seen as part of Total Quality Management programmes.[12]

- Controls can be concerned with the measurement and performance of day-to-day operational activities. This calls for more specific standards of performance and speedy corrective action.

Behavioural control and output control

Ouchi and Maguire suggest that the study of control in organisations includes selection and training, socialisation processes, bureaucracy, formalisation and the measurement of outputs.[13] From a study of retail department stores, they conclude that the control mechanism in an organisation is not a limited, single-purpose process. They refer to two independent forms of control that serve different functions:

- **Behavioural control** is based on direct personal supervision. This form of control appears more useful to the needs of individual managers in their attempts to control subordinates in one department or section. The use of behavioural control is responsive to the particular needs of the tasks, the abilities of the manager and the norms of the organisation.
- **Output control** is based on the measurement of outputs and the results achieved. This form of control serves the needs of the organisation as a whole and is used largely because of the demand for a quantifiable, simple measure of organisational performance.

Both types of control are important and they are not mutually exclusive. If controls over behaviour are applied without adequate attention to output controls this can lead to increased bureaucracy. An over-emphasis on formal rules and procedures may become more important in its own right rather than as a means to an end. People may behave as required by following the rules and regulations but important goals, such as, for example, providing effective customer service, may be overlooked.[14]

Control therefore can take a number of forms and can be categorised in a number of different ways.

CLASSIFICATION OF CONTROL SYSTEMS

Reeves and Woodward propose a classification of control systems based on seven case studies of differing industrial organisations.[15] They concluded that there was little likelihood of classifying control systems along a simple scale in one dimension, but from a large number of possible parameters they described two main aspects of control of particular relevance to the study of organisational behaviour:

- **personal–mechanical**; and
- **unitary–fragmented.**

Organisations might be positioned on a scale ranging from the extreme of completely personal hierarchical control to that of completely mechanical control; with administrative but impersonal control processes between the two extremes. This scale relates to how control is exercised within an organisation and the degree to which it is personal or impersonal. Impersonal control systems may be administrative or mechanical. Examples of administrative controls, which are based on formal standardised procedures, are production planning and cost control. An example of mechanical control is the automatic control system of machine tools

or continuous flow production plant which is built into the production process and operates through mechanical or electronic devices.

A second characteristic of management control systems, of importance in its behavioural effects, is the extent to which the various control systems are linked with each other and integrated into a single system of managerial control. Firms may be positioned on a scale ranging between the two extremes of a single integrated system of control and multi-system, fragmented control. Some firms attempt to relate the different control systems set for various departments into a unitary (integrated) system of managerial control. With multi-system control, standards of control are set independently by different functional specialists. People in the organisation are trying to satisfy a number of control criteria at the same time. For example, a particular task has to meet the demands of the production controller, the work study person, the personnel manager, the inspector and the cost accountant.

Control, technology and organisational behaviour

From a further analysis of the data collected from *Woodward*'s south Essex study of 100 manufacturing firms, clear links emerged between the original classification of technology and the above categorisation of managerial control systems (*see* Table 17.1).

Unit and small batch production firms tended to have unitary and mainly personal controls.

Process production firms tended to have unitary and mainly impersonal controls.

The similarities in some organisational characteristics between unit production firms and process firms identified in Woodward's south Essex study could be explained by the fact that in both groups unitary control systems predominated.

In the case of large batch and mass production firms, those with predominantly personal controls had similar organisational characteristics to unit firms; and those with predominantly mechanical controls had an organisation structure similar to process firms.

From the analysis, Reeves and Woodward suggest that control systems may be the underlying variable which links organisational behaviour and technology. The classification of control systems they propose might provide a better means of predicting certain facets of organisational behaviour than the classification of technology.

Table 17.1 **Relationship between control system and classification of technology**

	Control system A1 (%)	Control system B1 (%)	Control system B2 (%)	Control system A2 (%)
Unit and small batch production	75	25	–	–
Large batch and mass production	15	35	40	10
Process production	–	–	5	95
Total firms	28	21	18	33

(Reproduced with permission from J. Woodward, *Industrial Organization: Theory and Practice*, Second edition, Oxford University Press (1980) p. xxi.)

STRATEGIES OF ORGANISATIONAL CONTROL

Four particularly significant strategies of control in organisations are explained by *Child* (*see* Fig. 17.3):

- personal centralised;
- bureaucratic;
- output; and
- cultural.[16]

1 Personal centralised control
 1.1 centralised decision-taking
 1.2 direct supervision
 1.3 personal leadership: founded upon ownership or charisma, or technical expertise
 1.4 reward and punishment reinforce conformity to personal authority

2 Bureaucratic control
 2.1 breaking down of tasks into easily definable elements
 2.2 formally specified methods, procedures and rules applied to the conduct of tasks
 2.3 budgetary and standard cost-variance accounting controls
 2.4 technology designed to limit variation in conduct of tasks, with respect to pace, sequence and possibly physical methods
 2.5 routine decision-taking delegated within prescribed limits
 2.6 reward and punishment systems reinforce conformity to producers and rules

3 Output control
 3.1 jobs and units designed to be responsible for complete outputs
 3.2 specification of output standards and targets
 3.3 use of 'responsibility accounting' systems
 3.4 delegation of decisions on operational matters: semi-autonomy
 3.5 reward and punishment linked to attainment of output targets

4 Cultural control
 4.1 development of strong identification with management goals
 4.2 semi-autonomous working: few formal controls
 4.3 strong emphasis on selection, training and development of personnel
 4.4 rewards oriented towards security of tenure and career progression

(Reprinted with permission from Child, John, *Organization: A Guide to Problems and Practice*, Second edition, Paul Chapman (1984) p. 159.)

**Fig. 17.3
Four strategies of management control**

Personal centralised control

This is an approach often found in small owner-managed organisations. The approach is characterised by the centralisation of decision-making and initiative around a leadership figure. Control consists very largely of personal inspection to see that decisions are carried out, and the leader may spend a high proportion of time supervising the work personally. Once the organisation grows large enough to employ someone to undertake detailed supervision of everyday tasks, the locus of decision-making and close supervision will tend to become separated. A major criterion for the allocation of rewards and punishment is likely to be obedience to the leader's authority. The authority of the leader will usually rest upon the rights of ownership, special personal qualities (charisma) or technical expertise.

As organisations grow in size and technological complexity, a heavy centralised approach to control becomes increasingly difficult to maintain. In a large, complex organisation top managers will find increasing external demands on their time. In the development of an organisation, a combination of factors will move management away from personal centralised control towards bureaucratic control or output control.

Bureaucratic control

This approach to control is familiar in public sector organisations and in many other types of large organisations. The approach is based on the specification of how members should behave and carry out their work. There is an attempt to ensure predictability through formal job descriptions and procedures, the breaking down of tasks into constituent elements, and the specification of standard methods for the performance of tasks. Reward and punishment systems can be designed to reinforce this control strategy. Compliance can be rewarded by upgrading, improved status, favourable employment benefits and job security.

Bureaucratic control will make use of accounting control systems such as budgetary control (discussed later in this chapter) and standard cost variances. The bureaucratic strategy also permits delegation without loss of control. Managers can delegate routine decision-making within formally prescribed limits of discretion.

Output control

This approach relies upon the ability to identify specific tasks having a measurable output or criterion of overall achievement; for example, an end-product, a part manufactured to agreed standards, batch production or a sub-assembly. Once outputs or criteria for achievement have been identified, management can specify output standards and targets. Rewards and sanctions can be related to performance levels expressed in output terms. The efficiency of incentives will largely depend on the degree of trust in management's intentions to honour the relationship between performance and rewards.

Output control can make use of 'responsibility accounting' systems. The assignment of responsibility may be in terms of investment centres, profit centres or cost centres. Output control strategy is aimed at facilitating the delegation of operational decision-making without the need for bureaucratic controls or relying on close personal supervision. Once output standards have been agreed, subordinates can work with a 'semi-autonomous' relationship to management, free from detailed control over how tasks are carried out. Output control may be difficult to apply to certain activities, such as the legal department of a business organisation. Although it may be difficult to establish suitable and agreed measures of output, and it may be difficult for management to codify the activities involved, output control may be more appropriate than the application of a bureaucratic control strategy.

Cultural control

This approach tends to be exemplified by organisations offering professional services and staffed by professional people. The basis of cultural control strategy is the acceptance and willing compliance with the requirements of management, for example through strong professional identification and acceptance of the values and beliefs of the organisation. Provided members have the necessary skills and ability they can be given wide freedom of action in deciding how to undertake their responsibilities. There may not be any readily appropriate way of assessing the quality of output, especially in the short term, for example management development work of a personnel department.

There is likely to be careful selection, training and socialisation of staff in order to permit the use of semi-autonomous methods of working, with only limited formal controls. The combination of elements of cultural and output control could lead to self-managing units or teams with responsibility for completing projects and meeting agreed targets. This approach to control can only work with agreement on operating objectives and depends upon some shared culture among members of the organisation. Although a cultural control strategy may help identification with the objectives of corporate management, it is usually supported by substantial material inducements such as high salaries, fringe benefits and job security.

CHARACTERISTICS OF AN EFFECTIVE CONTROL SYSTEM

Whatever the nature or form of control there are a number of characteristic features of an effective control system. Control systems can have positive as well as negative effects. It is important therefore that they are designed and implemented in a constructive and rewarding way.

> Although they do not readily admit it, most people probably prefer some degree of control over their lives because it gives them some stability and contributes to their general welfare and safety. Nevertheless, the negative connotation of control still exists and is amplified by the ways in which controls have been traditionally set, implemented, and used in formal organizations.[17]

Hicks and Gullett state: 'Control systems should be understandable and economical, be related to decision centres, register variations quickly, be selective, remain flexible and point to corrective action.'[18] Developing the suggestion of Hicks and Gullett, we can identify a number of important characteristics of an effective control system.

Understandable For a control system to be meaningful, **it must be understood by those involved in its operation**. The purpose of the control system and the information it provides must be fully comprehensible to those who have to act on the results. The level of sophistication of a control system should be related to the nature of the activities involved and to the technical competence of the staff. For example, a detailed and sophisticated analysis of financial ratios may have little significance for an industrial shop-floor supervisor.

Information must be presented in a suitable format. If information is presented in a way which people do not understand they are likely to disregard it, and the full potential of the control system will not be realised. Equally, a too simplistic system of reporting which does little to help pinpoint the cause of deviations will not be of much value to the manager.

The control system should, wherever possible, yield objective information based on appropriate quantitative or qualitative units of measurement which cannot easily be questioned or subject to different interpretations and possible misunderstanding.

Related to decision centres Controls should **conform with the structure of the organisation and be related to decision centres responsible for performance**. Information should be supplied to those managers who have the responsibility for specified areas of activity

601

and who are capable of using this information to evaluate the degree of success in achievement of objectives: for example, the cause of excess expenditure in a manufacturing operation. Is this a result of increases in prices of raw materials? Is it because of the need to use substitute materials or suppliers? Is it because of problems with the manufacturing process? Or is it because of lower productivity by certain workers?

The information should enable managers to control their area of responsibility, and should be presented in a form which shows clearly when corrective action is necessary.

Reporting deviations quickly

An effective control system should **report deviations from the desired standard of performance as quickly as possible**. Ideally, indications of likely deviations should be discovered before they actually occur. It is important for deviations from the plan to be reported in good time so that corrective action to remedy the situation can be undertaken promptly. For example, information that the budget is likely to be overspent or underspent should arrive in sufficient time to enable the manager to do something about it and avoid drastic last-minute action.

Critical activities of the organisation

The control system should **draw attention to the critical activities which are important to the success of the organisation**. An unnecessary number of controls over comparatively unimportant activities are uneconomic and time-consuming; they can have a demoralising effect on staff and may possibly result in lack of attention to the key control points. Certain control points are more important than others. Careful control must be maintained in key result areas and in those activities which are crucial to the success of the organisation.

For example, a restaurant manager would need to have information on the number of orders taken at different times, and the number and type of meals provided, in order to deploy staff in the most effective manner. Information will also be needed to ensure adequate cash flow.

Flexibility

To be effective, **a control system must be flexible**. It must yield information which is not influenced by changes in other factors unconnected to the purpose of the control system. For example, a control system established five years ago, which specifies that reports to top management should be made whenever expenditure exceeds the budget by more than £x, is unlikely to be effective if no account has been taken of the effects of inflation. As prices rise over a period of time the excess expenditure will be an increasingly less serious matter.

Also, if the same amount is applied in all cases, high-spending departments may be subject to excessive control and low-spending departments not monitored closely enough. Control systems should not become an end in themselves. They should be designed to improve the operations of the organisation and be adaptable to changing environmental circumstances.

Nature of activity to which it relates

The control system should be **consistent with the objective of the activity to which it relates**. In addition to locating deviations from the planned standard of performance, the control system should be sophisticated enough to indicate ways in which performance can be improved.

For example, in the field of social services it may not be sufficient just to know that expenditure has been kept within the budget, without any underspending or overspending. It would be more helpful to know in what areas expenditure has

been incurred. It might be that the highest share of expenditure has gone to the financially better-off, who may be more knowledgeable of their rights and the procedures involved, than those who may be in greater financial need.

The control system should therefore address itself to causes of deviations rather than to symptoms. Controls may point to a number of possible problem areas for corrective action. Management will need to investigate these possibilities, and to determine the most appropriate form of corrective action which will deal with the causes of the deviation and solve the problems identified.

Continual review

Control systems should themselves **be subject to a continual review** to ensure that they are effective and appropriate in terms of the results they produce. They should not be too costly or elaborate, but should satisfy the characteristic features suggested above.

THE BALANCE BETWEEN ORDER AND FLEXIBILITY

Stewart refers to the classic dilemma that underlies the nature of control: finding the right balance for present conditions between order and flexibility. This involves the trade-off between trying to improve predictability of people's actions against the desirability of encouraging individual and local responsiveness to changing situations. The organisation may need a 'tight-loose' structure with certain departments or areas of work closely controlled ('tight'); whilst other departments or areas of work should be left fluid and flexible ('loose').[19]

Three main forms of control

According to Stewart, 'Control can – and should – be exercised in different ways'. She identifies three main forms of control.

- **Direct control by orders, direct supervision and rules and regulations**. Direct controls may be necessary, and more readily acceptable, in a crisis situation and during training. But in organisations where people expect to participate in decision-making, such forms of control may be unacceptable. Rules and regulations which are not accepted as reasonable, or at least not unreasonable, will offer some people a challenge to use their ingenuity in finding ways round them.
- **Control through standardisation and specialisation**. This is achieved through clear definition of the inputs to a job, the methods to be used and the required outputs. Such bureaucratic control makes clear the parameters within which one can act and paradoxically makes decentralisation easier. Provided the parameters are not unduly restrictive they can increase the sense of freedom. For example, within clearly defined limits which ensure that one retail chain store looks like another, individual managers may have freedom to do the job as they wish.
- **Control through influencing the way that people think about what they should do**. This is often the most effective method of exercising control. It may be achieved through selective recruitment of people who seem likely to share a similar approach, the training and socialisation of people into thinking the organisation's way, and through peer pressure. Where an organisation has a very strong culture, people who do not fit in, or learn to adapt, are likely to be pushed out, even though they may appear to leave of their own volition.

Stewart also refers to a second, related dilemma of finding the appropriate balance between centralisation, as a means of exercising control, and decentralisation. (Centralisation and decentralisation were discussed in Chapter 10.)

ASSUMPTIONS OF ORGANISATION AND MANAGEMENT

One view of control is based on the classical approach and traditional assumptions of organisation and management. Control is viewed as an essential feature of formal organisation and a hierarchical structure of authority. The traditional view assumes the amount of control is fixed. It is based on the use of routine procedures, and the exercise of rules and regulations in an attempt to create consistency and predictability in behaviour.

An alternative view of control is more in keeping with the human relations approach. Control is seen as a feature of interpersonal influence and takes place within a network of interaction and communication. **While the need for some form of control is constant, the extent and manner of control is variable. The exercise of control is an expression of management systems and styles of behaviour.**

In previous chapters we have discussed the general movement towards flatter organisation structures and the increasing importance of an integrating rather than a hierarchical or controlling style of management. The nature of management is moving away from an emphasis on getting results by the close control of the workforce and towards an environment of coaching, support and the devolution of power to the workforce. [20]

POWER AND MANAGEMENT CONTROL

Work organisations are not only systems of hierarchical structure, they are also systems of social relationships, status and power. Power is a complex and dynamic concept and difficult to define easily. At a broad level, power can be interpreted in terms of control or influence over the behaviour of other people with or without their consent. Sometimes power is interpreted in terms of the *extent* of the influence which can actually be exercised over other people, and sometimes it is taken to include influence over objects or things as well as people.

A more specific definition is given by *Morgan*, who sees power as 'the medium through which conflicts of interest are ultimately resolved. Power influences who gets what, when, and how'.[21] *Robbins* suggests that as power may exist but not be used it implies a potential that need not be actualised to be effective. Power is therefore a capacity or a potential. The most important aspect of power is probably dependency. 'A person can have power over you only if he or she controls something you desire.' [22]

Power is an inherent feature of work organisations and is often the underlying reality behind the decision-making process. It is central to the framework of order and system of command through which the work and activities of the organisation are carried out, for example through the operation of bureaucratic structures and the implementation of policies, rules and procedures. Lack of power and influ-

ence, and office politics, are among the main sources of managerial stress within organisations.[23]

The view of power as of functional importance is in keeping with a unitary approach to organisation. Management control is the predominant means by which the activities of staff are guided towards the achievement of organisational goals. The exercise of power is that which comes from a position of formal authority within the management structure of the organisation and which legitimises control over subordinate staff.

POWER, INVOLVEMENT AND COMPLIANCE

From a comparative analysis of complex organisations, *Etzioni* provides a classification of organisational relationships based on structures of control and the use of power resources as a means of ensuring compliance among members.[24] The Etzioni typology involves three dimensions: power; involvement; and the identification of kinds of power with kinds of involvement. Compliance is the relationship between the kinds of power applied by the organisation to control its members and the kinds of involvement developed by members of he organisation.

Power differs according to the means by which members of the organisation comply.

- **Coercive power** relies on the use of threats, or physical sanctions or force, for example, controlling the need for food or comfort.
- **Remunerative power** involves the manipulation of material resources and rewards, for example, through salaries and wages.
- **Normative power** relies on the allocation and the manipulation of symbolic rewards, for example, esteem and prestige.

Involvement is the degree of commitment by members to the organisation.

- **Alienative involvement** occurs where members are involved against their wishes. There is a strong negative orientation towards the organisation.
- **Calculative involvement** occurs where attachment to the organisation is motivated by extrinsic rewards. There is either a negative orientation or a low positive orientation towards the organisation.
- **Moral involvement** is based on the individual's belief in, and value placed on, the goals of the organisation. There is high positive orientation towards the organisation.

The identification of kinds of power with kinds of involvement

When considered together, nine logical types of organisational relationships and compliance result from this typology. (*See* Fig. 17.4.)

Based on this analysis, Etzioni suggests that a particular kind of power usually goes with a particular kind of involvement:

- coercive power with alienative involvement – relationship 1 (typified, for example, by prisons);
- remunerative power with calculative involvement – relationship 5 (typified, for example, by business firms);
- normative power with moral involvement – relationship 9 (typified, for example, by churches).

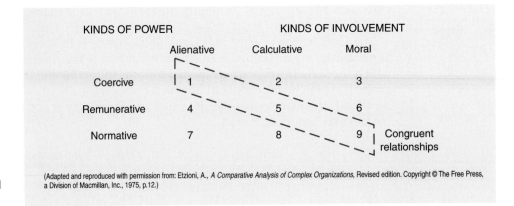

**Fig. 17.4
Organisational
relationships and
compliance**

The matching of these kinds of power and involvement is congruent with each other, and represents the most common form of compliance in organisations. The other six types of organisational relationships are incongruent. Etzioni suggests that organisations with congruent compliance structure will be more effective than organisations with incongruent structures.

PERSPECTIVES OF ORGANISATIONAL POWER

There are many potential sources of power which enable members of an organisation to further their own interests and which provide a means of resolving conflicts. Sources of organisational power include, for example: structure, formal authority, rules and regulations; control of the decision-making process; control of resources and technology; control of information or knowledge; trade unions and staff organisations; gender; and the informal organisation.[25]

Power can also be viewed in terms of the different levels at which it is constituted. *Fincham* looks at organisational power in terms of three types or levels of analysis: processual; institutional; and organisational.[26]

- At the **processual level** power originates in the process of daily interaction. The level of analysis is that of lateral relations between management interest groups and the basis of explanation is strategic. Processual power focuses on the 'micro-politics' of organisational life. It stresses power as negotiation and bargaining, and the 'enactment' of rules and how resources are employed in the power game.
- At the **institutional level** managerial power is seen as resting on external social and economic structures which create beliefs about the inevitability of managerial authority. Power is explained as being 'mandated' to the organisation. When managers seek to exercise power they can draw on a set of institutionally produced rules such as cultural beliefs about the right to manage.
- The **organisational level** stresses the organisation's own power system and the hierarchy as a means of reproducing power. Dominant beliefs, values and knowledge shape organisational priorities and solutions or reflect the interests of particular groups or functions. Those in authority select others to sustain the existing power structure. Organisational hierarchies transmit power between the institutional interests and the rules and resources governing action.

Culture as a source of power

All organisations have their own culture – which describes what the organisation is all about and 'the way things are done around here'. Culture is an important ingredient of managerial behaviour and organisational performance. Strong organisational cultures where individuals and the organisation share the same goals (for example IBM, Marks & Spencer and The Body Shop) will have a significant influence on power relationships, personal values and beliefs and the nature of organisational politics. (Organisational culture and climate are discussed in Chapter 20.)

PLURALISTIC APPROACH TO POWER

Power, however, arises not only from sources of structure or formal position within the organisation but from interpersonal sources such as the personality, characteristics and talents of individual members of the organisation. The exercise of power is also a social process which derives from a multiplicity of sources and situations. This suggests a more pluralistic approach and recognises power as a major organisational variable. Many different groups and individuals have the ability to influence the behaviour and actions of other people.

In Chapter 8 we discussed a classification of social power based on a broader perception of leadership influence. This includes not only legitimate power but also reward power, coercive power, referent power and expert power which may be exercised through all levels of the hierarchy.[27] Arguably, the most important and pervasive relationships in the organisation are those that do not rely on the exercise of formal power and position within the management structure. [28]

Recognition of the efficient use of human resources for business success together with advances in social democracy have highlighted the increasing importance of employee involvement and industrial partnership including the role played by trade unions. Where managers follow a unitary ideology and reject alternative sources of power and authority this can result in fear and stress associated with labour–management relationships. [29]

Empowerment of staff

In Chapter 15 we discussed how getting the best out of people and attempting to improve job satisfaction demands a spirit of co-operation and allowing people a greater say in decisions that affect them at work. Managers need to relinquish close control in favour of greater empowerment of employees. This gives members of staff a sense of personal power and control over their work and responsibility for making their own decisions.

Network of social relationships

Organisations function on the basis of networks of interdependent activities. A reality of organisational life is the vagaries of social relationships and office politics. Certain jobs or work relationships enable people to exercise a level of power in excess of their formal position within the structure of the organisation. A classic example is someone, perhaps a personal assistant or office manager, who fulfils the role of gatekeeper to the boss. There is an inherent danger with this type of role relationship that the boss may become too dependent upon the gatekeeper. Undertaking the responsibilities delegated by the boss and maintaining control can lead to the gatekeeper's misuse of their role and to an abuse of power.

Many people within organisations also have the ability to grant or withhold 'favours' within the formal or the informal interpretation of their job role – for example secretaries, caretakers, security staff and telephonists. Staff may exercise negative power – that is, 'the capacity to stop things happening, to delay them, to distort or disrupt them'.[30] A common example could be the secretary who screens and intercepts messages to the boss, delays arranging appointments and filters mail. Negative power is not necessarily related proportionately to position and may often be exercised easily by people at lower levels of the hierarchical structure. *Lerner* gives the following example:

> A retired gatekeeper who managed a large outpatient clinic gleefully confides that in her former position as head secretary she had felt like a madam of an exclusive house of ill repute. 'The part of my job I enjoyed the most was matching doctor with stenographer... I was in charge of the girls and the doctors frequently gave me gifts. If a doctor failed to reward me, he was assigned a girl less competent. If a girl defied me I assigned her to a doctor that she didn't like.'[31]

MOTIVATIONAL NEED FOR POWER

Power can be a positive source of motivation for some people (*see* the discussion on achievement motivation in Chapter 14). *McClelland* has examined the motivational need for power and believes that there are two major types of power: positive (social) power; and negative (personal) power. He suggests that the effective manager should possess a high need for **social power** directed towards the organisation, concern for group goals and helping members to achieve those goals, and exercised on behalf of people. Social power should be distinguished from the **negative personal power** which is characterised by satisfaction from exercising tight control over other people, and personal prestige and aggrandisement. [32]

There is often a fine line between the motivation to achieve personal dominance and the use of social power. It has to be acknowledged, however, that there are clearly some managers who positively strive for and enjoy the exercise of power over other people. They seek to maintain absolute control over subordinates and the activities of their department/section, and welcome the feeling of being indispensable. The possession of power is an ultimate ego satisfaction and such managers do not seem unduly concerned if as a result they are unpopular with, or lack the respect of, their colleagues or subordinate staff.

LIMITS TO THE FACILITATE-AND-EMPOWER PHILOSOPHY

Despite the general movement towards less mechanistic structures and the role of managers as facilitators there appears to be some reluctance especially among top managers to dilute or weaken hierarchical control. A recent study of major UK businesses suggests that there are mixed reactions to the new wave of management thinking. Whilst the prospect of empowerment can hold attractions for the individ-

ual employee, many managers are keen to maintain control over the destiny, roles and responsibilities of others. Beneath the trappings of the facilitate-and-empower philosophy the command-and-control system often lives on. [33]

BEHAVIOURAL FACTORS IN ORGANISATIONAL CONTROL SYSTEMS

Whatever the form or nature of the control system an essential feature underlying its success is the **need to consider the behavioural implications**.

> The broad objective of the control function is to effectively employ all the resources committed to an organization's operations. However, the fact that non-human resources depend on human effort for their utilization makes control, in the final analysis, the regulation of human performance.[34]

Control often provokes an emotional response from those affected by it. It should be recognised, therefore, that the activities of a management control system raise important considerations of the human factor and of the management of people.

The effectiveness of management control systems will depend upon both their design and operation, and the attitudes of staff and the way they respond to them. The manner in which control is exercised and the perception of staff will have a significant effect on the level of organisational performance.

Resistance to control systems

Whatever the extent of employee empowerment there is still a requirement for some form of management control, and this gives rise to a number of important behavioural considerations. We have seen that control systems can help fulfil people's needs at work and their presence may be welcomed by some members of staff. Often, however, control systems are perceived as a threat to the need satisfaction of the individual. Control over behaviour is resented and there is a dislike of those responsible for the operation of the control system. **Control systems provide an interface between human behaviour and the process of management.** Even when control systems are well designed and operated there is often strong resistance, and attempts at non-compliance, from those affected by them.

The amount of resistance is determined by both the nature of the control system and the characteristics of the individuals involved. For example, *Lawler* suggests that resistance to control systems is most likely to be present when:

- the control system measures performance in a new area;
- the control system replaces a system that people have a high investment in maintaining;
- the standards are set without participation;
- the results from the control system are not fed back to the people whose performance is measured;
- the results from the control system are fed to higher levels in the organisation and are used by the reward system;
- the people who are affected by the system are relatively satisfied with things as they are and see themselves as committed to the organisation;
- the people who are affected by the system are low in self-esteem and authoritarianism.[35]

OVERCOMING RESISTANCE TO MANAGEMENT CONTROL

Control systems are bound to be viewed with a certain amount of suspicion, and possible resentment, by members of staff. Therefore, if control systems are to be successful in leading to improved performance and organisational effectiveness, they require attention to factors which influence human behaviour.

There are a number of factors which can affect the successful implementation of management control systems, including:

- consultation and participation;
- motivation;
- groups and the informal organisation;
- organisation structure;
- leadership style and systems of management.

Consultation and participation

The manager should attempt to enlist the co-operation of staff and help them to feel that decisions which are taken are in their own interests. This calls for a high level of consultation and encouragement for staff to participate in the decision-making process. If staff are committed personally to particular objectives they are more likely to direct themselves and to exercise self-control over their level of performance. Staff should understand, and accept, the purpose and nature of control systems. This should help to make for better employee relations.

Motivation

Motivation is an important aspect in the operation of a control system. Lack of positive motivation can lead to frustrated behaviour resulting in lack of commitment to the aims of the organisation and poor job performance. This may lead to increased control.

People are influenced by the expected results of their actions. Motivation is a function of the relationship between effort expended and perceived level of performance, and the expectation that reward will be related to performance. People want to know how well they are performing. This places emphasis on the need for reporting of information and feedback, and the comparison of actual performance against planned targets.

Recognition given for a satisfactory level of attainment coupled with a suitable reward system, as integral parts of control, can do much to motivate staff and encourage improved performance. Emphasis should be placed on output controls of performance and achievement. No amount of management control will prove effective unless staff are positively motivated to achieve a high level of performance.

Groups and the informal organisation

The operations of groups and the informal organisation can influence the functioning of control systems. Informal group 'norms' and peer pressure can be one of the most powerful forms of control. It may be recalled that one of the findings of the bank wiring room experiment in the famous Hawthorne studies was that the group did not follow company policy on the reporting of production figures. Although actual production varied the workers officially reported a relatively standard amount of output each day, and in order to remain as a member of the informal group the supervisor acquiesced to this.

610

Membership of a harmonious and effective work group can be a source of motivation and job satisfaction. Socialisation can help create a feeling of commitment to the group and reduce the need for formal management control. Recall, also, the discussion on the value of group working as an approach to job design and improving job satisfaction (Chapter 15). With the development of autonomous work groups, members have greater freedom and wider discretion over the planning, execution and control of their own work.

In order to maintain co-operation and commitment of staff the manager must continually review at both the individual and group level the operation of the control system and the progress made in achieving objectives. This includes full participation of staff in discussions on the operation of control systems which affect them, on the difficulties and problems experienced, and on decisions concerning remedial action and future plans.

Organisation structure

The structure of an organisation and its pattern of management can affect the implementation of control systems. Organisation structure can be distinguished in terms of two divergent systems of management practice at extreme ends of a continuum – the **mechanistic** and **organic** systems.[36] These two systems imply differences in the total amount of control.

The **mechanistic** system is a more rigid structure and is appropriate to relatively stable conditions. It is characterised by specialisation, a clear hierarchical structure of authority, closely defined duties and responsibilities, and the downward flow of information. Organisations with a mechanistic structure are more readily suited, therefore, to the operation and implementation of traditional systems of control.

The **organic** system, however, is a more fluid structure and appears to be required for conditions of change and for uncertain environmental influences. This system is characterised by a network structure of control, authority and communication, the continual adjustment and redefinition of jobs and communication based on information and advice rather than instructions. New problems constantly arise and require actions which cannot be allocated among defined roles in the hierarchical structure. The effectiveness of control is more dependent upon individual involvement and commitment to the aims of the organisation. Traditional systems of control are therefore less suited to organisations with an organic structure.

The nature and form of management control systems are also influenced by specific features of organisational design: for example, the extent of divisionalisation and delegation, and the shape of the hierarchical pyramid structure, will affect the means of control over the behaviour of staff.

An example of this can be seen in Richard Branson's Virgin Group.

> The group's organizational structure reflects the decentralized arrangements at the top. Virgin's 2,500 employees worldwide work in small units of up to 80 people, each with its own director. In London alone there are 25 offices spread across the three divisions. 'People can dress as they feel comfortable, they work out of pleasant surroundings, and in small groups. There isn't a clock-in, clock-out mentality as there is in some companies, and because we have that attitude people are quite willing to work long hours.'[37]

Leadership style and systems of management

The exercise of control is an expression of leadership style and systems of management. The style of managerial leadership is a function of the manager's attitudes towards people, and assumptions about human nature and behaviour – for example *McGregor*'s Theory X and Theory Y.[38]

The central principle of Theory X is direction and control through a centralised system of organisation and the exercise of authority. By contrast, Theory Y is based on the principle of the integration of individual and organisational goals. People can learn to accept and to seek responsibility, and will exercise self-direction and self-control in the service of objectives to which they are committed.

The character of control processes is one of the organisational variables identified in *Likert*'s four-fold model of management systems: System 1 (exploitive–authoritative), System, 2 (benevolent–authoritative), System 3 (consultative) and System 4 (participative–group).[39]

In System 1 the major concern with regard to the performance of the control function is at the top hierarchical level in the organisation, the review and control functions are concentrated in top management, and there is an informal organisation opposing the goals of the formal organisation. In System 4 the concern for performance of control functions is spread throughout the organisation, review and control functions are carried out at all levels, and the formal and informal organisation share the same goals.

Likert found that in Systems 1 and 2 organisations, high performance goals by superiors, coupled with high-pressure supervision using tight budgets and controls, yield high productivity initially because of compliance based on fear. However, because of unfavourable attitudes, poor communications, lack of co-operative motivation and restriction of output, the long-term result is high absence and turnover, and low productivity and earnings. On the other hand, the nearer the behavioural characteristics of an organisation approach to System 4, the more efficiency improves. Organisational decisions are improved since they are based on more accurate information and there is greater motivation to implement the decisions.

Management by Objectives

A system of Management by Objectives may allow staff to accept greater responsibility and to make a higher level of personal contribution. Participation is inherent if Management by Objectives is to work well, and there is an assumption that most people will direct and control themselves willingly if they share in the setting of their objectives.[40]

The main features of Management by Objectives are: the setting of objectives; the specification of jobs and key tasks by discussion between the manager and staff; identification of key result areas; agreement on standards of performance; control, review and adjustment of objectives. The concept of Management by Objectives is therefore closely related to the general principles of a management control system.

Management by Objectives can be applied as a modern and effective method of control (*see* Table 17.2). It could, for example, be used in a positive and constructive way to provide a control system related to performance appraisal and career progression. However, there is a danger that if MBO is not implemented in a spirit of genuine trust, then the system will tend to be perceived simply as a control mechanism and may well result in reduced levels of performance.

Table 17.2 Management by Objectives as a control system

Activities in Management by Objectives	Management control system
Agree what you expect from me	Planning what is desired
	Specification of objectives and targets
Give me an opportunity to perform Let me know how I'm getting on	Establishing defined standards of performance
	Monitoring and reviewing actual performance
	Controlling information and feedback
Give me guidance where I need it	Comparing actual performance against planned targets
	What can be done to improve performance?
Reward me according to my contribution	Recognition of achievement
	Motivation for further improvement in performance
Control, review and adjustment	Taking corrective action

(Adapted and reproduced with permission from Humble, J. W., *Management by Objectives*, Management Publications Limited for the British Institute of Management (1972) p. 46.)

FINANCIAL AND ACCOUNTING SYSTEMS OF CONTROL

Management control systems are frequently thought of in terms of financial or accounting systems. The reasons for this are easy to understand.

- The stewardship of financial resources is of vital concern to the majority of organisations. In both private enterprise and public sector organisations there is an increasing need to demonstrate value for money expended. Control systems are often geared to highlight easily identifiable performance of sales, costs and profits.
- Organisational aims, objectives and targets are often expressed in financial terms and measured in terms of profitability. Results are measured and reported in financial terms.
- Money is quantifiable and is a precise unit of measurement. It is easily understood, and is often used as a common denominator and as a basis for comparison.
- Financial limits are easy to apply as a measure of control and easy to relate to. For example, the need for control is an integral part of the process of delegation. This control may easily be applied where, for example, a manager gives a subordinate the authority, without prior reference, to incur expenditure on certain items up to a given financial cost limit.

It is understandable, therefore, that so much attention is given to financial and accounting systems of control. Managers rely on accurate information systems as a basis of control and this information is frequently expressed in financial terms.

613

But accounting statements focus on only a limited area of activity. 'Thanks to the need for objectivity, everything in accounting statements is inward looking, concentrating on costs and based on the concept of capital maintenance.'[41] However, management control embraces far more than just financial or accounting considerations. It is concerned with the whole process of management: with the extent to which organisational aims are achieved and with improvement in performance. Control includes considerations of such factors as quality, judgement, consumer satisfaction, market share, social responsibilities, and the human factor and management of people.

Objective of profit maximisation

Although the objective of profit maximisation is undoubtedly of great importance, it is not by itself a sufficient criterion for the effective management of a business organisation. In practice, there are many other considerations and motivations which affect the desire for the greatest profit or maximum economic efficiency and the accompanying assumptions which underlie the economic theory of the firm.

The objective of profit maximisation must be considered over a period of time. It is also important to give full attention to the non-financial factors which affect organisational performance.

> A company can increase its short-term profit very easily. Cut down vital capital expenditures, reduce essential services, slash depreciation, and the return on investment will look splendid – for a time. The question is, for how long? . . . There is a point also to be made about non-financial factors, some of which indicate a great deal about the future performance of a company. Such factors as the industrial relations record, absenteeism, productivity performance, the ability or otherwise to meet deadlines, product quality and design and the extent to which customers are satisfied, are obviously eloquent pointers to the company's prospects, both for the present and the future.[42]

Consideration of behavioural factors

To what extent do financial and accounting systems of control take account of behavioural factors and motivate people to improve their performance?

Accounting control systems such as internal audit, management by exception and budgetary control tend to operate in a negative way and to report only on the unfavourable, or on favourable variances which may have adverse consequences, for example less spent than budgeted. 'Success' for the accounting staff may be equated with the 'failure' of other staff. As a result there is no specific recognition from management. There is only a limited sense of achievement or self-esteem for favourable performance or where no corrective action is required. There is little, if any, positive motivation.[43]

Budgets, for example, are accounting techniques designed to control costs through people. Budgets are used as a medium for personality expression and may also be used as a pressure device. Budgetary control can also be seen as imposing restriction on freedom of action by the individual.

> Budgetary control was originally intended to quantify liberty: The idea was that you said to a man, 'We are not going to tether you to this post any more. We are going to fix a financial fence, which you have agreed, and within this fence you can do whatever you like – trot, canter, gallop just as you please.' But the accountants got hold of budgetary control, and now it's universally regarded as just another form of head office restriction.[44]

Design and implementation

There is, of course, nothing wrong with the use of accounting systems of control such as internal auditing, management by exception and budgetary control, or with associated techniques such as time and motion studies. What needs to be considered is the manner in which these controls and techniques are applied, and the differences in use as a result of the attitudes adopted and the motives felt to be important in influencing behaviour.

Research by *Cammann* explored the moderating effects of subordinate participation in decision-making and subordinate job difficulty on their responses to different uses of control systems by superiors. The use of control systems for problem-solving was positively related to job satisfaction under conditions of low job difficulty and low participation. The use of control systems for goal-setting was positively related to satisfaction under conditions of high subordinate participation and high job difficulty. Results of the study indicate that responses to different uses of control systems will vary as a function of the contexts in which they are used.[45]

Hopwood distinguishes alternative approaches to information processing in terms of official or unofficial, and routine or non-routine. Unofficial strategies reflect attempts by non-senior members of the organisation to satisfy their own information needs. Official, routine approaches include most accounting systems. But 'even routine information systems can be designed to consciously encourage the exercise of self-control by organisational participants rather than merely facilitate the exercise of control by others'.[46]

Control systems can have positive as well as negative effects. Financial and accounting control systems, as with other forms of control, should be designed and implemented in a constructive and rewarding way. To do this, they must take account of individual, social and organisational factors which determine people's patterns of behaviour.

SYNOPSIS

■ There are varying connotations of the meaning of control. It is often interpreted in a negative manner to suggest direction or command, the restriction of behaviour or even exploitation of employees. However, control is not only a function of the formal organisation. It is also a function of interpersonal influence. Control is a general concept which is applied both to individual behaviour and organisational performance. Most people recognise the need for control and in certain circumstances may actually desire control.

■ Different approaches to organisation and management have illustrated different approaches to the nature of control. The essential elements in an organisational control system are: planning what is desired; establishment of standards of performance; monitoring actual performance; comparison with planned targets; and taking corrective action. Control is a general concept. It can serve a number of functions and take a variety of forms or classifications. There are also significant strategies of organisational control.

■ There are a number of important characteristics of an effective control system. The system should be understood, conform with the structure of the organisation,

report deviations quickly, draw attention to critical activities of the organisation, be flexible, consistent with the activity to which it relates and subject to continual review. If control systems are to be successful in leading to improved performance then attention must also be given to the factors which influence human behaviour. A classic dilemma that underlies the nature of control is finding the right balance between order and flexibility.

■ Work organisations are not only systems of hierarchical structure, they are also systems of social relationships, status and power. Power is an inherent feature of work organisations and an underlying reality behind the decision-making process. Organisations can be classified in terms of the relationship between power, involvement and the compliance of its members. The pluralistic approach, however, recognises power as a social process. Power is a major organisational variable which derives from a multiplicity of sources and situations.

■ Control systems can help fulfil people's needs at work and their presence may be welcomed. Often, however, control over behaviour is resented and perceived as a threat. The manager should, therefore, enlist the co-operation and commitment of staff, and provide for participation in the operation of control systems. The effective functioning of control systems is also influenced by: the motivation of staff; the operation of groups and the informal organisation; organisation structure; leadership style and systems of management.

■ Control systems are frequently thought of in terms of financial and accounting systems. Accounting control systems tend to operate in a negative way, and to give little specific recognition from management and only a limited sense of achievement. What needs to be considered is the manner in which financial and accounting control systems, as with other forms of control, motivate people to improve their performance. To do this, they must take account of individual, social and organisational factors which determine people's patterns of behaviour.

Review and discussion questions

1 Explain what you understand by the meaning of control. What do you see as the purposes of control in work organisations?

2 Outline how different approaches to organisation and management have viewed the nature of control. What are the essential elements of a management control system?

3 Detail, with your own supporting examples, the characteristic features of a good control system.

4 Discuss the importance of the concept of power to management and organisational behaviour. Provide examples of both unitary and pluralistic approaches to organisational power.

5 Explain the importance of behavioural implications of management control. What factors are likely to influence the amount of resistance to control systems?

6 Discuss what you see as the likely consequences of a manager exercising close personal supervision as a means of maintaining control over the work of subordinate staff.

7 Discuss the main factors which are likely to affect the successful implementation of organisational control systems. Suggest how MBO might be applied to help improve the process of control.

8 Why is it that many systems of control in work organisations tend to be financial or accounting in nature? To what extent do you think it is justified that they should be, and what other factors should be considered?

 Assignment 1

(i) For your own or some other organisation, identify:
 (a) the various areas of control of the activities of the organisation; and
 (b) the type and/or strategies of control systems adopted.

(ii) Examine a particular organisational control system of your choice and assess the extent to which it satisfies:
 (a) the essential elements of a control system; and
 (b) the characteristic features of a good control system.
 Give your views, with supporting reasons, on the apparent effectiveness of the control system, and the balance between order and flexibility.

(iii) Attempt to discover, and explain, a particular situation in which a management control system was welcomed by staff and/or where lack of a control system was the source of frustration to staff.

Assignment 2

THE ORGANISATIONAL POLITICS QUESTIONNAIRE

Answer each question 'mostly agree' or 'mostly disagree', even if it is difficult for you to decide which alternative best describes your opinion.

	Mostly agree	Mostly disagree
1. The boss is always right.	☐	☐
2. It is wise to flatter important people.	☐	☐
3. If you do somebody a favour, remember to cash in on it.	☐	☐
4. Given the opportunity, I would cultivate friendships with powerful people.	☐	☐
5. I would be willing to say nice things about a rival in order to get that person transferred from my department.	☐	☐
6. If it would help me get ahead, I would take credit for someone else's work.	☐	☐
7. Given the chance, I would offer to help my boss build some shelves for his or her den.	☐	☐
8. I laugh heartily at my boss's jokes, even if I do not think they are funny.	☐	☐
9. Dressing for success is silly. At work, wear clothing that you find to be the most comfortable.	☐	☐
10. Never waste lunch time by eating with somebody who can't help you solve a problem or gain advantage.	☐	☐
11. I think using memos to zap somebody for his or her mistakes is a good idea (especially if you want to show that person up).	☐	☐
12. If somebody higher up in the organisation offends you, let that person know about it.	☐	☐
13. Honesty is the best policy in practically all cases.	☐	☐
14. Power for its own sake is one of life's most precious commodities.	☐	☐
15. If I had a legitimate gripe against my employer, I would air my views publicly (for example, by writing a letter to the editor of a local newspaper).	☐	☐

	Mostly agree	Mostly disagree
16. I would invite my boss to a party at my home, even if I didn't like him or her.	☐	☐
17. An effective way to impress people is to tell them what they want to hear.	☐	☐
18. Having a high school or skyscraper named after me would be an incredible thrill.	☐	☐
19. Hard work and good performance are usually sufficient for career success.	☐	☐
20. Even if I made only a minor contribution to a project, I would get my name listed as being associated with it.	☐	☐
21. I would never publicly correct mistakes made by my boss.	☐	☐
22. I would never use my personal contacts in order to gain a promotion.	☐	☐
23. If you happen to dislike a person who receives a big promotion in your firm, don't bother sending that person a congratulatory note.	☐	☐
24. I would never openly criticise a powerful executive in my organisation.	☐	☐
25. I would stay late in the office just to impress my boss.	☐	☐

Details of scoring and interpretation of the Organisational Politics Questionnaire will be provided by your tutor.

╳ C A S E S T U D Y

The Omega organisation

You are the recently appointed Chief Executive of the Omega organisation. Your organisation is located in a large town and comprises five operating units and a head office with personnel, client service, management services and finance divisions. It employs a total of 5000 people.

The organisation has been successful in recent years. Clients report receiving good service and the financial performance of the organisation is good. The organisation has been run on centralised lines with tight financial controls applied by the Finance Division.

You have concluded that a more decentralised approach to management is needed, mainly to give unit managers greater discretion. The clients served by the five operating units have different and changing needs. You feel that greater discretion will allow a more flexible response to these various needs at unit level.

One of the ways you have decided to achieve decentralisation is to decentralise the management accounting function. Each operating unit will have a management accountant responsible to the unit General Manager for operational matters. The Finance Director will retain overall professional responsibility for the finance discipline, for financial accounting, planning and reporting. Unit management accountants will therefore report to the Finance Director for professional purposes but to the relevant General Manager for operational purposes.

In line with these changes, the Finance Director has proposed a number of changes to the role of the head office Finance Division. In particular, he wishes to encourage a more constructive and co-operative approach by finance staff to staff in other divisions. In the past, finance staff have identified inefficiencies in the utilisation of resources and generally called the various unit management teams to account. He wishes to move towards a more problem-solving style through which finance staff help others both to identify problems and develop solutions. As part of this, he wishes to see a change in the extent to which the Finance Division relies solely on traditional financial control techniques, often as a means of preventing change and limiting expenditure. Finally, he wishes to reduce the use of financial and accounting jargon.

These are significant organisational and professional changes. You accept the need for them and are fully committed to decentralisation. However, you are concerned about a number of issues.

Write a paper for circulation to your top management colleagues covering the following issues:

(a) What are likely to be the main problems and advantages of decentralised management accounting?
(b) What measures should be adopted to support the changed professional role for the Finance Division?
(c) What actions should be taken with the top management team (the General Managers of the five operating units, and the directors of the personnel, client service, management services and finance divisions) in preparation for the changes?

Notes and references

1. Mullins, L. J. 'Improving Management Control Systems', *Management Accounting*, vol. 61, no. 5, May 1983, pp. 30–2.
2. Tannenbaum, A. S. *Control in Organizations*, McGraw-Hill (1968) p. 3.
3. See, for example: Salaman, G. *Class and the Corporation*, Fontana (1981).
4. For a discussion on management control and an understanding of behaviour at work, see, for example: Johnson, P. and Gill, J. *Management Control and Organizational Behaviour*, Paul Chapman (1993).
5. For example, see: Mullins, L. J. and Banks, G. 'How Well am I Doing?', *Euhofa Journal*, Association Internationale des Directeurs d'Ecoles Hoteliers, Lausanne, Switzerland, no. 18, June 1986.
6. Lawler, E. E. 'Control Systems in Organizations', in Dunnette, M. D. (ed.) *Handbook of Industrial and Organizational Psychology*, Rand McNally (1976).
7. Robbins, S. P. *Essentials of Organizational Behavior*, Third edition, Prentice-Hall (1992) p. 6.
8. Fayol, H. *General and Industrial Management*, Pitman (1949) p. 107. See also: Gray, I. *Henri Fayol's General and Industrial Management*, Pitman (1988).
9. Gospel, H. F. and Littler, C. R. (eds) *Managerial Strategies and Industrial Relations*, Heinemann (1983).
10. See, for example, Blake, R. R. and Mouton, J. S. *The Managerial Grid III*, Gulf Publishing Company (1985).
11. Miner, J. B. *Management Theory*, Macmillian (1971).
12. Foster, M. and Whittle, S. 'The Quality Management Maze', *TQM Magazine*, vol. 1, no. 3, 1989, pp. 143–8.
13. Ouchi, W. G. and Maguire, M. A. 'Organizational Control: Two Functions', in Litterer, J. A. *Organizations: Structure and Behavior*, Third edition, Wiley (1980).
14. Robey, D. *Designing Organizations*, Third edition, Irwin (1991).
15. Reeves, T. K. and Woodward, J. 'The Study of Managerial Control', in Woodward, J. (ed.) *Industrial Organization: Behaviour and Control*, Oxford University Press (1970). See also: Introduction to Woodward, J. *Industrial Organization: Theory and Practice*, Second edition, Oxford University Press (1980).
16. Child, J. *Organization: A Guide to Problems and Practice*, Second edition, Harper and Row (1984).
17. Luthans, F. *Organizational Behavior*, Fifth edition, McGraw-Hill (1989) p. 547.
18. Hicks, H. G. and Gullett, C. R. *The Management of Organizations*, Third edition, McGraw-Hill (1976) p. 502.
19. Stewart, R. *Managing Today and Tomorrow*, Macmillan (1991).
20. See, for example: Gretton, I. 'Taking the Lead in Leadership', *Professional Manager*, January 1995, pp. 20–2.
21. Morgan, G. *Images of Organization*, Sage Publications (1986) p. 158.
22. Robbins, S. P. *Organizational Behaviour*, Sixth edition, Prentice-Hall (1993) p. 407.
23. *Managers Under Stress: A Survey of Management Morale in the '90s*, The Institute of Management, December 1993.
24. Etzioni, A. *A Comparative Analysis of Complex Organizations: On Power, Involvement and their Correlates*, Revised edition, Free Press (1975).
25. See, for example: Morgan, G. *Images of Organization*, Sage Publications (1986).
26. Fincham, R. 'Perspectives on Power: Processual, Institutional and Internal Forms of Organizational Power', *Journal of Management Studies*, vol. 29, no. 6, 1992.
27. French, J. P. and Raven, B. 'The Bases of Social Power', in Cartwright, D. and Zander, A. F. (eds) *Group Dynamics: Research and Theory*, Third edition, Harper and Row (1986).
28. See, for example: Ritti, R. R. *The Ropes to Skip and The Ropes to Know*, Fourth edition, Wiley (1994).

29. Bluen, S. D. and Barling, J. 'Psychological Stressors Associated with Industrial Relations', in Cooper, C. L. and Payne, R. (eds) *Causes, Coping and Consequences of Stress at Work*, Wiley (1988) pp. 175–205.

30. Handy, C. B. *Understanding Organizations*, Fourth edition, Penguin (1993) p. 131.

31. Lerner, P. M. 'Beware the Gatekeeper', *Amtrak Express*, July/August 1994, pp. 14–17.

32. McClelland, D. C. and Burnham, D. H. 'Power is the Great Motivator', *Harvard Business Review*, vol. 54, March–April 1976, pp. 100–10.

33. Ezzamel, M., Lilley, S. and Wilmott, H. 'Be Wary of the New Waves', *Management Today*, October 1993, pp. 99–102.

34. Reeser, C. and Loper, M. *Management: The Key to Organizational Effectiveness*, Scott, Foresman (1978) p. 437.

35. Lawler, E. E. 'Control Systems in Organizations', in Dunnette. M. D. (ed.) *Handbook of Industrial and Organizational Psychology*, Rand McNally (1976) p. 1274.

36. Burns, T. and Stalker, G. M. *The Management of Innovation*, Tavistock Publications (1966).

37. Foster, A. 'Virgin's New-Found Modesty', *Management Today*, March 1988, p. 57.

38. McGregor, D. *The Human Side of Enterprise*, Penguin (1987).

39. Likert, R. and Likert, J. G. *New Ways of Managing Conflict*, McGraw-Hill (1976).

40. Humble, J. W. *Management by Objectives*, Management Publications Limited for the British Institute of Management (1972).

41. Allen, D. 'There's More to Accountancy Than Accounting', *Administrator*, March 1992, p. 6.

42. Bhallacharya, K. 'Accountancy's Faulty Sums', *Management Today*, February 1985, p. 37.

43. Mullins, L. J. 'Behavioural Implications of Management Accounting', *Management Accounting*, vol. 59, no. 1, January 1981, pp. 36–9.

44. Prior, P. (in conversation with Strong, F.) 'Communicating: An Enthusiast's View', *Accountancy*, vol. 95, no. 1089, May 1984, p. 69.

45. Cammann, C. 'Effects of the Use of Control Systems', *Accounting, Organizations and Society*, vol. 1, no. 4, 1976, pp. 301–13.

46. Hopwood, A. G. 'Accounting and Organisational Behaviour', in Carsberg, B. and Hope, T. (eds) *Current Issues in Accounting*, Second edition, Philip Allan (1984) p. 269.

Part 7

THE PERSONNEL FUNCTION

18 PERSONNEL AND EMPLOYEE RELATIONS

The efficiency of staff and their commitment to the objectives of the organisation are fostered by good human relationships at work. This demands that proper attention be given to the personnel function and employee relations. The manager needs to understand how to make the best use of the human resources of the organisation. The promotion of good human relations is an integral part of the process of management and improved organisational performance.

 Learning objectives

To:

- Explain the nature of the personnel function, and contrast personnel management and human resource management;

- Analyse personnel policies and activities, and the organisation of the personnel function;

- Justify the personnel function as a shared responsibility;

- Examine the importance of training and development and the effective management of training;

- Explore the system of performance appraisal, methods of appraisal and potential problem areas;

- Explain the nature of employee relations, and reasons for attention to legal and behavioural dimensions;

- Recognise the importance of the personnel function and employee relations for organisational performance and effectiveness.

Worth thinking about

'Why is my job as human resource manager not given the full recognition it deserves?' . . . 'Because there is no clearly defined role or focus, for example you seem to be forever changing job titles. Until you can produce hard performance measures for your contribution is it any wonder line managers are sceptical and suspicious of your true value to the organisation?'

THE PERSONNEL FUNCTION

However the activities of management are identified, and whatever the nature of organisational processes, an essential part of the process of management is that proper attention be given to the personnel function. The effectiveness of any work organisation is dependent upon the efficient use of resources, in particular human resources. The human element plays a major part in the overall success of the organisation. There must be effective management of human resources – there must be an effective personnel function.

Personnel as a task or element function?

You will recall that in Chapter 10 we discussed the distinction between task functions – those basic activities related to the actual completion of the productive process or directed towards specific and definable end results; and element functions – those activities that are supportive of the task functions and an intrinsic part of the management process. In the majority of organisations the personnel function does not normally have any direct accountability for the performance of a specific end-task. Personnel is generally identified therefore as an element or support function.

In certain organisations, however, such as employment agencies, personnel is very much part of the 'productive' process and will be a task function. In other organisations, noticeably in service industries, the personnel function can also be closely associated with a task function. For example, in the hotel and catering industry many members of the workforce are in direct contact with the customer and are seen as being involved in achieving the objectives of the organisation. People are part of the finished product for which the customer is paying. Customer satisfaction is likely to be affected as much by the courtesy, helpfulness and personal qualities of the staff as by the standard of food and beverage, accommodation or other facilities. This places particular importance on the personnel function.[1]

PERSONNEL MANAGEMENT OR HUMAN RESOURCE MANAGEMENT

You will probably be aware that in recent years there has been an increasing tendency for use of the term 'human resource management' (HRM) to replace the term 'personnel management'. However, this change is subject to much debate and controversy.

For example, *Guest* suggests three ways in which human resource management has been used to distinguish it from traditional personnel management:

(i) simply to retitle personnel management to capture the new fashion;
(ii) to re-conceptualise and re-organise personnel roles, and the work of personnel departments; and
(iii) as distinctively different and offering a new approach for management.[2]

Guest goes on to describe some broad stereotypes which could be used to highlight the differences. Compared with personnel management, human resource management is concerned more with: a long-term rather than a short-term perspective; the psychological contract based on commitment rather than compliance; self-control rather than external controls; a unitarian rather than a pluralist perspective; an organic rather than a bureaucratic structure; integration with line management rather than specialist or professional roles; and maximum utilisation rather than cost-minimisation.

The nature of HRM

Torrington and Hall see the nature and degree of difference between personnel management and human resource management (HRM) as remaining 'largely matters of opinion rather than fact, and the similarities are much greater than the differences'.[3] They do, however, see a more substantive difference that needs to be explored.

Personnel management is 'workforce-centred', directed mainly at the organisation's employees. The people who work in the organisation are the starting point. Although indisputably a management function, personnel is never totally identified with management interests. Underpinning personnel management are the idea that people have a right to proper treatment as dignified human beings and the role of personnel management interventions in everyday manager–subordinate relationships.

Human resource management is 'resource-centred', directed mainly at management needs for human resources to be provided and deployed. There is greater emphasis on planning, monitoring and control, rather than mediation. Underpinning human resource management is the idea that this is much the same as any other aspect of management and an integral part of it which cannot be separated out for specialists to handle.

Horwitz discusses the ideological motivation of HRM as a managerial initiative which seeks to facilitate the achievement of organisational goals. The preferred focus is on individual rather than collective relations and the HRM theme positively seeks direct employee communication and involvement. The effectiveness of HRM in attempting to optimise co-operation and organisational loyalty, and a determination to impose new forms of management control, can arguably be viewed as a reformation of a strong unitarist managerial ideology.[4] (The unitary and pluralistic perspectives of work organisations are discussed later in this chapter.)

A critical analysis of HRM

From a critical analysis of human resources management, *Legge* detects three general differences between personnel management models and HRM models:[5]

- Personnel management is often seen as a management activity aimed at non-managers. HRM not only emphasises the importance of employee development but focuses particularly on development of the management team.
- In personnel management the role of line management is an expression of 'all managers manage people' with most specialist personnel work still implemented within line management's departments. HRM is vested in line managers as business managers responsible for the direction of all resources with personnel policies as an integral part of the pursuit of business strategy.
- Personnel management was not fully integrated with organisation development (OD) models and they were generally separate in the formal organisational sense. OD was often presented as a fringe benefit and not integrated with the personnel department. HRM emphasises management of the organisation's culture as the central activity for senior management and is more closely associated with organisational values and strategy.

Legge, however, believes that these differences are largely of meaning and emphasis rather than substance.

Goss believes that despite a decade of familiarisation it is difficult to clarify exactly what HRM is, where it differs from traditional personnel management or how important it will be for the future. The development of HRM can, however, be linked to a conjunction of socio-economic factors, particularly changes in international competition, the restructuring of industrial sectors and organisations, and a renewed confidence in the power of managers to manage. Goss suggests a framework for the nature and substance of HRM which encompasses three key themes: human relations psychology; strategic management theory; and doctrines of flexibility and quality management.[6]

No clear distinction

It can be argued that HRM is the elevation of personnel management to a more strategic level. It is not easy, however, to distinguish HRM from personnel management. And according to *Cuming*, for example, some argue that human resource management is just a new term for what most good personnel managers have already been practising. The extent to which personnel management has moved into another historical phase of human resource management is debatable.[7]

It seems reasonable to conclude that there is no clear distinction between personnel management and human resource management. The increasing emphasis on effective employee relations, and the importance of securing the involvement and commitment of staff to the aims of the organisation may, at least in part, be argued as justification for the change in title. It is difficult, however, to escape the thought that HRM is really little more than 'old wine in new bottles' and associated with personnel managers seeking to enhance their status and influence. Neither does it follow that human resource management, however it is described, will necessarily lead to a higher level of organisational performance than would be achieved with a traditional personnel management approach.

For ease of reference, therefore, we shall refer to personnel management and the personnel function.

PERSONNEL POLICIES, ACTIVITIES AND FUNCTIONS

Whatever the nature of the work organisation, a manager achieves results through the performance of other people. Recognition of the needs and wants of staff and of the nature of their grievances is a positive step in motivating them to perform well. The efficiency of staff, their commitment to the aims of the organisation, and the skills and attitudes they bring to bear on the quality of service offered are fostered by good human relationships. Success in the field of human relationships stems from good personnel policy and practice, and an effective personnel function.

Personnel policy and the effective management of people are influenced by the philosophy of top management and the attitudes which they bring to bear on relationships with staff, and the problems which affect them. Personnel policies should emanate from the top of the organisation. They should be defined clearly and communicated through managers and supervisors to staff at all levels.

Underlying philosophies

The formulation of personnel policies, and the implementation of personnel practices and procedures, should be based on underlying philosophies of managerial behaviour and employee relationships. Such philosophies should embrace:

- the recognition of people's needs and expectations at work;
- respect for the individual;
- justice in treatment and equitable reward systems;
- stability of employment;
- good working environment and conditions of service;
- opportunities for personal development and career progression;
- democratic functioning of the organisation; and
- full observance of all laws and codes of conduct relating to employment.

In overall terms, personnel policies can be seen to embrace:

- designing an effective organisation structure;
- staffing the structure with suitable people;
- defining work roles and relationships; and
- securing optimum working arrangements.

The objective is to develop and maintain a level of morale and human relationships which evoke willing and full co-operation of all persons in the organisation in order to attain optimum operational performance. This is the total concept of the personnel function.

Range of personnel activities

The range and scope of personnel activities are wide. This is illustrated by the definition of personnel management given by the (then) Institute of Personnel Management (now the Institute of Personnel and Development).

> Personnel management is that part of management concerned with people at work and with their relationships within an enterprise. Its aim is to bring together and develop into an active organisation the men and women who make up an enterprise and, having regard for the well-being of the individual and of working groups, to enable them to make their best contribution to its success. Personnel

629

management is also concerned with the human and social implications of change in internal organisation and methods of working, and of economic and social changes in the community.[8]

Personnel activities may be considered within the framework of the following broad headings:

- human resource planning and employment;
- salary and wage administration including related reward systems;
- organisational design and patterns of work;
- education, training and development;
- employee relations; and
- employee services, welfare, health and safety.

Inherent in these activities is the need to give proper regard and attention to employment legislation and other legal requirements. A system of human resource planning will provide the link between objectives and organisation structure, and clarification of personnel policies. It provides a framework within which personnel activities are planned and implemented. (Human resource planning is discussed in Chapter 19.)

ORGANISATION OF THE PERSONNEL FUNCTION

Smaller organisations may not justify a specialist personnel manager or a separate personnel department. But **it is still necessary to have an effective personnel function**, whether it is the responsibility of the owner or of a manager. Even in the smallest organisations, or in organisations where a specialist personnel department has not been established, there will be a need to recruit staff, to train them, to motivate and reward them, and to comply with the law relating to employment. Personnel work must still be carried out even if an organisation is too small to justify a separate department or chooses not to establish one.

Areas of specialisation

In the larger concerns, where more time is taken up with problems of organisation and the management of people, there is greater need for a specialist member of staff to whom are delegated full-time responsibilities for advising top management on human resource matters and for the development and implementation of clearly defined policies which permit consistent personnel practices. For example, high staffing costs together with increasing employment legislation suggest that greater attention must be given to the process of recruitment and selection. (Recruitment and selection is discussed in Chapter 19.) Other examples include:

- pressures for the exercise of a greater social responsibility towards staff;
- the general movement towards flexible working and employee involvement and empowerment;
- proposals from the European Union;
- government involvement in employment legislation and formal or informal incomes policies;
- developments in the applications of behavioural science;
- the role of the industrial tribunals, and the Advisory, Conciliation and Arbitra-

tion Service (ACAS) and other statutory bodies; and
- the role of trade unions and their officials.

These factors all combine to suggest that personnel management and employee relations are areas of increasing specialisation. *Tyson*, for example, suggests that the specialist personnel function emerged within the potential conflicts between capital and labour and is based on the need to mitigate the worst aspects of domination within the employment relationship.[9]

The personnel manager

Even where personnel work is established as a separate, specialist function, it is not easy to define closely the activities of the personnel department. The range of responsibilities varies from one organisation to another, as do the title and status of the head of the personnel department (for ease of reference we shall use the term personnel manager) and position in the management structure. In the larger organisations personnel activities might be divided between two or more specialists, so that it would be possible to have, for example, a personnel officer, training officer and employee relations adviser. Whatever the range of responsibilities, the personnel manager operates by consent, by delegated authority. How much consent is dependent upon the attitudes of top management, the role which they see the personnel specialist(s) performing and formal organisational relationships with 'line' managers.

Line managers

Line managers are departmental or unit managers with responsibility for the 'production' process – for the operational functions directly related to the purpose and aims of the organisation. They form a hierarchical level in the chain of command throughout the organisation structure. Line managers report directly to higher management for the activities within their own department and for its operational efficiency. There is unity of command, a clear line of authority and a direct boss–subordinate relationship between line managers and their staff. Line managers are responsible for the management of their own staff.

However, although line managers are specialists in their own area of work, they are not necessarily specialists on personnel matters. Just as line managers turn to specialists on legal and accounting matters and the use of the computer, so they will need help, guidance and specialist advice on personnel matters. For example, *Thomason* suggests that the personnel manager is probably the only specialist in the organisation whose role can be distinguished by the virtually exclusive concern with the management of human assets. All other managers will also have some direct concern with the management of physical assets.[10]

THE PERSONNEL FUNCTION: A SHARED RESPONSIBILITY

The Institute of Personnel Management definition draws attention to personnel management as part of the responsibility of all managers and supervisors. The personnel function is part of the generality of management.[11] The personnel manager, as a separate entity, operates in terms of a 'functional' relationship, that is as a specialist adviser on personnel matters and on the implementation of personnel policies through all departments of the organisation. It is the job of the

personnel manager to provide specialist knowledge and services for line managers, and to support them in the performance of their jobs.

In all other respects the personnel manager's relationship with other managers, supervisors and staff is indirect: it is an advisory relationship. It is the line managers who have authority and control over staff in their departments, and who have the immediate responsibility for personnel management, although there will be times when they need the specialist help and advice of the personnel manager. **If the personnel function is to be effective there has to be good teamwork, and co-operation and consultation between line managers and the personnel manager.**

This is made easier when top management, who retain ultimate responsibility for the personnel function, take an active part in fostering goodwill and harmonious working relationships among departments. It is important to have clear role relationships and to attempt to avoid difficulties with role incongruence or role conflict (recall the discussion in Chapter 6). Top management should agree clear terms of reference for the personnel manager within a framework of sound personnel policies. The effective management of people involves a partnership between managers and personnel specialists. Within this framework the personnel function can be seen as operating at two levels: the organisational level and the departmental level. (*See* Fig. 18.1.)

The organisational level

At the organisational level the detailed involvement of the work activities of several departments, available time, and the need for specialisation suggest that the personnel manager has a prominent role to play. The personnel manager is the main executor of personnel policies but acting in consultation with, and taking advice from, line managers.

On this basis the personnel manager would be concerned mainly with broader aspects of personnel policy and procedures which affect the organisation as a

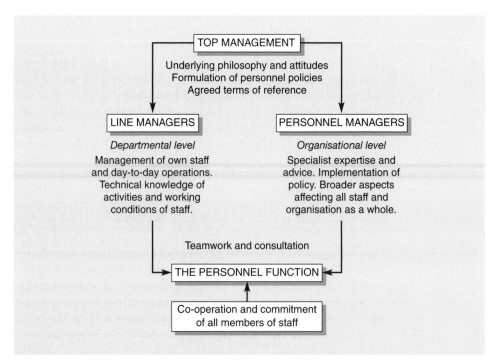

Fig. 18.1 The personnel function – a shared responsibility

632

whole or staff generally. This could include such activities as: human resource planning; job analysis and procedures for recruitment and selection; induction and training; problems of high labour turnover; consultations with trade unions or staff representatives; compliance with the law relating to employment; maintaining records and statistics; and liaison with outside bodies such as ACAS, employers' organisations, government agencies, training organisations and professional associations.

The department level

At the departmental or unit level the line managers might assume a prominent role for day-to-day personnel matters, with the personnel manager as adviser, and if necessary as arbitrator. Line managers would be more concerned, at least in the first instance, with the operational aspects of personnel activities within their own departments. For example: the organisation of work and allocation of duties; minor disciplinary matters; standards of work performance; safety; on-the-job training; communication of information; and grievances from staff. Line managers have the right and the duty to be concerned with the effective operation of their own department, including the well-being of their staff.

In this respect it could be said that **all line managers are their own personnel managers**. Line managers are on hand to observe directly the performance of their staff. They will actually see, and be directly affected by, for example, lateness of staff, unsatisfactory work, insufficient training, low morale, staff unrest, or poor planning of work duties and responsibilities. As an element function, personnel is an integral part of any managerial activity. It is the line managers who have the immediate responsibility for personnel management.

Decision by top management

The extent to which authority and responsibility for the personnel function is devolved to line managers is a decision for top management, and is likely to be influenced by the nature, culture, structure and characteristic features of the particular industry or organisation. For example, *Rocco Forte* has emphasised the importance of a caring and efficient personnel function to assist line managers in what is one of their primary responsibilities. The nature of Trusthouse Forte's business, with many separate units of differing size, location and mix of skills, means of necessity the personnel function is decentralised and prime responsibility has to be with line management.

> However, even if we have had a choice, I believe we would elect to put the prime responsibility for personnel on line management rather than on specialists. The nature of our work calls for active participation by management in day-to-day operations and they need to know that line management has the authority and responsibility for taking actions which vitally affect them in their work and in their working environment. The link therefore must be a direct one.[12]

Commitment of all members of staff

However, the responsibilities for personnel activities are shared, and whatever the respective roles of the personnel manager and line managers, the personnel function can only be effective if it is based and implemented on sound policies and procedures. If the personnel function is to be implemented successfully it also requires the co-operation and commitment of all members of staff, whatever their duties or positions within the organisation. The personnel function cannot be housed within one discrete department or as the sole responsibility of selected members of staff. It permeates all levels of the organisation and all phases of its operations.

It should be noted that in many countries managers are *required* to consult with representatives of the workforce on many personnel and employee relations matters. There are, in fact, some issues which have to be *determined jointly* by the personnel manager and worker representatives. This aspect of industrial democracy is discussed more fully later in this chapter.

Marks & Spencer's approach to personnel management

It is clear, then, that the personnel function is a shared responsibility among top management, line managers and supervisors, and the personnel manager. This can be illustrated by the enlightened approach of Marks & Spencer to personnel management.

The most distinctive elements of the Marks & Spencer approach to personnel management are precisely the following:

(1) 'Every manager a personnel manager'– that is, every member of staff with managerial or supervisory responsibilities is trained in, and expected to perform, a certain important personnel function.

(2) 'Every director a personnel director' – this implies that the personnel function – or more broadly, good human relations – is not seen by the board as something 'important but peripheral' but as central to the basic philosophy and approach of the entire business. Board members responsible for no matter what area share the common responsibility for ensuring that the personnel function is properly executed.

(3) A strong, well-trained team of personnel staff to provide support, training, guidance and advice to management of various levels and to ensure that personnel skills constitute an important element of all categories of managerial staff.[13]

TRAINING AND DEVELOPMENT

One major area of the personnel function of particular relevance to the effective use of human resources is training and development. Few people would argue against the importance of training as a major influence on the success of an organisation. Staff are a crucial, but expensive, resource. In order to sustain economic and effective performance it is important to optimise the contribution of employees to the aims and goals of the organisation.

The importance of training as a central role of management has long been recognised by leading writers. According to *Drucker*, for example, the one contribution a manager is uniquely expected to make is to give others vision and ability to perform. A basic operation in the work of the manager is to develop people and to direct, encourage and train subordinates.[14]

The general movement towards the downsizing of organisations and the nature of management moving towards the devolution of power to the workforce give increasing emphasis to an environment of coaching and support. Training is necessary to ensure an adequate supply of staff who are technically and socially competent, and capable of career advancement into specialist departments or management positions. There is, therefore, a continual need for the process of staff development, and training fulfils an important part of this process. Training should be viewed, therefore, as an integral part of the process of total quality management. (Management development is discussed in Chapter 21.)

The benefits of training

The purpose of training is to improve knowledge and skills, and to change attitudes. This can lead to many potential benefits for both individuals and the organisation. Training can:

- increase the confidence, motivation and commitment of staff;
- provide recognition, enhanced responsibility, and the possibility of increased pay and promotion;
- give a feeling of personal satisfaction and achievement, and broaden opportunities for career progression; and
- help to improve the availability and quality of staff.

Training is therefore a key element of improved organisational performance. Training increases the level of individual and organisational competence. It helps to reconcile the gap between what should happen and what is happening – between desired targets or standards and actual levels of work performance.[15]

MAIN STAGES OF TRAINING

From a study by the *East Hampshire Business Support Group* of almost a hundred organisations, *Fill and Mullins* report that training can be seen to pass through four main stages: output training; task training; performance training; and strategic training.[16]

- **Output training** is generally the province of small organisations which, on employing an individual or investing in a new machine, will endeavour to generate output as quickly as possible. The costs must be seen to be absorbed and the transaction completed in the shortest possible time, if only to justify the initial investment risk. This type of training is centred around the individual, is performed in-house and is only initiated when new equipment, products or persons are introduced into the organisation.
- **Task training** involves selected individuals being sent on short training or college-based courses. Health and safety regulations, manufacturers' familiarisation courses and the financing of vocational evening classes typify this type of training. From the introverted phase of output training, task training sees the first orientation as being to the joint needs of the individual and the organisation – the beginnings of an external view.
- **Performance training** arises when the organisation has grown substantially and becomes well-established. Training is now viewed positively with a single person for the first time formally designated as responsible for training. Plans and budgets are now some of the tools used to manage the training process. Training programmes become means by which the performance of individuals and the organisation can be controlled. Organisations choosing to adjust their quality can only do so effectively by embracing the training function. During this phase appraisal systems also become more established. These systems are used not only to evaluate the effectiveness of training received but also to anticipate future training requirements.
- **Strategic training** can be said to be reached when the organisation recognises and practises training as an integral part of the management of human resources, prepares organisational strategies, and plans training in the light of both individual and organisational needs. Strategic training is integral to the philosophy and culture of the organisation.

Training for the management of change

These four main stages of training need, however, to be related to the context of the external environment in which the organisation is operating. Different stages of training will be most appropriate at different times. There are a wide range of forces acting upon organisations and which make the need for change inevitable. Training for change is vital for the long-term survival of an organisation. Increasing emphasis is being placed both on the need for continuous training to support change and on training as a vital investment for the future.[17]

The Industrial Society points out that many unions are recognising the importance of training in relevant skills to sustaining the job security of their members. As a result they are seeking to bring training more centrally into the collective bargaining arena, with the setting up of joint training agreements. For some employers this may be an important route to developing a joint approach to managing change. Among the recommendations of the Society is that organisations should develop line managers' contribution to training. Organisations should ensure that individual managers at every level understand that leadership includes the responsibility for training and developing their staff and this will be a factor in their annual appraisal.[18] (The management of change is discussed in Chapter 20.)

Training and the small organisation

A significant and disturbing feature of the East Hampshire Support Group study was the negative attitude towards the benefits of training shown by many of the smaller organisations. Too often training is seen as a necessary expense to achieve output targets. It is not seen as providing long-term benefits or improving organisational performance. A common view of training was an activity undertaken by large corporate bodies who can afford it.

But training can benefit small organisations, for example, in helping to reduce skills shortages. *Jones and Goss* undertook a study of 26 small firms (between 15 and 125 workers) operating across a range of manufacturing and service industries in South Hampshire. There was evidence of a relationship between training provision and the extent of skills shortages. In the modern era of rapidly changing technology with increased emphasis on flexible working attitudes, job seekers are searching for employers who will offer them continued opportunities to develop and update their skills and experiences.[19]

THE MANAGEMENT OF TRAINING

Training should be viewed as an investment in people. This is important at any time, but particularly so with the increasing pace of technological, structural and social change. But training for its own sake achieves little. It must be real, operational and rewarding.

Training requires the co-operation of line managers, adequate finance and resources, time, skilled staff and a supporting appraisal system. There has to be a genuine commitment – from top management and throughout all levels of the organisation.

A planned and systematic approach

In order to secure the full benefits of successful training there must, therefore, be a planned and systematic approach to the effective **management of training**.[20]

- There must be **a clear commitment to training throughout all levels of the organisation**. This should include seeking the co-operation of line managers and, where appropriate, trade unions or staff representatives. Top management should set the scene by giving active support and encouragement to the training process, and through the provision of adequate finance, resources, time and skilled staff.

- There should be **an objective assessment of training needs** related to: (i) a vision of where the organisation is going; (ii) the need to be responsive to changes in external environmental influences; (iii) a comprehensive system of human resource planning; and (iv) a process of job analysis leading to the preparation of job descriptions and person specifications.

- It is important that **staff themselves should also feel a sense of involvement** and know how they can play their part in achieving the goals and objectives of the organisation. They should be given 'ownership and partnership' in the training process.[21]

- There should be **a clear set of objectives and a defined policy for training**. This will enable the design of a carefully planned programme of training. The programme should address such questions as: Who is to be trained and why? What should they be taught? How and where should the training be undertaken, and by whom? How will the training be assessed and evaluated? The expected results of training should be understood clearly and realistically and be seen as reasonably attainable. Wherever possible, desired objectives should be stated in behavioural terms such as: Exactly what, after training, should the trainee now be able to do?

- People cannot absorb properly a large amount of information at one time. **The training programme should therefore be planned carefully** and staggered over a reasonable period of time. Consideration should be given to the priority, loading and pacing of information; timing and sequence, common or related items; variety of subject matter and methods of presentation; review and consolidation.

- Consideration must be given to **the choice of the most appropriate methods of training**. These can include: business games, case studies, the incident method, assignments or projects; role-playing, in-tray exercises or simulation; lectures, seminars, programmed instruction; group discussions or exercises; coaching, job instruction and job rotation; delegation and allocation of special duties; training packages and audio-visual aids; internal courses, external courses and distance learning. The methods must be selected carefully according to the particular needs of the organisation and the employees. Guidance should be given on how to prepare for training and how to deal with the various material or situations presented.

- Consideration should also be given to **external courses and training opportunities linked to the educational system**.[22] These include General National Vocational Qualifications (GNVQs) which provide broad-based vocational education and training as a basis for employment or further study; and National Vocational Qualifications (NVQs) designed to provide improved employment opportunities and centred on standards of occupational competence. In addition there are qualifications from the Business and Technology Education Council (BTEC) which are essentially vocational in nature; and relevant professional, diploma and degree courses.

- Full regard should be given to **the training needs of those groups who are not currently active in the workforce**, including married women, ethnic minorities, older members of staff, and people with disabilities. Special consideration should

be given to the most appropriate methods of training for these groups of people. For example, recent research reveals that Britain's employers have a wide range of attitudes and policies towards older workers. While some maintain negative, stereotypical views about their capabilities and training, others are implementing positive, innovative policies towards this sector of the workforce.[23]

- There should be **an effective system of review and evaluation** including the on-going monitoring of progress, a supporting appraisal system and the maintenance of suitable training records. Evaluation should involve assessment by the trainers, line managers and supervisors, and the trainees. The review process should include identification of those areas to which greater attention should be given in future training programmes.

- Wherever possible **evaluation should be related to objective, measurable factors**, for example: increased output or sales; reduced scrap or wastage; fewer accidents at work; fewer errors or customer complaints. Other measurable factors may include reduced staff turnover, absenteeism or sickness. However, such measures are difficult to isolate in terms of a single cause and effect. The ultimate evaluation of training is, of course, the extent to which it contributes to improved organisational performance and effectiveness; and to the quality, job satisfaction and prospects of employees.

COMMITMENT TO TRAINING STANDARDS

If organisations are to pursue a positive policy of investing in people this demands that they demonstrate a continuous commitment to training standards. Training should be an integral part of business strategy. Employees, for their part, should receive positive recognition for good training achievements, through, for example, increased job satisfaction, higher wage rates and related systems of career progression.

Managers should be fully aware of the help and assistance available from government organisations and other bodies, for example Training and Enterprise Councils (TECs), which are intended to develop a close partnership between local employers and educational establishments in providing vocational education and training to meet local economic needs.

Successful training clearly offers potential benefits to the organisation and to employees. It can also be one of the most satisfying activities for the manager. But the extent to which the full rewards of training are realised depends on a planned and systematic approach.

Investors in People

One major obligation of the TECs was the launch of the initiative 'Investors in People' (IiP). This initiative seeks to reward organisations that achieve the prescribed training standard which allows them to display the IiP kitemark. IiP as a standard for training has been assimilated into BS 5750 and ISO 9000 as a standard of quality which is recognised nationally. The standard was based on UK organisations that had achieved a successful payback from investing in people.

IiP is underpinned by four principles. These are that the organisation

- makes a public commitment from the top to develop people in order to achieve business objectives;
- regularly reviews the training and development needs of people;

- takes action to train and develop people on recruitment and throughout their employment; and
- evaluates the investment in training and development to improve future effectiveness.

The focus is not on training and development *per se* but is purposefully aligned to business strategy so that training is directed more to the needs of the business. IiP is an approach which is approved by the TECs to a British Standard; the rationale behind it is that organisational success is dependent upon the effective development of human resources.

PERFORMANCE APPRAISAL

One way in which to review the performance and potential of staff is through a system of performance appraisal. It is important that members of the organisation know exactly what is expected of them, and the yardsticks by which their performance and results will be measured. A formalised and systematic appraisal scheme will enable a regular assessment of the individual's performance, highlight potential, and identify training and development needs. Most importantly, an effective appraisal scheme can improve the future performance of staff. The appraisal scheme can also form the basis of a review of financial rewards and planned career progression.

Performance appraisal is therefore a crucial activity of the personnel function and the management of human resources. A comprehensive appraisal system can provide the basis for key managerial decisions such as those relating to allocation of duties and responsibilities, pay, delegation, levels of supervision, promotions, training and development needs, and terminations. An overview of performance appraisal is given in Fig. 18.2.

(Appraisal as an element of a management development process is discussed in Chapter 21.)

Benefits of appraisal

An effective appraisal scheme offers a number of potential benefits to both the individual and the organisation.

- It can identify an individual's strengths and weaknesses and indicate how such strengths may best be utilised and weaknesses overcome.
- It can help to reveal problems which may be restricting progress and causing inefficient work practices.

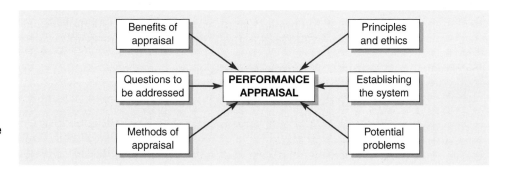

**Fig. 18.2
An overview of the performance appraisal system**

- It can develop a greater degree of consistency through regular feedback on performance and discussion about potential. This encourages better performance from staff.
- It can provide information for human resource planning, to assist succession planning, to determine suitability for promotion and for particular types of employment and training.
- It can improve communications by giving staff the opportunity to talk about their ideas and expectations, and how well they are progressing.

The process of appraisal can also improve the quality of working life by increasing mutual understanding between managers and their staff.[24]

Principles and ethics of performance appraisal

James suggests that performance appraisal has its roots in three well-substantiated psychological principles. People work/learn/achieve more when they are given:

(a) adequate feedback as to how they are performing, in other words knowledge of results;

(b) clear, attainable goals; and

(c) involvement in the setting of tasks and goals.[25]

These principles underpinning effective performance appraisal have wider relevance than simply improvements in individual performance. They are also concerned with the development of a participative organisational culture by contributing to the broader goals of creating satisfying, effective jobs, encouraging the involvement of people in the organisation, and the development of people.

James goes on to suggest that a performance system operated in an organisational context must, if it is to have any credibility, be based on clear ethical principles. These are particularly important to an involved culture where individual development, trust and openness are fundamental values. These principles would apply to both appraiser and appraisee:

- appraise on the basis of representative information;
- appraise on the basis of sufficient information;
- appraise on the basis of relevant information;
- make an honest appraisal;
- keep written and oral appraisals consistent; and
- present appraisal as opinion.

QUESTIONS TO BE ADDRESSED

The design and implementation of a successful appraisal system requires attention to a number of basic questions, including the following.

Who should be appraised?

Traditionally most appraisal schemes have been applied to staff in managerial, supervisory or administrative positions. There is, however, no reason why appraisal should not be applied to manual workers – especially skilled workers and those involved in technical duties. The increasing adoption of flexible working practices and harmonisation of conditions of employment, together with attempts to overcome the attitude of 'them and us', has prompted the extension of appraisal to cover all members of staff.

Who should undertake appraisal?

The usual practice is for appraisal to be carried out by the immediate manager or supervisor – as the person who allocates work and has the closest knowledge of the individual's duties and performance. There is, however, an argument in favour of appraisal at a higher level. This would extend the lines of communication and feedback. This may also help to demonstrate 'fair play' and to overcome problems of different managers/supervisors applying different standards of appraisal.

A third approach is for the immediate manager/supervisor to conduct the appraisal and write the report. Senior management are then asked to comment, to monitor the system, to review the consistency of reporting and to countersign as confirmation of approval. Appraisal can also be undertaken by a member of the personnel department, by peers, by subordinates, by assessment centres or by self-appraisal.[26] Another approach is the '360-degree feedback' which involves an appraisal and feedback system by those above, below and to the side of the member of staff; and internal or external customers. This approach is intended to provide feedback from all stakeholders in a person's performance.[27]

The removal of middle levels of management, flatter structures and greater empowerment of self-managed teams also have possible implications for who should undertake the appraisal process.

What should be the frequency of appraisals?

With the majority of schemes, staff receive an annual appraisal; and for many organisations this may be sufficient. However, the frequency of appraisal should be related to the nature of the organisation, the purpose and objectives of the scheme, and the characteristics of the staff employed. For some organisations, for example those operating in a dynamic, changing environment, more frequent appraisals may be called for. Also, more frequent appraisals may be appropriate for new members of staff, those recently promoted or appointed to a new position or for those whose past performance has not been up to the required standard.

Should there be an 'open' system of appraisals?

There is an argument which suggests that open reporting restricts managers from giving a completely honest and frank appraisal. However, the more staff see of their appraisal report – that is the more 'open' the system – the more they are likely to accept the process of appraisal. Staff are better able to check the consistency of the appraisal report with verbal feedback from the manager. With an open system of reporting, staff should be given the opportunity to sign the completed form and to add any comments on their perception of the accuracy of the assessment.

ESTABLISHING THE APPRAISAL SYSTEM

In order to establish a successful appraisal system, careful attention needs to be given to a number of important matters concerning its introduction and implementation.

The purpose and nature of the system

The purpose and nature of the appraisal system should be made clear. A successful system should establish a regular dialogue and lead to an improvement in manager–staff relationships. *Weitzel* sees performance appraisal as a power-sharing exercise. To succeed, it must be a co-operative, constructive endeavour with input

by both staff and the manager. The system should focus on the strengths and accomplishments of staff, rather than their faults and failures, and it should lead to a plan for the future development and progress of the individual.[28]

Commitment and support from top management

The system should not be perceived as something which is the prerogative of the personnel department or introduced for its benefit. Top management should be seen to own the system and be fully committed to the concept of appraisal. They should ensure full consultation with trade unions and staff representatives, and all managers and members of staff. Adequate provision will need to be made for the proper training of appraisers and there should be a reasonable time allowance for the activity. An effective administration system should aim to keep form-filling and paperwork to a minimum.

Related to corporate objectives

The appraisal system should not be viewed in isolation but in relation to the corporate objectives of the organisation, and designed to suit its culture and particular requirements. The system should be integrated with related personnel policies and practices such as human resource planning, and training and development programmes. A starting point is the process of job analysis. This identifies the purpose, and main duties and responsibilities of each job. From the job description can be determined the expected outcomes of the job, standards of performance and the criteria against which the appraisal will be based. (The process of job analysis is discussed in Chapter 19.)

Monitoring and follow-up action

The system needs to be monitored regularly to ensure that appraisals are being carried out properly and to obtain feedback from managers. The system should be kept under continual review and, where necessary, modified to meet changing environmental influences or the needs of the organisation. It is important to ensure that operation of the system and the criteria used for assessment satisfy all legal requirements, for example under the Sex Discrimination Act and the Race Relations Act. The system must be supported by appropriate follow-up action: for example, seeing that work plans or changes in duties and responsibilities actually take place, and that suitable arrangements are made to meet identified training or development needs.

Appeals procedure

As the main purpose of appraisals is to help staff improve their performance, an appeals procedure should only be used in exceptional circumstances. However, in order to help establish the credibility of the system and to maintain goodwill, it is necessary to establish a formal procedure which is clearly understood by all members of staff. Appeals should be made to a manager in a more senior position than the appraiser or sometimes to a representative committee. The appeals procedure should include provision for staff to be assisted, if requested, by a union or staff representative.

A checklist of points to be considered in establishing an appraisal system is given in Fig. 18.3.

Appraisal which consists simply of the employer's opinion of an employee is likely to be subjective, and biased by whether the boss likes or dislikes the person. But, since decisions regarding pay, prospects and promotion often rest on it, it is important that any assessment should be fair, and seen to be fair.

This checklist includes points to be borne in mind when designing or taking part in an an appraisal scheme.

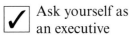 **Ask yourself as an executive**

1. Why do you need to have an appraisal scheme?
2. What methods are managers in your company already using to assess their staff?
3. Are the purposes of the scheme:
- to improve performance in the present job?
- to reward performance in the present job?
- to spot or develop those with potential for promotion?
- to reward those with potential for promotion?
4. What methods are managers in your company already using to assess their staff?
5. What say have people covered by the scheme had in its design and procedures?
6. How often should appraisal take place? Will this frequency vary with different levels and types of staff?

 Assessing past performance

7. Can performance on the job be fairly assessed in your company?
Should it be measured against:
- targets pre-set by the employee?
- targets pre-set by the boss?
- targets pre-set by both together?
- obvious personal qualities such as drive?
- obvious successes or failures?
8. Does the performance assessment point to training needs? What action is taken to meet these needs?
9. What are the most reliable indicators of likely success:
- personality?
- past performance?
- any others?
10. Who is best to assess an employee's potential:
- current boss alone?
- employee and employer together?
- and/or some other person, e.g. personnel officer?
11. Does the potential assessment highlight development needs?

 Appraisal and salary

12. What criteria are used for salary changes in your company? Are salary increases awarded for:
- average past performance?
- exceptional past performance?
- high future potential?

Ask yourself as an appraiser

13. Do I fully understand the appraisal scheme?
14. Am I giving undue weight to recent or memorable events?
15. Am I being influenced by personal likes or dislikes?
16. Am I expected to interview my staff? If so am I fully prepared for the interview and the possible outcomes, e.g. their responses to my comments?

Ask yourself as an appraisee

17. Do I feel that I am being asked questions about myself or my work and past performance on the job?
18. Have I had an opportunity of helping to set the work targets that I have been asked to meet?
19. Do I believe that I would work more effectively if I did have such an opportunity? Why?
20. Is there any connection between:
- my past performance and any increases in my salary?
- my past performance and any training courses that I am asked to attend?
- the work that I perform and my personal aims and ambitions?

Fig. 18.3 Checklist for appraisal scheme
(Reprinted with permission from *Professional Manager*, May 1994, p. 29.)

METHODS OF APPRAISAL

Appraisal systems can be used to measure attitudes, behaviour and performance. Measurement may be a combination of:

- 'quantitative' measures using some form of rating scale, such as, for example, (1) excellent, (2) good, (3) average, (4) below average, (5) unsatisfactory; and
- 'qualitative' measures involving an unstructured, narrative report on specific factors and/or overall level of behaviour and work performance.

An example of typical headings of an appraisal scheme are given in the appendix to this chapter. Details of the Abbey National Performance Review System are given at the end of Chapter 21.

Behaviourally anchored rating sales (BARS)

The use of behaviourally anchored rating scales (BARS) is an attempt to provide measurement scales that are directly related to the job being appraised. A sample group of managers/supervisors are asked to identify, independently, several key behavioural aspects of the job in question. The responses are then collated and returned to the same or a different group to agree examples of good, average or poor performance and to allocate a scale point for each example. Those examples which are consistently rated at the same point on the scale can then act as 'anchors' and provide behavioural examples for each point on the scale.[29]

Appraisers can then use the BARS as guidance against which to assess the expected behaviour of each person being rated. The number of categories in the rating scale will vary according to the particular nature of the job, but usually number between 5 and 9. There may also be a varying number of behavioural examples for each point on the scale.

The disadvantages with BARS are that they can be time-consuming and costly to construct, and require careful and detailed training in their correct use. They are also more likely to be appropriate only in larger organisations.

Achieving objectives

Another appraisal system is that of 'achieving objectives'. With this system, the manager agrees with members of staff set objectives at the beginning of the appraisal period. The appraisal is then based on the extent to which these stated objectives have been achieved. This method provides for participation by staff and also allows for at least some degree of self-appraisal. This method can be related therefore to a system of Management by Objectives (discussed in Chapter 13). It also suffers from the same potential problems.[30]

A major consideration with this method is the extent to which circumstances beyond the control of the individual, such as changes in environmental influences, make the achievement of objectives unrealistic. Objectives need to be continually reviewed and revised in accordance with changing circumstances. Comparison with achieving objectives may not, by itself, provide a detailed assessment of performance. Therefore, some appraisal schemes combine this method with the use of rating scales.

Performance 'agreement' or 'contract'

A variant of the 'meeting objectives' method is proposed by *Stein*. A good appraisal system could be the key by which companies get the most out of all their staff without making them feel exploited.[31] Stein puts forward an approach based on

the use of a performance 'agreement' or 'contract'. Members of staff create a succinct document, agreed with their superior, which sets out the individual's proposed contribution to the business plan of the organisation.

This document provides an agenda which can be referred to during the appraisal period and modified as necessary. This agenda serves as the basis of the appraisal judgement. Instead of rating performance in terms of a traditional five-box scale, as A, B, C, D or E, the question is simply: 'Has the plan been met?' This approach turns the appraisal system into a dialogue. The extent to which staff meet their contract also gives an indication of whether the business plan is realistic.

POTENTIAL PROBLEM AREAS

The effectiveness of any appraisal system relies heavily on the quality and reliability of assessment. Variations in the consistency of reporting standards can quickly lead to a feeling of dissatisfaction and injustice. There are many potential sources of rating errors including, for example, perceptual distortions such as stereotyping and the halo effect, discussed in Chapter 5. Where a senior manager has the opportunity to confirm the ratings and countersign the appraisal this may help to identify inconsistencies and those appraisers who appear to be too generous or too critical in their assessments.

Allowance for discretion

However well-designed the appraisal system it is not possible to apply a completely objective approach to every unique situation. The system should therefore always allow for at least a degree of discretion and personal judgement. The reporting system should give the appraiser an opportunity to record formally any necessary qualifications to the given ratings.

Managers' loss of expertise

As managers advance up an organisation they may become less expert in the day-to-day operations of their department/section and become more dependent on the team. 'Successful managers know how to get results out of others – they are not necessarily experts in their fields.'[32] In such cases subordinates may be their own harshest judges and this places emphasis on the importance of self-appraisal.

Emphasis on past performance

The appraisal may tend to concentrate too much on feedback on past performance and especially the recent past. The lapse of time between events which occurred early in the reporting period and completing the appraisal may lead to a distortion in the overall flavour of the report. Although reviewing past performance is an integral part of the appraisal system, it is even more important to concentrate attention on the changes required to bring about an improvement in future performance.

Regular review of performance

Finally, it is particularly important that a formal appraisal system does not result in managers failing in their responsibilities for reviewing performance on a day-to-day basis. Appraisal should not be limited to a formal event occurring once or twice a year but should be a continuous process of monitoring, feedback and review. There should be regular communications and contacts between managers and staff, and discussions of problem areas and plans for the future.

Fletcher suggests that approaches to performance appraisal need to change in line with organisational changes such as de-layering and the introduction of competency and total quality management. Instead of a standard, monolithic system, performance appraisal is evolving into a number of separate but linked processes applied in accordance with specific circumstances.[33]

EMPLOYEE RELATIONS

Sound personnel policies help to foster good employee relations. **Broadly defined, employee relations is concerned with the relationships between the policies and practices of the organisation and its staff, and the behaviour of work groups.**

The traditional view of 'industrial relations' has often been associated with institutions and rules relating to employment, and in particular with the activities of trade unions and their officials. Trade unions may be seen as existing, primarily, to promote the best interests of their members, and to improve their quality of working life and general standard of living. Through the process of collective bargaining, trade unions endeavour to improve their members' terms of employment and conditions of work.

Institutions and the process of interactions among them are clearly important but good management–staff relationships are not limited to trade unions and employment legislation. They also entail broader informal and social relationships, and the importance of the role of management.[34] For this reason the term 'employee relations' is now usually more favoured.

Employee relations policy

The nature and content of an employee relations policy will be influenced by such factors as:

- the type, nature and size of organisation;
- its structure and methods of operation;
- the nature of staff employed;
- arrangements for collective bargaining;
- the structure and strength of trade unions;
- preference of the parties for freedom of action from outside influences; and
- the philosophy of top management and their attitudes toward the management of employee relations.

To understand any employee relations situation it is necessary to take account of the institutions and parties involved, and their ideologies and motives.[35] It is necessary to consider not only the legal dimensions but also the behavioural dimensions.

UNITARY AND PLURALISTIC PERSPECTIVES

In the search for effective employee relations and a common commitment to the goals of the organisation, consideration should be given to contrasting approaches which present two major ways of perceiving work organisations; the unitary perspective and the pluralistic perspective. Whilst neither of the approaches can be

seen as 'right' or 'wrong', these contrasting views will influence the nature of employee relations and the management of human resources.

The unitary perspective

With the unitary perspective the organisation is viewed as an integrated and harmonious whole with managers and other staff sharing common interests and objectives. There is an image of the organisation as a team with a common source of loyalty, one focus of effort and one accepted leader. Conflict is perceived as disruptive and unnatural and can be explained by, for example, poor communications, personality clashes or the work of agitators. Trade unions are seen as an unnecessary evil and restrictive practices as outmoded or caused by trouble-makers.

Personnel policies and managerial development can be seen as reflecting a unitary ideology. *Horwitz*, for example, suggests that the unitary perspective views company and trade union loyalty as mutually exclusive. He raises the question of human resource management (HRM) as a reformation of a unitarist managerial ideology. Developments in HRM, in seeking to optimise co-operation and organisational loyalty, can be seen as imposing new forms of control. A managerial approach to facilitating organisational goals and the direct involvement of employees furthers a unitary perspective and can mask an underlying distaste for unionism.[36]

The pluralistic perspective

An alternative view suggested by *Fox* is the pluralistic perspective which views the organisation as made up of powerful and competing sub-groups with their own legitimate loyalties, objectives and leaders.[37] These competing sub-groups are almost certain to come into conflict. From the pluralist perspective, conflict in organisations is seen as inevitable and induced, in part, by the very structure of the organisation. Conflict is not necessarily a bad thing but can be an agent for evolution, and internal and external change.

Restrictive practices may be seen as a rational response from a group which regards itself as being threatened. The role of the manager would be less commanding and enforcing, and more persuading and co-ordinating. Fox suggests that the pluralistic perspective is a more realistic frame of reference. He argues the importance of viewing work situations through the different groups involved rather than attempting a wished-for unitary approach. According to *Horn*, 'these views were widely acceptable, particularly to trade unions, who saw this as legitimising their intervention into an increasing range of managerial prerogative areas'.[38] There are, however, relative shades of unitary and pluralistic perspectives, and both can co-exist within the same organisation.[39]

REGULATING THE EMPLOYMENT CONTRACT

A central feature of employee relations is managing through people and regulating the employment relationship.[40] Whether as individuals or members of a group, the actions and decisions of people are governed by a set of underlying rules. In the work organisation these rules are implemented within a structured hierarchy of authority and responsibility. But regulating behaviour between people at work is a complex process.

Legal and behavioural dimensions

Effective employee relations are founded on a combination of legal and behavioural dimensions. The legal dimension embodies observance of employment legislation, the formal contract of employment and codes of practice. The behavioural dimension embodies recognition of the individual, the social responsibilities of management and the psychological contract (discussed in Chapter 1). (*See* Fig. 18.4.)

Social responsibilities extend beyond terms and conditions of the formal contract of employment, and give recognition to the social and human needs of people at work. The recognition of social responsibilities should form an integral part of corporate strategy and regulating the employment relationship.

Legal dimensions

The work organisation has to operate within a system of legal rules and regulations. Legal dimensions regulate the relationship between employers and employees, provide individual rights for employees and strengthen the position of trade unions. Legislation and codes of practice lay down rules which govern patterns of behaviour to ensure that 'managers act reasonably in the circumstances'. Some managers view these rules with trepidation and avoid taking necessary action to discipline employees. Others are unaware of the rules or choose to disregard them, terminating contracts without due cause.

Either strategy is likely to result in behavioural problems among employees who will perceive avoidance or over-reaction as dysfunctional. A proper knowledge and understanding of the law, coupled with appropriate managerial action, can turn a potentially difficult situation into an opportunity to motivate staff and improve organisational effectiveness.

Although it is not the purpose of this book to consider detailed aspects of employment law, it is important to recognise the legal framework within which organisations function and which affects employee relations.

Traditionally, employee relations in Britain has been characterised by the concept of free collective bargaining between employees and employers. However, in recent years this philosophy has been underpinned by increasing amounts of

Fig. 18.4
Effective employee relations: the combination of legal and behavioural dimensions

employment law.[41] The substance of British laws is also increasingly being influenced by the impact of EU legislation. Until the 1960s the law governing terms and conditions was based almost entirely on the concept of the contract of employment and attracted little statutory intervention.

During the last two decades, however, this area of law has been significantly extended, introducing new statutory rights for both those in employment and those seeking employment. Employees can seek redress through a tribunal system, and have rights concerning a range of issues from relatively minor matters such as time off for public duties, to the more important employment protection rights such as the right not to be unfairly dismissed. The main statutory employment rights are now to be found in the Employment Protection Consolidation Act 1978, as amended by the Employment Act 1980, the Employment Act 1982 and the Trade Union Reform and Employment Rights Act 1993. In addition there is a considerable amount of anti-discrimination legislation affecting employment. The three main acts are the Equal Pay Act 1970 as amended, the Sex Discrimination Act 1975 as amended, and the Race Relations Act 1976.

Behavioural dimensions

Whilst the observance of legal rules and regulations is clearly a necessary part of effective employee relations this does not, by itself, make for a harmonious environment at work. Legal dimensions help to regulate the working relationships of people within the organisation. But rules and regulations do not by themselves ensure that disputes will be settled amicably. Human behaviour cannot be made to conform to prescribed rules and regulations just because such rules and regulations exist.

Employee relations can only be effective if sustained within a generally good relationship between management and staff, with a willing commitment from both sides.[42] Effective managers need to take note of both legal and behavioural perspectives, and to adopt a balanced view when making decisions that affect the employment relationship. Notwithstanding any legal obligations, the employer–employee relationship demands that attention be given to those factors which influence the behaviour of people at work, the psychological contract and the style of managerial behaviour.

For example, under the Employment Protection Act a general duty is placed on an employer to disclose, on request, to authorised representatives of independent trade unions information for the purposes of collective bargaining and which it would be good industrial relations practice to disclose. However, many organisations now consider the broader behavioural considerations and choose as a matter of policy to report fully, and in non-technical terms, wider details of their financial results and performance direct to all employees.

Another important example is the issue of discipline at work and in particular the process relating to termination of employment contracts. Managers need to be fully aware of the legal dimensions, including the criteria necessary before an employee can claim that they have been unfairly treated, the claims and procedures, the reasons that can constitute grounds for unfair dismissal proceedings and the remedies for unfair dismissal. But, in addition and equally important, managers also need to be aware of the possible behavioural consequences, including adverse effects on the motivation and morale of staff, and their future commitment and level of performance.[43]

POLICY ON HIV/AIDS

One particular aspect of employee relations policy of increasing significance is the attitude and response of organisations to people with AIDS. There are a number of factors that make the issue of HIV/AIDS relevant to the operation of organisational processes. These may be briefly classified under five headings: the epidemic and those affected; actual and perceived risk of transmission; the workplace as an arena of discrimination and prejudice; the workplace as an arena for support and assistance; work as a means of economic survival.[44]

The epidemic and those affected

The demographic profile of the epidemic has focused attention upon the micro- and macro-level consequences of infection for employment. Because most of those infected with HIV are in the age groups that have the highest level of economic activity – around half of all known infections are in those between the ages of 15 and 24 – the potential impact on various aspects of employment has always been an issue of concern to governments and employers.

Actual and perceived risk of transmission

Virtually all guidance and opinion makes clear that there is virtually no risk of transmitting HIV through normal workplace activity. Even in the field of medicine where there is a very small chance of transmission (usually from patient to medical worker rather than vice versa) this can be drastically reduced if standard procedures and precautions are followed. However, a low level of objective risk is not necessarily *perceived* or accepted as such, and the fear of contracting the virus from some forms of work-related activity can continue to exert an influence on employee behaviour.

The workplace as an arena of discrimination and prejudice

The most widely discussed HIV/AIDS issue within the workplace has been that of prejudice and discrimination against people with, or suspected of having, HIV/AIDS, be they employees or customers/clients of an organisation. This is an issue that has attracted comment around issues of legality, social justice, education and business ethics both in the USA and in Europe. However, in addition to action directed against people with HIV/AIDS as such, the arrival of the epidemic has also exposed pre-existing tensions and conflicts around issues of sexuality, race, and disability. The emergence of the epidemic has in many organisations fuelled homophobia and racism such that discrimination against homosexuals and those with presumed 'African connections' has been heightened by their being cast in the role of 'viral vector'.

The workplace as an arena for support and assistance

However, against the evidence of discrimination there is also the need to recognise that some employing organisations have been in the forefront of countering prejudice and providing practical assistance to people affected by the virus (through constructive policies and procedures) and support for health education aimed at preventing further infection. In the USA, for instance, considerable attention has been given to the activities of Levi Strauss in its open support for employees with HIV/AIDS, its contribution to AIDS support organisations, and its opposition to repressive legislation targeted at homosexuals.[45]

Work as a means of economic survival

However, for people with HIV infection employment is also likely to become increasingly significant as funding and support for health care become increasingly stretched, either as the result of a growing number of people ill with AIDS, as in many developing nations, or as the result of cuts in funding in some industrialised countries as the epidemic loses its political impetus and urgency. Already this is an issue in the USA, where contributions to health insurance through employment can have a crucial impact upon the nature and extent of care provided in the event of incapacity and, as European governments appear to be placing a greater emphasis on individual contributions to health care funding, such concerns are likely to spread, often meaning that people may need to remain in work for longer (perhaps at the expense of their long-term well-being) to ensure their health needs are met.

Development and operation of AIDS policy

From a survey of 118 organisations in both the private and public sectors, the Health and Safety Information Bulletin report that seven in ten respondents have a policy on AIDS. In particular, many large organisations, especially those in the caring professions and local authorities, have developed AIDS policies. In almost two-thirds of private companies, responsibility for operating the policy rests with the personnel department. There is widespread opposition to the introduction of HIV antibody tests for job applicants and employees. Most organisations claim not to discriminate against employees or job applicants who are HIV-positive and asymptomatic.[46]

However, as *Goss* and *Adam-Smith* have pointed out, the existence of a formal policy does not, of itself, guarantee that fair treatment will result. Their research into UK policy responses shows that while some may be 'constructive' (that is, providing for the interests of the person with HIV/AIDS as primary concern) others may be more 'defensive' in operation (having as their first objective the protection of organisational interests *from* the person with HIV/AIDS who is defined as a 'threat' to organisational effectiveness).[47]

THE RESPONSIBILITY FOR EMPLOYEE RELATIONS

It is sometimes suggested that in many organisations the responsibility for employee relations still lies with the line managers who are often sceptical or even hostile towards personnel ideas and techniques, and who frequently reject the concept of an employee relations policy because it hampers their work and limits their flexibility. For example, *Clegg* argues that:

> If line managers are left to handle industrial relations issues for themselves, the pressures of production are likely to lead to *ad hoc* and contradictory decisions . . .
> If a personnel policy is introduced to promote consistent decisions on industrial relations issues, its effectiveness may depend on granting authority to the personnel department to override the natural priorities of line managers.[48]

According to *Cuming*, however, the increase in employee relations legislation has resulted in a trend for personnel matters, particularly wage negotiations, to be transferred from line management to personnel departments. At the same time there has been a deterioration in management–worker relations in many places, and a failure to introduce changes in work methods necessary for effective competition and organisational effectiveness.

Personnel departments as such are clearly not to blame for these developments; much more guilty are those line managers at the highest level who have opted out of their most important function, that of managing people. They are especially blameworthy for allowing communication channels to become the province of personnel departments and trade union organisations, so that complaints are now frequently heard from first-line managers that they hear news of changes likely to affect them from their departmental shop stewards.[49]

Involvement of line managers

As with other aspects of the personnel function it is important that line managers are involved, at least to some extent, with employee relations. But there must be good communications and close consultation with the personnel department. There must be teamwork and a concerted organisational approach to the management of employee relations. This is made easier when top management, who retain ultimate responsibility for the personnel function, take an active part in fostering goodwill and co-operation between departments and with official union representatives. Top management should agree clear terms of reference for both the personnel manager and line managers within the framework of sound personnel policies.[50]

The shop steward

The shop steward, as an elective union representative of the employees, acts as spokesperson on behalf of the work group, initiates negotiations with management and may also be involved in grievance and disciplinary procedures. The shop steward will be responsible for communications with both full-time union officials and members about union matters and developments in working practices.

Shop stewards require knowledge of the trade union movement and its services, an awareness of the law relating to employment, and the role of ACAS and its tribunals. They also need an understanding of the policies and practices of the organisation, its structure, the role of managers, supervisors and personnel specialists, group situations; and how best to handle the problems affecting individual union members. Shop stewards are therefore an important part of the effective operation of the organisation. They undertake a range of activities broadly similar to those of managers and they require similar skills.

THE EFFECTIVENESS OF PERSONNEL MANAGEMENT

Proper attention to the establishment of sound personnel policies and to the operation of the personnel function, including employee relations, will help the development of good human relations. And good human relations will be a major influence on the efficiency of the workforce and the level of organisational performance and effectiveness. Full use should be made of personnel specialists, the involvement of line managers and modern methods of personnel management.

This of course will cost money. Cost is obviously a major consideration but should not be viewed in isolation. Not every activity of the organisation can be identified clearly as making a direct contribution to profitability. A balance must be kept between the more easily identified financial costs of the personnel function and the less readily apparent, but very important, long-term benefits which also make a positive contribution to organisational effectiveness and the achievement of objectives.

For example, *Tyson and Fell* consider the effectiveness of personnel management in terms of: (i) the effective individual practitioner; (ii) effective personnel roles and relationships; and (iii) the strategic development of the organisation.[51] *Cuming* suggests that every aspect of personnel management has an impact in two ways: one on organisational efficiency and the other on the individual employees concerned; and both should be considered in assessing the success of the personnel management function. Personnel managers can undertake a process of audit by a checklist to review methodically their whole range of activities by reference to acknowledged good practices.[52]

Marks & Spencer: human relations at work

According to *Lord Sieff*, good management is intimately connected with good human relations: the promotion of good human relations at work and efficient management are two aspects of the same thing. The attention paid to implementing a policy of good human relations at work has been an important factor in the profitable development of Marks & Spencer over the last 60 years.[53]

Lord Sieff also makes clear that the principle of implementing a policy of good human relations at work cannot be the responsibility of the personnel department (or the human resources department) alone. Such a policy will only be implemented if those at the top believe in it and set an example themselves. Good human relations involve a moral attitude, treating everyone whatever their position with respect, and caring about employees. All those down the line should do the same for those they manage. A policy of good human relations should apply to all concerned in and with the business.

INDUSTRIAL DEMOCRACY IN EUROPEAN COUNTRIES

It is appropriate at this point to examine the concept of statutory industrial democracy which is prevalent in many European countries. This will be of benefit to organisations contemplating expansion into the overseas market. It may also be noted that increasingly the European Union is seeking to harmonise employment practices among member states, and the whole notion of joint decision-making is already established in the majority of countries in western Europe.[54]

THE GERMAN SYSTEM

The German system of industrial democracy is the most comprehensive and has tended to be used by commentators as a model of its kind. The system comprises both the works council (*Betriebsrat*), and representation on boards of directors, the supervisory board (*Aufsichtsrat*) and the executive board (*Vorstand*).

The works council

Works councils exist in organisations covering all sectors of the economy including both the private and public sector. Works council representatives are elected by fellow workers. They do not, however, stand on behalf of trade unions, and in elections stress their individual qualities and experiences. The works council has three rights:

- **the right of information** – the works council has the right to be given information concerning the performance and future prospects of the organisation;
- **the right of consultation** – owners and managers must consult the works council over a range of strategic matters including investment, and the acquisition of new premises and the closure of existing units; and
- **the right of co-determination** – the works council has the power to formulate certain policies jointly with managers.

The third and most extensive power relates essentially to issues concerning the management of personnel including the working day, holiday arrangements, shift working, promotion, dismissal, and welfare and social facilities. As an example, the works council has the right to participate in the selection of new members of staff and can veto appointments. This power of veto is constrained, however, since it can only operate in the light of criteria agreed in advance. Nevertheless, the works council does take an active part in personnel management in German organisations.

Representation on boards of directors

The supervisory board may include employee representatives. In certain industries such as coal, iron and steel, workers make up 50 per cent of the membership of the board. In other sectors, one-third membership is common. The supervisory board has the power to appoint members of the executive board and can veto its decisions.

The composition of the executive board is most interesting in German organisations since it includes a labour director (*Arbeitsdirektor*). The labour director can only be appointed by a two-thirds majority of the worker representatives on the supervisory board. *French* shows how this director may be a worker representative, but equally may be a career personnel manager.[56] *Lawrence* suggests that increasingly personnel managers are labour directors and are thus represented on both boards of directors.[57]

Negotiation and discussion

It can be seen that in Germany, personnel managers are constrained by law from acting unilaterally, and are required to work jointly with the workforce representatives. Lawrence concludes that the personnel function in Germany is marked by a high degree of both legalism and formalism with laws, documents and written agreements being more salient than in Britain. The same author gives us a sense of the flavour of personnel management in that country as follows: 'the works council is an important reference point for the German personnel manager and much of his time is spent in negotiation or discussion with the council'.[58]

SYNOPSIS

■ An essential part of the process of management is that proper attention be given to the personnel function. Whatever the nature of the work organisation, success in the field of human relationships stems from good personnel policy and practice, and an effective personnel function. In recent years there has been an increasing tendency to use the term 'human resource management' to replace 'personnel management'. However, there is no clear distinction between the two and this change is subject to much debate and controversy.

■ Personnel policies and practices should be based on underlying philosophies of managerial behaviour and employee relations. The range and scope of personnel activities are wide and it is not easy to define closely the status or role of the personnel department. The personnel function is a shared responsibility among top management, line managers and supervisors, and the personnel manager. As an element function, personnel is part of the generality of management. The personnel function can be seen as operating at two levels, the organisational level and the departmental or unit level.

■ One major area of personnel work of particular relevance to the effective use of human resources is training and development. Training is a key element of improved performance and offers a number of potential benefits for both the individual and the organisation. Too often, however, training is seen as a low-priority activity, especially in many small organisations. In order to secure the full benefits of training there must be a planned and systematic approach to the effective management of training, and a continuous commitment to training standards.

■ One way to review the performance and potential of staff is through a formal appraisal system. An effective performance appraisal system offers a number of potential benefits but there are a number of important questions to be addressed. Consideration must be given to the design and implementation of the system, establishing the system, methods of appraisals and potential problem areas. It is particularly important that a formal appraisal system does not detract from the manager's responsibility for reviewing performance on a day-to-day basis.

■ Sound personnel policies help to foster good employee relations. The nature and contents of an employee relations policy will be influenced by a variety of factors and it is necessary to take account of the institutions and parties involved, and their ideologies and motives. There are two major and contrasting perspectives of work organisations, and the explanation and outcomes of conflict – the unitary and the pluralistic perspectives. These contrasting views influence the nature of employee relations and the management of human resources.

■ Effective employee relations and regulation of the employment contract are founded on a combination of legal and behavioural dimensions. It is important that line managers are involved, at least to some extent, with the responsibility for employee relations. The shop steward may also have an important role to play. Proper attention to the personnel function and employee relations will help the development of good human relations at work. Increasingly the European Union is seeking to harmonise employment practices among member states.

APPENDIX

Employee appraisal: example of a rating scales scheme

NAME	JOB TITLE	DATE OF APPRAISAL

LENGTH OF TIME IN POST	DEPARTMENT

OVERALL PERFORMANCE

The objectives of this section are to provide the employee with clear feedback about overall performance.

Check the box below which best summarises the employee's overall performance against work expectations. Your rating should consider: how well work assignments were achieved; how the employee went about achieving them; their difficulty; and what other results were achieved apart from planned assignments. When possible, take into consideration your experience with other employees in similar jobs and along the same factors. The rating scale includes three ranges of acceptable and one level of unacceptable performance, defined as follows:

Exceeded expectations Achievements consistently exceeded objectives or requirements. ☐

Achieved expectations Achievements consistently met the majority of objectives or requirements. In some areas, accomplishments may have exceeded work expectations, whereas in others, they may occasionally have slightly fallen short; however, the overall performance is acceptable for accomplishing objectives or requirements. ☐

Below expectations Achievements frequently did not meet several of the objectives or requirements. With improvements in designated areas of the development plan, this employee should perform at a more satisfactory achievement level. ☐

Not acceptable Achievements consistently fell below objectives or requirements. Counselling and/or disciplinary action should be considered unless improvement is shown. ☐

JOB DESCRIPTION (to be agreed with the employee)

Outline the main duties of the job and estimate the percentage of time which is taken up with each duty.

PERFORMANCE FACTORS

This section enables you to describe in more detail how the employee goes about achieving the results of the job by diagnosing relative strengths and weaknesses along different performance factors. For each factor use the COMMENT space to give specific examples, typical of this employee's performance, which illustrate the effectiveness rating given and any factors which have influenced performance.

Performance factors and definitions	Comments
1 Volume of work: Volume of work done compared with the job requirement.	
2 Quality of work: Accuracy and presentation of work.	
3 Knowledge of job: Understanding job procedures, equipment and methods, responsibilities and scope of duties.	

Performance factors and definitions	Comments
4 Dependability: The degree to which this person can be counted upon to do what is required in carrying out assigned tasks and to meet deadlines. Include comments on attendance and punctuality.	
5 Innovation: The degree to which methods and policies are continuously examined and suggestions made for new and better ones.	
6 Staff development: Consideration for subordinates shown; their performance planned, monitored, appraised and developed.	
7 Communications: Ability to convey verbal and/or written information.	
8 Teamwork: Work relationships established with fellow employees within and outside immediate work group.	

EFFECTIVENESS RATING SUMMARY

Performance factors	High	Medium	Low	Not acceptable
1 Volume of work				
2 Quality of work				
3 Knowledge of job				
4 Dependability				
5 Innovation				
6 Staff development				
7 Communication				
8 Teamwork				

Overall marking

Exceeded expectations	Achieved expectations	Below expectations	Not acceptable

Overall comments

Comments by senior manager

WORK IMPROVEMENT PLAN

This section enables you to construct a work improvement plan for the performance factors on which improvement is needed.

Performance Factor	Specific recommendations for improving employee's current job performance

Employee's comments _____

This appraisal has been reviewed and discussed with the employee:

Employee _____ Date _____

Manager _____ Date _____

Countersigning manager _____ Date _____

(Extracted with permission from *Employee Appraisal*, Advisory Booklet Number 11, ACAS, 1988.)

 Review and discussion questions

1 Critically analyse the extent to which you believe that 'human resource management' differs from 'personnel management'.

2 Discuss fully the range and scope of personnel activities within your own organisation. Explain the underlying philosophies of managerial behaviour which influence the implementation of personnel practices and procedures.

3 'Every director a personnel director, every line manager a personnel manager.' In the light of this statement discuss what you see as the role and functions of the personnel manager in a large business organisation.

4 How would you justify to a group of sceptical line managers a high level of financial provision for training? Explain the steps you would take in order to ensure the effective management of training.

5 What are the potential benefits for both the individual and the organisation from a formal system of performance appraisal? What questions need to be addressed in the design and implementation of an appraisal system?

6 Critically evaluate different methods of performance appraisal and discuss fully the potential problem areas.

7 Explain those factors which are likely to influence the nature and contents of an employee relations policy, and give specific examples from your own organisation. What is meant by the legal and behavioural perspectives of employee relations?

8 Discuss critically the extent to which line managers should be involved with the responsibility for employee relations. What arrangements exist in your own organisation? Where appropriate, explain the role of the shop steward.

 Assignment

For your own, or some other organisation well known to you, analyse the manner in which personnel work is undertaken.

(i) Explain fully arrangements for the sharing of the duties and responsibilities of the personnel function including employee relations, and detail clearly:
 (a) the role of top management; and
 (b) the means of co-operation and consultation between line managers and the personnel manager.
 Comment critically on the effectiveness of these arrangements.

(ii) Critically review the extent to which there is a planned and systematic approach to the **management of training**. In particular, examine:
 (a) arrangements made to provide for the training needs of special groups such as married women, ethnic minorities, older members of staff, and people with disabilities; and
 (b) the effectiveness of systems for the review and evaluation of training in the organisation.

Support your analysis with specific examples.

CASE STUDY 1

London Taverns Ltd

London Taverns Ltd is currently the largest independent public house operator in the UK with some 50 pubs, hotels and branded restaurants located within the radius of the M25. The last two years have seen a period of rapid expansion for the company and this is set to continue as the company plans to acquire at least a further 20 outlets either by one-off purchase or by small takeovers.

London Taverns Ltd was originally a family business; the founder's son is currently Chairman and Managing Director. A self-confessed 'maverick', he has an inherent suspicion of bureaucracy or any system which he feels will stifle initiative or the entrepreneurial culture of the company. This even extends as far as a reluctance to standardise a company staff application form.

At present the day-to-day operations of the company are overseen by a Finance Director and two area managers, with a further director handling development and acquisitions. The Managing Director's secretary is responsible for the majority of matters concerning recruitment and staff administration. Monthly and weekly wages are the province of the finance staff.

On-the-job training of trainees is the responsibility of each unit with some general training courses provided by an outside consultant. Since the demise of the Industrial Training Board, and the requirement to provide adequate training to qualify for levy exemption, even this minimal level of training has been reduced.

There exist no defined policies or procedures relating to personnel or training. Only a very few members of staff belong to a trade union. The Finance Director has frequently commented critically about the lack of a developed personnel function and on the need for standard systems, clear policy-making and longer-term strategic planning. In the past the Managing Director has not appeared very interested and has not been persuaded to take any positive action.

Recently, however, the company has experienced difficulties in recruiting and retaining both management couples and trainees of a suitable calibre. This has led to problems with some units which have had to rely on temporary managers. In addition, the company has been involved in two much publicised industrial tribunal hearings which they lost largely because of the handling of disciplinary matters relating to allegations of sex discrimination.

These problems, coupled with the continued plans for further expansion, have reluctantly persuaded the Managing Director to agree to the appointment of a full-time member of staff responsible for personnel matters. The Managing Director has resisted the designation of Human Resource Manager as 'too grand and likely to give the person ideas above their station' but rather grudgingly accepts the title of Personnel Manager.

The Finance Director feels strongly that it is important to have a clear picture about the new Personnel Manager's first priorities, the systems and policies for the company and the longer-term objectives for the appointment. The Managing Director, however, seems less concerned about these aspects and is more worried about the personality of the person to be appointed, and their position within the structure of the company.

The Managing Director has now engaged you, as an outside consultant, to advise on

the appointment of the Personnel Manager. He also expects you to provide him with a clear idea on the duties and responsibilities attached to the position, the first priorities, and the extent to which the person appointed should be involved in longer-term strategic policies and procedures.

(This case study has been prepared jointly with, and from original material supplied by, my colleague Karen Meudell.)

CASE STUDY 2

Note: *The general management principles contained within the case study are applicable to both the private and the public sector.*

A management consultant, J. Jones, was retained by Manfrithshire County Council to analyse the problems junior management were experiencing in obtaining the standards of performance expected from the staff. The council, which services a large catchment area, gave Jones complete freedom and access to all aspects of the organisation.

The County Council employs 8000 people within the following management structure:

> 80 employed at Senior Management grades;
> 150 employed at Middle Management grades; and
> 3200 employed at Junior Management grades (including supervisors and section leaders).

In order to identify the problems, Jones held a series of meetings with councillors and senior management, followed by a number of group discussions with junior and middle management.

Initially, Jones experienced considerable antagonism from junior management, especially from supervisors and section leaders; in fact certain supervisors expressed open hostility, being sceptical of a useful outcome from the inquiry.

A supervisor also expressed the view 'we have seen it all before and nothing beneficial ever appears from these surveys'.

Jones decided to hold a series of 'brainstorming' exercises (in strict confidence) within the context of the group discussions. The participants had 'complete freedom of expression' without fear of censorship or reprisal from senior management.

Jones then produced a report based on the meetings and group discussions. It included the following points:

- **Morale**

 It became quite apparent that the level of morale for all staff was extremely low. Cutbacks and lack of funding were to the forefront of the complaints, but there appeared to be a more sinister influence, which was the mistrust between staff and management. It was difficult to ascertain the reason, yet the mistrust was more evident at the junior level of management, especially amongst supervisors and section leaders.

 Staff generally viewed the supervisors as a level of managers who made a very poor attempt at managing their sections, with complete disregard for work practices and standards of performance. At the same time, supervisors said that their jobs had no explicit lines of authority which allowed specific decisions to be made. One supervisor described the job as 'general "dogsbody" and "whipping boy"', another observed that 'nobody wanted the supervisor's job'.

 The problems cited by the supervisors included: insufficient funding to achieve unrealistic targets; no recognition of their position; no formal job description; and no appropriate training for any level of staff.

- **Job security**

 Security of tenure was the underlying theme. Rumours were spreading throughout the council offices that massive redundancies were expected in the near future. The redundancy rumours concerned all levels of staff, but made particular reference to junior management. Another rumour was the possibility of some managers being replaced by younger employees with better qualifications and more formal training.

- **General**

 The problems manifested themselves in a high rate of labour turnover and high levels or absenteeism which, in addition to the above, were attributed to a modest wage system, no opportunity for personal development and poor working conditions.

The report made the following recommendations:

(1) introduce a more efficient training and development programme for all levels of staff;

(2) initiate a formal appraisal system ensuring feedback and recognition for junior management; and

(3) undertake a further investigation into absenteeism and turnover involving supervisors and section leaders, making such recommendations as necessary to solve the problem.

(a) As the consultant, what action would you expect to be taken with reference to the supervisors and section leaders for the implementation of your proposals?

(b) If you were Chair of Manfrithshire County Council, having read the report, what questions would you ask the Council's senior managers? What would you expect their response to be?

(c) How can the Council overcome the antagonism and scepticism which appeared during the initial stages of the behavioural investigation?

Notes and references

1. Mullins, L. J. *Hospitality Management: A Human Resources Approach*, Second edition, Pitman (1995).
2. Guest, D. E. 'Human Resource Management and Industrial Relations', *Journal of Management Studies*, vol. 24, no. 5, September 1987, pp. 503–21.
3. Torrington, D. and Hall, L. *Personnel Management: A New Approach*, Second edition, Prentice-Hall (1991) pp. 15–16.
4. Horwitz, F. M. 'HRM: An Ideological Perspective', *International Journal of Manpower*, vol. 12, no. 6, 1991, pp. 4–9.
5. Legge, K. 'Human Resource Management: A Critical Analysis', in Storey, J. (ed.) *New Perspectives on Human Resource Management*, Routledge (1989) pp. 19–40.
6. Goss, D. *Principles of Human Resource Management*, Routledge (1994).
7. Cuming, M. W. *The Theory and Practice of Personnel Management*, Seventh edition, Butterwoth-Heinemann (1993).
8. The Information and Advisory Services, Institute of Personnel Management.
9. Tyson, S. *Human Resource Strategy: Towards a General Theory of Human Resource Management*, Pitman (1995).
10. Thomason, G. F. *A Textbook of Personnel Management*, Fourth edition, Institute of Personnel Management (1981).
11. Mullins, L. J. 'The Personnel Function – A Shared Responsibility', *Administrator*, vol. 5, no. 5, May 1985, pp. 14–16.
12. Forte, R. 'How I See the Personnel Function', *Personnel Management*, vol. 14, no. 8, August 1982, p. 32.
13. Tse, K. K. *Marks & Spencer*, Pergamon Press (1985) p. 129.
14. Drucker, P. F. *People and Performance*, Heinemann (1977).
15. See, for example: Armstrong, M. A. *A Handbook of Personnel Management Practice*, Fourth edition, Kogan Page (1991).
16. Fill, C. and Mullins, L. J. 'The Effective Management of Training', *Industrial and Commercial Training*, vol. 22, no. l, 1990, pp. 13–16.
17. *The Challenge of Change: Case Studies in the Management of Survival, Transition and Transformation*, The Training Agency and The National Economic Development Office, 1990.
18. Webb, S. (ed.) *Training For Change*, Initiatives in Training and Development, no. 1, The Industrial Society, January 1989.
19. Jones, R. A. and Goss, D. M. 'The Role of Training Strategy in Reducing Skills Shortages: Some Evidence from a Survey of Small Firms', *Personnel Review*, vol. 20, no. 2, 1991, pp. 24–30.
20. Mullins, L. J. 'Successful Training – A Planned and Systematic Approach', *Administrator*, July 1991, pp. 4–5.
21. *Employment News*, The Department of Employment Newspaper, no. 191, November/December 1990.
22. See, for example: Baldwin, J. and Butchart, A. 'Training Opportunities Within the Education System', *Administrator*, January 1995, pp. 20–1.
23. 'Too Old at 25?', *Employment News*, The Department of Employment, no. 223, October 1993.
24. *Employee Appraisal*, Advisory Booklet Number 11, ACAS, 1988.
25. James, G. *Performance Appraisal*, Occasional Paper 40, ACAS Work Research Unit, March 1988.
26. See, for example: Torrington, D. and Hall, L. *Personnel Management: A New Approach*, Second edition, Prentice-Hall (1991) pp. 15–16.
27. See, for example: Ward, P. 'A 360-Degree Turn for the Better', *People Management*, 9 February 1995, pp. 20–2.

28. Weitzel, W. 'How to Improve Performance Through Successful Appraisals', *Personnel*, vol. 64, no. 10, October 1987, pp. 18–23.

29. See, for example: Fletcher, C. and Williams, R. *Performance Appraisal and Career Development*, Second edition, Stanley Thornes (1992).

30. Kane, J. S. and Freeman, K. A. 'MBO and Performance Appraisal: A Mixture That's Not a Solution', *Personnel*, vol. 63, no. 12, December 1986, pp. 26–36.

31. Stein, N. 'Remember, The Staff is the Bread of Life', *Management Today*, July 1991, pp. 58–60.

32. Willman, B. 'Appraisal's Seven Deadly Sins', *The British Institute of Administrative Management*, vol. 4, April 1991, p. 26.

33. Fletcher, C. 'Appraisal: An Idea Whose Time Has Gone?', *Personnel Management*, vol. 25, no. 9, September 1993, pp. 34–7.

34. For a more detailed discussion see, for example: Rollinson, D. *Understanding Employee Relations: A Behavioural Approach*, Addison-Wesley (1993).

35. See, for example: *Employee Relations for the Hotel and Catering Industry*, Seventh edition, Hotel and Catering Training Company, 1990.

36. Horwitz, F. M. 'HRM: An Ideological Perspective', *International Journal of Manpower*, vol. 12, no. 6, 1991, pp. 4–9.

37. Fox, A. *Industrial Society and Industrial Relations*, HMSO (1966).

38. Horn, C. A. 'Management Style', *Administrator*, vol. 6, no. 4, April 1986, p. 14.

39. See, for example: Purcell, J. and Sisson, K. 'Strategies and Practices in the Management of Industrial Relations', in Bain, G. S. (ed.) *Industrial Relations in Britain*, Blackwell (1983) pp. 95–120.

40. Mullins, L. J. and Peacock, A. 'Managing Through People: Regulating the Employment Relationship', *Administrator*, December 1991, pp. 32–3.

41. Peacock, A. and Mullins, L. J. 'Effective Employee Relations: Legal Dimensions', *Administrator*, March 1992, pp. 30–2.

42. Mullins, L. J. and Peacock, A. 'Effective Employee Relations: Behavioural Dimensions', *Administrator*, April 1992, pp. 12–13.

43. Peacock, A. and Mullins, L. J. 'Effective Employee Relations: Termination of Employment Contracts', *Administrator*, July 1992, pp. 23–4.

44. For a more extensive discussion, see: Goss, D. and Adam-Smith, D. *Organizing AIDS: Organizational Responses to the HIV Epidemic*, Taylor and Francis (1995).

45. Kohl, J., Miller, A. and Barton, L. 'Levi's Corporate AIDS Programme', *Long Range Planning*, vol. 23, no. 6 (1990) pp. 31–4; Kirp, D. 'Uncommon Decency: Pacific Bell responds to AIDS', *Harvard Business Review*, May 1989, pp. 140–51.

46. Industrial Relations Service, 'AIDS at the Workplace: 1', *Health and Safety Information Bulletin*, 186, 7 June 1991, pp. 2–8.

47. Goss, D. and Adam-Smith, D. 'Empowerment and Disempowerment: The Limits and Possibilities of Workplace AIDS Policy', in Aggleton, P., Davies, P. and Hart, G. (eds) *AIDS: Foundations For the Future*, Taylor and Francis (1994); Goss, D. and Adam-Smith, D. *Organizing AIDS: Organizational Responses to the HIV Epidemic*, Taylor and Francis (1995).

48. Clegg, H. A. *The Changing System of Industrial Relations in Great Britain*, Basil Blackwell (1980) p. 129.

49. Cuming, M. W. *The Theory and Practice of Personnel Management*, Seventh edition, Butterworth-Heinemann (1993) p. 22.

50. For a fuller discussion on the part played by line managers and personnel specialists in the management of human resources, see, for example: Storey, J. *Developments in the Management of Human Resources*, Blackwell (1992).

51. Tyson, S. and Fell, A. *Evaluating the Personnel Function*, Second edition, Stanley Thornes (1992).

52. Cuming, M. W. *The Theory and Practice of Personnel Management*, Seventh edition, Butterworth-Heinemann (1993).

53. Sieff, M. (Lord Sieff of Brimpton), *Management the Marks & Spencer Way*, Fontana Collins (1991).

54. French, R. 'Employee Relations in the New Europe', *Administrator*, November 1992, pp. 25–6.

55. French, R. 'Employee Relations: The German Experience', *Adminstrator*, January 1993, pp. 29–30.

56. French, R. 'The Development and Structuring of Personnel Departments in Britain and West Germany', Unpublished PhD Thesis, Nottingham Polytechnic, 1985.

57. Lawrence, P. 'The Personnel Function: An Anglo–German Comparison', in Brewster, C. and Tyson, S. (eds) *International Comparisons in Human Resource Management*, Pitman (1991) pp. 131–44.

58. *Ibid.* p. 134.

19 STAFFING THE ORGANISATION

Whatever the nature of an organisation, the effectiveness of its operations and functions inevitably depends very largely upon the staff it employs. All managers are concerned with the success of the personnel function in their own department and with the management of their staff. Managers should recognise the importance of a planned and systematic approach to staffing the organisation, and to the recruitment and selection of staff.

 Learning objectives

To:

- Explain the importance of, and main stages in, human resource planning;

- Examine the process of job analysis;

- Detail the main stages in a planned and systematic approach to recruitment and selection;

- Explore different methods of staff selection;

- Examine interviewing style and skills of interviewing;

- Suggest how the effectiveness of the recruitment and selection process might be evaluated;

- Recognise the importance to all managers of effective staff selection.

Worth thinking about

When you really think about it, the most important function in any organi-sation is effective recruitment and selection. Everything comes back to people. If you don't appoint staff with the right ability, temperament and willingness, all these fancy theories on motivation, empowerment and com-mitment etc. aren't likely to be much use.

THE CONCERN OF ALL MANAGERS

Most managers are likely to be faced with the frequent need to recruit and select staff. Effective resourcing of the organisation is a central part of the personnel function. As we discussed in Chapter 18, larger organisations may, perhaps, have a designated personnel manager and specialist personnel staff with responsibility for the administration of recruitment and selection procedures. But whatever the organisation of the personnel function, it is only right and sensible that managers and supervisors have at least some say in the appointment of their own staff or those staff whose work they have to supervise.

Unit managers/supervisors would be expected to consult with the personnel department and to seek specialist knowledge and advice. The recruitment and selection of staff can rightly be regarded as a specialist activity, but all managers and supervisors should be well acquainted with the basic procedures and skills involved. In smaller organisations it is likely that unit managers will have a greater responsibility for staffing the organisation.

The message for all managers is to:

- recognise the importance of recruitment and selection;
- assess the effectiveness of present policies and procedures; and
- improve methods, skills and techniques of selection.

The manner in which staff are appointed is a major factor in determining the quality of product produced and/or service offered, and the behaviour and perfor-mance of the workforce, and in meeting satisfactorily the objectives of the organisation.

Organisational context

Top management have overall control for personnel policies and final responsibil-ity for their success. The style and effectiveness of recruitment and selection are influenced by the underlying philosophy of top management and the attitude which is brought to bear upon the development and maintenance of a good work-ing climate in the particular organisation.

Procedures for recruitment and selection must themselves be put into an organ-isational context. The prerequisites of an effective recruitment and selection policy include:

- **the clarification of corporate objectives;**
- **design of an effective structure** – the allocation of work and network of jobs – in order to achieve these objectives; and
- **a system of human resource planning** – providing the link between objectives and organisation structure, and a framework within which personnel policies, including a systematic approach to recruitment and selection, are planned and operated.

HUMAN RESOURCE PLANNING

In recent years increasingly more attention has been given to the importance of planning human resources as well as other economic resources such as capital, materials, machinery and equipment. At both the national and the organisational level it is essential that human resources are utilised as effectively as possible. At the national level, the basic aim is to review performance in different industries in line with anticipated future economic growth. Government action is geared towards overcoming problems of overstaffing/understaffing and the movement (redeployment) of workers accordingly.[1] But our concern here is with human resource planning at the organisational level.

Human resource planning (HR planning) was previously described as manpower planning and has been defined as 'a strategy for the acquisition, utilisation, improvement and retention of an enterprise's human resources'.[2]

Whatever the nature of the organisation, HR planning should not be regarded in isolation but as an integral part of the broader process of corporate planning. HR planning is linked to the development of the organisation as a whole, and should be related to corporate objectives and to an organisation structure capable of achieving those objectives. It should also be related to the nature of the organisational culture and climate.[3]

The organisation will need to clarify the extent and scope of the HR plan; the target date, that is the length of the forecasting period; the types of occupations and skills for which forecasts are to be made; and the amount of information and detail required.

Main stages in HR planning

Whatever the scope and nature of the HR plan, it is possible to identify at least four main stages (*see* Fig. 19.1):

- **An analysis of existing staffing resources.** This requires an effective system of personnel records and a staffing inventory.
- **An estimation of likely changes in resources by the target date.** This includes consideration of changes and losses to the organisation; incremental improvements in staff performance and current programmes of staff development; and external environmental factors such as the likely availability of labour. This determines the **supply forecast.**
- **A forecast of staffing requirements necessary to achieve corporate objectives by the target date.** This determines the **demand forecast.**
- **A series of measures to ensure that the required staffing resources are available as and when required.** This reconciliation of supply and demand is the basis of the HR plan and the **personnel management action programme.**

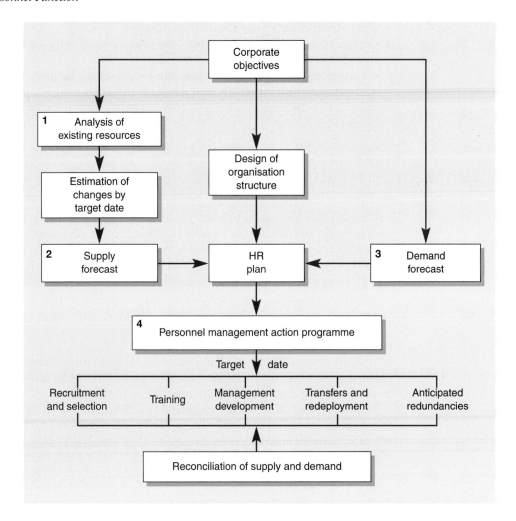

Fig. 19.1
Main stages in
human resource
planning

The HR planning process should also take account of broader environmental factors, such as: changes in population trends; patterns of employment, for example part-time workers; level of competition from other organisations for labour; changes in the educational system; government initiatives on employment, training or enterprise programmes, and employment legislation; developments in information technology and automation.

Concepts of
HR planning

The concepts of HR planning are basically straightforward and so are most of the methods involved. However, a number of more sophisticated statistical and quantitative techniques have been developed.[4] Computer programs are also available for more complex models of manpower planning.[5] These techniques can be helpful but should be applied only as appropriate to the amount of detail and accuracy required. What is most important is recognition of the need for effective HR planning to suit the requirements of the particular organisation.

THE VALUE OF HUMAN RESOURCE PLANNING

HR planning involves considerable uncertainty; it is not a science, and mistakes are bound to occur. However, the use of HR planning can assist organisations to foresee changes and identify trends in staffing resources, and to adopt personnel policies which help to avoid major problems. A human resource plan provides the trigger for a personnel management action programme aimed at reconciling differences between supply and demand. It provides a framework in which action can be taken to help overcome staffing difficulties facing the organisation. HR planning is a continuous process which seeks to ensure flexible resourcing related to internal and external environmental influences.

Effective HR planning can help anticipate potential future difficulties while there is still a choice of action. Forward planning should enable the organisation to develop effective personnel strategies related to such activities as: recruitment and selection; training and retraining; management development and career progression; transfers and redeployment; early retirements; wage/salary levels; anticipated redundancies; and accommodation requirements.

Coupled with good communications, and meaningful consultation and participation with staff involved, including where appropriate union and/or staff association representatives, effective HR planning should help alleviate potentially harmful effects to individual members of staff or to the performance of the organisation.

Overcoming HR problems

A survey of a range of 92 business organisations in the United Kingdom looked in detail at the steps taken to overcome human resource problems.[6] Almost 60 per cent of the organisations undertook formal HR planning and a further 10 per cent were considering its introduction. There was a correlation with number of employees. Less than half the organisations with under 4000 staff use HR planning, compared with 85 per cent of those above that size. For most organisations the planning process looked between two and five years ahead.

The five most important planning issues were identified as succession planning, recruitment problems, expected skills shortages, changing skills requirements, and retention difficulties. Improved selection procedures are seen as essential and 80 per cent of the organisations had established links with schools/higher education establishments to encourage young people to join them straight from education. Encouraging married women to return to work was also seen as important but less than 40 per cent had plans to encourage the number of women returners. Finally, 25 per cent were considering continuing employment beyond normal retirement age.

The report concluded that much greater priority needed to be given to human resource planning and management, since people will become central to the organisation's corporate plans. Organisations will need to restructure to make best use of available skills, and to develop human resources policies aimed at maintaining competitiveness in the labour market and to meet evolving employee aspirations. This will provide major challenges in terms of recruitment, selection, remuneration, training and development, and employee relations.

RECRUITMENT AND SELECTION OF STAFF

There are three important and fundamental considerations which should underlie the recruitment and selection of staff.

First, recruitment and selection should not be considered in isolation, that is simply finding someone to do a particular job, but in the context of the overall HR plan and personnel management action programme. For example, it will be necessary to investigate the potential of the persons appointed for training, development and future promotion; and their flexibility and adaptability to possible new methods, procedures or working conditions.

Second, it is necessary to consider not just technical competence and the ability to perform certain tasks but also, and equally important, sociability. It is necessary to consider how new members of staff will fit into the cultural and social structure of the organisation. There is nothing to be gained by appointing someone who although competent and technically efficient is unlikely to work in harmonious relations with other staff, customers or suppliers; or who is likely to upset the cohesiveness of work groups.

Indeed, if such is the case, there is plenty that the organisation can lose in terms of its overall performance and effectiveness. Sociability may be of particular significance in certain jobs or in certain types of organisations, but it is an important consideration in any work organisation. This is another reason for close involvement of the immediate head of department, and where appropriate the section leader/supervisor, in the recruitment and selection procedure.

Third, it is necessary to comply fully with all legal requirements relating to employment, to follow recommended codes of practice and to ensure justice and fair treatment to all applicants/candidates.

Staff turnover

One of the many adverse consequences of poor recruitment and selection is the possibility of a high level of staff turnover. Not only does this lead to increased direct costs, it also has a disruptive effect on the use of managerial time. In addition, a very important intangible cost is the effect of high staff turnover on the morale, motivation and job satisfaction of staff, and on the level of organisational performance and customer satisfaction.

The costs of high staff turnover are emphasised in a report from the hotel and catering industry.

> The costs of recruiting and engaging a new member of staff are considerable – not only the direct costs like advertising, agency fees, paperwork, interview time, but the many hidden or indirect costs. For example the expenses incurred in training and supervising new entrants, as well as those they are replacing, overtime that may have to be paid during staff shortages, an increase in wastage and losses while new staff settle in, customer irritation and low staffing morale if staff turnover is high.[7]

So what can be done to select the best available staff in the first place and to retain them for a reasonable length of time? **The need is for a planned and systematic approach.**

A planned and systematic approach

When selecting staff, managers should ask themselves two basic questions.

(i) If you do not know what you are looking for, how will you recognise a suitable person when you see one?

(ii) If you do not know what you want your staff to do, how can you judge their ability to do a good job, effectively train or develop them, or assess their performance?

The need is for a planned and systematic approach to recruitment and selection. (*See* Fig. 19.2.) Such an approach involves at least five main stages.[8]

- **The need to know about the job to be filled.** Is the job really necessary or can it be covered adequately by reorganising or reallocating other jobs? If the job is necessary what does it entail? What are the duties and responsibilities attached to the job?

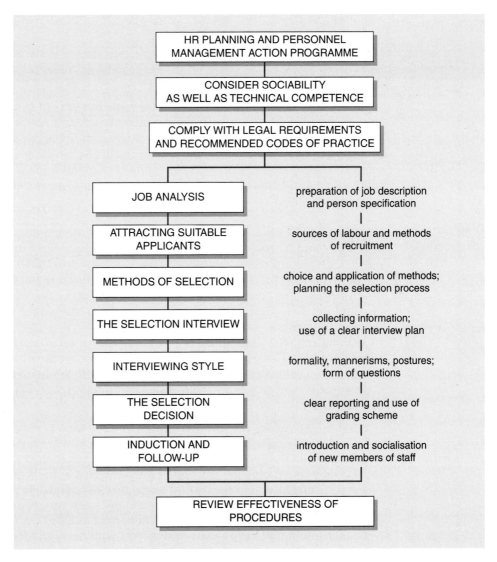

**Fig. 19.2
A systematic approach to recruitment and selection**

- **The need to know about the type of person to do the job**. What qualities and attributes are required for a person to perform the job effectively?
- **The need to know the likely means of best attracting a range of suitable applications**. Is it necessary to recruit outside the organisation? If so where are suitable applicants most likely to be found? Which are the best sources of labour and methods of recruitment?
- **The need to know how best to assess the candidates' likely suitability for the job**. How best to collect information about the candidates. How to plan the selection process. What are the most appropriate methods of selection?
- **The need for induction and follow-up**. How best to undertake the socialisation process. How to introduce new members of staff to the policies, procedures and working practices of the organisation.

Job analysis
Central to a planned and systematic approach is job analysis. The use of terms varies but it is generally agreed that job analysis is the total process by which you derive, first, a job description, leading to, second, a person specification.

JOB DESCRIPTIONS

A job description tells you about **the total requirements of the job**: exactly what it is; its purpose; what it entails; the duties, activities and responsibilities attached to it; and its position within the formal structure of the organisation. It may also include a note about any particular features of the working environment. The scope of the job description, and the amount of detail it gives, may vary among different jobs and different organisations. An example of a possible list of contents is given in Fig. 19.3.

Drawing up a job description
Sometimes a rider is added to the job description, often along the lines of 'Such additional and/or alternative duties as may be assigned by your head of department'. One can probably understand the reasoning behind such a statement and if the description is drawn up in terms of the general scope and level of the job, it might perhaps be considered appropriate. But where the description provides precise and detailed information about the job then one might well question the purpose and value of such a statement.

Although the job description is a valuable aid for recruitment and selection it should not be drawn up in such a rigid, bureaucratic manner as to imply a lack of flexibility, imagination or initiative on the part of the job-holder.

Townsend refers to job descriptions as straitjackets, and makes the following observation:

> Great for jobs where the turnover is high and the work is largely repetitive . . . (Insane for the more highly paid jobs.) Judgement jobs are constantly changing in nature and the good people should be allowed to use their jobs and see how good they are. At best, job description freezes the job as the writer understood it at a particular instant in the past. At worst, they're prepared by personnel people who can't write and don't understand the jobs. Then they're only expensive to prepare and regularly revise, but they're important morale-sappers . . . To be satisfying, a job should have variety, autonomy, wholeness and feedback. In other words, no job description.[9]

Job title (whether a new position or replacement appointment)

Department/section and location

Wage/salary range

Function of the department and main purpose of the job

Duties and responsibilities – including *ad hoc* or occasional requirements.
It may be appropriate here to give precise and detailed information. Or it may only be necessary to set out the general scope and level of the job, perhaps in terms of key result areas. Details may be quantified wherever possible. Duties and responsibilities can also be broken down into approximate percentage of time likely (or expected) to be devoted to each main activity over the average of, say, a week or month.

Specific limitations on authority – for example, in terms of financial expenditure or decisionmaking without prior approval of superior.

Responsible to – i.e., the job title of immediate superior.

Responsible for – i.e., the number and job titles of direct subordinates.

(Sometimes an organisation chart, or relevant extract, is included.)

Specific functional contacts – including main lateral communications and working relationships with staff in other departments/sections and contacts with external bodies.

Signature of head of department/section

Date job description prepared

Reference to indicate author of job description

Fig. 19.3 Possible list of contents for job description

Results-oriented job descriptions — There are, however, many ways in which a job description can be prepared. For example, instead of jobs being described traditionally in terms of the duties, tasks or activities to be undertaken, job descriptions can be written in terms of results. This should help to make people feel important and to let them know why they do what they do, why their work is important to the organisation and what it is intended to accomplish.[10] (*See* Fig. 19.4.)

PERSON SPECIFICATIONS

The person specification is an extension of the job description. It not only tells you about the job but also provides **a blueprint of the 'ideal' person to do that job**. The person specification details the personal attributes and qualities associated with successful performance of the job; for example, experience, technical skills, physical characteristics, health and appearance, motivation, intellectual ability, formal qualifications, personality and temperament, and any special requirements, such as the need for mobility. In drawing up the specification regard must be given to all legal requirements including the provisions of the Sex Discrimination Act 1975 and the Race Relations Act 1976.[11]

Patient Receptionist in a Dental Clinic	
Duty-oriented	*Results-oriented*
1. Greets patients and visitors and refers them to appropriate area.	1. Helps patients and visitors by greeting them and referring them to the appropriate area.
2. Notifies provider (dentist or hygienist) of patient's arrival, reviews adherence to schedule, and reminds provider of excessive delays.	2. Ensures that patient appointments are on schedule by notifying provider of patient's arrival, reviewing adherence to schedule, and reminding provider of excessive delays.
3. Anticipates patient's anxieties, answers questions, and maintains an orderly reception area.	3. Comforts patients by anticipating anxieties, answering questions, and maintaining an orderly reception area.
4. Schedules appointments in person or by telephone.	4. Optimises patients' satisfaction, providers' time, and treatment-room utilisation by scheduling appointments in person or by telephone.
5. Enters and retrieves patient scheduling data on a computer terminal while maintaining confidentiality.	5. Completes and updates scheduling files by entering and retrieving data on a computer terminal while maintaining confidentiality.
6. While stationed at the main desk: – Receives and redirects all incoming calls. – Operates the central paging and music system. – Monitors the hazard warning systems and notifies the appropriate person of deviations. – Opens and closes specified rooms and appliances while maintaining security precautions.	6. Provides centralised referral and control when stationed at the main desk by: – Receiving and redirecting all incoming calls. – Operating the central paging and music system. – Monitoring the hazard warning systems and notifying the appropriate person of deviations. – Opening and closing specified rooms and appliances while maintaining security precautions.
7. Responds to emergencies.	7. Assists patients in distress by responding to emergencies.
8. Performs other related duties which may be necessary from time to time.	8. Helps out when necessary by performing other related duties which may be necessary from time to time.

Fig. 19.4 Comparison of results-oriented and duty-oriented style of job description

Attention to equal opportunities

An important and fundamental feature of effective personnel policies and management is that of ensuring equal opportunities in employment. The Equal Opportunities Commission is an independent statutory equality body charged with enforcing, promoting and developing equality of opportunity between men and women. Its primary responsibilities include: to uphold the Sex Discrimination Act and Equal Pay Act; to work towards the elimination of discrimination; to review the working of equality legislation; and to act as an advisory and information service for the public.[12]

The Employment Department point out the need to make the most of the talents of all people and why equality of opportunity is good for business and a natural and integral part of good management practice. Successful employers tune

their personnel policies and practices to make the most of their present employees, and by recruiting the best available people to meet staff turnover and increased demands for labour in the future. The department has developed a Ten Point Plan to give practical advice to employers on how to offer equality of opportunity to people from ethnic minorities, women and people with disabilities. The principles also hold good for other groups such as older workers, or ex-offenders.[13]

A fairer deal at work

Continuing attention is being given to providing people with disabilities a fairer deal at work. For example, 21 top companies including B & Q, Rank Xerox and The Post Office have signed a ten-point agenda, conceived by the Employers' Forum on Disability, to give disabled people a fairer deal at work. The companies have pledged to take action in areas including active recruitment of people with disabilities, training existing staff through disability awareness programmes and adapting the working environment. Each company is building the action into their own equal opportunities policies.[14]

Preparation of a person specification

You are, of course, unlikely to find the perfect or absolutely ideal candidate. The person specification should therefore be written in a practical way and not unduly restrict the possible need for flexibility. The process of job analysis should provide you with a realistic set of objectives for the requirements of the job and the person to do it. It may be helpful to consider persons you have known to perform the job successfully and to analyse their attributes and qualities. 'Exit' interviews with staff can often yield useful information on the actual nature and requirements of the job.

A widely used classification for the basis of a person specification is the Rodger Seven Point Plan (discussed below). The headings in this plan, which may be related to both the job and the individual, are: Physical make-up; Attainments; General intelligence; Special aptitudes; Interests; Disposition; Circumstances.

DIFFICULTIES AND DISTASTES OF THE JOB

The person specification is even more meaningful if it includes the 'difficulties' and 'distastes' of the job.[15] Difficulties and distastes may often go together but this is not necessarily the case.

Difficulties are those aspects of the job which are regarded as particularly demanding or hard to perform competently. Examples, from the hotel and catering industry, might be the bar manager dealing with drunken or unruly guests; waiting staff serving a large number of unexpected customers arriving together; a washer-up scrubbing heavy copper pans; a receptionist dealing with complaints or awkward guests; section heads operating within budget limits. For the 'right' members of staff, however, *certain* difficulties might be seen as an attractive feature of the job. Some people may enjoy what they see as the challenge or responsibility that the difficulties of the job present.

Distastes are those aspects of the job or working conditions which are regarded as tedious or unpleasant. Examples might be waiting staff polishing silver before each service; a commis chef preparing the same vegetables for a standard menu; the kitchen porter emptying swill bins; cleaning staff changing soiled bed linen; restaurant staff unblocking the toilet. For some people, however, the 'easier'

aspects of the job might be disliked and seen as distastes; for example, because of the lack of variety, challenge or responsibility in the job, or because they prefer to be kept active.

Although these examples relate to the hotel and catering industry, the nature of difficulties and distastes for jobs in other organisations can readily be appreciated. And **effective managers should be well aware of the difficulties and distastes of particular jobs in their own department of their organisation.**

Concealing difficulties and distastes

Despite the temptation to paint the most attractive picture of the job, there is little to be gained from concealing the difficulties and distastes. If staff are appointed without full knowledge of the difficulties and distastes, or are not trained to deal with them, then once they find out what the job really involves they are likely to join the numbers who leave within a short period of time. This only adds to the 'induction crisis' and means starting the recruitment and selection process all over again! Even if staff do stay there is likely to be loss of goodwill, and an adverse effect on their attitude, job satisfaction and performance.

A study of insurance agents by *Weitz* showed that more realistic expectations about the job did not lower the number of applicants, but did reduce the six-month staff turnover rate.[16] One company introduced a revised recruitment booklet which gave attention to the less glamorous aspects of the job; for example, being turned down in a second interview after spending several hours preparing an insurance programme for a family, or being subjected to uncomplimentary and unwarranted comments about sales people.

Fifty agencies used the revised booklet and another 50 agencies continued to use the original booklet which emphasised only the positive aspects of the job. As many applicants were recruited for the job with the revised booklet as with the original booklet. But the number of agents recruited with the revised booklet and still employed after six months (71 per cent) was greater than the number recruited with the original booklet and still employed after six months (57 per cent).

Self-selection by applicants

If candidates are not prepared, or are unable, to accept the difficulties and distastes then clearly they should not be offered the job. It is preferable, however, that unsuitable potential applicants do not apply in the first place or that unsuitable candidates decide to withdraw their application before the selection decision. The other side of the recruitment and selection process is the applicants' assessment of you and your organisation. **The more information given to applicants the more self-selection there will be.** From the person specification can be distilled the job advertisement and further particulars available to inquirers.

Retention of staff

Staff are more likely to stay with your organisation for a reasonable time and provide a satisfactory standard of work if:

- the person specification paints a realistic picture;
- neither the organisation nor the job is oversold;
- the job and working conditions have been explained fully prior to their acceptance of the appointment;
- they understand exactly what will be expected of them including the difficulties and distastes of the job;

- their personal attributes and qualities match closely those required for successful performance of the job and/or potential future jobs;
- there is an effective induction and training programme; and
- the process of recruitment, selection and induction engenders realistic expectations, and the development of an appropriate psychological contract.

THE IMPORTANCE OF JOB ANALYSIS

From the person specification can also be drawn up the interview plan, including areas to be covered in assessing the candidate's willingness and ability to cope with the difficulties and distastes. Each of the headings in your interview plan can be related to the requirements of the job, and to the essential or desirable attributes and qualities looked for in the candidates.

The process of job analysis is, therefore, the basis of the recruitment and selection process. It provides guidelines for the objective assessment of applicants and aids the all-important selection decision. Upon appointment, successful candidates can be given a copy of, at least, the job description. New members of staff might be asked to sign and return a duplicate copy as an indication of their acceptance of its contents and requirements.

Basis for most staffing situations

The process of job analysis is not only an essential preliminary to effective staff selection; it is basic to most staffing situations. Job analysis provides the basis for performance review and appraisal, training, reward systems, staff development and career progression, and the design of working methods and practices. The study of difficulties and distastes helps provide a more thorough understanding of the jobs staff have to do and the working conditions under which they have to do them. Without such an understanding you are less able to assess the true performance of staff, including recognition of the shirkers and fiddlers.

A carefully prepared person specification is a focus for describing the requirements of the job, the working conditions, and the personal attributes and qualities necessary for successful performance. Any significant changes in the requirements of the job or the person to do it can be used as the basis for review of wage/salary rates, promotion prospects or training needs. Once agreed with the member of staff these changes can be formalised by incorporating them in a revised person specification.

ATTRACTING SUITABLE APPLICANTS

It is clearly important to know where suitable applicants are likely to be found, how best to make contact with them and to secure their application. This involves a thorough knowledge of sources of labour and methods of recruitment. The most appropriate means of attracting suitable applicants will depend upon the nature of the organisation, the position to be filled, and possibly the urgency of the need to make the appointment.

Among potential sources to be considered are: employment service job centres and agencies; career advisory offices; universities, colleges and schools; private

employment agencies; professional and executive appointments registers; ex-service organisations; personal introductions; and, of course, advertising. Another increasingly popular method is 'headhunting' or executive search. This involves direct contact with potentially suitable candidates, especially for senior or challenging appointments, to inquire about their interest in a particular job and where appropriate to attempt to elicit their 'application'.

Advertising

Vacancies may be advertised in the national and/or local press, professional or trade journals, and possibly on local commercial radio and television. Exhibitions and career conventions can also be considered under this heading. Advertising is expensive and it is important to be selective in the choice of media. Professional journals have the advantage that they are likely to attract the right kind of applicant in terms of qualifications and experience. But they may be particularly expensive, and there is usually some delay between placing the advertisement and publication date. With many organisations, and especially those in the public sector, it is customary to include an advertisement in the local press even for senior posts that are also advertised nationally.

The purpose of the advertisement is to attract suitable potential applicants and it should therefore contain the necessary information to secure their attention and interest. Careful consideration should be given to its design, layout and contents. For more senior appointments the advertisement might contain a named contact and telephone number for informal inquiries. This may help the process of self-selection. Also, for such appointments it is not usually possible to include sufficient information in the advertisement alone. In these cases, the 'please send for further details' procedure is useful.

Application form

The question of letters of application and/or specially designed, standard application forms, and preliminary, informal interviews must also be considered. Again, procedures will vary from organisation to organisation, and possibly with the nature of the vacancy. A common procedure is to invite inquirers to complete a standard application form (often, and preferably, typewritten) accompanied by a short, handwritten letter of application. Where appropriate a curriculum vitae (c.v.) may also be requested. Note Marks & Spencer's use of a computer program to screen application forms (*see appendix to this chapter*).

METHODS OF SELECTION

Methods of selection[17] involve the short-listing of applicants, collecting information (provided by other people) about the applicants, and the design and preparation of the selection process. The drawing up of the short-list can be undertaken by comparing applications against the information provided by job analysis, and consideration of the number of potentially suitable people applying for the position. After short-listing, selected applicants are referred to as 'candidates'.

Information provided about the applicants/candidates includes references and testimonials; university, college or school reports; service discharge documents; and possibly a medical report. Another possible source of information is from graphology – the analysis of the handwriting on the letter of application. However, despite

its popularity in certain European countries, the use and value of graphology is the subject of much scepticism in the UK.[18] Information provided by the candidates will come from the application form/letter of application, curriculum vitae and examples of past work, and during the course of the selection process.

There are a variety of methods which can be used in staff selection. These include: peer rating; in-tray exercises; selection tests and personality questionnaires; group exercises; assessment centres; and individual (one to one) or panel or board interviews. **The choice, combination and application of methods should be appropriate to the nature of the organisation; the position, tasks and responsibilities of the vacant job; and the number and nature of candidates.**

As an example, details of Marks & Spencer's selection process for management are set out in the appendix to this chapter.

Planning the selection process

Whatever selection process is adopted, it requires careful planning and preparation. Selectors must plan their work commitments to give adequate time and undivided attention to the candidates, free from interruptions or distractions. Time should be allowed to read carefully through all the papers and documents. A check should be made on the physical environment – accommodation, seating, facilities; arrangements for reception of candidates; and, where appropriate, arrangements for tea/coffee and lunch.

The manner in which the selection process is conducted is doubly important. It should, of course, be efficient in its own right to ensure that every effort is made to reach the 'best' decisions. Equally important, however, is that for most candidates the selection process is the first point of contact with the organisation. **The other side of the selection process is the candidates' assessment of you and your organisation.** Candidates will tend to judge the organisation by the manner in which the selection process is conducted, looking upon this as an indication of how it manages itself and its staff, and whether they would wish to work for the organisation.

Peer rating

Peer rating involves the candidates nominating other candidates, usually on the basis of a 'sociability' rating. It is sometimes known as 'buddy rating'. This was discussed in Chapter 7. Typical questions might be: 'Which of the other candidates would you choose to go on holiday with?' or 'If you had a personal problem (or a sensitive work problem) which of the other candidates would you choose to talk to?' Alternatively, negative or both positive and negative choices might be requested. Peer rating is clearly only appropriate if candidates are together long enough to become sufficiently well acquainted with each other; for example, if they are involved in a weekend selection programme.

In-tray (or in-basket) exercises

In-tray exercises are designed to simulate a state of affairs that participants can recognise as relevant to an actual working situation. Typically, the exercise presents a number of problems, and a range of material in the form of, for example, letters, memoranda, instructions and messages. Prepared plans of action may be disrupted by the receipt of further diverse communications. In-tray exercises require careful and detailed planning, and sufficient time needs to be allowed for their completion. They may be used as part of a group exercise or at an assessment centre (discussed below) but are often seen as being more useful as a training device.

683

SELECTION TESTS AND QUESTIONNAIRES

Much has been written about the value of selection tests and questionnaires and they are subject to a number of criticisms. It should be noted that the word 'test' is often taken to refer to measures of intelligence, achievement and developed abilities, and aptitude for particular tasks. Measures of interests, social attitudes, emotional stability or traits of personality are usually referred to as questionnaires or profiles, or similar. Answers are regarded as common or uncommon, typical or untypical, rather than right or wrong, good or bad. The word 'test' is therefore usually avoided in such measures, as in, for example, the Cattell 16PF Questionnaire (discussed in Chapter 4).

Objective tests which help to discover whether candidates are likely to possess the necessary skills for a job and to meet the demands made by the job can form a useful part of the selection process. Such tests help in the comparison of one candidate against another.[19]

Despite the debate about their value it does appear that an increasing number of larger organisations use tests as part of their selection procedures. It is, however, important to distinguish good tests from poor ones. The key point is 'that there must be a correlation between what the test measures and the skill or trait that it sets out to sample'. [20]

Personality questionnaires

The practical value of personality 'tests' has long been subject to much debate. According to *Barrett*,

> A dismal history has been recorded by personality tests. There have been a few scattered successes with some modern techniques, but on the whole the typical personality questionnaire, test, or inventory has not proved to be useful. In many of them, the 'right' answers (which exist despite the naive disclaimer that there are no right answers) are so obvious that everyone comes out a model of healthy adjustment. But even if all applicants were to answer each question with complete candor, the value of their answers for predicting success would still be in doubt because the complexities of human personality are as yet poorly understood.[21]

The potential usefulness of typical behaviour tests in personnel selection and placement is also questioned by *Dunnette*: 'Though widely used as aids in making selection decisions, the evidence regarding their accuracy for predicting job behaviour is far from impressive.'[22]

There is no test of completely general application and it is necessary to undertake a detailed study of the position for which a candidate is going to be tested. 'A test is only useful when one knows exactly what one is testing, and the minimum scores which will be needed in order to carry out the job. This is a particularly complicated problem where personality variables are concerned.'[23] There are still widespread doubts and criticisms about the use of personality tests, and continuing debate about their value in predicting performance at work.[24]

The use of selection tests

Great skill is required in the administering of tests or questionnaires and in the interpretation of results. This would probably entail the services of a consultant psychologist, which would add to the cost of the selection process. A suitable physical environment is also important. The possible reaction of candidates must

be considered. Some might find any form of 'test' something of an ordeal or regard it as an unpleasantness. A major concern with the majority of tests is the doubts about validity and lack of statistically proven reliability.

Another important consideration in the possible use of selection tests is whether they contravene the provisions of the Race Relations Act 1976 by having a discriminatory effect on a racial group which an employer cannot show to be justified. A degree of cultural bias in selection testing may be a potential source of unfair discrimination in employment decision-making.[25]

Even when selection tests *are* used, they should be part of a comprehensive selection process and applied in appropriate circumstances to supplement the interview, never as a substitute for it.[26]

GROUP EXERCISES

A group exercise is where a number of candidates are brought together and seen simultaneously by the selector(s). A number of group selection procedures are available, including discussions and debates, business games, command or executive exercises, and problem-solving exercises. The group may be leaderless or members may be allocated specific roles or briefs.

The group exercise is most effective when it simulates or resembles a practical 'real-life' situation which is reasonably representative of the task or type of situation that the person appointed might be concerned with in the organisation. The exercise might be guided or 'led' by a member of the selectors or by a nominated candidate, or it may be leaderless allowing the group to establish their own patterns of interaction.

Leaderless group discussions

A major possible criticism of 'techniques' such as leaderless group discussions (LGDs) is that they only highlight candidates who are proficient at that kind of activity rather than candidates who might be suitable for the job position. However, according to *Anastasi*, 'Validity studies suggest that LGD techniques are among the most effective applications of situational tests.'[27] The advantage of the group exercise is that it establishes a social situation. It enables candidates to demonstrate personal qualities and how well they are likely to get on with their peers. It provides a different slant on the candidates – as people in a working group.

The behaviour of candidates can be observed directly. A number of 'scoring' measures have been designed for LGDs (these were discussed in Chapter 7) and it is recommended that a set plan and observation sheet be used by the observer. This would assist in observing and rating each candidate's performance and allow a more meaningful interpretation of results. Note should also be made of body language, eye contact and other non-verbal clues. It is useful to have a short, informal discussion with the group at the end of the exercise. The observer could then explain any points arising from the exercise and candidates be given a chance to make any comments.

The value of group exercises

Sociability is an important consideration in the appointment of staff. An appropriate group exercise can be a valuable part of the selection process. It could be used, for example, in the appointment of a member of staff who has direct contact with

'customers' or who is the focal point for complaints and criticisms; or for staff who face frequent problem-solving situations or difficult tasks to accomplish. Group exercises are also commonly used in the selection of management trainees. However, the observer's own personality, values and attitudes can influence the categorisation of behaviour. There is therefore a need for trained observers and wherever possible it is advisable to use more than one observer for each group.

Assessment centres

The use of group exercises usually forms the central element of assessment centre selection. The centres provide an in-depth assessment of a group of broadly similar candidates, and aim to gauge the attributes and competencies required for a particular type of job. Group exercises are used in conjunction with business games and case studies, in-tray or other simulation exercises. These exercises may be supported by tests and questionnaires together with a variety of interviews in order to provide a range of contrasting but complementary activities. At the end of the various selection activities the observers agree on a cumulative rating for each candidate. The ratings are intended to match abilities and skills against specific requirements of the jobs to be filled. Assessment centres may also be used for training and development and promotion purposes. Assessment centres offer a number of potential advantages[28] but they can be costly and time-consuming and require careful planning,[29] and again they rely on trained observers.

THE SELECTION INTERVIEW

Despite its criticisms the interview is usually the central and indispensable element of the selection process, and the most widely used method of selection.[30] In order to make a fair assessment of candidates you must know what information is needed and how best to collect this from the interview. **A clear interview plan is necessary**. Probably the most popular example is the Rodger Seven Point Plan.[31] (*See* Fig. 19.5.) Although this plan was devised some years ago and is subject to challenge and interpretation of meaning, it serves to emphasise the importance of some clear plan and a *systematic* approach to selection.

Another well-known classification is the Munro Fraser Five Point Plan covering:

(i) **impact on others** – such as an individual's appearance, speech and manner;
(ii) **qualifications and experience** – the knowledge and skills required by different types of work;
(iii) **innate abilities** – the speed and accuracy with which an individual's mind works;
(iv) **motivation** – the kind of work that appeals to an individual and how much effort the individual is prepared to apply to it.
(v) **emotional adjustment** – the amount of stress involved in living and working with other people.[32]

Interview plan

Many organisations have their own interview plan/checklist. **The important thing is that some suitable plan is used, and that the plan is appropriate to the desired characteristics of the candidates**. The more structured the interview, the more effective it is likely to be.[33] Specific interview checklists may be drawn up for particu-

1. **Physical make-up**
 Are there any defects of health or physique that may be of occupational importance? How agreeable are appearance, bearing and speech?

2. **Attainments**
 What type of education? How well achieved educationally? What occupational training and experience had already? How well done occupationally?

3. **General intelligence**
 How much general intelligence can be displayed? How much general intelligence ordinarily displayed?

4. **Special aptitudes**
 Any marked mechanical aptitude, manual dexterity, facility in the use of words or figures, talent for drawing or music?

5. **Interests**
 To what extent are interests intellectual, practical–constructional, physically active, social, artistic?

6. **Disposition**
 How acceptable to other people? Influence on other people? Steady and dependable? Self-reliant?

7. **Circumstances**
 What are the domestic circumstances? What do the other members of the family do for a living? Are there any special openings available?

(Adapted from Rodger, Alec, *The Seven Point Plan*, Third edition, National Foundation for Educational Research (1970).)

Fig. 19.5
The seven point plan

lar appointments. An example of a checklist and rating scale for trainee social workers in a local authority is given in Fig. 19.6. **However, interviewers should avoid the impression of just 'going through a list'.** Candidates should be encouraged to do most of the talking and asked questions that will encourage them to describe experiences and develop ideas. Information under each heading of the interview plan can then be assembled as it is encountered and not in any set order. At the end of the interview all points in the plan should have been covered adequately.

Panel interview

If a panel, or board, interview is used the plan can serve as a basis of the division of questioning among selectors. It enables a clear allocation to be made of areas to be covered by each interviewer and the part which each is to play in the selection interview.

An advantage of the panel interview is that candidates may be seen simultaneously by a number of people who have an interest in the appointment. This would enable all aspects of the candidates' application to be explored and suitability for the appointment considered from both the technical competence and the broader organisational viewpoints. Typically, for example, the panel might include a member of top management, the head of department, the immediate supervisor and a member of the personnel department.

A disadvantage of the panel interview is that it tends to be a formal affair and sometimes rather intimidating to some candidates. Each additional member on the panel can add to the difficulties of putting candidates at ease and encouraging them to talk freely.

	X	1	2	3	4	5	Y
1.	Good bearing and address						Unprepossessing
2.	Health appears to be good						Doubtful if strong enough for social work
3.	Quick in intellectual grasp						Slow in intellectual grasp
4.	Expresses self well						Difficulty in expressing thoughts
5.	Shows resource and initiative						Might have difficulty in coping with the unexpected
6.	Personality seems warm						Seems cold
7.	Appears tolerant						Inclined to be rigid
8.	Response seems sensitive						Seems insensitive
9.	Inspires confidence						Does not inspire confidence
10.	Permissive						Inclined to be authoritative
11.	Likely to get on well with colleagues						Might not be able to co-operate well
*12.	Seems balanced and mature in relation to age						Seems immature
*13.	Has strong sense of responsibility						Sense of responsibility doubtful

1 X applies
2 tendency to X
3 average
4 tendency to Y
5 Y applies

Please tick appropriate box

*12 *Maturity of age*: This quality necessarily overlaps with others and might be regarded as a summing up, and an answer to the question – 'Is there promise of good all-round personal development?' Important considerations appear to be acceptance of one's own abilities and limitations; tolerance of opposition; variety of interests; resilience, humour and integrity.

*13 *Sense of responsibility*: Used in relation both to professional work and training. Important qualities seem to be a steady sense of value, forethought, consistency, persistence. Might be regarded as the answer to the question: 'Is this candidate likely to accept and fulfil reasonable conditions of training and employment and give good measure?'

Fig. 19.6
Ratings of selection panel for trainee social workers

Interview on the move

The traditional face-to-face interview can usefully be augmented by taking candidates round the organisation and conducting a two-way interview on the move. This will enable candidates to gain a fuller appreciation of the job, equipment and methods, and actual working conditions; to meet some of the staff and see them at work; and to ask further questions. The interview on the move will also aid the selectors' assessment of candidates by allowing them to observe what are likely to be more natural responses to actual situations.

INTERVIEWING STYLE

Candidates tend to copy the mannerisms and postures of the interviewer(s). A seating arrangement which is comfortable and allows some indication of informality helps the candidates to be more at ease and reduces the element of confrontation.

Skilled interviewers will know how to change their interview style and form of questions according to the different behaviour of candidates and the extent of their social skills. The type of question asked influences the candidate's reply. By using the right form of question you are better able to control the interview and the candidate's behaviour.

Interviewers should at all times show respect and good manners to candidates, be honest and behave ethically. Interview questions should observe equal opportunities principles and avoid any unfair discrimination.[34]

Types of questions

Interviewers should avoid the temptation to suggest possible answers to their own questions. They should also avoid 'leading' questions, that is questions which indicate the sort of response you expect to get and lead the candidate towards the 'right' answer. In most cases, a successful interview will contain a balance of open questions, direct or closed questions, and reflective remarks or questions.

Examples of leading questions

- Timekeeping is important in this job. Are you a good timekeeper?
- I guess you regret that now, do you?
- This is a very busy office and often we are short-staffed. Do you mind working under pressure?

Examples of open questions

- What made you decide to ...?
- Tell me about ...
- How did you happen to ...?

Examples of direct or closed questions:

- What grades did you receive in each of your subjects?
- Exactly how many staff report directly to you?
- How many months did you work with ...?

Examples of reflective remarks/questions
(These are helpful in correcting any misunderstandings and to show the candidates that they are being listened to attentively.)

- You appear to prefer working in a busy office.
- So you are interested in all outdoor sports?
- It seems that you do not respond well to personal criticism.

The purpose of the questions

Interviewers should probe the candidate and ask meaningful, searching and practical questions. Candidates should not be able to avoid particular questions or to give only a cursory reply. Interviewers should listen with care and note the way a candidate responds to a question. **Often this can tell you as much about the candidate as the actual answer to the question.** Candidates' reactions should be

noted, and interviewers need to be responsive to both verbal and non-verbal cues. **Understanding body language is an important feature of an interaction process such as selection interviewing.**[35]

All interviewers tend to have their own favourite questions, and sometimes very deep or philosophical questions are asked of candidates. For example: 'Tell me [pause] what do you do when you feel really lonely?' Usually such questions are avoided or the candidate tends to talk around the question, or to give only a superficial reply. The value of such questions seems doubtful, and in any case depends upon whether any meaningful interpretation can be placed on the answers given. **If any question is really worth asking in the first place, the interviewer should persevere and attempt to continue to tease out the information from the candidate.**

The interview involves an interaction of personalities and the perception of other people. Bear in mind the possibility of perceptual distortions and errors (such as the 'halo' effect and stereotyping) which were discussed in Chapter 5.

Towards the end of the interview, the interviewer might be expected to do more talking in explaining conditions of employment and in answering questions the candidate had been invited to ask. It is important to remember the other side of the selection process – the acceptance of you and your organisation by the candidate.

THE SELECTION DECISION

The selection decision is all-important and the culmination of the entire selection process. It should be as objective as possible and every effort should be made to reach the 'right' decision. This decision-making is greatly assisted by job analysis, a clear interview plan containing meaningful comments, and a meaningful grading scheme.

The need for good reporting
If the selection decision is to be effective, **good reporting as well as good interviewing is important.** The use of a grading scheme, for example, might introduce some degree of objectivity. It would encourage selectors to rationalise their comments and bring some level of uniformity to their assessment of candidates.

The description attaching to each grade should be carefully laid out, and the grading system and how to use it well known to all selectors. An example of a grading scheme is given below.

A **Outstanding candidate.** No weaknesses on technical competence or personal grounds. Could be appointed with confidence.

B **Above average candidate.** Many strengths and no serious weaknesses. Could be appointed with reasonable confidence.

C **Average candidate.** Strengths outweigh weaknesses. Could be appointed subject to any special comments noted on interview plan.

D **Below average candidate.** Number of weaknesses. Appointment doubtful. Normally a rejection (but acceptance might be possible subject to circumstances).

E **Definite rejection** (even if the only candidate). Weaknesses outweigh strengths to extent that appointment cannot be supported.

All five grades should be used and selectors should avoid the temptation to cluster candidates around the C grading. No pluses or minuses should be used.

It should always be borne in mind that there is the **N (number of candidates) + 1 option. That is that no appointment is made.** However much pressure there is to appoint a member of staff, it is clearly very short-sighted to appoint someone who is not really considered suitable or who is 'the best of a poor bunch'. Despite the costs, effort and time involved in going through another round of the selection process, it is in the long-term interests of the organisation to persist until a suitable candidate is found.

INDUCTION AND FOLLOW-UP

Induction involves the introduction of a new member of staff to the culture and environment of the organisation, its policies and practices and to other members of staff. Effective induction is a continuous process covering the first few months at work but it can be viewed as an extension of the recruitment and selection procedure starting with the selection process. Induction should include attention to rules and regulations, familiarisation with the culture and methods of operation of the organisation, and personal training and development needs.

The first impressions of an organisation and its managers are seldom forgotten. New members of staff face an unfamiliar environment and have to make a number of personal adjustments. A warm welcome, initial introductions, and a properly planned and designed induction programme will do much to reassure members, and aid their motivation and attitudes to their work performance.

Design of the induction programme

The induction programme should be designed to help new members of staff to familiarise themselves with their new environment, to settle easily into their new jobs and to establish harmonious working relationships with other members of staff. Induction should further the realisation of the psychological contract developed during recruitment and selection.

It is important to remember that people cannot fully absorb a large amount of information at one time, particularly in what could be a strange and initially uncomfortable situation. The induction programme should therefore be planned carefully and staggered over a reasonable period of time. It will also involve the active co-operation of managers, supervisors and colleagues.

COSTS OF THE SELECTION PROCESS

Cost is obviously a major consideration in any selection process. However, the costs should not be considered in isolation. They should be weighed against the costs of selection failure, either by the appointment of an unsuitable member of staff or by the rejection of a candidate who would have made a 'successful' member of staff. The financial costs of the selection process are immediately apparent and usually clearly identified, for example selectors' time and administrative expense. The contributions from an efficient and effective selection process and the benefits derived by the organisation are not readily apparent and less easy to identify.

Control is a vital part of a manager's job. Control over the performance of staff is not easy, nor is it achieved without cost. The more efficient the selection process, the easier the process of control and the lower the effort and expenditure. Teamwork and co-operation are necessary ingredients of a good staff and are more likely to be achieved the higher the stability of the labour force. Better staff morale leading to improved work performance and increased goodwill will improve the quality of products produced and/or service offered and assist in meeting satisfactorily the objectives of the organisation.

In the long term the costs of improving the selection process must be more than justified in improving the effectiveness of the organisation. Mistakes in selection are expensive, not only in the possible effects on staff morale and performance, but especially now that there is increased job security as a result of government legislation. To keep mistakes to a minimum the need is for a planned and systematic approach to recruitment and selection.

EFFECTIVENESS OF THE RECRUITMENT AND SELECTION PROCESS

We have said that the contribution from an effective selection process and the benefits derived by the organisation are not always readily apparent nor easy to identify. Over a period of time, however, some quantified measures might help to give a possible indication of its predictive validities and success. Examples are:

- staff turnover – especially in the short term or at the end of any probationary period of employment;
- labour costs;
- absenteeism/timekeeping;
- errors in work;
- breakages, scrap or waste;
- accidents at work;
- complaints, for example from clients or customers;
- promotions/staff development;
- discipline/grievance procedures;
- dismissals.

Information might also be obtained from: feedback from candidates; staff attitude surveys; performance appraisal schemes; exit interviews.

Other possible indicators might be:

- the number and quantity of applicants for positions in the organisation;
- the exercise of 'social' responsibilities, for example the employment of staff from government training schemes, registered disabled people or ethnic minorities;
- full compliance with all legal provisions and recommended codes of practice relating to employment.

However, it must be appreciated that it is always difficult to isolate a single variable. It is, of course, quite possible that a number of other factors, apart from recruitment and selection, contribute to, or are the main reasons for, favourable or unfavourable figures or indicators.

Basic principles *Drucker* makes the point that there is no magic to good staffing (and promotion) decisions and no such thing as an infallible judge of people. 'If I put a person into a job and he or she does not perform, I have made a mistake. I have no business blaming that person, no business invoking the "Peter Principle", no business complaining. I have made a mistake.'[36]

Drucker goes on to suggest five basic principles for matching jobs and people.

- **Think through the job requirements**. Job descriptions may last a long time and remain unchanged for many years. It is important to look at the nature of the job and what is at the heart of the job.
- **Look at the number of potentially qualified people**. Formal qualifications are a minimum for consideration because their absence disqualifies the candidate automatically. In order to make an effective decision the manager should look at three to five qualified candidates.
- **Think hard about how to look at these candidates**. The central question is the strengths each possesses and are these the right strengths for the job.
- **Discuss each of the candidates with several people**. All of us have first impressions, prejudices, likes and dislikes. We need to listen to what other people think.
- **Make sure the appointee understands the job**. After the appointee has been in a new job for three to four months, he or she should be focusing on the demands of that job rather than on the requirements of preceding jobs.

A crucial determinant of the success of recruitment and selection is how well the new member of staff adapts to the requirements of the organisation and makes an effective contribution to the development of the organisation.[37] Despite difficulties in evaluation, this should be an ultimate measure of the effectiveness of the recruitment and selection process.

SYNOPSIS

■ Whatever the structure of the organisation it has to be staffed with people of the right quality. Most managers are likely to be faced with the frequent need to recruit and select staff. Managers and supervisors should have at least some say in the appointment of their own staff or those staff whose work they supervise. Procedures for recruitment and selection must themselves be put into an organisational context. Human resource planning provides the link between corporate objectives and organisation structure, and is the basis of a personnel management action programme.

■ There are three important considerations which should underlie the recruitment and selection of staff: (i) the context of the overall human resource plan; (ii) how new members of staff will fit into the cultural and social structure of the organisation; and (iii) full compliance with all legal requirements. In order to select the best available staff, and to retain them for a reasonable length of time, the need is for a planned and systematic approach to recruitment and selection. Central to such an approach is the process of job analysis from which is derived, first, a job description, leading to, second, a person specification. The person specification is more meaningful if it includes the 'difficulties' and 'distastes' of the job.

■ It is important to have a thorough knowledge of sources of labour and methods of recruitment. There are a variety of methods which can be used in staff selection. The choice, combination and application of methods should be appropriate to the nature of the organisation, the vacant job and the number and nature of candidates. Whatever selection process is adopted, it requires careful planning and preparation. The other side of the selection process is the candidates' assessment of you and your organisation.

■ Group exercises, and selection tests and questionnaires may be used to supplement the interview. Despite its criticisms, the interview is usually the central and indispensable element of the selection process. A clear interview plan/checklist is necessary. If a panel or board interview is used the plan can serve as a basis for division of questioning among selectors. Skilled interviewers will know how to change their interview style and form of questions according to the different behaviour of candidates, and the extent of their social skills.

■ In most cases, a successful interview will contain a balance of open questions, direct or closed questions, and reflective remarks or comments. Interviewers should probe the candidate and ask meaningful, searching and practical questions. Interviewers should listen with care and note the way a candidate responds to a question. If the selection decision is to be effective, good reporting as well as good interviewing is important. The use of a grading scheme, for example, might introduce some degree of objectivity.

■ Cost is obviously a major consideration in any selection process. However, costs should be weighed against the costs of selection failure; the contributions from an efficient and effective selection process, and benefits derived by the organisation, should be taken into account. These benefits are not always readily apparent or easy to identify, but over a period of time some quantified measures might help to give a possible indication of the success of the selection process. However, there is no magic to good staffing decisions and no such thing as an infallible judge of people.

APPENDIX

Marks & Spencer plc: Selection process for management

We recruit centrally for management for both our stores and Head Office. The disciplines recruited are, for the stores, commercial, financial, personnel and general; for the Head Office, merchandising, selection, information technology, technology and specialists.

There are three main source areas: A Level entrants (or equivalent); graduates; and managers with experience.

For A Level entrants and graduates, the target jobs are 4/5 years into the company. Specialists and managers with experience are required to be operational sooner.

Over the years, we have developed a rigorous and sophisticated selection process to handle the thousands of applications we receive each year for a commensurately small number of vacancies (e.g. 8,500 graduate applications in 1995 for 270 vacancies).

This process operates in three stages:

- application form (initial screening);
- initial interview (interviewing to criteria); and
- Assessment Centre (graduates/A Level entrants only) or
- final board interview (managers with experience).

Selection criteria

All candidates are assessed against seven criteria which are a range of personal skills which we have identified as being essential for effective performance on the job. We have reviewed and refined these over the years (and continue to do so) to ensure that they reflect the changing requirements of our business and its culture. The seven criteria are the criteria for the business, whether it be a store or Head Office management position. There are, in addition, a small number of specialist criteria which are prerequisites for certain specialist Head Office roles. All interviewers share a common understanding of the selection criteria.

The application form and screening

The application form provides the first view of a candidate and as well as asking for biographical and academic information, asks for details of work experience and positions of leadership and responsibility held.

Screening is done through a bespoke computer program with built-in management controls, and the main objective is to select those candidates who should have an interview.

The initial interview

We have, for many years, used targeted interviewing (Interviewing to Criteria) and all our interviewers have had a minimum three-day intensive training in this skill.

Candidates at initial interview are assessed against five of the seven criteria. During the interview, through focused and probing questioning, which explores the candidates' past and present experiences, the interviewer seeks to determine the degree to which candidates possess these skills. Interest is focused on specific behaviour, i.e. what the candidate said and did in certain situations. Tests are administered at the interview for certain specialist Head Office roles and all candidates are asked to do some pre-work prior to attending the interview. The interviewer takes notes and afterwards separates the classification against criteria of the information gathered from the evaluation of that data to maximise objectivity.

The final evaluation and decision reflect both the quality of the information gathered against the criteria, and an awareness of what candidates will face at the next stage. Candidates are not compared with each other but against the standard required for the business.

The Assessment Centre

The Assessment Centre is a group evaluation where eight candidates come together to perform a series of management exercises designed to reflect the kinds of tasks/activities they are likely to face on the job, and which give them the opportunity to demonstrate the effective behaviours required for successful performance on the job.

Candidates at the Centre are assessed against all seven criteria in each exercise. Reliability is derived from the opportunity to observe the criteria in multiple situations (the exercises).

Objectivity is maintained as each assessor observes a different candidate in each exercise, so no one assessor is able to make a decision about a candidate without sharing information with the other assessors.

Each Centre runs with eight candidates, a Chairman, four assessors (one per two candidates) and four middle managers (not assessors) who interact with the candidates in a facilitation role in one exercise. The exercises consist of some group work, some individual work, analysis and report writing. No psychometric tests are employed. Centre design is reviewed regularly as are the exercises which have a limited shelf life.

Detailed evaluation conferences determine the decision to employ or reject, and information gathered at the Centre is used to compile a strength and development needs profile which is fed back to successful candidates on joining and used to focus initial training. Successful candidates also have a one-day attachment to either a store or Head Office (as appropriate) prior to a confirmation of offer to help them make an informed decision about acceptance.

Final board interview
(managers with experience only)

This follows the same format as the initial interview except that candidates are assessed against all seven criteria and the degree of probing is greater in keeping with the greater life and work experience of the candidates.

These candidates, if successful, will be expected to be operational at a management level within a far shorter time scale (3–6 months). They therefore must have relevant transferable skills.

(I am grateful to the Recruitment Department, Marks & Spencer, for providing the above information.)

 Review and discussion questions

1 Why is the recruitment and selection of staff the concern of all managers in an organisation? What are the prerequisites of an effective recruitment and selection policy?

2 Explain the importance of, and main stages involved in, organisational human resource planning. What do you understand by a personnel management action programme?

3 Explain (i) the fundamental considerations which should underlie the recruitment and selection of staff; and (ii) the basic stages in a planned and systematic approach to recruitment and selection.

4 Central to a systematic approach to staff selection is the process of 'knowing the job and the person to do it'. Explain how you would ensure this process is carried out effectively in a large organisation.

5 Assess the main methods of staff selection, *apart* from the interview, and give examples of when each method might be most appropriate.

6 Draw up (i) a suggested selection interview plan; and (ii) a suggested grading scheme for reporting the interview. Make clear the nature of the appointment to which your interview plan and grading scheme refer.

7 Discuss the main points to bear in mind in adopting an appropriate interviewing style. Give your own examples of the different types of questions that might be asked.

8 Suggest how the management of an organisation might attempt to evaluate the effectiveness of its recruitment and selection process. Give practical examples relating to your own organisation.

 C A S E S T U D Y 1

Sixth time lucky

Pink Passion Products Ltd.

Scene: The pleasantly appointed office of Pat Rennie, the Personnel Manager.

Players: The said Pat Rennie; secretary, Chris Lewis; and a very ruffled and agitated Production Manager, Tony Grey.

Time: The present.

Pat is discussing a job description with Chris when Tony bursts in, unannounced. He is waving a piece of paper in his hand.

Tony: He's done it. You wouldn't believe it was possible. Here it is, Crabtree's letter of resignation. A record this time. He stayed six weeks. (Pat takes the letter and reads it)

Pat: I remember interviewing him when he came for the job. He seemed really keen. According to this letter, he's got a more interesting job – he didn't mention money. Poor old Tony. You're certainly unlucky with your quality-control people. This is the fifth one you've lost in a twelvemonth isn't it?

Tony: It's too bad, Pat. I don't think we're getting the right sort of people applying for the job. Can't you make the advertisement more attractive next time so that we can have a better choice, at least?

Pat: I think the trouble is we've made the job sound too attractive. It's a routine job – just checking the tubs. But we've got to have a qualified person in the job.

Tony: Do everything you can, Pat, that's all I ask. This situation is getting ridiculous.

Pat: You can't say I haven't tried. I did some calculations last time we advertised this job. We've spent £1800 on advertisements alone in the last two years.
(As Tony goes through the door, Chris brings out the Job Description.)

Chris: Assistant Quality Control Manager – analyse ingredients in samples before they are used on the production line. M'm. Quite an important job. Some chemicals cause skin cancer don't they?

What advice would you offer Pat Rennie and Tony Grey in this situation?

 Assignment

In self-selected groups of 3 or 4, visit a large organisation or a large department of an organisation.

1 Investigate carefully the recruitment and selection process and comment critically on:
 (i) the nature of human resource planning and the extent to which it relates to, and aids, recruitment and selection;
 (ii) the extent and manner of the process of job analysis;
 (iii) measures taken to attract a range of suitable applicants;
 (iv) the application of different methods of selection;
 (v) the use of (a) an interview plan/checklist and (b) a grading scheme.

2 For a selected particular position within the organisation:
 (i) prepare your own detailed job description and person specification;
 (ii) detail what you believe are the particular difficulties and distastes of the job.

3 State clearly the recommendations you would make in order to help improve the effectiveness of the recruitment and selection process.

 # CASE STUDY 2

Wessex Computers

Wessex Computers has been running for five years now, and it is still virtually a 'one-man business' though there are 20 employees. While the firm sells books, magazines and small 'micro' games, its business is predominantly in microcomputers. Staff thus spend their time in selling computers and persuading clients that package programs are applicable to their business or in providing software packages to suit individual requirements. The employees are nearly all in the 20–25 age group, and very keen and interested in their jobs, obviously involved in learning a trade which has every prospect going for it in the years ahead. Every opportunity is taken to display their wares at computer shows and exhibitions and to help in running courses on micros in an effort to make people aware of the 'user-friendly' nature of the equipment.

The site of the main part of the business is in what was once a main shopping street but has now been bypassed, and is in fact a cul-de-sac. The premises consist of a small shop front with 600 square feet of shopping area in which are displayed microcomputers, books, computer games, calculators and standard software. Behind is a workroom, and above more workrooms and office space, in all 3000 square feet. Over the shop itself lived a tenant, who has just left the property so that another 1000 square feet has become available. The proprietor hopes to use this to solve the storage problems and to create one large room which can be used for setting up a permanent training section. His idea is to charge customers a moderate fee so that their employees can be taught how to run their computers. The staff currently consists of the proprietor, a secretary/bookkeeper, three receptionists/assistants and seven programmers/customer support staff. As this is a small organisation and somewhat overworked the specific tasks are flexible and depend on individual preferences.

The other part of the premises is about five miles away in Embridge; three years ago Wessex Computers won a local 'Enterprise' competition run by the corporation, for which the prize was this site rented at a reduced cost. It is used as working quarters for five programmers, two customer support staff involved in repairing and servicing the microcomputers and two administrative staff. Control of these staff and effective charging-out of their work to customers has not proved very satisfactory.

As far as Wessex Computers is concerned, some success has been achieved by lending out the microcomputers free of charge for about ten days or by renting them out at a minimal charge for a month or two so that customers have a chance to get acquainted with them. Ninety per cent of such clients end by buying the machine and to some extent the rental could be offset against the capital cost. The owner is considering going into the leasing business as potential buyers are worried about machines becoming quickly outdated; a financing company deals with the funding of this side of the business. Maintenance work has to be done at times, although most frequently problems are caused by either mishandling of floppy disks by the customers, or failure to read the instruction handbooks carefully. Staff have to spend about one or two hours with each customer teaching them to use the machines even though comprehensive instruction manuals are available.

Some six months ago, with everyone working particularly hard, the record keeping was neglected, and the overdraft increased rapidly. The bank became nervous and was only reassured when an independent accountant was called in to complete the year's accounts, and to produce a report and cash flow forecast for a few months ahead.

Among the accountant's remarks was the comment that the owner was working far too hard, for too many hours, trying to be sales manager, general manager and office manager. Obviously this pressure of work could not be maintained and some aspect of his work had to be shed. Since the least interesting part of the business for him was the 'paperwork', and the most interesting was selling microcomputers, meeting people and solving problems with them, he decided to appoint an office manager to take control of office procedures, in the most convenient way.

(a) Produce a job description and person specification for the appointment of the office manager.

(b) Prepare a press advertisement covering the vacancy and list other sources which could be used.

(c) Describe the methods of employment selection which could be used.

(Make clear any reasonable assumptions you feel are necessary.)

Notes and references

1. For a summary, see: The Employment Department Group *Just The Job*, September 1991.
2. Department of Employment *Company Manpower Planning*, HMSO (1974).
3. See, for example: French, W. L. *Human Resources Management*, Third edition, Houghton Mifflin (1994).
4. Civil Service Department *Some Statistical Techniques in Manpower Planning*, HMSO (1970).
5. See, for example: Tyson, S. *Human Resource Strategy*, Pitman (1995).
6. William Mercer Frazer Ltd. *Manpower Planning Survey Report*, August 1989.
7. *Employee Relations for the Hotel and Catering Industry*, Seventh edition, Hotel and Catering Training Company, 1990, p. 43.
8. See, for example: Mullins, L. J. 'Job Analysis – Know the Job and the Person to Do It', *International Journal of Hospitality Management*, vol. 4, no. 4, 1985, pp. 181–3.
9. Townsend, R. *Further up the Organisation*, Coronet Books (1985) pp. 115–16.
10. Plachy, R. J. 'Writing Job Descriptions that Get Results', *Personnel*, vol. 64, no. 10, October 1987, pp. 56–63.
11. For practical guidance see: Race Relations Employment Advisory Service *Positive Action: Promoting Racial Equality in Employment*, Employment Department Group, July 1994.
12. See, for example: Employment Department Group *Employment News*, no. 224, November 1993.
13. Employment Department Group, *Equal Opportunities: Ten Point Plan for Employers*, September 1994.
14. Employment Department Group, *Employment News*, no. 205, March 1992.
15. Rodger, A. and Cavanagh, P. 'Personnel Selection and Vocational Guidance', in Welford, A. T. *et al.* (eds) *Society: Problems and Methods of Study*, Revised edition, Routledge and Kegan Paul (1967).
16. Weitz, J. 'Job Expectancy and Survival', *Journal of Applied Psychology*, no. 40, 1956, pp. 245–7.
17. Some of the ideas expressed are based on the author's experience as a visiting selector for a number of organisations, including study of the selection process for long-term volunteers with the United Nations Association International Service.
18. See, for example: Fowler, A. 'An Even-Handed Approach to Graphology', *Personnel Management*, March 1991, pp. 40–3.
19. See, for example: Toplis, J., Dulewicz, V. and Fletcher, C. *Psychological Testing: A Practical Guide for Employers*, Institute of Personnel Management (1987).
20. Starkey, M. 'Testing the Tests', *Management Today*, May 1992, pp. 76–8.
21. Barrett, R. S. 'Guide to Using Psychological Tests', in Fleishman, E. A. (ed.) *Studies in Personnel and Industrial Psychology*, Revised edition, Dorsey Press (1967) p. 58.
22. Dunnette, M. D. *Personnel Selection and Placement*, Tavistock (1966) p. 63.
23. Kingston, N. *Selecting Managers*, BIM Management Survey Report no. 4, British Institute of Management (1971) p. 22.
24. Fletcher, C., Blinkhorn, S. and Johnson, C. 'Personality Tests: The Great Debate', *Personnel Management*, September 1991, pp. 38–42.
25. See, for example: Wood, R. 'Psychological Testing Free From Prejudice', *Personnel Management*, December 1992, pp. 34–7.
26. For further information on the use of selection tests see, for example: Torrington, D. and Hall, L. *Personnel Management: A New Approach*, Second edition, Prentice-Hall (1991).
27. Anastasi, A. *Fields of Applied Psychology*, McGraw-Hill (1964) p. 71.
28. Seegers, J. 'Assessment Centres for Identifying Long-Term Potential and for Self-Development', in Salaman, G. (ed.) *Human Resource Strategies*, Sage (1992) pp. 273–302.

29. Fowler, A. 'How to Plan an Assessment Centre', *Personnel Management Plus*, December 1992, pp. 21–4.
30. *IRS Recruitment and Development Report 17*, May 1991, IRS.
31. Rodger, A. *The Seven Point Plan*, Third edition (1970). Originally devised for the National Institute of Industrial Psychology; now available from the National Foundation for Educational Research.
32. Frazer, J. M. *Employment Interviewing*, Fifth edition, Macdonald and Evans (1978).
33. See, for example: Green, J. 'So You Think You Can Recruit Successfully?', *Administrator*, January 1992, pp. 36–8.
34. See, for example: Fletcher, C. 'Ethics and the Job Interview', *Personnel Management*, March 1992, pp. 36–9.
35. See, for example: Glaser, C. B. and Smalley, B. S. 'Four Minutes That Get You a Job', *Readers Digest*, January 1994, pp. 69–72.
36. Drucker, P. F. 'Getting Things Done: How to Make Good People Decisions', *Harvard Business Review*, vol. 4, July–August 1985, p. 22.
37. See, for example: Tyson, S. and Fell, A. *Evaluating the Personnel Function*, Second edition, Stanley Thornes (1992).

Part 8

IMPROVING ORGANISATIONAL PERFORMANCE

20 ORGANISATION DEVELOPMENT

Organisation development (OD) is concerned with the diagnosis of organisational health and performance, and the ability of the organisation to adapt to change. It involves the applications of organisational behaviour and recognition of the social processes of the organisation. The manager needs to understand the nature and importance of organisational culture and climate, employee commitment, and the management of organisational conflict and change.

 Learning objectives

To:

- Explain the meaning, nature and main features of OD;

- Examine the nature and importance of organisational culture;

- Specify the characteristics of organisational climate, staff morale and employee commitment;

- Assess the nature and sources of conflict, and strategies for managing organisational conflict;

- Explain the nature of organisational change and the forces of change;

- Explore reasons for resistance to change and examine the management of organisational change;

- Recognise the importance of organisational health and performance, and the ability of the organisation to adapt to change.

Worth thinking about

'I've been thinking about OD. It seems a strange subject to study because surely organisations can't develop.' . . . 'I suppose it depends on the strict use of words but it is the people who make up the organisation who are developing.' . . . 'So OD is really all about the actions, behaviour and performance of people?' . . . 'That's right!'

THE MEANING OF OD

Organisation development (OD) is a generic term embracing a wide range of intervention strategies into the social processes of an organisation. These intervention strategies are aimed at the development of individuals, groups and the organisation as a total system.

Because OD is a generic term there are many possible ways in which it can be defined. An example of a comprehensive definition of OD in the behavioural science sense of the term is given by *French and Bell*:

> Organization development is a long-term effort, led and supported by top management, to improve an organization's visioning, empowerment, learning, and problem-solving processes, through an ongoing, collaborative management of organization culture – with special emphasis on the culture of intact work teams and other team configurations – utilizing the consultant-facilitator role and the theory and technology of applied behavioural science, including action research.[1]

The broad nature of OD

In a very general sense, OD is concerned with attempts to improve the overall performance and effectiveness of an organisation. Essentially it is an applied behavioural science approach to planned change and development of an organisation.[2] In Chapter 1 it was suggested that the term 'organisational behaviour' is, strictly, a misnomer. The same caveat also applies to the term 'organisation development'. An organisation is made up of people. When we talk about organisation development it is important to remember that, in practice, we are referring to the development and performance of those **individuals and groups of people** who comprise the organisation.

TOPICS ASSOCIATED WITH OD

The broad nature of OD means that many interrelated topics could be included under this heading or 'label'.[3] Given the importance of people, topics that are normally included under the heading of organisational behaviour can also be seen as relevant to the study of OD. However, the emphasis of OD is more on the development of the organisation than the actual processes of organisation and

management. But even in this narrower interpretation many of the topics discussed in previous chapters such as, for example, socio-technical systems, the Leadership Grid (Managerial Grid), Management by Objectives, delegation, job design, T-groups and quality circles, may be seen as part of OD.

In this and the following chapter we look at selected, major topics which can be considered as central to, or closely associated with, the study of OD (*see* Fig. 20.1):

- organisational culture;
- organisational climate;
- employee commitment;
- organisational conflict;
- the management of change;
- management development; ⎫ These two topics are
- organisational effectiveness. ⎭ discussed in Chapter 21.

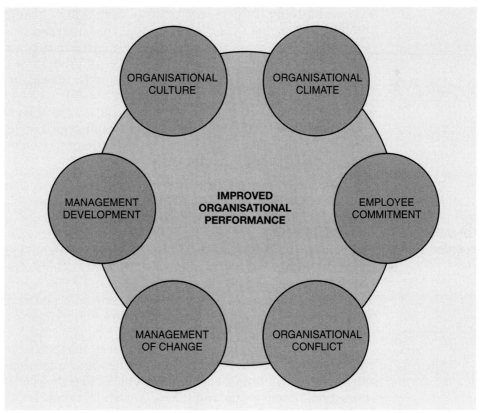

Fig. 20.1 Major topics associated with organisation development

The implementation of OD

In order to bring about effective change OD makes use of a number of approaches – often referred to as intervention strategies – including: survey research and feedback, T-groups, team building and grid training.

- **Survey research and feedback** involves the use of questionnaire surveys to help determine the attitudes of members to the functioning of the organisation. Results of the surveys are fed back to top management and then to work groups for interpretation and analysis. Group members participate in discussions on the implications of the information, the diagnosis of problems and the development of action plans to help overcome the problems identified.
- **T-groups (or sensitivity training)** involves small, unstructured, face-to-face groupings who meet without a planned agenda or set activities. Training is intended to concentrate on process rather than content: that is, on the feeling level of communication rather than the informational value of communication. With the guidance of the trainers, participants' patterns of behaviour become the focus of attention for the group. The objectives are usually to increase participants' sensitivity to the emotional reactions in themselves and others, their diagnostic ability, and their behavioural flexibility and effectiveness. (T-groups were discussed in Chapter 7.)
- **Team building** is the process of diagnosing task procedures and patterns of human interaction within a work group. The basic objective is to improve the overall performance of the organisation through improvements in the effectiveness of teams. Attention is focused on work procedures and interpersonal relationships, and especially the role of the leader in relation to other members of the group.
- **Grid training** is a development from the *Blake and Mouton* Managerial Grid approach (discussed in Chapter 13). An implied goal of grid training is that changes are aimed at attaining a 9,9 orientation (maximum concern for both production and people) on the Grid.[4]

An account of a joint UK/US investigation into team building as a mechanism of corporate change at Boots The Chemist is given in Appendix 1 to this chapter.

OD action-oriented

No two organisations are the same. Each organisation has its own types of problems and most appropriate remedies. OD is action-oriented and tailored to suit specific individual needs. It concerns itself with the examination of organisational health and the implementation of planned change. This may include training in interpersonal skills, sensitivity training, and methods and techniques relating to motivational processes, patterns of communication, styles of leadership and managerial behaviour.

Although an OD programme is legitimised by the formal system it focuses on both the formal and the informal system. The initial intervention strategy is usually through the informal system, which includes feelings, informal actions and interactions, group norms and values, and which forms part of the culture of an organisation.

Our concern in this book is not with the nature or value of OD programmes, *per se*, but with some of the major organisational processes that for convenience may be included under this heading.

ORGANISATIONAL CULTURE

Although most of us will understand in our own minds what is meant by organisational culture it is a general concept which is difficult to define or explain precisely. The concept of culture has developed from anthropology. Although people may not be aware consciously of culture it still has a pervasive influence over their behaviour and actions. There is, however, no consensus on its meaning or its applications to the analysis of work organisations.[5] The wide diversity of interpretations relating to OD gives rise to a large number of different definitions.[6] Also, there is sometimes confusion over the difference between the interpretation of organisational culture and organisational climate.

A popular and simple way of defining culture is: 'how things are done around here'. For example, *Atkinson* explains organisational culture as reflecting the underlying assumptions about the way work is performed; what is 'acceptable and not acceptable'; and what behaviour and actions are encouraged and discouraged.[7]

A more detailed definition is 'the collection of traditions, values, policies, beliefs, and attitudes that constitute a pervasive context for everything we do and think in an organisation'.[8] Culture is reinforced through the system of rites and rituals, patterns of communication, the informal organisation, expected patterns of behaviour and perceptions of the psychological contract.

Levels of culture

Schein suggests a view of organisational culture based on distinguishing three levels of culture: artifacts and creations; values and basic assumptions. [9]

- **Level 1: Artifacts**. The most visible level of the culture is artifacts and creations – the constructed physical and social environment. This includes physical space and layout, the technological output, written and spoken language and the overt behaviour of group members.
- **Level 2: Values**. Cultural learning reflects someone's original values. Solutions about how to deal with a new task, issue or problem are based on convictions of reality. If the solution works the value can transform into a belief. Values and beliefs become part of the conceptual process by which group members justify actions and behaviour.
- **Level 3: Basic underlying assumptions**. When a solution to a problem works repeatedly it comes to be taken for granted. Basic assumptions are unconsciously held learned responses. They are implicit assumptions that actually guide behaviour and determine how group members perceive, think and feel about things.

Schein suggests that the basic assumptions are treated as the essence – what culture really is; and values and behaviours are treated as observed manifestations of the culture essence.

TYPES OF ORGANISATIONAL CULTURE

There are a number of ways in which to classify different types of organisational culture. For example, developing the ideas of *Harrison*,[10] *Handy* describes four main types of organisational cultures: power culture; role culture; task culture; and person culture.[11]

- **Power culture** depends on a central power source with rays of influence from the central figure throughout the organisation. A power culture is frequently found in small entrepreneurial organisations and relies on trust, empathy and personal communications for its effectiveness. Control is exercised from the centre by the selection of key individuals. There are few rules and procedures, and little bureaucracy. It is a political organisation with decisions taken largely on the balance of influence.

- **Role culture** is often stereotyped as a bureaucracy and works by logic and rationality. Role culture rests on the strength of strong organisational 'pillars' – the functions of specialists in, for example, finance, purchasing and production. The work of, and interaction between, the pillars is controlled by procedures and rules, and co-ordinated by the pediment of a small band of senior managers. Role or job description is often more important than the individual and position power is the main source of power.

- **Task culture** is job-oriented or project-oriented. In terms of structure the task culture can be likened to a net, some strands of which are stronger than others, and with much of the power and influence at the interstices. An example is the matrix organisation. Task culture seeks to bring together the right resources and people, and utilises the unifying power of the group. Influence is widely spread and based more on expert power than on position or personal power.

- **Person culture** is where the individual is the central focus and any structure exists to serve the individuals within it. When a group of people decide that it is in their own interests to band together to do their own thing and share office space, equipment or clerical assistance then the resulting organisation would have a person culture. Examples are groups of barristers, architects, doctors or consultants. Although it is found in only a few organisations many individuals have a preference for person culture, for example university professors and specialists. Management hierarchies and control mechanisms are possible only by mutual consent. Individuals have almost complete autonomy and any influence over them is likely to be on the basis of personal power.

Four generic types of culture

From an examination of hundreds of business organisations and their environments, *Deal and Kennedy* categorise corporate cultures according to two determining factors in the marketplace:

- the degree of risk associated with the organisation's activities; and
- the speed at which organisations and their employees receive feedback on the success of decisions or strategies.

These factors give rise to four generic types of culture: the tough-guy, macho culture; the work-hard/play-hard culture; the bet-your-company culture; and the process culture.[12]

- **Tough-guy, macho culture** – an organisation of individualists who frequently take high risks and receive quick feedback on the right or wrong of their actions. Examples cited include police departments, surgeons, construction, cosmetics, management consulting and the entertainment industry. Financial stakes are high and there is a focus on speed. The intense pressure and frenetic pace often results in early 'burn-out'. Internal competition and conflict are normal, stars are temperamental but tolerated. A high staff turnover can create difficulties in building a strong cohesive culture.

- **Work-hard/play-hard culture** – characterised by fun and action where employees take few risks, all with quick feedback. There is a high level of relatively low-risk activity. Examples include sales organisations such as estate agents and computer companies, mass consumer companies such as McDonald's, office equipment manufacturers and retail stores. Organisations tend to be highly dynamic and the primary value centres on customers and their needs. It is the team who produce the volume, and the culture encourages games, meetings, promotions and conventions to help maintain motivation. However, although a lot gets done, volume can be at the expense of quality.
- **Bet-your-company culture** – where there are large-stake decisions with a high risk but slow feedback so that it may be years before employees know if decisions were successful. Examples include oil companies, investment banks, architectural firms, and the military. The focus is on the future and the importance of investing in it. There is a sense of deliberateness throughout the organisation typified by the ritual of the business meeting. There is a hierarchical system of authority with decision-making from the top down. The culture leads to high-quality inventions and scientific breakthroughs, but moves only very slowly and is vulnerable to short-term fluctuations.
- **Process culture** – a low-risk, slow-feedback culture where employees find difficulty in measuring what they do. Typical examples include banks, insurance companies, financial services, and the civil service. The individual financial stakes are low and employees get very little feedback on their effectiveness. Their memos and reports seem to disappear into a void. Lack of feedback forces employees to focus on how they do something, not what they do. People tend to develop a 'cover your back' mentality. Bureaucracy results with attention to trivial events, minor detail, formality and technical perfection. Process cultures can be effective when there is a need for order and predictability.

INFLUENCES ON THE DEVELOPMENT OF CULTURE

The culture and structure of an organisation develop over time and in response to a complex set of factors. We can, however, identify a number of key influences that are likely to play an important role in the development of any corporate culture. These include: history; primary function and technology; goals and objectives; size; location; management and staffing; and the environment.[13]

- **History** – the reason, and manner in which, the organisation was originally formed, its age, and the philosophy and values of its owners and first senior managers will affect culture. A key event in the organisation's history such as a merger or major reorganisation, or a new generation of top management, may bring about a change in culture. Corporate history can be an effective induction tool to assist a growth programme, and to help integrate acquisitions and new employees by infusion with the organisation's culture and identity.[14]
- **Primary function and technology** – the nature of the organisation's 'business' and its primary function have an important influence on its culture. This includes the range and quality of products and services provided, the importance of reputation and the type of customers. The primary function of the

organisation will determine the nature of the technological processes and methods of undertaking work, which in turn also affect structure and culture.

- **Goals and objectives** – although a business organisation may pursue profitability, this is not by itself very clear or a sufficient criterion for its effective management. For example, to what extent is emphasis placed on long-term survival or growth and development? How much attention is given to avoiding risks and uncertainties? Or how much concern is shown for broader social responsibilities? The organisation must give attention to objectives in all key areas of its operations. The combination of objectives and resultant strategies will influence culture, and may itself be influenced by changes in culture.

- **Size** – usually larger organisations have more formalised structures and cultures. Increased size is likely to result in separate departments and possibly split-site operations. This may cause difficulties in communication and inter-departmental rivalries with the need for effective co-ordination. A rapid expansion, or decline, in size and rate of growth, and resultant changes in staffing will influence structure and culture.

- **Location** – geographical location and the physical characteristics can have a major influence on culture: for example, whether an organisation is located in a quiet rural location or a busy city centre. This can influence the types of customers and the staff employed. It can also affect the nature of services provided, the sense of 'boundary' and distinctive identity, and opportunities for development.

- **Management and staffing** – top executives can have considerable influence on the nature of corporate culture. An example is the key role played by Lord Sieff when Chairman and Chief Executive of Marks & Spencer.[15] But all members of staff help to shape the dominant culture of an organisation, irrespective of what senior management feel it should be. Culture is also determined by the nature of staff employed and the extent to which they accept management philosophy and policies or pay only 'lip service'. Another important influence is the match between corporate culture and employees' perception of the psychological contract.

- **The environment** – in order to be effective the organisation must be responsive to external environmental influences. For example, if the organisation operates within a dynamic environment it requires a structure and culture that are sensitive and readily adaptable to change. An organic structure is more likely to respond effectively to new opportunities and challenges, and risks and limitations presented by the external environment.

THE IMPORTANCE OF CULTURE

Culture helps to account for variations among organisations and managers, both nationally and internationally. It helps to explain why different groups of people perceive things in their own way and perform things differently from other groups.[16] Culture can help reduce complexity and uncertainly. It provides a consistency in outlook and values, and makes possible the processes of decision-making, co-ordination and control.[17]

Culture is clearly an important ingredient of effective organisational performance. In their study of 62 American companies with outstandingly successful performance, *Peters and Waterman* draw attention to the importance of corporate culture.

Without exception, the dominance and coherence of culture proved to be an essential quality of the excellent companies. Moreover, the stronger the culture and the more it was directed to the marketplace, the less need was there for policy manuals, organization charts, or detailed procedures and rules. In these companies, people way down the line know what they are supposed to do in most situations because the handful of guiding values is crystal clear.[18]

Overt and covert culture

Egan refers to culture as the largest organisational control system which dictates how crazy or idiosyncratic people can be. Companies and institutions have both an overt and covert culture that influences both business and organisational behaviour.

The covert set can be quite dysfunctional and costly. Culture – the assumptions, beliefs, values and norms that drive 'the way we do things here' – is the largest and most controlling of the systems because it affects not only overt organisational behaviour but also the shadow-side behaviour... Culture lays down norms for the social system. In one institution you had to be an engineer to rise to the top. There was no published rule, of course, it was just the way things were. In one bank you could never be made an officer of the company if you wore polyester clothes. Culture tells us what kind of politics are allowed and just how members of an organisation are allowed to play the political game. [19]

Egan also distinguishes between the 'preferred culture' which serves the business and the 'culture-in-use'. This culture-behind-the-culture carries the real beliefs, values and norms that drive patterns of behaviour within the company. These remain unnamed, undiscussed and unmentionable and these covert cultures lie outside ordinary managerial control. The first step in changing such limiting behaviour features is to identify the preferred culture and to ensure that the company's way of operating effectively serves the business right now. [20]

Applications of organisational behaviour

At the heart of organisation development and improved performance is the need for effective management. It is the role of management to act as an integrating activity and to co-ordinate, guide and direct the efforts of members towards the achievement of goals and objectives. The process of management, however, does not take place in a vacuum but within the context of the organisational setting. Applications of organisational behaviour and the effective management of human resources are dependent therefore not only upon the nature of the industry or business, but also upon the characteristic features of the individual organisation – and its culture.

The pervasive nature of culture in terms of 'how things are done around here' and common values, beliefs and attitudes will therefore have a significant effect on organisational processes such as decision-making, design of structure, group behaviour, work organisation, motivation and job satisfaction, and management control.[21]

Brown suggests that organisational culture can be a powerful tool for improving performance and the key to effective leadership and organisational development. However, it is important that

Effective leadership and workable organization design and development programmes must be based on sensitivity to, and understanding of, culture. Excellent leaders are not merely aware of the organization's basic assumptions, they also know how to take action and mould and refine them. This process of cultural management appears to have been achieved through the skilful use of artifacts, stories, myths and symbolic actions to reinforce desired patterns of thought and behaviour.[22]

715

**Culture in
short-life
organisations**

The importance of culture raises interesting questions relating to its nature and influence in 'short-life' organisations – that is, organisations created to run for only a short period of time such as arts festivals or national garden festivals. [23] For example, how does culture develop when the organisation has little or no prior history, has short-term goals and objectives, and has only limited time for top management to exercise influence?

How do managers in such organisations attempt to inculcate culture? From a study of the Garden Festival Wales, *Meudell and Gadd* found that success in creating a culture occurred as a direct result of their recruitment and training initiatives. However, it is not only culture but climate that is important for organisational effectiveness. 'Rigorous training in customer care/corporate culture might produce an automatic "Have a nice day" but only the engendering of a suitable climate will encourage people to say it *and* mean it.'[24]

ORGANISATIONAL CLIMATE

Culture is a major factor in the appropriateness of management's methods of motivation. In addition to arrangements for the carrying out of organisational processes, management has a responsibility for creating a climate in which people are motivated to work willingly and effectively. Organisational climate is a general concept and difficult to define precisely. It is more something which is felt. It can be likened to our description of the weather and the way in which the climate of a geographical region results from the combination of environmental forces. Some of these forces are better understood than others.

Applied to organisations, climate can be said to relate to the prevailing atmosphere surrounding the organisation, to the level of morale, and to the strength of feelings or belonging, care and goodwill among members.

Climate will influence the attitudes which members of the organisation bring to bear on their work performance and personal relationships. The extent to which employees accept the culture of the organisation will have a significant effect on climate.

**The perception
of employees**

Whereas organisational culture describes what the organisation is about, organisational climate is an indication of the employees' feelings and beliefs of what the organisation is about. Climate is based on the **perceptions** of members towards the organisation.

> Organizational climate is a relatively enduring quality of the internal environment of an organization that (a) is experienced by its members, (b) influences their behavior, and (c) can be described in terms of the values of a particular set of characteristics (or attributes) of the organization.[25]

Climate also relates to the recognition of the organisation as a social system and the extent to which membership is perceived as a psychologically rewarding experience. It can be seen as the state of mutual trust and understanding among members of the organisation. For example, *Rentsch* suggests that 'one assumption of climate theory is that organizational members perceive and make sense of organizational policies, practices, and procedures in psychologically meaningful terms'.[26]

Characteristics of a healthy organisational climate

Organisational climate is characterised, therefore, by the nature of the people–organisation relationship and the superior–subordinate relationship. These relationships are determined by interactions among goals and objectives, formal structure, the process of management, styles of leadership and the behaviour of people.

Although similar types of organisations will share certain common features and norms, each organisation will have its own different and distinctive features. In general terms, however, a healthy organisational climate might be expected to exhibit such characteristic features as:

- the integration of organisational goals and personal goals;
- the most appropriate organisation structure based on the demands of the socio-technical system;
- democratic functioning of the organisation with full opportunities for participation;
- justice in treatment with equitable personnel and employee relations policies and practices;
- mutual trust, consideration and support among different levels of the organisation;
- the open discussion of conflict with an attempt to avoid confrontation;
- managerial behaviour and styles of leadership appropriate to the particular work situations;
- acceptance of the psychological contract between the individual and the organisation;
- recognition of people's needs and expectations at work, and individual differences and attributes;
- equitable systems of rewards based on positive recognition;
- concern for the quality of working life and job design;
- opportunities for personal development and career progression;
- a sense of identity with, and loyalty to, the organisation and a feeling of being a valued and important member.

If organisational climate is to be improved, then attention should be given to the above features. A healthy climate will not by itself guarantee improved organisational effectiveness. However, an organisation is most unlikely to attain optimum operational performance unless the climate evokes a spirit of support and co-operation throughout the organisation, and is conducive to motivating members to work willingly and effectively.

STAFF MORALE

Organisational climate will influence the level of morale and attitudes which members of the organisation bring to bear on their work performance and personal relationships. Morale, however, is another general concept which is difficult to measure objectively. A carefully designed and conducted attitude survey may help to establish the feelings of staff on factors contributing to organisational climate. When morale is low, and feelings of frustration or alienation are found to exist, it is important that positive action is taken to remedy the causes.

Morale has long been recognised as being of importance to the military. Critical incidents technique has been applied as a means of gauging morale levels.[27] To

simplify the mass of influences that must be taken into account in studying morale, *Gould* has suggested a summary model based on the three interrelated states of motivation, job satisfaction and group cohesiveness.[28] (*See* Fig. 20.2.)

Fig. 20.2
Model of morale

(Adapted from Gould, P. 'The Measurement of Morale', *Army Personnel Research Establishment Working Paper* 32/89 (1989).)

Key ingredients of morale

Morale can be viewed in terms of the mental attitudes which people have towards their tasks and responsibilities. *Petrick and Manning* suggest that before managers can start to improve morale they should review four main areas in which to develop the best possible attitudes in their staff.

- **A sense of importance in their job** – staff should have a feeling of meaning in the job, challenging and reasonably demanding assignments, and a sense of job accomplishment based on competent performance.
- **Teamwork among the staff** – there should be a sense of group pride and self-esteem, a high level of human interactions and good relations with co-workers, team effort and the support of other staff including supervisors and top management.
- **Management care about staff welfare** – staff should receive just rewards for their contribution and fair treatment for their efforts. There should be a clear statement of management goals and efforts to resolve genuine goal incongruence. Management should show concern for staff welfare, and attempt to create a feeling of mutual trust and respect with staff.
- **Economic rewards fair and individualised** – attention should be given to payment of sufficient wages and the fair distribution of wages. If fringe benefits are added management should attempt to meet individual needs and preferences. There should be opportunities for job advancement including promotion and cross-job postings.[29]

EMPLOYEE COMMITMENT

Among the factors which contribute to a healthy organisational climate, high morale and motivation, is the extent to which members of staff have a sense of commitment to the organisation. The extent of their commitment will have a major influence on the level of work performance.

The concept of commitment itself, and the manner in which it is actually created, is not easy to describe. There does, however, appear to be a growing acceptance of the notion of attachment and loyalty. Commitment may be defined in terms of the relative strength of the employee's identification with, and involvement in, a particular organisation.[30]

O'Reilly explains organisational commitment as 'typically conceived of as an individual's psychological bond to the organization, including a sense of job involvement, loyalty, and a belief in the values of the organization'.[31]

O'Reilly suggests three processes or stages of commitment:

* **compliance**, where a person accepts the influence of others mainly to obtain something from others, such as pay; this is followed by
* **identification**, in which the individual accepts influence in order to maintain a satisfying relationship and to feel pride in belonging to the organisation; which leads to
* **internalisation**, in which the individual finds the values of the organisation to be intrinsically rewarding and compatible with personal values.

A three-pillar model of commitment

Martin and Nicholls view commitment as encapsulating 'giving all of yourself while at work'. This entails such things as using time constructively, attention to detail, making that extra effort, accepting change, co-operation with others, self-development, respecting trust, pride in abilities, seeking improvements and giving loyal support.[32]

Based on case studies of 14 British companies, including Jaguar, Royal Bank of Scotland, British Steel, Pilkingtons, Rothmans, Raleigh, Schweppes and Burton, Martin and Nicholls present a 'model of commitment' based on three major pillars, each with three factors. (*See* Fig. 20.3.)

(i) **A sense of belonging to the organisation**
 This builds upon the loyalty essential to successful industrial relations. The sense of belonging is created by managers through ensuring that the workforce is:

 * informed
 * involved
 * sharing in success

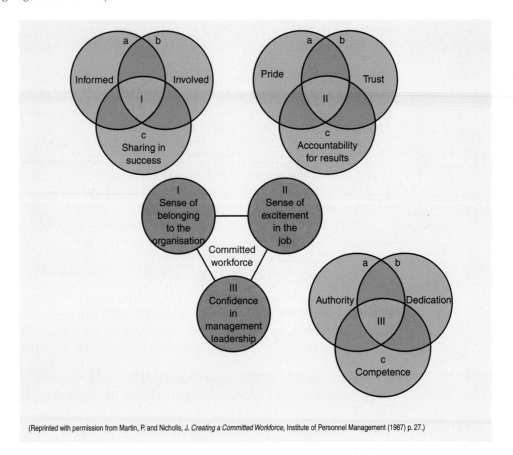

Fig. 20.3
The three-pillar model of commitment

(Reprinted with permission from Martin, P. and Nicholls, J. *Creating a Committed Workforce*, Institute of Personnel Management (1987) p. 27.)

(ii) **A sense of excitement in the job**
Improved results will not be achieved unless workers can also feel a sense of excitement about their work which results in the motivation to perform well. This sense of excitement can be achieved by appealing to the higher-level needs of:

- pride
- trust
- accountability for results

(iii) **Confidence in management**
The senses of belonging and excitement can be frustrated if workers do not have respect for, and confidence in, management leadership. This respect is enhanced through attention to:

- authority
- dedication
- competence

A large measure of the success of the companies studied derives from their management of people and from creating a climate for commitment. For example: 'If people feel trusted, they will make extraordinary efforts to show the trust to be warranted.' However, creating commitment is hard. It takes time, the path is not always smooth and it requires dedicated managers.

Comparison with United States experience

Martin and Nicholls suggest that the three pillars of their model apply equally well to the United States experience. The experience in creating commitment in Britain is paralleled closely by the experience in America with the quality of working life and employee involvement. A sense of belonging and being valued has been encouraged through collaborative agreements with unions, consultation and innovative reward systems. A sense of excitement in the job has been encouraged through semi-autonomous team working, participatory problem-solving and work restructuring.

Although it is difficult to draw cross-cultural comparisons of confidence in management, authority, dedication and competence appear to be as important in the USA as in Britain. According to Martin and Nicholls: 'The three-pillar model puts commitment into perspective. It shows how a wide variety of initiatives taken by management fit into a coherent picture, all pulling in the same direction and mutually reinforcing.'

Employee commitment makes a difference

Drennan suggests that most managers believe that with real commitment from staff the performance of their businesses could improve dramatically. Employee commitment does make a real difference. Not only does the performance of the organisation improve but it also becomes a better place to work.[33] Drennan proposes a number of definite steps that can be taken to improve employee commitment.

- Employees need to be clear about the direction in which the organisation is going. Goals should be made clear and simple, and translated into common action at every level of the organisation. Employees should understand the goals and be able to do something about them every day.
- It is vitally important that management also demonstrate full commitment to carrying through its own stated goals. Emphasis should be placed on teamwork and the involvement of all staff.
- Management must be prepared to spend time and effort on training and retraining (for example, as a result of new technology) for all employees including those doing the lowliest jobs.
- Managers and supervisors should clearly, visibly and constantly communicate information at every level on progress and actual performance against stated targets.
- Employees should be given a financial interest in the success of the company, for example, through share ownership. Companies with profit-sharing arrangements perform better and show positive changes in employee attitudes.

BEHAVIOURS WHICH DENOTE COMMITMENT

In a paper issued by ACAS, *White* draws attention to the effects of takeovers and mergers on employee commitment. Massive changes in the scale of some industrial and commercial concerns affect not only the ownership and organisation, but also the loyalty and attachment of people who work for them.[34] However, White suggests that employee commitment must have limits. If not, there is a danger of fanatical zeal or unquestioning compliance and it is rarely in the interests of an organisation to confine recruitment to people who appear willing to become committed to such an extent.

In contrast to 'involvement', White suggests three kinds of feelings or behaviours which denote 'commitment' to the organisation in which a person works:

- belief in, and acceptance of, the organisation itself and/or its goals and values;
- willingness to exert effort on behalf of the organisation above the contract of employment;
- desire to remain with the organisation.

Commitment is also always both **voluntary** and **personal**. It cannot be imposed, it cannot be initiated by others, and it can be withdrawn.

Commitment is reciprocated by the organisation

From a review of ways in which organisational policies can influence commitment, White concludes that a high level of employee commitment implies willingness to work for the organisation's benefit: but that its continuation depends on the reciprocal commitment by the organisation to its members.

> In the current industrial climate, there needs to be concern not only for producing goods or services, but also for the encouragement of innovative, exploratory and creative ideas that go beyond what can be prescribed for the job, and for the application to work of intuitive as well as explicit knowledge. These multiple objectives can only be achieved if managers consider with care exactly what kinds of commitment they are aiming for, and design policies and practices accordingly.[35]

THE MANAGEMENT OF ORGANISATIONAL CLIMATE

If organisational climate is to be improved, then attention should be given to the level of morale, the sense of involvement and strength of commitment of members. The climate created by managers will have a significant influence on the motivation and behaviour of employees.

The management of organisational climate is therefore an important means of improving productivity and standards of work performance. Similar types of organisations may share certain common features but each will have its own distinctive characteristics. Every organisation has its own climate, or internal environment or 'personality'.

ORGANISATIONAL CONFLICT

It might be expected that a healthy organisational climate would be reflected by complete harmony in working relationships, and loyalty and common commitment to the goals and objectives of the organisation. This view of work organisations as 'happy families' is perhaps a worthwhile and creditable ideal and as such appears to be implied by a number of management writers.

For example, *Drucker* makes the following point:

> Any business enterprise must build a true team and weld individual efforts into a common effort. Each member of the enterprise contributes something different, but they must all contribute towards a common goal. Their efforts must all pull in

the same direction, and their contributions must fit together to produce a whole – without gaps, without friction, without unnecessary duplication of effort . . . The manager must know and understand what the business goals demand of him in terms of performance, and his superior must know what contribution to demand and expect of him – and must judge him accordingly. If these requirements are not met, managers are misdirected. Their efforts are wasted. Instead of teamwork, there is friction, frustration and conflict.[36]

Such views appear to imply **a unitary perspective** of the organisation, as discussed in Chapter 18. The organisation is viewed as an integrated and harmonious whole. Conflict can be explained, for example, by poor communications, personality clashes or the work of agitators. But, if one accepts the views of, for example, the social action writers and the idea of **a pluralistic approach** to work organisations, then conflict among competing sub-groups will be seen as inevitable. Conflict is seen as an inherent feature of organisations and induced, in part, by the very structure of the organisation.

The radical perspective

The radical perspective is associated with the ideas of writers such as *Karl Marx* and the structuralist approach to organisations and management discussed in Chapter 2. It challenges the traditional view of conflict and sees organisations in terms of the disparity in power and control. Conflict is a feature of the unequal nature of organisational life and a means of bringing about change.[37] Collective bargaining is not seen as particularly helpful in a system stacked against the workers. Conflict is a natural part of the class struggle. The design of organisation structure, management systems and the choice of technology all form part of the struggle for power and control within the work organisation.

THE MEANING OF CONFLICT

Conflict, then, can be regarded as a reality of management and organisational behaviour. Most of us will understand what is commonly meant by organisational conflict and be aware of its existence and effects. Yet conflict is another term which can be defined and interpreted in a number of ways. For our purpose we can see conflict as **behaviour intended to obstruct the achievement of some other person's goals**. Conflict is based on the incompatibility of goals and arises from opposing behaviours. It can be viewed at the individual, group or organisation level.

Conflict and competition

The terms conflict and competition are often used synonymously. Conflict and competition do have common aspects. Both involve at least some degree of opposing behaviour and the belief that one party is attempting to deprive others of something which they value. But conflict can be seen to differ from competition.

- **Conflict situations** denote both incompatible goals *and* opposing behaviour.
- **Competition** may still arise when there is a greater commonality of goals and may involve only limited opposing behaviour, or even some co-operative behaviour. In competition, individuals or groups do not obstruct or interfere with each other in attempting to satisfy their goals.

An example of a conflict situation could be where two managers are in contest with each other to avoid compulsory redundancy. An example of competition could be members of staff vying for promotion. The unsuccessful members will not

lose their present level of pay, status or responsibilities; and they still have other options open, including the opportunity for promotion into some other position.

In **conflict situations** one or both of the parties may be drawn or forced into the confrontation. The situation may arise spontaneously with no ground rules and little knowledge of how far the situation could escalate. The outcomes are potentially dysfunctional for at least one of the parties.

In **competition** the parties are usually willing participants. Competition implies that certain ground rules apply and that there has been some prior planning by a higher authority.[38] Competition might, initially at least, be comparatively friendly. But if the situation develops into one of greater antagonism, and behaviour intended to obstruct the other person, then a conflict situation could develop.

CONTRASTING VIEWS OF CONFLICT

Common definitions of conflict tend to be associated with negative features and situations which give rise to inefficiency, ineffectiveness or dysfunctional consequences. The traditional view of conflict is that it is bad for organisations. Conflict is perceived as disruptive and unnatural, and represents a form of deviant behaviour which should be controlled and changed. Clearly, extreme cases of conflict in organisations can have very upsetting, or even tragic, consequences for some people and have adverse effects on organisational performance. Conflict situations can give rise to excessive emotional or physical stress.

Positive and negative outcomes

Conflict is not necessarily a bad thing, however. Properly managed, it can have potentially positive outcomes. It can be an energising and vitalising force in groups and in the organisation. Conflict can be seen as a 'constructive' force and in certain circumstances it can be welcomed or even encouraged. For example, it can be seen as an aid to incremental improvement in organisation design and functioning, and to the decision-making process. Conflict can be an agent for evolution, and for internal and external change. Properly identified and handled, it can help to minimise the destructive influences of the win–lose situation.

From a survey of practising managers, who reported that they spend approximately 20 per cent of their time dealing with conflict situations, *Schmidt* records a number of both positive and negative outcomes of conflict.[39]

Positive outcomes include:

- better ideas produced;
- people forced to search for new approaches;
- long-standing problems brought to the surface and resolved;
- clarification of individual views;
- stimulation of interest and creativity;
- a chance for people to test their capacities.

Negative outcomes include:

- some people felt defeated and demeaned;
- the distance between people increased;
- a climate of mistrust and suspicion developed;

- individuals and groups concentrated on their own narrow interests;
- resistance developed rather than teamwork;
- an increase in employee turnover.

Broad interpretation of conflict

The current view appears to recognise that conflict can be interpreted more broadly than in the traditional view. For example, *Townsend* sees conflict as a sign of a healthy organisation – up to a point.

> A good manager doesn't try to eliminate conflict; he tries to keep it from wasting the energies of his people . . . If you're the boss and your people fight you openly when they think you're wrong – that's healthy. If your people fight each other openly in your presence for what they believe in – that's healthy. But keep all the conflict eyeball to eyeball.[40]

Conflict, *per se*, is not necessarily good or bad but an inevitable feature of organisational life. Even if organisations have taken great care to try and avoid conflict it will still occur. Conflict will continue to emerge despite attempts by management to suppress it.

THE SOURCES OF CONFLICT

Much has been written about the implications of conflict as a social process. Whilst recognising the importance of this debate, it is not the intention here to enter into a detailed discussion of the ideologies of conflict. The important point is not so much whether competing sub-groups and conflict are seen as inevitable consequences of organisation structure, but how conflict, when found to exist, is handled and managed.

There are many potential sources of organisational conflict including the main ones summarised below.

- **Differences in perception**. We all see things in different ways. We all have our own, unique picture or image of how we see the 'real' world. Differences in perception result in different people attaching different meanings to the same stimuli. As perceptions become a person's reality, value judgements can be a potential major source of conflict. (The importance of perception was discussed in Chapter 5.)
- **Limited resources**. Most organisational resources are limited, and individuals and groups have to fight for their share; for example, at the time of the allocation of the next year's budget or when cutbacks have to be made. The greater the limitation of resources, then usually the greater the potential for conflict. In an organisation with reducing profits or revenues the potential for conflict is likely to be intensified.
- **Departmentalisation and specialisation**. Most work organisations are divided into separate departments with specialised functions. Because of familiarity with the manner in which they undertake their activities, departments tend to turn inwards and to concentrate on the achievement of their own particular goals. When departments need to co-operate with each other this is a frequent source of conflict.

Differing goals and internal environments of departments are also a potential source of conflict. For example, a research and development department is more likely to be concerned with the long-run view and, confronted with pressures for new ideas and production innovation, the department is likely to operate in a dynamic environment and with an organic structure. A production department, however, is concerned more with short-term problems such as quality control and meeting delivery dates. The department tends to operate in a more stable environment and with a bureaucratic structure.

- **The nature of work activities.** Where the task of one person is dependent upon the work of others there is potential for conflict; for example, if a worker is expected to complete the assembly of a given number of components in a week but the person forwarding the part-assembled components does not supply a sufficient number on time. If reward and punishment systems are perceived to be based on keeping up with performance levels, then the potential for conflict is even greater.

 If the work of a department is dependent upon the output of another department a similar situation could arise, especially if this situation is coupled with limited resources; for example, where the activities of a department, whose budget has been reduced below what is believed necessary to run the department efficiently, are interdependent with those of another department, who appear to have received a more generous budget allocation.

- **Role conflict.** A role is the expected pattern of behaviours associated with members occupying a particular position within the structure of the organisation. In practice, the manner in which people actually behave may not be consistent with their expected pattern of behaviour. Problems of role incompatibility and role ambiguity arise from inadequate or inappropriate role definition and can be a significant source of conflict. (Role conflict was discussed in Chapter 6.)

- **Inequitable treatment.** A person's perception of unjust treatment, such as in the operation of personnel policies and practices, or in reward and punishment systems, can lead to tension and conflict. For example, according to the equity theory of motivation (discussed in Chapter 14) the perception of inequity will motivate a person to take action to restore equity, including changes to inputs or outputs, or through acting on others.

- **Violation of territory.** People tend to become attached to their own 'territory' within work organisations; for example, to their own area of work, or kinds of clients to be dealt with; or to their own room, chair or parking space. Jealousy may arise over other people's territory; for example, size of room, company car, allocation of a secretary or other perks; through access to information; or through membership of groups. A stranger walking into a place of work can create an immediate feeling of suspicion or even resentment because people do not usually like 'their' territory entered by someone they do not know, and whose motives are probably unclear to them.[41]

 Ownership of territory may be **conferred formally**, for example by organisation charts, job descriptions or management decisions. It may be **established through procedures**, for example circulation lists or membership of committees. Or it may **arise informally**, for example through group norms, tradition or perceived status symbols. The place where people choose to meet can have a possible, significant symbolic value. For example, if a subordinate is summoned to a meeting in a manager's office this might be taken that the manager is sig-

nalling higher status. If the manager chooses to meet at the subordinate's place of work, or on neutral territory, this may be a signal that the manager wishes to meet the subordinate as an equal.

If a person's territory is violated this can lead to the possibility of retaliation and conflict. For example, in *Woodward*'s study of management organisation of firms in this country (discussed in Chapter 10) she comments on the bad relationships between accountants and other managers. One reason for this hostility was the bringing together of two quite separate financial functions.

> People concerned with works accounting tended to assume responsibility for end results that was not properly theirs; they saw their role as a controlling and sanctioning one rather than as a servicing and supportive one. Line managers resented this attitude and retaliated by becoming aggressive and obstructive.[42]

- **Environmental change**. Changes in an organisation's external environment, such as shifts in demand, increased competition, government intervention, new technology or changing social values, can cause major areas of conflict. For example, a fall in demand for, or government financial restrictions on, enrolments for a certain discipline in higher education can result in conflict for the allocation of resources. If the department concerned is a large and important one, and led by a powerful head, then there could be even greater potential for conflict.

Other potential sources of conflict

There are many other potential sources of organisational conflict, including:

- **individual** – such as attitudes, personality characteristics or particular personal needs, illness or stress;
- **group** – such as group skills, the informal organisation and group norms;
- **organisation** – such as communications, authority structure, leadership style, managerial behaviour.

The possible sources of conflict have been summarised by *Bryans and Cronin* as:

1. Differences between corporate and individual goals.
2. Conflicts between different departments or groups within the organization.
3. Conflict between the formal and informal organization.
4. Conflict between manager and managed.
5. Conflict between individual and job.
6. Conflict between individuals.[43]

STRATEGIES FOR MANAGING CONFLICT

Although a certain amount of organisational conflict may be seen as inevitable, there are a number of ways in which management can attempt to avoid the harmful effects of conflict. Many of these ways have been discussed in previous chapters. The strategies adopted will vary according to the nature and sources of conflict outlined above.

- **Clarification of goals and objectives**. The clarification and continual refinement of goals and objectives, role definitions and performance standards will help to avoid misunderstandings and conflict. Focusing attention on superordi-

nate goals, that are shared by the parties in conflict, may help to defuse hostility and lead to more co-operative behaviour.

- **Resource distribution**. Although it may not always be possible for managers to increase their allocated share of resources, they may be able to use imagination and initiative to help overcome conflict situations; for example, making a special case to higher management; flexibility in virement headings of the budget; delaying staff appointments in one area to provide more money for another area.

- **Personnel policies and procedures**. Careful and detailed attention to just and equitable personnel policies and procedures may help to reduce areas of conflict. Examples are: job analysis, recruitment and selection, job evaluation; systems of reward and punishment; appeals, grievance and disciplinary procedures; arbitration and mediation; recognition of trade unions and their officials.

- **Non-monetary rewards**. Where financial resources are limited, it may be possible to pay greater attention to non-monetary rewards. Examples are job design; more interesting, challenging or responsible work; increased delegation or empowerment; flexible working hours; attendance at courses or conferences; unofficial perks or more relaxed working conditions.

- **Development of interpersonal/group process skills**. This may help to encourage a better understanding of one's own behaviour, the other person's point of view, communication processes and problem-solving. It may also encourage people to work through conflict situations in a constructive manner.

- **Group activities**. Attention to the composition of groups and to factors which affect group cohesiveness may reduce dysfunctional conflict. Overlapping group membership with a 'linking-pin' process, and the careful selection of project teams or task forces for problems affecting more than one group, may also be beneficial.

- **Leadership and management**. A more participative and supportive style of leadership and managerial behaviour is likely to assist in conflict management; for example, showing an attitude of respect and trust; encouraging personal self-development; creating a work environment in which staff can work co-operatively together. A participative approach to leadership and management may also help to create greater employee commitment.

- **Organisational processes**. Conflict situations may be reduced by attention to such features as: the nature of the authority structure; work organisation; patterns of communication and sharing of information; democratic functioning of the organisation; unnecessary adherence to bureaucratic procedures, and official rules and regulations.

- **Socio-technical approach**. Viewing the organisation as a socio-technical system, in which psychological and social factors are developed in keeping with structural and technical requirements, will help in reducing dysfunctional conflict.

ORGANISATIONAL CHANGE

An organisation can only perform effectively through interactions with the broader external environment of which it is part. The structure and functioning of the organisation must reflect, therefore, the nature of the environment in which it is operating. Factors such as uncertain economic conditions, fierce world competition, the level of government intervention, scarcity of natural resources and rapid

developments in new technology create an increasingly volatile environment. In order to help ensure its survival and future success the organisation must be readily adaptable to the external demands placed upon it. The organisation must be responsive to change.

Change also originates within the organisation itself. Much of this change is part of a natural process of ageing; for example, as material resources such as buildings, equipment or machinery deteriorate or lose efficiency; or as human resources get older, or as skills and abilities become outdated. Some of this change can be managed through careful planning; for example, regular repairs and maintenance; choice of introducing new technology or methods of work; effective human resource planning to prevent a large number of staff retiring at the same time; management succession planning; training and staff development.

But the main pressure of change is from external forces. The organisation must be properly prepared to face the demands of a changing environment. It must give attention to its future development and success.

The nature of change

Change is a pervasive influence. We are all subject to continual change of one form or another. **Change is an inescapable part of both social and organisational life.** The effects of change can be studied over different time scales, from weeks to hundreds of years, and they can be studied at different levels. Change can be studied in terms of its effects at the individual, group, organisation, society, national or international level. However, because of its pervasive nature, change at any one level is interrelated with changes at other levels, and it is difficult to study one area of change in isolation. But our main focus of attention is on the management of organisational change.

Organisational change can be initiated deliberately by managers, it can evolve slowly within a department, it can be imposed by specific changes in policy or procedures, or it can arise through external pressures. Change can affect all aspects of the operation and functioning of the organisation.

Planned organisational change

Most planned organisational change is triggered by the need to respond to new challenges or opportunities presented by the external environment, or in anticipation of the need to cope with potential future problems; for example, intended government legislation, a new product development by a major competitor or further technological advances. Planned change represents an intentional attempt to improve, in some important way, the operational effectiveness of the organisation.

The basic underlying objectives can be seen in general terms as:

- modifying the behavioural patterns of members of the organisation; and
- improving the ability of the organisation to cope with changes in its environment.

Behaviour modification

A programme of planned change and improved performance developed by *Lewin* involves the management of a three-phase process of behaviour modification:

- **unfreezing** – reducing those forces which maintain behaviour in its present form, recognition of the need for change and improvement to occur;
- **movement** – development of new attitudes or behaviour and the implementation of the change;
- **refreezing** – stabilising change at the new level and reinforcement through supporting mechanisms, for example policies, structure or norms.[44]

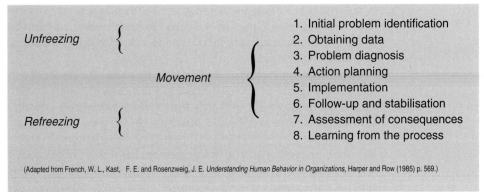

**Fig. 20.4
Stages in a planned-change effort**

(Adapted from French, W. L., Kast, F. E. and Rosenzweig, J. E. *Understanding Human Behavior in Organizations*, Harper and Row (1985) p. 569.)

French, Kast and Rosenzweig list eight specific components of a planned-change effort related to the above process.[45] (*See* Fig. 20.4.)

A systems approach to organisational change

One strategy of change is through the adoption of a systems approach. The organisation can be viewed as a system and analysed in terms of its major interrelated variables (sub-systems). The variables can be identified in a number of ways including: task, technology, structure, people and management. (The organisation as a system and the identification of sub-systems were discussed in Chapter 3).

In practice, change in any one variable is likely to involve changes in the other variables. The implementation of change can be approached, therefore, in terms of a choice of strategies relating to modifications of the task, the technology, the structure, the people or the management. Applying a systems approach involves managers understanding the interrelationships among all major variables (sub-system) of the organisation.

Overlooking the systems nature of organisations can result in the failure of even well-conceived change programmes.

No unit is an island, and changes planned for one part of an organisation invariably have knock-on effects on the other parts. It is crucial in planning any changes to be aware of the likely impact of those changes on other parts of the organisation. If a change has an unanticipated effect on a unit, a considerable amount of resistance to the change will develop. It is better to consider the effects of any changes with all the units concerned and to plan the changes in consultation with them to minimise the adverse effects.[46]

THE FORCES OF CHANGE

There are a wide range of forces acting upon organisations and which make the need for change inevitable. These forces of change can be summarised under five broad headings: changing technology; knowledge explosion; rapid product obsolescence; changing nature of the workforce; and quality of working life.[47]

- **Changing technology.** The rate of technological change is greater now than at any time in the past; for example, advances in information technology, automation and robotics.

- **Knowledge explosion**. The amount of knowledge is increasing continually; for example, the number of people in some form of education, the number of scientific journals and new books. With this knowledge explosion, knowledge in a particular field quickly becomes outdated or obsolete.
- **Rapid product obsolescence**. Changes in consumer preferences, together with rapidly changing technology, have shortened the life-cycle of many products and services. Many products and services available today did not exist a few years ago and many do not remain available for long.
- **Changing nature of the workforce**. This includes changes in the composition of the working population, broader educational opportunities, part-time working, changes in family lifestyles, and equal opportunities.
- **Quality of working life**. Increased importance attached to the quality of working life has drawn attention to the satisfaction of people's needs and expectations at work; and to such factors as frustration and alienation, job design and work organisation, and styles of managerial behaviour. It has also drawn attention to relationships between the quality of working life and employee commitment, levels of work performance and productivity.

Changes in organisations and management

Organisations must be responsive to the external environment of which they are part. And changing organisations will affect the nature of managerial work. *Stewart*, for example, describes how changes in organisations affect the kinds of jobs that managers have to do and the nature of their lives and careers.[48]

- **The changing nature of business** – the growth of service industries and the decline of manufacturing industries; more frequent changes in ownership through acquisition by another company including more foreign-controlled companies; public sector organisations affected by privatisation; the increasing globalisation of international companies.
- **Changes in the composition of the workforce** – a higher proportion of staff employed for their knowledge rather than their brawn or skill; a declining number of school-leavers and an increasing number of older workers; the employment of more women; an increasing number of part-time members of staff including better opportunities for women to return to work.
- **Changes within organisations** – many organisations becoming smaller, although some are larger because of acquisitions; greater flexibility in the use of labour including distance working; changing relationships with staff including those engaged as sub-contractors, self-employed or agency temporaries; greater entrepreneurial activity in looking for new products and business opportunities.

As a result of these changes, Stewart suggests that older managers now work for very different kinds of organisations from those in which they first became managers. Although hierarchies of authority will continue to exist in large organisations they will be shorter and there will be wider networking. There will be a smaller number of middle managers but with more responsible roles. Managers' jobs are more complex and demanding, and managers' careers are much less predictable. But managers now have a greater choice in their work and careers.

RESISTANCE TO CHANGE

Despite the potential positive outcomes, change is often resisted at both the individual and the organisational level. Resistance to change – or the thought of the implications of the change – appears to be a common phenomenon. People are naturally wary of change. 'Among many there is an uneasy mood – a suspicion that change is out of control.'[49]

Resistance to change can take many forms and it is often difficult to pinpoint the exact reasons for the resistance. The forces against change in work organisations include: ignoring the needs and expectations of members; when members have insufficient information about the nature of the change; or if they do not perceive the need for change. Fears may be expressed over such matters as employment levels and job security, de-skilling of work, loss of job satisfaction, wage rate differentials, changes to social structures and working conditions, loss of individual control over work, and greater management control.

Individual resistance

Some common reasons for individual resistance to change within organisations include the following:

- **Selective perception**. People's own interpretation of stimuli presents a unique picture or image of the 'real' world and can result in selective perception. This can lead to a biased view of a particular situation, which fits most comfortably into a person's own perception of reality, and can cause resistance to change. For example, trade unionists may have a stereotyped view of management as untrustworthy and therefore oppose any management change however well founded might have been the intention. Managers exposed to different theories or ideas may tend to categorise these as either: those they already practise and have no need to worry about or those that are of no practical value and which can be discarded as of no concern to them.
- **Habit.** People tend to respond to situations in an established and accustomed manner. Habits may serve as a means of comfort and security, and as a guide for easy decision-making. Proposed changes to habits, especially if the habits are well established and require little effort, may well be resisted. However, if there is a clearly perceived advantage, for example a reduction in working hours without loss of pay, there is likely to be less, if any, resistance to the change, although some people may, because of habit, still find it difficult to adjust to the new times.
- **Inconvenience or loss of freedom.** If the change is seen as likely to prove inconvenient, make life more difficult, reduce freedom of action or result in increased control, there will be resistance.
- **Economic implications**. People are likely to resist change which is perceived as reducing either directly or indirectly their pay or other rewards, requiring an increase in work for the same level of pay or acting as a threat to their job security. People tend to have established patterns of working and a vested interest in maintaining the status quo.

- **Security in the past**. There is a tendency for some people to find a sense of security in the past. In times of frustration or difficulty, or when faced with new or unfamiliar ideas or methods, people may reflect on the past. There is a wish to retain old and comfortable ways. For example, in bureaucratic organisations, officials often tend to place faith in well-established ('tried and trusted') procedures and cling to these as giving a feeling of security.
- **Fear of the unknown**. Changes which confront people with the unknown tend to cause anxiety or fear. Many major changes in a work organisation present a degree of uncertainty; for example, the introduction of new technology or methods of working. A person may resist promotion because of uncertainty over changes in responsibilities or the increased social demands of the higher position.

Organisational resistance

Although organisations have to adapt to their environment, they tend to feel comfortable operating within the structure, policies and procedures which have been formulated to deal with a range of present situations. To ensure operational effectiveness, organisations often set up defences against change and prefer to concentrate on the routine things they perform well. Some of the main reasons for organisational resistance against change are as follows:

- **Maintaining stability**. Organisations, especially large-scale ones, pay much attention to maintaining stability and predictability. The need for formal organisation structure and the division of work, narrow definitions of assigned duties and responsibilities, established rules, procedures and methods of work, can result in resistance to change.
- **Investment in resources**. Change often requires large resources which may already be committed to investments in other areas or strategies. Assets such as buildings, technology, equipment and people cannot easily be altered. For example, a car manufacturer may not find it easy to change to a socio-technical approach and the use of autonomous work groups because it cannot afford the cost of a new purpose-built plant and specialised equipment.
- **Past contracts or agreements**. Organisations enter into contracts or agreements with other parties, such as the government, other organisations, trade unions, suppliers and customers. These contracts and agreements can limit changes in behaviour; for example, organisations operating under a special licence or permit, or a fixed-price contract to supply goods/services to a government agency. Another example might be an agreement with trade unions which limits the opportunity to introduce compulsory redundancies, or the introduction of certain new technology or working practices.
- **Threats to power or influence**. Change may be seen as a threat to the power or influence of certain groups within the organisation, such as their control over decisions, resources or information. For example, managers may resist the introduction of quality circles or worker-directors because they see this as increasing the role and influence of non-managerial staff, and a threat to the power in their own positions. Where a group of people have, over a period of time, established what they perceive as their 'territorial rights', they are likely to resist change.

THE MANAGEMENT OF ORGANISATIONAL CHANGE

As we have seen, people tend to be resistant to change. It is important, therefore, for management to adopt a clearly defined strategy for the initiation of change.[50] The successful management of change is an increasingly important managerial responsibility. New ideas and innovations should not be perceived as threats by members of the organisation. The efforts made by management to maintain the balance of the socio-technical system will influence people's attitudes, the behaviour of individuals and groups, and thereby the level of organisational performance and effectiveness.

Understanding of human behaviour

The effective management of change must be based on a clear understanding of human behaviour at work. Most people are not detached from their work but experience a range of emotional involvements through their membership of the organisation. People may also be concerned about the effects of change including the possible loss of financial needs, security, status or self-esteem. Organisational change can result in a feeling of a lack of identity, a lack of involvement, a lack of direction and a lack of affection.[51]

Most people feel threatened and disoriented by the challenge of change. Emotions such as uncertainty, frustration or fear are common reactions. It is understandable therefore that people often adopt a defensive and negative attitude, and demonstrate resistance to change.

Elliott explains change as a complex, psychological event. The power of change needs to be respected and managed. Managing change places emphasis on employee (and customer) needs as the highest priority. To be successful, organisations need a dedicated workforce and this involves the effective management of change. But not everyone reacts to change in the same way. Change impacts each person differently and management must accept the individual nature of change.

For example, senior managers responsible for initiating a restructuring may be filled with great expectations. They do not see the sense of resistance and find it hard to accept the negative impact of change. But the change may mean inconvenience, uncertainty and loss for other people. Loss and grief are just as normal reactions to change as are excitement and anticipation.[52]

Style of managerial behaviour

One of the most important factors in the successful implementation of organisational change is the style of managerial behaviour. In certain situations, and with certain members of staff, it may be necessary for management to make use of hierarchical authority and to attempt to impose change through a coercive, autocratic style of behaviour. Some members may actually prefer, and respond better, to a directed and controlled style of management. (Recall, for example, the discussion on Theory X and Theory Y styles of managerial behaviour in Chapter 13.)

In most cases, however, the introduction of change is more likely to be effective with a participative style of managerial behaviour. If staff are kept fully informed of proposals, are encouraged to adopt a positive attitude and have personal involvement in the implementation of the change, there is a greater likelihood of their acceptance of the change.

With the participative change cycle, a significant advantage is that once the change is accepted it tends to be long lasting. Since everyone has been involved in the development of the change, each person tends to be more highly committed

to its implementation. The disadvantage of participative change is that it tends to be slow and evolutionary – it may take years to implement a significant change. An advantage of directive change, on the other hand, is speed. Using position power, leaders can often impose change immediately. A disadvantage of this change strategy is that it tends to be volatile. It can be maintained only as long as the leader has position power to make it stick. It often results in animosity, hostility, and, in some cases, overt and covert behavior to undermine and overthrow.[53]

An example of a mind map giving a summary outline of 'introducing change' is presented in Fig. 20.5.[54]

HUMAN AND SOCIAL FACTORS OF CHANGE

Activities managed on the basis of technical efficiency alone are unlikely to lead to optimum improvement in organisational performance. A major source of resistance to change arises from the need of organisations to adapt to new technological developments.[55] The following discussion on how to minimise the problem of change centres on the example of the impact of information technology. The general principles, however, apply equally to the management of change arising from other factors.

- **An important priority is to create an environment of trust and shared commitment, and to involve staff in decisions and actions which affect them**. There is a considerable body of research and experience which demonstrates clearly the positive advantages to be gained from participation. Government encouragement has come through the Employment Act 1982 which requires all companies with more than 250 employees to report annually on steps taken to introduce, maintain or develop arrangements of employee consultation and involvement, information sharing, employee share schemes and related matters. It is important to remember, however, that the implications of information technology will need to be faced even by small organisations.

- **There should be full and genuine participation of all staff concerned as early as possible, preferably well before the actual introduction of new equipment or systems**. Information about proposed change, its implications and potential benefits should be communicated clearly to all interested parties. Staff should be actively encouraged to contribute their own ideas, suggestions and experiences, and to voice openly their worries or concerns. Managers should discuss problems directly with staff and handle any foreseen difficulties in working practices or relationships by attempting to find solutions agreed with them. The use of working parties, liaison committees, steering groups and joint consultation may assist discussion and participation, and help to maintain the momentum of the change process.

- **Team management, a co-operative spirit among staff and unions and a genuine feeling of shared involvement will help create a greater willingness to accept change**. A participative style of managerial behaviour which encourages supportive relationships between superiors and subordinates, and group methods of organisation, decision-making and supervision, are more likely to lead to a sustained improvement in work performance. A system of Management by Objectives (MBO) may allow staff to accept greater responsibility and to make a

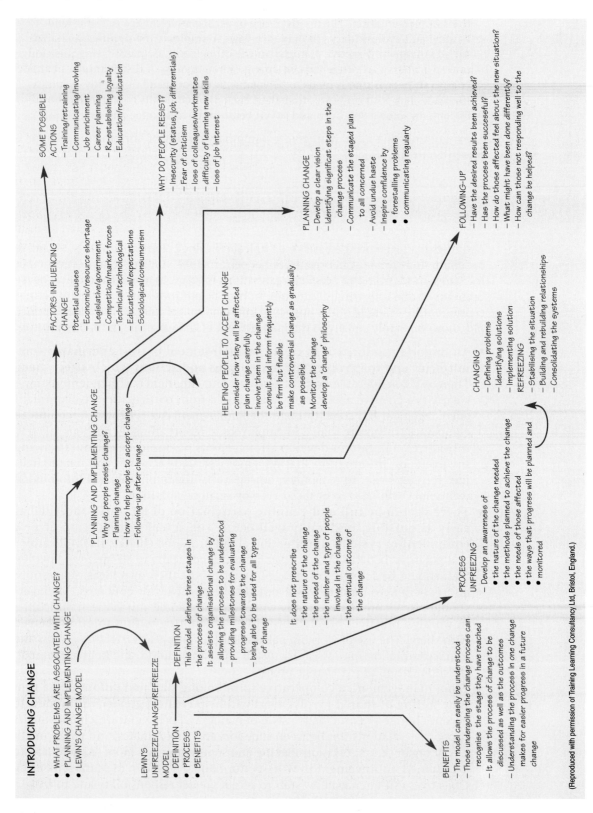

INTRODUCING CHANGE

● WHAT PROBLEMS ARE ASSOCIATED WITH CHANGE?
● PLANNING AND IMPLEMENTING CHANGE
● LEWIN'S CHANGE MODEL

SOME POSSIBLE ACTIONS
– Training/retraining
– Communicating/involving
– Job enrichment
– Career planning
– Re-establishing loyalty
– Education/re-education

PLANNING AND IMPLEMENTING CHANGE
– Why do people resist change?
– Planning change
– How to help people to accept change
– Following-up after change

WHY DO PEOPLE RESIST?
– Insecurity (status, job, differentials)
– Fear of criticism
– loss of colleagues/workmates
– difficulty of learning new skills
– loss of job interest

FACTORS INFLUENCING CHANGE
Potential causes
– Economic/resource shortage
– Legislative/government
– Competition/market forces
– Technical/technological
– Educational/expectations
– Sociological/consumerism

HELPING PEOPLE TO ACCEPT CHANGE
– consider how they will be affected
– plan change carefully
– involve them in the change
– consult and inform frequently
– be firm but flexible
– make controversial change as gradually as possible
– Monitor the change
– develop a 'change' philosophy

PLANNING CHANGE
– Develop a clear vision
– Identifying significat steps in the change process
– Communicate the staged plan to all concerned
– Avoid undue haste
– Inspire confidence by
 ● forestalling problems
 ● communicating regularly

FOLLOWING-UP
– Have the desired results been achieved?
– Has the process been successful?
– How do those affected feel about the new situation?
– What might have been done differently?
– How can those not responding well to the change be helped?

CHANGING
– Defining problems
– Identifying solutions
– Implementing solution

REFREEZING
– Stabilising the situation
– Building and rebuilding relationships
– Consolidating the systems

LEWIN'S
UNFREEZE/CHANGE/REFREEZE
MODEL
● DEFINITION
● PROCESS
● BENEFITS

DEFINITION
This model defines three stages in the process of change
It assists organisational change by
– allowing the process to be understood
– providing milestones for evaluating progress towards the change
– being able to be used for all types of change

It does not prescribe
– the nature of the change
– the speed of the change
– the number and type of people involved in the change
– the eventual outcome of the change

PROCESS
UNFREEZING
– Develop an awareness of
 ● the nature of the change needed
 ● the methods planned to achieve the change
 ● the needs of those affected
 ● the ways that progress will be planned and monitored

BENEFITS
– The model can easily be understood
– Those undergoing the change process can recognise the stage they have reached
– It allows the process of change to be discussed as well as the outcomes
– Understanding the process in one change makes for easier progress in a future change

(Reproduced with permission of Training Learning Consultancy Ltd, Bristol, England.)

Fig. 20.5 Summary outline of introducing change

higher level of personal contribution. Participation is inherent if MBO is to work well, and there is an assumption that most people will direct and control themselves willingly if they share in the setting of their objectives.

- **As part of the pre-planning for new technology there should be a carefully designed 'personnel management action programme'.** The development of information technology together with the growth of service organisations may, in the longer term, lead to the creation of new jobs. However, it must be recognised that the extra efficiency of new technology and automation can result in the more immediate consequence of job losses. The action programme should be directed to a review of: recruitment and selection; natural wastage of staff; potential for training, retraining and the development of new skills; and other strategies to reduce the possible level of redundancies or other harmful effects on staff. Where appropriate, arrangements for a shorter working week, and redeployment of staff with full financial support, should be developed in full consultation with those concerned. If job losses are totally unavoidable, there should be a fair and equitable redundancy scheme and provision for early retirement with protected pension rights. Every possible financial and other support should be given in assisting staff to find suitable alternative employment.

- **The introduction of incentive payment schemes may help in motivating staff by an equitable allocation of savings which result from new technology and more efficient methods of work.** Incentive schemes may be on an individual basis, with bonuses payable to each member of staff according to effort and performance; or on a group basis, where bonus is paid to staff in relation to the performance of the group as a whole. An alternative system is 'measured day work' Staff receive a regular, guaranteed rate of pay in return for an agreed quantity and quality of work based on the capabilities of new equipment and systems. Management may also be able to negotiate a productivity bargain with unions. By accepting changes in work methods and practices, staff share in the economic benefits gained from the improved efficiency of information technology and automated systems.

- **Changes to the work organisation must maintain the balance of the socio-technical system.** Increased technology and automation may result in jobs becoming more repetitive and boring, and providing only a limited challenge and satisfaction to staff. It is important, therefore, to attempt to improve the quality of work, to remove frustration and stress from jobs, and to make them more responsible and interesting. Actual working arrangements rely heavily on the informal organisation and effective teamwork. Groups and teams are a major feature of organisational life and can have a significant influence on the successful implementation of change.[56] New working practices should take account of how best to satisfy people's needs and expectations at work through the practical application of behavioural science.

- **Careful attention should be given to job design, methods of work organisation, the development of cohesive groups, and relationships between the nature and content of jobs and their task functions.** The introduction of new technology has also highlighted the need to give attention to the wider organisational context including the design of technology itself, broader approaches to improved job design, employee involvement and empowerment, the development of skills and problem-solving capacity, and the effective management of change.

Responsiveness to change The successful implementation of new work methods and practices is dependent upon the willing and effective co-operation of staff, managerial colleagues and unions. Continued technological change is inevitable and likely to develop at an even faster rate. Managers must be responsive to such change. Attention must be given not only to products and processes but to people. The full, potential benefits of information technology and automation will only be realised if the management of change takes proper account of human and social factors, as well as technical and economic factors.

THE MANAGEMENT OF NEW TECHNOLOGY

The successful management of change is a key factor of organisational effectiveness (which is discussed in the following chapter). A major aspect of change facing all industrial organisations is the management of new technology.

> Industry is a term embracing a diverse range of activities aimed at wealth creation and each sector will have different objectives, needs and approaches. This diversity makes it impossible to find a single model of technology management which can be applied to all to ensure a successful outcome. However, a common thread that should run through all industrial sectors is an awareness of the opportunity for wealth creation provided by advances in science and technology, and a willingness to ensure their application and exploitation.
> *Sir Richard Sykes, deputy chairman and chief executive of Glaxo Holdings plc.*[57]

An account of managing new technology in organisational contexts is given in Appendix 2 to this chapter.[58]

SYNOPSIS

■ Organisation development (OD) is concerned with the diagnosis of organisational health and performance, and adaptability to change. OD is a generic term embracing a wide range of intervention strategies into the social processes of an organisation. It involves the application of organisational behaviour. The broad nature of OD means that many interrelated topic areas could be included under this heading. In order to bring about effective change OD makes use of a number of approaches, or intervention strategies. It is action-oriented and tailored to suit individual needs.

■ Applications of organisational behaviour and the effective management of human resources are dependent upon organisational culture and climate. Organisational culture helps to explain how things are performed in different organisations.

Culture is, however, a general concept, and difficult to explain precisely. It develops over time and in response to a complex set of factors. Organisations have both an overt and covert culture. The pervasive nature of culture has an important effect on organisational processes and performance.

■ Organisational climate is based on the perception of members towards the organisation, and can be seen as the state of mutual trust and understanding among members of the organisation. Climate influences the attitudes which staff bring to bear on their work performance and personal relationships. A healthy organisational climate might be expected to exhibit a number of characteristic features. Among the factors which contribute to a healthy climate are staff morale and the extent to which employees have a sense of commitment to the organisation.

■ It might be expected that a healthy organisational climate would be reflected by complete harmony in working relationships, but conflict is a reality of management and organisational behaviour. There are contrasting views of conflict and it can be seen to have both positive and negative outcomes. There are many potential sources of organisational conflict related to individual, group, organisational and environmental factors. Although a certain amount of conflict may be seen as inevitable, the important point is how conflict is handled and managed. Managers need to adopt appropriate strategies for dealing with the harmful effects of conflict.

■ Organisations operate within an increasingly volatile environment. Change is a pervasive influence and an inescapable part of social and organisational life. There are a wide range of forces acting upon organisations which make the need for change inevitable. One strategy of change is through the adoption of a systems approach. Despite the potential positive outcomes, change is often resisted at both the individual and the organisational level. It is important, therefore, for management to adopt a clearly defined strategy for the initiation of change, including attention to the human and social factors of change.

APPENDIX 1

Organisational culture change: The BCM Story

I From the traditional organisation to the team concept

For many organisations the 'old' ways of doing business simply cannot continue if the company is to survive in today's global market. For many years organisations thrived and prospered by focusing their efforts on their 'core' competencies – basically doing one thing and doing it very well. The organisation needed to support this business focus tended to emphasise issues such as structure, procedures and loyalty to the organisation. A hierarchical structure, with layers of management each responsible for a specific area of the business was very effective in this environment.

For example, in a traditional manufacturing environment each producing unit had a supervisor – responsible for organising and controlling both the flow of work and the people doing the work. The training programmes developed to support these supervisors tended to focus on issues such as effective employee discipline, evaluating employees, and other skills designed to improve the supervisor's skill at doing the job. Little or no attention was paid to developing the supervisors' skills in areas such as interpersonal communications and working with other people.

The speed of communication and transportation, coupled with the emergence of many former 'colonial' states as major competitors in the world economy has caused a dramatic shift in the environment of manufacturing throughout the world. The scale of this change may very well be viewed by historians as being of at least the magnitude of the Industrial Revolution, and possibly even greater in its scope and impact on the workplace.

II Change at BCM

Boots The Chemist (BTC) is a long-established company, well known in the high street for its retailing activity serviced by in-house production facilities – a typical vertically integrated company. This integrated relationship allowed the production people to concentrate on technical excellence, rather than seeking outlets for their production in the open market.

In the late 1980s and early 1990s Boots underwent a major reorganisation, splitting the business into strategic business units (SBUs). This split the retail, health care and manufacturing functions of Boots into separate divisions, and required each SBU, including Boots Contract Manufacturing (BCM), to function as a stand-alone profit centre.

Top management at BCM began the process of becoming a profit centre by conducting an exhaustive analysis of the organisation and of the needs of their new customers. Customers were seeking flexibility and reliability in their producers to make the competitive difference when seeking a supplier of products. Benchmarking surveys of other organisations throughout the UK and other countries suggested five major new strategies for BCM, all of which have required initiative, drive and patience. The first was to turn the organisation into one that was totally customer-focused. Second, as good customer service has become of paramount importance in retaining and developing BCM's customer base, there was a need to develop cross-functional processes to improve product development and reduce customer lead times. The third strategy was to establish Key Performance Indicators in order to challenge the organisation's effectiveness. This is being driven through all levels of the organisation, across all functions, and represents the commitment to continuously improve business performance. Fourth, there was room to improve production efficiency through investment in new plant. This was done. But to support this investment in new plant and equipment also required tapping the talents and enthusiasm of the people. In order to achieve this fifth goal, it was decided to move the

organisation in the direction of teamworking. This approach offered new answers to old problems, involved employees in every level of the production process, and released management from merely controlling the minute-by-minute activities of the workforce.

Three decisions made early in the process were critical to the teambuilding that was to follow. First, it was decided that the 'supervisors' – brought up on a diet of 'direct and control' – were unlikely to be the team leaders of the future. It was not that their skills for the job were wrong, just that the environment had changed and those skills were now obsolete. A completely new set of competencies was developed for the team leaders, and an assessment centre was designed to select people for these key positions.

The second decision was to align the production and engineering management functions within each department by assigning technicians to each team. Before teamworking, engineering and production had two entirely independent management structures at the department level, and only came together at the factory level. Thus the impact of losing all the 'craft/apprenticeship' heritage was the most devastating element of teamworking for the technicians to come to grips with. In addition, the majority of the technicians had to undergo more technical training so that they could truly become multi-skilled. For some of the fitters this has required a substantial amount of additional training.

The third decision had major ramifications for the packaging floor. Previously there had been six separate pay grades, with assignment to the grades being based on the skill level required for each position. So many grades tended to create confusion and competition within each department. The decision was made to simplify the grading structure by concentrating on three grades, and to provide training opportunities to upgrade over time.

III Teambuilding at BCM

Paralleling the revolution in the structure of the organisation has been a major revolution in the field of training and development. BCM has been very supportive of employee development programmes, including programmes such as basic reading skills and a formalised NVQ framework available to all employees. While traditional training methods are fine for teaching these 'skills', they do not fully address the specific issues that BCM needed, including taking responsibility for one's own actions, empowerment, and learning to value each other's contributions. One increasingly popular method of training has been the use of 'experiential' methods. Experiential (or experience-based) training focuses on 'learning by doing'. For example, to train a group in problem-solving methods, traditional training would probably include a video on problem-solving, followed by a lecture on the steps to solving a problem. A creative trainer might finish with a case study or 'hands-on' problem for the group to solve. Some participants would learn a lot, but some would learn very little because they were not engaged in the process.

An experiential training programme would emphasise the involvement of *all* participants right from the start. The group would be given an activity which required them to actually solve a problem. In this way the group would 'learn' as they actually did the activity. Failure would cause them to replan, while success would allow them to begin to develop a process for team problem-solving that works and is transferable to the work setting.

BCM management chose an experiential programme to provide core teamwork training for both team leaders and the teams themselves. The specifics of the programme are described below. The overall programme is large – over 60 programmes will be run in a period of approximately one year.

Some issues crucial to the overall success of the teambuilding programme take place immediately after the training sessions are over. The teams generally meet with their manager the day after the programme to discuss those work issues identified during training and to help 'verify' to the team the belief that things can move forward

TEAM LEADER PROGRAMMES

Outcomes
- Develop management skills.
- Understand the difference between supervision and team leadership.
- Become a team themselves.
- Practise the skills of team leadership, inlcuding:
 - The value of people's contribution to the group;
 - Improving communication skills;
 - Developing group planning and problem-solving skills;
 - Learning to take responsibility for one's own actions.

Description
- Length – four days.
- Participants – department team leaders (6), immediate managers (2) and department engineer.
- Team leaders all come from one department.
- Location – hotel (they spend three nights at the hotel).
- Methodology – experiential – following Kolb's Learning Cycle.

Day 1
- Set the scene for the four days.
- Agree on ground rules for risk-taking and feedback.
- Become familiar with experiential process and theory through the use of several experiential activities.

Day 2
- Three experiential activities ranging in length from 1 1/2 to 3 hours each.
- In-depth review of each activity by the team.
- Feedback for the team leader responsible for each activity.
- Theory building by the team to uncover what works well for them.
- Linking of activities to actual situations encountered at BCM.
- Managers do not 'control' the activities, but are encouraged to act as a 'coach' to the team leader in charge of each activity. Managers also facilitate discussion during the feedback sessions.
- Participants maintain a 'learning log' to record key learning points and relate these to actual work situations where possible.
- Final activity – completion of Belbin self-perception questionnaires.

Day 3
- Results of self-perception questionnaires to teams and individuals.
- Discussion of how to best use the range of roles and to cover deficiencies noted from questionnaires.
- Completion of three experiential activities and follow-up as per day 2.
- Final activity – complete observer forms for each other to build on the self-perception information.

Day 4
- Feedback and discussion of updated team profile.
- Final 3-hour experiential activity, focusing on team process and outcomes, is conducted.
- Teams are encouraged to identify how they will maintain their 'leader team' back at work. The maintenance of the 'leader team' has been shown to be an important criterion for success of the 2-day 'team programme'.
- Development of a 'take-away' product which can be used to link the 2-day team programme to the leader programme. This can be a 5-minute video, a mission statement, or something of the team's choosing.
- Final activity – development of an individual action plan by each team leader.
- Department Manager reviews the 'take-away' product and the individual action plans, and closes the overall programme.

TEAM PROGRAMMES

Outcomes
- Learn the advantages and process of teamwork.
- Become a team themselves.
- Practise the skills of teamwork inlcuding:
 - The value of people's contribution to the group;
 - Improving communication skills;
 - Developing group planning and problem-solving skills;
 - Learning to take responsibility for one's own actions.

Description
- Length – two days.
- Participants – all members of the team and the team leader. Overall size varies from 8 to 20 or more, depending on the production environment.
- Location – the hotel where the team leader attended the programme (they spend one night at the hotel, which becomes a sort of team training home).
- Methodology – experiential – following Kolb's Learning Cycle.

Note: Most departments consist of six production teams, but some contain as few as two, and some as many as eight teams. The team programmes immediately follow the team leaders' programme, so that all teams are trained within a four-week period.

Day 1
- Set the scene for the two days.
- Divide the large team into sub-teams of 5 or 6 to assure maximum involvement in each phase of training (team leader moves from team to team).
- Complete three short (30–40 minutes) experiential tasks.
- In-depth review of each exercise by the team focusing on: how the team is functioning, the need for clarity of purpose, the value of planning, and the value of each individual's contribution to the exercise.
- Final task – group plans a project and commits the plan to paper. Groups then swap plans and each group 'tries' to complete the plans given them by one of the other groups.
- Debriefing of the final event – looking at the complexities of communication and the need to take responsibility for the quality of our own, rather than judge the actions of others.

Day 2
- Large-scale, full group exercise led by the team leader fills the morning. The team leader participated in a similar exercise during the team leader course, but the 'packaging' of this one is different. The focus of this exercise is on managing complex jobs in a dynamic environment with a large team. This exercise is the critical phase of the entire programme, and forces the team to focus on: clearly understanding the requirements of the task; planning; communication; quality; and personal responsibility.
- Review of exercise. This focuses on what each individual could have done differently to take responsibility for moving the team forward, rather than leaving it up to the team leader.
- The parallel of this exercise to the *new* work setting is clearly discussed during the debriefing process.
- Brainstorming exercise. The afternoon begins with small group sessions to identify work issues which need to be dealt with. These range from maintaining the level of training to day to day operational issues to organisational questions. The team is encouraged to take responsibility for those issues it can deal with, and to refer issues to the team leader when needed. The managers close the session, and discuss those issues which need management's attention.

by connecting issues and learning from the course to the workplace. This is a critical 'first step' in bringing the skills taught during training back to the work setting. Follow-up training is also a critical part of the teambuilding process. Two full-time facilitators have been appointed. Their main focus has been working with management helping them to take ownership of the whole process, both before and after the team-building event.

IV Evaluating the programme

One of the key elements of the teambuilidng programme is evaluation. While many organisations talk about teambuilding, and a number of organisations even spend a lot of money for training programmes, very few organisations *commit* themselves to seriously evaluate them. BCM has made this commitment,

Working with an independent research and evaluation team from the University of Wisconsin in the USA, each team receives evaluations at two intervals after the initial programme. These evaluations focus on a number of key teambuilding behaviours, including decision-making, empowerment, trust, communication, and problem-solving. In addition to team evaluations, evaluations are also done by department and plant, and there is an overall evaluation for the entire programme.

While the programme is still on-going, the results to date suggest that it has been very effective in achieving its goals. Some examples of this success include:

- at least 10 per cent improvement in efficiency on some lines;
- up to 50 per cent more suggestions from team members;
- team members developing their own NVQs;
- cost savings with initiatives worked through in detail by the teams; and
- improving customer satisfaction and reducing wastage through visits to customers and suppliers.

In addition, it is important to note that a number of issues do seem to impact upon the success of the programme. Preliminary results suggest that factors such as previous position (technical or production) and the gender make-up of the group appear to have a significant effect on the teambuilding efforts.

Conclusion

Boots Contract Manufacturing is dealing with an all too common organisational problem with a unique teambuilding training programme, and has decided to make a serious effort to evaluate that programme. While it is too early to see the overall effect on the bottom line of the organisation, many positives have already been seen by an organisation going through the upheaval of change.

(I am grateful to John Campbell, Executive and Staff Training Ltd; Julian Page, Boots The Chemist; and Richard J. Wagner, University of Wisconsin-Whitewater, USA, for providing this information.)

APPENDIX 2

Managing new technology in organisational contexts[59]

The focus here is upon new technology (that is, microelectronics and microprocessors) as used in adopting organisations in: (a) design/ engineering/production processes (or Advanced Manufacturing Technology – AMT); (b) information capture, storage, transmission, analysis and retrieval (IT); (c) the provision of services to customers, clients or patients; and (d) products themselves. We will not be looking at the original design and development of the technology itself (hardware and software), but it should be borne in mind that social processes impinge upon and are built into the technology which emerges from design and development, and they therefore influence the nature of the technology which emerges.[60]

A final qualification: *new* technology does not mean 'new' in the sense of 'just become available'. Much AMT, for example, has been around for over 40 years, but it may not be adopted by a particular company until, say, 1996: it is not this fact which takes it 'new'. Diffusion rates for new technology not only vary across different organisations, but the core technology challenges have also changed over time. *Friedman and Cornford*, for example, identify four main phases of computer systems development. Phase 1 (1940s to mid-1960s) was dominated by hardware problems; phase 2 (mid-1960s to early 1980s) was dominated by software problems; the current phase (3) is centred on user relations and is in a process of transition to phase 4, which looks likely to be focused upon the exploitation of the strategic potential of new technology.[61]

Adoption and introduction of new technology

Let us now turn to examine the adoption and introduction of new technology into organisations. The starting point is the recognition that new technology is inherently flexible because of the following characteristics: (a) compactness, (b) low energy use, (c) decreasing cost in relation to processing power (over time more processing power has been packed into less space at a lower unit of cost), and (d) the programmability of the software.

This flexibility allows those organisational actors who participate in new technology adoption and introduction a good deal of choice with regard to the purposes for which, the ways in which, and the internal contexts within which the technology is deployed. This means that new technology utilisation is likely to be strongly influenced by the associated adoption and introduction decisions and the perspectives, objectives and strategies of the people involved.[62] It follows that, in order to understand what has occurred in a particular application, we need to know who these people were.

At the same time, the particular features of the technology *per se* will have an effect upon what is possible (for example, in terms of job design) and aspects of the inner context of the organisation could act as constraints upon choice. It is also important to distinguish between the two main phases of adoption and introduction, for it is during the first phase that there is available the greatest amount of room for manoeuvre with regard to objectives, strategies and processes of involvement.[63] By the time the second phase – introduction – is reached, the majority of the key decisions will probably already have been made, with respect to matters such as labour requirements (numbers of staff, hours of work), skill, experience and knowledge required, payment and grading, and linkages into other installations of new technology inside or outside the organisation.

Therefore, if certain staff are *not* involved during the adoption phase, their chances of influencing the process, and thus imprinting their preferences upon the above sort of matters, are not good. Fig. 20.6 outlines the stages involved in new technology adoption and introduction.

The adoption phase

The adoption phase concerns those social processes and events which precede the actual

introduction of the new technology into the organisation. Here is the main opportunity for the exercise of choice, or, to put it another way, the widest design space. Key issues at initiation include whose idea it was to introduce the new technology, their job and background, and the source(s) of the idea. Progression/feasibility involves the more detailed work which follows, including a search for further information, looking at what competitors are doing with the technology, and bringing in other expertise.

It is at the investment decision stage that the sponsors of the proposal either get the go-ahead from senior managers to invest in the technology, or have to resubmit or abandon the idea. It involves an assessment and comparison of the costs and benefits of the proposal, and projections about returns from the investment; investment appraisal techniques are available to facilitate this work. Planning and systems design consists of a more detailed consideration of such matters as which supplier(s) to use and their selection, preparation for the introduction (for

example, training and communication), and changes to operating procedures in readiness.

The above may appear to imply that the adoption process is inherently rational and systematic. This is by no means necessarily the case, for, on the one hand, it is an ideal-typical model in the Weberian sense,[64] and, on the other, all organisations do not have to go through all the stages exactly as delineated here. In any event, the stages and processes of adoption (and introduction for that matter) are iterative and inherently **political** and **social**, with all that this implies.

The introduction phase

Turning to the introduction phase, whilst stage 5 (*see* Fig. 20.6) is self-explanatory, it should be noted that it is at stage 6 that the users of the new technology come to understand its capabilities and limitations, and may for the first time imprint *their* objectives and knowledge upon its utilisation.[65] The nature and extent of the opportunity users have here will depend in part upon the earlier decisions which were taken by other

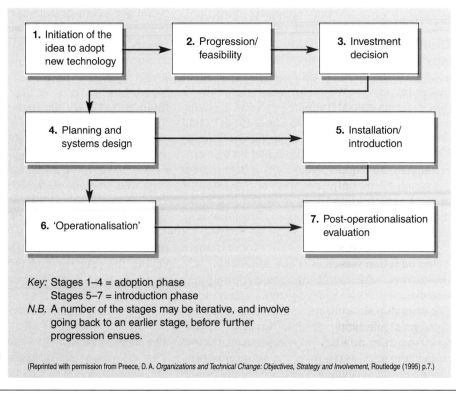

**Fig. 20.6
Stages in new technology adoption and introduction**

Key: Stages 1–4 = adoption phase
Stages 5–7 = introduction phase
N.B. A number of the stages may be iterative, and involve going back to an earlier stage, before further progression ensues.

(Reprinted with permission from Preece, D. A. *Organizations and Technical Change: Objectives, Strategy and Involvement*, Routledge (1995) p.7.)

actors, but they are likely to have at least a modicum of discretion about operating the technology; indeed, it is in the organisation's interests that they *do* have some discretion at the job level in order that the potential of the technology is realised, given its inherent flexibility, and the imperative for many contemporary organisations to be responsive to customer requirements and competitor actions.

Finally, it is important that an evaluation of new technology adoption and introduction takes place, in order that the organisation learns from its experience and is in a position to pass on that learning in subsequent introductions of new technology. It is not unusual, however, for little or no evaluation to occur in practice (often due to social and political factors).

Case studies

On the basis of case studies conducted in two engineering companies and two building societies over the period 1986–93 (and the work of other researchers), the following observations can be made about some of the key social and organisational issues associated with the adoption and introduction of new technology:

1. By the early 1990s new technology had become an everyday, taken-for-granted, aspect of operations: it was the purposes for which and the ways in which it was used which were seen as the crucial issues.
2. The wider external contexts of these organisations exerted an important influence upon the quality and direction of new technology utilisation. In the engineering companies 'contexts' included not only the former, but also the inter-organisational contexts of corporate–division and division–division relationships. For example, the particular form of new technology introduced and the timing of introduction was dictated to one company by the corporate head office and/or the manufacturing head office. At the other, a changed ownership structure resulted in more encouragement and support being given to investment in what was now solely an engineering group of companies, as contrasted to the previous situation where engineering was just one division of a diversified group of companies.
3. Internal contexts form an important backdrop to, and influence upon, the nature of and outputs from the new technology adoption and introduction processes. Examples of aspects of inner context found to be of importance included organisation structuring, employment relations, personnel practices and policies, modes of control and communication, employee involvement in technological and other changes, and job design/redesign.
4. Managers and other actors in the technological change process typically had a 'constellation' or wide range of objectives, and a variety of strategies at the corporate/business/organisational, labour, and manufacturing/technology levels for achieving those objectives. What is more, the objectives and strategies which were chosen were associated with the orientations and backgrounds of the people who had participated in the objective-setting and strategy-formulation processes. This usually meant managers and technical specialists at the adoption and introduction phases, but an involvement (typically rather limited) of affected staff (or 'users') at the implementation stage, largely through communication and consultation. A deeper and somewhat earlier involvement of users has been found to occur in certain European countries as compared to the UK, particularly in Denmark and Germany.[66]
5. Thus:

> The success . . . of the new technology adoption process depends upon the appropriateness and quality of the non-technological changes which go hand in hand with the technical changes *per se*, and upon the social, economic and organisational contexts into which that technology is in due course introduced. There is much to be said, then, for not only *studying* new technology adoption through an interdisciplinary perspective, but also for managing the process of its adoption in a way which is sensitive to, and knowledgeable about, the multi-faceted nature of new technology.[67]
>
> David Preece

 Review and discussion questions

1 Explain what you understand by the meaning and nature of organisation development (OD).

2 Suggest how you would attempt to explain the concept of organisational culture. What factors might influence the development of culture?

3 Discuss the importance of organisational culture for effective organisational performance. Give practical examples from your own organisation.

4 What do you understand by organisational climate and what do you think are its main characteristic features? From your own organisation, give examples of features that have contributed to and/or detracted from a healthy climate.

5 Explain the concept of employee commitment and suggest how it might actually be created. Give examples of factors which have contributed to your own strength of commitment in a work situation.

6 To what extent do you accept the view that conflict is an inevitable feature of management and organisational behaviour? Suggest how management can attempt to avoid the harmful effects of conflict.

7 Discuss, with supporting practical examples, some of the major changes confronting organisations and management today. What is the need for planned organisational change?

8 Why do people in organisations tend to resist change? Explain instances of resistance to change in your own organisation and the effectiveness of management strategies to overcome the resistance.

CASE STUDY 1

The Wakewood organisation

The Wakewood organisation comprises seven units, each of which has been managed autonomously over the last five years. Each unit is managed by a General Manager and comprises one or more product/service departments and other staff departments. Each unit is, in effect, an autonomous division of Wakewood.

The Chief Executive has managed the organisation from a small headquarters building using a participative style. He has become increasingly concerned about the performance of one of the seven units. The unit employs 700 people and accounts for 20% of Wakewood's activities. He perceives the following internal and external pressures on this unit and believes that the General Manager responsible for it cannot deal with the problem. The Chief Executive has been unable to devote much time to this unit during the last years because of other pressures on his time. During the last four years, he has achieved significant changes and improvements in other units within the organisation. This has absorbed much of his time but has created a very positive reputation for him throughout Wakewood. He is seen as up-to-date and concerned for his employees.

External pressures
Increasing client/customer dissatisfaction
New technology
Increasing competition in the provision of the products/services provided
Rapidly increasing costs

Internal pressures
Fear of change
Limited management skills in the introduction of change
Lack of experience with new technology
Low productivity and quality
Poor staff morale

The unit is managed by a General Manager with functional managers responsible to the General Manager for three product/service departments, an administration department, finance and a small personnel department.

The General Manager has worked with Wakewood for 18 years now. His approach to managing the unit has been always to control costs and activities fairly tightly and to concentrate on developing an efficient and professional team working for him. He has paid little or no attention to the needs of clients. There has been a growing number of complaints from clients about the service provided by the unit. Long waits are often involved and staff are said not to handle clients too well.

New computer technology is being deployed by Wakewood. However, progress in this unit has been slow. The General Manager seems largely disinterested and the staff reluctant to adapt. However, the pressure to introduce the technology is strong. Staff costs are high and many routine tasks seem likely to be capable of computerisation.

The Chief Executive wishes to introduce marketing and quality audit ideas into the unit as a means of responding to some of the pressures identified above. Moreover, he believes that new technology must be introduced over the next few years, particularly in the product/service departments. To do so he has concluded that three major problems must be faced, as follows:

(i) attitudes to change and the organisation must be changed;
(ii) attitudes to, and knowledge of new technology, must be improved dramatically;
(iii) the organisation structure must be reviewed in order to introduce marketing and quality audit ideas into the unit.

You have been asked to advise on how to proceed. Outline a strategy for change designed to achieve the following objectives:

(a) to prepare people for change, convincing them that significant organisational changes are needed;
(b) to plan and monitor a programme of organisational change;
(c) to help people at all levels in the unit cope with the problems of change;
(d) to achieve improvement in the unit's performance.

(You may deal with this case study from *either* a private sector *or* a public sector perspective. If you adopt a public sector standpoint you can interpret 'marketing and quality audit ideas' to mean to develop an approach in which concern for the client and the quality of services provided becomes more important than previously.)

CASE STUDY 2

Rudmore Press Limited

Rudmore Press was founded in the early 1960s by the current Managing Director, Tony Stone, and his friend and partner, Roger Preston. The original company was housed in a large shed in Tony's garden and start-up capital to buy the first hand-operated printing press was provided by his parents. From this inauspicious beginning, the company expanded into its own premises in the early 1970s and then again in the mid-1980s to a purpose-built factory and warehouse. The company provides a wide range of printing work to local businesses and operates in a highly competitive market.

In the beginning, lack of working capital caused much work to be contracted out, but a policy of continuing investment meant that the company has now been able to equip its premises with the latest colour printing presses and computerised typesetting facilities. This has enabled most work now to be completed in-house, a service which has been enhanced by joining forces with two small independent lithographic companies who run the in-house plate-making services from Rudmore's premises. Modern production facilities are underpinned by a comprehensive warehouse system housing guillotines and folding and cutting machines, together with a computerised dispatch system which produces and co-ordinates all customer documentation.

The original two-man team was joined in the late 1970s by Gerry Farr to oversee production; shop-floor and supervisory staff were taken on as business levels demanded. Rapid growth during the middle and late 1980s meant that the company seriously had to review its organisation structure. Gerry Farr was promoted to Works Director; Roger Preston moved from Works Manager to Marketing Director to reflect the need which the company had identified to seek out new markets; and Tony's wife, Anthea, was brought in to the company on a part-time basis to oversee administration and personnel. Additionally, a Quality Controller, Joyce Baker, was appointed to lead the initiative to obtain the International Standards Organisation (ISO) 9000 Approved Quality Standard Certificate.

Tony is a dynamic Managing Director who realises that the organisation is still very much in an embryonic state of development. A highly intelligent and charismatic figure, well known in the local community, he believes in allowing people to manage their own functions and becomes frustrated when they appear to be failing to do so. Passionately believing in his company, he always seems to know what is going on. He works long hours, often appearing to tackle several important tasks at once, and sets himself, and others, tight deadlines and seemingly impossible objectives. He has received little formal management training and recognises this possible shortfall in his development, but never seems to find the time to undertake a course of study. He feels that he has a moral and financial obligation to Roger, his original partner who is now a major shareholder.

Conversely, Roger is an introverted individual who is devoted to his wife and family. He believes that the company has grown too quickly for his own personal comfort. He feels most at home when getting his hands dirty on one of the presses and doesn't really want to be the Marketing Director. Indeed, he isn't really sure

what the job involves except that Tony had told him that he is to search out new markets and improve sales. Tony had also recently asked him to recruit and manage a small sales team, a task which Roger had inwardly dreaded.

Gerry Farr is very much a 'hands on' manager who began his career as a printer. He feels happiest when he is on 'his' shop floor rather than in the boardroom. Tony has identified a management course for Gerry to attend but Gerry is resisting it on the grounds of pressure of work. On this note, Gerry feels than he works very hard, often putting in more hours than the other three, and sometimes feels resentful that, unlike the others, he has no shareholding in the company.

Tony's wife, Anthea, has been co-opted into the company to bring some order to the administrative function. Calm and capable, she is the perfect foil for her husband's management style. Freely admitting that, having trained as an infant teacher, she has little related experience, Anthea is nevertheless ready and willing to learn whatever is needed in order to drive the organisation forward. She does not see her role as a permanent one and eventually wants to return to what she considers as her main role, that of looking after her husband and children.

Communication within the company is informal and more likely to take the form of conversations with individuals rather than written memoranda. Likewise there are few, if any, laid-down policies or procedures other than those in place in the dispatch department and warehouse. If systems are needed, they are added on an *ad hoc* basis. Staff at all levels of the organisation also seem to be recruited by this same approach. Tony, who has recently read an article in a management magazine on the subject, is proud that the organisation is adopting what he terms 'the contingency approach'. This view is not shared by Roger who, liking order and discipline, prefers to know exactly what is expected of him, nor by Gerry who just wants to be allowed to get on with production unhindered by what he terms 'Tony's meddling'.

As Rudmore entered the 1990s, Tony Stone realised that major changes were needed if the company was to continue its planned expansion. He applied for, and was awarded, a government grant which enabled him to appoint a team of consultants to undertake an analysis of the organisation and report back to him with their recommendations.

Tony's first comment to the consultants was: 'the four of us have been together for a long time now but I can't seem to motivate them any more'. When the consultants interviewed the other key members of the organisation they repeatedly heard comments along similar lines: 'Everything was OK when we were a very small company and everyone knew what everyone else was doing. Since we started to expand we're no longer a team and Tony has become a bit of a bully. He either sets us targets which are impossible or treats us like idiots. We are no longer a team but a group of people working in a dictatorship.'

One of Anthea Stone's main concerns was to the effect that there is a growing problem of authority and accountability which has come with expansion of the company. In the consultants' discussions with Roger, he made the comment that: 'I think one of the main problems is that the staff have the wrong attitude and approach for what I am trying to achieve.'

As a member of the consultancy team you are required to prepare a report indicating clearly:

(i) the factors to be considered in your analysis of the organisation;
(ii) which of these factors should be given the highest priority, together with your supporting reasons;
(iii) how your ideas and recommendations might best be implemented; and
(iv) the relevant theoretical or other models you would bear in mind.

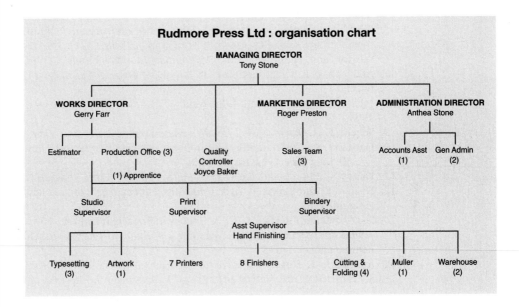

Rudmore Press Ltd : organisation chart

(This case study has been prepared jointly with, and from original material supplied by, my colleague Karen Meudell.)

Notes and references

1. French, W. L. and Bell, C. H. *Organization Development: Behavioral Science Interventions for Organization Improvement*, Fifth edition, Prentice-Hall (1995) p. 28.
2. See, for example: Mumford, E. 'Helping Organizations Through Action Research: The Sociotechnical Approach', *Quality of Work Life*, vol. 3, nos 5–6, September–December 1986, pp. 329–44.
3. For example, see: Pritchard, W. 'What's New in Organisation Development', *Personnel Management*, vol. 16, no. 7, July 1984, pp. 30–3.
4. Blake, R. R. and Mouton, J. S. *The Managerial Grid III*, Gulf Publishing Company (1985).
5. See, for example: Smircich, L. 'Concepts of Culture and Organizational Analysis', *Administrative Science Quarterly*, 28, 1983, pp. 339–58.
6. See, for example: Brown, A. D. *Organisational Culture*, Pitman (1995).
7. Atkinson, P. E. 'Creating Cultural Change', *Management Services*, vol. 34, no. 7, 1990, pp. 6–10.
8. McLean, A. and Marshall, J. *Intervening in Cultures*, Working Paper, University of Bath, 1993.
9. Schein, E. H. *Organizational Culture and Leadership: A Dynamic View*, Jossey-Bass (1985).
10. Harrison, R. 'Understanding Your Organization's Character', *Harvard Business Review*, vol. 50, May/June 1972, pp. 119–28.
11. Handy, C. B. *Understanding Organizations*, Fourth edition, Penguin (1993).
12. Deal, T. E. and Kennedy, A. A. *Corporate Cultures: The Rites and Rituals of Corporate Life*, Penguin (1982).
13. See, for example: Handy, C. B. *Understanding Organizations*, Fourth edition, Penguin (1993); and McLean, A. and Marshall, J. *Cultures at Work*, Local Government Training Board, October 1988.
14. Kransdorff, A. 'History – A Powerful Management Tool', *Administrator*, October 1991, p. 23.
15. See Sieff, M. (Lord Sieff of Brimpton), *Management the Marks & Spencer Way*, Fontana Collins (1991).
16. Potter, C. C.'What is Culture: And Can It Be Useful For Organisational Change Agents?', *Leadership and Organization Development Journal*, vol. 10, no. 3, 1989, pp. 17–24.
17. Gorman, L. 'Corporate Culture – Why Managers Should Be Interested', *Leadership and Organization Development Journal*, vol. 8, no. 5, 1987, pp. 3–9.
18. Peters, T. J. and Waterman, R. H. *In Search of Excellence*, Harper and Row (1982) pp. 75–6.
19. Egan, G. 'The Shadow Side', *Management Today*, September 1993, p. 37.
20. Egan, G. 'Cultivate Your Culture', *Management Today*, April 1994, pp. 38–42.
21. See, for example: Pheysey, D. C. *Organizational Cultures: Types and Transformations*, Routledge (1993).
22. Brown, A. D. 'Organizational Culture: The Key to Effective Leadership and Organizational Development', *Leadership and Organization Development Journal*, vol. 13, no. 2, 1992, pp. 3–6.
23. Mullins, L. J., Meudell, K. and Scott, H. 'Developing Culture in Short-Life Organizations', *International Journal of Contemporary Hospitality Management*, vol. 5, no. 4, 1993, pp. 15–19.
24. Meudell, K. and Gadd, K. 'Culture and Climate in Short-Life Organizations: Sunny Spells or Thunderstorms?', *International Journal of Contemporary Hospitality Management*, vol. 6, no. 5, 1994, pp. 27–32.
25. Tagiuri, R. and Litwin, G. H. (eds) *Organizational Climate*, Graduate School of Business Administration, Harvard University (1968) p. 27.
26. Rentsch, J. R. 'Climate and Culture: Interaction and Qualitative Differences in Organizational Meanings', *Journal of Applied Psychology*, vol. 75, no. 6, 1990, p. 668.

27. Malcolmson, J. 'Critical Incidents Techniques as a Means of Gauging Morale Levels', *Army Personnel Research Establishment*, Working Paper 28/90, May 1990.

28. Gould, P. 'The Measurement of Morale,' *Army Personnel Research Establishment*, Working Paper 32/89, 1989.

29. Petrick, J. A. and Manning, G. E. 'How To Manage Morale', *Personnel Journal*, vol. 69, no. 10, October 1990, pp. 83–8.

30. Coopey, J. and Hartley, J. 'Reconsidering the Case for Organisational Commitment', *Human Resource Management Journal*, vol. 1, no. 13, Spring 1991, pp. 18–32.

31. O'Reilly, C. 'Corporations, Culture and Commitment: Motivation and Social Control in Organizations', in Steers, R. M. and Porter, L. W. (eds) *Motivation and Work Behavior*, Fifth edition, McGraw-Hill (1991) pp. 242–55.

32. Martin, P. and Nicholls, J. *Creating a Committed Workforce*, Institute of Personnel Management, (1987).

33. Drennan, D. 'How To Get Your Employees Committed', *Management Today*, October 1989, pp. 121–9.

34. White, G. *Employee Commitment*, ACAS Work Research Unit, Occasional Paper no. 38 (October 1987).

35. *Ibid.* pp. 17–18.

36. Drucker, P. F. *The Practice of Management*, Heinemann Professional (1989) p. 119.

37. Salaman, G. *Class and Corporation*, Fontana (1981).

38. French, W. L., Kast, F. E. and Rosenzweig, J. E. *Understanding Human Behavior in Organizations*, Harper and Row (1985).

39. Schmidt, W. H. 'Conflict: A Powerful Process for (Good or Bad) Change', *Management Review*, 63, December 1974, pp. 4–10.

40. Townsend, R. *Further Up the Organisation*, Coronet Books (1985) p. 39.

41. See, for example: Ardrey, R. *The Territorial Imperative*, Collins (1967) (Ardrey suggests that principles of territory which motivate animal behaviour can also be applied to society).

42. Woodward, J. *Industrial Organization: Theory and Practice*, Second edition, Oxford University Press (1980) p. 113.

43. Bryans, P. and Cronin, T. P. *Organization Theory*, Mitchell Beazley (1983) p. 103.

44. Lewin, K. Field *Theory in Social Science*, Harper and Row (1951).

45. French, W. L., Kast, F. E. and Rosenzweig, J. E. *Understanding Human Behavior in Organizations*, Harper and Row (1985).

46. Wilson, B. 'The Challenge of Change', *Industrial Management and Data Systems*, November/ December 1987, p. 21.

47. Hellreigal, D., Slocum, J. W. and Woodmann, R. W. *Organizational Behavior*, Fifth edition, West Publishing (1989).

48. Stewart, R. *Managing Today and Tomorrow*, Macmillan (1991).

49. Toffler, A. *Future Shock*, Pan Books (1970) p. 27.

50. See, for example: Burnes, B. *Managing Change: A Strategic Approach to Organisational Development and Renewal,* Pitman (1992).

51. Tessler, D. 'The Human Side of Change', *Director*, vol. 43, no. 3, October 1989, pp. 88–93.

52. Elliott, R. D.'The Challenge of Managing Change', *Personnel Journal*, vol. 69, no. 3, March 1990, pp. 40–9.

53. Hersey, P. and Blanchard, K. *Management of Organizational Behavior*, Fifth edition, Prentice-Hall (1988) pp. 342–3.

54. Training Learning Consultancy Ltd, Bristol, England.

55. Mullins, L. J. 'Information Technology – The Human Factor', *Administrator*, vol. 5, no. 8, September 1985, pp. 6–9.

56. See, for example: Coghlan, D. 'Managing Organizational Change through Teams and Groups,' *Leadership and Organization Development Journal*, vol. 15, no. 2, 1994, pp. 18–23.

57. Sykes, R. 'The Management of Technological Change', *Professional Manager*, November 1994, p. 6.

58. I am grateful to my colleague, David Preece, University of Portsmouth, for contributing this account.

59. This appendix has been written by David Preece. The material used in this extract is discussed in much more detail in Preece, D. *Organizations and Technical Change: Objectives, Strategy and Involvement*, Routledge (1995).

60. On the social and economic contexts of technology-design, see, respectively: MacKenzie, D. and Wacjman, J. (eds) *The Social Shaping of Technology*, Open University Press (1985); Clark, P. and Staunton, N. *Innovation in Technology and Organization*, Routledge (1989).

61. Friedman, A. and Cornford, D. *Computer Systems Development: History, Organization and Implementation*, Wiley (1989).

62. For a strong advocacy of this position, see: Buchanan, D. and Boddy, D. *Organizations in the Computer Age: Technological Imperatives and Strategic Choice*, Gower (1983).

63. See Preece, D. *Managing the Adoption of New Technology*, Routledge (1989).

64. For an outline and review of Weber's ideal type of bureaucracy, see: Albrow, M. *Bureaucracy*, Macmillan (1970).

65. For illustrations of how this opportunity has been taken up in practice see, for example: Wilkinson, B. *The Shopfloor Politics of New Technology*, Heinemann (1983); Clark, J., McLoughlin, I., Rose, H. and King, R. *The Process of Technological Change: New Technology and Social Choice in the Workplace*, Cambridge University Press (1988).

66. For empirical data on this, see: Daniel, W. and Millward, N. 'Personnel Management and Technical Change: The Findings from the WIRS Series', in Clark, J. (ed.) *Human Resource Management and Technical Change*, Sage (1993); Gill, C. and Krieger, H. 'The Diffusion of Participation in New Information Technology in Europe: Survey Results', *Economic and Industrial Democracy*, 13 (3), 1992.

67. Preece, D. *Organizations and Technical Change: Objectives, Strategy and Involvement*, Routledge (1995) p. 235.

21

MANAGEMENT DEVELOPMENT AND ORGANISATIONAL EFFECTIVENESS

Every work organisation is concerned with being effective. Upon the attainment of its aims and objectives rests the success and ultimate survival of the organisation. The quality of management is central to organisation development and improved performance. There are, however, a multiplicity of variables which impinge upon organisational effectiveness. The manager needs to understand the importance of improving the overall performance and effectiveness of the organisation.

 Learning objectives

To:

- Explain the importance of effective management to organisation development;

- Detail an integrated model of managerial behaviour and development;

- Explain the main features and requirements of the management development process;

- Examine the importance and effectiveness of management education, training and development;

- Assess the nature of organisational effectiveness and basic attributes for organisational success;

- Outline criteria for an evaluation of organisational effectiveness;

- Recognise the importance of management development, and attempts to improve organisational performance and effectiveness.

Worth thinking about

'Despite all my studies of organisational behaviour it is difficult to find single, right answers to problems at work. And managing people now seems to be more complex than I ever thought. So what's the point?' . . . 'But don't you see – that's exactly why it's important to study management and organisational behaviour – and how much you've already learned!'

THE IMPORTANCE OF EFFECTIVE MANAGEMENT

Previous chapters of this book have emphasised the importance of management as an integrating activity which permeates every facet of the operations of the organisation. Management is the cornerstone of organisational effectiveness, and the contribution to economic and social needs of society. This applies as much to public sector and service organisations as to any other industry. The quality of management is one of the most important factors in the success of any organisation. Managers need a balance of technical, social and conceptual knowledge and skills, acquired through a blend of education and experience. There is, therefore, a continual need for managerial development. The organisation must ensure the development of both present and future managers.

THE MEANING AND NATURE OF MANAGEMENT DEVELOPMENT

There is no single, agreed definition of management development. A common view is that whereas training is concerned with the achievement of effective performance in the manager's present job, development is concerned with preparing the manager for expected changes in the job, or for an anticipated future job or role. However, management development is likely to include at least an element of training.

A more general interpretation views management development as an integral part of the process of organisational development. Management development is not only concerned with improvement in the effectiveness of individual managers, it is also concerned with an improvement in management performance as a whole and with improvement in organisational effectiveness.[1] Yet attention to the development of team management skills and team performance tends to be a neglected area of management development.[2]

Details of five significant B & Q employee policies and practices that seek to develop the management skills, abilities and staff resources required for the successful growth of the company are given in Appendix 1 to this chapter.

The public sector and small business organisations

Management development is equally as important for the public sector as it is for private enterprise organisations. For example, the (then) Local Government Training Board has drawn attention to the need for local authorities to have managers of the highest quality to manage the enormous changes confronting local government and to the provision of management development activities.[3]

Some suitable form of management development is also important for the small business organisation. However, there is evidence to suggest that small business education in Britain is currently underdeveloped and needs to extend beyond its present traditional 'training' orientation.[4]

A climate of coaching, empowerment and support

An environment of rapid change, technological innovations and increasing business competitiveness has highlighted the growing importance of management development. In particular, the general movement towards greater employee involvement and making things happen through people has emphasised an integrating rather than a controlling style of management. In addition to personal competence in their own areas of specialisation, the nature of management requires a climate of coaching, empowerment and support.[5]

For example, *Clarke* refers to the changing role of the manager and suggests that the manager of the future will have to master three specific roles, or survival skills – leader, coach and facilitator.

- **The role of leader** involves the skills of focusing on the wider picture, involving employees in implementation, and establishing an environment in which people can operate and have enough space for creativity.
- **The role of coach** involves the skills of creating an environment where change can thrive, and bringing abilities to the surface by building up confidence and building upon capabilities.
- **The role of facilitator** involves the skills of moving the organisation forward and achieving continuous improvement in performance, encouraging the growth of new ideas and bringing the best out of employees.[6]

AN INTEGRATED MODEL OF MANAGEMENT DEVELOPMENT

The wide variety of organisational settings found within the work situation makes special demands upon its managers. There is a dichotomy between the application of general management theory in influencing the behaviour and performance of managers, while at the same time accepting the need for individuals to manage according to situational demands. Particular models of managerial behaviour applied to specific types of organisations have little relevance, and if anything provide a constraint on the need for an open and fluid interpretation of management development.

Using accumulated knowledge of management theory, *Mullins and Aldrich* have constructed an integrated model of managerial behaviour and development. The model relies on basic management and behavioural theories for its structure, and situational demands for its adaption.[7] (*See* Fig. 21.1.)

759

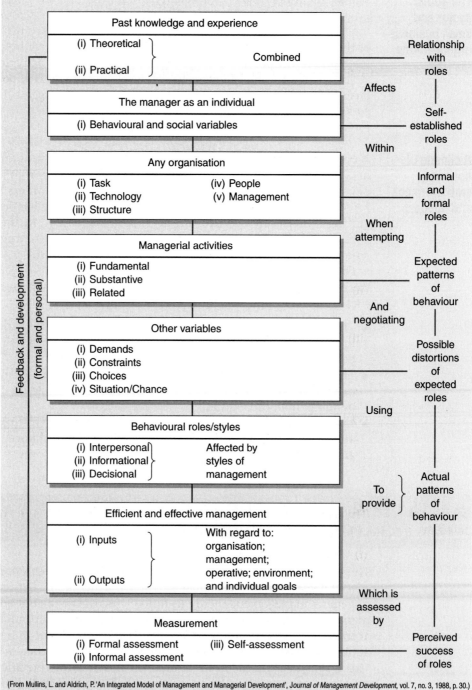

**Fig. 21.1
An integrated
model of managerial
behaviour and
development**

(From Mullins, L. and Aldrich, P. 'An Integrated Model of Management and Managerial Development', *Journal of Management Development*, vol. 7, no. 3, 1988, p. 30.)

Past knowledge and experience

Development involves a combination of knowledge and varied experience. These are seen as taking place through a combination of both theoretical and practical involvement. The advancement of human relations skills is ideally seen as stemming from deliberate and constructive self-development.

The manager as an individual

Behavioural and social variables provide a framework for conceptualising behaviour in organisations, and include:

- Links with other individuals and groups within and outside the organisation. These links may be formal or informal.
- Personality and people perception.
- Values.
- Attitudes.
- Opinions.
- Motivation: needs and expectations.
- Intelligence and abilities: learning and skill acquisition and the assimilation and retention of past knowledge and experiences.[8]

Any organisation

The organisation can be analysed in terms of five main interrelated sub-systems. Two of these, people and management, can be considered within the context of the 'behavioural and social variables' above.

(i) **Task** – includes the goals and objectives of the organisation, the nature of its inputs and outputs, and work to be carried out during the work process.

(ii) **Technology** – describes the manner in which the tasks of the organisation are carried out and the nature of the work performance. The materials, techniques and equipment used in the transformation or conversion process.

(iii) **Structure** – defines the patterns of organisation and formal relationships among members. The division of work and co-ordination of tasks by which any series of activities can be carried out.

(iv) **People** – the nature of the members undertaking the series of activities as defined by the behavioural and social variables.

(v) **Management** – is therefore the integrating activity working to achieve the 'tasks', using the 'technology' through the combined efforts of 'people' and within the formal 'structure' of an organisation. This involves corporate strategy, direction of the activities of the organisation as a whole and interactions with the external environment.

Managerial activities

This area of the model attempts to synthesise common views on the basic activities and processes of management.

(i) **Fundamental activities**
- Managers can be seen to set and **clarify goals and objectives**. For instance Management by Objectives.
- A manager **plans**, examining the past, present and future; describing what needs to be achieved and subsequently planning a course of action.
- A manager **organises**, analysing the activities, decisions and relationships required. Classifying and dividing work, creating an organisation structure and selecting staff.
- A manager **motivates and develops** people, creating a team out of the people responsible for various jobs while directing and developing them.
- A manager **measures**, establishing targets and measurements of performance, focusing on both the needs of individuals and the control demanded by the organisation.

(ii) **Substantive activities**
 - Communication
 - Co-ordination
 - Integration
 - Having responsibility
 - Making decisions

These permeate the fundamental activities and are therefore no less important. Substantive activities are inherent in the process of management and are simply more descriptive of how the work of a manager is executed.

(iii) **Related activities** include, for instance, the personnel function. Personnel policies help determine the efficient use of human resources and should therefore emanate from the top of an organisation, be defined clearly and be communicated through managers at all levels to their staff.

Other variables *Stewart* has developed a model based on studies of managerial jobs which it is suggested provides a framework for thinking about the nature of managerial jobs and about the manner in which managers undertake them.[9]

(i) **Demands** are what anyone in the job has to do. They are not what the manager ought to do but only what must be done.

(ii) **Constraints** are internal and external factors limiting what the manager can do.

(iii) **Choices** are the activities that the manager is free to do but does not have to do.

'Chance' is one of the factors which determine dominant Managerial Grid style: where, for instance, a manager has no experience of, or sets of assumptions about, how to manage a particular situation.[10]

Behavioural roles and styles According to the contingency approach, the task of the manager is to identify which style, role or technique will in a particular situation, in particular circumstances, within a particular organisation and at a particular time contribute best to the attainment of corporate, managerial, social and individual goals.

The activities of managers can be classified into ten interrelated roles.[11]

- **Interpersonal roles** – relations with other people arising from the manager's status and authority. These include **figurehead, leader** and **liaison** roles.
- **Informational roles** – relate to the sources and communication of information arising from the manager's interpersonal roles. These include **monitor, disseminator** and **spokesperson** roles.
- **Decisional roles** – involve making strategic, organisational decisions based on authority and access to information. These include **entrepreneurial, disturbance handler, resource allocator** and **negotiator** roles.

It is emphasised that this set of roles is a rather arbitrary synthesis of a manager's activities. These roles are not easy to isolate in practice but they do form an integrated whole. As such, the removal of any one role affects the effectiveness of the manager's overall performance.

This area has strong links with *Miner*'s 'role expectations and expected pattern of behaviours' theory which is adopted in the model.[12]

The variables already described within the model will determine which form of management is appropriate in any given situation. For example, *McGregor*'s Theory X and Theory Y attempt to develop a predictive model for the behaviour of individual managers.[13] Most managers have a natural inclination towards one basic style of behaviour, with an emergency or 'back-up' style. The dominant style is influenced by one or several of the following: organisation, values, personal history and chance.[14]

Another influential model of management style is centred on 'exploitive authoritative', 'benevolent authoritative', 'consultative' and 'participative group' systems. These systems can then be related to a profile or more specific organisational characteristics.[15]

Efficient and effective management

Managerial efficiency can be distinguished from managerial effectiveness.[16]

- **Efficiency** is concerned with doing things right and relates to **inputs** and what a manager does.
- **Effectiveness** is concerned with doing the right things and relates to **outputs** of the job and what the manager actually achieves.

Performance is related to the goals of the organisation and the informal and formal goals of all its individual participants, including managers. The need to take into account external, environmental variables must not be forgotten.

Measurement

Managerial effectiveness is a difficult concept either to define or to measure. Managerial effectiveness cannot be measured simply in terms of achievement, productivity or relationships with other people. The manager must be adaptable in adopting the appropriate style of behaviour which will determine effectiveness in achieving the output requirements of the job. What is also important is the manner in which the manager achieves results, and the effects on other people.

Managerial effectiveness may be assessed in three ways:

(i) **Formal assessment** – the pursuit of the systematic development of managers is not possible without the support of an appraisal scheme providing for periodic assessment on the basis of the best obtainable objectivity. An assessment form is often used as a valuable aid to objectivity and covers, among other areas: personal skills, behaviour and attitudes; performance in the allocated role; management knowledge and competence; and performance related to potential. Assessment should point out strengths and weaknesses and suggest ways of resolving the latter.

(ii) **Informal assessment** – may be given as advice by other managers, or by the behaviour and attitudes of staff. The willingness to accept a manager's authority will manifest itself through the strength of motivation and therefore measured levels such as staff turnover, incidence of sickness, absenteeism and poor time-keeping.

(iii) **Self-assessment** – the more managers understand about their job and themselves the more sensitive they will be to the needs of the organisation. Sensitivity should also extend to the needs of members. This understanding cannot come simply from studying the results of formal appraisals. Managers must be receptive to the reactions of others and focus consciously on their own actions to try and develop an understanding of what specifically they do and why.[17]

Feedback and development

There are two basic kinds of feedback: intrinsic and augmented.[18]

- **Intrinsic feedback** – includes the usual visual and kinaesthetic cues occurring in connection with a response; for example, the perception of other people's visual reactions towards a management style in a given situation.
- **Augmented feedback** – may be concurrent or terminal, and may occur with performance or after it. The frequency, details and timing of each illustrate the differences between the two; for example, continuous, interim reviews as part of a system of Management by Objectives, compared with the annual performance appraisal interview.

Feedback is largely associated with the measurement area of the model but should be seen as part of the manager's development package. The specific elements in the programmes for individual managers are determined by a variety of circumstances including the outcome of periodic appraisals.

Stewart has commented on the move towards a more individual approach to management development. There should be a greater emphasis on the individual's own setting and needs, and the growing interest in promoting self-development encourages the individual to adopt general management theories to his or her particular needs.[19] This has more recently been extended by the idea of 'mentoring' – a process of nurturing the growth of other people within their jobs – and by the allocation of senior management to support the development of individual juniors within the organisation. Mentoring is part of a self-managed learning process.[20]

MANAGEMENT DEVELOPMENT PROCESS

The process of management development should be related to the nature, objectives and requirements of the **organisation as a whole**. A prerequisite of management development is **effective human resource planning** coupled with procedures for **recruitment and selection**.

Programmes of management development should be designed in accordance with the culture and specific requirements of the particular organisation, and the demands of particular managerial jobs.[21] There should be a clear management development policy together with regular reviews of individual performance and a programme of career progression.

Management development policy

The execution of management development activities should be part of a continuous, cumulative process and take place within the framework of a clear management development policy. Such a policy should include responsibility for:

- the implementation, standardisation and monitoring of management development activities including selection and placement, performance appraisal, potential appraisal, career planning and remuneration;
- the availability of finance and resources, and operational support including training, counselling and problem-solving;
- the motivation and stimulation to continue with management development activities at the operational level; and
- the evaluation and review of policies, procedures and systems.[22]

Performance review

An essential feature of management development is performance review, which was discussed in Chapter 18. The systematic review of work performance provides an opportunity to highlight positive contributions from the application of acquired knowledge, skills, qualifications and experience. An effective system of performance review will help identify individual strengths and weaknesses, potential for promotion, and training and development needs. A key activity is **Management by Objectives** (MBO) which attempts to relate organisational objectives to individual performance and development through the involvement of all levels of management.

For example, the Abbey National Performance Review System allows staff to take control of their own career development. It provides a framework for:

- agreeing objectives and standards of performance;
- measuring results against objectives;
- pinpointing strengths and weaknesses; and
- identifying and meeting training and development needs.

Details of the Abbey National Performance Review System are given in Appendix 2 to this chapter.

Training and learning

Management development also requires a combination of **on-the-job-training**, through, for example, delegation, project work, coaching and guided self-analysis, trial periods and simulation; and **off-the-job-learning**, through, for example, external short courses, or study for a Diploma in Management Studies or MBA qualification. This training and learning should be aimed at providing a blend of technical competence, social and human skills, and conceptual ability.

One of the most basic dilemmas faced by designers of courses and by trainers is the balance between theory and practice; between what may be considered as theoretically desirable and what participants perceive as practically possible to implement. Practising managers may be sceptical of what they regard as a theoretical approach but it is worth remembering the contention that: 'there is nothing so practical as a good theory'.[23] It is also important to achieve an appropriate balance between the assimilation of knowledge information and the development of skills in order to do something.

Action learning

A particular and increasingly popular approach to management development courses is through action learning. Typically, this involves a small self-selecting team undertaking a practical, real-life and organisational-based project. The emphasis is on learning by doing with advice and support from tutors and other course members.[24] Action learning is, therefore, essentially a learner-driven process. It is designed to help develop both the manager and the organisation, and to find solutions to actual problems. For example, *Inglis and Lewis* maintain that action learning aims to increase the number of possible solutions through the involvement of non-experts and posing basic questions such as: what are we trying to do? what is stopping us? what can we do about it?[25]

Feedback

Whatever the nature of a management development programme, one of the most important requirements of any learning process is **the need for effective feedback**. Without feedback there can be no learning. Feedback should be objective,

specific and timely and give a clear indication of how other people perceive behaviour and performance. Wherever possible there should be supporting evidence and actual examples.

Succession planning and career progression

Management succession planning aims to ensure that a sufficient supply of appropriately qualified and capable men and women are available to meet the future needs of the organisation. Such men and women should be available readily to fill vacancies caused through retirement, death, resignation, promotion or transfer of staff, or through the establishment of new positions.

Allied to management development and succession planning should be a programme of **planned career progression**. This should provide potential managers with:

- training and experience to equip them to assume a level of responsibility compatible with their ability; and
- practical guidance, encouragement and support so that they may realise their potential, satisfy their career ambition and wish to remain with the organisation.

Career progression should involve individual appraisal and counselling. However, care should be taken to avoid giving staff too long or over-ambitious career expectations. If these expectations cannot be fulfilled, staff may become disillusioned and frustrated.

Requirements of a management development programme

The requirements of a management development programme have been identified as providing:

- an effective method of defining expected results from managers;
- the continuous improvement in the performance of managers;
- the recruitment and retention of suitable calibre staff;
- first-class training, for tomorrow's jobs as well as today's at lower cost;
- a reliable means of judging the performance of managers;
- a flexible succession plan for the future staffing of the organisation;
- the motivation of managers and fair rewards in relation to results achieved;
- improved flow of communications up, down and across the organisation.[26]

SELF-DEVELOPMENT

An important part of the process of improving the performance of managers is self-development. Part of being an effective manager is the responsibility to further one's own development. A significant factor affecting the success of self-development is the extent to which individual managers take advantage of development opportunities around them. This demands that the manager must be able to identify clearly real development needs and goals, to take responsibility for actions to reach these goals and recognise opportunities for learning.[27]

Self-development has to be self-initiated. But if this is to be a realistic aim it requires an organisational climate that will encourage managers to develop themselves and the active support of top management. Managers need sufficient authority and flexibility to take advantage of situations which are likely to extend their knowledge and skills. Superiors should be prepared to delegate new and challenging projects including problem-solving assignments.

MANAGEMENT EDUCATION, TRAINING AND DEVELOPMENT

The importance of management education, training and development in this country was highlighted by two major reports, sponsored by the (then) British Institute of Management, published in 1987. The *Constable and McCormick Report*, and the *Handy Report* both drew attention to the low level of management education and development of British managers in absolute terms and also relative to major international competitors. The reports note the need for managers with an appropriate knowledge of languages, cultures and business environments of our trading partners.

THE CONSTABLE AND McCORMICK REPORT

The first report, *The Making of British Managers*, examines the development of managers in Britain and warns that many managers need broad professional training and education if they are to compete successfully.[28]

There is widespread recognition of effective management as a key factor in economic growth. But Britain's 2.75 million managers lack the development, education and training opportunities of their competitors in other countries. The majority of people entering management roles each year have no prior formal management education and training.

Recommendations for action

The report listed 23 recommendations for action, centred on four main areas.

(i) Ensuring an adequate flow of educated and trained entrants into management.

(ii) Providing a new Diploma in Business Administration to be taken by young people during their first three to four years of work after higher education. The diploma should be the primary qualification for membership of BIM (now the Institute of Management), but it should not be created by a simple repackaging of the existing Diploma in Management Studies.

(iii) Growth in MBA programmes should be concentrated on flexible and modular programmes, integrated with career development and work experience. Provision for open and distance learning should be expanded for both the diploma and the MBA.

(iv) Management development should be a career-long process with both internal and external training. There should be co-operation among employers, academic and professional institutions, government and individual managers. A credit transfer system should be established covering both academic courses and company programmes.

The report recommends that the government should be responsible for the costs of expanding the infrastructure of university and college management schools. Two new management teacher training programmes should be established and employer organisations should encourage managers to teach part-time.

767

THE HANDY REPORT

A second report, *The Making of Managers: A Report on Management Education, Training and Development in the United States, West Germany, France, Japan and the UK*, questions why enterprises in these other countries are economically more successful than those in Britain, and whether there is something special about the particular contribution by management.[29] Although there are differences in the approach taken to management development by the other countries, overall there is a much more positive approach than in this country. The main similarity is that, in the four competitor countries, most managers have been educated to a higher level than British managers. In contrast to other professions, for example medicine, law and accountancy, there is no clear, relevant and prestigious route into management in Britain.

The report warns that in future technical and functional skills alone will not be enough. Managers will require business knowledge, and human and conceptual skills. Main proposals in the report include the following:

(i) A move to a two-part qualification, on the professional model, with periods of early study leading to a preliminary qualification, followed by work experience interleaved with more specialised study leading to a full qualification, which could be a (revised) MBA.

(ii) For management development there could be a 'Development Charter' setting out a code of good practice including, for example, a personal development plan for every manager and a system for experience-based learning. Major organisations should commit themselves to the charter and form a charter group to set examples, take initiatives and help disseminate good practice.

A ten-point agenda

The report outlines a ten-point agenda for Britain based on the best aspects of management education, training and development in the other countries. The agenda includes: educating more people more broadly, if possible up to first degree level; encouraging some form of work experience to be undertaken as part of this education; establishing a tradition of apprenticeship or 'articles of management'; encouraging good practice in management development by promoting larger organisations as trendsetters; improving co-operation in training between companies, and between companies and business schools; establishing an information base on the provision of management education.

A key conclusion of the report is that, by comparison with the other countries, Britain has yet to find an appropriate form of management education to suit its culture. Many more of the managers in the four competitor countries have benefited from formal, systematic policies for continuous education and development.

THE MANAGEMENT CHARTER INITIATIVE (MCI)

The Constable and McCormick Report and the Handy Report were instrumental in the creation of the Management Charter Initiative in 1988. The MCI was founded

by leading British organisations including Shell, IBM and BP with the support of the government, the CBI, and the (then) British Institute of Management to improve the performance of UK organisation by improving the quality of managers. It has championed the competence-based approach to management development with the emphasis on whether managers can actually do their jobs, and assessment against national Management Standards.

DEVELOPMENTS IN MANAGEMENT EDUCATION

Leo Murray, director of Cranfield School of Management, and *Graham Milborrow*, director of professional development services, BIM, have reviewed developments in the field of management education since publication of the Constable and McCormick Report and the Handy Report.

The Management Charter Initiative has had only a relatively small impact on British industry and the effects of the new approach to training have yet to show their full impact. However, there is a growing awareness of the value of management development within organisations. The number of MBA programmes and graduates has expanded enormously. There is also a robust movement within management development with greater attention to the notion of competence – the ability to perform the activities within an occupation to the standard expected in employment. A growing number of organisations use the competency-based approach to management development.

Impetus to the new management development initiatives has been given by changes in the business environment. Organisations are getting 'flatter'. There is less development upwards and more expertise is expected at any one level. The new developments link management training directly to the bottom line of the firm. Human resource development is now becoming a key feature of business development. Management development is now concerned with improving the whole person and not just some of their skills.[30]

Encouraging trend in management development and training

However, recent research by the MCI indicates that management training has become a priority and that an encouraging trend has been firmly established with training higher on the corporate agenda. MCI conducted a study among those responsible for management development and training in a representative sample of 507 UK organisations employing 21 or more people.[31] Almost 70 per cent of the organisations surveyed regard an investment in management development as justified in terms of business benefits of improvements in efficiency, productivity and quality of work.

The survey focused on changes in attitudes to management training and development in organisations over the last three years. The biggest trend was that training now had to be justified in terms of benefits to the organisation. Other main trends were the use of a wider variety of training techniques and media, and that management training has also become more practical and less academic. Awareness of MCI has remained steady. The use of the standards for management development or training programmes has increased significantly.

MANAGEMENT DEVELOPMENT TO THE MILLENNIUM

A recent major research survey into management development, conducted by the Institute of Management, shows that managers in the next century will have to be good at:

- strategic planning;
- responding to and managing change;
- total quality management;
- verbal communication;
- coaching others; and
- delegating responsibility.

The research involved in-depth interviews with 30 of Britain's most senior managers followed by a questionnaire to 5000 practising managers. [32]

The major challenges managers foresee are contracting-out, de-layering and empowerment. Managers will have to draw on the brainpower of all employees and trust them by letting them make their own decisions. Almost four in ten believe that by 2001 most work will be carried out in multi-disciplinary teams but the skills required to manage this way are still in their infancy. However, the survey found that individuals have recognised the need for continuous, lifelong training. Nearly 90 per cent of those surveyed believe there will be an increased need to acquire new work-related skills. They realise that to improve their employability they must have transferable skills.

Challenges facing management

The report identifies six challenges facing management:

- organisations must recognise that investment in management development contributes directly to long-term competitiveness;
- managers must commit themselves to lifelong learning;
- senior managers must provide commitment and leadership;
- providers must recognise and respond to the diverse training and development needs of their customers and users;
- standards must be accepted and qualifications transferable; and
- a more coherent infrastructure for management development must be created.

Female ways of managing more appropriate

The report concludes that in order not to become a dinosaur the manager as we know him will have to change. He will no longer be The Boss but will be a team leader who will need to earn the respect of all people. And the people will not necessarily be in the same building, town or even country because e-mail and fax will replace meetings and memos. And he is just as likely to be a she because female ways of managing will be more appropriate in the millennium. These female attributes include teamworking, consensus management, negotiating, the ability to handle several projects at a time and interpersonal skills. Male managers face extinction by 2001!

THE NATURE OF ORGANISATIONAL EFFECTIVENESS

The underlying theme of this book has been the need for organisational effectiveness and the role of management as an integrating activity. Organisational effectiveness, however, is affected by a multiplicity of variables. For example, *Handy* identifies over 60 factors that impinge on any one organisational situation and which illustrate the complicated nature of the study of organisational effectiveness.[33] (*See* Fig. 21.2.)

Efficiency and effectiveness

Organisations need to be **efficient** in doing the right things, in the optimum use of their resources and in the ratio of outputs to inputs. But organisations must also be **effective** in doing the right things and in their outputs related to some specific purpose, objective or task. **Performance** should be related to such factors as increasing profitability, improved service delivery or obtaining the best results in

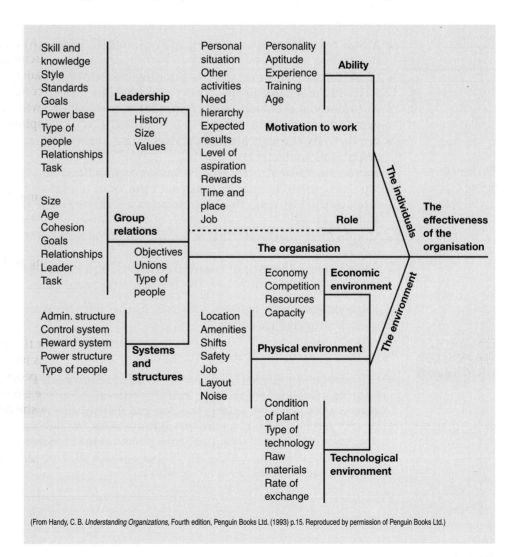

Fig. 21.2 Some factors affecting organisational effectiveness

(From Handy, C. B. *Understanding Organizations*, Fourth edition, Penguin Books Ltd. (1993) p.15. Reproduced by permission of Penguin Books Ltd.)

important areas of organisational activities. Organisations must also ensure that they meet satisfactorily, or exceed, the demands and requirements of customers, and are **adaptable** to specific requirements, changes in the external environment and the demands of the situation.[34]

In analysing effective organisations, *Dunderdale* argues that an organisation can be separated into two parts or structures – one a definitive structure present in every company, the other caused by human intervention. Each part can then be examined. Essentially the effectiveness of an organisation depends on how accurately human design matches the structure of organised behaviour.[35]

THE PETERS AND WATERMAN STUDY

In their study of 62 American companies with outstandingly successful performance, *Peters and Waterman* identify eight basic attributes of excellence which appear to account for success:[36]

- **A bias for action**; that is, being action-oriented and with a bias for getting things done.
- **Close to the customer**; that is, listening and learning from the people they serve, and providing quality, service and reliability.
- **Autonomy and entrepreneurship**; that is, innovation and risk-taking as an expected way of doing things.
- **Productivity through people**; that is, treating members of staff as the source of quality and productivity.
- **Hands-on, value driven**; that is, having well-defined basic philosophies and top management keeping in touch with the 'front lines'.
- **Stick to the knitting**; that is, in most cases, staying close to what you know and can do well.
- **Simple form, lean staff**; that is, simple structural forms and systems, and few top-level staff.
- **Simultaneous loose-tight properties**; that is, operational decentralisation but strong centralised control over the few, important core values.

The companies were marked, above all, by the 'intensity itself' which stemmed from their strongly held beliefs.

The McKinsey 7-S framework

From their research Peters and Waterman report that:

> any intelligent approach to organizing had to encompass, and treat as interdependent, at least seven variables: structure, strategy, people, management style, systems and procedures, guiding concepts and shared values (i.e. culture), and the present and hoped-for corporate strengths or skills. We defined this idea more precisely and elaborated what came to be known as the McKinsey 7-S Framework. With a bit of stretching, cutting and fitting, we made all seven variables start with the letter S and invented a logo to go with it.[37]

(*See* Fig. 21.3.)

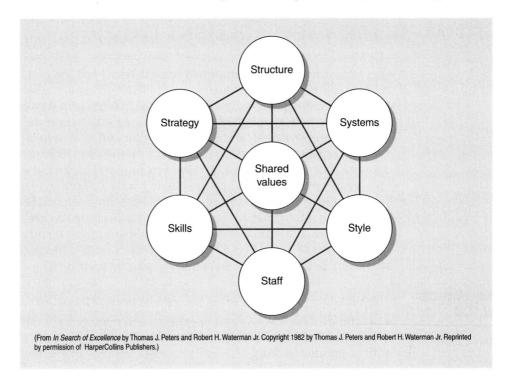

**Fig. 21.3
The McKinsey
7-S framework**

(From *In Search of Excellence* by Thomas J. Peters and Robert H. Waterman Jr. Copyright 1982 by Thomas J. Peters and Robert H. Waterman Jr. Reprinted by permission of HarperCollins Publishers.)

The importance of innovation

A key factor in organisational effectiveness is the successful management of change. Diagnosing and solving organisational problems involves the interaction of a multiplicity of factors influencing an organisation's ability to change and its proper mode of change.[38]

A common thread among the successful companies is **innovation**. A common characteristic of excellently managed companies is that they tend to have a flexible organisation structure. In contrast to bureaucracies, the attributes of successful, well-managed companies included open communications, informality, participative decision-making and freedom of expression. The flexible nature of organisation led to a bias for quick action rather than inertia, and emphasis was placed on risk-taking and innovation.

When looking at management excellence itself, Peters and Waterman chose a double meaning for 'innovation'.

> In addition to what might normally be thought of – creative people developing marketable new product and services – . . . *innovative companies are especially adroit at continually responding to change of any sort in their environments.*[39]

When their environments change, innovative companies change too. As a whole culture, they innovate to meet changes in the needs of their customers, the skills of competitors, the mood of the public, forces of international trade or government regulations. The concept of innovation defined the task of the truly excellent manager or management team. Companies that appeared to have attained that kind of innovative performance were the ones Peters and Waterman labelled as 'excellent companies'.

TOTAL QUALITY MANAGEMENT (TQM)

One particular approach to improved organisational performance and effectiveness is the concept of Total Quality Management (TQM). There are numerous definitions of TQM. These definitions are generally expressed in terms of: **a way of life for an organisation as a whole, committed to total customer satisfaction through a continuous process of improvement, and the contribution and involvement of people.**

The successful organisation should as a matter of policy be constantly seeking opportunities to improve the quality of its products and/or services and processes. The organisation must also couple quality with a required level of productivity. TQM represents a total system and as such increasingly embraces quality circles (discussed in Chapter 15) as a broader means of addressing the demands for quality.[40] However, *Heller*, while recognising improvement in the quality revolution, raises doubts as to how far TQM is 'total' and how far it is truly affecting management and the quality of management. Total quality is a long journey.[41]

Key elements of TQM

The key elements of TQM have been identified by *Pentecost* as:

- a **total process** involving all operations and management units in the organisation, and led from the top;
- the **customer as king** with every strategy, process and action directly related to satisfying customers' needs;
- a greater emphasis on **rational information collection and analysis** using modern technology where appropriate;
- an emphasis on a different approach to looking at the **costs of poor quality** by examining all processes in the organisation which add to costs;
- a greater **involvement of people**, recognising that they are a great untapped resource in most companies;
- **teamwork** as crucially important, involving multi-discipline and multi-level working to solve problems and to meet customers' needs; and
- the requirements for **creative thinking** and the ability to think beyond the immediate job or work environment.[42]

Caulkin sets out 'maps' contrasting the old model and the new model for a quality voyage (*see* Fig 21.4).[43]

Public sector and service organisations

The search for a TQM culture is also of increasing significance for public sector organisations. In local government, tight financial constraints and the requirements of compulsory competitive tendering help to emphasise the demands for quality.[44] Managers in all public sector organisations are likely to be involved increasingly with the concepts and application of TQM.[45] Attention to quality can also be seen to be of particular significance in service organisations, for example within the hospitality industry. TQM can provide a strategic focus in the search for a culture of total quality service.[46]

The importance of people

TQM emphasises the importance of people as the key to quality. Human resource management and quality management are converging to give total quality. It is lack of communications and awareness that causes failures and costs. There has

	Old model	New model
Objective	Growth (sales, earnings, ROI)	Total customer satisfaction to achieve profitable growth
Production	Long runs, economies of scale	Short runs, small lots, quick changeover
Production aims	Low cost, high efficiency	Quick response
Inventory	Just-in-case, buffer	Just-in-time, zero
People	Liability to be reduced where possible; specialised for repetitive tasks; 'do what you're told'; recruit from outside	Asset to be invested in; multi-skilled for flexible tasks; 'do what you think'; home grown
System v. people	People made to fit system, sub-optimisation	System made to fit people, optimising system
Quality v. cost	Trade-off; one or the other	Highest quality equals lowest cost
Quality management	Inspection, rework, allowances, warranty	Prevention, right first time, no inspection
Structure	Vertical, 'functional silos'	Process, cross-functional, networking
Management	Hierarchical, short spans of control, turf conscious	Flat, large spans of control, 'empowering'
Suppliers	Adversaries; many to play off against each other	Long-term partners; few
Customers	Short-term exploitative relationships	Long-term relationships; joint action teams
Change	Resists and puts off change	'Divine discontent'; welcomes change; continuous

(Reproduced with permission from Caulkin, S. 'TQM 1: The Road to Peerless Wigan', *Management Today*, March 1994, p. 30.)

Fig. 21.4 Maps for a quality voyage

been too much reliance on systems. Although systems are necessary, they are only as effective as the people who design them.[47]

TQM requires the creation of a corporate identity and a supportive environment. It involves setting the highest standards for quality at lowest costs; effective training including teambuilding throughout the organisation; integrating systems and technology with people; and the motivation, participation and commitment of staff at all levels of the organisation.[48]

TQM and the Quality of Working Life

James puts forward the contention that TQM initiatives will not succeed unless rooted in a supportive Quality of Working Life (QWL) culture.

world standards of organisational effectiveness are not achievable without fully developed and committed people at all levels within an organisation. New technologies, new systems, and new concepts may, of themselves, produce some improvement in effectiveness and hence competitiveness but even in the short term the improvement will be stunted without an organisation culture which engenders commitment of people across the organisation.[49]

The aim of a QWL culture is to create a fear-free organisation in which employee involvement is pursued vigorously. It generates a high degree of recipro-

cal commitment between the needs and development of the individual, and the goals and developments of the organisation. A QWL cultural underpinning anchors the development of total quality and is essential to a successful TQM strategy. (The Quality of Working Life was discussed in Chapter 15.)

MANAGEMENT SERVICES AND TECHNIQUES

In the search for improved organisational effectiveness there is an increasing range of specialist skills to help managers, whether in business, public sector or other organisations. When striving to achieve the goals and objectives of the organisation there are a number of 'tools' which can assist the manager in organisational processes and the execution of work. Many of these tools come under the heading of management services and techniques. These services and techniques aid management by providing relevant information to enable improved decision-making and more effective control. (*See* Fig. 21.5.)

The meaning of management services and techniques

'Management services' and 'management techniques' tend to be overworked terms and there are considerable differences in the interpretations placed upon them. Although it is not the purpose here to explain the particular tools of management, it is important to understand what is implied by the terms management services and management techniques.

One simple approach is to regard management services as the generic term covering the grouping of a number of specialist, advisory activities or services to management. It is the emergence of various new specialisations and techniques which has given rise to the term management services. In ideas of 'hierarchical' levels, management services might be regarded as the more comprehensive and

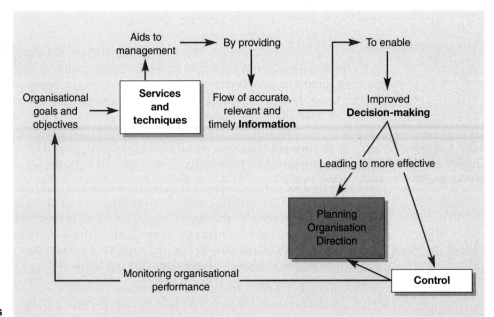

**Fig. 21.5
The role of management services and techniques as part of a control process**

embracing term covering aids to management in the broader sense; while management techniques are particular specialisations and skills for dealing with individual problems.

On this basis computerisation, organisation and methods, management information systems, programme budgeting and management accounting could be quoted as examples of management services. Simulation, critical path analysis, discounted cash flow, and cost–benefit analysis could be quoted as examples of management techniques. However, terminology is confused. There is no clear distinction between the use of the word services or of the word techniques. The two words are often used synonymously or interchangeably. There are different connotations in different publications and different organisations, and varying interpretations on the range of activities properly placed under each heading.[50]

The use of management techniques

Whatever the debate on terminology, the important thing is the use of techniques as aids to the process of management and the execution of work. Many techniques are based on a high level of mathematics or statistics, and they have been surrounded with an aura of mystique and glamour. Because of their apparent complexity many techniques may seem to the manager to lack practical application. Some techniques are by their nature complex and not easy to describe in simple terms. This may further confuse the manager. There is, therefore, the danger of using sophisticated techniques for their own sake when simpler methods might be just as satisfactory.

The manager will not usually be expected to have a detailed technical knowledge of all the individual techniques. This is a job for the specialist. The manager should, however, be aware of their main features, advantages and limitations; and have sufficient understanding of how different techniques might be applied to help the process of management and organisation development. The responsibility for the implementation of these techniques should rest with the manager. An understanding of management services and techniques will aid the activity of management, including the control process, and help to improve organisational effectiveness.

ASSESSING ORGANISATIONAL EFFECTIVENESS

Based on experience in a broad range of organisations, *Steele* suggests nine questions to help managers assess the performance of their companies. These questions have been submitted to approximately 125 different groups of managers from all industries – manufacturing, banking, retail and general commerce. Although the questions are not exhaustive and not intended to be a panacea, there has been full agreement that they are a reasonable list of questions for assessing organisational effectiveness.

1. What is the attitude to change?
2. What is the degree of trust in the management's view of the workforce, is there a THEM and US mentality?
3. Really a manifestation of Question 2 – How much management information, especially financial, is communicated?
4. How visible and accessible is management, especially top management?

5. What is the atmosphere like in the organisation?
 Focusing on more specific areas to help identify the quality of an organisation's atmosphere:
 (i) What do people believe about the organisation?
 (ii) How much control exists?
 (iii) Is there a fear of failure?
 (iv) Do people feel free to talk back?
 (v) Is there a fun atmosphere in the organisation?
6. How frequently are people rewarded and recognised?
7. What is the posture and prowess of the first point of customer contact?
8. Is customer service actively measured and the results communicated widely?
9. Do people have an appropriate purpose?[51]

A RANGE OF DIFFERENT CRITERIA

There is a wide range of interrelated individual, group, organisational and environmental influences on behaviour in work organisations, and therefore many different criteria which might be applied as part of an attempt to assess organisational performance and effectiveness. In addition to those discussed in the last two chapters, we can mention some examples that have been discussed in previous chapters of this book.

Open systems framework

An organisation may be analysed in terms of an open systems framework: inputs; the series of activities involved in the transformation or conversion process: outputs; interactions with the environment; and performance of the system (organisation) in achieving its aims and objectives. The organisation may also be examined in terms of interrelated sub-systems, for example tasks to be undertaken, technology employed, formal structure, behaviour of people and the process of management. The state of the sub-systems will reflect upon the effectiveness of the organisation as a whole.

Key areas of performance and results

The extent to which the goals of the organisation are pursued in accordance with an underlying ideology, codes of behaviour, sets of principles, and ethical and organisational foundation. The effectiveness of an organisation might be assessed against *Drucker's* eight key areas in which objectives need to be set in terms of business performance and results: market standing; innovation; productivity; physical and financial resources; profitability; manager performance and development; worker performance and attitude; and public responsibility.

Design of organisation structure

One of the most significant factors which determine effective organisational performance is the correct design of structure. Part of the attempt to gauge organisational effectiveness could involve a review of structure to assess the extent to which it aids the process of management and the execution of work. In particular, does the structure harmonise with organisational goals and objectives, and maintain the balance of the socio-technical system? How flexible is the structure and how effective is the 'fit' between structure, systems of management, the behaviour of people and situational variables?

Profile of organisational characteristics

The overall effectiveness of an organisation could also be gauged against *Likert*'s profile of organisational characteristics, and the extent to which these meet the fundamental concepts of System 4 (participative group) management practices, that is: the principle of support relationships; group decision-making, and methods of organisation and supervision; and high performance aspiration for all members of the organisation. The human organisation and operation of the firm can be examined in terms of the relationships among causal, intervening and end-result variables.

The role of management

There are also a number of criteria which could be applied, more specifically, to an evaluation of the essential nature and role of management. The activities of management could be judged, for example, against *Bourn*'s set of ten interrelated activities; against *Mintzberg*'s set of ten integrated roles which comprise the essential functions of a manager's job; or against *Kotter*'s key activities of agenda-setting and network-building. Style of management could be assessed, for example, by the *Blake and McCanse* Leadership Grid in terms of an appropriate mixture of concern for production and concern for people.

Managerial effectiveness

This could be gauged against *Stewart*'s checklist of questions for managers. It can be evaluated by *Reddin*'s three-dimensional model of managerial behaviour: task orientation, relationship orientation and the demands of the situation; or by *Langford*'s criteria of: the manager's work; the manager himself/herself; the manager's relationship with other people; the manager as part of the organisation; and a single overall criterion of general effectiveness. In more general terms managers are judged not just on their own performance but by the actual results achieved by subordinate staff.

Organisational control systems

The effectiveness of organisational control systems can be gauged by the extent to which they draw attention to the critical activities which are important to the overall success of the organisation. To what extent do control systems provide an effective means of checking progress to determine whether the objectives of the organisation are being achieved, and help lead to an improvement in performance? Are structures of control congruent with power and involvement, and the means of ensuring compliance among members?

ORGANISATION AUDIT

A programme of organisation audit (or management audit) involves a review of the operations of the organisation as a whole and an examination of the full range of management activities, including the effective use of human resources. Organisation audit is concerned with the identification of problems which are encountered in achieving organisational goals and disparities between strategy formulation and policy decisions, and actions necessary for their successful implementation.

Such a review may be undertaken by members of the organisation, external consultants on organisation and management, or a combination of both internal members and external consultants. Organisation audit tends to be concerned more with the current state of the organisation, and with what must be done now in order to meet set objectives and targets. But an organisation must also be properly prepared to face the demands of a changing environment. It must give attention to its future development and success.

SYNOPSIS

■ The quality of management is one of the most important factors in the success of any organisation. There is, therefore, a continual need for managerial development as an integral part of the process of organisation development. Using accumulated knowledge of management theory it is possible to construct an integrated model of managerial behaviour and development. Attention needs to be given to the process of management development, including performance review and management by objectives, training and learning, management succession planning and career progression.

■ Two major reports sponsored by the British Institute of Management have highlighted the importance of, and shortcomings in, management education, training and development in Britain, and were instrumental in the establishment of the Management Charter Initiative. There is now a growing awareness of the importance of management development and human resource development but the effects of the new approach to management education have yet to show their full impact. A recent major research survey draws attention to the need for managers to acquire new skills. The managers will no longer be The Boss but a team leader. The report also concludes that female ways of managing will be more appropriate in the millennium.

■ There are a multiplicity of variables which impinge on any one organisational situation and which illustrate the complicated nature of the study of organisational effectiveness. In their study of 62 American companies with outstandingly successful performance, Peters and Waterman identify eight basic attributes of excellence. One approach to organising is the McKinsey 7-S framework of interdependent organisational variables – structure, strategy, skills, staff, style, systems and shared values. A key factor in organisational effectiveness is innovation and the successful management of change.

■ One particular approach to improved organisational effectiveness is Total Quality Management (TQM). The successful organisation should as a matter of policy be constantly seeking opportunities to improve the quality of its products and/or services and processes. People are the key to quality and if TQM initiatives are to succeed they should be supported by a Quality of Working Life culture. The appropriate use of management services and techniques can aid the process of management and execution of work, and help to improve organisational effectiveness.

■ Based on experience in a broad range of organisations, Steele suggests nine questions to help assess organisational effectiveness. There are, however a wide range of interrelated individual, group, organisational and environmental influences on behaviour in work organisations. Accordingly there are many different criteria which might be applied in attempting to assess organisational performance and effectiveness.

■ An organisation may be analysed in terms of an open systems framework; it may be assessed in terms of key areas of performance and results, or against a profile of organisational characteristics. There are also a number of criteria which could be applied more specifically to an evaluation of the role of management and managerial effectiveness. A programme of organisation audit involves a review of the operations of the organisation as a whole. However, in addition to concern for the current state of the organisation, attention must be given to its future development and success.

APPENDIX 1 QWL CASE STUDY SERIES

B & Q – 'Who cares wins'

Matching and developing staff to meet the business needs of the 1990s

'Who cares wins' is more than a slogan at B & Q, financially the most successful company in the Kingfisher Group. Starting from one humble store in Southampton in 1969 the company is now the UK's largest national DIY chain of 280 stores and garden centres, with 15,000 employees, well over 10 million square feet of selling space and a turnover of £900 million in 1990.

This article describes five significant B & Q employee policies and practices that seek to develop the management skills, abilities and staff resources required for the successful growth of the company. The employment practices covered by the article are:

1. Assessment Centres and staff competency.
2. Staff selection (pyschometric testing) and retention.
3. Staff development and training.
4. Customer service.
5. Work scheduling.

Strategy

The present company strategy is to grow from its existing DIY market base and to extend its interests in the much bigger field of professional repairs, maintenance and home improvement. This will create new opportunities for the company and its staff but requires major changes in planning, structure, organisation and employee attitudes. Additionally, the company is seeking to further improve its business performance. To successfully manage both these objectives creates strong pressures on the company's management skills and staff resources.

1. Assessment Centres – staff competency

As a rapidly expanding organisation, opening several new stores a year, B & Q have a requirement for a smooth, credible career structure for staff to progress through the company. Improved appraisal and selection systems were needed to identify individual abilities within the organisation and adequately match the skills available against the requirements of the positions to be filled.

B & Q decided that their use of Assessment Centres for managers could assist in achieving these aims. They saw that employees attending these centres could build on their individual strengths and reduce identified weaknesses. Assessment Centres were also seen as good training vehicles to help achieve the company's aim of 'profit through people'.

After a period of using the Assessment Centres, the company *undertook the largest valuation study into assessment centres ever conducted by a retail organisation.* They sought to evaluate how their managers performed in their jobs and compared the results with the employees' performance during the assessment tests. The results of the evaluation study confirmed the value of the Assessment Centres, and a number of improvements were then introduced to fine tune the centres.

A further advance was made when the Development (Assessment) Centres were made available to Head Office staff.

Competencies

As an extension to the work done on Assessment Centres they also examined the tasks and competencies required for managerial and department proficiency. In all, through interviews with Senior Managers some *700* critical incidents were gathered from which 23 major competencies were isolated and linked to a scale of values. They potentially provide an excellent management tool for matching the jobs and ability of the management workforce spread throughout the UK. With further development, they can fill management vacancies quickly and effectively; rejuvenate and motivate those who are not

making the most of their abilities, and identify achievers and 'square pegs'.

2. Staff selection (psychometric testing) and retention

Many retail stores and shops in the UK have a high staff turnover and a high percentage (some 60 per cent in many large retail outlets) of part-time staff. Poor customer service, a low motivated staff, badly trained in product knowledge and selling skills are among the problems identified.

B & Q made a detailed examination of its labour turnover figures. The company further examined its recruitment, selection, training and induction practices. It considered staff expectations, personality attributes, career progression, and a possible 'over sell' when staff were recruited by Store Managers. B & Q made a job and organisational analysis at store level. In addition, the company sent a detailed questionnaire to 3000 former employees and considered the 1000 forms returned. A working party of store personnel, training and regional staff was set up to study the whole question of labour turnover and to make recommendations to bring about improvements. The working party issued a further questionnaire which went to 1000 staff covering 24 stores. The replies included concerns about training, job satisfaction, repetitive work, communications, pay and working conditions. These replies confirmed the target areas to attack, the first target being the selection of employees.

Psychometric testing

The company conducted a pilot exercise of psychometric testing. The tests covered numeracy, personality, checking and understanding of information. The company compared these tests with the actual results achieved through the previous method of selection by interview. B & Q also carried out a validation exercise which produced signs of encouraging trends in staff retention rates. These positive results confirmed the value of psychometric tests for selection and it was decided to apply these tests to all store applicants.

B & Q also built an extensive training network with facilities at most stores for a training centre.

All stores follow a comprehensive and monitored induction programme for new employees and provide a facility for distance learning courses. The attainment of the National Retail Certificate is encouraged.

Equal opportunities

B & Q have endeavoured to remove all forms of discrimination so that all capable staff are able to progress through to management positions. In the past, female employees were under-represented at store and district managerial levels and the company took steps to rectify this position. Women, employed initially in junior general assistant positions, are now appointed to all managerial grades in growing numbers. The company set a target that at least 50 per cent of graduates recruited should be female. A large proportion of all department managers and supervisors are women; some were appointed while still in their teens. Many B & Q press advertisements are specifically targeted for career-minded 'but not necessarily academically qualified' women.

B & Q were also the first major retail group to open a store completely staffed by employees aged over 50. The company were extremely satisfied with the calibre and the number of applications (600 applied) for the posts. The subsequent trading position, retention of staff, low absenteeism and high standards of customer service confirmed the success of this bold venture. Previously, all employees retired at 60 years of age. The company now offers an 'over 60 contract' which is also available to external applicants.

The company ensures positive vetting and comparison with competitors on salaries, bonus and pension. It also addresses significant shortfalls in organisational and environmental conditions. These items can form part of the agenda of B & Q's 'Regional Consultative Committees', the National Committee being chaired by the Personnel Director. The membership is composed of representatives of every grade of store and district staff. By these and other measures the company's labour turnover figure has reduced by 8 per cent over the last two years.

3. Staff development and training

Mention has been made of the company's comprehensive store induction programme; their extensive and well equipped Training Centres and Store Trainers based either in the District or Store. The company also employ Regional Training Officers to conduct regional training and oversee and assist Store Trainers.

The company ensures each employee receives induction and further retail training. *An individual training programme is designed for each member of the staff* and monitored at store level. The Store Training Centre contains an impressive number of well produced booklets on a large variety of subjects. Laser discs and a full range of videos on retail-related topics are now provided. Computerised Interactive Videos which teach, ask questions and mark the answers also play an important part in B & Q training.

These and other forms of open learning are seen by the company as an ideal, cost-effective vehicle to suit B & Q's structure and personnel. It provides a standard message and maintains consistency across a wide geographical area. It caters for shift patterns of working and is sufficiently flexible to meet company and individual needs. It is of major assistance in supplementing the on-site and off-site training given to new staff when a new store is being opened. The open learning facility enables the company to respond to demands on its training resources. It provides the means whereby employees at all levels can come together under the trainer for official training sessions during work time periods. Or, it can provide a method by which employees in their own free time can, if they so desire, further their own study – a facility of great benefit when such staff are of disparate educational backgrounds and learning speeds.

4. Improving 'customer service'

In 1989, B & Q was concerned that the number of complaints from its customers was rising and undertook the task of examining ways by which customer service standards could be improved.

A vital step in bringing about greater customer service was to encourage from store management and staff a greater sense of responsibility for their store's performance. To implement this required a cultural change. Managers were allowed the greatest freedom possible with authority to manage their staff, stock levels, and the merchandising of some goods etc. To assist this change process motivational training was introduced with every manager attending a two-day course. A new appraisal system was implemented and greater emphasis placed upon objectives that would improve customer service.

A high profile customer care programme was established and given full support and encouragement by the Directors and the Chief Executive who took a significant personal interest.

A 'customer care' training module was produced and the rules of the 'Best Store' competition were amended to place greater emphasis on customer service. 'Mystery' B & Q shoppers rewarded stores and store personnel for high customer service performance. Sales and service 'Employees of the Month' competitions for each store were developed, with qualifying stages at District and Regional level, culminating in a national 'Employee of the Year'. Bonuses were paid by Store Managers from their budgets to employees who, from the customers' own comments or letters, were said to have made an outstanding service contribution to the customer.

Areas of work demand, staff availability and suppliers' delivery times were examined to avoid, where possible, time constraints – constraints that could lead to poor customer service when staff had difficulty in meeting conflicting demands on their time.

Help line

A major venture was the introduction of the B & Q 'Help line' to provide assistance and advice to customers. The company also took serious note of the desire by many customers for improved standards of product knowledge from B & Q staff. An extensive training programme was established to raise these standards.

These and other developments have substantially raised standards in customer care but the

company continues to review these and other alternatives. The employment at depots of specialist DIY consultants and the employment in stores of older, more experienced staff are but two of the features in this area that have gained B & Q national prominence.

5. Work scheduling

Utopia for many managers is to supply the demands of labour, materials and sales at the precise time they are required: a situation very difficult to achieve in any labour-intensive, variable, demanding work situation. In an attempt to minimise shortages and surpluses and to retain the skilled labour required to cope with a fluctuating product demand, a number of organisations 'average out' their demand peaks and troughs. They can then seek to employ a sufficient number of staff to meet that *average*.

The B & Q 'Work Scheduling' programme seeks to provide a far more accurate and cost-effective method of matching staff numbers with the fluctuating requirements of the business. The aim is to provide the correct number of staff of the required skills at the *precise moment* they are needed!

B & Q believe the key to reducing conflicting work pressures and priorities is to predict accurately the number and type of staff required to carry out the stores' functions. Accurate predictions require massive and complex statistical information gathering. B & Q's investigation has demonstrated that it is possible to predict the number of specific items likely to be sold *and* the *time* of day when they would most probably be sold. In establishing the specific item, its weight, size and the product knowledge required to sell it can also be calculated. Establishing customer demand in detail simplifies pre- and re-ordering and the supply and replenishing of shelves at the most appropriate time. It facilitates the planning of the best time for good housekeeping and merchandising within the store area and the correct staff skills to be employed to carry out those tasks. Accurately predicting sales on an individual store and time basis reduces over and under ordering of stock, reduces costs and prioritises delivery from the warehouse while improving budget control and *customer satisfaction*. The statistical information obtained can also be utilised to estimate the appropriate time required for staff to complete a work task.

Benefits of work scheduling

The evidence gained has already demonstrated the cost-effectiveness uses to which work scheduling can be put. It has also shown that customer demand and staff resources can be adjusted to provide a 'best fit'. Establishing what and when work will be required and the staff time needed to complete it satisfactorily, makes discussions on minimum labour and skill requirements possible. Such periods can be a few hours a day, employing the appropriate staff for the *time* of the day required.

The benefits of work scheduling are seen to be an improved supply of goods on the shop floor and better and higher skill coverage for the customer. Greater product security at peak times can also be attained. For the staff, establishing accurate work times for the completion of tasks creates the possibility of additional bonus payments or time allowances for their earlier completion. The greater opportunity for short work periods, and annual hours arrangements at mutually convenient times, permits the employment of skilled and non-skilled employees from sections of the population who would have found it inconvenient in the past. Reducing waste in time and resources can lead to greater company profitability, expansion and improved career prospects for its employees.

B & Q are winning because they care about their customers *and* staff.

Terry Quinlan
Work Research Unit

(Reprinted with permission from *ACAS Work Research Unit*, News and Abstracts, no. 108, Autumn 1991, pp. 10–12.)

APPENDIX 2

Abbey National Performance Review System

FOREWORD FROM JOHN KING
HUMAN RESOURCES DIRECTOR

Dear colleague,

As individuals, we all have a vital part to play in the success of Abbey National. Our track record is excellent, thanks largely to the efforts of all our staff. As a company, we value our staff highly, and believe that the individual's contribution to the continuing success of the business deserves to be recognised and rewarded.

That philosophy is reflected in our performance-related pay scheme, and in our performance review system, which are designed to encourage personal development and excellence, in line with our business objectives.

Our performance review system has attracted long-standing recognition in the industry at large, but in keeping with our culture, which encourages open debate, fairness, and a continuing commitment to improvement, we have recently introduced some refinements to the scheme, which will enhance it still further. These changes take account of the views expressed by staff and managers. As a result, the system now focuses more closely on the needs of the business, the way these relate to the individual's job as a whole, and on meeting associated training and development needs.

In order to maintain our competitive edge, we must be adaptable. For the individual, that means cultivating a flexible approach to work, and a clear understanding of how key job responsibilities contribute to the success of the business as a whole. The performance review system aims to foster an environment in which people are given support and encouragement to develop their talents to the full. This in turn will allow Abbey National to deliver quality products and high standards of customer service, and to position ourselves as the outstanding financial services company in the UK.

INTRODUCTION

The Performance Review system is a way of helping staff to improve the quality of their contribution to their branch, centre or department, and to the company as a whole. It allows managers and staff to take control of their work and career development. It provides a framework for measuring results and identifying and meeting training and development needs. It also forms the basis for rewarding staff for work well done.

In response to suggestions and comments from managers and staff, a number of changes have been made to the scheme. The purpose of doing this is to make it fairer, by looking at the whole range of tasks associated with a job rather than setting isolated objectives. The result is that individual ratings will reflect performance more accurately. The changes are also designed to help the individual evaluate his or her performance and training requirements on an on-going basis, in the context of the overall needs of the business.

Finally, the changes address the need for an easy-to-use method of monitoring progress and achievement. The changes and the way the system now operates can be briefly summed up as follows:

- Rather than setting objectives for the year, the employee and his or her manager will meet to draw up a Performance Agreement in January for the year ahead.
- The individual's progress will be regularly reviewed throughout the year, and a formal interim review will take place in June. This will measure progress against the Performance Agreement, paying particular attention to identifying and meeting any resulting training or development needs.
- In December, an appraisal review will take place where the individual will be given a performance rating (the five ratings definitions

used in the past will continue to apply). This rating is a major factor in determining the individual's pay for the following year.

This is a detailed guide to the system, and should help you to get the most out of it, whether as a person whose performance is being reviewed, a manager conducting a review, or as a manager who has to countersign a number of reviews.

How the system works

1. Performance Agreement
The Reviewer and Reviewee develop a Performance Agreement.

2. Informal Reviews
Reviewer and Reviewee check on progress and alter the Performance Agreement as necessary.

3. Preparation for Interim Review
Reviewer provides a pre-interview form to Reviewee and agrees a date for the review. Reviewer and Reviewee both consider:

- performance over the review period;
- the effectiveness of training and development received;
- the training and development required in the future.

4. Interim Review
Reviewer and Reviewee discuss performance to date and update the Performance Agreement as necessary. The meeting will focus on any training and development received in the last 12 months, and the planning of training and development for the next 12 months.

5. Appraisal Form
Written up and signed by the Reviewer and then the Reviewee; countersigned by the Reviewer's manager.

6. Administration
Copies of the complete form are given to the Reviewer and the Reviewee, and the original appraisal form should be sent to the Personnel Department.

7. Informal Reviews
Reviewer and Reviewee check on progress and alter the Performance Agreement as necessary.

8. Preparation for End-of-Year Review
Reviewer provides a 'pre-interview form to Reviewee and agrees a date for the review. Reviewer and Reviewee both consider performance over the review period. Reviewer discusses *proposed* ratings with his/her line manager to ensure consistency.

9. End-of-Year Review
Discussion of performance to date and additional activities undertaken. Reviewer awards rating. Discussion of key competencies which have affected performance, and identification of personal qualities.

10. Appraisal Form
Written up and signed by the Reviewer and then the Reviewee; countersigned by the Reviewer's manager.

11. Administration
Copies of the complete form are given to the Reviewer and the Reviewee, and the original appraisal form should be sent to the Personnel Department, together with a copy of the Performance Agreement.

12. Appeals Process
Staff who do not believe their rating reflects their performance can use the Appeals Process.

PERFORMANCE AGREEMENTS

At the start of the year, the manager and the member of staff meet to draw up a Performance Agreement for the coming year. The Agreement sets out the job the individual will need to do if the business plan for the year is to be achieved. It identifies priorities, and forms a bridge between the business plan and the individual's job description. It should be challenging but achievable.

Once the Agreement has been produced it will form a basis for continuous self-monitoring. Each month, the individual can record the progress made against each accountability.

The way in which Performance Agreements are written is important. The process should be participative; both the manager and the employee should take an active part in the discussion, and provide input to the document. The Performance Agreement process may be carried out on a one-to-one basis or, in the case of 'generic' jobs, as a group exercise, to help ensure consistency between jobs that are the same, or very similar.

Generic Performance Agreements should be modified to meet individual needs or local circumstances. A group approach to writing generic Performance Agreements saves time, and can be a very constructive teambuilding exercise. It gives the team the opportunity to hear about the manager's vision for the year ahead, to share their ideas and concerns, and to add to the year's agenda. Last but not least, individual team members are encouraged to make a strong commitment to supporting each others' efforts to achieve the team's overall goals.

The more effort that goes into defining Performance Agreements, the easier it will be for individuals and managers to monitor, review and reward progress.

Performance Agreements are made up of three elements: accountabilities, key tasks and measures of success.

Accountabilities

Accountabilities describe the areas of work for which the individual is responsible, and what needs to be achieved. The individual's success in meeting his or her accountabilities will impact upon the success of the wider business area.

- The range of accountabilities set out in the Performance Agreement should relate to the *whole* job, including:
 - *The achievement of business results;*
 - *The management of resources;*
 - *The achievement of quality standards;*
 - *Staff or team responsibilities;*
 - *The achievement of personal objectives, e.g. to meet personal development priorities.*
- Accountabilities should be expressed in the form of a short definition, e.g:
 - *To ensure customer service differentiates us from competition;*
 - *To provide a comprehensive administrative service;*
 - *To complete X project.*
- There should probably be no more than four to six accountabilities for each job holder.
- Employees doing the same job should have the same accountabilities.
- In most jobs, accountabilities should not change much from year to year.

Accountabilities = What Needs to be Achieved.

Key Tasks

Key tasks are the activities and projects the individual must undertake in order to meet their accountabilities.

- Key tasks should be expressed in terms of activities and tasks to be undertaken, e.g:
 - *By processing new savings applications.*
- Key tasks should relate specifically to the achievement of a given accountability, e.g:
 - *Accountability.*
 To provide a comprehensive administration service.
 - *Key Tasks:*
 By opening correspondence,
 By distributing correspondence,
 By typing correspondence, etc.
- Key tasks will include some new, better and different things that need to be done, e.g:
 - *By becoming competent at operating 'x' system.*
- Key tasks will include 'maintenance' tasks that are essential for meeting an accountability, e.g:
 - *By monitoring customer service standards;*
 - *By preparing a monthly report.*
- People doing the same job will have many of the same key tasks.
- There will always be some individual key tasks which relate to personal development or to particularly technical or specialised jobs.

Key Tasks = How Each Accountability Is To Be Met.

Measures of Success

Measures of success are yardsticks designed to help the employee and his/her manager judge whether his/her performance is matching up to expectations. Measures of success may be expressed in terms of:

- Business targets, e.g.:
 - *£x sales per month.*
- Milestones, or specific stages that must be reached during the course of a project, e.g.:
 - *Draft proposals prepared by x date.*
- Deadlines, e.g.:
 - *Specific dates work is required by.*
- Customer service standards, e.g.:
 - *Applications to be processed within x days.*
- Staff performance standards, e.g.:
 - *To input x applications per day.*
- Personal skill improvements, e.g.:
 - *Where an individual needs to develop their business knowledge or learn a new skill, the standards required and the time scales for development should be identified,*
 - *Where an individual needs to improve their skills in a particular competency, it may be appropriate to seek a measured improvement against one of the Supervisory/Middle Management competency scales.*

Measures of success should be INDIVIDUAL and should take into account local circumstances, and the individual's level of skill, length of service and input.

Key tasks and measures of success will need to be agreed at the beginning of the year.

REGULAR REVIEWS

If our organisation is to remain competitive, staff and managers must strive to work together more effectively. Reviews are a means to this end. They give staff an opportunity to assess their progress against their Performance Agreement, to discuss training needs and plan the development of their skills, and to improve the quality of their work.

Areas for discussion

The purpose of holding reviews is to enable individual members of staff and their managers to assess how they can work together more effectively. The issues discussed will be those identified in the Performance Agreement, but could also include:

Workloads/targets

Are they sufficient and varied enough to challenge and motivate?

Communication

Is communication adequate between the employee and the manager? Could it be improved to help the employee with his or her work?

Job-related knowledge

Is the individual up-to-date with product knowledge, technical skills and business developments?

Competencies

Do the individual's competency levels suggest the need for more development in his or her current role, or is the individual concerned almost ready to take on a bigger job?

Career aspirations

What can the employee do to progress towards the achievement of his or her career plan, and how can the manager help?

The areas chosen for detailed discussion will depend on the individual's current level of performance, confidence, training and development needs, motivation and aspirations.

Frequency

The manager's role is to give each individual feedback on an on-going basis. It is up to each business area to decide the frequency of reviews. The Retail Branch Network, for example, tends to have monthly reviews. In other areas, the minimum number of two reviews a year, i.e. June and December, is appropriate. Managers and staff should also take into account individual circumstances when agreeing the number of discussions which should take place.

Preparation

Before the review meeting both the manager and employee should think through the ideas and actions that have contributed to effective working. They should also give some thought to those areas where performance has fallen below the standards required, and possible reasons for this. For example, what factors, skills and abilities have affected the individual's performance at work, and what action could be taken to improve performance?

Both the manager and the employee should provide some examples of the work which has been done during the period under review.

The individual's Performance Agreement record should help both the manager and the individual structure their thoughts in preparation for the review. In particular, progress against accountabilities and key tasks will help identify:

- which skills need to be refined or developed;
- areas in which the manager and employee could operate more effectively together;
- obstacles to fulfilment of the Agreement.

It is advisable that both the manager and employee prepare by updating the Performance Agreement in advance of the review meeting.

Other documents which could be useful in these reviews include:

- the individual's career management profile;
- the individual's training plan;
- the Staff Performance Pre-interview form.

There may be some occasions during a review where areas of performance which need improvement are identified. In this situation, it may be appropriate to put together a Recovery Agreement. This document can be used in subsequent performance reviews, and may be incorporated into the Performance Agreement.

INTERIM REVIEWS

Individual performance will be reviewed half-way through the year. The employee and the manager can discuss performance for the first 6 months against the Performance Agreement. In addition,

they should review any training received in the last 12 months and identify any training planned for the next year. The Interim Review should be conducted in the following way:

1. Achievement towards the accountabilities identified in the Performance Agreement should be discussed and summarised on the first page of the Interim Review form.
2. Any other achievements should be discussed and recorded.
3. Any changes to the Performance Agreement should be discussed and summarised on the form.
4. Any other comments or factors affecting performance should be discussed and recorded on the form.
5. Any training and development needs identified during the past 12 months, the activities undertaken to meet these needs, and evidence of success should be discussed and recorded.
6. Any training and development required for the next 12 months should be discussed and recorded, together with any activities planned to help the employee meet his/her training and development needs. In addition, the criteria for success should be agreed and recorded on the form.

THE END-OF-YEAR REVIEW

The End-of-Year Review should be conducted in the following way:

- **The accountabilities identified in the Performance Agreement should form the basis of the discussion.** The manager and the employee should consider what achievements have contributed to the employee meeting his or her accountabilities, and any other factors which have played a part. The discussion should be summarised on the first page of the Year End Performance Review form.
- The employee and the manager should also identify and discuss any **additional activities** which have been undertaken by the individual.

- THE INDIVIDUAL'S **OVERALL RATING** SHOULD BE DISCUSSED AND RECORDED ON THE FORM IMMEDIATELY FOLLOWING THE DISCUSSION OF THE TWO ITEMS ABOVE

 To encourage the individual to discuss the key competencies which have affected his/her performance during the last 12 months more freely, it is important that the rating is awarded after discussion of accountabilities and activities. The rating must reflect the individual's achievement against accountabilities over the past 12 months. The five ratings are defined below.
- Key competencies which have influenced the employee's performance should be discussed, and recorded on the form, together with supporting examples.
- Personal qualities (both positive and negative) which the individual displays should be identified, discussed and recorded on the form, together with examples.

The success of the meeting will depend on the openness of the participants and the quality of feedback. Staff can only develop their potential by increasing their awareness of their strengths and weaknesses. Quality feedback is essential to this process.

RATING DEFINITIONS

Overall rating

This is the rating which reflects an individual's performance over the past 12 months. It measures the employee's success in fulfilling his or her Performance Agreement. The overall rating falls into one of the following five categories:

Exceptional

Measures of success for priority accountabilities were substantially exceeded, and overall performance was exceptional in most respects.

All other accountabilities were achieved to the agreed standard. All job requirements were maintained. Working beyond normal job requirements, the individual made a significant contribution to the business.

Highly Effective

Measures of success for priority accountabilities were exceeded.

All other accountabilities were achieved to the agreed standard. All job requirements were maintained. A significant contribution was made to the department or area.

Effective

Measures of success for accountabilities achieved to the required standard, taking into account all the circumstances. All job requirements were maintained.

Less than Effective

Measures of success for some priority accountabilities were not met, or all accountabilities were met, but were below the agreed standard. Basic job requirements were maintained.

Unacceptable

No priority accountabilities were met, or accountabilities were well below the required standard. Basic job requirements were not maintained.

Rating Guidelines

Choosing an accurate rating involves an element of managerial judgement. While the rating definitions are quite specific, circumstances must be taken into account as well. For example, a member of staff who achieved all major accountabilities, but did not exceed them, might still in some circumstances merit a 'highly effective' rating, if the person conducting the review knows that:

- the Performance Agreement was particularly challenging;
- the individual had to overcome major obstacles which were not foreseen at the time the Performance Agreement was originally drawn up;
- the individual initiated activities which had a significant impact on the business while still maintaining effective performance of their accountabilities.

RECOVERY AGREEMENTS

Regular, planned reviews will help to identify performance which falls below standard as soon as possible. Recovery – getting performance back on track – is the joint responsibility of the employee and his or her line manager.

The Human Resources Division is committed to supporting both the line manager and the individual in cases of under-performance. A Recovery Agreement has been designed to help the line manager and individual to manage performance shortfalls. It is best used as soon as a performance issue has been identified.

Business areas using Performance Agreements so far found that a structured Recovery Agreement, in conjunction with a Training Action Plan, have been useful in helping staff to manage a successful improvement in their performance.

It is important that performance issues are addressed immediately. Of course, different parts of the business use different methods to identify performance goals. Equally, under-performance can be addressed using a variety of methods. **For advice and guidance on the best way of addressing performance issues, please contact your Personnel Manager.**

THE APPEALS PROCESS

Occasionally, the manager and the individual under review may be unable to agree on the rating to be awarded at the end-of-year Performance Review meeting. In these rare cases, there is a Performance Review Appeals Process to resolve any issues that arise. The Appeals Process consists of three stages, and attempts, in the first instance, to resolve issues at a local level. In order to ensure that matters are dealt with promptly and efficiently, each stage must be completed within a given time scale.

Anyone requiring clarification or help with the Appeals Process should contact their local Personnel Manager.

MANAGEMENT AND CLERICAL COMPETENCIES

Competencies are the skills and business knowledge used in a job, which affect the way in which accountabilities are achieved. They are an important part of the Review Form, because they provide information to help individuals identify their strengths and weaknesses.

ONLY THOSE COMPETENCES WHICH HAVE HAD AN EFFECT ON PERFORMANCE SHOULD BE DISCUSSED DURING THE REVIEW, AND EXAMPLES SHOULD BE RECORDED ON THE FORM.

Competencies fall into two groupings: management and supervisory, and clerical. An outline of these is given below.

The clerical competency groupings are as follows:

- job knowledge;
- planning and organising;
- consistency of work standards;
- relationships/working with others;
- customer service.

Management and supervisory competencies
Abbey National has a Career Management Profiling System which is available to staff in or aspiring to grades 4–10. The system provides individuals with the opportunity to review their skills with their manager, by using Career Management Profile forms in conjunction with competency definitions. The Career Management Profile system helps staff to identify their strengths and weaknesses, and prepare plans for the future development of their skills.

A full review of competencies does not form part of the year-end appraisal, but a summary of the way in which competencies have affected performance during the year should be recorded on the end-of-year appraisal form. A completed profile form may be very helpful in identifying training needs at the mid-year review.

Information about using the system is available from your Personnel Manager. Career Management Profile forms and competency definition booklets are available from your local Personnel Manager.

The company has identified some key competency areas which are present in all management and supervisory jobs.

The management and supervisory competency groupings are:

- **problem analysis and decision-making:** (1) judgement; (2) assimilating information;
- **achieving results:** (3) prioritisation; (4) planning; (5) monitoring and control; (6) liaising/networking;
- **focus on service:** (7) including improvement; (8) customer service internal/external; (9) quality standards;
- **communication:** (10) oral; (11) written;
- **working with others**: (12) teamworking/team management; (13) development; (14) feedback; (15) openness;
- **personal impact:** (16) influencing; (17) self-assertion; (18) positive focus.

Other factors which could be considered are:

- business knowledge;
- information management;
- policy and law.

Note: *technical competence and any other relevant factors should also be considered where this is appropriate.*

GIVING FEEDBACK

Giving quality feedback is important in any job, whether you are a manager or a member of staff. You can improve your technique with practice, and by remembering a few simple rules. Here are some suggestions to bear in mind:

1. Give the feedback as soon as possible after the event.
2. Be clear about what you want to say in advance. Rehearse and/or write down what you are going to say.
3. Check that the person you are talking to understands what you say, by asking him or her to rephrase your comments.
4. 'Own' the feedback, i.e. begin with an 'I' statement like 'I thought' or 'I felt'. This indicates to the other person that you realise you are expressing your own personal view, and that other people might think differently.
5. Start with the positive.
6. Select priority areas; avoid giving too much feedback at any one time because the person will not take it all in – particularly if it's negative.
7. Be specific: what exactly did the person say or do? Give examples. Focus on the behaviour rather than the person – this is less likely to put him or her on the defensive if you are raising negative points.
8. Offer alternatives: don't simply criticise if you give negative feedback. Try to give examples of what could have been done differently, and how the person receiving the feedback could work on changing his or her performance.
9. Leave the person with a choice as to whether or not to act on the feedback.

RECEIVING FEEDBACK

1. Ask for clarification if you do not fully understand the feedback.
2. Keep contact with the person giving you feedback.
3. Encourage the person giving you feedback to be specific.
4. Avoid arguing, denying, justifying.
5. Separate the 'content' of the feedback from the 'process' of giving feedback.
6. Be aware of how you are responding.
7. Remember that you have a choice about how to respond to feedback.
8. Let the person giving you feedback know how you are using or have used it.

(*Source:* Extracted form Abbey National Performance Review System Booklet, 1994. I am grateful to Jim Smart, Group Personnel Policy Manager, Abbey National plc, for permission to reprint this information.)

Review and discussion questions

1 Discuss fully the importance of effective management to organisation development.

2 Outline the main elements of an integrated model of managerial behaviour and development. Use this model to examine the nature of management development in your own organisation.

3 Detail the main features in the process of management development. What are the main factors to consider in the implementation of a successful management development programme?

4 What are your views on the nature of management education, training and development in Britain? Comment critically on the apparent effectiveness of management education, training and development in your own organisation.

5 Summarise clearly what you believe are the main factors which affect organisational effectiveness.

6 Discuss the relevance and applications to organisational effectiveness of :
 (i) Total Quality Management; and
 (ii) management services and techniques.
 Support your discussion with practical examples.

7 Explain what you see as the main attributes for organisational success and give examples from your own or some other organisation. Discuss the importance of innovation as a key factor in organisational effectiveness.

8 Detail the questions you would ask, and the specific criteria you would apply, in attempting to evaluate the performance and effectiveness of your own organisation.

Assignment

Imagine you are the managing director or chief executive of your organisation, and complete the following checklist.

	Yes	No	Maybe
(a) **Structure** Does your organisation have:			
(1) an outdated structure, for example: geared to forgotten objectives, old markets, retired top managers;	☐	☐	☐
(2) an over-extended structure, for example: no adaptation to business growth, technical change or to the competition;	☐	☐	☐
(3) changed organisational objectives, but structure and staffing basically unchanged;	☐	☐	☐

	Yes	No	Maybe

(4) formal structure which is an impediment to business performance, and out of touch with reality;

(5) flexibility, adaptability and delegation impeded by bureaucracy or detailed built-in procedures?

(b) Managerial staffing

Does your organisation have:

(6) unclear top management succession; or does it offer only a 'Hobson's Choice' for several senior positions;

(7) a general and unduly heavy loss of managers, especially the younger or better ones;

(8) quite numerous examples of badly under-employed managers in 'non-jobs';

(9) development clearly held back by a lack of good people;

(10) fairly widespread managerial job dissatisfaction and frustration;

(11) managerial vacancies frequently difficult to fill, from either within or outside the organisation?

(c) Performance

Does your organisation have:

(12) poor organisational performance, due to ineffective management controls;

(13) poor performance because of a generally low level of managerial competence for present-day tasks;

(14) poor performance which arises from blurred or badly drawn managerial responsibilities;

(15) widespread overburdening of managers, which undermines performance;

(16) extensive waste of managerial time, for example in board meetings, committees, working groups;

(17) widespread delays in obtaining either decisions, or the information needed to make decisions;

(18) frequent failure to seize opportunities, or to react speedily to new challenges?

Use the completed checklist and your own analysis to highlight the priorities for reviewing your organisation.

Compare and discuss your responses with colleagues. What overall conclusions do you draw?

Although the object of this exercise is to help you master this section of your study, it is hoped that this approach and checklist will be of some interest and value to you in the practical management situations which you face in your job – either now or in the future.

Notes and references

1. See, for example: Cole, G. A. *Management: Theory and Practice*, Third edition, DP Publications (1990).
2. McCowen, P. and McCowen, C. 'Teaching Teamwork', *Management Today*, September 1989, pp. 107–11.
3. *Going For Better Management*, Local Government Training Board, 1988.
4. Goss, D. M. 'Management Development and Small Business Education: The Implications of Diversity', *Management Education and Development*, vol. 20, part 1, 1989, pp. 100–11.
5. See, for example: Gretton, I. 'Taking the Lead in Leadership', *Professional Manager*, January 1995, pp. 20–2.
6. Clarke, K. 'Survival Skills for a New Breed', *Management Today*, December 1993, p. 5.
7. Mullins, L. J. and Aldrich, P. 'An Integrated Model of Management and Managerial Development', *Journal of Management Development*, vol. 7, no. 3, 1988, pp. 29–39.
8. Payne, R. and Pugh, D. S. 'Organizations as Psychological Environments', in Warr, P. B. (ed.) *Psychology at Work*, Penguin (1971).
9. Stewart, R. *Choices for the Manager*, McGraw-Hill (1982).
10. Blake, R. R. and Mouton, J. S. *The Managerial Grid III*, Gulf Publishing Company (1985).
11. Mintzberg, H. *The Nature of Managerial Work*, Harper and Row (1973).
12. Miner, J. B. *Management Theory*, Macmillan (1971).
13. McGregor, D. *The Human Side of Enterprise*, Penguin (1987).
14. Blake, R. R. and Mouton, J. S. *The Managerial Grid III*, Gulf Publishing Company (1985).
15. Likert, R. and Likert, J. G. *New Ways of Managing Conflict*, McGraw-Hill (1976).
16. Drucker, P. F. *The Effective Executive,* Heinemann Professional (1988); Reddin, W. J. *Managerial Effectiveness*, McGraw-Hill (1970).
17. Mintzberg, H. *The Nature of Managerial Work*, Harper and Row (1973).
18. Ribeaux, P. and Poppleton, S. E. *Psychology and Work: An Introduction*, Revised edition, Macmillan (1983).
19. Stewart, R. *The Reality of Management*, Second edition, Pan Books (1986).
20. Mumford, A. 'What's New in Management Development', *Personnel Management*, vol. 17, no. 5, May 1985, pp. 31–2; Zey, M. G. 'Mentor Programs: Making the Right Moves', *Personnel Journal*, vol. 64, no. 2, 1985, pp. 53–7.
21. See, for example: Nixon, B. and Pitts, G. 'W. H. Smith Develops a New Approach to Developing Senior Managers', *Industrial and Commercial Training*, vol. 23, no. 6, 1991, pp. 3–10.
22. Mathison, C. S. 'Establishing The Management Development Function', *The British Journal of Administrative Management*, April/May 1992, pp. 8–11.
23. See, for example: Hinton, I. 'Learning to Manage – And Managing to Learn' *Industrial and Commercial Training*, vol. 16, no. 3, 1984, pp. 10–16.

24. For example, see: Kable, J. 'Management Development Through Action Learning', *Journal of Management Development*, vol. 8, no. 2, 1989, pp. 77–80.

25. Inglis, S. and Lewis, B. 'Action Learning – The Key to the Competitive Edge', *Professional Manager*, May 1994, pp. 16–17.

26. Humble, J. W. *Management by Objectives*, Management Publications Limited for the British Institute of Management (1971).

27. For further details on self-development, see: Pedler, M., Burgoyne, J. and Boydell, T. *A Manager's Guide to Self Development*, Third edition, McGraw-Hill (1994).

28. *The Making of British Managers* (the Constable and McCormick Report), British Institute of Management (1987).

29. *The Making of Managers: A Report on Management Education, Training and Development in the United States, West Germany, France, Japan and the UK* (the Handy Report), National Economic Development Office (1987).

30. 'Management Education Challenge – Five Years On', *Management News*, The Newspaper of the British Institute of Management, no. 84, February 1992.

31. *Management Development in the UK: 1994 – Market Research Report*, MCI, June 1994.

32. *Management Development to the Millennium*, Institute of Management, July 1994.

33. Handy, C. B. *Understanding Organizations*, Fourth edition, Penguin (1993).

34. For a fuller discussion see, for example: Baguley, P. *Improving Organizational Performance: A Handbook For Managers*, McGraw-Hill (1994).

35. Dunderdale, P. 'Analysing Effective Organisations', *Professional Manager*, September 1994, pp. 23–5.

36. Peters, T. J. and Waterman, R. H. *In Search of Excellence*, Harper and Row (1982).

37. *Ibid.* p. 9.

38. Waterman, R. H., Peters, T. J. and Phillips, J. R. 'Structure Is Not Organization', *Business Horizons*, June 1980, pp. 14–26.

39. Peters, T. J. and Waterman, R. H. *In Search of Excellence*, Harper and Row (1982) p. 12.

40. See, for example: Hill, S. 'Why Quality Circles Failed But Total Quality Management Might Succeed', *British Journal of Industrial Relations*, vol. 29, no. 4, 1991, pp. 541–68.

41. Heller, R. 'Putting the Total into Total Quality', *Management Today*, August 1994, pp. 56–60.

42. Pentecost, D. 'Quality Management: The Human Factor', *European Participation Monitor*, Issue no. 2, 1991, pp. 8–10.

43. Caulkin, S. 'TQM 1: The Road to Peerless Wigan', *Management Today*, March 1994, pp. 28–32.

44. See, for example: Stewart, J. and Walsh, K. *The Search for Quality*, Local Government Training Board (1989).

45. For example, see: Morgan, C. and Murgatroyd, S. *Total Quality Management in the Public Sector*, Open University Press (1994).

46. As an example, see: Hubrecht, J. and Teare, R. 'A Strategy for Partnership in Total Quality Service', *International Journal of Contemporary Hospitality Management*, vol. 5, no. 3, 1993, pp. i–v. This provides an account of the application of TQM in Scott's Hotels Ltd.

47. Lammermeyr, H. U. 'Human Relationships – The Key to Total Quality Management', *Total Quality Management*, vol. 12, no. 2, 1991, pp. 175–80.

48. For details of the core concepts of TQM see, for example: Bank, J. *The Essence of Total Quality Management*, Prentice-Hall (1992).

49. James, G. *Quality of Working Life and Total Quality Management*, ACAS Work Research Unit Occasional Paper no. 50, November 1991.

50. Mullins, L. J. 'Understanding Management Services and Techniques', *Industrial Management & Data Systems*, January/February 1983, pp. 3–7.

51. Steele, M. *Assessing Organisational Effectiveness*, Cranfield School of Management, Working Paper 5/88, 1987.

Conclusion

This book has presented a managerial approach to organisational behaviour. It has been concerned with interactions among the structure and operation of organisations, the process of management and the behaviour of people at work. The underlying theme has been the need for organisational effectiveness and the importance of the role of management as an integrating activity.

No single book could hope to have covered adequately all aspects of such a wide and multi-disciplinary field of inquiry. In order to attain a reasonable level of depth, therefore, this book has concentrated on selected topics of particular relevance to problems of organisation and management in work situations, and which meet the needs of the intended audience.

The book has reflected how the general movement towards flatter structures, flexible working and greater employee involvement has placed increasing emphasis on an integrating rather than a hierarchical/controlling style of management.

It is hoped that this book has provided you with an improved understanding of management and organisational behaviour, and the nature of the people–organisation relationship. It is also hoped that the book has encouraged you to be more aware of, and sensitive to, the organisational factors and management processes influencing the behaviour and performance of people at work.

LAURIE J. MULLINS

Name index

This index consists of people; names of organisations are in the Subject Index.

SUBJECT INDEX